THE ELGAR COMPANION TO CONSUMER RESEARCH AND ECONOMIC PSYCHOLOGY

D0756841

The Elgar Companion to Consumer Research and Economic Psychology

Edited by

Peter E. Earl

Professor of Economics
Lincoln University
Canterbury, New Zealand

and

Simon Kemp

Associate Professor of Psychology
University of Canterbury
Christchurch, New Zealand

Edward Elgar
Cheltenham, UK • Northampton, MA, USA

Published by
Edward Elgar Publishing Limited
Glensanda House
Montpellier Parade
Cheltenham
Glos GL50 1UA
UK

Edward Elgar Publishing, Inc.
136 West Street
Suite 202
Northampton
Massachusetts 01060
USA

A catalogue record for this book
is available from the British Library

Library of Congress Cataloguing in Publication Data
The Elgar companion to consumer research and economic psychology /
    edited by Peter E. Earl and Simon Kemp
        Includes index.
        1. Consumers—Research.   2. Consumer behavior.   3. Economics—
    –Psychological aspects.   I. Earl, Peter E.   II. Kemp, Simon.
HF5415.32.E48   1999
658.8'342—dc21   98–38240
                                                                          CIP

ISBN 1 85898 554 4 (cased)
       1 84376 060 6 (paperback)

Printed and bound in Great Britain by MPG Books Ltd, Bodmin, Cornwall

Contents

Contents

Contents

Contributors to This Volume and Their Entries

Ainslie, George, Veterans' Administration Medical Center, Coatesville, PA, USA
Psychological Discount Rate

Allen, Michael W., Psychology, Victoria University of Wellington, P.O. Box 600, Wellington, New Zealand
Poverty, Psychology of

Arnett, Dennis B., Marketing, Texas Tech University, P.O. Box 42101, Lubbock, TX 79409, USA
Philosophical–Methodological Foundations

Ball, Sheryl B., Economics, Virginia Polytechnic and State University, Blacksberg, VA 24061, USA
Experimental Economics

Beckmann, Suzanne C., Economics and Business Administration, Copenhagen Business School, Struenseegade 7–9, DK-2200 Copenhagen, Denmark
Ecology and Consumption; Emotions and Consumer Behaviour

Belk, Russell W., Marketing, David Eccles School of Business, Kendall D. Garff Building, University of Utah, Salt Lake City, UT 84112, USA
Money

Berno, Tracy, Psychology, Human Sciences Division, P.O. Box 84, Lincoln University, Canterbury, New Zealand
Tourism, Psychology of

Berry, Christopher J., Politics, University of Glasgow, Glasgow G12 8QQ, Scotland, United Kingdom
Needs and Wants

Bloch, Brian, International Business, University of Auckland, Private Bag 92019, Auckland 1, New Zealand
Speculation

Block, Lauren G., Marketing, Stern School of Business, New York University, New York, NY 10012, USA
Fear Appeals and Persuasion

Bolle, Friedel, Institut für Volkswirtschaftstheorie, Europa Universität Viadrina, Postfach 776, 15207 Frankfurt (Oder), Germany
Trust

Burgoyne, Carole B., Psychology, Washington Singer Laboratories, University of Exeter, Exeter EX4 4QG, United Kingdom
Gifts

Burt, Christopher D.B., Psychology, University of Canterbury, Private Bag 4800, Christchurch, New Zealand
Organizational Culture and Profitability

Burton, Scot, Marketing, College of Business Administration, University of Arkansas, Fayetteville, AR 72701, USA
Vanity

Caginalp, Gunduz, Mathematics, University of Pittsburgh, 507 Thackeray Hall, Pittsburgh, PA 15260, USA
Experimental Asset Markets

Cameron, Judy, Educational Psychology, 6–102 Education North, University of Alberta, Edmonton, Alberta, T6G 2G5, Canada
Rewards and the Myth of Performance Decrements

Choi, Young Back, Economics and Finance, St John's University, Jamaica, NY 11439, USA
Conventions

Cox, Anthony D., Marketing Indiana University School of Business, 801 West Michigan Street, Indianapolis, IN 46202, USA
Shoplifting

Cox, Dena, Marketing Indiana University School of Business, 801 West Michigan Street, Indianapolis, IN 46202, USA
Shoplifting

Dabholkar, Pratibha A., Marketing, University of Tennessee, 307 Stokely Management Center, Knoxville, TN 37996, USA
Expectancy Value Models

Darity, William A. Jr, Economics, University of North Carolina at Chapel Hill, Chapel Hill, NC 27514, USA
Unemployment and Well-Being

Dawar, Niraj, Marketing, Richard Ivey School of Business, University of Western Ontario, London, Ontario N6A 3K7, Canada
Brand Equity; Perceived Quality

Dhar, Ravi, Marketing, Yale School of Management, Yale University, 135 Prospect Street, New Haven, CT 06511, USA
Choice Deferral

Dowling, Grahame R., Marketing, Australian Graduate School of Management, University of New South Wales, Sydney, NSW 2052, Australia
Consumer Innovativeness; Perceived Risk

Duggan, Michael, Department of Psychology, Victoria University of Wellington, P.O. Box 600, Wellington, New Zealand
Share Markets and Psychology

Earl, Peter E., Economics, Commerce Division, P.O. Box 84, Lincoln University, Canterbury, New Zealand
Cognitive Dissonance; Personal Construct Theory

Ehrenberg, Andrew, Centre for Research in Marketing, South Bank Business School, South Bank University, London Road, London SE1 0AA, United Kingdom
Brand Loyalty

Elffers, Henk, Centre for Sociolegal Tax Research, Erasmus University, Rotterdam, P.O. Box 1738, 3000 DR Rotterdam, The Netherlands
Tax Evasion

Endres, A.M., Economics, University of Auckland, Private Bag 92019, Auckland 1, New Zealand
Smith, Adam; Utility Theory

Fletcher, Garth, Psychology, University of Canterbury, Private Bag 4800, Christchurch, New Zealand
Attribution Theory

Ford, J.L., Economics, University of Birmingham, P.O. Box 363, Edgbaston, Birmingham B15 2TT, United Kingdom
Expectations

Foxall, Gordon R., Consumer Psychology, Cardiff Business School, Cardiff University, P.O. Box 920, Cardiff CF1 3XP, United Kingdom
Behaviourism

Friese, Susanne, Lehrstuhl für Konsumtheorie und Verbraucherpolitik (530/1) Universität Hohenheim, D-70593 Stuttgart, Germany
Addictive Buying

Friestad, Marian, Marketing, College of Business Administration, University of Oregon, Eugene, OR 97405, USA
Persuasion

Furnham, Adrian, Psychology, University College London, Gower Sreet, London WC1E 6BT, United Kingdom
Culture Shock

Gilleard, Christopher, Psychology, Springfield Hospital, Tooting SW17 7DJ, United Kingdom
McClelland Hypothesis

Goldsmith, Arthur H., Economics, Washington and Lee University, Lexington, VA 24450, USA
Unemployment and Well-Being

Gould, Stephen J., Marketing, Baruch College, The City University of New York, New York, NY 10010, USA
Introspective Research; Protocol and Cognitive Response Analysis

Groenland, Edward A.G., Economic Psychology, Tilburg University, P.O. Box 90153, 5000 Le Tilburg, The Netherlands
Saving

Güth, Werner, Institut für Wirtschaftstheorie, Humboldt-Universität zu Berlin, Spandauer Str. 1, D-10178 Berlin, Germany
Game Theory

Hirschman, Elizabeth C., Marketing, School of Business, Janice H Levin Building, Livingston Campus, Rutgers University, Piscataway, NJ 08854, USA
Hedonic Consumption

Hisrich, Robert D., Weatherhead School of Management, Case Western Reserve University, Enterprise Hall, 10900 Euclid Avenue, Cleveland, OH 44106, USA.
Entrepreneurship and Innovation

Holbrook, Morris B., Marketing, Graduate School of Business, 504 Uris Hall, Columbia University, New York, NY 10027, USA
Howard, John A.

Hudson, Stephen M., Psychology, University of Canterbury, Private Bag 4800, Christchurch, New Zealand
Addiction, Theories of

Hunt, Shelby D., Marketing, Texas Tech University, P.O. Box 42101, Lubbock, TX 79409, USA
Philosophical–Methodological Foundations

John, Deborah Roedder, Marketing, University of Minnesota, Minneapolis, MN 55455, USA
Children's Consumer Behaviour

Kagel, John H., Experimental Economics Laboratory, University of Pittsburgh, Pittsburgh, PA, USA
Animal Experiments in Economics

Kahneman, Daniel, Psychology, and the Woodrow Wilson School of Public and International Affairs, Princeton University, Princeton, NJ 08544, USA
Heuristics and Biases

Kemp, Simon, Psychology, University of Canterbury, Private Bag 4800, Christchurch, New Zealand
Inflation; Utility of Public Goods

Kirchler, Erich, Psychology, University of Vienna, Gölsdorfgasse 3/6, 1010 Vienna, Austria
Household Decision Making

Kleine, Susan Schultz, College of Business Administration, Bowling Green State University, Bowling Green, OH 43402, USA
Possessions

Klumb, Petra L., Abt für Gerontopsychiatrie, Freie Universitaet Berlin, Nussbaumallee 38, 14050 Berlin, Germany
Time Use

Koslow, Scott, Marketing, School of Management, University of Waikato, Private Bag 3105, Hamilton, New Zealand
Conjoint Analysis

Laaksonen, Pirjo, Marketing, Faculty of Business Administration, University of Vaasa, PO Box 700, 65101 Vaasa, Finland
Involvement

Langer, Ellen J., Psychology, Harvard University, William James Hall, 33 Kirkland Street, Cambridge, MA 02138, USA
Illusion of Control

Lavin, Marilyn, Marketing, School of Business and Economics, University of Wisconsin–Whitewater, Whitewater, WI 53190, USA
Soap Opera

Lea, Stephen E.G., Psychology, Washington Singer Laboratories, University of Exeter, Exeter EX4 4QG, United Kingdom
Credit, Debt and Problem Debt

Lewis, Alan, Economic Psychology, School of Humanities and Social Sciences, University of Bath, Claverton Down, Bath BA2 7AY, United Kingdom
Morals, Markets and Green Investing

Lichtenstein, Donald R., Marketing, College of Business Administration, University of Colorado, Boulder, CO 80309, USA
Vanity

Lodewijks, John, Economics, University of New South Wales, Sydney, NSW 2052, Australia
Anthropology and Consumer Behaviour

Lutz, Mark A., Economics, University of Maine, 5774 Stevens Hall, Orono, ME 04469, USA
Dual Self; Humanistic Perspective

Lux, Kenneth, Clinical and Consulting Psychologist, Steven Mills Professional Building, 1441 Hotel Road, Auburn, ME 04210, USA
Dual Self

Maani, Sholeh A., Economics, University of Auckland, Private Bag 92019, Auckland 1, New Zealand
Labour Supply; Work Effort

MacFadyen, Alan J., Economics, University of Calgary, 2500 University Drive NW, Calgary, Alberta T2N 1NS, Canada.
Well-Being

Mayer, Robert N., Family and Consumer Studies, University of Utah, Salt Lake City, UT 84112, USA
Consumer Protection

Mengüç, Bülent, Marketing, Commerce Division, P.O. Box 84, Lincoln University, Canterbury, New Zealand
Search Processes

Miller, Christopher M., Marketing, Thunderbird: The American Graduate School of International Management, 15249 N. 59th Ave, Glendale, AZ 85306, USA
Fashion

Mollenkopf, Diane, Marketing, Commerce Division, P.O. Box 84, Lincoln University, Canterbury, New Zealand
Congruity Theory

Moore, Kevin, Psychology, Human Sciences Division, P.O. Box 84, Lincoln University, Canterbury, New Zealand
Leisure, Psychology of

Moore, Vanessa, Marketing, Commerce Division, P.O. Box 84, Lincoln University, Canterbury, New Zealand
Congruity Theory

Muthoo, Abhinay, Economics, University of Essex, Wivenhoe Park, Colchester, CO4 3SQ, United Kingdom
Rationality in the Face of Uncertainty

Nelson, Paul, Marketing, William E Simon Graduate School of Business Administration, University of Rochester, Rochester, NY, USA
Multiattribute Utility Models; Positioning

Netemeyer, Richard G., Marketing, E.J. Ourso College of Business, Louisiana State University, Baton Rouge, LA 70803, USA
Vanity

Ng, Sik Hung, Psychology, Victoria University of Wellington, P.O. Box 600, Wellington, New Zealand
Poverty, Psychology of

O'Curry, Suzanne, Economics, College of Business, DePaul University, 1 E. Jackson Boulevard, Chicago, IL 60604, USA
Budgeting and Mental Accounting

Olekalns, Mara, Management and Industrial Relations, University of Melbourne, Parkville, Victoria 3052, Australia
Negotiation

Ozanne, Julie L., Marketing, R.B. Pamplin College of Business, Virginia Polytechnic and State University, Blacksberg, VA 24061, USA
Hermeneutics

Peñaloza, Lisa, Marketing, College of Business, University of Colorado, Campus Box 419, Boulder, CO 80309-0419, USA
Acculturation

Phelps, Charlotte, D., Economics, School of Business and Management, Temple University, Philadelphia, PA 19122, USA
Altruism

Porter, David, Humanities and Social Sciences, California Institute of Technology, Pasadena, CA 91125, USA
Experimental Asset Markets

Quiggin, John, Economics, The Faculties, Australian National University, ACT 0200, Australia
Utility

Rajendran, K.N., Marketing, University of Northern Iowa, Cedar Falls, IA 50614, USA
Reference Price

Richins, Marsha L., Marketing, College of Business and Public Administration, University of Missouri, Columbia, MO 65211, USA
Material Values

Roland-Lévy, Christine, Laboratoire de Psychologie Sociale, Université Rene Descartes Paris V, 28 Rue Serpente, F-75270 Paris Cedex 06, France
Economic Socialization

Rook, Dennis W., Marketing, Marshall School of Business, University of Southern California, Los Angeles, CA 90089, USA
Impulse Buying; Ritual

Routh, David A., Psychology, University of Bristol, 8 Woodland Rd., Bristol BS8 1TN, United Kingdom
Lay Economic Beliefs

Schoormans, Jan, Consumer Research, Faculty of Industrial Design, Jaffalaan 9, 2628 BX Delft, The Netherlands
Consumer Knowledge

Scott, Linda M., Advertising, University of Illinois at Urbana–Champaign, Urbana, IL 61801, USA
Images in Advertising; Women in Advertising

Scriven, John, Centre for Research in Marketing, South Bank Business School, South Bank University, London Road, London SE1 0AA, United Kingdom
Brand Loyalty

Sent, Esther-Mirjam, Economics, 426 Decio Hall, University of Notre Dame, Notre Dame, IN 46556, USA
Satisficing

Shafir, Eldar, Psychology, and the Woodrow Wilson School of Public and International Affairs, Princeton University, Princeton, NJ 08544, USA
Heuristics and Biases

Singer, Alan E., Management, University of Canterbury, Private Bag 4800, Christchurch, New Zealand
Escalation of Commitment; Rationality, General Theory of

Singer, Ming, Psychology, University of Canterbury, Private Bag 4800, Christchurch, New Zealand
Fairness

Smith, Vernon L., Economic Science Laboratory, Karl Eller Graduate School of Management, University of Arizona, Tucson, AZ 85721, USA
Experimental Asset Markets

Spash, Clive L., Department of Land Economy, University of Cambridge, 19 Silver Street, Cambridge, CB3 9EP, United KIngdom
Contingent Valuation

Stacey, Barrie G., Lincoln Gerontology Centre, LaTrobe University, Bundoora, Victoria 3083, Australia
Growing Old

Stern, Barbara B., Marketing, Ackerson Hall, Newark Campus, Rutgers University, Newark, NJ 07102, USA
Literary Explication and Deconstruction

Sujan, Mita, Marketing, Smeal College of Business Administration Pennsylvania State University, University Park, Pittsburgh, PA 16802, USA
Bettman, James R.

Tay, Richard S., Economics, Commerce Division, P.O. Box 84, Lincoln University, Canterbury, New Zealand
Discrete Choice Models

Trivedi, Minakshi, Marketing, State University of New York at Buffalo, Jacobs Management Center, PO Box 604000, Buffalo, NY 14260, USA
Variety-Seeking Behaviour

Troilo, Gabriele, Marketing, SDA Bocconi (Business School of Bocconi University) via Bocconi 8, 20136 Milan, Italy
Collecting

Twomey, Paul J., Economics, King's College, Cambridge, United Kingdom
Habit

Tyszka, Tadeusz, Psychology, Polish Academy of Sciences, Podlesna 61, PL 00-967 Warsaw, Poland
Transformation in Eastern Europe

Vandekerckhove, Marie M.P., Ableilung Psychologie, Universität Bielefeld, 33501 Bielefeld, Germany
Conspicuous Consumption

Van Raaij, W. Fred, Economics and Psychology, Erasmus University, P.O. Box 1738, 3000 DR Rotterdam, The Netherlands
History of Economic Psychology

Venkatesh, Alladi, Marketing, Graduate School of Management, University of California at Irvine, Irvine, CA 92717, USA
Postmodernism and Consumption

Veum, Jonathan R., Research Economist, Bureau of Labor Statistics, Room 4945, 2 Massachusetts Avenue, NE, Washington, DC 20212, USA
Unemployment and Well-Being

Walker, Michael, Psychology, University of Sydney, Sydney, NSW 2006, Australia
Gambling

Ward, Colleen A., Social Work and Psychology, National University of Singapore, Kent Ridge, Singapore, 119260
Cross-Cultural Research

Ward, Tony, Psychology, University of Canterbury, Private Bag 4800, Christchurch, New Zealand
Addiction, Theories of

Wärneryd, Karl-Erik, Stockholm School of Economics, P.O. Box 6501, 113 83 Stockholm, Sweden.
Katona, George

Webley, Paul, Psychology, Washington Singer Laboratories, University of Exeter, Exeter EX4 4QG, United Kingdom
Children's Saving

White, Judith B., Psychology, Harvard University, William James Hall, 33 Kirkland Street, Cambridge, MA 02138, USA
Illusion of Control

Wicklund, Robert A., Ableilung Psychologie, Universität Bielefeld, 33501 Bielefeld, Germany
Cognitive Dissonance; Conspicuous Consumption

Wilkes, Robert E., Marketing, College of Business Administration, Texas Tech University, Lubbock, TX 79049, USA
Household Life Cycle

Introduction

The related fields of consumer research and economic psychology draw principally on two different traditions of research — marketing and psychology — which are generally reported in two different sets of journals and books. Hence, the two have largely proceeded independently of each other, although of late — and particularly within economic psychology — there has been a conscious effort to try to bring them together. We, the editors, rather reflect this division in our backgrounds: Peter Earl initially trained as an economist but during his doctoral studies expanded his interests into marketing and management; Simon Kemp's training is in psychology. We hope that readers will find this Companion a useful contribution to this task of integration. Certainly we found the task of editing it helped broaden our individual horizons.

Consumer research and economic psychology are similar in their intellectual foundations, but differ in other respects. Consumer research is perhaps the more tightly focused field, as it has a more closely defined subject area, although, as this Companion shows, it features an enormous diversity of approaches to studying it. Economic psychology has a less well-defined subject area (see the entry on the History of Economic Psychology for an overview), and indeed consumer research could be thought of as a subset of this larger study. However, consumer research has generally been the more intensively researched area. Luckily, the history of separation between the business school and psychological traditions finds no parallel in a separation between consumer research and economic psychology, and the two areas are quite closely related. Hence, at the outset of this project we rejected any attempt to try to separate the different entries in this Companion into separate consumer research and economic psychology categories.

In planning this book, we had in mind principally the needs of the advanced undergraduate or graduate student in departments of business administration, economics, marketing and psychology, but we hope that many established researchers and practitioners in these fields will also find the book a guide that can be usefully and frequently consulted. With this in mind, we have tried to ensure that a broad range of topics were covered, including some that appear to have been little reported in either the main consumer research or the main economic psychology journals. Each entry contains a brief overview of an area of research and interest, and a brief list of some of the important journal articles and books that have been written on the topic. We also hope that both researchers who have been trained largely in economics and those who have been trained largely in psychology will find entries that suggest to them that the other tradition has something worthwhile to report.

Many established researchers are likely to notice omissions in the titles featured in this Companion. It is, of course, inevitable that a work of this kind will not be complete, although we have done our best, aided by the suggestions of others, to ensure that at least the majority of the most important topics have been covered. But we should also like to remind readers that not finding an entry you are looking for under a particular or related title does not necessarily mean that the Companion contains nothing on the topic. To aid the initial search for relevant material we have chosen to include an index, rather than rely on a system of cross-referencing as some previous Companions in this series have done.

Writers and researchers on Consumer Research and Economic Psychology come from a variety of different areas. Psychologists, economists, marketers and business administrators are all well-represented in this Companion, and there are contributions from scholars with backgrounds in law, mathematics, medicine, philosophy, sociology, anthropology and education as well. Although there are a number of common themes linking many of the entries in this Companion — the idea of rationality is an important example — we believe that many readers will be struck rather more by the diversity of the theories, methods, ideas and approaches represented by the different entries. We, like many of those who work in Consumer Research and Economic Psychology, find this diversity and the intellectual stimulation that results from it one of the attractions of the area. We find it an exciting area and hope you will too.

Individual entries in this Companion have been written by scholars and researchers with knowledge and expertise in the particular topic. We think we have been fortunate that so many of those we asked to write entries were able to find the time to do so, and that the writers took pains to make their particular specialities comprehensible to the nonspecialist. This helped to make the editing an easier task for us, and, much more important of course, we believe it has made the completed book more accessible to its readers. We are also indebted to many contributors for suggesting entries to cover gaps in our original plan.

In addition to thanking the contributors, we wish to express our gratitude to a number of other people who offered their help. Some researchers who could not contribute themselves were able to suggest expert colleagues who could. Most of the articles were transmitted electronically and we are grateful to Annette Brixton, Ann Christie, Gerard Mesman and Robyn Daly for helping to keep this process going.

PETER E. EARL AND SIMON KEMP

Acculturation

Acculturation is defined as the general process of adaptation to one culture by persons of another culture. Consumer acculturation studies examine cultural adaptation processes mediated by, and expressed in, the marketplace. Cultures, like markets, extend beyond borders of the nation, in the form of familial ties and other social networks, remittances, corporations and trade. Fundamental to acculturation is interaction with another culture, and the changes that result. Measurement issues revolve around definitions of the culture and calibrations of its changes. Often there are both distinctions and overlaps of nationality, social class, race, ethnicity and region.

Historically, acculturation studies are inexorably linked to the rise of the modern nation state and the use of social scientific studies in the formation of public policy. The degree to which immigrants have integrated into the host society has been a central concern of social scientists. Immigration has served as a logical testing ground for the health and identity of the nation. Particularly in US and other nations where immigration has played a key role in the formulation of the national culture and character, immigration studies have sought to understand the interactions of agents from various levels and sectors of the economy, and from various national and subcultural groups. Immigrant studies have provided a rich area for the development of theories of cultural interaction and community formation, as people from various nations confront other people and their respective ways of life.

Yet, while acculturation has most commonly been studied in the form of immigrant adaptation, intercultural interaction and change may also be stimulated *intranationally* by physical relocation, social mobility, and conversion to another belief system, and *internationally* by tourism, trade, employment, conquest and colonization. In the contemporary world, intercultural interaction and change are stimulated as much by subcultural and international conflicts, themselves the result of ongoing historical events, as by market phenomena. As the economy becomes more global, attention shifts to the market as a cultural agent triggering interaction and change and fostering intercultural harmony and conflict. Market factors include the movement of people, products, services and companies related to international labour and trade, as well as differences in the economic health and standard of living of particular nations. Intercultural relations are then viewed against the backdrop of economic exchanges.

Acculturation processes
Studies of acculturation have drawn from and extended more general work on social learning. To our understanding of modelling, reinforcement and social interaction dynamics has been added processes of movement, translation and

adaptation. Acculturation processes are initiated by movement, both literally, as in physical relocation, and figuratively, as in changes in one's social circles, activities and values. The latter changes can entail upward as well as downward social mobility, depending upon the reception of the person's skills in the new labour market, and differences in the standard of living between the two nations. Translation processes are characterized by substantial code-switching activities as the new codes of the host culture are acquired in relation to those of the previous culture, with some difficulty due to the tacit nature of cultural knowledge and the experiential qualities of cultural learning. Adaptation processes involve the simultaneous yet gradual depositioning and repositioning of life worlds as one detaches from a previous way of life and adjusts to living in the new cultural context.

Acculturation is understood as a function of individual and cultural characteristics and agents of influence. Motivations include improving oneself and the lives of one's children, fleeing economic and political persecution, reuniting family, and corporate relocation. Individual experiences differ along the sociodemographics of age, social class, and ethnic and national identity, in addition to language ability, intercultural contact and generation. Further, the more similar the national cultures, the less intense and the more rapid the adaptation process. Yet, some adaptation is often required even in nations that share cultural customs, such as language, as the result of accompanying differences in market customs, such as store hours, meal times, and product and service availability.

Substantively, the focus of acculturation studies has been on cultural values, gender and familial roles, influences on decision making, information processes, media behaviour and purchasing patterns. Agents of influence include family, peers, stores, and religious and educational institutions.

Outcomes include assimilation of the new culture, maintenance of the old, the formation of new hybrid cultural forms, the resistance to one or more cultures, and segregation, the physical separation of the cultures. Notably, social theoretical models of immigrant adaptation have reflected the social and historical conditions of their time. In the US, for example, as earlier waves of European migrants have been supplanted with movements of people from Latin America and Asia, assimilation models have been replaced by those emphasizing bicultural adaptation, resistance and segregation.

Models of assimilation emphasize the ways in which an immigrant/minority group takes on behaviours of the mainstream, or dominant culture. Yet, assimilation is increasingly recognized as only part of the story; with its ideological functions challenged in reifying the mainstream culture by reducing the immigrant culture to its caricature. The assimilation model dominated in the eighteenth and nineteenth centuries, but by the mid-twentieth century a shift of terms had occurred in popular discourse away from the melting pot, in which one group ultimately blends into the mainstream culture and loses its sense of its original culture, to the salad bowl, in which each of the cultures maintains its integrity, even as together they constitute the whole.

Maintenance entails immigrants' reproduction of their culture of origin. Interestingly, some behaviours which appear characteristic of assimilation are more accurately classified as maintenance, provided that their interpretation and use affirm the original culture. An example is the use of the automobile and telephone by Mexican immigrants in the US, which ironically maintained their strong family ties to members both in the US and in Mexico. At issue are the meanings and cultural orientations given particular products, services and market customs, as they may serve to reshape one's sense of previous national identity.

An important feature of acculturative change is that it is bidirectional, comprising active and passive changes directed both towards and away from the origin and host cultures by both immigrants and residents. Examples of public policies limiting language, other cultural expressions, and use of social services by immigrants suggest limits on the tolerance and acceptance by a host culture of its others, and are often associated with adverse economic circumstances. Ironically, these measures often foster the formation of social movements designed to strengthen the identity and agency of members of the excluded group.

Resistance centres on the rejection of aspects of host and/or origin cultures. Such resistance signifies a marked agency and self-determination *vis-à-vis* both cultures, which is of interest to researchers, particularly its changes over generations. Both immigrants and subcultural minorities share a differential positioning on the border between two cultural worlds, as they learn to traverse and position themselves with respect to both. Further, the previously mentioned salad bowl model of cultural adaptation reflects the concerted efforts of subcultural groups, including indigenous peoples in many parts of the world, to resist assimilation into a larger, mainstream, and often consumption-based culture.

Finally, segregation marks the physical limits of cultural acceptance and the particular mechanisms of separation. Social domains often occupy physical space, and as such, cultural insights are generated from attention to spatial groupings. Examples include physical segregation in housing, and clientele concentration and specialization in shopping centres which cater to particular ethnic groups comprising immigrants and their descendants. Of interest are the ways in which ethnic tensions are exacerbated or lessened by the market, as many of the civil rights struggles in the US in the 1960s were carried out in the marketplace. Similarly, tensions between Blacks, Koreans and Latinos in the early 1990s in Los Angeles took the form of urban riots in shopping centres.

Socio-historical contexts

Acculturation processes are most usefully viewed within their historical and socio-cultural contexts. As an example, the history and socio-demographics of Mexican and Indian immigrants to the US differ substantially, although both are minority subcultures.

Until 1847 the southwestern US was Mexican territory, and to this day the descendants of the early Mexicanos continue to live in the area, although they have also dispersed in lesser concentrations throughout the country. The history of Mexican immigration entails citizenship for those Mexicans living in the southwestern US in 1847, transportation to work in the fields and factories at various times between 1942 and 1960, recurring deportations and discrimination, and the recent inclusion of their descendants in affirmative action programmes, which are currently being dismantled. In contrast, India gained independence from Britain in 1947, yet while Indian immigrants to the US have been primarily highly skilled professionals, they, too have experienced racial discrimination in the US, and are included within some affirmative action programmes under the larger category of Asians.

Numbers relative to the whole are also significant; the number of Mexican immigrants is estimated at one million annually, while Indian immigrants are estimated in the tens of thousands. For reasons of numbers, geographic concentration and historical presence, the Latino market is a full service market in its own right, with a longstanding historical tradition denied in its recent 'discovery' by major corporations. A necessary anchor of consumer acculturation is the larger economic phenomenon of micro-niching, that is, the accessibility and profitability of small population segments. Also important is the distinction between first-generation immigrants and subsequent generations, as generally the two groups reside in close proximity.

Implications

Cultural artefacts and behaviours are appropriated on an increasingly large scale by consumers and corporations with and without the participation of people from the originating culture as the market extends beyond national borders. In a world where firms and consumers are increasingly aligned with multiple cultures, scholars debate whether anything is sacred and/or culturally unique any more. Examples include Mexican firms selling to Mexicans in the US, Anglos buying Mexican foods and dancing salsa, and Anglo firms selling to Mexicans. Of concern are perceptions and fears of the impending loss of cultural identity and authenticity. This is especially the argument of conservative literary and cultural scholars reacting to the plethora of hybrid cultural forms. In this sense acculturation studies have come full circle, from their elitist origins as cultural refinement, to the more modern sense of nationality and ethnicity, to the most recent postmodern sense of class and lifestyle subcultures and purchase choices.

Concerns of cultural homogenization are raised in response to the accumulation of power among multinational corporations throughout the world and speculation concerning the corresponding loss of power by the nation state. Materialism, industrialism, environmental destruction, pollution and social alienation are some of the negative externalities attributed to the hegemony of Western culture at a time when national powers are being curbed. In fact, the unification of Europe, the North American Free Trade Agreement (NAFTA), and the Association of South East Asian Nations (ASEAN) may well be understood as extensions of national sovereignty and economic power in a world where national borders are increasingly called into question.

Other concerns centre on the role of business in separating groups of people. The issue is whether marketers, by offering products and services tailored to those outside a cultural mainstream, enable them to maintain cultural distinctions. Thus, concerns of the cultural divisiveness of the market are raised as more and different consumer subcultures are incorporated within it.

Ultimately, the market both integrates and separates. First, in its integrative function the market assembles various people under a particular rubric. The group then attains a cultural legitimation of sorts as a market, with the people within it granted a particular form of consumer sovereignty. The market separates as an artefact of market practices treating subsegments as unique and apart from the rest, and in the limits of consumer sovereignty. Neither structurally nor procedurally is the market necessarily democratic, as consumers are afforded the right to buy, but without any guarantee of civic participation. Nevertheless, the calls for free markets and democracy continue juxtaposed and unabated. It remains to be seen how capitalism and democracy coexist — acculturation studies indicate fairly sophisticated mechanisms in the market for the reproduction of cultural values.

LISA PEÑALOZA

Bibliography
Bhabha, H.K. (1994) *The Location of Culture*, London, Routledge.

Buell, F. (1994) *National Culture and the New Global System*, Baltimore, MD, Johns Hopkins University Press.

Cornelius, W., Martin, P. and Hollifield, J. (1994) *Controlling Immigration: A Global Perspective*, Stanford, CA, Stanford University Press.

Costa, J. and Bamossy, G. (1995) *Marketing in a Multicultural World*, Thousand Oaks, CA, Sage.

Featherstone, M. (ed.) (1990) *Global Culture: Nationalism, Globalization and Modernity*, London, Sage.

Gilly, M., Peñaloza, L. and Kambara, K. (1997) 'The Role of American Identity in

5

Expatriates' Consumer Adjustment', presented to the Association for Consumer Research, 16–19 October, Denver, Colorado.

Light, I. (1972) *Ethnic Enterprise in America: Business and Welfare Among Chinese, Japanese and Blacks*, Berkeley, CA, University of California Press.

Mattelart, A. (1979) *Multinational Corporations and the Control of Culture*, Brighton, Harvester Press.

Peñaloza, L. (1994) 'Atravasando Fronteras/Border Crossings', *Journal of Consumer Research*, **21**: 32–54.

Peñaloza, L. (1995) 'Immigrant Consumers: Marketing and Public Policy Considerations in the Global Economy', *Journal of Public Policy and Marketing*, **14**: 83–94.

Wilson, R. and Dissanayake, W. (eds) (1996) *Global/Local: Cultural Production and the Transnational Imaginary*, Durham, NC, Duke University Press.

Addiction, Theories of

In this entry we consider the contribution an economic perspective can make to the explanation of addictive behaviour. Because of space limitations we base our discussion on the work of Becker (Becker and Murphy, 1988; Becker, 1992) who has developed an influential and promising economic model of addictive behaviour. Becker constitutes but one of a number of writers who provide analyses that stress that addictive behaviour may well be rational — for example, Taylor (1986) makes extensive use of Solomon and Corbit's (1974) opponent process model. We first describe the key features of addictive behaviour and briefly sketch the prominent etiological models and current theoretical directions in the area. Next, the basic assumptions of Becker's economic model of addiction are outlined and their applicability to the area evaluated. Finally, we consider the implications of this approach for future theoretical and empirical research. We use alcoholism as a prototypical example of an addictive disorder.

Traditional models of addiction

Broadly speaking there are currently two major types of etiological theories of addiction, disease models and learning models. The disease model of addiction is essentially based on a construct of *the dependency syndrome* (Davison and Neale, 1996). This consists of a constellation of behavioural patterns and problems resulting from addictive behaviour that are thought to constitute a syndrome. For example, the crucial elements of alcohol dependency involve a narrowing of the drinking repertoire, increased salience of drinking in the life of the individual, increased awareness of compulsion to drink, increased tolerance to the effects of alcohol, repeated withdrawal symptoms, relief from or avoidance of withdrawal symptoms by further drinking, and the rapid reinstatement of dependency after a period of abstinence.

The basic assumption is that individuals suffering from alcoholism have an inbred susceptibility for drinking that is beyond their control. The emphasis is on uncontrollable biochemical factors thought to be the basis of addiction, for example, malfunctioning neurotransmitter and/or opiate systems, while psychological variables are thought to be causally irrelevant in leading to alcoholism (Davison and Neale, 1996). The disease process is viewed as irreversible and progressive, and treatment is thought to require complete and utter abstinence, although in more recent genetic-developmental models, risk and symptoms are seen as fluctuating (Tarter and Vanyukov, 1994). Drug availability and exposure to even the smallest amount of alcohol is believed to result in an inevitable loss of control. This model is still widely adhered to in most alcohol treatment agencies, especially in North America.

The medical model draws upon adoption studies, twin studies and biological studies (for example, effect of alcohol on transmitter systems) for experimental support, although it has a number of well-documented weaknesses (Davison and Neale, 1996; Marlatt and Gordon, 1985). It has been criticized for creating an 'all- or-nothing' cognitive set, and neglecting the important role of psychological variables such as expectations in the development of addiction. Additional difficulties include its inability to accommodate the research finding that controlled drinking is a common outcome in diagnosed alcoholics or to explain why commonalties appear to exist in the different addictions. Finally, a medical model is unable to explain why many individuals can recover from addictions without help, or why research has failed to uncover clear evidence of disease progression: a basic assumption of the classical disease model. Additionally problem behaviours such as addictive buying (see the entry in this volume) and gambling (Rosenthal, 1992) are remarkably difficult to explain with reference to biological substrates.

In contrast to the medical model, the learning approach defines addictive behaviour as a *repetitive habit pattern* that increases the risk of disease, and/or associated personal and social problems (Davison and Neale, 1996; Marlatt and Gordon, 1985). Addictive behaviour is hypothesized to serve a function for an individual and to be maintained by its reinforcing consequences. In a sense it functions to help individuals cope with problematic situations or emotions. Such behaviour is often experienced subjectively as a loss of control, is difficult to curtail or stop, and is typically characterized by immediate gratification (short-term rewards) and delayed negative effects (long-term costs). There is a de-emphasis on diagnosis, which forces the clinician to consider the client from a more individual perspective.

The learning model rejects the disease model's claim that fixed person factors lead to the development of substance disorder. Rather, it suggests that a combination of social learning history and current experiential factors contribute to an individual's use of a substance. Addiction problems are hypothesized to be acquired and maintained through cultural norms, modelling, social reinforcement, anticipated effects, direct experience of the substance as rewarding or punishing, and physical dependency. Direct experience with a substance is hypothesized to be positively reinforced by factors such as its (initial) euphoric properties, and negatively reinforced by reduced levels of anxiety or tension. The use of an addictive substance is thought to vary along a continuum beginning in adolescence and progressing to normal use and/or episodes of abuse, abstinence or controlled use throughout the adult life cycle. As learning events vary over time within individuals and from one individual to another, so too would their use of the substance. The continued high levels of consumption can result in physical and psychological dependence. In addition, the impact of the environment can lead to increased stress (for example, increased marital conflict) which can lead to further drug use. Recovery from addiction depends on the learning of alternative coping skills. Consequently, treatment programmes based on learning models often promote the goal of moderation.

The learning model draws support for its assumptions from controlled drinking research and experimental studies demonstrating the important causal role of cognitive and other psychological variables in individuals' responses to alcohol priming. It also has a number of weaknesses. It fails to account for the role of demonstrated biological and genetic factors in addictive disorders. Recent research suggests that addictive disorders such as alcoholism are heterogeneous in nature and comprise a number of distinct disorders, some having a primarily genetic or physiological basis and others a primary psychological basis (Tarter and Vanyukov, 1994). A final consideration is that a controlled drinking outcome is not possible for everyone. Why is this the case?

As stated above there is increasing evidence that addictions such as alcoholism represent a heterogeneous disorder and contemporary thinking suggests that neither of the above opposing perspectives are likely to provide a satisfactory explanation of their development and maintenance (for example, Donovan and Marlatt, 1988). Instead, it is argued that a complete account of addiction will probably need to include cultural/social factors (for example, norms, availability of alcohol), psychological variables (for example, expectations, skill deficits, learning experiences), and biological factors (for example, genetic predisposition, different degrees of tolerance).

An economic model of addiction

According to Becker's model, addicts are rational agents who attempt to maximize their future utility by engaging in addictive behaviour. Individuals may decide to take an addictive substance or engage in an addictive behaviour because they reason that the advantages of doing so are greater than the future consequences of abstaining. People may become addicted because they are unhappy but may anticipate that if they did not consume the addictive goods their mood would be even worse. When the price of a good (for example, addictive substance) falls, there is likely to be an increase in addictive behaviour. The price of an addiction also involves psychological costs, for example, emotional stress, as well as money.

Two key assumptions of Becker's model are that addictions evolve out of habits (persistent behaviours reflecting preferences) and that there is a positive relationship between past and current consumption. When past consumption is weighed more heavily than present consumption, an individual is likely to have an addiction. Consumption refers to the engaging in an addictive behaviour, for example, smoking, drinking alcohol, or eating binge foods. Habits develop out of childhood experiences and constrain the development of desires and preferences. Those created as a child usually persist into adulthood, for example, coping strategies such as emotional avoidance. Habits are hypothesized to be harmful if increased present consumption lowers future utility (that is, has an overall negative effect on future well-being or happiness), for example, adversely affecting an individual's health or relationship.

Another key idea is that of discounting or trading off future rewards or utility for current ones. The stronger an addiction or habit, the greater the rate at which the future or past is discounted. This essentially translates into a greater preference for short-term rewards at the expense of longer-term ones. Arguably, a person is more likely to engage in harmful behaviours if he or she discounts future consequences. It is important to keep in mind that this is not viewed as irrational; it is simply a question of deciding that addiction offers a more promising way of maximizing well-being. According to Becker, when considering utility, agents also take into account intrapsychic variables such as emotional states. For example, a person may decide to drink alcohol in order to reduce or extinguish a negative mood state, or to boost their sense of confidence and sense of personal control. Some individuals may be more present-orientated than others and therefore have greater potential to discount future consequences, resulting in lower utility calculations for some behaviours, for example, abstaining from alcohol. Peer pressure or external pressures can increase the demand for a good and transform a habit into an addiction. An increase in past consumption can lead to a smaller increase in full price if an individual heavily discounts the future. This means that a person is more likely to purchase and consume the addictive goods, for example, alcohol.

A habit may evolve into an addiction simply by a process of exposure. A consequence of taking certain drugs or engaging in addictive behaviours is that a person may pay less attention to future consequences. This leads to an increased

9

valuing of present utility at the expense of future consequences, and subsequent further discounting of future utility: a self-perpetuating addictive cycle. Habits by virtue of their well-entrenched nature are typically performed in an automatic, unthinking manner, and are relatively resource free. This means that little effort is required to make a decision or to execute an action: savings that increase a behaviour's utility.

Goals or standards of comparison play an important role in Becker's model. Any calculation of utility will involve a comparison of current consumption with the future or past. It is the relative discrepancy that is important not the absolute level. For example, individuals with a high standard of living are likely to be dissatisfied if their lifestyle either becomes only marginally better or becomes worse. However, for those with a low standard of living, any improvement is likely to result in increased satisfaction. Tolerance means that levels of consumption are less satisfying when previous consumption has been greater. If a person has consumed higher levels of an addictive good in the past, then he or she would be less satisfied consuming the same level of goods in the present.

It is necessary to take into account a person's capital and earnings when considering the cost of goods and the future utility of actions. From a psychological perspective, this includes their coping skills, support levels, the quality of their intimate relationships, and factors such as motivation. This highlights the importance of considering an individual's particular circumstances when calculating the utility of actions. For example, drunkenness is much more harmful in some jobs than in others, or to some relationships rather than others. To a degree, it is dependent on other people's preferences and expectations. Stressful life events might lower the utility of staying off drugs in the future and raise the utility of addictive behaviours (for example, an addiction might be seen as a way of managing grief), similar to a lowering of the price of addictive goods. Therefore, anticipated future stress may increase current consumption if the person thinks that indulging in an addictive behaviour in the future will be beneficial to him or her.

From a treatment perspective a crucial issue concerns the anticipated costs of attempting to change an addiction for an individual. This will involve evaluating current options, the strength of influence of past habits, and whether or not it is worth the effort to attempt to change. A person may decide to end an addiction when he or she expects a large short-term loss in utility (including costs of adjustment) will be offset by even larger gains in the long term. When contemplating the utility of change, a rational addict will appraise the pros and cons of the various options and decide to peruse the option that promises to maximize his or her rewards.

Conclusions

Becker's economic model of addiction represents an intriguing contribution to the addictive behaviour literature. It is consistent with the newly developed self-regulation approach by virtue of its assumption that addiction represents goal-directed behaviour. Similarly, it contrasts with the disease and learning models' emphases on biological or psychological deficits, and instead hypothesizes that addictive behaviour could reflect misregulation processes rather than a loss of control. It also emphasizes the importance of appetite-based processes and claims that addiction may help individuals maximize their utility in some circumstances. It has some similarities with both classical models and stresses the importance of experience and context while also accepting that the pharmacological effects of addictive substances can contribute to the addictive process.

From a critical perspective it has difficulty accounting for the addictive paradox, where people feel compelled to engage in addictive behaviour, but also appear to be implementing behaviour directed towards other goals (Ainslie, 1992). That is, people appear to be using their addiction as a way of coping with, or solving, certain problems, for example, using alcohol to reduce social anxiety. Becker's approach also appears to have problems accounting for the conflicting goals or preferences that are typically associated with addictive disorders.

This model also appears to need supplementing by additional psychological theories. For example, it requires an additional theory to account for the impact of stress and mood on preferences and decision making. Put simply, why are people under stress more inclined to discount future consequences and focus preferentially on immediate rewards? According to modern information-processing theories, when individuals are stressed they tend to experience increased negative cognitions and therefore are likely to evaluate their options in a biased way (Wells and Matthews, 1994). This is partly a function of mood congruent effects where the valance of a particular mood can lead to the preferential recall of information and memories. Also, when people are stressed and experiencing cognitive overload they tend to rely on information-processing short cuts or heuristics (Wells and Matthews, 1994). This can lead to a number of inferential errors and subsequent adaptation problems.

Despite these shortcomings we suggest that economic models offer an exciting perspective on the way addictions develop and are maintained. It challenges the received view that addiction is inherently irrational and involves loss of control by an individual. We may well be more in charge of our own problems than has been apparent! In our view, future research into addictive behaviour could benefit from incorporating economic models into the theoretical picture.

TONY WARD AND STEPHEN M. HUDSON

Bibliography

Ainslie, G. (1992) *Picoeconomics*, New York, Cambridge University Press.

Baumeister, R.F., Heatherton, T.F. and Rice, D.M. (1994) *Losing Control: How and Why People Fail at Self-Regulation*, San Diego, CA, Academic Press.

Becker, G.S. (1992) 'Habits, Addictions, and Traditions', *Kyklos*, **45**: 327–46.

Becker, G.S. and Murphy, K.M. (1988) 'A Theory of Rational Addiction', *Journal of Political Economy*, **96**: 675–700.

Davison, G.C. and Neale, J.M. (1996) *Abnormal Psychology* (revised 6th edn), New York, John Wiley & Sons.

Donovan, D.M. and Marlatt, G.A. (eds) (1988) *Assessment of Addictive Behaviors*, New York, Guilford Press.

Marlatt, G.A. and Gordon, J.R. (eds) (1985) *Relapse Prevention: Maintenance Strategies in the Treatment of Addictive Behaviors*, New York, Guilford Press.

Rosenthal, R.J. (1992) 'Pathological Gambling', *Psychiatric Annals*, **22**: 72–8.

Solomon, R.L. and Corbit, J.D. (1974) 'An Opponent Process Theory of Motivation: Temporal Dynamics of Affect', *Psychological Review*, **81**: 119–45.

Tarter, R.E. and Vanyukov, M. (1994) 'Alcoholism: A Developmental Disorder', *Journal of Consulting and Clinical Psychology*, **62**: 1096–1107.

Taylor, L.D. (1986) 'Opponent Processes and the Dynamics of Consumption', in MacFadyen, A.J. and MacFadyen, H.W. (eds) *Economic Psychology: Intersections in Theory and Application*, Amsterdam, Elsevier: 135–62.

Wells, A. and Matthews, G. (1994) *Attention and Emotion: A Clinical Perspective*, Exeter, Lawrence Erlbaum Associates.

Addictive Buying

First mentioned in the psychiatric literature in the 1920s, in recent years addictive buying has been put on the research agenda again since it has become a prevalent problem in modern Western societies. Estimates are that between 1 and 5 per cent of the general population are addicted to buying (see, Faber and O'Guinn, 1992; Lejoyeux et al., 1996; Scherhorn, Reisch and Raab, 1990).

This form of buying has been defined as having an addictive propensity and/or compulsive trait, arising from persistently assailing, repetitive motive(s) to buy which are mostly irresistible, pleasurable and/or relieving, but will ultimately cause harm to the individual and/or others (Nataraajan and Goff, 1991; O'Guinn and Faber, 1989).

Most authors refer to this deviant form of consumer behaviour as compulsive buying. But this may not be the best terminology to use, as Scherhorn (1990) first emphasized. In 1994, Schlosser et al. showed empirically that, on the one hand, addictive buying shares many superficial similarities with obsessive compulsive disorders, such as being repetitive and problematic; on the other hand, the behaviour has many characteristics in common with other impulse control disorders such as pathological gambling or binge eating. At present, researchers are still unclear about the relationship between this form of buying behaviour and obsessive–compulsive and impulse-control disorders. Since obsessive–compulsive or impulse-control disorders refer to specific neurotic syndromes, whereas addiction is the overall term consistent with any neurotic style, it seems most appropriate to use the more general term 'addiction' for the observed buying phenomena.

Following the definition by the World Health Organization, addictive behaviour can be identified by six characteristics. Addicts rely on an external source (i) to compensate for an inner deficit or, as others have expressed it, an empty self (ii). Over time the addict becomes dependent on this external source (iii). Dependency in this context means that alternative sources for the gratification of genuine needs are missing. Therefore, the addict feels an irresistible urge to repeatedly engage in the behaviour (iv). Since the underlying 'true' need is never satisfied by the addictive behaviour, the addict feels the need to increase the dosage (v), and if restrained from it experiences withdrawal symptoms (vi) (Scherhorn et al., 1990).

The addictive buying experience
For the specific case of buying addiction, the experience can be described as follows: most buying addicts rely on buying as an external source of mood modification and as a reaction to stress, unpleasant emotions or situations which they seek to avoid. The driving force behind the addiction is not the purchased objects *per se*, but the symbolic properties of the shopping experience. For example, addicted buyers use the experience to receive recognition and acceptance through the attention from sales personnel; as an occasion to fantasize and to escape into a dream world; or as a way to feel powerful and grandiose while spending money (Scherhorn et al., 1990). For many women, going on a shopping spree signifies freedom; freedom from their assigned roles and the freedom to just be (by) themselves. For others receiving the fully packed bags with the purchased items is the driving force behind the addiction. It provides them with the sensation of inner fullness. Once the bags are opened and unpacked, however, this sensation disappears. The purchased items are only of marginal importance to addicted buyers. Some hope to receive compliments and the desired recognition when using the items or giving them away as presents.

Almost all addicted buyers report irresistible urges, uncontrolled needs or mounting tension that they feel can only be relieved by buying (see Lejoyeux et al., 1996). Often they try to resist the impulse and at times several days go by between experiencing the drive and the reaction upon it. Hence, there can be an element of planning in addictive buying, and not all addictive buying is impulsive and spontaneous.

13

The shopping location is mostly chosen purposefully and addicted buyers often specialize in a certain range of shops and items. Multiple purchases of the same item are common. Some addicted buyers get a kick out of finding good bargains, others only buy in exclusive and expensive shops. Overall, the likelihood of engaging in buying is higher during mild to moderate depressive episodes. Where they shop and what they shop for is generally related to their particular or desired self-image. This is evident in addictive buyers hoping to reduce subjectively-felt self-discrepancies and 'to feel more like the person they want to be' through buying.

The buying experience itself is described as pleasurable and is compared to a 'high', a 'buzz' or a 'rush'. Typically, after the buying episode feelings of guilt, anxiety and shame over the buying are experienced. In most studies, addicted buyers describe their buying as causing significant financial or personal problems. Financial problems range from addicted buyers owing $5000 on average for purchases they attribute to addictive buying, to losing their homes because mortgage payments fall behind (Schlosser et al., 1994; compare Lejoyeux et al., 1996). Personal problems include severe depression, feelings of guilt, suicidal tendencies, anxiety, and breakup of relationships or marriages. But despite these problems, at this stage, addicted buyers are unable to stop their behaviour pattern since they have become dependent on it.

Generally speaking, for a person to become dependent on a behaviour, two criteria must be fulfilled — the behaviour must be reliable and predictable. Buying meets these criteria. The buying addict can be almost certain that the buying experiences will give pleasurable feelings, at least momentarily, and that this is the case every time he or she engages in it. This intermittent positive effect is a powerfully influential factor and reinforces the behaviour. Thereby thoughts about long-term negative consequences such as mounting debts are repressed or ignored (Orford, 1985).

Profile of an addicted buyer
With regard to age, income, education, marital status or geographical locations, so far only small or inconsistent differences have been found between 'normal' and addicted buyers. However, numerous studies have shown that addicted buyers have lower self-esteem than average (for example, O'Guinn and Faber, 1989; Scherhorn et al., 1990); and higher levels of depression (Scherhorn et al., 1990; Valence, d'Astous and Fortier, 1988). Moreover, they attain higher scores on a general test of obsessive–compulsiveness (O'Guinn and Faber, 1989; Scherhorn at al., 1990). Others studies have shown that major mood, anxiety, substance use, eating and impulse-control disorders are more prevalent among addicted buyers than they are in the general population (see Black, 1996). Another distinction is that addicted buyers are more materialistic than average,

but not more possessive. Their attitude to material things indicates a strong belief that consumption and the acquisition of consumer goods is an important route to success, happiness and self-definition.

Both women and men can become addicted to buying, but the percentage of women is higher. From a large random sample of the West German population, a 60:40 ratio was estimated; in other studies it has been as much as 90:10. The more extreme ratios are likely as a result of methodological artefacts of the ways the samples were constructed (see Faber and O'Guinn, 1988; Scherhorn et al., 1990). Nevertheless, addiction to buying can be regarded as more likely to appeal to women. For women, shopping is a significant aspect of their 'work', and the construction and maintenance of their self-identities are more likely to depend on it. In addition, fashion ideals strongly influence how the 'ideal' woman is supposed to look. This pushes many women towards buying items like clothes and cosmetics in the hope of achieving this idealized image. This is especially true for women who are addicted to buying. They focus primarily on buying clothes, shoes, jewellery and cosmetics. In addition they frequently buy household goods, books, magazines and groceries — those categories of items that are closely linked to their sense of self. A parallel pattern can be observed in addicted male buyers. They buy mainly technical appliances, things for the car, sports equipment, antiques, clothes and other prestige items — generally items in accordance with their image of an 'ideal' man.

Socialization into buying addiction

Buying addiction often has its roots in childhood and adolescence. Addicted buyers are more likely to come from families with a history of addictive behaviours and mental disorders (Lejoyeux et al., 1996; Black, 1996), and family types that are close and authoritarian (Faber and O'Guinn, 1988). They were socialized to appear to get along with others and to give in to people's desires rather then to express their own opinion. As children, the later buying addicts often tried hard to please their parents but failed (Faber and O'Guinn, 1988). Some were spoiled by an overcaring parent or subject to inconsistent parental behaviour. Independent of parenting style, a very common experience for all addicted buyers was that instead of love, time and attention, they received money and presents. The genuine need for tenderness and bodily nearness remained unsatisfied (Scherhorn et al., 1990). In summary, family circumstances were not very favourable for the buying addict to develop a healthy and stable sense of self during childhood (for example, Faber and O'Guinn, 1988; Krueger, 1988). In addition, their receipt of money or gifts as a replacement for love and attention constituted a first model to equate the gratification of non-material needs such as love, attention and approval with material goods. A well-established observation through all studies is that the main motivation for addicted buyers to engage in buying is to enhance self-esteem and to restore a depleted sense of self. They hope to achieve this through the above 'add-on' functions of buying, but an activity like buying can never fulfil this expectation over the long run. The underlying genuine non-material need cannot be satisfied. This results in the buying addict trying even harder by increasing the frequency of buying. McElroy et al. (1994) report a range of one to 30 episodes a month, with occurrences varying from one to seven hours in duration. In extreme cases the buying addict experiences withdrawal symptoms such as headaches, fever and dizziness when restrained from buying (Scherhorn et al., 1990).

Differences between 'normal' and addicted consumers

It has been argued in the literature that seeking immediate gratification from buying may also be a motive for 'normal' consumers (d'Astous and Trembly, 1988). The question has been posed whether addicted buyers are different from 'normal' consumers and whether there exists a continuum. Some of the main psychological and biographical differences have been presented above, the most important being feelings about one's self-worth. Nonaddicts have a fairly stable sense of self and even though they may engage in buying to correct temporary imbalances such as mood shifts, for them buying is but one means of achieving this. Addicted buyers reach a point where buying remains the only alternative, becomes difficult to control and leads to severe consequences and life disruption. Thus, it can be inferred that the urge to buy lies on a continuum and exists in the general population of consumers, and only when certain conditions and circumstances are present do people become addicted to it.

Treatment suggestions

Several suggestions for helping individuals overcome pathological buying behaviours have been put forward. These range from therapies in the psychoanalytical and psychodynamic tradition (for example, Krueger, 1988) to cognitive behaviour therapy (Elliott, 1994) and psychiatric treatment (see Black, 1996). Knowledge about the appropriateness and success of these therapies is limited. This is largely the result of an acceptance problem since, unfortunately, the addicted buyer is often treated like the alcoholic of the 1920s when alcoholism was not yet recognized as a problem and jokes about the town drunk abounded. But this does not mean that there is no help available at all. In recent years a number of self-help groups have been founded across the US and in some European countries, from which people can benefit from the understanding and support given by others who are afflicted with similar problems.

SUSANNE FRIESE

Bibliography

Black, D.W. (1996) 'Compulsive Buying: A Review', *Journal of Clinical Psychiatry*, **57** (supplement 8): 50–55.

d'Astous, A. and Trembly, S. (1988) 'The Compulsive Side of "Normal" Consumers: An Empirical Study', in Avlonitis, G.J., Papavasiliou, N.K. and Kouremenos, A.G. (eds) *Marketing Thought and Practice in the 1990s*, Volumr 1, Athens, The Athens School of Economic and Business Science: 657–69.

Elliott, R. (1994) 'Addictive Consumption: Function and Fragmentation in Postmodernity', *Journal of Consumer Policy*, **17**:159–79.

Faber, R.J. and O'Guinn, T.C. (1988) 'Compulsive Consumption and Credit Abuse', *Journal of Consumer Policy*, **11**: 109–21.

Faber, R.J. and O'Guinn, T.C. (1992) 'A Clinical Screener for Compulsive Buying', *Journal of Consumer Research*, **19**: 459–69.

Krueger, D.W. (1988) 'On Compulsive Shopping and Spending: A Psychodynamic Inquiry', *American Journal of Psychotherapy*, **62**: 574–84.

Lejoyeux, M., Adès, J., Tassain, V. and Solomon, J. (1996) 'Phenomenology and Psychopathology of Uncontrolled Buying', *American Journal of Psychiatry*, **153**: 1424–529.

McElroy, S.L., Keck, P.E., Pope, H.G., Smith, J.M.R. and Strakowski, S.M. (1994) 'Compulsive Buying: A Report of 20 Cases', *Journal of Clinical Psychiatry*, **55**: 242–8.

Nataraajan, R. and Goff, B.G. (1991) 'Compulsive Buying: Towards a Reconceptualization', in Rudmin, F.W. (ed.) 'To Have Possessions: Handbook on Ownership and Property' (Special Issue), *Journal of Social Behavior and Personality*, **6**: 307–28.

O'Guinn, T.C. and Faber, R.J. (1989) 'Compulsive Buying: A Phenomenological Exploration', *Journal of Consumer Research*, **16**: 147–57.

Orford, J. (1985), *Excessive Appetites: A Psychological View of Addictions*, Chichester, John Wiley.

Scherhorn, G. (1990) 'The Addictive Trait of Buying Behaviour,' *Journal of Consumer Policy*, **13**: 33–51.

Scherhorn, G., Reisch, L. and Raab, G. (1990) 'Addictive Buying in West Germany: An Empirical Study', *Journal of Consumer Policy*, **13**: 355–87.

Schlosser, S., Black, D.W., Repertinger, S. and Freet, D. (1994) 'Compulsive Buying: Demography, Phenomenology, and Comorbidity in 46 Subjects', *General Hospital Psychiatry*, **16**: 205–12.

Valence, G., d'Astous, A. and L. Fortier, L. (1988) 'Compulsive Buying: Concept and Measurement', *Journal of Consumer Policy*, **11**: 419–33.

Altruism

Altruism can be defined as individual behaviour that helps another at personal cost. Two sets of questions have been asked by researchers about the phenomenon. The first set concerns the kind of person who exhibits altruistic behaviour. Is there an altruistic personality? If so, does it have a genetic component? Does it have a learned component?

The second set of questions concerns the kinds of situations that produce altruistic behaviour. Here it is useful to distinguish between micro and macro behaviour. At the micro or individual level of analysis, a situational cue arouses a person's latent motive to help. At the macro level of analysis, a situational cue causes altruistic and selfish people to jointly produce helping behaviour.

The altruistic personality

Experimental evidence is consistent with the hypothesis that there is an altruistic personality. Central to this personality is the capacity for empathy. A brief description of an experiment with subjects who were college students is illustrative. Carlo et al. (1991) manipulated the emotional evocativeness and ease of escape from a situation that offered the possibility of helping a woman in distress. Students with high scores on dispositional altruism assisted most when it would have been easy for them to forgo helping her. They were particularly sensitive to her distress cues.

In the nature–nurture debate about the origins of empathy, Eisenberg (1992) is sceptical about evidence of a genetic origin and favours the case for nurture. She concludes: 'In general, cultures and families are likely to produce prosocial children when cooperation, helpfulness, generosity, and harmony are valued and modeled, children are loved and treated with respect, and the similarity of diverse groups of people is emphasized' (p.144). In other words, empathy is learned in early childhood. Piliavin and Charng (1990) are more open to the evidence on genetic origins of empathy and cite several studies conducted during the 1980s which present evidence for both genetic and learned components.

Situations that produce altruistic behaviour

Piliavin and Charng also surveyed the literature on situational determinants of altruistic behaviour. Surprisingly, the best-known situational effect in the literature that affects the likelihood of an individual's response to a call for help is 'the bystander effect', not the emotional evocativeness of the call. An individual is less likely to respond if he or she believes that there are others who will. He or she is also less likely to respond if the perceived personal cost is high.

These findings suggest that selfish and altruistic personalities coexist and that selfish personalities constitute the majority in the population at large. The terms on which the two kinds of personalities interact — competitive or cooperative — depend on the arena in which they interact. Organizations and groups circumscribe the arena. The literature contains models of interaction in several kinds of organizations: the family, the firm, governmental and nongovernmental organizations. Each person selects membership in different structures for different purposes.

Models of organizational and group behaviour

The family

Becker (1981; 2nd edn, 1991) developed a model of mating and a model of interaction between altruists and egoists within the family. In the marriage market, he postulated that altruists were likely to marry altruists. However, they might have some selfish offspring. In any case, the altruistic patriarch could motivate cooperative behaviour within the family by a system of financial rewards and penalties. To illustrate: if a 'rotten kid' hurt his sister, the altruist would reduce the kid's allowance and compensate his sister. The altruist's utility was dependent on the utility of the family members. By maximizing his own utility, he would bind the members of the family together.

The majority of contemporary economic research on altruism in the family is devoted to testing and exploring variations on Becker's theories. Frank (1988) constructed a model that explained how altruists could find and marry each other in a society where altruists and egoists coexist. He hypothesized that genetic and/or cultural conditioning of emotional reactions made it possible for altruists to recognize each other and cited social psychological research findings on Thematic Apperception Tests (TATs) to support his hypothesis.

A TAT is a personality test based on imaginative stories written in response to word or picture cues. Motives are measured by scoring the stories for themes. Frank used the TAT motive for intimacy to measure altruistic motivation. Individuals who measured high on this motive were highly successful economically and in marriage. They had established long-term stable cooperative relationships.

Frank also tested his model with a prisoner's dilemma game (PDG). In his experiment, he allowed the players to interact socially before playing the game and asked that they predict their partner's behaviour: cooperate or defect. The percentage of cooperative predictions was greater than would be expected by chance. He inferred that by reading telltale signs such as facial expressions and tone of voice, cooperators were able to find others they could trust.

In a PDG, altruism is defined as playing the cooperative strategy. The game dramatizes the conflict between individual and social welfare and the importance of establishing trust between potential cooperators. PDGs have been used for over twenty years to study altruistic behaviour: see Collard (1978) and Stark (1995).

Phelps (1988, 1991) tested Becker's hypothesis that the altruistic patriarch maximizes his utility. She used the TAT motive to affiliate to measure altruistic motivation and family income to measure the money value of the altruist's utility. Psychologists think that the affiliation motive taps both positive and negative valences of the desire to be helpful. They believe that the negative valences stem from deprivation of affection and feelings of guilt for not having maintained friendships.

The tests, based on cross-section data from the US in 1957 and 1976, resulted in rejecting Becker's hypothesis. The data for 1957 revealed polarized altruism; that is, after controlling for human capital variables, men with altruistic motivation had both the highest and the lowest family incomes. By 1976, polarized altruism had disappeared. Men with power motivation had the highest family income.

Phelps's results are consistent with the hypothesis that the moral dimension (guilt) is measured by the motive to affiliate and that the moral dimension inhibits the pursuit of economic power. Her results can be read as a test of Etzioni's (1988) theory of moral obligation.

Phelps found other evidence of altruistic bonds in the family. Altruistic men were more likely to share child-care time equally with their wives than power-motivated men. Altruistic wives were more likely to participate in the labour force than wives with other motivation, but power-motivated wives outranked them in earnings (Phelps, 1995). Furthermore, altruistic wives were more likely than power-motivated wives to report that their children's achievements were a source of their satisfaction. Such parental behaviours are consistent with the evolutionary survival of altruism. However, she also found that the offspring of divorce are less likely to be altruistic than the offspring of intact families, a result with gloomy implications for the evolution of altruism (Phelps, 1998).

Altonji, Hayashi and Kotlikoff (1992) did another kind of test of the evolutionary success of altruism. They used food consumption and resource data for parent–offspring pairs from the Panel Study of Income Dynamics to test the hypothesis that the families were altruistically linked. They rejected the hypothesis after finding no evidence of an intergenerational budget constraint. However, their test was flawed because it did not include an empirical measure of the parents' motivation. It did not distinguish between selfish and altruistic parents. In fact, Becker postulated that selfish parents would not use their income to bind the family together.

The Firm
Simon (1993) based a theory of cooperative behaviour in the firm on the concept of bounded rationality. He argued that human beings tend to follow group norms because they have incomplete information and limited capacity to process the information they do have. That group norms induce altruistic behaviour is also a dominant theme in the sociology literature (again, see Etzioni, 1988). Simon thinks that group loyalty is a factor determining the evolutionary success of a

firm. Loyalty to a group provides the basis for cooperation within it, and hence for the organization to make adjustments necessary for survival in a turbulent environment.

The government

Although governmental organizations are formed to deliver public goods, history is filled with examples of public servants who used public office for selfish purposes. The checks and balances built into democratic governments are history's response to the need to monitor opportunism. The mechanisms that enable democracy to survive are the same as those that nourish the evolution of altruism. Although the neoclassical theory of voting behaviour dominates the literature on governmental behaviour, a new perspective is emerging. For example, Rasinski and Rosenbaum (1987) provided evidence of altruistic voting.

Nongovernmental organizations (NGOs)

Meyer (1995) developed a model of interaction between altruists and egoists in NGOs and applied the model to two case studies in environmental protection. The terms of the interaction in both cases were cooperative.

These cases can also be explained by Etzioni's (1988) theory of encapsulated competition. The formation of the NGOs helped to segregate economic power from political power and to increase the probability that the capsule, Planet Earth, will survive. The NGOs facilitated the transfer of funds from for-profit firms to groups engaged in conservation. The NGOs have been in existence sufficiently long to test the hypothesis of the New Institutional Economics that asymmetric information and uncertainty lead to self-interest seeking with guile (opportunism). However, evidence of opportunism has not emerged. It is possible that the reason for this is that altruists within the groups monitor the behaviour of egoists. Another possibility is that both altruists and egoists are bound by a moral obligation to preserve the ecology.

Piliavin and Charng (1990) provided a bibliography on altruistic behaviour in other nongovernmental organizations. They distinguished between two broad kinds of behaviour: gifts of time and money. 'The commonest form of voluntary action in the United States is the donation of money to charitable causes.' They listed the top three causes: religion, education and health.

CHARLOTTE D. PHELPS

Bibliography
Altonji, J.G., Hayashi, F. and Kotlikoff, L.J. (1992) 'Is the Extended Family Altruistically Linked? Direct Tests Using Micro Data', *American Economic Review*, **82**: 1177–98.

Becker, Gary S. (1981; 2nd edn, 1991) *A Treatise on the Family*, Cambridge, MA, Harvard University Press.

Carlo, G., Eisenberg, N., Froyer, D., Switzer, G. and Speer, A.L. (1991) 'The Altruistic Personality: In What Contexts is it Apparent?', *Journal of Personality and Social Psychology*, **61**: 450–58.

Collard, D. (1978) *Altruism and Economy: A Study in Non-Selfish Economics*, New York, Oxford University Press.

Eisenberg, N. (1992) *The Caring Child*, Cambridge, MA, Harvard University Press.

Etzioni, A. (1988) *The Moral Dimension: Toward a New Economics*, New York, Free Press.

Frank, R.H. (1988) *Passions Within Reason: The Strategic Role of the Emotions*, New York, W.W. Norton.

Meyer, C.A. (1995) 'Opportunism and NGOs: Entrepreneurship and Green North–South Transfers', *World Development*, **23**: 1277–90.

Phelps, C.D. (1988) 'Caring and Family Income, *Journal of Economic Behavior and Organization*, **10**: 83–98.

Phelps, C.D. (1991) 'The Disappearance of Polarized Altruism', *Journal of Economic Behavior and Organization*, **15**: 91–113.

Phelps, C.D. (1995) 'Wives' Motives and Fertility', *Journal of Economic Behavior and Organization*, **27**: 49–67.

Phelps, C.D. (1998) 'Gender Differences in the Long-Term Economic Consequences of Parental Divorce', forthcoming in *Journal of Economic Behavior and Organization*.

Piliavin, J.A. and Charng, H.-W. (1990) 'Altruism: A Review of Recent Theory and Research', *Annual Review of Sociology*, 16: 27–65.

Rasinski, K.A. and Rosenbaum, S.M. (1987) 'Predicting Citizen Support of Tax Increases for Education: A Comparison of Two Social Psychological Perspectives', *Journal of Applied Social Psychology*, **17**: 990–1006.

Simon, H.A. (1993) 'Altruism and Economics', in a symposium held at the 1993 meetings of the American Economic Association: 'The Economics of Altruism', *American Economic Review*, **83(2)**: 156–61.

Stark, O. (1995) *Altruism and Beyond: An Economic Analysis of Transfers and Exchanges Within Families and Groups*, Cambridge, Cambridge University Press.

Animal Experiments in Economics

Experimental studies of animal behaviour in economics have been predominantly devoted to investigating the neoclassical paradigm of individual choice behaviour — the Slutsky–Hicks theory of consumer demand and labour supply behaviour and expected utility theory. The original motivation for these experiments was twofold. First, there was a need to establish a clear connection between the primitive economic concepts underlying neoclassical models of individual choice and the data used to test these models. This is difficult to establish with field data because predictions of the model break down when applied to aggregate time series or cross-sectional data (the kind of data usually available to economists), except under very restrictive assumptions about preferences (assumptions which are not satisfied even for simple animal consumers; Kagel, Battalio and Green, 1995). Second, the study of laboratory animals permits precise, well-controlled *experiments* to investigate elementary principles of microeconomic theory using outcomes of real consequence with well-motivated subjects. With human subjects it is often impossible or too expensive to study certain economic phenomena under relevant conditions with real outcomes of significant value.

An obvious first question involved in such a research programme (for an economist at least) is whether there is any basis for supposing that the kinds of 'rational' hedonistic calculations that underlie economic models apply to typical laboratory animals such as rats and pigeons. (In addition, a question for psychologist collaborators is whether economic theory had any new, interesting insights into animal behaviour.) It did not take long to find ample evidence collected by experimental psychologists and behavioural biologists that animals do indeed respond to the basic cost–benefit calculations underlying economic theory. We then set about devising our own experiments to test more precisely many of the implications of the theory. In operationalizing the theory we adopted the experimental methodology developed by operant psychologists, without necessarily endorsing their theoretical framework.

Initial questions focused on the negativity of 'own substitution effects' for income-compensated price changes in a two-commodity world (Kagel et al., 1975). We employed Slutsky-compensated price changes: after first determining baseline consumption levels, the relative prices of the two commodities are changed while income is simultaneously adjusted so that the consumer is still able to purchase baseline levels of both goods. To the extent that the two goods are substitutable and consumers' preferences are 'consistent' over time, the theory predicts *increased* consumption of the good whose relative price is *decreased* and *reduced* consumption of the good whose relative price is *increased*. In these experiments we used a 'vending machine' paradigm in which rats were studied in a Skinner box equipped with two response levers. Presses on one lever would deliver a predetermined amount of commodity *A* (water or root beer) and presses on the other lever would deliver a predetermined amount of commodity *B* (Noyes food pellets or Tom Collins mix). Since for the particular consumers in question — rats — handling and exchanging money or tokens is a time-consuming behaviour to learn, the 'income constraint' was operationalized as the number of lever presses allowable in an experimental session. Thus 'prices' are naturally defined in terms of the amount of the commodity delivered for a lever press, and prices are varied by changing the amount of the commodity delivered per press. (See Kagel et al., 1995, for more detailed discussion of the underlying theory along with descriptions and results from alternative procedures used to operationalize the theory.)

Remarkably enough, the results from these experiments were overwhelmingly consistent with the neoclassical theory. In experiments in which rats' daily intake of food and water were the commodities to be 'purchased' during the experimental session, 86 per cent of all income-compensated price changes reduced consumption of the good whose relative price increased, and the median price elasticity of demand was –0.08 (Kagel et al., 1995). Although price elasticities were relatively small, there were occasions when the ratio of food to water consumption showed substantial changes, and these were accompanied by significant weight changes. (Apparently, internal metabolic changes could not compensate for the changes in food intake.) In experiments where rats chose between nonessential commodities such as root beer and Tom Collins mix, with *ad libitum* access to food and water, 100 per cent of the income-compensated price changes resulted in reduced consumption of the good whose relative price increased, and the median price elasticity was –0.59. The marked differences in price elasticities are entirely consistent with a priori assumptions about differential degrees of substitutability between essential and nonessential commodities.

We also conducted experiments with income-constant price changes. In this research, relative prices are changed but income is held constant. With 'normal' goods (goods whose consumption covaries positively with income changes) the predictions are that consumption should decrease with price increases, and that there should be larger (absolute) price elasticities than under income-compensated price changes. These predictions were verified in both essential and nonessential commodity experiments. In contrast, for inferior goods, consumption moves inversely to price changes. Consequently, when real income is reduced because of a price increase, consumption of an inferior good can go up or down depending on whether the magnitude of the income effect exceeds or falls short of the substitution effect. In the former case we have a Giffen good whose consumption actually increases when its price rises. This counterintuitive prediction of the theory has been virtually impossible to confirm using field data, but has been supported in the laboratory (Battalio, Kagel and Kogut, 1991; Hastjarjo, Silberberg and Hursh, 1990). Indeed, the primary difficulty in identifying a Giffen good was in devising a commodity that was strongly inferior and took up a relatively large portion of the budget, as is required by the theory.

These results (arguably) provide the first real tests of neoclassical demand theory. Some economists have embraced the results to support extensions of economic theory beyond its traditional purview of market behaviour, for example, to such diverse areas as love and marriage, medieval agriculture, and crime and punishment. Resistance to such extensions often revolves around the view that these behaviours are dominated by nonrational considerations. Consequently, extending economic theory to such presumably 'nonrational' agents as laboratory animals provides rather striking support for the theory, and indirectly, for these other extensions of the theory (although our experiments provide virtually no insight into the auxiliary hypotheses required in these applications regarding the detailed nature of preferences, such as the relative size of income and substitution effects).

Another major goal of the animal research is to experimentally evaluate competing theoretical explanations. Alternative explanations include random behaviour models drawn from the economics literature (Becker, 1962), optimal foraging models from behavioural biology, and, most directly, rival explanations from animal psychologists (for example, the matching law; Herrnstein, 1970). After all, this particular exercise in economic imperialism tramples most directly on psychologists' turf, adapting their experimental technologies to the study of economic behaviour.

Although these jousts have yet to yield a unifying behavioural heuristic underlying the animals' behaviour, advances have been made. Random behaviour models have been soundly disconfirmed. The matching law and melioration theory have been called into question: for complimentary goods such as food and water, response ratios move *inversely* to obtained reinforcement ratios, a result consistent with economic theory, but not the matching law (Rachlin et al., 1981). Although a consensus has yet to emerge, it seems safe to say that such fundamental economic concepts as income and substitution effects will be essential elements in the experimental and theoretical analysis of choice between qualitatively different reinforcers.

One should have no illusions about what these results imply about the 'rationality' or 'optimality' of animals' choices. Behaviour is deemed rational/optimal in the sense that it is consistent with the axioms of the Slutsky–Hicks theory of consumer behaviour. However, an economist's notion of optimality differs fundamentally from that of the biologist. For the economist, preferences are taken as given, and are not subject to dispute. As long as the consumer obtains his or her most preferred consumption bundle subject to his or her budget constraint, behaviour is optimal even if these preferences produce consumption patterns detrimental to the consumer's health. In contrast, for the biologist, optimality means maximizing inclusive fitness. As such, optimizing with respect to preferences that are detrimental to inclusive fitness would be treated as suboptimal. Of course, inclusive fitness becomes difficult to define once one incorporates uncertainty or distinctions between long- versus short-run survival requirements. And the biologist is keenly aware that evolutionary processes respond neither so finely nor so rapidly to environmental shifts that inclusive fitness might never be fully maximized.

Questions naturally arise concerning the usefulness of experiments with animal subjects for understanding human behaviour. In using animals to better understand human behaviour we take as our starting-point that there is behavioural as well as physiological continuity across species. This notion of behavioural continuity is well established in psychology and behavioural biology, both of which have well-developed subdisciplines that incorporate animal experiments. Given that experiments with laboratory animals provide a means to investigate elementary microeconomic principles, the question becomes: 'If basic economic principles do not apply to the relatively simple choice situations involved in these experiments, then how can they be relied upon to account for behaviour in substantially more complex situations?'.

In studying consumer demand and labour supply behaviour of rats and pigeons we are not studying the behaviour of simplified humans. The behaviour of a given species is constrained by its ecological niche, which is distinctive to the species in question. As such, there can be no general answer to the species extrapolation problem. Rather, the presumption is that a theory that works well across species has a greater likelihood of being valid and useful than one that works well with only one, or a limited set of, species.

Experimental studies with animals have gone beyond looking at simple principles of economic behaviour and have begun to address more complicated social issues. How does one go from testing general principles of economics to social issues such as the disincentive effects of welfare programmes for the poor? Is it not one thing to use animal experiments to test general theoretical principles in economics — such as the effects of income-compensated wage changes — but altogether different to argue that these results have implications for income-leisure decisions of humans? The answer to this is, we think, both yes and no. After all, it is the Slutsky–Hicks theory's prediction that income-compensated wage decreases will reduce labour supply that underlies economists' concern about the potential disincentive effects of welfare on labour supply (see Kagel et al., 1995: 101–3 and references cited.) Consequently, experimental verification of this basic principle would seem, to us at least, to heighten these concerns. On the other hand, the size of any disincentive effect depends crucially on the substitutability of income for leisure and how much leisure increases in response to increases in unearned income. And laboratory experiments in general, no less experiments with pigeons and rats, may have precious little to tell us about the likely magnitudes of such effects in relevant field settings.

JOHN H. KAGEL

Bibliography

Battalio, R.C., Kagel, J.H. and Kogut, C.A. (1991) 'Experimental Confirmation of the Existence of a Giffen Good', *American Economic Review*, **81**: 961–70.
Becker, G.S. (1962) 'Irrational Behavior and Economic Theory', *Journal of Political Economy*, **70**: 1–13.

Hastjarjo, T., Silberberg, A. and Hursh, S.R. (1990) 'Quinine Pellets as an Inferior Good and a Giffen Good in Rats', *Journal of the Experimental Analysis of Behavior*, **53**: 263–71.

Herrnstein, R.J. (1970) 'On the Law of Effect', *Journal of the Experimental Analysis of Behavior*, **13**: 243–66.

Kagel, J.H., Battalio, R.C. and Green, L. (1995) *Economic Choice Theory*, New York, Cambridge University Press.

Kagel, J.H., Battalio, R.C., Rachlin, H., Green, L., Basmann, R.L. and Klemm, W.R. (1975) 'Experimental Studies of Consumer Demand Behavior Using Laboratory Animals', *Economic Inquiry*, **13**: 22–38.

Rachlin, H., Battalio, R., Kagel, J.H. and Green, L. (1981) 'Maximization Theory in Behavioral Psychology', *The Behavioral and Brain Sciences*, **4**: 371–417 (with commentaries).

Anthropology and Consumer Behaviour

A small number of well-known economists such as George Akerlof, Kenneth Arrow, Amartya Sen and Albert Hirschman have operated at times on the borderline between economics and anthropology. The work of George Akerlof demonstrates how integrating certain findings, particularly different behavioural assumptions, from anthropology (as well as from psychology and sociology) directly into the economist's models can solve problems that otherwise have baffled economists. Akerlof spent a year in India, read much cultural anthropology and has written papers on the caste system, loyalty filters and gift exchange. Kenneth Arrow has also acknowledged his interest in the work of anthropologists including Margaret Mead, Ruth Benedict and Franz Boas, and is particularly concerned about differences in performance among ethnic groups, or how cultural diversity or homogeneity affects productivity (see Swedberg, 1990).

Similarly, the work of anthropologists has demonstrated the variety and diversity of economic behaviour and the role of cultural analysis in explaining the shaping of value, taste and consumer demand. Whereas psychology focuses on individuals, their personality, motivation and disorders, and the voluntary bonds between people, the anthropologist sees consumer behaviour as part of a social process where cultural norms determine consumption patterns and saving decisions. Individuals have social obligations and their reference group imposes values on what is and what is not acceptable consumer behaviour. Human needs are themselves socially determined. Yet there is a wide diversity of social environments with varying consumption rituals so that commodities convey status and rank and can be used as weapons of exclusion to limit their accessibility to certain classes of consumers (Douglas and Isherwood, 1996).

The unique contribution that anthropologists provide is prolonged, intensive and detailed on-the-spot observation of how people actually behave. This contrasts sharply with economists who have been content to see the homogeneous actions of rational economic actors and rely on universal explanations of economic behaviour. Partly, this reflects a choice of research methodology which underlies the relation between economics and other social sciences that work with the more empirical aspects of social phenomenon. Frank Knight (1941: 252–4) expresses this distinction clearly, stating that economics:

> as a science of principles, is not, primarily, a descriptive science in the empirical sense at all . . . Indeed, economics is the only social science which effectively uses inference from clear and statable abstract principles, and especially intuitive knowledge, as a method. In contrast with it, all other social sciences are empirical . . . The relationship between observation, induction from observations, and inference from 'a priori' principles forms the very pivot of the problem of collaboration between the social sciences, and specifically of collaboration between economic theory and the 'quasi-empirical' sciences of history, sociology, and anthropology, including institutional — one might say anthropological — economics.

Methodological differences are important but in practice economists and anthropologists concentrate on different types of markets, pursue different types of questions and use different forms of appraisal. Anthropologists describe the actual characteristics of marketplaces in the Third World or peripheral markets in industrial nations such as the underground economy and illegal transactions. Historically, the discipline of anthropology devoted its attention to the countries being opened up by European colonial expansion where the economy merged with religion and kinship, and in which money, markets and sometimes economic rationality itself were regarded as intrusive. When they focused on industrialized countries they adopted the role of scavenger, picking up matters of peripheral or residual interest to economists: entrepreneurial motivation, collective bargaining, ethnic and gender segregation, social mobility, ideology, trust and altruism.

As economists worked in the marketplace among orderly and rational individuals, anthropologists examined markets where goods are not standardized, the value of goods is frequently incomparable, and the very process of buying and selling is part of the consumption package. Participating in the market itself provides entertainment, and purchases may be incidental or irrelevant to this process. Anthropologists were among the first to uncover informal sector economic activities and other markets variously called black, parallel and fragmented. Fragmented markets, for example, lead to differing prices prevailing for the same goods, services or factors, even if there are no government controls imposed on the market. Work on informal sector activities has now made us more aware of the interdependence of decision making and the role of interlinked markets (for example, the supply of labour to a landlord may be contingent on access to loans and goods from the same landlord).

With respect to the purchase of consumer goods in the market, anthropological work is characterized by a number of themes. Initial concerns related to the rampant consumerism in the Third World. The insistent demand for Western goods by the local peoples was seen as leading to the loss of their own culture and indigenous arts and crafts, in addition to the exploitative conditions of debt-peonage. Attention was given to the sort of new products being introduced into local markets and the effects on changing consumer tastes and preferences in luxury-embodied directions. The impacts on health and inequality were also noted (infant milk formula is a classic example: see Meade and Nason, 1991).

Subsequent work has queried whether the locals are passive victims or active and creative participants in consumerism. Western consumer goods can express the changes in the balance of power between young and old, they can be used to demonstrate prestige and symbolize the escape from the existing social hierarchy. Closer study of the way foreign goods are integrated into autonomous systems of consumption often reveals a creative response to goods in terms of developing new styles of dress so that 'Western goods provided new and increased opportunities for both technological and symbolic innovation' (Humphrey and Hugh-Jones, 1992: 51, 59).

A dominant theme in the anthropological literature is the elaborate set of exchange arrangements found in societies and that economic activities cannot be understood without the specific cultural context. Hence, any analysis of behaviour should give room to cultural peculiarities and complexities. The literature has concentrated on ceremonial exchange (the gift) and on sharing and hierarchical redistribution as well as formalized trades and monetized commodity market exchange. With gift exchange, objects pass between people bound together by social ties and the exchange underwrites social relations, whereas with commodity exchange people can act more as free agents.

It is often claimed that economic activities are embedded in social relations and reciprocity is a common mode of exchange. The kind of relationship between two people determines how they should behave towards each other, which goods and services they can exchange, and what terms of exchange are appropriate. This largely explains why people prefer one mode of transaction over another, why they consider some people better exchange partners than others, and why some material goods cannot be exchanged at all or only in kind. Reciprocal transactions involve the exchange of material goods or services, and serve to create and maintain social relations. People attempt to create long-term social exchange relationships and seek exchange partners who can provide them with the resources they lack, and thereby make provisions to cope with contingencies.

Economists abstract from considerations relating to preference formation, and the impact of social institutions on choice, as they concentrate on the workings of the market mechanism and the signals prices convey with regard to resource allocation. For anthropologists, the terms of exchange in transactions depend on the quality of social relations between the exchange partners. Exchange is analysed within the historical, cultural and political context of the society involved. The focus is always on a specific type of economy, based on distinctive types of social relations, and characterized by a specific combination of modes of exchange. An individual's wants and the types of exchange they create will be culturally defined in particular ways.

For anthropologists, what happens in markets is a serious social process and transactions are guided by considerations of kinship, place of residence, hierarchical status, degree of trust and nationality of traders. Supply and demand factors affect prices but so do a variety of social factors such as religion, status indicators of buyers, traditional norms of just price and even the eagerness of women traders not to sell out quickly because the marketplace is a source of entertainment and social intercourse. The 'Kula ring' was often used as an example that participants may derive more value from participating in exchange than from the intrinsic worth of what they receive.

In this context of social relations the treatment of debt is particularly interesting. In some developing economies, individuals feel very positive about having debts. There may be a general state of mutual indebtedness in the community with a very high proportion of viable householders indebted, and many creditors are also debtors. Individuals are involved in chains of reciprocal obligations and they repay their debts according to the relationship with their creditor. The kind of relationship between the lender and the borrower affects not only the terms of credit, but also the chance of repayment. Debt can be seen as a natural condition, everyone with an idle balance lends it out, and people do not think in terms of the net balance of debit or credit. Indeed, the terms debtor or creditor are often meaningless as are interest rates because borrowing is apt to be timeless.

In some rural settings it is not unusual to save most of one's wealth in non-monetary forms (livestock, jewellery). This saving strategy is to diminish one's holdings of liquid cash, and thereby the associated constant claims of relatives and neighbours, without appearing selfish. When it comes to seeking loans it is relatives and ties of ethnicity that are exploited. Lenders rely heavily on informal social sanctions for repayment. Complex negotiations and calculations are features of the credit acquisition process and it is deeply embedded in religion and culture. In markets where there is a lack of contract enforcement, ill-defined property rights, and a scarcity of collateral, informal sector lenders limit their loans to a small number of individuals who are personally known to the lender and by market interlinking. The latter refers to linking the loan with other transactions such as selling the output to the lender, or providing labour services to, or buying inputs from, the lender. A wide range of monthly interest rates can then emerge, depending on the type of loan and the relationship established with the borrower.

To illustrate these issues in a specific region, economic behaviour in the South Pacific has often baffled economists. Sociocultural behaviour discourages private initiative and saving while promoting immediate consumption. This system requires a person with savings to make them available to any family or village members upon request. It is also frequently mentioned that Pacific Islanders are attracted to entrepreneurship only when they have migrated to a different island where the social obligations are not a burden for them. These practices appear inimical to greater productivity and growth and economists have interpreted them as either irrational or constraints on development that need to be released. Alternatively, they can be interpreted as an attempt by Islanders to maximize collective welfare through a harmonious balance of traditional socio-cultural and material welfare. What to economists are perceived as impediments to growth are to Pacific Islanders fundamental components of their distinctive national culture and identity, and highly valued.

Many anthropologists see the human economy as embedded and enmeshed in economic and noneconomic institutions. Economic behaviour in turn is structured by a complex set of forces, duties and obligations and units of society are examined rather than the atomistic individual producer/consumer. The limits on individual autonomy mean that consumption is channelled in particular ways so that custom and tradition enforce a restricted consumption system. This then opens up the issue of whether people act because of their culture or is culture determined by the ways in which people act? That is, are people encased in a set of customs (a determinist concept of culture) or are they free to shape or mould their environment. Some contemporary formalist anthropologists try to depict institutions as the products of rational choice and regard individual behaviour as responsive to self-interest rather than obedient to social norms.

Much of the preceding discussion and the literature has focused on 'primitive' economies and not on the arguably richer applicability of anthropological ideas to traditional economic concerns. It has been argued that barter, for example, is not a feature of primitive economies only but a contemporary phenomenon covering both large- and small-scale transactions. Similarly, gift exchange is not an archaic relic of the past but prominent today (Humphrey and Hugh-Jones, 1992) and moneyless transactions seem to be on the rise, harking back to earlier anthropological discussions of special and general purpose money. Multiplex relationships — long-term relationships between traders over various commodities and services — also seem to be prominent in contemporary discussions.

It is the precise description of data in which anthropologists immerse themselves that is the distinguishing feature of the profession and this insistence on descriptive realism makes ethnographic studies so attractive to those disillusioned by the excessive abstraction and high theory of modern consumer theory. Anthropological research incorporating the heterogeneity of purchasing and consumption constraints adds much of value to our understanding of economic (and noneconomic) behaviour.

JOHN LODEWIJKS

Bibliography

Bohannan, P. and Dalton, G. (eds) (1962) *Markets in Africa*, Evanston, IL, NorthWestern University Press.

De Marchi, N. and Morgan, M.S. (eds) (1994) *Higgling: Transactors and Their Markets in the History of Economics*, Durham, NC, Duke University Press.

Douglas, M. and Isherwood, B. (1996) *The World of Goods: Towards an Anthropology of Consumption*, New York, Routledge (originally published in 1978, New York, Basic Books).

Humphrey, C. and Hugh-Jones, S. (eds) (1992) *Barter, Exchange and Value: An Anthropological Approach*, Cambridge, Cambridge University Press.

Knight, F.H. (1941) 'Anthropology and Economics', *Journal of Political Economy*, **49**: 247–68.

Lodewijks, J. (1994) 'Anthropologists and Economists: Conflict or Cooperation?', *Journal of Economic Methodology*, **1**: 81–104.

Meade, W.K. and Nason, R.W. (1991) 'Toward a Unified Theory of Macromarketing: A Systems Theoretic Approach', *Journal of Macromarketing*, **11**: 72–82.

Schneider, H.K. (1974) *Economic Man: The Anthropology of Economics*, Salem, WI, Sheffield Publishing Company.

Swedberg, R. (ed.) (1990) *Economics and Sociology: Redefining Their Boundaries, Conversations with Economists and Sociologists*, Princeton, NJ, Princeton University Press.

Attribution Theory

Attribution theory is broadly concerned with understanding how lay people predict, explain and control their social worlds. The fact that these three aims (explanation, prediction and control) are equivalent to standard scientific aims is not accidental, as attribution theory explicitly adopts a model of the lay social perceiver as 'naive scientist'. However, the primary goal of attribution theory is with describing and explaining the cognitive structures and processes involved in the layperson's causal explanations for human behaviour (Ross and Fletcher,

1985). In short, attribution theory is a scientific psychological theory that seeks to explain folk psychological explanations.

Attribution theory (which is a generic term) became one of the most dominant approaches within social psychology in the 1970s and 1980s, and was based on the classic attribution theories of Heider (1958), Jones (Jones and Davis, 1965), Kelley (1967), and Weiner (Weiner et al., 1972). However, it is important to understand that the classic statements of attribution theory, and associated research, predated the emergence of social cognition within social psychology. In contrast to attribution theory, social cognition is more obviously a child of modern cognitive psychology — a pedigree that is clearly evident in social cognition's focus on general features of social information processing (such as encoding, storage and retrieval of information) and its appropriation of methodologies and concepts from cognitive psychology. Accordingly, attribution theory has been heavily influenced in the last 15 years by recent developments in social psychology, most notably by the rise of social cognitive approaches.

Attribution theory, in both its classic and more contemporary versions, has been exported, developed and tested within a wide range of applied domains including consumer research and economic psychology. Various reviews of attribution research in the consumer and economic domain have been published including Mizerski, Golden and Kernan (1979), Van Raaij (1986) and Folkes (1988). Attribution research in consumer and economic psychology has covered a wide range of topics including the effects of advertising, lay inferences about advertisers' motives, lay attributions for product purchases, product failures and unemployment. I shall briefly describe the research examining attributions for unemployment to illustrate the contributions that such applied research has produced.

The classic attribution statements all assume that the internal–external dimension is a key causal dimension (among others including stability). Research on the perceived causes of unemployment supports this assumption, with the well-replicated finding that perceived causes for unemployment fall either into an internal category (for example, lack of effort, lack of ability), or into an external category (for example, luck, government policies) (for reviews see Feather, 1990; and Lewis, Webley and Furnham, 1995). Research has found that (i) unemployed people make more external attributions for unemployment than employed people (for example, Furnham, 1982a); (ii) unemployed people who make more uncontrollable attributions (either internal or external) tend to become more depressed (for example, Feather and O'Brian, 1986), and (iii) conservative prior belief systems are associated with making more internal attributions for unemployment, such as laziness or lack of ability (for example, Feather and O'Brian, 1986; Furnham, 1982b).

The research on unemployment thus illustrates some key themes that are consistent with a wide array of other attribution research. First, prior beliefs, expectations, or cognitive styles influence the fashion in which attributions are made. Second, attributions tend to be organized around causal dimensions such as internality or stability. Third, the nature of attributions can have important psychological consequences for the individual.

One advantage of such applied research is that it can uncover important features of the attribution process that are not so readily revealed using standard laboratory-based tasks. For example, Furnham and Hesketh (1989) compared attributions for unemployment in Great Britain and New Zealand, two countries that have much in common politically, socially and historically. As expected, they found that unemployment in New Zealand tended to be explained via internal rather than external societal causes, whereas in Great Britain the reverse was the case. The most obvious explanation concerns the different unemployment rates in the two countries at the time the studies were completed: 12 per cent in Great Britain and 4 per cent in New Zealand. Consistent with Kelley's (1967) attribution theory, the higher base rate of unemployment in Britain apparently encouraged attributions to the external situation, as compared to New Zealand.

A central point illustrated by this study is that lay attributions do not operate in a social vacuum, divorced from physical and social reality. As Feather (1990: 127) put it:

> the explanations that people give for events such as poverty and unemployment can be understood not only as products of cognitive processing but as social products as well. . . . The views about social reality that emerge involve integrated systems of beliefs, attitudes, and values that have some consistency about them and that are important in social judgment, social interaction and self-definition. . . . Their reality is a psychological reality that may involve both accurate and inaccurate inferences from the social world as it exists.

One of the findings noted above was that unemployed people make more external attributions for unemployment than do employed people. Two plausible explanations for this finding seem likely. Unemployed people may be motivated to avoid attributing the causes to themselves in order to maintain a positive self-image. Conversely, unemployed folk may know more unemployed people than do employed people, and generally be more knowledgeable concerning the difficulty of obtaining a job. Thus, attributional differences between employed and unemployed people could result from both groups making rational inferences from their own available knowledge bases.

The two styles of explanation just advanced for attribution differences in employed versus unemployed people reprise a general argument that has been played out many times in psychology concerning the nature of the social perceiver. Indeed, a key argument in consumer and economic psychology has concerned whether the layperson is best thought of in rational terms or as a biased and flawed cognizer. Precisely the same argument has occupied central stage in attribution theory, social psychology, and more recently in cognitive science (see Fletcher, 1995). As previously noted, the classic statements in attribution theory assumed that laypeople were like scientists both in terms of their aims (explanation, prediction and control) and in relation to the rationality of their attribution processes. However, by the 1980s, under the burgeoning influence of social cognitive approaches, the layperson came to be seen as a flawed and hopelessly biased cognizer, motivated by the need to maintain a positive self-concept rather than in terms of striving for the truth (see Fletcher, 1995).

More recently, a rough consensus has emerged that stresses the ability of humans to be both — or either — self-serving and biased or rational and scientific. Which cognitive style is adopted depends on a multitude of conditions including individual differences, motivating conditions, memory and attentional demands, social context and so forth (see Fletcher, 1995). The same conclusion will almost certainly apply to attribution processes in consumer and economic spheres. For example, a consumer may buy a brand of toothpaste (a low-cost decision) because of an unthinking acceptance of the message that using this brand is associated with having a successful life and being wildly attractive to the opposite sex. On the other hand, observing sexy models draped over cars may have minimal influence on a car-buying decision (a high-cost decision) compared to the careful analysis of more mundane information (such as gas consumption and reliability).

As noted in Feather's (1990) comment cited previously, laypeople (like scientists) can produce both accurate and inaccurate attributions. Indeed, there has recently been a strong resurgence of interest in mainstream psychology concerning the causes and consequences of accuracy in social judgements (see Fletcher, 1995). This issue has been studied very little in consumer and economic psychology. However, given the important consequences attendant on the truth or otherwise of our attributions and other judgements, this topic may well become an important one in this domain

In the last decade or so, research concerned solely with attribution processes has waned considerably in mainstream psychology, and in applied areas including consumer and economic psychology. However, in my view this has not occurred because of doubts about the importance of explanatory cognitive processes. Rather, psychologists, partly under the influence of social cognitive approaches, have sought to incorporate attribution processes into more general social cognitive theories (see, for example, Fletcher and Thomas, 1996). The same tendency is apparent in consumer and economic psychology, with attempts being made to incorporate attribution theory into more general theoretical accounts (for example, Feather, 1990; Lewis et al., 1995). Along with this theoretical development, an increasing amount of research is being published which measures attributions as simply one variable among other variables, rather than treating attributions as the central focus of the research. Examples include Hunt and Keaveney's (1994) research on consumers' responses to price rebates, and the work of Tripp, Jenson and Carlson (1994) on the effects of endorsement of products by celebrities.

Five postulates were central to Heider's pioneering attributional account published four decades ago (see Ross and Fletcher, 1985). First, Heider argued that psychologists can learn a great deal from folk psychology. In Heider's words, the ordinary person 'has a great and profound understanding of himself and other people which, although unformulated or only vaguely conceived, enables him to interact with others in more or less adaptive ways' (Heider, 1958: 2). Second, Heider argued that a fundamental principle of human social cognition was the need to perceive and represent the underlying invariant properties of the social world, even in the face of transitory and evanescent social phenomena. Third, Heider stressed the importance of the distinction between intentional and unintentional behaviour . Fourth, he claimed that internal and external classes of causal attribution form the key causal dimension. Fifth, Heider suggested that perceived covariation between cause and effect is fundamental to the attribution process.

Since Heider's seminal work, attribution theory and the standing of Heider's five postulates have waxed and waned. Literally thousands of related empirical studies have been done (a computer literature search revealed that 7534 academic articles in the last 23 years had the word 'attribution' in the title or abstract), including a good number in consumer and economic psychology. In my view, the sustained empirical and theoretical battering that attribution theory has sustained has cemented in place the pivotal status of Heider's five postulates, and more generally confirmed the key role played by lay explanations in human behaviour and cognition. These conclusions are no less true for the field of consumer and economic psychology.

GARTH FLETCHER

Bibliography

Feather, N.T. (1990) *The Psychological Impact of Unemployment*, New York, Springer-Verlag.

Feather, N.T. and O'Brian, G.E. (1986) 'A Longitudinal Study of the Effects of Employment and Unemployment on School-Leavers', *Journal of Occupational Psychology*, **59**: 121–44.

Fletcher, G.J.O. (1995) *The Scientific Credibility of Folk Psychology*, Mahwah, Lawrence

Erlbaum.

Fletcher, G.J.O. and Thomas, G. (1996) 'Close Relationship Lay Theories: Their Structure and Function', in Fletcher, G.J.O. and Fitness, J. (eds) *Knowledge Structures in Close Relationships: A Social Psychological Approach*, Hillsdale, NJ, Erlbaum: 3–24.

Folkes, V.S. (1988) 'Recent Attribution Research in Consumer Behavior: A Review and New Directions', *Journal of Consumer Research*, 14: 448–565.

Furnham, A.F. (1982a) 'Explanations for Unemployment in Britain', *European Journal of Social Psychology*, 12: 335–52.

Furnham, A.F. (1982b) 'Why are the Poor Always With Us? Explanations for Poverty in Britain', *British Journal of Social Psychology*, 21: 311–22.

Furnham, A. and Hesketh, B. (1989) 'Explanations for Unemployment in Great Britain and New Zealand', *Journal of Social Psychology*, 129: 169–81.

Heider, F. (1958) *The Psychology of Interpersonal Relations*, New York, Wiley.

Hunt, K.A. and Keaveney, S.M. (1994) 'A Process Model of the Effects of Price Promotions on Brand Image', *Psychology and Marketing*, 11: 511–32.

Jones, E.E. and Davis, K.E. (1965) 'From Acts to Dispositions: The Attribution Process in Person Perception', in Berkowitz, L. (ed.) *Advances in Experimental Social Psychology*, Volume 2, New York, Academic Press: 219–66.

Kelley, H.H. (1967) 'Attribution Theory in Social Psychology', in Vine, D.L. (ed.) *Nebraska Symposium on Motivation*, Lincoln, NB, University of Nebraska Press: 192–238.

Lewis, A., Webley, P. and Furnham, A. (1995) *The New Economic Mind: The Social Psychology of Economic Behaviour*, Hemel Hempstead, Harvester Wheatsheaf.

Mizerski, R.W., Golden, L. and Kernan, J.B. (1979) 'The Attribution Process in Consumer Decision Making', *Journal of Consumer Research*, 6: 123–40.

Ross, M. and Fletcher, G.J.O. (1985) 'Attribution and Social Perception', in Lindzey, G. and Aronson, E. (eds) *The Handbook of Social Psychology* (3rd edn), New York, Random House: 73–122.

Tripp, C., Jensen, T.D. and Carlson, L. (1994) 'The Effects of Multiple Product Endorsement by Celebrities on Consumers' Attitudes and Intentions', *Journal of Consumer Research*, 20: 535–47.

Van Raaij, F. (1986) 'Causal Attributions in Economic Behavior', in MacFadyen, A.J. and MacFadyen, H.W. (eds) *Economic Psychology: Intersections in Theory and Application*, Amsterdam, North-Holland: 353–79.

Weiner, B., Heckhausen, H., Meyer, W.U. and Cook, R.C. (1972) 'Causal Ascriptions and Achievement Behavior: Conceptual Analysis of Effort and Reanalysis of Locus of Control', *Journal of Personality and Social Psychology*, 21: 239–48.

Behaviourism

Behaviourism is a philosophy of psychology concerned with the implications of explaining behaviour without causal resort to unobservables, be they mental, neural or hypothetical. Behaviourists do not necessarily deny the existence of thinking, feeling and physiology, or even the proximal capacity of these factors to influence behaviour; but they understand behaviour to be ultimately a function of environmental variables. This emphasis on explaining as much behaviour as possible by reference to the environment shares some characteristics with the economist's idea of rationality (compare Lewin, 1996), although some important differences are mentioned below.

The behaviourist programme, announced early in the twentieth century by John Watson, was in part a reaction to the introspectionism with which psychology was then rife. Watson's (1924) aim was to develop psychology as a branch of natural science, the goal of which was the objective prediction and control of behaviour. His explanations relied on the classical conditioning demonstrated by Pavlov in which a previously neutral stimulus comes to exert similar power to elicit a response to that exerted by a stimulus with which it is repeatedly paired. The mechanistic approach of the stimulus–response psychology which resulted from this marriage was largely rejected by some subsequent neo-behaviourists such as Tolman and Hull who attempted to account for complex behaviours by positing cognitive or hypothetical intrapersonal events to mediate stimuli and responses (Chiesa, 1994; Smith, 1986; Zuriff, 1985). The *radical behaviourism* proposed by B.F. Skinner (1974) resolutely refused to embrace both intervening variables and hypothetical constructs of this kind.

Despite Watson's contributions to American advertising following his academic career, and the easy accommodation of early behaviourism into the pervasive cognitivism, this entry concentrates on Skinner's operant behaviourism, which is particularly appropriate for the analysis of consumer and other economic activity since it portrays behaviour as instrumental. Economic action, like much complex behaviour, *operates* on the environment, producing consequences which influence its future rate of occurrence in similar circumstances. Operant behaviour has long been the subject of laboratory experimentation in which the elements of the 'three-term contingency' — consequential stimuli, response and the discriminative stimuli that signal the consequences contingent on performing the response — can be unambiguously specified. Hence the basic explanatory device of operant behaviourism:

$$S^d \longrightarrow R \longrightarrow S^{r/a} \tag{1}$$

where S^d is a discriminative stimulus, R is a response, and $S^{r/a}$ the reinforcing or aversive outcomes of the response.

Operant behaviour is sensitive to its contingent consequences: when it is emitted more frequently, those consequences are said to be reinforcing and, when its rate is diminished, they are called punishing. The rate at which reinforcement is presented (the 'schedule of reinforcement') determines how quickly and resistantly behaviour is learned. When a response is reinforced every time it occurs ('continuous reinforcement'), the behaviour is quickly learned but extinguishes equally rapidly when reinforcement ceases. Physical responses such as turning a switch to produce light are best learned in this way. However, when not every response is reinforced ('intermittent reinforcement'), the behaviour may take longer to learn but it also extinguishes slowly. Moreover, different patterns of intermittent reinforcement, varying according to the fixed or variable time intervals that separate reinforcers, or the fixed or variable ratio of responses to a single reinforcement, produce and maintain distinct patterns of responding (Ferster and Skinner, 1957).

Operant behaviourism proposes that behaviour results from two sources: contingency-shaping and rule-governance. Behaviour which is acquired directly through such sensitivity to its consequences is known as *contingency-shaped* behaviour; the behaviour of nonhumans is apparently entirely of this kind. Human behaviour, however, need not be shaped in this way: if it were, learning to drive a car would be so (literally!) hit and miss that few if any would survive to get their licence. The fact that so many people in fact become safe drivers attests to the capacity of human behaviour to be instructed or *rule governed*. Despite criticisms of behaviourism as a method of explanation confined to contingency shaping, radical behaviourists have long incorporated the role of rules, as verbal descriptions of contingencies, in their analyses (Hayes, 1989). The ability of this approach to deal with the phenomena of reasoning and thought, long imagined to be the province of cognitivists, actually provides the mainspring of current intellectual progress in operant psychology. The character of operant behaviour as contingency sensitive remains; although rules may override the contingencies for a time, empirical work shows that the ultimate source of behavioural control lies in the environment. Nevertheless, although in both cases the contingencies themselves have been held to provide ultimate control of human behaviour, the interpretation of complex human behaviour has in fact increasingly relied upon theoretical entities located within the individual.

Recent formulations deny that any but the simplest human behaviours can be considered entirely contingency shaped — tapping one's fingers absentmindedly, for instance. The impossibility of operant conditioning occurring in humans without conscious awareness has long been noted, casting doubt on whether the word 'conditioning' is justified or useful. Most if not all human behaviour is influenced by rules that specify setting–response–outcome contingencies which, at the most basic level, arise from the verbal behaviour of others.

Beyond the laboratory, where this scientific explanation is not feasible, operant psychology relies on *interpreting* complex behaviour in terms derived from the simpler experimental setting where the variables are more amenable to control. Operant interpretation is most clearly seen in its account of the private events such as thinking and feeling which nonbehaviourists generally interpret as cognition and affect. Operant psychology interprets these acts as behaviours under the control of environmental events. Thoughts and feelings may act as discriminative stimuli for verbal and nonverbal behaviours but they are not 'initiating causes'. Private verbal behaviours include reasoning as in the analysis of situations and abstracts from the rules that will guide one's further behaviour.

Economic behaviour as operant

These elements suggest an operant interpretation of economic behaviour in which the number of responses represents the money which the consumer of commodities 'purchased' must give up, reinforcers are products and other provisions of the marketing system, and the schedule of reinforcement is the exchange rate of one in terms of the other (the 'price'). The behaviour of rats and pigeons readily conforms on this basis to the requirements of ordinal microeconomic theory and that of human employees and consumers can also be interpreted in this way (Kagel, 1988). The experimental analysis of economic behaviour is establishing itself as a unique approach to behavioural economics (Green and Kagel, 1996).

The question of whether such behaviour displays maximization remains controversial, if this behaviour is defined as the maximization of total utility or reinforcement. Analysts such as Rachlin (1989) have argued for maximization but Herrnstein (1997; see also Davison and McCarthy, 1986) proposes on the basis of extensive experimental evidence that 'matching' is the rule. Indeed, Herrnstein (1990) bases a penetrating critique of rational choice theory on these empirical results. What is 'matching'? When animals are presented with two schedules, they allocate their responses in proportion to the availability of reinforcement. The end result is matching rather than maximization and the process that leads to it is *melioration*: at any given time, an individual performs that behaviour which produces the greater or greatest local reinforcement. Empirical work on both maximization and melioration has been remarkable for its positing a *molar* conception of behaviour. Whereas *molecular* explanations of behaviour attempt to identify the precise environmental stimuli responsible for each and every response, molar conceptualizations relate *rates* of response to *rates* of reinforcement. Hull's (1952) theory of behaviour is molecular; it traces reaction potential ($_sE^R$) to drive (D), stimulus intensity (V), incentive (K) and habit strength ($_sH^R$) thus:

$$_sE^R = D \times V \times K \times {_sH^R}. \tag{2}$$

Herrnstein's matching equation, by contrast, represents response frequencies (B_i) as a function of reinforcement frequencies (R_i) thus:

$$B_1/(B_1 + B_2) = R_1/(R_1 + R_2). \tag{3}$$

Within this framework, maximization emerges as a special case of matching.

Alhadeff (1982) points out that any consumer behaviour meets with both reinforcing and aversive consequences. He portrays purchase behaviour as a vector of these two strengths or probabilities which are a function of the current consumer behaviour setting as it is primed by the consumer's learning history. The strength of approach depends upon reinforcer effectiveness (which is, in turn, a function of the consumer's level of deprivation), the schedule of reinforcement (and here we must add, to Alhadeff's analysis, the possibility that multiple schedules will be in operation in nonlaboratory settings), reinforcer delay (the length of time by which reinforcement has followed the response in the past; the longer this interval, the weaker the response), the quantity of signalled reinforcement, and the quality of signalled reinforcement. The strength of escape depends, *inter alia*, upon how aversive the loss of money is to the consumer who must pay for the product (and this is itself a function of the reaction of others to previous purchases by the individual), the past results of losing the positive generalized reinforcer, money, and the result of having been prevented from acquiring other reinforcers as a consequence of having bought a particular product, the length of delay between the purchase and such punishing consequences, the quantity and quality of the money surrendered, and the reinforcement schedule. The strength of escape will also reflect any negative consequences of using the brand in question in the past: an ill-fitting collar, an uncomfortable driving seat and poor after-sales service, all increase the probability of escape next time the brand is considered.

Behaviourist interpretation of consumer behaviour
An operant interpretation of consumer behaviour in its full complexity of marketing orientation and exchange requires a broader understanding of radical behaviourism (Foxall, 1990, 1997). This recognizes Skinner's demonstration that much human and animal behaviour can be explained, predicted and controlled by reference to its consequences (operant behaviour) rather than accepting the exclusive philosophical basis of this paradigm (Catania and Harnad, 1988).

The prediction of consumer behaviour requires an idea of the context in which the person is given an opportunity to behave (Foxall, 1997). This context has two dimensions: time and place. Time is represented by the consumer's learning history; place, by the behaviour setting, which consists of the physical and social discriminative stimuli that indicate the outcomes of emitting specific consumer behaviours. The intersection of these temporal and spatial variables defines the *consumer situation*. Learning history is an elusive variable in the case of adult consumers; it can be reconstructed to some extent by observation and questioning such as the various attitude theories require. But whatever an individual *says* about his or her past, present and future behaviour, it is necessary to know the structure of the current behaviour setting in order to interpret this verbal behaviour. Contextual interpretation reconstructs the meaning of consumer behaviour by examining the intersection of learning history and setting.

The somewhat abstract concept of the consumer situation is made more operational in terms of the *scope* of the behaviour setting (CBS). CBS scope is the extent to which the discriminative stimuli in the setting (that is, the neutral physical and social stimuli that compose the setting, as given meaning by the consumer's learning history) compel the performance of a particular response. (Incidentally, the study of addictive buying, compulsive gambling, and involuntary drug use are central components of behavioural economics in this tradition: see Ainslie, 1992; Green and Kagel, 1996). The interpretation is not a mechanistic stimulus–response notion, however; it employs a molar view of response rate. That is, the setting stimuli do not automatically evoke a given response in the individual whose learning history is appropriate; rather we need to look for a rate of response correlated with a rate of exposure to the setting stimuli. The rate of response is under the control not simply of the setting variables but of the consumer's history of reinforcement for similar behaviour in similar settings previously encountered. There is no reason to expect an automatic motivating intersection of learning history and setting variables. Hence the molar approach.

The scope of the consumer behaviour setting has a direct bearing on the probability of a particular purchase or consumption response's being emitted, and may be influenced in two ways: either by an increase in the monopoly power of the supplier, or by the supplier's reducing some of the costs otherwise borne by the consumer (a hotel mini bar reduces the inconvenience of having to fetch drinks and snacks from a store, for instance; the financial costs levied by the provider may actually be higher than those the store would charge; moreover, the propinquity of the food and drink may also increase the likelihood of their consumption).

When the individual lacks a relevant learning history and therefore rules for performing a given behaviour, decision making is required. In the cognitive depictions of this, consumer behaviour is said to be preceded by 'deliberative processing' or 'systematic processing' or the 'central route to persuasion'. In a radical behaviourist interpretation, such behaviour is governed by 'other rules' embodying the social pressures that give rise to the 'subjective norms' of multiattribute models. lacking a learning history, the consumer uses other rules as a surrogate. As the consumer develops experience, a history of reinforcement and punishment prompts the generation of self–rules which take the place of others' formulations of the situation. Finally, the consumer's behaviour is characterised by apparent spontaneity as the discriminative stimuli that compose the behaviour setting evoke self-rule-governed responses. These correspond to the peripheral route to persuasion, the spontaneous processing and the heuristic processing of the cognitive models.

Marketing management in behavioural perspective

Marketing management thus aims to modify the two main variables that influence consumer behaviour. First, managerial marketing attempts to influence the scope of behaviour settings, making the purchase of whatever the marketer offers more likely (whether this refers to spending on buying a product or consuming a service such as depositing money in a savings account) and making other responses (such as leaving the store, buying or consuming an alternative offering) less probable. Obvious examples are the provision of credit facilities for consumers who cannot afford the full cash outlay immediately, changing consumers' moods through in-store music, using advertising to promise desirable reinforcers contingent upon buying and using the item, and so on. Second, marketers manage the reinforcements available to consumers, particularly by controlling the schedules on which reinforcers are presented, and increasing the quantity or quality of reinforcers. Hence, special promotions may increase brand loyalty, at least for as long as the promotion lasts, using schedules that make additional rewards (extra merchandise, entry in prize draws, cash inducements and so on) contingent upon an increase in the rate of purchase.

This view extends the price-dominated economic analysis of consumer behaviour and the limited experimental analyses characteristic of operant behavioural economics. Price represents only one of the instruments by which supply is accommodated to demand (and by which suppliers seek to accommodate demand to supply) in a complex market system. Hence the need for a more sophisticated interpretation of complex economic behaviour which depicts the nonprice elements of the marketing mix — the product, promotion and distribution — as well as price by means of the three-term contingency. The mix elements can be specified in operant terms and incorporated into a situational analysis of purchase and consumption. To do this is to recognize that all four elements of the marketing mix are essential components of the consumer situation, presenting discriminative stimuli and reinforcers which guide purchase behaviour, for example, in the retail setting, and subsequent consumption.

Product

A product class is a set of reinforcers which shapes and maintains specific purchase and consumption behaviours. Brands are distinguished by the discriminative stimuli that differentiate them from competitors; these discriminative stimuli feature in both product and nonproduct marketing mix elements. The attributes of a product or service contain discriminative stimuli announcing the reinforcement that will result from the performance of specified purchase and consummatory responses. Packaging and product shapes, brand names and labels also perform these functions by enabling the consumer to discriminate his or her behaviour, purchasing the brands of which he or she has positive experience and avoiding the others. These effect a partial closure of the consumer behaviour setting, making the purchase of the brand in question more probable and seeking to exclude consideration of alternatives. Goods also contain the reinforcing stimuli that make further purchase more probable.

Price

Price information contains both positive and aversive stimuli. For most consumers, price is aversive, and effectively closes the setting by excluding wouldbe consumers or limits severely the amount which can be bought and consumed. The payment of this price is the major immediate aversive consequence of purchase. However, for consumers who are reinforced by conspicuous consumption, a high price may actually be a prerequisite of purchase, a discriminative stimulus which signals high levels of reinforcement contingent upon the possession and use of the item. The price still closes the setting given the reinforcement history of such consumers and their current financial status (ability to pay or obtain credit). For many consumers price is an indicator of quality: for them a relatively high price may similarly lead to discriminated purchasing.

Promotion

Marketing communications like advertising and point-of-sale promotions provide rules, promises, suggestions, prompts and other abbreviated descriptions of the contingencies of consumer behaviour. They are generally elements of the consumer behaviour setting which they close in the sense of encouraging purchase and consumption of one brand within the product class at the expense of its competitors. However, when advertising and other marketing communications are designed to promote a new brand in an existing product class, they may have the effect of opening the consumer behaviour setting by offering novelty. They encourage rule-governed consumer behaviour which is not initially dependent upon the actual consequences contingent upon purchase and consumption so much as those (such as the approbation of others) which are contingent upon rule following. However, they are effective only if the consumer has a tendency to behave already in the specified way — that is, a learning history which predisposes him or her towards rule conformity.

Place
Time and place and utilities consist in discriminative stimuli that signal the availability of the reinforcing and punishing properties of the remainder of the marketing mix. The components of a retail outlet portray its downmarket, value laden or plush ambience which in turn prefigure the probable prices of the merchandise, the level of customer service which can be expected, the quality of the products and services on offer, and so on. Time utilities indicate the usefulness of the items purchased in the context of the consumer's overall sequence of consumption behaviours. Timing is a central element in determining the usefulness of what is on offer to the consumer. Retail outlets are consumer behaviour settings which encourage *or deter* purchase; consumption contexts are consumer behaviour settings which encourage *or deter* usage.

GORDON R. FOXALL

Bibliography
Ainslie, G. (1992) *Picoeconomics: The Strategic Interaction of Successive Motivational States within the Person*, Cambridge, Cambridge University Press.
Alhadeff, D.A. (1982) *Microeconomics and Human Behaviour*, Berkeley, CA, University of California Press.
Catania, A.C. and Harnad, S. (eds) (1988) *The Selection of Behaviour: The Operant Behaviorism of B.F. Skinner. Comments and Consequences*, Cambridge, Cambridge University Press.
Chiesa, M. (1994) *Radical Behaviorism: The Philosophy and the Science*, Boston, MA, Authors Cooperative.
Davison, M. and McCarthy, D. (1986) *The Matching Law: A Research Review*, Hillsdale, NJ, Erlbaum.
Ferster, C. and Skinner, B.F. (1957) *Schedules of Reinforcement*, New York, Appleton-Century.
Foxall, G.R. (1990) *Consumer Psychology in Behavioural Perspective*, London and New York, Routledge/International Thompson Business Press.
Foxall, G.R. (1997) *Marketing Psychology*, London, Macmillan.
Green, L. and Kagel, J. H. (eds) (1996) *Advances in Behavioral Economics,*. Volume 3, Norwood, NJ, Ablex.
Hayes, S.C. (ed.) (1989) *Rule-Governed Behaviour: Cognition, Contingencies, and Instructional Control*, New York, Plenum.

Herrnstein, R.J. (1990) 'Rational Choice Theory: Necessary but not Sufficient', *American Psychologist*, **45**: 356–67.

Herrnstein, R.J. (1997) *The Matching Law: Papers in Psychology and Economics*, edited by H. Rachlin and D.I. Laibson, New York, Russell Sage Foundation; Cambridge, MA, Harvard University Press.

Hull, C.L. (1952) *A Behaviour System*, New Haven, CT, Yale University Press.

Kagel, J. (1988) 'Economics According to the Rats (and Pigeons Too): What Have We Learned and What Can We Hope to Learn?', in Roth, A.E. (ed.) *Laboratory Experimentation in Economics*, Cambridge, Cambridge University Press.

Lewin, S.B. (1996) 'Economics and Psychology: Lessons for Our Own Day from the Early Twentieth Century', *Journal of Economic Literature*, **34**: 1293–323.

Rachlin, H. (1989) *Judgment, Decision and Choice: A Cognitive/Behavioral Synthesis*, New York: Freeman.

Skinner, B.F. (1974) *About Behaviorism*, New York, Knopf.

Smith, L.D. (1986) *Behaviorism and Logical Positivism: A Reassessment of the Alliance*, Stanford, CA, Stanford University Press.

Watson, J. (1924) *Behaviorism*. New York, W. W. Norton.

Zuriff, G.E. (1985) *Behaviorism: A Conceptual Reconstruction*, New York, Columbia University Press.

Bettman, James R.

Professor James R. Bettman did his doctoral work in operations research in the Administrative Science department at Yale University. His dissertation, however, carried out in 1967–68, was on consumer behaviour. He followed two consumers around a grocery store as they shopped over a six to eight week period. He asked them to think aloud while they were shopping, tape recorded these verbalizations, and then interpreted these data to develop decision net models of their choice processes. He began his research and teaching career at the University of California at Los Angeles in 1969 as assistant professor. In 1970, he published an article in the *Journal of Marketing Research* which proposed a general model of decision and choice (Bettman, 1970). The 1970 framework was further fleshed out in his 1979 book, *An Information Processing Theory of Consumer Choice*. The ideas embodied in this book were far ahead of their time, both in terms of their ingenious methods for studying choice processes and in their views about choice, notably that choice is both adaptive (strategies people use depend upon the task) and constructive (decision strategies may be constructed or made up on the spot instead of being available in memory and simply implemented).

In his efforts to understand the *process* of choice, Bettman's use of methodology has been eclectic. His dissertation was almost anthropological in character, although the bulk of his information-processing work is experimental.

In general, his coding and analysis of thought protocols from consumer choice episodes, with choice strategies analysed as sequences of elementary information, is far more detailed than the analysis obtained from typical studies of consumer information processing. This approach to choice data is reflected in his much-cited and -used coding scheme for verbal choice protocols (Bettman and Park, 1980). He has also examined choice processes inductively. He has used information integration approaches in which the pattern of each individual's choice responses over varying information inputs is examined using analysis of variance to determine decision rules (Bettman, Capon and Lutz, 1975). To trace decision processes, and especially to understand why decision processes are contingent on task environments, he has used a computer-based information display that employs a computer mouse to control information acquisition. This acquisition system measures both the sequence and timing of information gathering in several different types of task environments (this is referred to in Payne, Bettman and Johnson, 1993).

To select Bettman's most influential ideas is difficult. However, he has had an indisputable impact on the field of consumer behaviour through his work on choice heuristics, his advocacy of an important role for memory in consumer choice and, possibly most notably, his formulation of choice processes as both contingent and constructive.

The dominant view in consumer behaviour before Bettman's work on choice heuristics was that brand attitudes (conceptualized as a weighted sum of attributes) predict brand choice. In the early 1970s, Bettman forcefully argued that consumers do not necessarily process by brand, use compensatory rules or choose the 'best'. He detailed several different choice strategies in Chapters 7 and 8 of his 1979 monograph. These describe how consumers may process by attribute, how attitudes and choice may be independent in that overall evaluations *may* be derived during the choice process but may *not* be central to choice, and how consumers may use hybrid strategies that continually shift as the choice process unfolds. These notions revolutionized research on consumer choice.

Another of Bettman's enduring contributions to consumer behaviour was his emphasis on the role of memory in decision making. Bettman's thesis on consumer memory is embodied in Chapter 6 of his 1979 book. Here he outlines the significant implications of the differences between recall and recognition, information organization at encoding, retrieval cues in the environment and the match of incoming information to stored expectations for understanding consumer behaviour, and also derives important public policy implications.

Bettman's focus on memory also led him to make the important distinction between stored choice rules that are retrieved from memory and simply implemented to make a choice, and decision strategies that are constructed or made up on the spot. This constructive view of choice implies that individuals will be sensitive to their environments and change their processing to utilize what they have learned about the structure of the choice task. This further implies that the resulting heuristics will be very sensitive to specific salient features of the choice task. Thus decision makers are necessarily adaptive (Payne, Bettman and Johnson, 1988, 1993).

Bettman's investigation of adaptive decision making spans more than two decades and includes his early work on the effects of information presentation format on acquisition strategies (Bettman and Kakkar, 1977). His current work focuses more on strategy selection in decision making. He and his coauthors argue that two major goals of decision makers, which help us to understand which strategy an individual will use in any given situation, are the desire to make a good decision and the desire to conserve cognitive effort (Payne et al., 1993). Individuals select strategies based upon tradeoffs between the accuracy a given strategy might attain in a particular choice environment and the cognitive effort required to execute the same strategy in that choice environment. Thus, they postulate that this accuracy/effort tradeoff approach provides a useful conceptual framework for understanding contingent decision processes. Further, they argue that constructive processing is consistent with the accuracy/effort viewpoint in the sense that on-the-spot shifts in direction are based upon local, momentary accuracy/effort assessments.

Much research on consumer information processing is 'cold' cognition. 'Hot' constructs such as feelings and emotions are given little emphasis. Bettman's most recent interests attempt to redress this balance. In one recent stream of research, Bettman reexamines the concept of risk (see Luce, Bettman and Payne, 1997). Although his early work examined perceived risk, he and others characterized risk cognitively rather than at a more visceral level. In his current research on individuals' reactions to decision making under stress, he establishes a link between risk and stress and recognizes not only that stress may be externally imposed (for example, through time pressure, waiting lines and so on) but also that individuals can generate stress and emotion (for example, feelings of great uncertainty, even worry or anxiety generated by anticipation regarding the outcomes) while making a decision. The work of Bettman and his colleagues appears to indicate that the stress generated during a decision leads to both more extensive and more attribute-based strategies (Luce et al., 1997).

Bettman also argues that in the accuracy/effort perspective on consumer choice, in general, consumer information processing researchers have taken a relatively narrow view of the sorts of benefits and costs considered by consumers. Taking a broad, functional perspective of the role of consumer behaviour in people's lives, Bettman considers the importance of nostalgia, and specifically the importance of savouring memories of the past as a deeper concern that individuals may have when they make their consumer choices. He proposes that one way that advertisements can evoke emotions and feelings is to cue the retrieval of product-related autobiographical memories. In one set of studies he shows empirically that the extent of transfer of autobiographical affect to brand evaluations depends upon the degree to which the advertisement forges a link between the brand and the autobiographical memory. Further, in the presence of such a brand–autobiographical memory link the presence or absence of more concrete product benefits is ignored (Sujan, Bettman and Baumgartner, 1993).

Bettman's current research thus recognizes the importance of emotion in decision making. His work highlights both the role of emotion in the decision *process* and emotion as an integral part of what products and brands mean to consumers and thus as a valued *outcome*.

Bettman's contributions to information processing and decision-making research, consumer behaviour and marketing in general have been recognized through numerous teaching, research and service awards. He was coeditor of the *Journal of Consumer Research* from 1981 to 1987. He was the 1979 winner of the Harold M. Maynard Award for significant contributions to marketing theory and thought, and elected a Fellow of the American Psychological Association in 1981. He presently is the Burlington Industries Professor of Business Administration at the Fuqua School of Business, Duke University. He was the Duke University Scholar/Teacher of the Year in 1988 and also won the North Carolina National Bank Faculty Award at the Fuqua School of Business, Duke University, in the same year. He became a Fellow of the American Psychological Society in 1991. He was elected as Fellow in Consumer Behaviour by the Association for Consumer Research in 1991, and in 1992 he was the recipient of the Paul D. Converse Award for outstanding contributions to the theory or science of marketing.

MITA SUJAN

Bibliography

Bettman, J.R. (1970) 'Information Processing Models of Consumer Behavior', *Journal of Marketing Research*, 7: 370–76.

Bettman, J.R. (1979) *An Information Processing Theory of Consumer Choice*, Reading, MA, Addison-Wesley.

Bettman, J.R., Capon, N. and Lutz, R.J. (1975) 'Cognitive Algebra in Multi-attribute Attitude Models', *Journal of Marketing Research*, 12: 151–64.

Bettman, J.R., and Kakkar, P. (1977) 'Effects of Information Presentation Format on Consumer Information Acquisition Strategies', *Journal of Consumer Research*, 3: 233–40.

Bettman, J.R. and Park, C.W. (1980) 'Effects of Prior Knowledge and Experience and Phase of the Choice Process on Consumer Decision Processes: A Protocol Analysis',

Journal of Consumer Research, **7**: 234–48.

Luce, M.F., Bettman, J.R., and Payne, J.W. (1997) 'Choice Processing in Emotionally Difficult Decisions', *Journal of Experimental Psychology: Learning, Memory, and Cognition*, **23**: 384–405.

Payne, J.W., Bettman, J.R. and Johnson, E.J. (1988) 'Adaptive Strategy Selection in Decision Making', *Journal of Experimental Psychology: Learning, Memory, and Cognition*, **14**: 534–52.

Payne, J.W., Bettman, J.R. and Johnson, E.J. (1993) *The Adaptive Decision Maker*, Cambridge, Cambridge University Press.

Sujan, M., Bettman, J.R. and Baumgartner, H. (1993) 'Influencing Consumer Judgments via Autobiographical Memories: A Self-Referencing Perspective', *Journal of Marketing Research*, **30**: 422–36.

Brand Equity

A Toyota sells for more than a Geo, even though the two cars are identical and roll off the same production line; Swatch watches command large market shares, despite being priced at a premium relative to competitors and imitators; and many purchasers of Levi's jeans would not be seen wearing any other brand. These types of customer behaviour are attributed to the draw of brand equity. The equity vested in a brand is often the most important asset a firm owns. The value of a brand to a firm resides in its ability to draw customers, justify a price premium, and keep customers loyal. Customer-based brand equity captures the psychological basis for these advantages, and is defined as 'the differential effect of brand knowledge on consumer response to the marketing of the brand' (Keller, 1993: 8). Brand knowledge consists of brand awareness and brand image. For example, historical knowledge of the performance of Toyota versus Geo cars may be the basis for consumers' willingness to pay a premium for the Toyota over the Geo. Similarly, the imagery associated with Levi's (youth, confidence, authenticity and americana) may be at the root of the staunch loyalty to the brand. Brand awareness relates to the ease with which a brand is recalled or recognized. Brand image is a set of perceptions about a brand as reflected in the brand 'associations held in consumer memory' (Keller, 1993: 3). These associations include attitudes towards the brand, perceptions of quality and other idiosyncratic associations with other nodes in consumer memory. Other authors also include in the definition the behavioural outcomes of brand equity such as loyalty or intentions to purchase (Aaker, 1991).

A variety of measures of brand equity have been proposed. Some of these measures focus on the behavioural outcomes of brand equity such as customer loyalty to a brand or willingness to pay a premium, while others focus on the measurement of psychological components of brand equity such as perceptions of quality, and brand awareness and attitudes. The former types of measures tend to employ scanner panel data or a form of tradeoff analysis to estimate the extent to which customer purchase behaviour or preferences can be attributed to brand equity (Kamakura and Russell, 1993). The latter measures focus on understanding the psychological antecedents of brand equity and assume that these have an impact on customer behaviour (Agarwal and Rao, 1996).

Recognition of the value of brand equity as an asset for a firm suggests a need to demonstrate how this asset generates a return. This is perhaps best reflected in the ability of the firm to extend the brand to new products. The assumption behind the managerial decision to extend a brand is that the benefits of brand awareness and a positive brand image can be carried over to a new product category. The expected benefits of brand extension include lower advertising and awareness-building investments, and ease of positioning. A large body of research on brand extensions lends support to this assumption but also provides some caveats. For example, brand associations do transfer to new products which are similar in attributes or proximate in concept (Aaker and Keller, 1990; Park, Milberg and Lawson, 1991). Associations may also transfer to distant extensions, provided the original brand is of a high quality or extensions occur in sequential order (Dawar and Anderson, 1994; Keller and Aaker, 1992). Distant extensions may be perceived as a better fit when the existing brand is broad, in as much as it already represents a variety of products (Boush and Loken, 1991). However, the cognitive structure of broad brands can have an important impact on the specific brand associations brought to mind when evaluating an extension and consequently may affect perceptions of fit. For example, brands such as Honda, Nike and Levi's which are broad brands, are nevertheless, strongly associated with a single-product category. On the other hand, brands such as Bic, Siemens and Kraft may be associated with a number of different product categories. Contextual cues on cognitive structure can have a significant impact on the extendibility of brands (Dawar, 1996).

The ability of brand equity to generate a return has also been demonstrated at a 'macro' or firm level by examination of the impact of brand-related variables on the firm's market share, or stock market valuation. Findings suggest that brand extensions provide both greater market share and advertising efficiency than new brands (Smith and Park, 1992). A qualification to this finding is that brand extensions do better when they are late rather than early entrants into a market (Sullivan, 1992). Perceived quality, which is considered an important element of the brand associations, has been shown to be related to stock market valuation (Aaker and Jacobson, 1994). Further, brand extension announcements have been shown to interact with existing brand attitudes and familiarity (which are elements of brand equity), to affect stock market returns (Lane and Jacobson, 1995).

Brand equity continues to generate substantial research. Of significant interest are questions about the impact of firm actions on brand equity. Little is known about which firm actions generate brand equity or the effects of, say, new product announcements, organizational structure changes, price changes, strategic alliances, or product recalls on brand equity. Yet these firm actions can have dramatic effects on brand equity, which is one of the most important corporate assets. Further, questions still remain about the impact of brand equity on certain aspects of consumer behaviour. For example, can brand equity create inertia in brand switching?

NIRAJ DAWAR

Bibliography

Aaker, D.A. (1991) *Managing Brand Equity: Capitalizing on the Value of a Brand Name*, New York, Free Press.

Aaker, D.A. and Jacobson, R. (1994) 'The Financial Information Content of Perceived Quality', *Journal of Marketing Research*, **31**: 191–202.

Aaker, D.A. and Keller, K.L. (1990) 'Consumer Evaluations of Brand Extensions', *Journal of Marketing*, **54**: 27–41.

Agarwal, M.K. and Rao, V.R. (1996) 'An Empirical Comparison of Consumer-Based Measures of Brand Equity', *Marketing Letters*, **7**: 237–47.

Boush, D.M. and Loken, B. (1991) 'A Process Tracing Study of Brand Extension Evaluation, *Journal of Marketing Research*, **28**: 16–28.

Dawar, N. (1996) 'Extensions of Broad Brands: The Role of Retrieval in Evaluations of Fit', *Journal of Consumer Psychology*, **5**: 189–207.

Dawar, N. and Anderson, P.F. (1994) 'The Effects of Order and Direction on Multiple Brand Extensions', *Journal of Business Research*, **30**: 119–29.

Kamakura, W.A. and Russell, G.J. (1993) 'Measuring Brand Value with Scanner Data', *International Journal of Research in Marketing*, **10**: 9–22.

Keller, K.L. (1993) 'Conceptualising, Measuring, and Managing Customer-Based Brand Equity', *Journal of Marketing*, **57**: 1–22.

Keller, K.L. and Aaker, D.A. (1992) 'The Effects of Sequential Introduction of Brand Extensions, *Journal of Marketing Research*, **29**: 35–50.

Lane, V. and Jacobson, R. (1995) 'Stock Market Reactions to Brand Extension Announcements: The Effects of Brand Attitude and Familiarity', *Journal of Marketing*, **59**: 63–77.

Park, C. Whan, Milberg, S. and Lawson, R. (1991) 'Evaluation of Brand Extensions: The Role of Product Feature Similarity and Brand Concept Consistency', *Journal of Consumer Research*, **18**: 185–93.

Smith, D.C. and Park, C. Whan (1992) 'The Effects of Brand Extensions on Market Share and Advertising Efficiency', *Journal of Marketing Research*, **29**: 296–313.

Sullivan, M. (1992) 'Brand Extensions: When to Use Them', *Manaement Science* , **38**: 793–806.

Brand Loyalty

Brand loyalty is a topical topic. We discuss briefly (i) how far there is such a thing, (ii) what form it takes, (iii) how it can be predicted, and (iv) some practical applications.

Four questions for the reader to answer are:

Tick one box per row

	Yes	No	Don't know
1. Is there such a thing as 'loyalty'?	( )	( )	( )
2. Is loyalty the same for different brands?	( )	( )	( )
3. Are loyalty levels predictable?	( )	( )	( )
4. Are 100 per cent-loyal buyers well worth having?	( )	( )	( )

People typically give different answers. For Question 1 perhaps 25 per cent say 'Yes', 35 per cent 'No', and 20 per cent 'Don't know/all depends' (with the remaining 20 per cent apparently not knowing that they didn't know). There is little consensus. But for Question 4 people invariably answer 'Yes: 100 per cent-loyalty is a good thing'.

Our own answers are clear 'Yeses' for Questions 1 to 3, but an emphatic '*No!*' for Question 4. Our reasons are:

Q1 There are many different loyalty-related measures (see Technical appendix). Yet they all vary together and hence reflect/measure the same thing, 'loyalty'.
Q2 The degree of loyalty for brands of the same size has been found to be much the same, in more than 50 different product categories or services.
Q3 The loyalty measures follow regular patterns and are predictable, as we shall see.
Q4 No: 100-per-cent-loyal buyers are few and they buy little.

In practice few consumers are by nature either monogamous (near-100 per cent loyal) or promiscuous. They are mostly *polygamous*. They have steady ongoing relationships with several serious partners, one usually consumed more often than others. And only occasionally do they try out a new relationship or drop an established one. Loyalty can therefore be defined as an ongoing propensity to buy the brand, usually as one of several. This predicts all the customary brand performance measures (for example, buying rates) without presuming any deep commitment.

A classic example

To illustrate, Table 1 gives the annual penetrations and average rates of buying of the eight leading US instant coffee brands. The penetrations differ greatly, by a factor of four, from 24 per cent buying Maxwell House down to 6 per cent buying Maxim. But the buying rates differ far less (they are all about 3, from 3.6 just down to 2.6 or so).

Table 1: Brand Penetration and Purchase Rates

US Annual	Market share percentage	Percentage buying		Average purchase per buyer	
		O	T	O	T
Any Instant	100	67	–	6.7	–
Maxwell House	19	24	**27**	3.6	**3.1**
Sanka	15	21	**23**	3.3	**3.0**
Tasters Choice	14	22	**21**	2.8	**2.9**
High Point	13	22	**20**	2.6	**2.9**
Folgers	11	18	**17**	2.7	**2.8**
Nescafé	8	13	**14**	2.9	**2.7**
Brim	4	9	**7**	2.0	**2.6**
Maxim	3	6	**6**	2.6	**2.6**
Other brands	13	20	**21**	3.0	**2.9**
Average brand	11	17	**17**	2.8	**2.8**

Note: O = Observed; **T** = Theoretical Dirichlet predictions.

Source: MRCA.

Together these two measures make up the brand's sales. Sales = Penetration X Average purchase rate. Market shares (sales) therefore differ mainly by how many customers you have, and hardly at all by how 'loyal' they are (unless the penetration is *very* high). This has been found widely, as mentioned.

None the less, the purchase rates in Table 1 *do* decrease slowly with market share (with an exception, not too dramatic, for Brim at 2.0). This decrease is a near-universal pattern known as double jeopardy (DJ): a small brand has fewer buyers and these buy it somewhat less often. This is not only widely observed but also predicted by the Dirichlet theory. (DJ is not a case of lower 'brand equity' — that the small brand is *weak* — but merely a statistical selection effect relating to the brand's size, as outlined in the appendix).

A theoretical model
These results are all predictable from a single 'split-loyalty' model, named after Dirichlet, a mathematician. The Dirichlet is basically defined for steady-state markets. It assumes that a consumer tends to have steady propensities to buy each of a small repertoire of brands, with differing probabilities. But the model does not imply that the market *has* to be steady (it only predicts what the market is like when it *is* steady (which in practice it does tend to be). But the predictions are also robust to departures from strict stationarity: they benchmark the regular patterns that occur and pinpoint the deviations.

To calibrate the model only three simple numerical inputs for the product category are required: How many consumers bought it, on average how often (for example, 67 per cent in Table 1 buying any instant coffee, on average 6.7 times in a year), and how many brands they bought (on average 1.7).

For each *brand* only its market share has to be specified. The model then gives the theoretical predictions as in the tables here. The fit is typically close, with correlations of more than 0.9 (see also Ehrenberg, 1988; Ehrenberg and Uncles, 1998).

Some applications
Some practical applications of the generally steady buying rates as in Table 1 are as follows:

New brands
One can predict that any new brand of US instant coffee will be bought at an average purchase rate of about three (once sales have 'settled down'). This is because *all* the coffee brands in Table 1 are bought about three times. For the new brand to differ in this respect its attributes would have to differ more from those of the existing brands than these differ from each other (and the marketing plan did not say that).

How sales increase
Any existing brand — Nescafé, say — can double its sales, since some of the existing brands clearly have done so in the past (they now differ greatly in size). But a brand cannot grow by making its existing buyers buy it twice as often (for

example, about six times in the year) because no brand has ever shown such a deviation from the norm.

Instead, a doubled Nescafé would have to have almost twice as many buyers. (That is what is also found in practice.) The model therefore dictates how sales can increase, which helps in setting and evaluating targets and in determining means and ends.

Private labels

The Table 1 type of results provide benchmarks for assessing private labels (that is, 'store brands'). In practice, their loyalty is much like that of manufacturers' brands (for example, Bound and Ehrenberg, 1997).

Deviations

In Table 1, Brim had a low purchase frequency (2.0, instead of the predicted 2.6). This had not occurred in the previous year, so that the deviation was not a property of the brand as such (for example, 'low brand equity' perhaps). Instead, it must have been a momentary upset in the market, such as a fire in a warehouse – 'bad' – or a short-lived promotional influx of once-only buyers – 'good', presumably. This could have been pinpointed by analysing the background data (if it had still been available).

More patterns

Additional patterns in consumers' buying behaviour which are also predicted by the Dirichlet theory include:

The '80:20' rule

Traditionally, a brand's 50 per cent heaviest buyers are said to account for about 80 per cent of its sales, and its 50 per cent lighter ones for only about 20 per cent. This occurs broadly for each of the coffee brands listed in Table 1 (with a DJ effect of slightly more light buyers for the smaller brands). In the model even the very light buyers are, however, still loyal to the brand: they buy it again but infrequently (for example, more than a year later).

One hundred per cent-loyal buyers

Unlike most people's expectations, 100 per cent-loyal or near-100 per cent-loyal buyers are *not* important to one's sales: there are few of them — see Table 2 below — and they are not heavy buyers. This is predictable and can hardly be changed. (Many people are misled over this because in *short* time periods the proportion of 100 per cent loyals is necessarily vastly higher: in a week, say, most people buy coffee at most once and hence buy only one brand then).

Multibrand buying

Nearly all of a brand's customers are therefore multibrand buyers over a year or so. This is so even under steady market conditions. Typically, the customers of Nescafé in Table 1 buy *other* brands about twice as often (on average six times, versus only about three purchases of Nescafé itself). Nescafé's 'share of customers' category requirements' (SCR) is therefore as low as about 30 per cent (3/9): 'Your customers are mostly other brands' customers who occasionally buy you'.

The theoretical model implies, and the empirical data support it, that such multibrand buyers are none the less loyal to their brands, that is, they go on buying each brand with more or less steady propensities. People may buy different brands for different end users or different end uses, for example, mid-morning versus after-dinner coffee. Or just because most brands are very much alike anyway but they want *some* variety of choice but still find having a *small* repertoire of habitual brands convenient.

The Duplication of Purchase Law

Which specific other brands your customers also buy is predictable. With equally substitutable brands, the proportion of buyers of brand A who also buy brands B, C or D varies directly with B, C and D's overall market penetrations.

In Table 1 far more people bought Maxwell House than Maxim (24 per cent and 6 per cent). In line with that, about four times as many customers of any *other* brand also bought Maxwell House than Maxim (as for Nescafé in Table 2 below.) However, some markets are more or less heavily 'partitioned' — for example, ground versus instant coffee, or leaded and unleaded gasoline as an extreme example (Ehrenberg and Uncles, 1998). There is then much more switching in each such submarket, but the Duplication of Purchase Law (and the Dirichlet model generally) still holds in each.

Brand performance audits

The Dirichlet theory provides benchmarks for many different loyalty criteria. Table 2 illustrates this for Nescafé, a brand with an eight per cent share in the US at the time.

The observed figures seem potentially threatening — less than three Nescafé purchases per Nescafé buyer, and over half of its customers buying the brand only once in the year! However, the figures are in fact much as predicted. Like most brands most of the time, Nescafé was behaving normally for an 8 per cent brand in that market:

1. Nescafé customers grew from about 1 per cent of the population in a week to 13 per cent in the year (that is, from less than 1 million to about 13 million

Table 2: A Brand Performance Audit (Nescafé in the US with an 8 per cent market share)

	O	T	
Percentage buying in a week	1	**1**	
Percentage buying in a year	13	**14**	
Purchases per buyer	2.9	**2.7**	
Percentage buying once 46		**49**	
Percentage buying 5+	12	**18**	
Q by Q repeat percentage	48	**48**	
100-per-cent-loyal percentage	15	**13**	
100-per-cent-loyal rate	3.3	**1.8**	(low)
Category rate	10	**10**	
Category SCR	29	**27**	
Percentage of buyers who also bought:			
Maxwell House	48	**41**	
Tasters Choice	35	**31**	
Folgers	34	**26**	
Brim	15	**11**	
Maxim	8	**9**	
Other	40	**31**	

Note: O = Observed, **T** = Theoretical. Annual unless stated.

Source: MRCA.

US households).
2. On average they bought the brand only three times a year.
3. Half bought it just once in the year, and only one in six more than once a quarter.
4. No more than 50 per cent of those buying it in one quarter bought it again in the next.
5. Only 15 per cent of Nescafé's annual buyers were 100 per cent loyal.
6. They bought only at about the brand's *average* rate of purchase (about

three).

7. Buyers of Nescafé made as many as ten purchases of *any* instant coffee in the year, a 'share of category requirements' or SCR of only about 30 per cent (2.9/10).

8. *Which* other brands Nescafé buyers also bought was mostly in line with their market shares or penetrations, as shown by the predictions (a correlation of 0.99).

Such norms also show up submarkets and isolated deviations, and provide benchmarks for interpreting *dynamic* markets (for example, Ehrenberg and Uncles, 1998). The prediction of the 100-per-cent-loyal buyers' buying rate at 1.8 is however low, but this recurs more generally (e.g. Table 3 in the appendix) — it is a *general* failing of the model and of no diagnostic value.

Conclusions

These results lead to five main conclusions:

1. Different loyalty-related measures mostly vary together: hence there is 'loyalty'.
2. Individual consumers generally have 'split-loyalty' portfolios of several habitual brands.
3. Loyalty levels differ little between brands of the same size.
4. But smaller brands inherently have slightly lower loyalty measures (double jeopardy).
5. What distinguishes a large brand from a smaller one is therefore how many customers each has, not how often they tend to buy it (unless penetration is already very high).

The patterns and predictive Dirichlet theory outlined here are much the same for different brands and products. This provides simple and near-universal benchmarks for assessing the loyalty levels in one's market and auditing the performance of one's brands.

In the model, brands are seen as similar and substitutable: 'Brands are Brands'. Maxwell House, Nescafé and so on, are all coffee, not dishwashing liquid. But brands are also distinct, that is, they have their unique names and packaging ('The product with a name') and very different market shares.

And in practice even similar brands can and do also differ in 'minor' aspects. For example, nuances of flavour, texture, the bottle top or the car-door handle, being out of stock more often and so on. Such minor differences are usually not copied by the competition or explicitly featured in the advertising. Consumers can therefore notice them (if at all) only after having tried the brand

— a typical example of attitude change *following* a change in behaviuor (for example, Barnard and Ehrenberg, 1998).

All in all, the main driver of market share is not variations in aspects of loyalty but large differences in market penetration – the number of customers you have. This is determined not by any single factor but by the marketing mix and how well it is applied.

Technical appendix
We elaborate here briefly on some of the technicalities.

Different loyalty measures
There is a great variety of different loyalty-related measures (as was in part illustrated by Table 2). For example:

1. *Repeat-buying* Asking 'What percentage of buyers of X bought it again next time?' is one commonsense measure. But different people's successive purchases quickly get out of step with each other and also with happenings in the marketplace (some specific promotion or advertising campaign and so on).

    An alternative is *period-to-period* repeat buying, for example, of those buying X in the first period, what percentage bought X again in the second period. This gives a plethora of different numbers, for periods of different lengths (weeks, months, quarters and so on), and also for how such repeat-buyers bought in each such period.

    A third approach is how often people buy in just *one* time period. This gives yet further numbers. For Nescafé, say, it is just over one for buyers in a single week, about three times per quarterly buyer as in Table 2, about eight in a year, etc.

2. *Multibrand buying* Loyalty-related measures at 'right angles' to repeat buying are how much your customers buy your brand rather than *other* brands (its SCR). This again varies: almost all in a week, less than a third in a year (for example, 3.6/15 in Table 3), and so on.

    A complementary measure is how many of your customers are 100 per cent loyal to it (very high in a week, very low in a year) and how often *they* buy. Another set of related measures is *which* other brands your customers also buy, that is, which appear either more or less competitive.

3. *Attitudes* Yet a different approach to loyalty is attitudinal: how much consumers say they *like* the brand, would buy it in future, and/or perhaps feel *committed* to it. Or how many have specific positive attribute beliefs about the brand ('Good value for money', 'Tastes nice' and so on).

    The good news is that all these different measures tend to correlate

Brand Loyalty

highly (with some specific exceptions) and therefore reflect much the same thing, loyalty.

The generalizability of the patterns

The various loyalty patterns outlined here hold for each brand in more than fifty products, from soap to soup, for different countries and years, and also for store-choice, doctors' prescriptions, cars, petrol and so on. Table 3 illustrates this some for basic performance measures across a dozen categories. Such patterns and model predictions can be checked by anyone with available panel-type data.

Table 3: Annual performance measures for the eight leading brands

	Brand share O	Percentage buying O		Packages per buyer O		Percentage buying once O		100 per cent loyal* buyers O		rate O		Category purchases per buyer O	
		O	T	O	T	O	T	O	T	O	T**	O	T
Any brand	100	(83)	**(83)**	(11)	**(11)**	12	**13**	100	**100**	11	**11**	11	**11**
First	(27)	46	**48**	4.6	**4.5**	36	**36**	20	**15**	4	**3**	13	**13**
Second	(19)	36	**37**	4.1	**4.0**	40	**41**	15	**12**	4	**2**	14	**14**
Third	(12)	26	**27**	3.7	**3.6**	47	**45**	10	**10**	4	**2**	15	**14**
Fourth	(9)	24	**23**	3.3	**3.4**	50	**47**	10	**9**	4	**2**	14	**15**
Fifth	(7)	16	**18**	3.7	**3.3**	46	**48**	11	**9**	3	**2**	15	**15**
Sixth	(5)	15	**14**	3.0	**3.3**	55	**50**	9	**8**	3	**2**	15	**15**
Seventh	(4)	13	**13**	3.2	**3.3**	55	**50**	8	**8**	3	**2**	15	**16**
Eighth	(3)	8	**9**	3.9	**3.2**	55	**52**	7	**8**	3	**2**	16	**16**
Average	(8)	(23)	**23**	3.7	**3.6**	48	**46**	11	**10**	3	**2**	15	**15**

Notes: ( ) = Inputs to the model. * Percentage of brand purchase. **Consistently low (see text). Observed O and Theoretical **T**, for individual brands across a dozen product categories – see text.

Sources: Nielsen, IRI, AGB, GK, TCI.

Double jeopardy

The DJ phenomenon is that a small brand is bought relatively less often by its few buyers. This is compared with a large brand which is bought somewhat more often by its much more numerous buyers. DJ is merely a 'statistical selection effect', which applies to *any* small brand just because it is small.

To see in brief how DJ comes about, consider a big brand *A* and a small brand *B* which are very similar except for their size. Buyers of *A* buy as much of the total product category (say coffee) as do buyers of *B*, which is typical.

The vast majority of buyers of each brand are, however, multibrand buyers in a year (only some 10 per cent or so are 100 per cent-loyal — see Tables 2 and 3). But buyers of the large *A* will buy the small *B* relatively seldom because *B* is not bought much anyway (it is small). Hence the *A* buyers will be buying *A* itself relatively often (to satisfy their total coffee needs).

In contrast, buyers of the small *B* will buy the big brand *A* relatively often (because *A* is big and therefore is generally bought more). They will therefore buy *B* itself less often. That is the double jeopardy effect explained.

Guide to the bibliography

The fuller Dirichlet story has been outlined in Ehrenberg and Uncles (1998). The basic text is Ehrenberg (1988). A training exercise on analysing scanner-panel purchasing data is Ehrenberg, Uncles and Carrie (1994).

The evidence on consumers' attitudes to brands is consistent with the Dirichlet assumption of directly substitutable brands being seen as similar by their users (Barnard and Ehrenberg, 1998). How advertising works for such brands is discussed in Ehrenberg, Barnard and Scriven (1998).

As more general background, Engel, Blackwell and Miniard (1995) is the classic consumer behaviour text. Lilien, Kotler and Sridhar Moorthy (1992) review a wide range of marketing models.

Guadagni and Little (1983) is the prime paper on the logit model, probably the most widely discussed market-share model in the last ten or fifteen years. But logit modelling differs fundamentally from the Dirichlet approach. Thus it seeks to predict changes in market share from a variety of marketing-mix inputs (including a 'loyalty' measure). In contrast, the Dirichlet predicts a variety of brand performance measures (as shown here) from market shares as the only brand-specific inputs. Again, logit modelling is thought to apply to dynamic markets, while the Dirichlet is basically defined for steady-state or 'stationary' markets (although it is robust to dynamic market movements).

ANDREW EHRENBERG AND JOHN SCRIVEN

Bibliography

Barnard, N.R. and Ehrenberg, A.S.C. (1998) 'Attitudes to Brands', JOAB Report 7, London, South Bank University.

Bound, J.A. and Ehrenberg, A.S.C. (1997) 'Private Label Purchasing', Admap 375.

Ehrenberg, A.S.C. (1988) *Repeat-Buying: (A) Facts and Theory*, London, Arnold; New

York, Oxford University Press.

Ehrenberg, A.S.C., Barnard, N.R. and Scriven, J.A. (1998) 'Advertising is Publicity not Persuasion', R&D I Research Report, London, South Bank University.

Ehrenberg, A.S.C. and Uncles, M.D. (1998) 'Understanding Dirichlet-Type Markets', R&D I Research Report, London, South Bank University.

Ehrenberg, A.S.C., Uncles, M.D. and Carrie, D. (1994) *Armed to the Teeth*, Cranfield, European Case Clearing House (M94–005: 594–039–1).

Engel, J.T., Blackwell, R.D. and Miniard, P.W. (1995) *Consumer Behavior* (8th edn), Orlando, FL, Dryden Press.

Guadagni, P.M. and Little, J.D.C. (1983) 'Logit Model of Brand Choice Calibrated on Scanner Data', *Marketing Science*, **2**: 203–38.

Lilien, G., Kotler, P. and Sridhar Moorthy, K. (1992) *Marketing Models*, Englewood Cliffs, NJ, Prentice-Hall.

Budgeting and Mental Accounting

All consumers face the problem of allocating their income to expenditures, whether a homemaker juggling bills, savings and investments or a child deciding how to spend an allowance. For most consumers, attractive ways to spend money far outnumber the available resources. Thus, allocating income to expenditures involves planning and prioritizing expenses, as well as the application of self-control.

How do consumers make and follow budgets? Typical household budgets are based on income and expenses that occur on a regular, recurring schedule. Expenses for shelter, utilities, food and so on are allocated from the regular budget. Any discretionary income can be consumed or saved according to whatever personal rules or habits the consumer has adopted. Several issues complicate this seemingly simple process, however.

One of the most basic assumptions of economics is that money is fungible — that is, money has no labels attached to it. Thus, money from any source should be put to whatever use maximizes a consumer's utility. However, many consumers seem to treat money derived from different sources as though it belonged to separate accounts. Another assumption is that financial decisions should be based on overall wealth, yet many consumers mentally segregate portions of their assets for reasons of self-control.

Standard economic approaches

An approach to budgeting based on the standard theory of consumer choice would posit that consumers allocate their income to the uses that maximize utility. Strotz (1957) proposed that consumers make budgets by maximizing utility for different categories of spending separately. This idea was formalized as a 'utility tree', with separate branches for each category of the budget.

Spending within each branch was assumed to be independent of every other branch, although Strotz himself noted that 'actual expenditure decisions do not correspond exactly to this pattern' (p. 271). Income source or amount did not play a role in this approach, except as a budget constraint.

The life-cycle consumption function hypothesis suggests that younger consumers will borrow against future earnings and older consumers will spend any excess resources they have accumulated, although much empirical evidence contradicts the hypothesis. Such real-world phenomena as excess credit card debt and the market for rent-to-own consumer goods (which leads to paying highly inflated overall prices in small chunks) are evidence that consumers are not always rational utility maximizers. The increase in the number of consumers who turn to credit counselling services for help to manage their budgets indicates that personal financial management is a challenge to many.

What is mental accounting?

Mental accounting is a term applied to several phenomena associated with evaluations of transactions and spending decisions. These phenomena include categorization of one's budget into topical accounts, designation of some resources 'off limits' as a self-control measure, reliance on reference points such as price paid to assess value of an asset, and using monetary resources differently depending on where they originate, the amount received, and how frequently they are obtained. The phenomena of mental accounting present a serious challenge to economic theories based on a rational consumer.

Richard Thaler (1980) applied prospect theory (Kahneman and Tversky, 1979) to the evaluation of transactions, suggesting that consumers derive utility from the merits of a deal beyond that derived from a purchased good or service. Consumers are seen as likely to evaluate a deal not in terms of the overall budget, but in relation to the context of the specific transaction. Transaction utility is determined by the difference between what a consumer expects to pay for a product (reference price) and the actual price. When the difference is positive, the consumer feels that he or she has a good deal, but when the difference is negative, the consumer may experience 'sticker shock' (Winer, 1986). According to prospect theory, losses loom larger than gains, so prices that are higher than expected have a greater negative impact on consumers than the positive impact associated with lower than expected prices.

Thaler suggested that consumers engage in 'hedonic editing' as a way to maximize transaction utility, separating the outcomes of some transactions, but combining the outcomes of others. For example, a consumer who experiences two gains derives the most utility from thinking about them separately and generally prefers to experience them on different days. In contrast, a consumer who experiences two losses is likely to prefer to integrate the losses into a single experience. These predictions are derived from the shape of the value function of prospect theory, which is steeper in the domain of losses than in the domain of gains.

Assessing utility in the context of a specific transaction can lead to such anomalous behaviour as travelling 20 minutes to save five dollars on a 15-dollar item, but not making the trip to save the same amount on an item priced at 150 dollars. A classic example of mental accounting is Kahneman and Tversky's (1984) theatre ticket problem. Subjects were asked to imagine that they had plans to go to the theatre, but discovered on their arrival that they had (i) lost the ticket, valued at $10.00 or (ii) lost $10.00 in cash. Only 12 per cent of subjects in the lost ticket condition would purchase a new ticket, compared to 54 per cent in the lost cash condition ($n = 200$). Kahneman and Tversky explained the difference by suggesting that subjects encoded the lost ticket as an expense in an entertainment category, while the lost cash had not yet been assigned. Thus, subjects in the lost ticket condition would feel that they were paying $20.00 to see a $10.00 play, while subjects in the lost cash condition would consider the ticket purchase separately from the lost money, although the net effect on the budget is identical for both conditions.

Several different factors appear to contribute to mental accounting of income and expenses. These include timing, labelling, amount and the consumer's reference budget. The process of mental accounting has been described as framing of gains and losses (Kahneman and Tversky, 1984) as well as a variant of categorization (Henderson and Peterson, 1992; Heath and Soll, 1996; O'Curry, 1997). Whether framing or categorization is the process, differential salience of attributes of income and expenses affects mental accounting.

Timing

Hirst, Joyce and Schadewald (1994) showed that consumers prefer the term of a loan to match the useful life of the item purchased with the loan. Prelec and Loewenstein (1997) found similar results, showing that consumers preferred to prepay items such as vacations or parties, but would pay for durable goods on credit. They point out that part of the appeal of credit cards may be to disconnect payment from consumption. Gourville and Soman (1997) showed that consumers are more likely to mentally depreciate sunk costs that have been incurred a long time prior to consumption of benefits than when the same costs are incurred closer to the time of consumption.

In a somewhat different vein, Shefrin and Thaler (1988) suggested that consumers tend to categorize money into three types of mental accounts based on when money is received and when it is to be used: current income, assets and future income. Current income is the most 'spendable' while future income, such as retirement investments, is deemed untouchable. They suggested that self-control issues lead to this sort of mental accounting. By mentally segregating portions of wealth, consumers can enjoy current consumption while alleviating the risk of bankrupting themselves in a seemingly distant future. Income taxes and retirement plans (both public and private) are usually funded by withholding from paypackets to ensure sufficient funds for compliance. Ironically, many American consumers are thrilled to receive a large income tax refund in the spring, although this means that they have given the government an interest-free loan.

Labelling

Mentally labelling income and expenses can lead to different spending patterns, such as spending gift money or windfalls on fun expenses such as entertainment (O'Curry, 1997; Henderson and Peterson, 1992) or cutting back on spending in one discretionary category based on prior spending in that category, rather than overall resources and preferences. Heath and Soll (1996) showed that expenses are assigned to category budgets on the basis of how prototypical an expense is for the category. They show that further spending in a category is less likely when a typical expense has been incurred than when the expense is atypical. For example, spending money on a concert ticket is a fairly typical entertainment expense, while spending money on a costume rental is not. Subjects who were asked to imagine that they had spent money on a ticket indicated that they would spend less for additional entertainment than subjects who were asked to imagine that they had spent the same amount on a costume rental.

Another issue in labelling is whether or not income or expenses are anticipated or not. Income for most households is received either monthly or bi-weekly, although many variations exist. The usual budget is based on predictable income and expenses. Unexpected income is often spent differently from income that is fully anticipated. Arkes et al. (1994) reported that windfall gains are more likely to be spent than other money, and argue that windfalls are more 'spendable' because they are unanticipated.

Amount

Amount appears to interact with both timing and labelling in determining disposition of income. Several researchers have found that the marginal propensity to consume windfall income decreases with the amount of the windfall, perhaps because large amounts are particularly salient (Keeler, James and Abdel-Ghany, 1985). Conversely, small amounts are discounted as too trivial to think about. Charities make use of this idea when they encourage donations by describing the amount in terms of cost per day, rather than annual cost. Interestingly, consumer budget advisers often encourage clients to think about expenses in annual terms in order to recognize the true cost of seemingly trivial daily expenses.

Irregular income, such as sales commissions or tips, can be difficult to manage because of variability. Tips present a dual problem for personal financial management because they are received daily and are in the form of cash. Consumers who are paid irregularly report spending more in a period when they have earned more, rather than saving excess earnings to smooth consumption later (O'Curry, 1997). Understanding how consumers think about their budgets is important to both managers and public policy makers. Response to tax cuts or price changes will often be very different from what a standard economic model would predict.

SUZANNE O'CURRY

Bibliography

Arkes, H.R., Joyner, C.A., Pezzo, M.V., Nash, J.G., Siegal-Jacobs, K. and Stone, E. (1994) 'The Psychology of Windfall Gains', *Organizational Behavior and Human Decision Processes*, **59**: 331–47.

Gourville, J.T. and Soman, D. (1997) 'Payment Depreciation: The Effects of Temporally Separating Payments From Consumption', Working Paper, Harvard Business School.

Heath, C. and Soll, J. (1996) 'Mental Budgeting and Consumer Expenses', *Journal of Consumer Research*, **23**: 40–52.

Henderson, P.W. and Peterson, R.A. (1992) 'Mental Accounting and Categorization', *Organizational Behavior and Human Decision Processes*, **51**: 92–117.

Hirst, D.E., Joyce, E.J. and Schadewald, M. (1994) 'Mental Accounting and Outcome Contiguity in Consumer Borrowing Decisions', *Organizational Behavior and Human Decision Processes*, **58**: 136–52.

Kahneman, D. and Tversky, A. (1979) 'Prospect Theory: An Analysis of Decision Under Risk', *Econometrica*, **47**: 263–91.

Kahneman, D. and Tversky, A. (1984) 'Choices, Values, and Frames', *American Psychologist*, **39**: 341–50.

Keeler, J.P., James, W.L. and Abdel-Ghany, M. (1985) 'The Relative Size of Windfall Income and the Permanent Income Hypothesis', *Journal of Business and Economic Statistics*, **3**: 209–15.

O'Curry, S. (1997) 'Income Source Effects', Working Paper, Department of Marketing, DePaul University, Chicago, IL 60604.

Prelec, D. and Loewenstein, G. (1997) 'The Red and the Black: The Mental Accounting of Savings and Debt', Working Paper, Sloan School of Management, Massachusetts Institute of Technology.

Shefrin, H.M. and Thaler, R. (1988) 'The Behavioral Life-Cycle Hypothesis', *Economic Inquiry*, **26**: 609–43.

Strotz, R.H. (1957) 'The Empirical Implications of a Utility Tree', *Econometrica*, **25**: 269–80.

Thaler, R. (1980) 'Toward a Positive Theory of Consumer Choice', *Journal of Economic Behavior and Organization*, 1: 39–60.

Winer, R.S. (1986) 'A Reference Price Model of Brand Choice for Frequently Purchased Products', *Journal of Consumer Research*, **13**: 250–56.

Children's Consumer Behaviour

The history of research into children's consumer behaviour spans the last 25 years, with conceptual and empirical papers covering a broad range of topics. The beginning of the field was marked by the appearance of a few articles in the 1960s, followed by a rapid growth period in the 1970s and early 1980s. Research waned somewhat in the mid to late 1980s, but rebounded in the 1990s. Today, interest in children's consumer behaviour comes from many groups, including academic researchers, business and marketing managers, public interest groups and government agencies.

Throughout the years, several topics have dominated research on children's consumer behaviour. The most attention, by far, has been directed at the issue of children's understanding of and response to television advertising. Smaller, but substantial, bodies of literature have also accumulated in studying how children interact with their parents to influence purchases and, more generally, how children become socialized as consumers. A common thread across these different literatures, reviewed below, is a focus on identifying and understanding differences that occur between children of different ages in an attempt to understand the developmental progression from child to adult consumer.

Understanding of and response to television advertising

The impetus for most of the academic research in this area can be traced to public policy concerns about the fairness of advertising to children that surfaced in the 1970s. In fact, in 1978, the Federal Trade Commission (FTC), an agency of the US government, charged that advertising to children was inherently unfair because young children do not have the requisite cognitive abilities to distinguish between television programming and television commercials, to identify the persuasive intent of television commercials, and to understand that advertising is not always truthful. Based on these charges, the FTC forwarded a proposal banning television advertising to children under the age of eight and restricting advertising for some products to children under the age of twelve.

Research published in the 1970s and early 1980s focused on providing empirical evidence relevant to these public policy concerns. Most of the studies used a survey approach, asking children of different ages a variety of questions pertaining to their understanding and knowledge of advertising. Researchers found that there were age differences in children's understanding of and reactions to television advertising. Young children, under the age of eight, were found to be less adept at distinguishing television commercials from programmes, less knowledgeable about advertising's persuasive intent, placed more trust in the truthfulness of advertising, and were generally less 'savvy' about television advertising than were older children and adults (see Robertson

69

and Rossiter, 1974). More recent data, gathered by researchers during the 1980s with more age-appropriate and nonverbal methods of questioning children, indicate that young children probably understand more about television advertising than prior survey approaches suggest, although they are clearly less knowledgeable than older children (see Macklin, 1985).

Several experimental studies also examined children's responses to television advertising, investigating whether advertising could indeed change children's preferences and choices. Although limited in number, these experimental investigations clearly demonstrate that children can be persuaded by television advertising and that exposure to advertising can affect children's preferences and product choices (see Goldberg, Gorn and Gibson, 1978). Importantly, this research also suggests that television advertising may overpower longstanding product preferences that children hold, especially younger children (see Roedder, Sternthal and Calder, 1983).

A final set of literature addresses the long-term impact of television advertising on children. The question here is whether long-run exposure to television advertising for certain types of products (for example, sugared cereal, candy, medicine) might permanently alter children's perceptions and usage of these products. Concern over the possibility that television advertising might have a detrimental effect on children's nutritional well-being or contribute to heightened over-the-counter and illicit drug use led researchers to examine the correlation between long-run exposure to television advertising and these consumption behaviours in the late 1970s and early 1980s. Results from these investigations suggest little or no correlation between long-run exposure to television advertising and basic consumption behaviours, although this conclusion is tempered by the fact that a relatively small number of studies exist on this topic. More recently, researchers have turned their attention to the long-run effects of cigarette advertising, with stronger results that tie television advertising for cigarettes to product preferences.

Parent-child purchase interaction

In their role as consumers, children not only make direct purchases with their own money but also influence purchases within their families. Acknowledging this important context, researchers have examined how children interact with their parents, how children attempt to influence their parents, how parents respond to influence attempts, and how successfully children influence purchasing of all types of products. The predominate findings are that children are very involved and quite influential participants in family consumer decision making, primarily influencing the purchase of child-orientated items (for example, toys, fast-food restaurants) but with some influence on more traditionally adult-oriented items (for example, cars, vacations) (see Mangleburg,

1990). Children make product requests from early ages, with younger children requesting more frequently and making more direct requests from their parents.

Children develop more sophisticated techniques for influencing their parents as they mature, and parents, in turn, seem to acknowledge the fact that older children should have an important voice in purchase decisions. As they mature, children learn new and more successful negotiating strategies to woo their parents. Parents, in response, acquiesce more often to older children's requests and often actively seek to involve them in purchasing situations. Although conflicts are inevitable at times, and result in some frustration on the part of children and parents alike, it is also true that conflicts appear to function as learning opportunities for parents to impart important consumer values, especially for older children and adolescents.

Consumer socialization

Many of the concerns about television advertising and marketing to children suggest the need to know more about how children learn to become consumers. That is, we needed to understand how children acquire consumer concepts and skills, such as learning about the nature and purpose of advertising, learning about money and prices, and learning how to gather information and evaluate products.

Some of the most basic questions were tackled by early research in the area. Using survey methods, researchers found that children become more knowledgeable about sources of product information and types of product information as they mature, as well as using more of this information in making product choices as they grow older (see Ward, Wackman and Wartella, 1977). Subsequent research built upon these findings by uncovering other sources of developmental differences, observing that abilities to learn information from shopping experiences and incorporate specific product information into overall preferences developed as children moved from early to middle childhood. During this same period, children were also found to be developing an awareness of the symbolic nature of products, learning that certain items convey status or prestige on those who own them (see Belk, Bahn and Mayer, 1982).

Consumer socialization does not take place in a vacuum, but involves important relationships among children, their families, and their peers. Although findings from this line of inquiry differ somewhat across studies, the general sense is that families and peers can both play an important role in consumer socialization. The importance of family in the learning process varies by the type of family communication pattern, with socio-orientated and participatory communication patterns contributing more to the socialization process. Peers play an increasingly important role as children enter adolescence, with peers becoming influential sources of information about brands and the symbolic nature of consumption (see Churchill and Moschis, 1979).

Conclusion

After 25 years, children's consumer behaviour continues to be an important area for academic and business research. Concerns about advertising and marketing to children continue even today, especially in the light of questions about the effects of cigarette and alcohol advertising on the consumption of these substances by underage consumers. On a different front, marketing and advertising practitioners continue to be interested in children as a potential and growing market for goods and services. In addition, parents and educators continue to be interested in how to convey the basic knowledge and skills that are necessary for becoming an informed consumer. Many questions in this area have been answered, but many more remain as fodder for future research.

DEBORAH ROEDDER JOHN

Bibliography

Belk, R.W., Bahn, K.D. and Mayer, R.N. ((1982) 'Developmental Recognition of Consumption Symbolism', *Journal of Consumer Research*, **9**: 4–17.

Churchill, G.A. and Moschis, G.P. (1979) 'Television and Interpersonal Influences on Adolescent Consumer Learning', *Journal of Consumer Research*, **6**: 23–35.

Goldberg, M.E., Gorn, G.J. and Gibson, W. (1978) 'TV Messages for Snacks and Breakfast Foods: Do They Influence Children's Preferences?', *Journal of Consumer Research*, **5**: 73–81.

Macklin, M.C. (1985) 'Do Young Children Understand the Selling Intent of Commercials?', *Journal of Consumer Affairs*, **19**: 293–304.

Mangleburg, T. (1990) 'Children's Influence in Purchase Decisions: A Review and Critique', in Goldberg, M.E., Gorn, G. and Pollay, R.W. (eds) *Advances in Consumer Research*, **17**, Ann Arbor, MI, Association for Consumer Research.

Robertson, T.S. and Rossiter, J.R. (1974) 'Children and Commercial Persuasion: An Attribution Theory Analysis', *Journal of Consumer Research*, **1**: 13–20.

Roedder, D.L., Sternthal, B. and Calder, B. (1983) 'Age Differences in Attitude-Behavior Consistency in Children', *Journal of Marketing Research*, **20**: 337–49.

Ward, S., Wackman, D. and Wartella, E. (1977) *How Children Learn to Buy: The Development of Consumer Information Processing Skills*, Beverly Hills, CA, Sage.

Children's Saving

Saving is of great theoretical interest to psychologists (who have mostly been interested in delay of gratification and individual intertemporal choice) and economists (who have concentrated on explaining variations in saving across the lifecycle). It is also of great practical interest to those who want to sell savings accounts, such as banks and building societies, and to governments, who want to encourage saving in general. But despite the fact that, as Maital (1982) put it, 'learning to wait begins in childhood', children's saving has to date received only very limited empirical study. Demos (a left-leaning UK think-tank) recently commissioned a review of policy-relevant research on saving and, in the absence of good quality data on the link between childhood and adulthood saving, was reduced to using commonsense ideas on what the link might be and how to encourage the latter.

But although there is not a lot of information on children's saving, what there is comes from a wide range of sources, including surveys, interview studies, laboratory experiments and role plays. What does this information tell us?

Most basically, it is clear that there are age-related changes in the level and forms of saving in childhood. Forty years ago, Dickins and Ferguson (1957) found that saving increased with age. Most children in the age groups they investigated (seven and eleven) said that they were saving for a special purpose, with Christmas presents being the most common target. In their much larger survey of children's consumer practices, Ward, Wackmann and Wartella (1977) also found that saving increased with age. Furnham and Thomas (1984) put more flesh on this bare-bones account. They reported that older children saved because they anticipated a generalized need for money in the future (rather than for concrete targets) and were more likely to use a savings account.

But why do these age differences occur? Is it that older children simply have more money or have different levels of access to bank accounts or is it something more interesting?

The series of studies of children's saving carried out by Webley and his colleagues (Webley and Lewis, 1987; Webley, 1988; Sonuga-Barke and Webley, 1993; Webley, Levine and Lewis, 1993) suggest that a number of processes are involved. Three of their studies involved a savings board game. Having earned tokens on an operant task, children played a game which presented them with a range of problems similar to those faced by children in the real economy. These included temptation (passing a sweet shop full of desirable goodies) and external threat (a relatively kindly robber who took just one token each time a child passed by). The details of the board game varied from study to study but each had a toy shop from which the child had selected his or her preferred toy (the long-term target that they were saving for) and a bank, which was one possible strategy for solving the problems with which they were faced. In another study, children took part in a play economy situated in a suite of four rooms, in which a variety of economic activities (such as going to a video arcade, a café, the bank) as well as free activities (a library, a drawing room) were available. Money was given out in the form of 'daily' pocket money and the children had to save over a 'week' to obtain their chosen toy (a day equalled a ten-minute time period).

Two further studies looked at parents' influence on children's saving (through a series of open-ended interviews) and how savings institutions encourage children's saving (through an analysis of promotional and marketing material).

These studies give us some insight into the development of saving behaviours (strategies and decisions) and saving beliefs (attitudes and beliefs). By age six, children know that saving is a good thing: they have picked up, presumably from their parents, the notions that self-control, patience and thrift are virtuous although most parents claim not to be teaching the purpose of saving or instilling the value of thrift. But although six-year-olds have learned that saving is a 'good thing' they do not like it very much. Some see money saved as money lost. They also do not save very well. For example, in one of the board game studies, children could use the bank to deposit money before encountering the robber or the temptation of the sweet shop. In this study, the major improvements in performance occurred between the ages of six and nine. At age four the use of the bank was essentially random. Six-year olds did save, but only because they thought they ought to. The older children, on the other hand, perceived the value of saving as a strategy to protect one's assets from threats from the inside (temptation) and outside (the robber). These findings were also mirrored in the play economy. Again six-year-olds showed a limited ability to save (about half saved not at all) and many equated putting money in the bank with spending, so that money in the bank was money lost.

Most nine-year-olds and all twelve-year-olds can save, if need be, but have also developed a range of other strategies for dealing with their financial affairs, most of which involve techniques for getting more money out of their parents. So saving is not seen as good *per se*, but one possible way of achieving a goal. In the play economy, this was seen in the older participants, some of whom attempted to manipulate the experimenter to make up the difference between the amount that they had saved and the amount that they needed to buy their target toy.

Accounts of the development of economic cognition have consistently isolated an early stage where economic actions are explained in social terms. Similarly, in these studies of saving, the six-year-olds said that they saved because it was a good thing and described the robber as 'that naughty man'. In one board game where children had the option of spending more tokens on something socially neutral (a ferry) or having fewer tokens robbed, the younger participants tended to choose the more expensive ferry (socially better but economically worse) whereas the older ones opted to brave the robber (socially worse but economically better).

Thus it seems as if children initially learn the behaviour of saving as they

74

pick up from their parents the notion that it is socially good, but they do not know what it is for. It is functionless. Children subsequently learn that saving is one strategy among many that can be used to solve economic psychological problems.

This account of children's saving leaves much unsaid. In particular, it says nothing about the origins of individual differences in saving (and how these might relate to the marked cross-cultural differences in savings rates), the relationships between childhood saving and childhood money management or the role parental practices play in fostering saving. These issues remain to be explored.

PAUL WEBLEY

Bibliography

Dickins, D. and Ferguson, V. (1957) *Practices and Attitudes of Rural White Children Concerning Money* (Technical Report no. 43), Mississippi State College, MS, Agricultural Experimental Station.

Furnham, A.F. and Thomas, P. (1984) 'Pocket Money: A Study of Economic Education', *British Journal of Developmental Psychology*, **2**: 205–12.

Maital, S. (1982) *Minds, Markets and Money*, New York, Basic Books.

Sonuga-Barke, E.J.S. and Webley, P. (1993) *Children's Saving*, Hove, Erlbaum.

Ward, S., Wackmann, D.B. and Wartella, E. (1977) *How Children Learn to Buy*, London, Sage/

Webley, P. (1988) '"Money for Spending and Money for Saving": Parental Views About Children's Saving', in Vanden Abeele, P. (ed.) *Psychology in Micro and Macro Economics: Proceedings of the 13th Annual Colloquium of IAREP*, Brussels.

Webley, P., Levine, R.M. and Lewis, A. (1993) 'A Study in Economic Psychology: Children's Saving in a Play Economy', in Maital, S. and Maital S.L. (eds) *Economics and Psychology*, Cheltenham, Edward Elgar: 61–80.

Webley, P. and Lewis, A. (1987) 'Saving Behaviour: Some Research in Progress', in Olander, F. and Grunert, K.G. (eds) *Understanding Economic Behaviour: Proceedings of the 12th Annual Colloquium of IAREP*, Aarhus.

Choice Deferral

The focus of most research in consumer behaviour and decision making has been on understanding how people choose among a given set of alternatives. While most studies force subjects to choose among a set of alternatives that are provided, consumers in the real world also have the option of seeking new alternatives and deciding whether to choose at all. Recent research suggests that the composition of the choice set and the precise nature of the task influences the likelihood of choice deferral. The standard economic framework suggests that the decision to not choose should be based on the attractiveness of the alternatives, and on perceived marginal costs and benefits of searching for more information. In addition, research in psychology suggests that consumers may defer deciding when the choice is stressful. Conceptually, choice deferral may then be influenced by contextual factors that alter the attractiveness of the decision outcomes as well as the difficulty of making the best choice. This issue is particularly interesting if one assumes that consumers do not have well-defined preferences — for example, when choosing products of which they have little experience — but rather construct them based on the alternatives provided. Here, I examine how task and contextual factors can be manipulated to influence choice attractiveness and choice difficulty and consequently choice deferral (see also the earlier discussion in Dhar, 1997a).

One reason why a decision maker may not choose is that none of the available alternatives is viewed as being attractive. It could be argued that this refusal option is just an expression of preferring the current possession (that is, money), and therefore does not undermine the validity of a model that would treat no-choice as just another option. Yet, recent research suggests that the attractiveness of an alternative is influenced by comparison with other alternatives and that the *same* alternative may be viewed as more or less attractive depending upon the choice context in which it is embedded. To illustrate how the choice context may influence decision attractiveness, consider an alternative that is presented as a part of a 'unique-good' pair such that the two alternatives have unique-good features but share their bad features. As indicated by the feature-matching model (Houston and Sherman, 1995), the unique (good) features of the alternatives receive greater attention and the shared (bad) features are under-weighted in the choice process. The alternatives are thus likely to appear attractive. The reverse is the case when the alternative is presented as part of a 'unique-bad' pair such that this alternative now shares its good features but differs on the bad features with the new alternative. In this case, it is the bad features that carry greater weight in the choice process.

Note that if consumers are confronted with a forced choice between two alternatives, it is entirely reasonable to ignore the attractiveness of their shared features. In contrast, when the no-choice option is also available, the extent to which the attractiveness of the alternatives varies with the context can affect the likelihood of making a choice as opposed to not choosing and wanting to see other options. This may be true even when the options in the unique-bad choice set are objectively as attractive as the options in the unique-good choice set. This proposition was recently tested by Dhar and Sherman (1996) by altering the choice set provided, such that either the good or the bad features were unique, and thus were seen as central and important. Subjects were first shown a set of alternatives, each of which had some good and some bad features. They were told that they would have to decide between random pairs of alternatives that were drawn from the initial set. They were also that told they had the option of not choosing the two alternatives that were shown and to look for another option. Subjects were then shown choice sets consisting of two relatively equally attractive alternatives. In some of the choice sets, the two alternatives shared their bad features and had unique-good features (unique-good pairs). In a second case, the two alternatives shared their good features and had unique bad features (unique-bad pairs). Consistent with the notion that unique features are overweighted relative to shared features, Dhar and Sherman (1996) found that the propensity to choose was significantly greater for the unique-good pairs compared to the unique-bad pairs, even though the alternatives in both conditions were matched for attractiveness.

The refusal option discussed above comes into play after the alternatives have been evaluated. A different reason why the exact timing of choice may vary is the uncertainty about the universe of available alternatives. The two most common reasons why choices may be postponed is to consider additional sources of information as well as to sample more of the alternatives that are available. When the alternatives vary on several attributes, the decision of when to stop searching is complicated by the notion of conflict and preference uncertainty. In many choice situations, the consumer may be uncertain about which of the alternatives is most preferred while not being certain that he or she wants them equally. Although value-based theories imply that two alternatives where none has a decisive advantage are equally likely to be selected, the indecision in such situations may result in a tendency to avoid commitment by not choosing at all. This is consistent with some previous research (and anecdotal evidence) that suggests that people do not like to choose at random but prefer to resolve the uncertainty in a manner that provides a justification for their choice (Elster, 1980). The need for justification can arise as much from being able to account for one's choices to an external audience or to justify to oneself why certain actions were more desirable than others (for additional reasons, see Shafir, Simonson and Tversky, 1993).

Recent research examined the effect of the relationship among the alternatives provided on choice deferral. In the typical study, subjects were shown a choice set with either two relatively equally attractive alternatives (high conflict) or a choice set where one alternative dominated the other (low conflict). These studies find that the percentage of subjects who choose is greater when they are presented with a choice set containing a dominated alternative than when they are presented with two relatively equally attractive alternatives (Tversky and Shafir, 1992; Dhar, 1997b). Luce (in press) suggests that the readiness to choose is further moderated by the ease with which consumers can make tradeoffs among the different attributes. She demonstrates that choice among equally attractive alternatives led to greater deferral when the alternatives consisted of attributes that were rated as being high on tradeoff difficulty. More generally, the findings suggest that the no-choice option is also preferred to a difficult choice between alternatives even in cases in which each alternative, by itself, may be chosen.

If the decision to defer choice is influenced by the lack of a compelling reason to act, one might predict that when the option of choosing more than one alternative is available, it should increase the likelihood of making a choice. This was tested in a study where the subjects were shown the same two attractive alternatives but the task was modified to allow the choice of a single item or both items, in addition to the no-choice option (Dhar, 1997b). Consistent with the notion that subjects in the 'single item' condition are more likely to be undecided, Dhar found that choice incidence was higher for subjects who were given the option of choosing both items than for subjects who could choose only a single item. The treatment of the no-choice option as a less risky alternative to choosing when one is uncertain which option to choose also suggests an interaction between decision accountability and choice deferral. Dhar and O'Curry (1996) looked at the effect of accountability on choice deferral when subjects were shown a set of two equally attractive alternatives, or a set where one alternative dominated the other. Consistent with the notion that the no-choice option may be viewed as a safe option, subjects in the high accountability condition were more likely to defer choice when the choice set contained two relatively equally attractive alternatives than when one alternative dominated the other.

The studies described so far focused on the effect of the relationship among the alternatives provided on choice deferral (that is, equal attractiveness or relative dominance). Choice deferral among the same alternatives may also be influenced by the different decision rules that consumers employ for choosing among available alternatives. Studies in forced choice typically find that individuals adopt different decision rules in different choice situations, potentially leading to differences in outcomes (Payne, Bettman, and Johnson, 1992). To the extent that different decision rules also result in a different degree of decision difficulty, the readiness to choose may also vary across the different rules. One reason why decision strategies may lead to differences in choice deferral is the notion that choice timing is influenced by the individual's confidence in his or her chosen option. Since the degree of confidence in the decision is influenced by the number of reasons available for and against each alternative, decision rules that involve the explicit consideration of the pros and cons of competing alternatives result in a lower decision confidence compared to decision rules for which the advantages of one option are not explicitly traded off against the advantages of competing alternatives. Thus, using a rule such as the additive-difference rule that generates both advantages and disadvantages for the alternatives, should reduce decision confidence and, consequently, should increase choice uncertainty and deferral. To the extent that a rule decreases decision difficulty by establishing a decisive advantage for a single alternative, it should increase the tendency to choose. For example, the lexicographic decision rule implies that the decision maker chooses based on the most important attribute on which one, and only one, alternative is better than all the other alternatives.

The effect of different decision rules on decision difficulty, and consequently choice incidence, was examined recently by Dhar (1996). Two different manipulations were used to influence the preferred mode of decision processing. In one study, the same set of equally attractive alternatives was presented either sequentially or simultaneously. Consistent with the idea that attribute tradeoffs are more likely in the simultaneous presentation condition which would increase decision difficulty, choice deferral was higher when the alternatives were presented simultaneously. A second study asked subjects in different treatment conditions to use specific decision rules to determine their most preferred alternative. They were then asked to decide between choosing this alternative and looking for other options. Consistent with the notion that choice difficulty differs across rules, subjects were more likely to defer choice when they were asked to use the additive difference rule than when they were asked to use the lexicographic rule. Note that the attractiveness of the outcomes can also vary across rules and potentially influence deferral (Earl, 1986: 179–88). For example, if consumers make choices by comparing the options relative to some aspirational cutoffs, they may end up 'in two minds' because they are unclear what cutoff levels it would be appropriate to use and can see that the options may look less or more attractive depending on the level of such cutoffs.

Much of consumer research has focused on the final moment of choice, rather portraying consumers as decisive and never prone to procrastination or hesitation. By contrast, the recent research summarized here has addressed consumer decision making when the no-choice option is also provided. The attractiveness of the decision outcomes and the difficulty of choosing among the alternatives provided were proposed as two key factors that determine the decision to defer choice. A number of studies described how these underlying factors can be modified and contribute to choice deferral. Overall, the results suggest that the timing of choice is sensitive to some of the same task and contextual factors that have previously been shown to influence relative preference ordering in forced choice (Simonson and Tversky, 1992). More generally, the narrow focus on the immediate context seems to hinder creativity in considering a broader set of alternative actions that are generally available but not explicitly provided to the decision maker.

The research on choice deferral has several interesting implications for marketers. Because few products achieve dominance in the marketplace, the choice of a comparative brand also implicitly determines the nature of tradeoffs that consumers are asked to make. Thus, comparing one's brand to a relatively inferior one not only increases market share but also may increase the size of the market that is ready to purchase. In a similar vein, marketers could encourage consumers to consider the different advantages of their product in relation to a competitor rather than competitors' disadvantages in relation to their product. Advertising wars that focus on giving reasons for not buying competing products (for example, side effects of aspirin) may prove counterproductive and result in not purchasing at all. The studies also suggest that providing a large variety of options may not always increase total purchase. Some evidence suggests that the confusion of choosing among increasing variety of brands may provide an edge to manufacturers or retailers with narrow offerings.

The focus on choice deferral also has some theoretical implications. In contrast to the neoclassical theory of choice that assumes stable preferences, the notion of preference uncertainty and choice difficulty suggests interesting implications for consumer behaviour. Intuitively, one can think of several situations where choice proliferation may result in decision delay, especially when the cost of delay is low. A related issue that arises is whether consumers alter the decision-making process and choose to limit their choice by taking into account the aversiveness that may be experienced at the final moment of choice. After all, full freedom entails the freedom to bind oneself, and to reduce one's range of choice (Schelling, 1984). If constraints on choices can increase welfare, consumers will be motivated to manufacture constraints where none exist. A doctoral candidate may restrict the schools that he or she visits in order to minimize future regret. Voters may pass term limits in order to deny themselves the choice of electing incumbents, and thus eliminate the anticipated conflict of not voting for an incumbent. Of course, it is entirely likely that the decision between imposing a choice restriction and a desire to maintain a full repertoire of options is itself seen as a difficult choice leading to indecision.

RAVI DHAR

Bibliography
Dhar, R. (1996) 'The Effect of Decision Strategy on the Decision to Defer Choice', *Journal of Behavioral Decision Making*, **9**: 265–81.
Dhar, R. (1997a) 'Context and Task Effects on Choice Deferral', *Marketing Letters*, **8**: 119–30.
Dhar, R. (1997b) 'Consumer Preference for a No-Choice Option', *Journal of Consumer Research*, **24**: 215–31.
Dhar, R. and Nowlis, S. (1996) 'Consumer Choice and Decision Delay Under Time

Pressure: The Role of the Choice Set Composition', Working Paper, Yale School of Management.

Dhar, R. and O'Curry, S. (1996) 'Decision Difficulty and Accountability', Working Paper, Yale School of Management.

Dhar, R. and Sherman, S.J. (1996) 'The Effect of Common and Unique Features on Consumer Choice', *Journal of Consumer Research*, **23**: 193–203.

Earl, P.E. (1986) *Lifestyle Economics: Consumer Behaviour in a Turbulent World*, Brighton, Wheatsheaf Books.

Elster, J. (1980) 'The Nature and Scope of Rational-Choice Explanation', in Davidson, D. (ed.) *Essays on Action and Events*, Oxford, Clarendon Press.

Houston, D.A. and Sherman, S.J. (1995) 'Cancellation and Focus: The Role of Shared and Unique Features in the Choice Process', *Journal of Experimental Social Psychology*, **31**: 357–78.

Luce, M.F. (in press) 'Choosing to Avoid: Coping with Negatively Emotion-laden Consumer Decisions', *Journal of Consumer Research*.

Payne, J.W., Bettman, J.R. and Johnson, E.J. (1992) 'Behavioral Decision Research: A Constructive Processing Perspective', *Annual Review of Psychology*, **43**: 87–131.

Schelling, T.C. (1984) *Choice and Consequence*, Cambridge, MA, Harvard University Press.

Shafir, E., Simonson, I. and Tversky, A. (1993) 'Reason-Based Choice', *Cognition*, **49**: 11–36.

Simonson, I. and Tversky, A. (1992) 'Choice In Context: Tradeoff Contrast and Extremeness Aversion', *Journal of Marketing Research*, **29**: 281–96.

Tversky, A. and Shafir, E. (1992) 'Choice Under Conflict: The Dynamics of Deferred Decision', *Psychological Science*, **3**: 358–61.

Cognitive Dissonance

Cognitive dissonance theory (hereafter, CDT) was proposed by Festinger (1957) and, over forty years later, it continues to attract considerable interest (the most up-to-date, all-encompassing reference source is Harmon-Jones and Mills, forthcoming). It is usually cast within the same conceptual school as other consistency theories, such as Heider's balance-theory analysis of attitudes and cognitive organization, or Osgood and Tannenbaum's theory of congruity and attitude change (see Steinbruner, 1974: 99). But there is a deciding element in CDT that sets it apart from the other consistency formulations, an element that has led to its immense expansion, both in theoretical tests and in direct applications. This is the idea that cognitive dissonance is a motivated state, and one which drives the person to regain cognitive consistency by taking the path that is *least* resistant to change.

Festinger defined dissonance as the existence of nonfitting relations among cognitions. After noting that people experience cognitive dissonance because they are not in control of the information they receive and because many things tend to be a mixture of contradictions, Festinger (1957: 3) advanced two basic hypotheses:

1. The existence of dissonance, being psychologically uncomfortable, will motivate the person to try to reduce the dissonance and achieve consonance.
2. When dissonance is present, in addition to trying to reduce it the person will actively avoid situations and information which would increase the dissonance.

His book elaborated these hypotheses and many subsidiary ones, and a lesser-known volume reporting experimental investigations of them appeared some years later (Festinger, 1964). It is not surprising that attempts have been made to frame economic behaviour in terms of strategies aimed at reducing cognitive dissonance. Many of Festinger's own illustrative scenarios actually concern economic situations, such as the trials of car ownership, employment choices, decisions not to give up smoking, or even minor decisions about whether to continue on a picnic expedition in the face of gathering clouds. Many of his scenarios complement those used in the literature on escalation of commitment which challenges orthodox economic thinking on the significance of sunk costs.

The application of Festinger's notion to such economic contexts illustrates how a simple cognitive inconsistency principle is insufficient to account for the phenomenon. For instance, suppose that people voluntarily switch from normal telephones to cellular telephones, knowing full well that there may be some enhanced chance of incurring brain cancer. There is a cognitive inconsistency between, on the one hand, having adopted cellular telephones on the basis of their advantages and, on the other hand, knowing the health risks. CDT is unique in predicting that dissonance *reduction* will be guided by whatever cognition is *least* resistant to change. As Festinger (1957: 28) puts it,

> The maximum dissonance that can possibly exist between any two elements is equal to the total resistance to change of the less resistant element. The magnitude of dissonance cannot exceed this amount because, at this point of maximum possible dissonance, the less resistant element would change, thus eliminating the dissonance.

As the theory has evolved (Brehm and Cohen, 1962; Wicklund and Brehm, 1976), research and applications have assumed that a decision or behavioural commitment carries with it a built-in resistance to change. This implies that the cognitive efforts of individuals will concentrate on supporting or rationalizing the commitment, on discounting or neglecting all cognitions that contradict the chosen course of action. The latter are then assumed to be *less* resistant to change than the cognitions that are congruent with the commitment.

If would-be cellular phone users find it easier to argue away the health risks — for example, 'I'm never on the phone for long periods, so I doubt I'd be at much risk' — than to dismiss more immediate threats to their social or business lives arising from sticking to the old technology, then CDT predicts they will become users of cellular phones and seem untroubled by brain cancer risks. Such predictions challenge conventional economic thinking by suggesting that people may avoid facing up to the fact that life is full of opportunity costs and by suggesting that they will be prone to try to gather information that will enable them to rationalize away the sacrifices that they have made as a result of committing themselves to particular courses of action. Furthermore, CDT seems to run counter to the idea of 'given preferences', for it suggests that once people have made commitments to particular courses of action they will tend to re-evaluate alternatives in the direction of favouring the chosen schemes or disfavouring the rejected ones (Elster, 1983).

The economics of reducing cognitive dissonance
The incorporation of dissonance-reducing behaviour into economic models does not require the abandonment of the assumption that decision-makers choose by weighing up costs and benefits. Rather, it requires the recognition that dissonant thoughts about the wisdom of a prior choice impose a *mental* cost and hence that a person may be prepared to incur other costs up to this level if this is the price that must be paid to avoid dissonance. Although people can reduce dissonance by discarding some beliefs and replacing them with others that fit better with those that are retained, this strategy is by no means guaranteed to be costless once one has 'made up one's mind'. It is here that the notion of commitment matters as an anchoring point for the direction to be taken in dissonance reduction.

If a chosen commodity is turning out to be rather disappointing, one could in principle avert the whole dissonance-arousal and dissonance reduction process simply by admitting — at least to oneself — that a mistake has been made and ceasing to expect the product to perform so well. But, as simple and rational as such a solution may appear, the Festinger (1957) and Brehm and Cohen (1962) versions of CDT, as well as later versions (see Harmon-Jones et al., 1996; Harmon-Jones and Mills, forthcoming) imply that the tension state would remain. When commitments are made on the basis of careful thought, decision makers by implication lay open to challenge their views of themselves in terms of decision-making competence. Thus, it may be impossible to lower expectations of further performance by a product one has chosen without also downgrading one's self-assessed capacities as a decision-maker. In terms of the person's way of viewing the world, the latter could carry very troubling 'implications' (Earl, 1992). Compared with the mental costs of self-reappraisal, it may be far easier to reappraise the product's performance 'through rose-tinted spectacles' or to dismiss the significance of aspects of it whose performance is undeniably poor. Mental costs of acquiring new perspectives and reframing ideas about things in terms of these perspectives are additional to any pecuniary costs associated with liquidating prior commitments to commodities in imperfect markets. The uncertainty associated with costs of trying to find a new way of looking at things may further encourage a decision maker to continue to struggle along with his or her existing, ill-matched beliefs. In short: if people are to be induced to revamp their expectations and change course, they need to become aware of opportunities that offer compensation for both mental and commodity-related costs of change. Admitting error is far easier when one has access to a means of explaining how the error was made which does not reflect poorly on one's capabilities as a decision maker.

In placing the decision maker's competence as a chooser at the centre of the analysis, such a perspective is portraying the state described by Festinger as an involved, motivated one, not a cognitively cold matter of information processing. This is consistent with the recent findings of researchers such as Harmon-Jones and his colleagues. For example, it has been found that dissonance reduction is not observed when people are convinced that the discomfort after a decision is due to other causes than their own dissonance-producing actions. Likewise, when the role of external pressure on a person to perform a dissonance-arousing act has been investigated, it has been found that dissonance will be maximized if the deciding person is convinced that the basis of choice lies within one's own person. If there is a strong outside inducement, the rationalization process, and hence the restoring of cognitive consistency, is thereby circumvented.

Pre-choice versus post-choice dissonance
In Festinger's view of decision making, switches between different sets of ideas *can* be achieved without any bother *prior* to choice: it is as if, during the process of evaluating alternatives, a chooser's mindset takes the form of putty, capable of being moulded into a variety of shapes. It may be kept in this form as long as fear of dissonance leads to choice being deferred (Festinger, 1957: 31). However, while potential scenarios are being rehearsed, the difficulty of escaping dissonance may eventually lead to an impulsive choice that at least stabilizes the situation and cuts short a seemingly endless information-gathering process (Festinger, 1964: 5, 154–5). At the moment of choice it is as if the putty mindset is at least partially hardened: commitment is made not merely to a particular course of action and its associated commodities but also to a particular set of expectations. Thenceforth, the decision maker will be prepared, up to a point, to incur costs of gathering information that neutralizes challenges to the chosen mindset, as well as costs necessary to avoid confronting such challenges in the first place — such as avoiding particular social encounters and making selective use of information sources within a particular medium.

The fact that choice is often a lengthy process and takes place in a social setting stands as something of a qualification to Festinger's focus on post-choice dissonance reduction. If a person is thinking aloud in the presence of social referents about possible bases for reaching a decision, there is the risk that points made at this stage will be raised subsequently by the audience as a basis for criticizing the eventual choice, on the ground that it is inconsistent with what was previously said. Although the person may expect memories to fade as time passes, a perceived need to appear consistent may drive a commitment towards particular options and a 'sour grapes' approach to others that are having to be ruled out to meet this need (compare Elster, 1983) before a decision is finally reached.

As Steinbruner (1974: Ch. 4) stresses, uncertainty will make it easier for people to avoid cognitive dissonance at the time of making up their minds. Complexity of the decision problem may also make it easier for a seemingly dissonance-free decision to be reached: the boundedly rational decision maker may fail to see that dissonance would arise from the detailed following through of implications of arguments used in justifying the choice. Later, these inconvenient implications may surface and generate the sort of behaviour predicted by Festinger.

Applications

The history of CDT research suggests that applications are limited only by the prerequisite that the process in question must begin with a relatively free decision. Given this point of departure, there are two broad realms of application to consumer and economic behaviour. The first of these, following Brehm (1956) is often called 'free choice'. These are the ostensibly unconstrained decisions among consumer products or other courses of action. In such cases there may be a short-lived regret phase just after the decision (Festinger, 1964), in which the chosen alternative is subject to doubt. This regret is typically superseded by a rationalizing effect — a spreading apart of the chosen and unchosen alternatives in subjective attractiveness. The strength of such effects will then be multiplied by the importance of the decision, for example, the monetary value of the products.

The second realm of application is called 'forced compliance' or, sometimes, 'induced compliance'. Here, the respondents do not choose the companions, consumer goods or political actions that they find the most appealing; rather, their choices result from subtle social pressures — such as an experimenter's coaxing, a friend's advice, or a salient advertisement. Once again, the effects are the sorts of seemingly irrational cognitive adjustments described above. However, when researchers in this area encounter peculiarly contrived-looking justifications of actions, they might do well to be mindful of Garfinkel's (1967: 113–14) provocative view that often people make choices without any idea of what their 'real' reasons are and simply construct justifications after the event on the basis of the most likely looking explanation they can muster. (Of course, what looks 'likely' may depend on how events are unfolding following such choices.)

In the hands of economists, CDT has been used to make sense of a wide variety of behaviours that might otherwise prove puzzling. It has typically been used to give a path-dependent dimension to economists' tales.

It was swiftly applied in development economics by Hirschman (1965), who argued that the kinds of societies most likely to develop rapidly would be ones that are prone to let their motivation to solve their problems outrun their understanding of how to do so. Having plunged headlong into attempting to promote development they would ignore noncognitive 'barriers' such as poor natural resource endowments. Thus they might achieve more than somewhat better endowed societies that tend to avoid tackling problems unless easy solutions seem available.

Maital (1982: 142–3) used CDT to explain why, despite believing that 'debt is wrong', American consumers were happily getting themselves deeper into debt with the aid of credit cards: since credit cards can be used merely as a means of payment rather than for their extended credit facilities, people can use them without having to admit to themselves that they are getting into debt; they can tell themselves that they will make full payments when the next statement arrives. This scenario is extended by Etzioni (1986: 179–80) to suggest the possibility of a kind of 'thin end of the wedge' effect where a successful dissonance reduction strategy enables a person to dodge an inconsistency between one of his or her actions and his or her normal moral constructs. Etzioni stresses that moral dilemmas are often irreversible, discontinuous and prone to involve threshold effects. He comments that 'Taking out the first loan, for people who feel being in debt is a moral evil, is different from extending it or taking out a second one'. If people initially tell themselves that they are using their credit cards as debit cards but then end up using their cards' extended credit facilities, they can no longer construe themselves as the sort of people who do not get into debt (although, as long as they meet their monthly payments obligations, they can still claim not to be living beyond their means). Having, so to speak, lost their virginity as debtors and come to see that the situation does not entail the nasty implications that they expected, they may become avid users of finance as a powerful device for avoiding dissonance. (Note how the euphemistic phrase 'using finance' may itself have rather nicer connotations than 'being in debt'.) The sources of finance that they now use may include hire purchase, overdrafts and personal loans that they used to shun because, unlike credit cards, such arrangements necessarily involved an admission that one was borrowing.

Tendencies to speculate have also been explored with the aid of CDT. Kaish

(1986) has used the analogy of skaters on a frozen pond to explain how participants in a bull market may justify ignoring warnings that a crash is imminent because asset prices have become dangerously divorced from levels implied by underlying fundmentals: someone having a great time skating may see others joining him or her on the pond and yet justify ignoring warnings about the danger of the ice cracking by reminding him- or herself how cold it has been lately and how thick, therefore, the ice must be (for a related discussion of the effects of dissonance on stock-purchasing behaviour, see Klausner, 1984: 71–5).

The best-known and most rigorous of economic applications of CDT is the work of Akerlof and Dickens (1982), which considers, among other things, the role for compulsory old age insurance (since people may feel uncomfortable contemplating themselves in retirement and therefore avoid considering things, such as life assurance schemes, that bring such thoughts to mind) and safety legislation (since people who view themselves as smart may choose to ignore the dangers of their well-paying but hazardous work environments). One of the important suggestions made by Akerlof and Dickens is that attempts to reduce dissonance in the past may affect preferences in the present. Their specific example concerns attitudes towards the purchase of newly invented safety equipment. Workers may have resolved the conflict between suggestions that their work environment is dangerous and their views of themselves as 'smart guys' by turning a blind eye to the dangers and telling themselves that their pay reflects their smartness, not the probability of injury at work. Having convinced themselves that their jobs are not particularly dangerous, they will be less interested than new recruits will be in buying the newly available safety equipment.

For marketers, CDT carries the implication that a major role for advertisements is to set minds at ease *after* purchases have been made. Furthermore, attempts to reduce dissonance will affect the information that one will gather about possibilities even if these activities do not lead consumers to discover new ways of looking at the world and new attributes of significance. This may mean that, when the time comes to replace a product, the person is looking at a field that has already been narrowed down in a biased way.

PETER E. EARL AND ROBERT A. WICKLUND

Bibliography

Akerlof, G.A. and Dickens, W.T. (1982) 'The Economic Consequences of Cognitive Dissonance', *American Economic Review*, **72**: 307–19.

Brehm, J.W. (1956) 'Postdecision Changes in the Desirability of Alternatives', *Journal of Abnormal and Social Psychology*, **52**: 384–9.

Brehm, J.W. and Cohen, A.R. (1962) *Explorations in Cognitive Dissonance*, New York, Wiley.

Earl, P.E. (1992) 'On the Complementarity of Economic Applications of Cognitive Dissonance Theory and Personal Construct Psychology', in Lea, S.E.G., Webley, P. and Young, B.M. (eds) *New Directions in Economic Psychology*, Aldershot, Edward Elgar: 49–65.

Elster, J. (1983) *Sour Grapes: Studies in the Subversion of Rationality*, Cambridge, Cambridge University Press/Paris, Editions de la Maison des Sciences de L'Homme.

Etzioni, A. (1986) 'The Case for a Multiple-Utility Conception', *Economics and Philosophy*, **2**: 159–84.

Festinger, L. (1957) *A Theory of Cognitive Dissonance*, Stanford, CA, Stanford University Press.

Festinger, L. (ed.) (1964) *Conflict, Decision, and Dissonance*, Stanford, CA, Stanford University Press.

Garfinkel, H. (1967) *Studies in Ethnomethodology*, Englewood Cliffs, NJ, Prentice–Hall.

Harmon-Jones, E., Brehm, J.W., Greenberg, J., Simon, L. and Nelson, D.E. (1996) 'Evidence that the Production of Aversive Consequences is Not Necessary to Create Cognitive Dissonance', *Journal of Personality and Social Psychology*, **70**: 5–16.

Harmon-Jones, E. and Mills, J. (forthcoming) *Cognitive Dissonance Theory 40 Years Later: Revival with Revisions and Controversies*, Washington, DC, American Psychological Association.

Hirschman, A.O. (1965) 'Obstacles to Development: A Classification and a Quasi-Vanishing Act', *Economic Development and Cultural Change*, **13**: 385–93.

Kaish, S. (1986) 'Behavioral Economics in the Theory of the Business Cycle', in Gilad, B. and Kaish, S. (eds) *Handbook of Behavioral Economics*, Volume B, Greenwich, CT, JAI Press: 31–49.

Klausner, M. (1984) 'Sociological Theory and the Behavior of Financial Markets', in Adler, P.A. and Adler, P. (eds) *The Social Dynamics of Financial Markets*, Greenwich, CT, JAI Press.

Maital, S. (1982) *Minds, Markets and Money: Psychological Foundations of Economic Behavior*, New York, Basic Books.

Steinbruner, J.D. (1974) *The Cybernetic Theory of Decision*, Princeton, Princeton University Press.

Wicklund, R.A. and Brehm, J.W. (1976) *Perspectives on Cognitive Dissonance*, Hillsdale, NJ, Erlbaum.

Collecting

The word 'collecting' is derived from the Latin word 'colligere', meaning to gather. One can therefore deduce that the term 'collecting' refers to the methodical collection of objects. Such a broad definition is at odds, however, with the common significance evoked by the word.

It is commonly thought that a selective ability lies behind collecting. A collector does not gather objects at random, but only seeks those items which seem likely to serve his or her purposes. This means that a collector has his or her own, not necessarily explicit, criteria for comparing the objects which attract his or her attention. It is on the basis of these criteria that the collector selects the objects which he orf she perceives as worth collecting.

Collecting is also associated with considerable knowledge about the genre to which objects belong. Selection ability is generally considered a consequence of the collector's experience, gained through study, exchanges with other enthusiasts, participation in fairs and exhibitions, and the act of collecting itself. All these factors make the collector an expert who can make an accurate judgement of the value of the objects to be selected.

Collecting is attributed with the capacity to provide considerable self-gratification. Collectors are perceived as taking pride in their own collections, in their willingness and ability to describe and exhibit the pieces in their possession, in their awareness of the importance of the collecting activity, and in their considerable employment of financial and time resources for the continuous enrichment of their collections.

These characteristics which common knowledge generally attributes to collecting emphasize some peculiarities of the activity in comparison with the simple gathering of objects. Collecting can, therefore, be seen as the process of selection, acquisition and care of a series of related objects, with the aim of providing self-gratification for the individual involved.

On this basis it is possible to distinguish between collecting and similar activities such as accumulating and hoarding (Baekeland, 1981; Belk et al., 1988; Baudrillard, 1994: 22). The difference is due to the fact that these other activities usually lack the selective ability; thus, dissimilar objects are accumulated because they may one day be useful (it is enough to think here of the quantity and type of goods stored in the lofts or basements of many houses). These activities may also lack the specialized knowledge about objects; value is attributed to them solely in terms of their usefulness or the amount someone will pay for their acquisition (it is easy here to remember the small junk and second-hand shops where one can find objects of every kind). Again, these activities may lack the element of self-gratification in gathering, other than obtaining money in exchange for the objects, or some value associated with the goods other than their value in use.

Given its peculiarities, collecting, and the personalities of collectors themselves, have attracted the attention of scholars in different fields. Psychiatrists and psychologists were among the earliest to be interested in studying collecting behaviour, and their interpretations provide a rather negative idea of the collector figure (Baekeland, 1981; Muensterberger, 1994; see Formanek, 1991, and Olmsted, 1991, for a review). The collector is seen as an individual with an immature personality, with markedly childish characteristics. Seen in terms of the Freudian theory of psychosexual development, collecting behaviour was associated with the individual in the anal phase of development — the accumulation and care of objects, the reluctance to part with pieces from a collection were interpreted as a surrogate of the pleasure experienced by a baby learning to retain its faeces and the sense of loss when evacuating its bowels. Another interpretation has seen collecting as a sign of the individual's remaining in the oral phase of development, for whom the acquisition of objects in the collection is a surrogate of the pleasure experienced by a baby in feeding itself. Collecting behaviour was also associated with aggression rather than with the libido. In this interpretation the process of searching for missing pieces and the pleasure in gathering and acquiring them would be the equivalent of the instinctive behaviour of pursuing and catching prey. The collector figure has also been seen as having obsessive, addictive and compulsive behaviour traits, associated with the process of the continuous increase of the collection and the desire underlying the process itself, which are the signs of a distorted, immature and sometimes disturbed personality. It is not by chance that many of the clinical cases analysed in the psychological studies of collecting (Baekeland, 1981; Muensterberger, 1994) concern adults who suffered in infancy from privation, lack of affect or trauma.

The psychological interpretation of collecting has become more positive in recent years, thanks to the contributions of scholars in other fields such as anthropology, ethnography and consumer behaviour. The progressive social and institutional acceptance of the phenomenon has probably also contributed to this change of view (Mukerji, 1978; Olmsted, 1991). The motivations underlying collecting have been gradually revealed (Formanek, 1991; Olmsted, 1991): for example, the wish to preserve history and maintain a sense of continuity with the past, to invest resources, to deepen one's own knowledge, and to employ leisure time in an enjoyable way.

Collecting is now commonly seen, like other phenomena, as a way of possessing goods through which the individual constructs his or her own self-image and extended self (Belk, 1988), thus establishing his or her own identity and place in a social and cultural context. Collecting provides self-gratification and self-worth on one side, and on the other, social acceptance and legitimacy for highly cultural aspects (although this depends to a great extent on the subject matter of the collection).

The interpretation of collecting as a particular form of possession has stimulated the interest of scholars of consumer behaviour (see Belk et al., 1988, for a review). This has led to the distinction between consumer–collector and normal consumer traits, making the consumer–collector a figure of considerable interest in the interpretation of ever more diffused consumption phenomena. Using the traditional subdivision of cognition, affect and behaviour employed in consumer behaviour analysis, one can highlight the characteristics of the consumer–collector (Guerzoni and Troilo, 1998).

At the cognitive level the collector is an extremely creative consumer. While, generally, the characteristics of a product category are affected by producer choices, collectors instead make a subjective definition of the boundaries of the category of objects making up their collection. While an ordinary individual cannot make discerning judgements within the category 'old French stamps', a collector can use distinctive criteria for these objects, which can be used to establish innumerable subcategories. Temporal categories are also defined creatively; the concepts of new and old, of antique and modern, are not defined according to traditional standards so much as according to subjective and consistent one relating exclusively to the selection criteria of the collection.

At the level of affect, the collector has a marked propensity to pleasure, to self-gratification, to search for fun and enjoyment in all the activities connected with forming the collection. The process of research, the discovery of a piece and the care taken of it, give the collector a satisfaction similar to that deriving from the acquisition of the object. Further, the symbolic and aesthetic value of the good is clearly greater than its value in use or value in exchange. In so far as the former is concerned, the object is generally 'divested of its function and made relative to a subject' (Baudrillard, 1994: 7). The pieces of a collection are rarely used for their original function. More often, they are simply possessed, or rather cared for, admired and exhibited just for self-gratification. In so far as value in exchange is concerned, this is generally regarded as nil, because no price can estimate the affective value that an object has for the owner. It rarely happens that pieces, much less the whole collection, are sold. It is more common for them to be given away, Maecenas-like — in which case the right price is not expressible in money as much as in glory or eternal gratitude. They can also be bequeathed after death, although there is a series of problems that collectors are familiar with, connected to this (Belk et al., 1988).

The collector has some special characteristics at the level of behaviour as well. Above all, he or she is a serial consumer. The acquisition of pieces for the collection only makes sense within the collection itself: it is the series which gives value to the individual good. The 'missing piece' has a value not as such, but because its absence reduces the value of the whole collection. This element highlights another factor — rising marginal utility. In contradiction of a classical law of economics, the collector does not experience falling utility as a function of the growing number of pieces owned. Just the opposite happens — utility rises exponentially because of the logic of the series, so that as the collection increases in size the value of the missing pieces also increases. The price elasticity of demand of the collector is sharply reduced as a collection nears completion. Because of the logic of the series and rising utility, the missing piece has such a high affective value that it cannot be expressed in money terms — the final piece of the collection gives value to the whole collection.

Considering the cognitive, affective and behavioural levels together, one can see the final significant characteristic of the consumer–collector: what happens when the collection is finished, when the final piece has been bought? This is a situation in which the collector does not tend to find him- or herself. When the series is nearly finished (behaviour), the emotional involvement (affect) is very high but it contains symptoms of disappearance. At this point the collector usually makes a creative redefinition of the boundaries of the collection so as to widen or deepen it (learning), and to give the chance of beginning a new series.

GABRIELE TROILO

Bibliography
Baekeland, F. (1981) 'Psychological Aspects of Art Collecting', *Psychiatry*, **44**: 45–59.
Baudrillard, J. (1994) 'The System of Collecting', in Elsner, J. and Cardinal, R. (eds) *The Cultures of Collecting*, London, Reaktion Books.
Belk, R.W. (1988) 'Possessions and the Extended Self', *Journal of Consumer Research*, **15**: 139–68.
Belk, R.W., Wallendorf, M., Sherry, J., Holbrook, M. and Roberts, S. (1988) 'Collectors and Collecting', *Advances in Consumer Research*, **15**: 548–53.
Formanek, R. (1991) 'Why They Collect: Collectors Reveal Their Motivations', *Journal of Social Behavior and Personality*, **6**: 275–86.
Guerzoni, G. and Troilo, G. (1998) 'Silk Purses out of Sows' Ears. Mass Rarefaction of Consumption and the Emerging Consumer–Collector', in Bianchi, M. (ed.) *The Active Consumer*, London, Routledge.
Muensterberger, W. (1994) *Collecting: An Unruly Passion*, Princeton, NJ, Princeton University Press.
Mukerji, C. (1978) 'Artwork: Collection and Contemporary Culture', *American Journal of Sociology*, **84**: 348–65.
Olmsted, A.D. (1991) 'Collecting: Leisure, Investment or Obsession?', *Journal of Social Behavior and Personality*, **6**: 287–306.

Congruity Theory

Background: self-image research

Do consumers buy goods because of what they do (functional value), or because of what they mean (symbolic value)? The answer to this question is at the heart of congruity research, and the larger domain of self-image research. Self-image theory (sometimes referred to as self-concept theory) focuses on the link between an individual's perception of self and the symbolic value of the brands/products an individual purchases (Loudon and Della Bitta, 1988).

Self-image is theorized to be a multi-dimensional construct, comprising *actual* self-image and *ideal* self-image (Lamone, 1966), *actual social* self-image and *ideal social* self-image (Hughes and Guerrero, 1971), to name four of the more commonly researched dimensions. To understand these various dimensions of self-image, consider a young female academic who teaches in blue jeans every day, until the university administration imposes a dress standard such that the young lecturer must now appear in front of the classroom in a suit each day. While the lecturer's preference is to wear jeans because they are comfortable and casual, much like her teaching style (actual self-image), the lecturer wishes she felt more comfortable in the required suits (ideal self-image). She realizes, however, that her fellow colleagues think she is much too casual in her approach and dress (actual social self-image). So, wearing a suit helps her blend in and be more accepted by her colleagues (ideal social self-image).

An individual's self-image is expected to affect behaviour in such a way that his or her perception of self will be enhanced through the consumption of goods as symbols (Grubb and Grathwohl, 1967). Sirgy (1982) has identified five major themes in self-image research:

1. the relationship between self-image and socio-psychological factors (for example, the impact of factors such as gender, social class, conservative/ liberal views, religious convictions, on self-image);
2. consumer behaviour as a function of the match between self-image and the individual's perception of a product image (known as congruity);
3. consumer behaviour as a direct function of the effects of self-concept *per se* (that is, not looking for any match/interaction with product images);
4. product image as a function of consumer behaviour (for example, 'I use *X* product; I am this kind of person; therefore, the product image has to be like me');
5. self-image as a function of behavioural effects.

Of these research themes, self-image/product-image congruity has received the most empirical support. Early work in this area focused on testing Grubb and Grathwohl's (1967) theory, known as the 'self-congruity hypothesis'. This hypothesis implies that, in some forms of consumer behaviour, a consumer seeks to express his/her self-image by seeking out products whose images match his/her self-image. Early empirical work in this area focused on testing the self-congruity hypothesis relative to the actual self-image, and found general support for the theory (Grubb and Hupp, 1968; Birdwell, 1968; Grubb and Stern, 1971). This research theorized that when a person's actual self-image ('I am a casual person') is consistent with the individual's product image ('blue jeans are casual clothes'), actual congruity is high, thus enhancing purchase motivation. Conversely, when a person's actual self-image does not match the individual's product image, actual congruity is theorized to be low, resulting in low purchase motivation.

Several weaknesses of the early work were noted. First, it predicted behaviour post-purchase (Evans, 1968). This argument was based on the theory of cognitive dissonance, such that a consumer may alter his/her attitudes towards the product after purchase in order to increase satisfaction with the purchase. Second, the hypothesis was seen to be quite naive. Empirical research had dealt only with *actual* self-image, and totally ignored other factors contributing to purchase decisions. Hughes and Guerrero (1971), for example, argued for a more complex conception of self-image. They suggested that purchases may reflect ideal self-image (especially if one's actual self-image is negative), or social self-image, in which one projects an image perceived to be desirable to others.

Congruity research throughout the 1970s therefore focused on other dimensions of self-image, trying to explain the circumstances in which each dimension was most salient. Three streams of research evolved, focusing on the use of moderating variables to explain the differential effects of actual self-image and ideal self-image; situational views of self-image; and the simultaneous effects of actual and ideal self-image (Sirgy, 1985a).

Sirgy's interactive congruity theory
Sirgy (1982, 1985b) advanced congruity research by focusing on the inter-relationship between actual congruity and ideal congruity, and their combined effects on a consumer's purchase motivation. Actual congruity exists when a person's actual self-image matches his/her product image. Ideal congruity refers to a match between an individual's ideal self-image and his/her product image. Sirgy's (1985b) congruity theory posits four discrete conditions that are theorized to activate varying levels of self-esteem and self-consistency motivation in a purchase situation. While congruity is hypothesized to motivate purchase intentions or purchase avoidance, such motivation is driven by the mediating constructs of self-esteem and self-consistency. Self-esteem motivation refers to an individual's need to behave so as to maintain and/or enhance self-esteem, whereas self-consistent motivation refers to an individual's need to behave in a way consistent with his/her self-perception. Table 1 indicates the theorized relationship of each of the four conditions of actual- and ideal-congruity interaction on purchase motivation, as mediated by self-consistency and self-esteem motivations.

The four cases above are listed in predicted strength of purchase motivation. Condition 1, in which both actual and ideal congruity are high, is argued to produce the greatest purchase motivation, since consumption would satisfy both self-esteem and self-consistency. Conditions 2 and 3 are considered to produce a conflict of purchase motivation, and condition 4 is argued to produce the lowest purchase motivation. Recent congruity research has generally adopted Sirgy's (1985a) interactive congruity model, since it explains the combined effects of actual and ideal congruity on purchase motivation in terms of the self-concept. Sirgy (1985b) found that both actual congruity and ideal congruity have a positive and additive effect on purchase motivation. However, several criticisms can be raised about this model. First, the four cases are described as discrete conditions, and do not allow for various degrees of match between self-image and product image. When a consumer falls into the grey area between discrete conditions, there is no interpretation of the congruity/purchase motivation relationship. Second, it is not clear why Case 2 would be a stronger predictor of purchase motivation than Case 3, when both are predicted to cause conflict in an individual's purchase motivation. While Sirgy's congruity theory attempts to provide an explanation of the salience effects of actual- and ideal-self-image, the theory does not provide clear guidance in predicting purchase motivation.

Table 1: The four conditions of Sirgy's interactive congruity theory

Case	Condition	Self-consistency motivation	Self-esteem motivation	Purchase motivation
1	High actual congruity/ High ideal congruity	+	+	Approach
2	Low actual congruity/ High ideal congruity	−	+	Conflict
3	High actual congruity/ Low ideal congruity	+	−	Conflict
4	Low actual congruity/ Low ideal congruity	−	−	Avoidance

Source: Adapted from Sirgy (1985b).

Several other criticisms have emerged about congruity research in general. The first is that self-concept studies have tended to be based on atheoretical notions that consumers are motivated to approach those products which match their self-perceptions. Self-concept research needs to focus on describing when and how congruity motives are activated and explain the process by which consumers compare themselves with product images. Another criticism has been that congruity research needs to develop a better understanding of the combined effect of actual and ideal congruity on purchase behaviour. Research to date has been equivocal in its findings in this regard, and the use of moderating variables to explain differential effects has been particularly lacking in a theoretical approach. For example, an explanation of the relative salience of ideal congruity and actual congruity may depend on an individual's level of self-esteem. When an individual has low self-esteem, and therefore a need to enhance self-esteem, ideal congruity would more likely be the relevant predictor of purchase motivation. However, when an individual has high self-esteem, and therefore seeks to maintain self-esteem, actual congruity would probably be the stronger predictor of purchase motivation. Thus, self-esteem, as a moderating construct, could explain some of the difference between Case 2 and Case 3 in Sirgy's model.

A third area of criticism about congruity research lies with methodological issues, which have further hindered theory development (Sirgy, 1982). Measurement of self-image and product image has been problematic, making it difficult to measure the 'congruity' or match between them. Three standard measurement approaches have typically been used to measure self-image and product image: the use of semantic differential scales (using bipolar adjectives to describe one's self); Q-method, based on personality associations with products; or modified personality inventories. These traditional approaches are problematic because they treat every individual alike, with a predetermined set of values and characteristics against which congruity is assessed. None of these approaches is fundamentally designed to provide insight into an individual's world view, or one's perception of self or the products he or she encounters. Instead, these traditional methodological approaches reduce congruity theory to nothing more than another form of trait theory. On top of the measurement problems noted, empirical testing of congruity theory has also been hindered by the methods used to calculate congruity. The traditional method of determining congruity is based on the mathematical discrepancy between a subject's perception of the product image and his/her perception of self-image. Marketers use the resulting congruity 'score' to position their brands using the most congruous images that are also different enough from the images communicated about competing brands. However, the use of discrepancy scores to measure congruity has arguably contributed to the poor explanatory power of congruity models. Discrepancy scores do not incorporate any reference to the psychological congruity experience of the individual respondents, and inappropriately presume that a consumer invariably uses a compensatory decision rule, in which he or she sums up, in a piecemeal additive fashion, the match between a given product image and his/her self-image (Sirgy et al., 1997).

Recent developments in congruity research

Congruity researchers have tried to overcome these shortcomings in recent work. Traditionally, two competing approaches (multiattribute models and congruity models) have been used to understand and predict consumer buying behaviour. Multiattribute attitude models, based on expectancy-value theory, generally involve utilitarian or performance-related (functional) attributes in predicting consumer attitude or purchase intentions towards a particular brand. In contrast, congruity models have focused on the value-expressive and symbolic attributes of products in trying to predict consumer behaviour (Sirgy et al., 1991). Congruity models are based on the 'match' between an individual's self-image and value-expressive attributes of a given product, whereas multiattribute models are based on cognitive-processing activities assessing the importance of various attributes. While both research approaches are designed to predict consumer behaviour, and can be used by marketers to position their product brands, until recently little work has considered the role of these two models respective to each other. In Sirgy et al. (1991), self-congruity (based on self-image models including actual-, ideal-, social- and ideal social-self-congruity) and functional congruity (based on utilitarian criteria found in multiattribute models, such as belief-evaluation, belief-importance and ideal-point models) are both found to be direct predictors of consumer behaviour. However, functional congruity is found to be a much stronger predictor of behaviour than self-congruity, while self-congruity is found to have a 'biasing' effect on functional congruity. This suggests that the two models can play different roles in consumer decision making situations. Marketers can use self-concept communication to enhance a consumer's functional evaluation of a brand. Thus, congruity research and multiattribute research can be considered to be complementary, rather than competing models of consumer behaviour.

To overcome the methodological limitations of previous congruity research, Sirgy et al. (1997) suggest new measurement methods of self-image congruence. First, to overcome the problems inherent in traditional discrepancy scores, a direct measure of self-image congruence in relation to an individual's attitude and brand intention is recommended. Allowing respondents to assess self-attributes and product attributes that are personally meaningful ensures that individual respondents are associating with relevant images. This has been successfully attempted in recent research on congruity theory in advertising (Moore, 1996). This approach enables congruity research to become part of a larger stream of thought in which an individual's belief system (worldview) is said to be made up of a system of constructs by which he or she classifies and makes sense of the world, and which then forms the framework which guides an individual's behaviour and decision making.

Second, by using a global measure, instead of a combination of dimension-based measures, congruity theory can be bridged to other theoretical approaches to decision making. Such a methodological approach is argued to be more appropriate than the traditional compensatory decision rules, based on the current realization that self-image congruence may be a 'holistic, *gestalt*-like perception' (Sirgy et al., 1997: 232), rather than 'a multi-dimensional, piecemeal process' (p. 231). While individuals are said to assess congruity on self-meaningful attributes or constructs, previous research has failed to explore the possibility that such decisions are made by way of conjunctive or other noncompensatory decision - making approaches. Sirgy et al.'s (1997) work is the first to move congruity theory beyond the compensatory decision-making framework. Results of several tests indicate that the new methods tap self-congruency more directly and completely, with less measurement error than previous measures. These measurement improvements mean that self-concept congruency can be a better predictor of consumer behaviour than previously thought.

Conclusion

Congruity theory has developed out of work in self-image research, which considers the role of 'self' in predicting an individual's consuming behaviour. Early research was groundbreaking in its attempts, but overly simplistic in nature, by only considering a unidimensional aspect of self: the actual self. As the construct evolved into multidimensional elements, congruity 'theory' began to take shape. A major advance was made with Sirgy's (1980, 1982, 1985b) development of the interactive congruity theory, which considered both actual and ideal selves and their interactive effect on a consumer's purchase motivation. The conceptual base of the theory was further solidified when Sirgy et al. (1991) provided a stronger theoretical base by demonstrating the role of both congruity models and multiattribute (functional approaches) models in predicting consumer behaviour. More recently, further advances have been made in congruity research with the refinement of several methodological problems, thereby strengthening the validity of the measures and the predictive power of the models.

DIANE MOLLENKOPF AND VANESSA MOORE

Bibliography

Birdwell, A.L.E. (1968) 'The Influence of Image Congruence on Consumer Choice', *Journal of Business*, **41**: 76–88.

Evans, F. (1968) 'Automobiles and Self Imagery: Comment', *Journal of Business*, **41**: 445–59.

Grubb, E.L. and Grathwohl, H.L. (1967) 'Consumer Self Concept, Symbolism, and Market Behaviour', *Journal of Marketing*, **31**: 22–7.

Grubb, E.L. and Hupp, G. (1968) 'Perceptions of Self, Generalised Stereotypes, and Brand Selection', *Journal of Marketing Research*, **5**: 58–63.

Grubb, E.L. and Stern, B. (1971) 'Self-Concept and Significant Others', *Journal of Marketing Research*, **8**: 382–5.

Hughes, G. and Guerrero, J.L. (1971) 'Automobile Self-Congruence Models Reexamined', *Journal of Marketing Research*, **8**: 125–7.

Lamone, R.P. (1966) 'The Use of Semantic Differential in a Study of Self Image, Product Image and Prediction of Consumer Choice', Unpublished PhD thesis, University of Washington, Seattle, WA.

Loudon, D.L. and Della Bitta, A.J. (1988) *Consumer Behaviour: Concepts and Applications* (3rd edn), New York, McGraw–Hill.

Moore, V. (1996) 'The Effectiveness of Idealised Advertising Images: A Congruity Analysis', Unpublished MCM thesis, Lincoln University, New Zealand.

Sirgy, M.J. (1980) 'Self-Concept in Relation to Product Preference and Purchase Intention', in Belleur, V.V. (ed.) *Developments in Marketing Science*, Volume 3, Marquette, MI, Academy of Marketing Science: 350–54.

Sirgy, M.J. (1982) 'Self-Concept in Consumer Behaviour: A Critical Review', *Journal of Consumer Research*, **9**: 287–300.

Sirgy, M.J. (1985a) 'Self-Image/Product-Image and Consumer Decision-making', *International Journal of Management*, **2**: 49–63.

Sirgy, M.J. (1985b) 'Using Self Congruity and Ideal Congruity to Predict Purchase Motivation', *Journal of Business*, **13**: 195–206.

Sirgy, M.J., Grewal, D., Mangleburg, T.F., Park, J., Chon, K., Claiborne, C.B., Johar, J.S. and Berkman, H. (1997) 'Assessing the Predictive Validity of Two Methods of Measuring Self-Image Congruence', *Journal of the Academy of Marketing Science*, **25**: 229–41.

Sirgy, M.J., Johar, J.S., Samli, A.C. and Claiborne, C.B. (1991) 'Self-Congruity Versus Functional Congruity: Predictors of Consumer Behavior', *Journal of the Academy of Marketing Science*, **19**: 363–75.

Conjoint Analysis

Marketers need to make choices about the kinds of features and attributes with which to configure their products and the price at which to sell those features and attributes. For example, a firm that produces equestrian helmets must make decisions whether to make the outer shell plastic or leather, whether to make the helmet thin or thick or whether to offer it in sizes based on head circumference alone or combinations of both head circumference and width. Economic theory elegantly speaks to the fact that consumers prefer more of a good to less, but less so to how one might translate theoretically based indifference and demand curves to actual information about consumers' willingness to pay for those goods (see Lancaster, 1966). One method by which one can collect high-quality information for marketing decisions is by applying conjoint analysis (see Ratchford, 1975; 1979).

To introduce conjoint analysis for the general reader, I shall first explain what it is; I also consider the perspective of those who develop and use conjoint analysis-based techniques by comparing and contrasting the approach with similar specialties. This is followed, finally, by a discussion of current trends in the conjoint analysis research tradition.

So what exactly is conjoint analysis?

Conjoint analysis is an experimental tradition focused on finding the value of particular attributes. Usually it is focused on products that marketers wish to sell, and subjects know that they are being studied. A simple example of conjoint analysis is presented by Hair, Anderson and Tatham (1987) and a portion of it is repeated here.

Assume a marketer is introducing a new brand of laundry detergent and is considering how to design the packaging. There are two attributes or features of the package that could be altered. First, the package could have a clear plastic window through which one could see the detergent or it may be plain cardstock. Second, the package could use a blue and white colour scheme or a red and white colour scheme. The interested manager could have four boxes of detergent made up such that each combination of window and colour is represented. Two hundred detergent buyers then rate each of the four detergent boxes on a 100-point scale for a total of 800 ratings, four per subject.

Let us first consider one individual subject. The rating of each of the four boxes can be viewed as four separate observations. The rating for each box becomes the dependent variable. The design of the box can be converted into independent variables by the following method. One can create a new variable called 'Window' such that it equals +1 when the plastic window is present, but −1 when only cardstock is used. Also one can create a second variable called 'Colour' such that it equals +1 when the colour scheme is blue and white, but −1 when the colour scheme is red and white. If one regresses the rating for each box on the two variables, one can determine if 'Window' or 'Colour' has a significant effect on the subject's responses.

This procedure can be repeated on the remaining 199 subjects and estimates of subjects' preference can be estimated using the regression parameters, 200 for 'Window' and 200 for 'Colour'. These parameter estimates can be plotted on a two-by-two graph to give some idea of the distribution of preferences and allow some identification of potential segments. However, the next issue is aggregating across subjects. Sometimes analysts perform a regression involving all subjects in the same model of all 800 ratings. This approach works well when most subjects are similar, but if half prefer the blue and white colour scheme and half the red and white, then this method will show that each preference cancels out the other. Indeed, the method of aggregating individual subject's ratings is still the subject of active research.

Another issue arises when one wants to add additional variables other than just the two of 'Window' or 'Colour'. A third variable can be added to the box design, for example, whether or not the box has an easy pour handle or not. In this case, there are eight different combinations of window, colour scheme and handle that can be designed and the experiment can proceed much like the four-box example. However, this approach becomes cumbersome when the number of manipulated variables exceeds four or five. Therefore, conjoint analysis experiments frequently employ fractional factorial designs to study large numbers of independent variables.

Hair et al. (1987) develop more detailed examples. Several other readings in the same book also explore the approach. The studies noted above and discussed in more detail in Hair et al. are called *full profile*, because subjects are allowed to see a number of options of product configurations at one time. Full-profile techniques always use statistical techniques such as regression to infer attribute importance ratings. They are also the most commonly used.

Other variations of conjoint analysis are *self-explicated weight* models. These models use some kind of direct input from subjects such that they report in a structured manner the value and desirability of product attributes. Rarely do marketing researchers use self-explicated weights by themselves and more commonly they apply them in conjunction with full-profile models. Green and Krieger (1996) and Srinivasan and Park (1997) provide recent examples of using self-explicated and full-profile models in combination, or as they are generally referred to, *hybrid* models.

The variety of hybrid models is staggering, but even more models are on the horizon with yet another class of conjoint analysis models. This new category, *choice conjoint analysis* models, is compared to traditional conjoint analysis models by Elrod, Louviere and Davey (1992). Choice conjoint analysis differs from other forms of conjoint analysis because subjects do not rate all the options presented to them. Instead, they choose only the most desired product. From a series of such choices, possibly aggregated across a number of subjects, attribute importance can be assessed.

The conjoint analysis approach also makes a number of important assumptions. The major one is that consumers are thinking in a compensatory manner in their decision making, rather than on the basis of, say, an intolerant set of priorities or a highly specific checklist of required features (compare Earl, 1986). In other words, with regard to the equestrian helmet example above, the approach assumes that a vegetarian will accept a leather cover on the helmet if the price is low enough to compensate for the cover not being made of a preferred non-leather material. If a vegetarian will not accept leather under any conditions, then the assumptions of the model do not hold.

Comparisons with other specialities: conjoint analysis versus multiattribute utility theory and discrete choice modelling

To understand better how a conjoint analysis modeller thinks, it may be helpful to review how conjoint analysis differs from related specialities. Two to be considered here are multiattribute utility theory (MAUT) and discrete choice modelling, both of which have full-scale entries elsewhere in this book.

MAUT

This speciality is the larger tradition out of which conjoint analysis evolved and it assumes that the preference for an object is related to the sum of its attributes' ratings weighted by the desirability of each attribute. In their review of the area, von Winterfeldt and Edwards (1986: Ch. 7) give a simple example of how five military rifles with different effective ranges and weights could be compared. The focus in MAUT is how to use decision models to improve the quality of decisions and to model underlying preferences. The methodological structure of MAUT is needed to focus thought rationally, so as to solve difficult problems.

The self-explicated weight approach to conjoint analysis borrows heavily from MAUT, and some authors find it difficult to tell the difference between them. However, conjoint analysis is more focused on determining how large numbers of people give a small amount of thought to products that a marketer might develop, as opposed to MAUT applications where a small number of decision makers give a great deal of thought to an important issue. The major difference is that conjoint analysis researchers are more tied to experimentation and MAUT researchers focus more on in-depth elicitation of preference whether by depth interview, survey or other means.

Both types of researchers, if given the choice, would choose good data over good statistical models, and they centre on how to extract useful information from willing and cooperative subjects. Both types of researchers occasionally cut methodological corners, but they generally are aware of it when they do so. Although conjoint analysis and MAUT researchers work on different kinds of problems, they are philosophical kindred.

Discrete choice models

In contrast to MAUT, conjoint analysis researchers share discrete choice modelling's estimation techniques and substantive problems, but not its philosophy. McFadden (1986) explored possible overlaps on how discrete choice models could be used in conjoint analysis settings, but as the choice conjoint analysis subspeciality was developed by researchers such as Louviere (Elrod et al., 1992) and his colleagues, conjoint analysis and discrete choice models grew further apart rather than closer.

The basic idea behind discrete choice modelling is that given the observed choices that consumers make among certain brands, one may infer unobserved preferences and the value of various marketing promotional vehicles, such as coupons or advertising. These researchers observe purchase histories over long periods of time to construct sequences of purchases which they aggregate across the population and estimate via logistic regression and other highly technical methods. The focus of discrete choice modelling research is usually on the technique or substantive findings rather than on the data, which is assumed to be secondary. Few choice researchers have considered the size or effect of measurement error on discrete choice models.

Choice conjoint analysis has excited conjoint analysis researchers not because of its technical elegance, but because of its realism. Many conjoint analysis researchers dislike the traditional methods of conjoint analysis (called *ratings based* because all products combinations presented are rated) because consumers do not typically rate all products seen on shop shelves. However, the similarities of choice conjoint analysis and discrete choice modelling end there.

Choice conjoint analysis researchers are appalled at the biases introduced by using observational data and instead place their faith in the experimental tradition common to other conjoint analysis modellers. For example, in Koslow (1994), I take a conjoint analysis measurement perspective and consider some major failings of observational choice data and therefore discrete choice models. I consider two consumers, one who buys the same brand of detergent week after week for a 14-week observation period and a second consumer who also buys every week, but usually switches among brands to choose the one that is on special price reduction or coupon.

For the first consumer, one can predict what the consumer will purchase in future weeks, but as to the cause of such behaviour, one can only guess. Any number of hypotheses can be floated and because there is no variance in the purchase history, any number of *post hoc* reasons could be advanced. For the second consumer, one can be more specific about the reasons for choosing one brand over another (that is, lower price), but one cannot determine what will be purchased next because one does not know what will be on price promotion in the next period. Thus, observational discrete choice models are faced with a tradeoff between prediction and causality. They may do one or the other, but never both.

The tradeoff between causality and prediction does not exist for choice conjoint analysis because the independent variables can be manipulated experimentally so as to identify both prediction and causality simultaneously. The discrete choice modeller, however, finds the use of experimentation a departure from the realism of observed choices. For example, to gain the improved variance characteristics of orthogonal experimental designs, conjoint analysis researchers often have to create options that are not feasible, dominate

103

over other alternatives, or otherwise confuse subjects. Therefore, it is the adherence to the experimental approach that differentiates the conjoint analysis researcher from the discrete choice modeller.

Recent trends: the growing maturity of conjoint analysis research

Over the last thirty years, conjoint analysis research has matured and a number of trends are identified by Carroll and Green (1995); additional ones were apparent when I subsequently conducted an analysis of citations. In the late 1960s and early 1970s, the conjoint analysis speciality included only a small group of specialist researchers, but today conjoint analysis is recognized as one of the major streams of quantitative marketing research, with multiple sessions at major marketing conferences. The composition of conjoint analysis research has also changed over time. Less than a dozen years ago, almost 90 per cent of research published on conjoint analysis in major refereed journals was focused on improving the technique and was aimed at the specialist researcher. A mere 10 per cent was focused on applications. As of 1996, about 60 per cent of conjoint analysis articles in those journals were focused on applications of conjoint analysis to substantive problems and only 40 per cent were focused on methodology.

Over the same period, the number of conjoint analysis papers appearing in print has remained constant, which means that the pace of methodological paper production has more than halved. Considering that the number of methodological researchers working in this field has been increasing greatly and the number of papers falling, the potential for any one researcher to affect the field is therefore reducing quickly. The time when a single researcher could have a major influence on the conjoint analysis speciality is over and conjoint analysis has reached Kuhn's (1962) 'normal science' stage of academic research. In fact, it has proved difficult for later researchers to overturn several research traditions established early on in the conjoint analysis tradition.

For example, several researchers have advocated that LINMAP, MONANOVA and other techniques are the appropriate methods for estimating many conjoint analysis models. However, most computer packages still use ordinary least squares (OLS) routines to estimate parameters, which occasionally results in biased estimation of conjoint analysis parameters. Recent developments using hierarchical Bayes techniques or latent class models have failed to revolutionize the field despite being superior estimation techniques. Applications now dominate the research agenda for conjoint analysis research and the needs of applied conjoint analysis users drive successful research programmes. Purely technical innovations in conjoint analysis fail to excite reviewers today outside a small group of technically orientated journals, and many researchers have followed the strategy of couching methodological research topics in terms of interesting applied settings. For example, many new hybrid models are justified on their ability to handle more attributes than full-profile techniques. The focus on applications also gives centre stage to a small group of statistical programmes that are ubiquitous in recent conjoint analysis efforts.

Carmone and Schaffer (1995), in a recent review of major commercial conjoint analysis statistical packages, find them lacking from a methodological researcher's point of view. However, most of the packages are well positioned for the applied researcher who lacks conjoint analysis expertise, thus making them dangerous weapons in some instances. If the measure of a technique's influence is the extent to which it is abused, then conjoint analysis may soon join the esteemed ranks of regression and factor analysis.

Conclusion

Over the last third of a century, the development of conjoint analysis stands as one of the clear successes of consumer and marketing research. Conjoint analysis might also be one area in which consumer and marketing research might export ideas to other academic areas. For example, the approach can be applied to contingent valuation and other difficult economic problems. It might also be applied to political choice if one makes the assumption that issues stances in political manifestos can be treated as product attributes. Overall, conjoint analysis is something about which we feel we know a great deal that is relevant both theoretically and practically, indeed, one of the few areas about which we can make such a claim.

SCOTT KOSLOW

Bibliography

Carmone, F.J. and Schaffer, C.M. (1995) 'New Books in Review', *Journal of Marketing Research*, **32**: 113–20.

Carroll, J.D. and Green, P.E. (1995) 'Psychometric Methods in Marketing Research: Part 1, Conjoint Analysis', *Journal of Marketing Research*, **32**: 385–91.

Earl, P.E. (1986) *Lifestyle Economics*, Brighton, Wheatsheaf.

Elrod, T., Louviere J.J. and Davey, K.S. (1992) 'An Empirical Comparison of Ratings-Based and Choice-Based Conjoint Models', *Journal of Marketing Research*, **29**: 368–77.

Green, P.E. and Krieger, A.M. (1996) 'Individualized Hybrid Models for Conjoint Analysis', *Management Science*, **42**: 850–67.

Hair, J.F., Anderson, R.E. and Tatham, R.L. (1987) *Multivariate Data Analysis with Readings* (2nd edn), New York, Macmillan.

Koslow, S. (1994) 'The Illusion of Quantitative Information in Consumer Choice Research: Data, Models, and the Limits of Knowledge' in Brooksbank, R. (ed.) *Proceedings to the 1994 New Zealand Marketing Educators' Conference*, Hamilton, New Zealand, University of Waikato.

Kuhn, T.S. (1962) *The Structure of Scientific Revolutions*, Chicago, IL, University of Chicago Press.

Lancaster, K.J. (1966) 'A New Approach to Consumer Theory', *Journal of Political Economy*, **74**: 132–57.

McFadden, D. (1986) 'The Choice Theory Approach to Marketing Research', *Marketing Science*, **5**: 275–97.

Ratchford, B.T. (1975) 'The New Economic Theory of Consumer Behavior: An Interpretive Essay', *Journal of Consumer Research*, **2**: 65–75.

Ratchford, B.T. (1979) 'Operationalizing Economic Models of Demand for Product Characteristics, *Journal of Consumer Research*, **6**: 76–85.

Srinivasan, V. and Park, C.S. (1997) 'Surprising Robustness of the Self-Explicated Approach to Customer Preference Structure Measurement', *Journal of Marketing Research*, **34**: 286–91.

von Winterfeldt, D. and Edwards, W. (1986) *Decision Analysis and Behavioral Research*, Cambridge, Cambridge University Press.

Conspicuous Consumption

Modern thinking about the concept of conspicuous consumption is generally associated with Veblen (1899), although similar notions were in evidence in earlier economic writings by Adam Smith, John Rae and Alfred Marshall (see Mason, 1981, 1998). Veblen's concept was used to stand for the signalling of class or status. 'Consumption' referred explicitly to the acquisition of the unnecessary, the superfluous. 'Conspicuous' denoted the display component, making those superfluous acquisitions ostentatious within the community that the person values. Veblen referred to the unproductive consumption of goods as 'honourable', indicative of prowess, or human dignity. To consume only what is necessary for subsistence, by contrast, indicates absence of socially recognized prowess or status.

As described by Leibenstein (1950), a 'Veblen effect' arises where a consumer's demand for a good arises at least in part from the price other people believe has been paid for it: expensive-looking goods are attractive to potential buyers because they are more likely to impress others. However, he suggested that social interdependence of individuals' demand functions is further complicated by 'bandwagon effects' — in which the demand for a good is positively associated with the number of consumers already seen to be buying it — and 'snob effects' — in which willingness to pay for a good is positively associated with its uniqueness, which increases the attention drawn to its owner. Leibenstein showed how interactions between these three effects arising from the social dimension of choice can produce unusually shaped demand curves (for example, a backward-sloping S-shape). However, beyond this economist's perspective, there are other seeming paradoxes within the conspicuous consumption arena, which we shall now examine more closely.

Acting in congruence with existing symbols

One process of acquisition of goods in Veblen's writings is a socially mediated consistency phenomenon. One begins with a recognized symbol — that is, something that brings its possessor a subjective sense of being socially adapted, well off, perhaps better than others. Often these existing symbols can take the concrete form of inherited social rank, occupation or political status. The next step is that the community will expect the person with those symbols further to reflect them on a material level. Thus a doctor or symphony conductor would be expected by the relevant community to manifest the material side of that social status. The higher the person is in the social status hierarchy, for example, then the more that costly, exclusive goods are to be collected and exhibited.

This linear assumption obviously needs to be differentiated. For one thing, the reference group will not automatically accord high status to a person who possesses a high quantity of material prestige objects, nor is the cost of the object *per se* the index that wins the person recognition and confirmation as a recognized member of the better group. Over and above the actual price/quantity of prestige possessions, it is a matter of giving the impression that one has decoded the meaning of 'good taste' from the reference group's perspective (see Earl, 1998). Thus for a person who is in the process of climbing to an aspired-to social clique or level, hazards are entailed (Mason, 1981: 110–11). Each time a material component of an aspired-to position is acquired, the person risks the possibility of its falling flat and being seen as simply ostentatious or garish, and of seeming not to possess the overall capacity to act and behave as a member of that sought-for reference group.

Compensation for lack of existing symbols

A second perspective is based on a rather different assumption. The person's experienced *lack* of symbolic evidence for an aspired-to status is the starting-point, leading to the accumulation and display of unnecessary possessions. Drawing on Max Weber, Hamilton (1977) observes that the content and style of consumption are components of status competition. This is a competition with significant others, in terms of ideas and material goods, to substantiate one's status claims. This is consistent with the popul99ist writings of Stanley and Danko (1996), who observe that those who simply have high incomes tend towards conspicuous consumption, whereas some people with established wealth actively avoid displaying it through their consumption behaviour.

'Claims' is the deciding element here, in that consumption and display, owing to one's own experiencing of lack of symbols, are to be observed primarily in those realms to which the person is highly committed (Wicklund and

Gollwitzer, 1982). An example from Wicklund and Braun (1987) concerns two samples of lawyers, differing in terms of their membership status *vis-à-vis* the occupational group *attorney*. One group was an established sample of attorneys in a metropolitan area; the other consisted of law students from the same city. When asked the simple question, 'Do people perceive you as a lawyer or a potential lawyer and, if so, why?', 40 per cent of the established attorneys answered positively, while 84 per cent of the law students claimed to be recognizable as a lawyer. In short, a desire to be recognizable as a member of the aspired-to group accompanies an actual falling-short of attainment.

One can also examine the thesis by looking at more concrete material displays. Braun and Wicklund (1989), investigating business majors in a series of studies, began with the variable of insecurity in one's business studies. For example, in one study this meant that the students found their major difficult, and in a further study subjects were encouraged to think that they were not accomplishing enough towards their chosen occupational goals. The more insecure the participants felt about their future occupational status, the more that they emphasized the prestige character of their vacation spots.

Compensation for lack of intrinsic satisfaction

We assume that the relationship of the person to the work, play and social environments can tell us something about another underlying basis of the compensation process. Active intrinsic engagement with and within the environment leads to experiencing satisfaction with the activity, in and of itself. In this sense, people place themselves intrinsically within the confines of the tasks of social situations. They act freely, and tensions and goals carry them through their work and social relations. Consumption is then necessary to underlie or develop a natural expansion of one's personal identity. Consumption in this sense is a manifestation, or disclosure, of the sense of self, rather than being directed to the public demand for self-presentation. This kind of fit to the environment gives the person a sense of personal satisfaction, which in turn is part of the experience of identity.

However, if this intrinsic kind of person or task involvement is lacking, the spontaneous tension (compare Lewin, 1926) and corresponding satisfaction are missing. A condition then results whereby the person's orientation becomes external and *instrumental,* or *extrinsically motivated.* The lack of intrinsic involvement, and corresponding tension within the environment, facilitate an extrinsic, product-orientated focus.

We assume, in accord with Kasser and Ryan (1993), that low social and individual satisfaction facilitate a materialistic orientation. Kasser and Ryan even found that people with strong, central aspirations for financial success are more anxious and have less general well-being. Another case is based on Belk's (1985) earlier work: Richins (1994) and Richins and Dawson (1992) have developed a scale to operationalize a materialistic orientation. High materialism correlates with envy of others, less pleasure or joy, and lack of satisfying relations. The phenomenon is one of people whose falling short in intrinsic, satisfying engagement with others is accompanied by an emphasis on the importance of material accumulation.

Consumption as enjoyable/instrumental

The possession of a seemingly superfluous prestige object does not always have to reflect one of the two processes just described. Csikszentmihalyi and Rochberg-Halton (1981) and Goode (1978) bring in an important third perspective. This is the possibility that the possession and use of consumer goods can be enjoyable in and of themselves, *and* that those goods can be directly instrumental to the person's everyday goals and satisfactions. Expensive products can often be the most effective tools or instruments, the longest-lasting, comfortable, and fitting for the person's endeavours. Violin music in fact sounds better on a Stradivarius; hand-tailored suits can be more durable and comfortable. To the extent that the expensive, apparently ostentatious object in fact enhances the person's performance or enjoyment, it is difficult to speak of strategic, or socially-dictated, conspicuous consumption.

Conspicuous consumption as making oneself attractive

Another basis for displaying the material side of the social interaction is a highly pro-social one, and generally overlooked in discussions of conspicuous consumption. We do not begin with the person's own needs, lacks, or responsiveness to social expectations, but rather the starting-point is the person's attentiveness to what the other could find agreeable. If a person is highly involved in a romantic partner, for example, then certain displays will lead to pleasure and to emotional reactions from the other.

People who try to make themselves appealing for their partners are implicitly and explicitly communicating their perspectives on, and understandings of, the other person, what the partner might appreciate, and what could make them smile, or bring them to experience certain positive emotions. However, a somewhat charming 'Woody Allen' effect could be generated if they try to make themselves attractive in a way that totally bypasses their partners' tastes or emotional readiness. Worse still, there could be a subtle distancing effect, as though the person has a limited understanding of, and is not really attuned to, the other party. The finer aesthetic perspective taking, instead, facilitates an extra stimulation of the interaction by a certain 'we-feeling', a sense of commonality.

Conclusion

Conspicuous consumption, as a special case of symbolically representing oneself to the community, has manifold psychological meanings. The mere fact of a person's possessing valued material goods, as well as displaying that possession, is insufficient to inform us as to which psychological function is being served by those goods. The psychological task is to look into the displaying person's background and environment, to tease out the sense — for example, compensating, or making oneself attractive for others — of the particular act of apparent conspicuous consumption.

ROBERT A. WICKLUND AND MARIE M.P. VANDEKERCKHOVE

Bibliography

Belk, R.W. (1985) 'Materialism: Trait Aspects of Living in the Material World', *Journal of Consumer Research*, **12**: 265–80.

Braun, O.L. and Wicklund, R.A. (1989) 'Psychological Antecedents of Conspicuous Consumption', *Journal of Economic Psychology*, **10**: 161–87.

Csikszentmihalyi, M. and Rochberg-Halton, E. (1981) *The Meaning of Things*, New York, Cambridge University Press.

Earl, P.E. (1998) 'Marketing as Information Economics', in Macdonald, S. and Nightingale, J. (eds) *Information and Organisation: A Tribute to the Work of Don Lamberton*, Amsterdam, Elsevier.

Goode, W.J. (1978) *The Celebration of Heroes: Prestige as a Control System*, Berkeley, CA, University of California Press.

Hamilton, G.G. (1977) 'Chinese Consumption of Foreign Commodities: A Comparative Perspective', *American Sociological Review*, **42**: 877–91.

Kasser, T. and Ryan, R.M. (1993) 'A Dark Side of the American Dream: Correlates of Financial Success as a Central Life Aspiration', *Journal of Personality and Social Psychology*, **65**: 410–22.

Leibenstein, H. (1950) 'Bandwagon, Snob and Veblen Effects in the Theory of Consumers' Demand', *Quarterly Journal of Economics*, **64**: 183–207.

Lewin, K. (1926) 'Untersuchungen zur Handlungs- und Affekt-Psychologie. II: Vorsatz, Wille und Bedürfnis', *Psychologische Forschung*, **7**: 330–85.

Mason, R. (1981) *Conspicuous Consumption*, Farnborough, Gower.

Mason, R. (1998) *The Economics of Conspicuous Consumption*, Cheltenham, Elgar.

Richins, M.L. (1994) 'Special Possessions and the Expression of Material Values', *Journal of Consumer Research*, **21**: 522–33.

Richins, M.L. and Dawson, S. (1992) 'A Consumer Values Orientation for Materialism and Its Measurement: Scale Development and Validation', *Journal of Consumer Research*, **19**: 303–16.

Stanley, T.J. and Danko, W.D. (1996) *The Millionaire Next Door*, Atlanta, GA, Longstreet.

Veblen, T. (1899) *The Theory of the Leisure Class*, New York, Macmillan.

Wicklund, R.A. and Braun, O.L. (1987) 'Incompetence and the Concern with Human

Categories', *Journal of Personality and Social Psychology*, **53**: 373–82.
Wicklund, R.A. and Gollwitzer, P.M. (1982) *Symbolic Self-completion*, Hillsdale, NJ, Erlbaum.

Consumer Innovativeness

For decades scientists and public policy makers have been interested in why some people adopt new ideas, products and services and others do not. Even when an innovation has obvious advantages, it is often rejected by many people who could benefit from its use. Researchers in the disciplines of cultural anthropology, education, geography, industrial economics, marketing, medical sociology and rural sociology are working in this area. In 1995, it was estimated that there had been approximately 4000 publications which dealt with one or more aspects of the diffusion of innovations (Rogers, 1995).

To ground the following discussion about consumer innovativeness in its theoretical context, it is necessary first to outline briefly what is meant by the diffusion of innovations. Then the focus will shift to the concept of consumer innovativeness as it has been studied within the discipline of marketing, in particular consumer behaviour.

The diffusion of innovations

Diffusion is the process whereby information about an innovation is communicated among the members of a social system over time. Traditionally, researchers focus on five main elements of this definition — the innovation, the person, the communication channels, the social system, and the time taken for the innovation to be adopted or rejected. An innovation can be a new idea, practice, product or service (IPPS). People can be characterized by their innate predisposition to accept new IPPSs. This personality trait is often related to other traits such as risk aversion, self-confidence and novelty seeking. Communication about the innovation can occur through various channels; most often these are mass media and/or interpersonal. The social system can be a marketplace (for example, consumers or organizations) or a community (for example, families in a town, scientists in a research laboratory), and can comprise individuals, groups, and (in)formal organizations. Time in diffusion studies is of two types. One is decision-making time, namely, the time it takes for an individual member of the social system to make an adoption or rejection decision. (This is discussed more fully in the next section.) The other is the time it takes the innovation to diffuse, or spread through the social system. This diffusion time is often measured as the rate of adoption of the innovation, and is often related to both an innovation and imitation effect (Bass, 1969). Gatignon and Robertson (1985) and Rogers (1995) provide good reviews of the hundreds of studies done on each of these elements.

This paradigm is also presented as a contingency model in Figure 1. (The perspective taken is that of an individual potential adopter.)

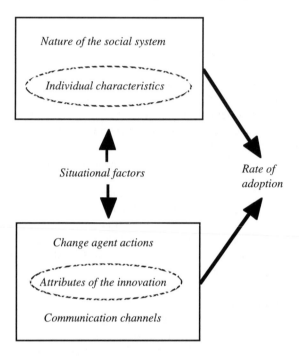

Figure 1: Factors affecting innovation diffusion

The top portion of Figure 1 shows that individuals have a number of characteristics which will predispose them to be more or less receptive to an innovation. These individual characteristics may be mitigated by the nature of the social system in which the individual is a member. For example, in a study of the diffusion of women's fashion, Dowling and Midgley (1988) found that some women acted as innovative communicators (high fashion interest, high opinion leadership, high purchase frequency of new clothesand so on) while others were more concerned about the role of fashion in their social context. The bottom portion of Figure 1 identifies three external factors which affect the success or otherwise of an innovation: (i) the attributes of the innovation (for example, its cost — both dollar cost and switching costs, brand image, relative advantage, compatibility with the individual's current life situation, perceived difficulty to understand and use, ability to trial on a limited basis, and social relevance), (ii) the effectiveness of the change agent's promotion activities, and (iii) the effectiveness of the communication channels used. Current and unanticipated situational factors moderate the fit between an individual's motivation to adopt and the desirability of the innovation. For example, the current and anticipated wealth of a person can have a big effect on his or her ability to buy many new products.

Consumer innovativeness is a key individual characteristic which has been shown to affect the time taken for an individual to make an adoption or rejection decision relative to the times taken by other members of the social system. In recent years there have been two competing views about how this individual characteristic should be conceptualized and measured.

Consumer innovativeness

Innovativeness has traditionally been defined as 'the degree to which an individual or other unit of adoption is relatively earlier in adopting . . . than other members of a (social) system' (Rogers, 1995: 252). This is a time- and behaviour-based definition as opposed to a trait- or attitude-based definition. On the assumption that most adopter distributions follow a bell-shaped curve over time and approach normality, the mean and standard deviation are used to classify adopters as: innovators (the first 2.5 per cent to adopt), early adopters (the next 13.5 per cent), early majority (34 per cent), late majority (34 per cent), laggards (last 16 per cent to adopt). Researchers using this typology have searched for a set of personal characteristics which discriminate between the individuals in each group. For example, Rogers suggests that the salient value of innovators is that they are venturesome; early adopters seek respect from their peers; the early majority are deliberate; the late majority sceptical; and the laggards traditional. These types of descriptions are questionable, however, because they do not incorporate situational contingencies and the descriptors are confounded by the product knowledge, and level of product category usage of the individual.

The Rogers/traditional approach has one major strength and one major weakness. Its strength is that innovativeness is simple to measure — who adopts and when do they adopt. Even with this measure, however, it is possible to misclassify people if care is not exercised when specifying the first point in time when an individual could adopt. For example, the clock starts running when each individual first becomes aware of the innovation, not when it first appears in the market. The critical weakness of this, or any time-based measure of innovativeness is that in order to assign each individual to the correct adopter group, the researcher has to wait until the diffusion pattern is complete in order to calculate the mean time (and standard deviation) of adoption.

If used with care for historical analysis, the traditional measure of innovativeness is not a great problem. For agents wishing to engineer change however, it is practically useless. The change agent must use the diffusion pattern of a very similar innovation, if there is one, to forecast which individuals will belong to each adopter category.

Midgley and Dowling (1978) exposed this weakness in the time-based measures of innovativeness. In its place they proposed that individual innovativeness is better defined and measured as a trait-attitudinal disposition to adopt innovations. In particular, they suggested that the crucial factor which differentiates the innovators from the later adopters is the individual's reliance on the support of other people before they make an adoption or rejection decision. Innovators make their adoption decisions more independently of the opinions of other individuals. In Figure 1, this is represented by enclosing the 'individual characteristics' element of the diffusion process within the 'social system' context. Moreover, the Midgley–Dowling measure of innovativeness is a contingency approach to modelling innovativeness because an individual's innovative predisposition interacts with the spread of social messages concerning the innovation. They have used this approach successfully to show that an individual's predisposition to innovate is modified by socially transmitted messages about the innovation, as well as by other situation-specific factors (Midgley and Dowling, 1993).

The key insight here is that the social context can mediate how and when individuals make new product adoption decisions and the effects of marketing variables (for example, advertising) on this decision making. To understand these relationships more fully, researchers have studied the patterns of information seeking (for example, Midgley, 1983), social ties and interpersonal communication (Brown and Reingen, 1987), risk perception (Dowling and Staelin, 1994), consumer susceptibility to interpersonal influence (Bearden, Netemeyer and Teel, 1989), the identification of opinion leaders Leonard-Barton, 1985), and peer group influence and consumption visibility (Fisher and Price, 1992).

The value of innovative predisposition type measures of innovativeness is that they can be used before the launch of an innovation to identify innovators and early adopters so that the appropriate channels of communication can be chosen and other marketing strategies developed. They can also be used after the launch to evaluate whether the innovation's launch strategy was effective to the extent that it was able to initially target the more innovative adopters. This is important because diffusion research has a broad pragmatic appeal in helping change agents in a variety of areas to market new IPPSs.

GRAHAME R. DOWLING

Bibliography
Bass, F. (1969) 'A New Product Growth Model for Consumer Durables', *Management*

Science, **15**: 215–27.

Bearden, W.O., Netemeyer, R.G. and Teel, J.E. (1989) 'Measurement of Consumer Susceptibility to Interpersonal Influence', *Journal of Consumer Research*, **15**: 473–81.

Brown, J.J. and Reingen, P.H. (1987) 'Social Ties and Word-of-Mouth Referral Behavior', *Journal of Consumer Resarch*, **14**: 350–62.

Dowling, G.R. and Midgley, D.F. (1988) 'Identifying the Coarse and Fine Structures of Market Segments', *Decision Sciences*, **19**: 830–47.

Dowling, G.R. and Staelin, R. (1994) 'A Model of Perceived Risk and Intended Risk Handling Activity', *Journal of Consumer Research*, **21**: 119–34.

Fisher, R.J. and Price, L.L. (1992) 'An Investigation into the Social Context of Early Adoption Behavior', *Journal of Consumer Research*, **19**: 477–86.

Gatignon, H. and Robertson, T.S. (1985) 'A Propositional Inventory for New Diffusion Research', *Journal of Consumer Research*, **11**: 849–67.

Leonard-Barton, D. (1985) 'Experts as Negative Opinion Leaders in the Diffusion of a Technological Innovation', *Journal of Consumer Research*, **11**: 914–26.

Midgley, D.F. (1983) 'Patterns of Interpersonal Information Seeking for the Purchase of a Symbolic Product', *Journal of Marketing Research*, **20**: 74–83.

Midgley, D.F. and Dowling, G.R. (1978) 'Innovativeness: The Concept and Its Measurement', *Journal of Consumer Research*, **4**: 229–42.

Midgley, D.F. and Dowling, G.R. (1993) 'A Longitudinal Study of Product Form Innovation: The Interaction Between Predispositions and Social Messages', *Journal of Consumer Research*, **19**: 611–25.

Rogers, E.M. (1995) *Diffusion of Innovations*, New York, Free Press.

Consumer Knowledge

The ability to learn and to store information plays a role in many psychological processes. Differences in the amount, content and organization of the information stored in the memory are known to affect decision-making processes. In the field of consumer psychology, knowledge, or more specifically consumer or product knowledge, has received much attention because it influences consumers' decision processes such as the comprehension and evaluation of product information.

Consumer knowledge defined
Consumer knowledge is the information about a product stored in consumers' long-term memory. In their seminal paper Alba and Hutchinson (1987) indicate that consumer knowledge is a multidimensional construct characterized by a familarity and an expertise dimension. Familiarity is defined as the number of product-related experiences that have been accumulated. This dimension covers information about the relationship between the self and the product. Expertise is

defined as the ability to perform product-related tasks and is related to information about specific product aspects that consumers have in their memories.

Consumer knowledge is reflected in the consumer's cognitive structure. In consumer research, cognitive structure refers to both the amount and the content of information and to the way this information is organized. The consumer literature that more or less reflects the general psychological knowledge and memory literature, indicates that a number of profound differences exist between the cognitive structure of those who have product knowledge, the expert consumers, and those who do not have such knowledge, the nonexpert consumers.

A first difference between expert and nonexpert consumers concerns the amount of available information. Experts have been found to store more product information; they simply know more. For example, they know more products in a certain market. Furthermore, the kind of information stored differs between experts and nonexperts. Experts generally process more detailed product information than nonexperts. They have more knowledge about specific product models. Research further shows that experts have stored in memory more thoughts and feelings about and experiences with products.

Second, the way in which information is organized in memory is found to differ with product knowledge. Nonexpert consumers use relatively simple structures to organize their limited information. In contrast, it is suggested that the knowledge structure of more knowledgeable individuals is more sophisticated; experts are able to organize information both more specifically and abstractly. In terms of categorization theory this means that product familiarity results in an increased ability to categorize products not only at the basic level, but also at subordinate and superordinate levels. Studies in the consumer field indicate that consumer experts use more subcategories than nonexperts. In practice this means that nonexpert consumers categorize, for example cars, into basic-level categories only: family cars and sports cars. In addition to this basic-level categorization, experts use subcategories: they divide sports cars according to German and Italian design.

It has further been found that experts can structure their knowledge using more superordinate, abstract categories. This is consistent with the idea that abstraction processes develop out of the need for cognitive economy. Because experienced consumers have more detailed, concrete, product information structured in more dimensions, they have a greater need to form abstract knowledge dimensions. Often, abstract knowledge dimensions subsume more concrete (basic-level) dimensions. Thus the use of abstract dimensions allows expert consumers to organize seemingly different objects according to more general principles or product aspects. In contrast, nonexpert consumers apply more concrete, sensory-level product aspects that are known to be related to the use of basic-level dimensions. For example, an art expert will immediately recognize and connect the hand of Picasso to a painting and a sculpture exhibited in a museum, while an art novice will see the painting and the sculpture as two completely different objects.

The advantage of consumer knowledge in information processing

The richness and the more sophisticated organization of the product information of expert consumers provides them with a number of information-processing advantages. Knowledge gives people the opportunity to impose structure on to a situation and consequently to react more adequately to this situation. As a result, expert consumers are likely to evaluate and decide more quickly than nonexperts. Furthermore, the richness of the information available gives experts more flexibility in evaluating an object: they can interpret a product in more than just one way. The expert might think: this Italian design sports car is beautiful, but does it also have the high quality of engine that the German one has?

The availability of detailed information and the ability to use subcategories give the expert consumers the opportunity to make finer distinctions between products. It is for this reason that the experts have a greater ability to discriminate between relevant and irrelevant product aspects. Furthermore, they can use more stricly defined dimensions in decision making, and do this with greater reliability.

The richness of information also influences the quality and quantity of consumers' product-related inferences. Based on the richer product information in memory, experts are able to make more complex inferences. For example, both positive and negative product consequences are inferred by experts. Furthermore, consumer experts avoid the use of 'nonreliable' inferences more frequently than nonexperts do. A nonreliable inference is an inference about a product aspect based on another product aspect, when a direct relation between the two product aspects does not always exist, for example, the inference that a car with an innovative design is also by definition innovative in its technological aspects.

Finally, consumer knowledge influences the understanding and learning of new information. The richness of knowledge available to consumers enhances the learning of new information in consumers in terms of both quality and speed (Johnson and Russo, 1984). An explanation for this learning advantage is that the ability of expert consumers to structure information on more abstract levels gives them the opportunity to integrate new information with existing information more easily.

Effects of expertise on the consumer decision-making process

A product expert can be seen as somebody who has the knowledge required to select an appropriate product for a particular usage situation. In the case of consumer behaviour, product knowledge is therefore often linked to the underlying decision-making process. Differences in expertise are found to influence the different stages in the process. We shall discuss the effect of expertise during the stages of product information search and product evaluation.

In many instances, consumers start product decision processes by searching for product information. A number of studies indicate that these search processes are influenced by product knowledge. In her influential paper, Brucks (1985) discusses these studies. As indicated above, knowledge results in a different way of structuring information, giving the individual the ability to formulate a number of different questions about a product. Because the more knowledgeable consumers have more questions that need to be answered, a positive linear relation exists between the knowledge available and the amount of search conducted. For real experts, however, this will not hold: all their questions are already answered. In the case of real experts a negative relationship is found: more product knowledge leads to less search behaviour.

Based on these ideas, an inverted U-shaped relationship between knowledge and search behaviour is suggested. In this model consumers with moderate knowledge levels search the most. The positive slope of the curve can be explained by the greater ability to ask more questions and to encode new information that comes with increasing knowledge. The negative slope of the curve can be explained by the greater ability of experts to ignore irrelevant information, and by their already high level of knowledge: experts simply do not need to search for information any more. In addition, Moorthy, Ratchford and Talukdar (1997) report a study that underscores the inverted U-shaped curve. They show that search behaviour is related not only to the available knowledge, but also to the perceived uncertainty about existing knowledge, the so-called subjective knowledge. If this subjective knowledge increases, and consequently perceived uncertainty decreases, the extent of the search process decreases as well.

A second important part of the consumers' decision-making process is product evaluation. Consumers are believed to judge products using an extended evaluation process. A number of different products are evaluated with regard to different product aspects. Product knowledge influences this process on a number of points. First, the number of attributes taken into account in the evaluation is influenced by knowledge. Both consumers with low knowledge levels and experts use only a limited number of aspects. The first group simply because they have very few product aspects available, the experts because they need only a limited number of (abstract) product aspects in order to make a reliable evaluation. Consumers with relatively moderate knowledge levels use the greatest number of product aspects in the evaluation process, probably because they more or less know the importance of the different aspects, but are not yet able to integrate the available information.

Not only do the number of aspects differ, but also the nature of the aspects used and the way they are weighted in the evaluation process differ between experts and nonexperts. Nonexperts have a tendency to evaluate a product based on direct concrete product attributes and on extrinsic information such as price and brand name. Nonexperts also have a greater tendency to incorporate into the evaluation process product aspects that are based on non-reliable inferences. Experts use more abstract aspects, like the quality of a product and they use reliable, information based, inferences. Mitchell and Dacin (1996) show that experts weight the importance of product aspects used in the evaluation. In contrast, nonexperts do not weight aspects but use them in a nominal way: they either do or do not take them into consideration.

The differences indicated between experts and nonexpert consumers result in differences with respect to the quality of the evaluation process, a difference that is also recognized in product-testing situations by Schoormans, Ortt and de Bont (1995). However, the difference in quality is more pronounced when the evaluation process is more complex, as in the case of evaluating really new products compared with the case of evaluating 'simple' redesigns. Spence and Brucks (1997) also show that the differences in information-handling quality between experts and nonexperts are less pronounced when simple problems are at stake.

Product knowledge is found to be correlated with a preference for innovative products; to be able to be an innovator, a certain degree of expertise is required. In daily practice the product evaluations and consumer behaviour of innovators differ from the mainstream, and are therefore salient. This salience is likely to evoke scornful remarks about the expertise of the innovators from those who find it uncomfortable to admit the superficiality of their own knowledge: note the treatment commonly accorded to those who always come up with the latest and most advanced hi-fi products, or the 'pretentious' wine connoisseur who utters the most incomprehensible qualifications with regard to a simple glass of wine.

Consumer knowledge assessment

The fact that knowledge influences consumers' behaviour directly but also via the perceived uncertainty about decisions has generated more elaborate definitions of consumer knowledge. According to a number of authors, product knowledge should include the amount of accurate information held in the memory as well as self-perceptions of product knowledge. In the assessment of consumer knowledge this has led to two measures: objective measures of knowledge and subjective or self-assessed measures of knowledge. According to Park, Mothersbaugh and Feick (1994), objective knowledge is related to the amount of stored product information. Subjective measures relate more to earlier experiences with the product. A number of studies show that both knowledge measures are correlated only weakly. This leads to the conclusion that the two measures are related to two different aspects of consumer knowledge. In an ideal situation, objective knowledge should be assessed by measuring all those elements that make up consumer knowledge. This requires complex, time-consuming in-depth interviews. Instead, Brucks (1985) proposes a number of relatively simple methods to assess objective product knowledge. She proposes a method in which subjects have to mention product aspects, to discriminate a set of related products on criteria such as price and brand, or answer a multiple-choice scale consisting of questions regarding separate product aspects. This last method is used by many authors. Subjective product knowledge is often assessed with a few simple items, measuring how much the subject thinks he or she knows about a product in general, related to friends, and related to experts.

Conclusion

Research on product knowledge has given us important insights into the ability of expert and nonexpert consumers to evaluate products. The cognitive structures of experts enables them to search for relevant information, to make accurate product evaluations and consequently to make the right product choices. Nonexperts perform at a lower level in all three ways, but only when the evaluation situation (or the product) is complex.

JAN SCHOORMANS

Bibliography

Alba, J.W. and Hutchinson, J.W. (1987) 'Dimensions of Consumer Expertise', *Journal of Consumer Research*, 13: 411–54.

Brucks, M. (1985) 'The Effects of Product Class Knowledge on Information Search Behavior', *Journal of Consumer Research*, 12: 1–16.

Johnson, E.J. and Russo J.E. (1984) 'Product Familiarity and Learning New Information', *Journal of Consumer Research*, 11: 542–50.

Mitchell, A.A. and Dacin, P.A. (1996) 'The Assessment of Alternative Measures of Consumer Expertise', *Journal of Consumer Research*, 23: 219–39.

Moorthy, S., Ratchford, B.T. and Talukdar, D. (1997) 'Consumer Information Search Revisited: Theory and Empirical Analysis', *Journal of Consumer Research*, 23: 263–77.

Park, C.W., Mothersbaugh, D.L. and Feick, L. (1994) 'Consumer Knowledge Assessment', *Journal of Consumer Research*, 21: 71–82.

Schoormans, J.P.L., Ortt, R. J. and de Bont, C.J.P.M. (1995) 'Enhancing Concept Test Validity by Using Expert Consumers', *Journal of Product Innovation Management*,

12: 153–62.

Spence, M.T. and Brucks, M. (1997) 'The Moderating Effect of Problem Characteristics on Experts' and Novices' Judgments', *Journal of Marketing Research*, **34**: 233–47.

Consumer Protection

Imagine being appointed as your country's Director of Consumer Protection. You have no formal training or experience in the field of consumer protection, but you are smart and open-minded. You studied economics as an undergraduate, obtained a master's in business administration, and spent the last two decades working for various medium- and large-sized firms. You have familiarized yourself with the various laws and regulations you will enforce, but you consult a consumer behaviour expert to answer three questions: (i) 'What exactly is consumer protection and what are my major policy options?'; (ii) 'What can I do to help consumers protect themselves?'; and (iii) 'Will there be situations in which I will have to decide what is in the best interests of consumers?'.

Definition and policy options

Consumer protection is defined as the government's effort to enhance the economic well-being of consumers. Consumer protection policies can be implemented by government bodies at the local, state, national and even international levels. These policies can be divided into those that influence consumers (i) *indirectly* by altering the way in which firms interact with each other (for example, antitrust policies) and (ii) *directly* by changing the way in which firms interact with consumers. Consumer research and economic psychology is most relevant to the latter set of policies.

Government policies that protect consumers directly by altering the way in which they interact with firms can be further subdivided into those that (a) *facilitate* consumer decision making through education or information disclosure and (b) *preempt* choice by forcing firms to provide and consumers to accept prescribed levels of quality and or price. Mandating that food comes labelled with nutritional information would be an example of an information disclosure policy, while banning certain food additives, colourings or preservatives controls the choices of producers and consumers. In providing overall protection for consumers, the two approaches of choice facilitation and choice preemption can be blended. A choice between the two approaches must often be made, though, in addressing a particular consumer problem. For example, should a state, province or nation require that motorcyclists wear helmets or just mandate a warning sticker on new motorcycles? Should a nation ban air conditioners and water heaters that fall below some certain minimal level of energy efficiency, or should it just require that these appliances bear labels allowing consumers to see their relative energy inefficiency?

The choice between choice facilitation and preemption will often hinge on the basic assumptions made about how consumers behave in a particular market. If consumers are assumed to be eager to process new information, undaunted by uncertainty, adaptive to new situations, and minimally affected by each other's actions, then choice facilitation will likely be the preferred strategy. If consumers are considered poorly informed, immobilized by uncertainty about the future, creatures of habit, and strongly influenced by the decisions of others, then choice preemption may be warranted.

Information search and processing

Economic theory asserts that consumers will not endlessly gather ('search') and manipulate ('process') information in an effort to come up with the perfect decision, for this would be far too costly in terms of their time, money and mental energy. Choice facilitation strategies of consumer protection presume, though, that consumers are willing to search for and process information that they believe will markedly improve their decisions. The question then becomes: under what conditions are consumers most likely to engage in information search and processing activities and are these conditions readily met in a given situation in which consumer protection is being considered?

Economic models suggest that information search and processing will occur when they generate net benefits, that is, their (marginal) benefits exceed their (marginal) costs. This implies that search and processing will be greatest when the potential gains are great (for example, big ticket items like cars and houses) and/or when the costs are minimal (for example, easily comprehended information is provided at the point of sale). Further, economic theory suggests, almost by definition, that consumers are more likely to search and process when a good's features can be ascertained before purchase ('search good') than when it is necessary to try a good before being able to judge its quality ('experience good').

Studies of information search and processing have validated predictions from economic theory but have also generated additional insights. The strongest finding is that vast differences exist among consumers, making it difficult to generalize about consumer search and processing behaviour. Some differences are rooted in demographic characteristics such as age, education and socioeconomic status. Other differences are based on prior knowledge of a product category or level of interest in it.

Clearly, there is a great deal of variation among consumers in their information and search activities. From a consumer protection perspective, however, the key question is whether, for a given product class, there is a sufficiently large number of consumers who are motivated and able to determine the 'best' brands (in terms of quality per dollar). These expert consumers — whether called market mavens, opinion leaders, or information seekers — are capable of disciplining markets and individual firms such that consumers who use little or no information in their decisions are still able to rely on minimal levels of product performance and a positive correlation between price and quality. Bloom (1989: 171) writes: 'Unfortunately, determining whether a market has a sufficient number of experts to experience a self-correction promises to be a difficult task'. He proposes three indicators that expert consumers exist in large enough numbers to police the market for other consumers: (i) sellers seem to acknowledge the existence of experts by giving them special attention in promotional campaigns, customer relations programmes and regulatory monitoring activities; (ii) word of mouth seems to be prevalent between experts and nonexperts; and (iii) large numbers of consumers seem to react strongly to either good or bad publicity about sellers. Markets for automobiles, stereo equipment, major appliances and personal computers probably qualify for these conditions.

Types of information and information formats

In addition to showing who is likely to obtain and use consumer information, and under what circumstances, research addresses the types of information that are most useful to consumers and the best formats for presenting information. The strongest test of the value of a particular type of consumer information is its ability to change consumer behaviour as measured in the marketplace. For example, Russo et al. (1986) found in a field experiment that presentation of negative information (in this case, sugar content of breakfast cereals) increased the market share of low-sugar cereals, although presentation of positive information (that is, vitamins and minerals) had no market impact. Warning labels for saccharin were capable of reducing the sale of diet soda, at least in the short run, and several studies confirmed the ability of feedback on energy use to encourage energy conservation. As further testimony to the power of consumer information, a negative rating on a car's safety from a product-testing magazine like *Consumer Reports* can lead to a precipitous decline in sales; just ask the makers of the Suzuki Samurai or the Isuzu Trooper.

In a review of fifty product information programmes, Russo and LeClerc (1991) found that both the provision of new information (benefits) and the reduction of the effort (costs) required to obtain information can be successful in changing consumer behaviour. Among programmes aimed at reducing consumer effort, Russo and LeClerc could not find a connection between the degree of effort reduction (crudely measured) and the level of programme success. Their review of research confirms the economic tenet that information disclosure programmes can be successful across a variety of product types as long these programmes increase the net benefits of information search and use.

Further support for the value of choice facilitation strategies as a means of consumer protection comes from a somewhat unlikely source — studies of government policies to permit greater latitude to advertisers. One set of studies documents the beneficial effects on food purchases of allowing manufacturers to make health claims (Ippolito and Mathios, 1994). Another set of studies argues for the beneficial impact of the US Federal Trade Commission's decision to relax restrictions on cigarette advertising. This relaxation encouraged firms to develop and promote low tar and nicotine brands, thereby increasing the market share of less dangerous cigarettes (Calfee, 1986).

Presenting the right type of information is important, but so is presenting information in the right format. The best evaluation studies of information disclosure policies have been conducted in the field under real-world conditions. The best format studies, in contrast, have been conducted in the controlled conditions of the laboratory. Not surprisingly, the most consistent finding is that conspicuous disclosures are better than less conspicuous ones. The most research attention for a single type of information has addressed the question of how best to design nutrition labels. Should labels rely on text only or pictures and graphs as well? Should absolute values be presented (for exmaple, 6 grams of fat per serving) or should amounts be placed in the context of a daily diet? Should nutrients be listed in order of their familiarity to consumers or in terms of their importance as determined by dietary experts? Should nutrients be listed from good (for example, fibre and protein) to bad (for example, fat and sodium) or from bad to good?

A great deal of research has also been directed to the problem of designing effective warnings. Studies of warning formats have covered tobacco products, alcoholic beverages, fresh produce, pharmaceutical products, medical devices, toxic household chemicals, chain saws and lawn mowers. Reviews of existing knowledge have been commissioned by the Department of Health and Human Services (*Review of the Research*, 1987) and the National Academy of Science (*Improving Risk Communication*, 1989). Substantial agreement has been reached about optimal wording (for example, danger versus warning versus hazard), colour, warning placement, and use of symbols to complement text. Yet, empirical studies continue to challenge even the most basic assumptions about the effectiveness of warnings, especially when they involve attempts to dissuade people from engaging in behaviour that presents risks but yields substantial benefits (for exanple, smoking, driving under the influence of alcohol, or operating a tool without a cumbersome safety mask). Consequently, choice facilitation strategies may give way to product use limitations and even bans.

Limitations of choice facilitation strategies

There is abundant evidence that consumer information — when properly presented — can change consumer behaviour for the better. This change, in turn, can stimulate improvements by manufacturers and retailers, thereby improving the welfare of information users and non-users alike. Nevertheless, choice facilitation is not a cure-all for consumer protection problems. There is at least anecdotal evidence that consumers can become sensitized to warnings when too many items carry warnings. Warnings may carry inadvertent and counterproductive messages. A warning directed at pregnant women that smoking can lead to low birth weight might be misinterpreted to mean that smoking during pregnancy prevents excessive weight gain.

Choice facilitation through information provision has been challenged in two more fundamental ways. First, choice facilitation is criticized by many consumer advocates as ignoring the fact that many consumers do not fit the model of the educated, well-informed, deliberate consumer that lies behind choice facilitation strategies. Consumers suffer from a variety of vulnerabilities that preclude them from using information to its fullest. The most obviously vulnerable group of consumers is children. Some research has shown that young children view advertising in fundamentally different, and more positive ways, from adults, thereby making them more easily influenced (Kunkel and Roberts, 1991). Other researchers have argued that young children are less naive than they seem and that they can be taught to view advertising more sceptically and critically. In any event, few people would argue that young consumers would be sufficiently protected by allowing them to see R-rated movies without an adult as long as they have been warned about the movie's sex, profanity and violence, or by pointing out the nutritional labels on candy bars.

Children are not the only group of vulnerable consumers for whom choice facilitation may be an insufficient consumer protection (Andreasen, 1993). For example, consumers with limited education may have difficulty deciphering the information about kilowatt hours on energy efficiency labels or annual percentage rates on loan applications. Recent immigrants from less-developed countries may not understand the pictorial elements on warnings and care instructions, even though these pictures are specifically designed to overcome language differences. Of course, consumers who are addicted to cigarettes, alcohol, or even their credit cards cannot be expected to respond to information disclosures.

Second, choice facilitation is criticized by those who believe that consumers are prone to 'information overload' and seek ways whenever possible to find shortcuts through their consumer decisions through the use of heuristics. The concept of information overload has fascinated and divided consumer researchers since it was first introduced in the 1970s by Jacob Jacoby and his colleagues.

125

While it is indisputable that there are finite limits to the amount of information consumers can effectively use (and, one might add, afford to acquire), substantial disagreement exists about the nature of those limits, to what extent the limits can be expanded, and whether information disclosures mandated as consumer protection would fall within or outside those limits. Seemingly supportive of information load is the low level of search reported by many consumers, even for expensive items (Olshavsky and Granbois, 1979). Consumers often rely on heuristics such as 'you get what you pay for' and 'you can trust well-known brand names' to avoid the costs of information search and use. In response, advocates of information provision policies point to research that suggests information quality, not quantity, is the real impediment to better decisions.

Choice preemption as an alternative to choice facilitation
Many of the limitations of choice facilitation are the strengths of choice preemption. Most notably, choice preemption can be an appropriate response to consumer vulnerability. Literally, paternalism involves adults preempting the decisions of children, as when laws take away the right of teenagers to buy alcohol or tobacco products or the right of toddlers to ride in cars without seat restraints. Yet, paternalism and choice preemption pervade many consumer protection policies directed at adults; these policies are based on the idea that people misperceive risk. Choice preemption justifies policies that require motorists to use seat belts and lawnmower manufacturers to provide a 'dead man's' switch that makes it impossible to leave the motor running without holding the handle. Choice preemption also provides the rationale for prohibiting people access to certain drugs without a physician's prescription and shutting down Ponzi schemes such as those that recently jolted investors in Albania and Romania.

Choice preemption is also capable of taking into account 'externalities', whereas choice facilitation does not. Externalities are byproducts of buyer–seller transactions that affect third parties who are not directly involved in the transaction. Externalities can be positive, but they are of most concern when they are negative, as in the case of air pollution or noise or higher medical insurance costs due to the reckless behaviour of other people. By their very nature, externalities are effects that would not impinge on even fully informed decision makers and therefore are typically ignored. Choice preemption forces the internalization of externalities, as when pollution and noise control equipment is mandated in new cars or when helmets are required for motorcyclists.

Indeed, if information overload is a pervasive problem, choice preemption might sometimes be justified and welcomed by consumers. For instance, when long-distance telephone service was deregulated in the 1980s in the United States, consumers were given the opportunity select a carrier other than AT&T.

126

Many people complained about the difficulty of this choice; if they failed to select a carrier within a given time period, they were randomly assigned a new one. Similarly, few patients want doctors to explain the benefits, contraindications, precautions, side effects and adverse reactions associated with each possible medication; patients want doctors to make the choice for them. This may explain why direct-to-consumer advertising of prescription drugs is banned in most countries other than the US. Still, consumer protection policies involving choice preemption are far more likely to be defended on the basis of consumer vulnerability or externalities than information overload.

Before concluding, a major problem of choice preemption strategies should be noted. In addition to the serious objection that such strategies limit freedom of choice, research suggests that consumers may adapt to choice preemption in unexpected and potentially counterproductive ways. Like squeezing a balloon, strategies that reduce consumer risk by limiting certain choices can lead to compensating behaviour that restores the original level of risk exposure. For example, Peltzman (1975) and later Peterson and Hoffer (1994) presented evidence compatible with the idea that motorists drive more recklessly when their cars carry new safety features. A 'lulling effect' has also been proposed whereby people let down their guard in the presence of safety features. Similarly, people may simply pull harder on their cigarettes or smoke more cigarettes when tar and nicotine levels are reduced, and people may react to the purchase of special energy-conserving air conditioners by running their machines for more hours during the day or at lower temperatures. Although the extent of risk compensation can be easily overstated, there is a grain of truth to the argument. At least for some people, choice preemption leads to adaptive behaviour that leaves the consumer no better protected than before a choice was taken away.

Conclusion

Consumer protection often entails a choice between policies that facilitate choice or preempt it. Policy makers, in evaluating their options, have to assess which approach is more likely to be effective given the types of consumers and types of products involved. Consumers can be encouraged to gather and use information, but only up to a point. Some consumers will quickly suffer from information overload; others will be too vulnerable to make decisions for themselves. Virtually all consumers will make decisions without regard to the indirect effects of their behaviour. Yet, choice preemption strategies may have unanticipated effects as well. Consumers may engage in risk-compensating behaviour, putting efforts at protecting consumers back where they started. Research suggests that the safest path for policy makers is to ensure that there are enough well-informed consumers to create incentives for sellers to offer products and services that are safe, with quality reflective of their price, and backed up with effective redress

127

mechanisms.

ROBERT N. MAYER

Bibliography

Andreasen, A.R. (1993) 'Revisiting the Disadvantaged: Old Lessons and New Problems', *Journal of Public Policy and Marketing*, **12**: 270–75.

Bloom, P.N. (1989) 'A Decision Model for Prioritizing and Addressing Consumer Information Problems', *Journal of Public Policy and Marketing*, **8**: 161–80.

Calfee, John E. (1986), 'The Ghost of Cigarette Advertising Past', *Regulation*, **10**: 35–45.

Improving Risk Communication (1989) Washington, DC, National Academy Press.

Ippolito, P.M. and Mathios, A.D. (1994) 'Information, Policy, and the Sources of Fat and Cholesterol in the US Diet', *Journal of Public Policy & Marketing*, **13**: 200–217.

Kunkel, D. and Roberts, D. (1991) 'Young Minds and Marketplace Values: Issues in Children's Television Advertising', *Journal of Social Issues*, **47**: 57–72.

Olshavsky, R.W. and Granbois, D.H. (1979) 'Consumer Decision Making — Fact or Fiction?', *Journal of Consumer Research*, **6**: 93–100.

Peltzman, S. (1975) 'The Effects of Automobile Safety Regulation', *Journal of Political Economy*, **83**: 677–725.

Peterson, S.P. and Hoffer, G.E. (1994) 'The Impact of Airbag Adoption on Relative Personal Injury and Absolute Collision Insurance Claims', *Journal of Consumer Research*, **20**: 657–62.

Review of the Research Literature on the Effects of Health Warning Labels (1987) Report submitted by the Assistant Secretary for Health, Department of Health and Human Services, June.

Russo, J.E. and LeClerc, F. (1991) 'Characteristics of Successful Product Information Programs', *Journal of Social Issues*, **47**: 73–92.

Russo, J.E., Staelin, R., Nolan, C.A., Russell, G.J. and Metcalf, B.L. (1986) 'Nutrition Information in Supermarkets', *Journal of Consumer Research*, **13**: 48–70.

Contingent Valuation

Many aspects of the environment have values which have no explicit market price. Neoclassical economics recommends such nonmarket goods and services be given a pseudo-market or shadow price in order to correct for market failure. Such prices may then enter a cost–benefit calculus or a welfare economic assessment. One method of pricing an environmental good is to create a hypothetical or contingent market, that is, the contingent valuation method (Hanley and Spash, 1993 review the complete range of methods).

The basic format of the contingent valuation method simply requires that individuals are asked their willingness to pay or willingness to accept compensation for an environmental quality or quantity change. For example, a new road may be planned which will destroy a local woodland and the survey might be framed so as to ask how much you would be willing to pay to prevent this development or how much compensation you would require to allow the road to proceed. In practice, the willingnes-to-pay format has been preferred but often without good reason, as explained in a review of problems by Knetsch (1994). Knetsch, in collaboration with Kahneman (Kahneman and Knetsch, 1992), has also raised concerns about the extent to which contingent valuation focuses upon one aspect of the environment and how varying the inclusiveness of the issue creates a bias. On the basis of this effect, contingent valuation has been characterized as measuring a moral motivation to contribute to a good cause rather than the valuation of environmental goods and services. The problem is variously termed as 'part–whole bias', the 'warm-glow effect' and 'embedding'.

The contingent valuation method has been controversial both within and outside the economics profession. As a tool of cost–benefit analysis the conduct of the survey should be in accordance with microeconomic welfare theory. However, results have been extrapolated and transferred beyond their original context, and aggregated without considering the violation of *ceteris paribus*. For example, recently the world's ecosystems have been priced largely on the basis of summing values from any contingent valuation studies the authors could find regardless of comparability or micro-theoretic constraints. Psychologists have criticized survey practice and there have been a range of biases identified which have been controlled for by redesign and refinement of the survey instrument. Despite these damage-limitation exercises, the contingent valuation method has become a target for concerns about any monetary valuation of the environment with philosophers raising issues of incommensurability, environmental ethics and citizens' values.

Historical overview

Contingent valuation was suggested by Ciriacy-Wantrup in 1947 and first applied by the US National Park Service in 1958 (see Mack and Myers, 1965). More frequently cited is the second application by Davis (1963); carried out in 1961 as part of his doctoral dissertation, the contingent valuation assessed the value of woodlands in the State of Maine. Initially, little attention was paid to these developments, with only a few studies by academics (in 1965 and 1969). However, this changed with the work of Weisbrod (1964) and Krutilla (1967), which brought attention to 'nonuse' values. These became classified as maintaining an option to use environmental services (option value), preserving the environment for future generations (bequest value), and a concern that aspects of the environment persist regardless of current or future human uses (existence value). Nonuse values have become central to the justification for using contingent valuation because this is currently the only method by which they can be evaluated.

Throughout the 1970s, contingent valuation studies in the US increased in frequency, although the technique remained largely of academic interest. In the 1980s and 1990s, studies took place first in Europe and then in less-developed economies, and became increasingly connected to government decision making. A bibliography in 1992 listed almost one thousand contingent valuation studies worldwide.

The exponential growth in the use of the contingent valuation method has several roots. In the 1980s, governments in Europe and the US were politically right wing and in favour of expanding the realm of market pricing. In the US, cost–benefit analysis returned to the public policy arena with President Ronald Reagan's executive order 12291 in 1981, and in 1986 the contingent valuation method was incorporated into the Department of Interior's regulations for measuring the damages associated with oil spills and hazardous wastes. In the UK the government's emphasis on monetary valuation increased and by 1988 the Department of the Environment was sponsoring work by environmental economists and supporting contingent valuation for both project and policy appraisal.

There were also two volumes produced which promoted the contingent valuation method. Cummings, Brookshire and Schultze (1986) conducted a critical assessment of the technique which, while raising many problems, gave an academic credibility to contingent valuation by involving economists and psychologists of high standing, such as Kenneth Arrow and Daniel Kahneman. This book also recommended a set of working conditions for a good contingent valuation. A further boost to the general ease of applying contingent valuation was given by Mitchell and Carson (1989), who provided a widely used manual of contingent valuation for those wishing to avoid the obvious pitfalls.

As the use of contingent valuation has increased so has the debate between supporters and detractors. Sagoff (1988), a philosopher, has critically attacked contingent valuation and in particular what he terms the 'Wyoming experiment' of the late 1970s and early 1980s. He sees the technique as economists venturing into the political realm, which he regards as totally separate. Applications to Kakadu National Park in Australia and the assessment of damages arising from the Exxon Valdez oil spill in Alaska created public controversy. In the latter case, the State of Alaska funded contingent valuation studies to estimate damages. Meanwhile, Exxon funded a considerable amount of work attacking the contingent valuation method (Hausman, 1993). A panel of experts was convened by the National Oceanic and Atmospheric Administration (NOAA) to fight pressure from Exxon coming via the Bush administration. The panel, which included Nobel laureates Kenneth Arrow (Exxon consultant) and Robert Solow (State of Alaska consultant), gave qualified support for contingent valuation.

They produced guidelines which suggest that there is one correct approach to conducting a good contingent valuation study (that is, methodologically similar to Cummings et al.). Blind adoption of the NOAA guidelines has become a defence of the validity of specific work, although this denies methodological pluralism and ignores the wider debate and controversy.

Stages in conducting contingent valuation

There are several stages to conducting a contingent valuation study: survey design, pre-testing; the main survey; estimating willingness to pay and/or willingness to accept; regression analysis; data aggregation and final assessment. Survey design requires framing a realistic decision concerning the environment where the monetary question to be asked is accepted as a possibility that the individual might face. Thus, several decisions must be taken by the analyst: a reason for the payment; how funds will be raised (the bid vehicle — for example, taxation of trust fund); the arrangements for and regularity of payments. The technique for bid elicitation may be an open-ended question (with or without a bidding card), a dichotomous choice, or a bidding game. Also, at this stage information on physical changes will be summarized and the method of their description chosen (such as text, graphics or maps).

Because of the sensitivity of responses to the information supplied, the pre-testing of the survey has become of increasing importance. This can be conducted via a simple small sample test run to see if respondents have problems or special sections can be included to pick out the occurrence of difficulties. A focus group is another method now in use for pre-testing. The pre-test will enable the identification of problems in the framing of the decision problem as well as divergence between encoding and decoding of information.

The conduct of the main survey can be done using several variations. The in-house interview is now most favoured, although expense often results in street surveys, telephone interviewing or mail shot. Early surveys, and academic ones, have used student interviewers, but the preference is for a market survey company with professionally trained personnel. The sample is often 'quota' (that is, requiring a sample selected on the basis of population characteristics such as balance of age, sex and education) as this is less expensive than a random sample (a random element may be included, for example, random walk method). The sample is also often weighted in terms of the local or regional population, which is seen as politically more important to the decision and likely to have strong direct economic connections to the outcome.

Typically, median bids are less than mean bids so both are reported, At this stage the treatment of 'protest bids' becomes problematic and these are often omitted from the mean calculation. Protest bids are zero bids given for reasons other than a zero value being placed on the resource in question. For example, a respondent may refuse any amount of compensation for loss of an environment which he or she regards as unique or a species which he or she feels should be protected at all costs. Respondents may refuse to state a willingness-to-pay amount because they reject the survey as an institutional approach to the problem, or because they have an ethical objection to the tradeoff being requested — which might be described as a lexicographic preference (Spash and Hanley, 1995). Another potential problem is the 'outlier' who bids a very large amount and so has a strong influence on the mean. This should be regarded as a problem only when the bid is unlikely to occur because the individual lacks the income to pay or would actually accept a much lower amount. In this case the respondent would be acting strategically, so creating a bias.

Regression analysis of the factors explaining the bids is used to test construct validity, that is, do the socio-economic variables have the expected signs, is the function statistically significant? Other relationships can also be investigated at this stage. In general, this bid curve analysis has tended to be of academic interest only.

The method of aggregating data across time and space is of more immediate practical interest. Several decisions need to be made which include determining: the relevant population, the method of aggregation from the sample bid, and the time period or discounting procedure. Aggregation on the basis of individual valuations will result in some double counting because households tend to contribute once rather than on the basis of each individual member. However, getting individuals to respond as heads of household can create problems for respondents

Final reflection upon the contingent valuation study can include convergent validity, and success of repeatability where there exist other similar studies. Several studies have been conducted which simultaneously conduct contingent valuation and another method of valuation (for example, travel cost or hedonic pricing), but these can compare only the direct use benefits. The overall success of the exercise will also become apparent as the results are being analysed, for example, a high number of protest bids. There are several specific problems which are recognized as possible causes of bias, some of which have been mentioned: strategic bias, design bias (choice of bid vehicle, prompting a bid). More problematic is the impact of information as this is by necessity restricted but can have serious influence upon the resulting bids.

Kahneman and Knetsch (1992) raised the problem, noted earlier by others, of embedding in the contingent valuation context. There is continuing disagreement as to whether survey redesign can help. This problem arises when the component parts of an individual's valuation are assessed separately and when summed found to exceed the valuation placed upon the whole. Contingent valuation studies commonly find this part–whole bias, also termed embedding, and it has been attributed by some to valuation of the moral satisfaction from contributing to a worthy cause ('warm glow'). The counter reaction has been that the contingent valuation surveys finding embedding are flawed in some way which creates the part–whole bias, and that this can be corrected by careful survey design. However, some experimental evidence for the existence of part–whole bias for private goods outside of the contingent valuation context now exists. Thus, the problem may lie with economic preference theory rather than merely with the contingent valuation method.

Contingent valuation in future
The extent to which the contingent valuation method can be generalized is easily overstated. According to Cummings et al. (1986), contingent valuation works best in only a limited range of circumstances. They consider that the most important rules are that respondents must understand and be familiar with the 'commodity' to be valued; respondents have prior valuation and choice experience with respect to the 'commodity'; uncertainty about the operation of the hypothetical market is low; willingness to pay is used as a conservative estimate in preference to willingness to accept compensation. However, the quantitative results of violating these conditions remains largely unspecified, and the reasoning behind some of the rules dubious.

The NOAA panel guidelines include: use of willingness to pay; in-house interviews on a random sample; full information on the resource change (including information on substitutes) and checks for understanding; closed-ended referendum formats (dichotomous choice); reinforcing budget restrictions; and careful pre-testing. They have also recommended the halving of any resulting price, which raises questions about the derivation and credibility of this particular set of rules. Perhaps the panel of five economists and one sociologist was the wrong group of experts to address the issue?

A more general problem is the extent to which any one set of rules can dictate innovative interdisciplinary research. The NOAA guidelines have not resolved the debate around contingent valuation because they assume a technical solution in the modernist tradition. The rules try to impose a set behavioural model upon individuals (economic rationality) and reject divergent behaviour. Yet this 'irrational' behaviour is some of the most interesting in terms of insights into what motivates individuals and the potential for the political success or failure of environmental policy. There is a fundamental methodological divergence between the approach of contingent valuation practitioners who try to find evidence in support of their a priori model in the neoclassical economic tradition, and those who allow the data to inform them as to the possible variety of human motivation and behaviour. The future of contingent valuation is potentially rich if it is developed as a method of empirical investigation into environmental valuation rather than an exercise in producing the one true price.

CLIVE L. SPASH

Bibliography

Ciracy-Wantrup, S.V. (1947) 'Capital Returns from Soil Conservation Practices', *Journal of Farm Economics*, **29**: 1188–90.

Cummings, R.G., Brookshire, D.S. and Schulze, W.D. (eds) (1986) *Valuing Environmental Goods: An Assessment of the Contingent Valuation Method*, Totowa, NJ, Rowman & Allanheld.

Davis, R. (1963) 'Recreation Planning as an Economic Problem', *Natural Resources Journal*, **3**: 239–49.

Hanley, N. and Spash, C.L. (1993) *Cost–Benefit Analysis and the Environment*, Cheltenham, Edward Elgar.

Hausman, J.A. (ed.) (1993) *Contingent Valuation: A Critical Assessment*, Amsterdam. North-Holland.

Kahneman, D, and Knetsch, J.L. (1992) 'Valuing Public Goods: The Purchase of Moral Satisfaction', *Journal of Environmental Economics and Management*, **22**: 57–70.

Knetsch, J.L. (1994) 'Environmental Valuation: Some Problems of Wrong Questions and Misleading Answers', *Environmental Values*, **3**: 351–68.

Krutilla, J.V. (1967) 'Conservation Reconsidered', *American Economic Review*, **57**: 777–86.

Mack, R.P. and Myers, S. (1965) 'Outdoor Recreation', in Dorfman, R. (ed.) *Measuring Benefits of Government Investments*, Washington, D.C., The Brookings Institute.

Mitchell, R. and Carson, R. (1989) *Using Surveys to Value Public Goods: The Contingent Valuation Method*, Washington, DC, Resources for the Future.

Sagoff, M. (1988) *The Economy of the Earth*, Cambridge, Cambridge University Press.

Spash, C.L. and Hanley, N. (1995) 'Preferences, Information and Biodiversity Preservation', *Ecological Economics*, **12**: 191–208.

Weisbrod, B.A. (1964) 'Collective Consumption Services of Individual-Consumption Goods', *Quarterly Journal of Economics*, **78**: 471–7.

Conventions

Conventions are the recognizable patterns of behaviour shared by a group of people, ranging from a family to a large society. Conventions denote all regularities in individual behaviour that tend to be maintained without explicit formal sanctions. There are other words that overlap with conventions, namely, customs, norms, mores, folkways and so on. Conventions — reflecting expectations of individuals who have evolved to be more or less mutually consistent — reduce much uncertainty concerning human interaction and enable people to live under a system of coordination and cooperation. People often underestimate the force with which the human mind craves predictability and the ability with which human beings can attain predictability under most unlikely situations. The urge to generate conventions rests on the fact that without conventions which enable human beings to behave as if things are more or less predictable, human action would be impossible. In all areas of human action and interaction, we observe conventions and, as a consequence, a degree of predictability (see Heiner, 1983). Indeed, much of our daily expectations (and our actions based on them) would be impossible except for the modes of behaviour that are best described as conventional. Yet, despite its importance, the study of conventions is a neglected area.

The ubiquity of conventions

Conventions, with varying degrees of normative implications, are prevalent in any ongoing relationship. Conventions are easily observed in any ongoing social relations — ranging from languages and etiquette, to the sense of justice (see Hume, 1965: 483). Although economists commonly underestimate the place of conventions in economic activities, business practices are riddled with conventions. For example, it is widely recognized that the pricing of assets depends upon conventional decisions on what should be factored into their value and what should be excluded from consideration (see Keynes, 1936: 149–58). Also, the top economic forecasters as a group seem to follow certain conventions by together erring greatly in calling every recent deviation a turning-point (see Linden, 1991: 68). The neglect of the role of conventions in human action results in a deficient understanding of social and economic processes. It can result in costly mistakes when one is confronted with the issue of bringing about a change, for example, the transformation of former socialist countries, or the adoption of a Western- style constitution in a less-developed country.

Origins of conventions

Most of the familiar conventions on which we base our daily actions have obscure origins because they are outcomes of the attempts by disparate individuals in a group to deal with their own surroundings, including other individuals. But individuals learn to behave conventionally: individuals — who experiment to arrive at methods most serviceable for survival, imitate the successful examples and avoid the failed examples, care about relevant others' reactions, and judge others and react to them by their own standards — tend to acquire over time certain regularities in their behaviour and come to expect similar regularities in others. Through conventions, therefore, much of inherent uncertainty is contained. Those who do not behave conventionally, that is, deviants, tend to frustrate others' expectations, meet their disapproval, and fare rather poorly. Their behaviour or practices will then be taken up as examples to shun.

It is easy to see how conventions may emerge in a 'coordination game' — for example, a situation where people could drive either on the left or on the right. Here, individuals, with nothing more than precedents and imitation of viable examples, are perfectly capable of generating conventions with which they can stabilize mutual expectations and coordinate their activities. Thanks to their ability to experiment and learn, people tend to generate conventions even in a prisoner's dilemma game (where people could benefit from cooperation but also there are incentives not to cooperate) if it is a recurrent one (see Axelrod, 1984).

The fact that conventions are products of human action and interaction should not lead us to conclude that they are arbitrary or even artificial, something that can be created at will. Rather, conventions should be regarded as the very basis of human action and knowledge.

Stability and inertia

If conventions are enabling by their stability, they are also constricting by their inflexibility. The majority of people in society conform to conventions. However, the nonconformist tendency is ever present. It exists, in part, because learning takes time. In addition, people learn different things and some people learn more quickly than others. At any moment in a community (defined as a group of people interacting closely in some capacity), there is bound to be a number of people who have not quite learned to conform to conventions. The majority of these will in due time become conventionalists, as they will learn from their experiences that the world is ruled by conventions (or else will eke out a marginal existence). Therefore, the ever-present deviants are in the minority and on the margin.

Each deviant, however, represents a new way of doing things. Although many of them may not be as good as the conventional, it is possible that some of them could be better. The new possibilities that deviants represent are significant, especially in the light of the fact that, although most conventionalists constantly encounter events and experience things, they often do not see the necessity of having to revise their way of seeing the world or doing things, but instead prefer to acquire great proficiency in fitting the observations and experiences into a familiar perspective, or telling soothing tales. A deviant is an individual with a different perspective and therefore may see things of significance where conventionalists see none, or recognize the possibility of new combinations that the majority, with their conventional blinders, neglect. Therefore, the stability of the regime of conventions, in which deviants are suppressed, implies social inertia and possibly missed opportunities.

This is not to deny the possibility that people can improve their lives within the context of existing conventions, but to underline the fact that people tend to ignore the possibility of improvement by abandoning the existing conventions and adopting a new one. This is because constant revision of expectations and behaviour is not consistent with the nature of convention itself, that is, a means of reducing uncertainty.

Consider, for example, a firm whose production method has proved viable. As far as management is concerned, this is the way to do business, and the firm is committed to this successful convention. Time brings change, however, and suppose now some new ways of doing things dawn on individual workers, engineers, or outside advisers and so on. However, it takes a lot to overthrow a convention. Although decision makers in firms have more discretionary power than many traditional authorities, they are largely influenced by firm conventions or 'corporate cultures'. Decision makers are thus liable to make mistakes (see Earl, 1984), whether in the sense that one may regret them *ex post*, or in the sense that one may have acted differently if a different corporate culture had prevailed. These mistakes, far from being the consequence of calculated risks (or the result of trembling hands), are often the systematic sort that derive from a certain mind-set. The employees most likely to be promoted to posts of decision making are those who seem most successful according to the firm's established standards or criteria, that is, the conventions prevalent in the firm. Corporate decision makers are therefore perhaps least likely to deviate from the very conventions that have been the benchmarks of their success (Schoenberger, 1997). Moreover, if decision makers are willing to entertain an innovative idea, the success of its execution will depend upon how much cooperation can be garnered from subordinates, suppliers and consumers, and these groups are themselves accustomed and loyal to existing conventions. In brief, conventions are very thoroughly entrenched, especially in firms with good track records. Stability and inertia go hand in hand.

The process of change
Inflexibility in the face of change creates the possibilities both of neglected opportunities and of entrepreneurial discovery (see Choi, 1993). Therefore, the stability of conventions, together with spontaneous learning sets in motion the process of endogenous change, for the opportunities neglected by conventionalists tend to grow over time as people simultaneously (but unsystematically) learn from their daily experiences. That is, the gap between the actual and the potential (in other words, the neglected opportunities) tends to grow over time. As the gap becomes bigger with the passage of time, it becomes easier to discover. Consequently, the probability of some deviants successfully innovating should increase with time; it is harder not to notice what is growing larger and more distinct over time. The impetus for social change, therefore, is given by individuals intending to exploit the opportunities that others ignore.

The process of change is accelerated in a market economy where individuals have greater freedom to start a venture that strikes their fancy and greater security based on private property rights. The entrepreneur believes that he or she can gain over and above the customary expectations. He or she must see what others do not because of their conventional blinders. He or she claims to know more than we do, perhaps not in words, but in actions that speak louder than words. The entrepreneur has the conviction that he or she can expose our ignorance, parochialism and undue inhibitions. Of course, many will fail, as evidenced by the countless startup firms that go bankrupt each year. But sooner or later, some will succeed.

Entrepreneurial success is often met by emulation. Once enterprising individuals achieve outstanding success by exploiting these possibilities through innovative — and therefore unconventional — practices, they may become role models. Even strong loyalty to conventions must eventually yield to persistent forces of change, or succumb to them; institutional inertia may hold these forces at bay for a while. In due course, the innovative practices will become routine and conventional, not necessarily because they tend to degenerate over time, but rather because they tend to become so widely accepted that people are seen as conforming to them. After acquiring another set of conventional blinders, they ignore new information that crops up over the years. Again, the potential gains grow, thus preparing the ground for the next round of innovations and changes.

The market encourages entrepreneurial discovery of opportunities and innovations. We can view this process as one of social learning. The competitive urge to exploit opportunities ignored, or at least not yet captured, by others is a stronger incentive to keep our information up to date and handy than even the best-meaning of teachers can provide. The prospect of becoming extinct unless we learn the lesson can fix our attention more closely than the sternest of taskmasters. (This process works best if people's urge to protect the status quo, or to promote their interests, by political means or by force, is not given a free reign.)

This market process of learning may appear lamentably chaotic and undisciplined. But the market process of social learning involves contributions from everywhere and everyone. A more 'disciplined' process would require a plan, which is at best the product of a few brains in a few places (see Hayek, 1945). Innovation is possible under any system, but in a market system the pace of innovation is much quicker: by limiting the impediments and inhibitions tradition attaches to deviation, and through the protection of private property rights, a market system encourages innovators and arbitrageurs to exploit opportunities as far as they are able. Surely here lies the explanation for the higher rates of innovation and rapid economic development observed under capitalism than under feudalism or socialism.

From the perspective of conventions, the story of modern economic and social development is but a continual process in which the market has successfully expanded and invaded the domain once exclusively ruled by conventions through entrepreneurial exploits. The market has been truly dynamic, its consequences far-reaching, and this process of expansion continues before our very own eyes. Only by taking the perspective of conventions as general social tendencies generated by disparate individuals, can one begin to appreciate the multifaceted dynamism of the market processes.

YOUNG BACK CHOI

Bibliography

Axelrod, R. (1984) *The Evolution of Cooperation*, New York, Basic Books.
Choi, Y.B. (1993) *Paradigms and Conventions: Uncertainty, Decision Making, and Entrepreneurship*, Ann Arbor, MI, University of Michigan Press.
Earl, P.E. (1984) *The Corporate Imagination: How Big Companies Make Mistakes*, Armonk, NY, M.E. Sharpe.
Hayek, F.A. (1945) 'The Use of Knowledge in Society', *American Economic Review*, **35**: 519–30.
Heiner, R.A. (1983) 'The Origin of Predictable Behavior', *American Economic Review*, **73**: 560–95.
Hume, D. (1965) *A Treatise on Human Nature*, Oxford, Clarendon Press.
Keynes, J.M. (1936) *The General Theory of Employment, Interest, and Money*, New York, Harcourt, Brace.
Linden, D.W. (1991) 'Dreary Days in the Dismal Science', *Forbes*, 21 January: 68–71.
Schoenberger, E. (1997) *The Cultural Crisis of the Firm*, Cambridge, MA, Blackwell.

Credit, Debt and Problem Debt

Credit and debt both involve paying for goods or services some significant time after receiving them. In accountancy terms, the two are simple mirror images of each other: if I am under contract to pay you money, the money is a credit as far as you are concerned and a debt as far as I am concerned; you are my creditor and I am your debtor. In discussing people's behaviour, however, we need to draw a distinction between credit and debt, and we need to add a category of problem debt. The following distinctions more or less correspond to the way these words are used in everyday speech, and although they are not followed universally in the literature on the economic psychology of credit and debt, they are consistent with most researchers' usage. In this entry, then, we use *credit* for situations involving an arrangement for deferred payment, agreed between buyer and seller: examples include a house mortgage, the use of what is known in North America as instalment credit and in the UK as hire purchase, borrowing money from a door-to-door moneylender to buy the week's groceries, or paying

139

monthly or quarterly for utilities received daily. *Debt*, on the other hand, is a situation where payment has been deferred by the buyer without the seller's agreement. Very commonly it results from default on a credit agreement, but it could also result from failure to make any other regular payment, such as a rent, or a payment incurred unintentionally, such as a fine. Finally, in *problem* or *crisis debt*, people have debts that they cannot meet, either now or in the reasonably foreseeable future.

Everyday speech is affected by the strong negative connotations of debt. As advertisements for financial services recognize, people prefer to say that they have taken on a credit arrangement rather than that they have gone into debt, and we label our credit/debt behaviour in the self-serving ways that are predicted by attribution theory. Everyday experience also shows that we avoid acknowledging debts: for example, if asked whether they have any debts, people may reply that they do not, and subsequently say that they have a house mortgage, or outstanding balances on credit cards. Concepts of debt and understandings of its causation can be complex (Lea, Walker and Rooijmans, 1992). They tend to be strongly influenced by debt status: people who are debt free attribute debt to fecklessness and mismanagement of money, while those who have debts are more likely to explain them in terms of external circumstances, though they may revert to internal attributions when accounting for other people's debts (Walker, 1997). Those who have debts are less disapproving of debt in general than those who are debt free. The direction of causality here is disputed, but Davies and Lea (1995) claim that data on student debt imply that attitudes change after debt has been incurred, presumably in order to maintain internal consistency, as suggested by cognitive dissonance theory and many other social psychological accounts of attitude change.

Theoretically speaking, incurring debt is the opposite of saving: it is an example of intertemporal choice. Life-cycle theories of saving of the type pioneered by Modigliani and Brumberg (1954) predict that people should incur debt at certain times in their lives, if they have rational expectations of higher future income. Given the oft-noted tendency for people to save less than simple economic theories predict (Fisher, 1930), we might expect that people would incur more debt than predicted, and that the economic psychology of debt would be dominated by the problem of explaining why. In practice, however, a broad tendency towards overindebtedness has not been observed. There are some general 'irrationalities' about people's behaviour towards debt; for example, people make consistent errors in judging the cost of credit arrangements, paying too much attention to weekly repayments and too little to total cost (Ranyard and Craig, 1993, 1995); some of these problems may well be accounted for by the difficulties of the arithmetic of compound interest. Most psychological studies of credit and debt, however, have been concerned with more differential issues:

why do some people take on credit, incur debts, and get into debt crisis, when other, apparently similar, people do not, and have there been secular changes in willingness to get into debt, and if so, why?

Issues of credit and debt played a prominent part in Katona's early work on the economic psychology of gross consumer demand in the economy. Katona (1975: 271ff.) noted that willingness to enter into new credit agreements was one of the marks of a high level of consumer confidence. It is at the same time one of the engines of economic expansion, since if banks and other financial institutions lend consumers money to finance new purchases, that tends to expand the money supply in the economy. Katona also noted that willingness to take on credit did not just vary across time periods for the population as a whole, but also varied within the population. It was not concentrated among those with the lowest incomes, but rather among those with higher incomes and an expectation that their incomes would increase further.

When we consider debt rather than credit, however, the available evidence is that it is concentrated among people with low incomes and high necessary expenditures, for example, because they have young children (Berthoud and Kempson, 1992; Lea, Webley and Levine, 1993; Lea, Webley and Walker, 1995b). Studies of the psychology of debt, and especially crisis debt, therefore tend to overlap with studies of the psychology of poverty. In some cases, debtors' incomes may be low not absolutely, but relative to their 'reference group', the occupational or social group they feel they belong to and whose consumption pattern they therefore adopt (for example, Sullivan, Warren and Westbrook, 1989). That is not to say that there are no debtors with high incomes, either absolutely or relatively. However, it is likely that this group are more or less delinquent, and correspondingly difficult to recruit into a research study by traditional psychological methods. Low response rates have bedevilled studies even of low-income debtors (for example, Lea et al., 1993, 1995b). For psychologists, the interesting question has often been whether there are social, psychological and behavioural factors that would predict who does or does not get into either debt or crisis debt, over and above the obvious economic factors such as income and needs for expenditure. Many factors have been suggested, including attitudes towards debt (for example, Lea et al., 1993; Davies and Lea, 1995), broader attitudinal factors such as locus of control (those with a more external locus of control being thought more likely to get into debt: see Livingstone and Lunt, 1992a; Tokunaga, 1993), personality (a disproportionate number of extroverts have been found among bankrupts: see Little, 1989), patterns of consumer behaviour (especially consumption preferences and issues concerning necessities and luxuries: see Livingstone and Lunt, 1992b; Walker, 1997), reference groups (especially basing one's consumption style on a group of higher typical income than one's own: Lea et al., 1995b) and styles and strategies of money management (for example, Lea et al., 1993, 1995b; Lea, Webley and Bellamy, 1995a). Evidence in favour of each of these have been found in at least some surveys. Although none of them is entirely reliable, reports (including self-reports) of poor money management among debtors are a particularly recurrent theme, although it has been argued that they should be looked at relatively to the financial problems poor people face, which few people would be able to overcome (Walker, 1997; Lea et al., 1997).

The social and psychological factors in debt may help explain explain two demographic tendencies that have consistently been found in surveys of attitudes and behaviour towards debt. In population surveys, older people report less debt than younger ones (Lea et al., 1993), and among young people, especially but not only students, women are less likely to be in debt than men (for example, Peters, 1987; Davies and Lea, 1995; Lea et al., 1995a). The reason that the latter trend is not seen in population surveys is almost certainly that it is masked by the massive differences in typical income and family circumstances between men and women. Popular accounts of these trends include a generational shift in attitudes, with the generations who have grown up through the credit expansion of recent decades more tolerant of debt than older people, and differences in money management skills, with women and older people budgeting more systematically. However, we have already noted that there are problems in interpreting the direction of causality in relation to attitudes towards debt, and the same issues arise for the other psychological variables listed here. As regards money management, most studies have relied on self-reports of quality and techniques of people's budgeting, and it is likely that people who find themselves in debt will deduce that they must be poor money managers; alternatively, it has been suggested that chronic imbalance between income and the expenditure needs of a family may induce 'learned helplessness' (Walker, 1997). Similarly, it is likely that some of the distinctive patterns of consumer behaviour found among debtors are consequences rather than causes of their financial situation; for example cigarette purchasing, often high among debtors (for example, Lea et al., 1995b), represents almost the only attainable luxury for the poor, and smoking also serves to alleviate the stress that debt undoubtedly induces. In some cases the economic approach may be more productive: for example, low debt among the old is what would be expected from life-cycle theory.

Studies that have compared 'normal' debt with crisis debt (for example, Lea et al., 1993, 1995b) have generally found that the same factors contribute to each, but are, as would be expected, more intense and numerous in cases of problem debt. A further concern has been how to help people who are in a debt crisis. Standard advice is to contact creditors at the earliest stage, but debtors do not report that this is helpful, preferring family, friends, and independent agencies such as Citizens' Advice Bureaux (Lea et al., 1995b). The most helpful strategy

142

for recovering from a debt crisis seems to be to take on regular payment plans such as standing order or direct debit arrangements, or deductions at source from social security payments. These are unpopular with debtors before they have tried them, but acknowledged as successful when used (Walker, 1997).

Except in relation to people's understanding of credit plans, which Ranyard and Craig (1995) interpret in terms of the theory of mental accounts, little effort has yet been made to bring the recent practical studies of debt to bear on the theoretical issues raised at the beginning of this entry. Self-serving attributional processes are clearly recognizable in interview studies with debtors and in attitudes to and beliefs about debt in nondebtors. The ubiquity of self-attributions of poor money management among debtors is an exception to this trend, and perhaps the more striking because of that. It may be at this level that we see the dominance of short- over long-term considerations, expected on theoretical grounds: it is not that people choose to get into debt in order to achieve instant gratification, but rather that they do not embark early enough, or realistically enough, on the forbidding task of planning a very tight budget, and are unwilling to risk the loss of liquidity involved in committing themselves to regular payment plans. Future progress in the economic psychology of debt seems likely to depend on getting a tighter theoretical grip, without losing the pragmatic and socially applicable emphasis of the recent empirical research. It will also be important to find ways of getting more comprehensive samples, both to give greater assurance that current results on low-income debtors are reliable, and also so that theoretically interesting groups such as wealthy debtors can be studied.

STEPHEN E.G. LEA

Bibliography

Berggren, N. (1997) 'Rhetoric or Reality? An Economic Analysis of the Effects of Religion in Sweden', *Journal of Socio-Economics*, **26**: 571–96.

Berthoud, R. and Kempson, E. (1992) *Credit and Debt: The P.S.I. Report*, London, Policy Studies Institute.

Davies, E. and Lea, S.E.G. (1995) 'Student Attitudes to Student Debt', *Journal of Economic Psychology*, **16**: 663–79.

Fisher, I. (1930) *The Theory of Interest*, New York, Macmillan.

Katona, G. (1975) *Psychological Economics*, New York, Elsevier.

Lea, S.E.G., Burgoyne, C.B., Jones, S.M. and Beer, A.J. (1997) 'An Interview Study of the Psychology of Poverty', in *The XXII International Conference of Economic Psychology*, Valencia, Promo/Libro, Vol. 2: 955–67.

Lea, S.E.G., Walker, C.M. and Rooijmans, J.G. (1992) 'The Concept of Debt: An Experimental Investigation', in Brüggelambert, G. et al. (eds) *Economic Psychology and Experimental Economics*, Rieck, Eschborn/Taunus.

Lea, S.E.G., Webley, P. and Bellamy, G.W. (1995a) 'Student Debt: A Psychological Analysis of the UK Experience', in Nyhus, E. and Troye, S.V. (eds) *Frontiers in*

Economic Psychology, Bergen, Norges Handelshøyskole, Vol.1: 430–44.

Lea, S.E.G., Webley, P. and Levine, R.M. (1993) 'The Economic Psychology of Consumer Debt', *Journal of Economic Psychology*, **14**: 85–119.

Lea, S.E.G., Webley, P. and Walker, C.M. (1995b) 'Psychological Factors in Consumer Debt: Money Management, Economic Socialization, and Credit Use', *Journal of Economic Psychology*, **16**: 681–701.

Little, C. (1989) 'Personality Correlates of Debting Behaviour: Two Studies', Economic Psychology Research Group Internal Report no. 89/19, University of Exeter.

Livingstone, S. and Lunt, P. (1992a) 'Predicting Personal Debt and Debt Repayment: Psychological, Social and Economic Determinants', *Journal of Economic Psychology*, **13**: 111–34.

Livingstone, S.M. and Lunt, P. (1992b) 'Everyday Conceptions of Necessities and Luxuries: Problems of Cultural Relativity and Moral Judgement', in Lea, S.E.G., Webley, P. and Young, B.M. (eds) *New Directions in Economic Psychology*, Aldershot, Edward Elgar.

Modigliani, F. and Brumberg, R. (1954) 'Utility Analysis and the Consumption Function: An Interpretation of Cross-Sectional Data', in Kurihara, K.K. (ed.), *Post-Keynesian Economics*, New Brunswick, NJ, Rutgers University Press.

Peters, J.F. (1987) 'Youth, Family and Employment', *Adolescence*, **22**: 456–73.

Ranyard, R. and Craig, G. (1993) 'Estimating the Duration of a Flexible Loan: The Effect of Supplementary Information', *Journal of Economic Psychology*, **14**: 317–35.

Ranyard, R. and Craig, G. (1995) 'Evaluating and Budgeting with Instalment Credit — An Interview Study', *Journal of Economic Psychology*, **16**: 449–67.

Sullivan, T.A., Warren, E. and Westbrook, J.L. (1989) *As We Forgive Our Debtors,* New York, Oxford University Press.

Tokunaga, H., (1993) 'The Use and Abuse of Consumer Credit: Application of Psychological Theory and Research', *Journal of Economic Psychology*, **14**: 285–316.

Walker, C.M. (1997) 'The Psychology of Debt in the 1990s', Unpublished PhD thesis, University of Exeter.

Cross-Cultural Research

Science aspires to be universal. It relies upon empirical research for the formulation of laws and principles which are stable over time and across cultures. While this may not prove problematic for the physicist, it presents a greater challenge to the social scientist. An atom may respond in a predictable fashion from Athens to Zanzibar, but human behaviour is considerably more complex and strongly influenced by social and cultural factors. What implications does this have for consumer research and economic psychology? The strong emphasis placed on empirical investigations in industrialized European and American cultures necessarily calls into question the generality of existing constructs and propositions. Cross-cultural studies, however, can broaden our empirical horizons and provide a useful tool for evaluating the universality of social science theory. They can also contribute to the solutions of practical problems pertaining to consumer behaviour, marketing, management and economic development.

One method for testing the cross-cultural generality of established concepts, laws and principles is replication studies. Within the realm of economic psychology a good example is provided by Waines's (1984) research on the development of economic concepts in Egyptian children. Waines studied 180 boys between 7 and 13 years old who differed in socioeconomic background and employment experience. The children were asked questions about the meaning of rich and poor, the value of money and its relationship to buying and selling, and the concept of inequality. The study reported evidence of a developmental trend towards more complex and differentiated constructs which was consistent with the findings from Western industrialized nations. Comparing these results with cross-cultural research from other countries such as Malaysia, Italy, Australia and the United States, the author argued in favour of convergence in the developmental sequence of the acquisition of economic concepts. She also interpreted the findings within the broader framework of cross-cultural research on cognitive maturation which suggests a universal sequence of development but culture-specific variation in developmental rates and levels.

Cross-cultural replication studies do provide interesting and useful information; however, there are limits to what these studies can actually tell us. If, for example, we successfully replicate findings in a new cultural context, this does give us greater confidence in the universality of theory. Still, one must ultimately ask the question 'At which point have we provided enough information to establish universality?'. After ten cultures? After 100? The answer might be guided more by the types of cultures used in replication studies than by the actual number of comparisons. A representative sample of world cultures would be convincing. Even a selection of extremely diverse cultural groups would be persuasive; a collection of a few Western European cultures would tell us very little. A more significant problem with replication studies, however, is that of interpreting negative results. If the replication appears to be successful, there is no discernible problem, and the findings may be taken to contribute to universal theory-building. If, however, the results do not replicate, the findings may be very difficult to interpret. Is the failure due to measurement problems? Indeed, cross-cultural replications are extremely complicated to conduct because they must meet strict methodological demands of conceptual, stimuli, functional, linguistic and metric equivalence. Alternatively, is the failure due to culture-bound aspects of the theory under investigation? In these cases it is difficult, if not impossible, to draw conclusions with confidence.

Theory-driven research, which relies on the careful selection of comparative cultures, is a more powerful method for testing the universality of basic principles in economic psychology. Investigations of reward allocation and distributive justice clearly illustrate this approach. Social psychological theory concerning the distribution of monetary assets has been largely dominated by the equity principle. The theory states that allocation of rewards should reflect the inputs and outputs of group members, in short, that individuals should receive rewards in relation to the amount of their respective contributions. While there are a number of factors which may affect the operation of the equity rule, research suggests that equity is the major organizational principle in the distribution of financial assets, so much so that in the mainstream social psychological literature it is often referred to as the equity 'norm'. Cross-cultural psychologists, however, have noted an individualistic bias in the equity principle and have proposed that the operation of other principles, particularly those of equality and need, may exert more potent influences on the allocation of monetary rewards and the perceptions of fairness in collectivist cultures.

One method for investigating this proposition involves the identification of two or more groups that vary along the continuum of individualism–collectivism for the cross-cultural comparison of resource allocations. Murphy-Berman et al. (1984), for example, selected American (individualist) and Indian (collectivist) subjects for comparisons of the allocations of bonuses and pay cuts to work colleagues. Their research revealed that Indians, compared to Americans, assigned higher bonuses and lower pay cuts to needy colleagues. In addition, their financial resource allocations were less affected by merit and equity. Comparative studies have also been undertaken with Chinese, Japanese and Korean subjects. Leung and Bond (1984) found that Chinese subjects in Hong Kong operated more on the equality principle than Americans when monetary rewards were shared among friends. Similarly, Leung and Iwawaki (1988) reported that collectivism was associated with a stronger preference for equality and a weaker preference for equity in their study of American, Korean and Japanese students. Overall research suggests that in comparative studies between Asian countries and the United States, collectivist subjects rely more on equality and less on equity for ingroup reward allocations. Accordingly, these findings call into question the cross-cultural generality of an equity 'norm'.

In addition to replication studies and theory-driven research, cross-cultural investigators also contribute to a wider body of knowledge in economic psychology through exploratory investigations. Hofstede's (1984) cross-cultural study of work-related values exemplifies this approach. In this large-scale project, data were gathered from employees of a well-known multinational organization. The study included more than 100 000 workers sampled from 40 countries across North America (US, Canada, Mexico), South America (for example, Argentina, Chile, Peru), Europe (for example, Norway, Spain, Switzerland), Africa (South Africa), the Middle East (Iran, Israel), Asia (for

146

example, India, Japan, Hong Kong) and the South Pacific (Australia, New Zealand). Ecological factor analysis of the cross-cultural survey data revealed the emergence of four independent domains of work-related values: power distance (inequality in power and influence), uncertainty avoidance (intolerance of uncertainty or ambiguity), individualism (egocentrism or self-orientation) and masculinity (instrumentality). Hofstede then examined the relationship between the four value domains and macro social, economic and political factors. Using GNP (gross national product) as an indicator of wealth, he reported a significant negative correlation (–0.65) between wealth and power distance (the greater the status differentials in organizations, the lower the level of economic development) and a significant negative correlation (–0.30) between wealth and uncertainty avoidance (the greater the tolerance of ambiguity, the higher the level of economic development). More impressive, however, was the substantial positive correlation (0.82) between individualism and wealth.

Hofstede's work on values has attracted considerable attention in cross-cultural studies; however, both Hofstede and his critics have acknowledged the potential limitations of the research. Of particular concern are the sample bias (Euro-American cultures are overrepresented, and Africa is underrepresented) and the cultural origins of the measurement instruments. As a complement to this research and in efforts to move towards a more universal psychology, Michael Bond and colleagues developed a Chinese Values Survey and administered the research instrument to university students in 22 countries (Chinese Culture Connection, 1987). Although the data base was considerably smaller than Hofstede's cross-cultural sample, it managed to tap respondents in North America (United States, Canada), South America (Brazil), Eastern and Western Europe (for example, Poland, Netherlands, Sweden), Africa (Zimbabwe, Nigeria), Asia (for example, Bangladesh, Singapore, South Korea) and the South Pacific (Australia, New Zealand). Ecological factor analysis of the survey responses revealed a four-factor structure in the cross-cultural data: integration, moral discipline, Confucian work dynamism and human-heartedness. Bond noted that there was conceptual and empirical overlap between these factors and Hofstede's dimensions. For example, integration was significantly related to both power distance and individualism, and human-heartedness correlated highly with masculinity. However, Confucian work dynamism did not significantly relate to any of the Hofstede dimensions. In addition, GNG (gross national growth) was strongly correlated with Confucian work dynamism (0.70) across the 22 countries. Bond has speculated that Confucian work dynamism may constitute an 'Oriental' dimension of values and that the results of his study lend further credence to the post-Confucian hypothesis of economic vitality in East Asian societies in the mid-twentieth century.

Finally, cross-cultural research may be undertaken to answer very specific questions about practical matters related to economic psychology and consumer behaviour. Applied research of this type is generally conducted with comparative samples of various ethnic or cultural groups within a single country; there are rarely attempts to generalize the findings across ethnic, cultural or national boundaries. Who buys what? Lee and Um (1991) found that the ownership of cars and stereo equipment is greater for Korean Americans than for Anglo-Americans. Who buys more? Gentry, Jun and Tansuhaj (1995) confirmed that Chinese Thais own more consumer durables than either Thais or Muslim Thais. Which factors affect spending? Saegert, Hoover and Hilger (1985) reported that Mexican Americans are more price conscious and prefer familiar stores to a greater extent than do Anglo Americans. This type of research is particularly useful in identifying target groups and strategic approaches for marketing and advertising.

These are but a few examples of cross-cultural research. Admittedly, cross-cultural studies in economic and consumer psychology are still in their infancy; nevertheless, they have a strong potential to contribute to the development of the field by critically assessing the limits of existing theory and by correcting ethnocentric biases in contemporary research. In an ever-shrinking world this is an important contribution.

COLLEEN A. WARD

Bibliography

Chinese Culture Connection (1987) 'Chinese Values and the Search for Culture-free Dimensions of Culture', *Journal of Cross-Cultural Psychology*, **18**: 143–64.

Gentry, J.W., Jun, S. and Tansuhaj, P. (1995) 'Consumer Acculturation Processes and Culture Conflict', *Journal of Business Research*, **32**: 129–39.

Hofstede, G. (1984) *Culture's Consequences — International Differences in Work-Related Values*, Beverly Hills, CA, Sage.

Lee, W.-N. and Um, K.-H.R. (1991) 'Ethnicity and Consumer Product Evaluation: A Cross-Cultural Comparison of Korean Immigrants and Americans', *Proceedings, Association for Consumer Research*.

Leung, K. and Bond, M.H. (1984) 'The Impact of Cultural Collectivism on Reward Allocation', *Journal of Personality and Social Psychology*, **47**: 793–804.

Leung, K. and Iwawaki, S. (1988) 'Cultural Collectivism and Distributive Behavior', *Journal of Cross-Cultural Psychology*, **19**: 35–49.

Murphy-Berman, V., Berman, J., Singh, P., Pachauri, A. and Kumar, P. (1984) 'Factors Affecting Allocation to Needy and Meritorious Recipients: A Cross-cultural Comparison', *Journal of Personality and Social Psychology*, **46**: 1267–72.

Saegert, J., Hoover, R.J. and Hilger, M.T. (1985) 'Characteristics of Mexican–American Consumers', *Journal of Consumer Research*, **12**: 104–9.

Waines, N.O. (1984) 'Development of Economic Concepts among Egyptian Children', *Journal of Cross-Cultural Psychology*, **15**: 47–64.

Culture Shock

The term 'culture shock' implies that the experience of a new culture (national, corporate, departmental) is an unpleasant surprise or shock, partly because it is unexpected, and partly because it may lead to a negative evaluation of one's own culture. Like 'jet-lag', 'culture shock' is a term used by the layperson to explain, or at least label, some of the more unpleasant consequences of travel to foreign parts.

Defining the term
An anthropologist, Oberg (1960), is the first to have used the term. In a brief and largely anecdotal article, he mentions at least six aspects of culture shock:

1. *Strain* due to the effort required to make necessary psychological adaptations.
2. A *sense of loss and feelings of deprivation* in regard to friends, status, profession and possessions.
3. Being *rejected* by/and or rejecting members of the new culture.
4. *Confusion* in role, role expectations, values, feelings and self-identity.
5. *Surprise, anxiety*, even *disgust* and *indignation* after becoming aware of cultural differences.
6. *Feelings of impotence* due to not being able to cope with the new environment.

The flavour of Oberg's observations may be gathered from this quotation:

> Culture shock is precipitated by the anxiety that results from losing all our familiar signs and symbols of social intercourse. These signs or cues include the thousand and one ways in which we orient ourselves to the situations of daily life: when to shake hands and what to say when we meet people, when and how to give tips, how to give orders to servants, how to make purchases, when to accept and when not to refuse invitations, when to take statements seriously and when not.
>
> Some of the symptoms of culture shock are: excessive washing of the hands; excessive concern over drinking water, food, dishes, and bedding; fear of physical contact with attendants or servants; the absent-minded, far-away stare (sometimes called the 'tropical stare'); a feeling of helplessness and a desire for dependence on long-term residents of one's own nationality; fits of anger over delays and other minor frustrations; delay and outright refusal to learn the language of the host country; excessive fear of being cheated, robbed, or injured; great concern over minor pains and irruptions of the skin; and finally, that terrible longing to be back home, to be able to have a good cup of coffee and a piece of apple pie, to walk into that corner drugstore, to visit one's relatives, and, in general, to talk to people who really make sense. (Oberg, 1960: 176)

Cleveland, Mangonc and Adams (1960) offered a similar analysis relying heavily on the personal experience of travellers, especially those at two extremes of the adaptation continuum, individuals who act as if they had 'never left home' and those who immediately 'go native'.

Researchers since Oberg have seen culture shock as a normal reaction, as part of the routine process of adaptation to cultural stress and the manifestation of a longing for a more predictable, stable and understandable environment. Many researchers have attempted to improve and extend Oberg's definition and concept of culture shock. Alternative terms used have been *culture fatigue*, *language shock, role shock* and *pervasive ambiguity*. In doing so, different researchers have simply placed the emphasis on slightly different problems — language, physical irritability, role ambiguity — rather than actually helping to specify how or why or when different people do or do not experience culture shock.

Bock (1970) has described culture shock as primarily an emotional reaction that follows from not being able to understand, control and predict another's behaviour. When customary social behaviour no longer seems relevant or applicable, people's usual behaviour becomes 'unusual'. Lack of familiarity with both the physical setting (design of homes, shops, offices) as well as the social environment (etiquette, ritual) have this effect, as do the experiences with, and use of, time. This theme is reiterated by all the writers in the field. Thus a person is anxious, confused and apparently apathetic until he or she has had time to develop a new set of cognitive constructs to understand and enact the appropriate behaviour (Furnham and Bochner, 1986; Furnham, 1996).

Writers about culture shock have often referred to individuals' lacking points of reference, social norms and rules to guide their actions and understand others' behaviour. This is very similar to the attributes studied under the headings of *alienation* and *anomie*, which include powerlessness, meaninglessness, normlessness, self- and social estrangement and social isolation.

In addition, ideas associated with *anxiety* pervade the culture-shock literature. Observers have pointed to a continuous general 'free-floating' anxiety which affects normal behaviour. Lack of self-confidence, distrust of others and mild psychosomatic complaints are also common. Furthermore, people appear to lose their inventiveness and spontaneity and become obsessively concerned with orderliness, hence the concern for cross-cultural training programmes (Ptak, Cooper and Brislin, 1995).

Most investigations of culture shock have been descriptive, in that they have attempted to list the various difficulties that sojourners experience and their typical reactions. Less attention has been paid to explaining who will find the shock more or less intense (for example, the old or the less educated); what determines which reaction a person is likely to experience; how long he or she remains in a period of shock, and so forth. The literature suggests that all people will suffer culture shock to some extent, which is always thought of as unpleasant and stressful. This assumption needs to be empirically supported. In theory, some people need not experience any negative aspects of shock; instead they may seek out these experiences for enjoyment (Furnham and Bochner, 1986).

For instance, Adler (1975) has stated that although culture shock is most often associated with negative consequences, it may, in mild doses, be important for self-development and personal growth. Culture shock is seen as a transitional experience with can result in the adoption of new values, attitudes and behaviour patterns:

> In the encounter with another culture, the individual gains new experiential knowledge by coming to understand the roots or his or her own ethnocentrism and by gaining new perspectives and outlooks on the nature of culture . . . Paradoxically, the more one is capable of experiencing new and difficult dimensions of human diversity, the more one learns of oneself. (Adler, 1975: 22)

Thus, although different writers have put emphases on different aspects of culture shock there is, by and large, agreement that exposure to new cultures is stressful. Fewer researchers have seen the positive side of culture shock either for those individuals who revel in exciting and different environments or for those whose initial discomfort leads to personal growth.

The shape of curves
Since Oberg (1960), it has been fashionable to describe the 'disease' of culture shock in terms of a number of stages. Oberg listed four stages of shock:

1. *Honeymoon stage* An initial reaction of enchantment, fascination, enthusiasm, admiration and cordial, friendly, superficial relationships with hosts.
2. *Crisis* Initial differences in language, concepts, values, familiar signs and symbols lead to feelings of inadequacy, frustration, anxiety.
3. *Recovery* The crisis is resolved by a number of methods such that the person ends up learning the language and culture of the host country.
4. *Adjustment* The sojourner begins to work in and enjoy the new culture, although there may be occasional instances of anxiety and strain.

Others have proposed five stages in the development of culture shock, while some have proposed a nine-stage sequence, and some a three-stage sequence. But there are numerous problems with these simple descriptive studies:

Is the order of stages invariant? Must all strangers be passed through or can some be skipped by some individuals? In order to classify individuals, key indicators of each stage are needed, indicators that many vary with the culture of origin or be indicative of more than one stage, reflecting superficial adjustment in an early stage but a true 'coming to terms' with the new culture in a later stage. (Church, 1982: 542)

One of the more interesting consequences of these stagewise theories is the debate on the U-curve or V-curve (See Figure 1). The idea of the U-curve has been attributed to Lysgaard (1955). He concluded from his study of more than 200 Norwegian Fulbright scholars in the United States that people go through three phases: initial adjustment, crisis and regained adjustment. Nowhere in the paper does Lysgaard describe the shape of the U, though he does imply that the period of adjustment took about twenty months with some point after between six and 18 months being the bottom of the U. The idea is quite simple: if one traces the sojourners' level of adjustment, adaptation and well-being, they gradually decline but then increase again. The W-curve is an extension, which found that once sojourners return to their home country they often undergo a similar re-acculturation process, again in the shape of a U, hence the double U that is W. This partly explains why six months after returning 'home', culture travellers become dissatisfied, say that home has changed and that they want to go back to the 'foreign' country they left.

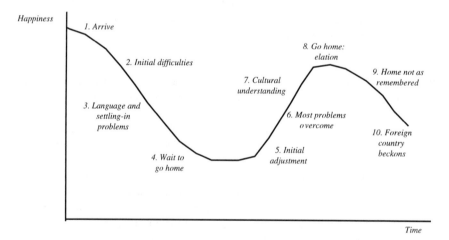

Figure 1: The U- and W-curve hypothesis

It is partly the appealing nature of the thesis, but also the vagueness in the initial description, that has led so many researchers to study this particular topic.

But support for the U-curve is weak, inconclusive and overgeneralized. For instance, not all sojourners start off in the phase of supposed adjustment, elation and optimism — some are unhappy, depressed and anxious right from (if not before) the beginning. Second, some never become depressed or anxious, enjoying the experience and adjusting to the culture right from the start. Third, where there are U-curves, they are of dramatically different shape— some are flat, others tall, and all are fairly irregular.

Some sojourners never learn the new culture or develop reciprocal role relationships with their hosts. Other sojourners do acquire the social skills of the new society and develop genuine contacts with their hosts. The rate of culture learning is not uniform across sojourners, but depends on a range of contact variables. This may explain why the U-curve is not supported in some studies, since some individuals may not experience it, such as sophisticated travellers who immediately become full participants, and hence never exhibit curve drop. Likewise, there are some very poor culture learners who fail ever to participate in their new society, and whose curve of satisfaction would therefore never rise.

Business sojourners
According to the Swedish researcher Torbiorn (1982), companies have three basic motives in posting people to foreign countries: the *control* function — to ensure that operations in other countries are being carried out as planned and to secure staff loyalty; the *know-how* function — to provide technological and administrative services; and the *contract/coordination* function — to evaluate and transmit salient information between company operations. For Torbiorn, overseas businesspeople are required both to act in accordance with the expectations of the parent company and also to fulfil local expectations, the two often being incompatible. Problems with these professional roles include: unclear, ambiguous or even incompatible expectations on the part of the parent company; communication difficulties; a clash between company and personal interests and values; uncertainty about the future; and problems with the adjustment of their spouse and family.

In a large study, Torbiorn set out to establish the determinants of business expatriate satisfaction. In doing so, he questioned more 1000 Swedish businessmen and businesswomen in 26 host countries. He looked at their personal circumstances (age, education, status); motives for moving abroad; who initiated the move; previous overseas experience; the name of the country they came from and the country they moved to; their chosen lifestyle; and spouse satisfaction. Among his findings were that men adapt better than women, and better-educated better than less-well-educated people; that the motive for moving most strongly associated with adjustment was 'special interests in the particular host country'; that previous overseas experience had no effect on adjustment;

that expatriates who spent most of their free time with host-country nationals were happier on average than those who turned to their own countrypeople; and that the satisfaction of the spouse was a major factor in determining adjustment.

Despite all this information, Torbiorn admits being unable to explain business expatriates' satisfaction and adjustment totally. Happiness of spouse was by far the most important factor, followed by various features of the external environment such as food and climate. Women tended to feel more isolated than men, which in turn greatly affected the man's satisfaction. A number of cultural barriers — religion, language and socioeconomic development — were good predictors of the business people's happiness, adjustment and lifestyle, and hence showed enormous variance between countries; the more the barriers, the less the satisfaction.

Studies such as Torbiorn's have important implications for the selection, training and management of businessmen and businesswomen and their families as they move from country to country (de Verthelyi, 1995). For instance, their study suggests the desirability of selecting people with interpersonal skills and high scores on assertiveness. Similarly, flexible, multidimensional and fairly extensive training programmes can help to ensure not only adaptation but efficiency in the job.

Culture shock and economic psychology

The research on culture shock overlaps with various other topics in economic psychology. For instance, the study of the psychology of unemployment (Furnham, Lewis and Webley, 1995) is concerned with adaptation to change and the psychology of loss. There are also various U-curve descriptions in that literature. Further, the culture shock literature is also highly germane in circumstances of rapid economic transition such as that currently found in Eastern Europe. Here, the environment changes around people who do not themselves move, giving a powerful sense of culture shock. Indeed, whenever people have to adapt to change — be it through organizational restructuring or downsizing, through relocation, through becoming voluntarily unemployed or retiring, or through living in politically or economically turbulent times — they often experience the classic symptoms of culture shock so graphically described in the specialist literature in the field.

ADRIAN FURNHAM

Bibliography

Adler, P. (1975) 'The Transitional Experience: An Alternative View of Culture Shock',. *Journal of Humanistic Psychology*, **15**: 13–23.
Bock, P. (ed.) (1970) *Culture Shock: A Reader in Modern Anthropology*, New York, Knopf.

Church, A. (1982) 'Sojourner Adjustment', *Psychological Bulletin*, **91**: 540–72.

Cleveland, H., Mangone, G. and Adams, J. (1960) *The Overseas Americans*, New York,: McGra- Hill.

de Verthelyi, R. (1995) International Students' Spouses: Invisible Sojourners in the Culture Shock Literature', *International Journal of Intercultural Relations*, **19**: 387–411.

Furnham, A. (1996) 'Culture Shock, Homesickness and Adaptation to a Foreign Culture', in van Tilburg, M. and Vugerhoets, A. (eds) *Acculturalism, Stress and Homesickness*, Tilburg, University of Tilburg Press.

Furnham, A. and Bochner, S. (1986) *Culture Shock*, London, Methuen.

Furnham, A., Lewis, A. and Webley, P. (1995) *The New Economic Mind*, Hemel Hempstead, Harvester-Wheatsheaf.

Lysgaard, S. (1955) 'Adjustment in a Foreign Society', *International Social Science Bulletin*, **7**: 45–51.

Oberg, K. (1960) 'Culture Shock: Adjustment to New Cultural Environments', *Practical Anthropology*, **7**: 171–82.

Ptak, C., Cooper, J. and Brislin, R. (1995) 'Cross Cultural Training Programs: Advice and Insights from Experienced Trainers', *International Journal of Intercultural Relations*, **19**: 425–33.

Torbiorn, I. (1982) *Living Abroad: Personal Adjustment and Personnel Policy on Overseas Settings*, Chichester, Wiley.

Discrete Choice Models

> One of the most important developments in econometrics in the past ten years has occurred in the area of qualitative response (QR) or discrete models .... I believe that QR models are so important in economics that every applied researcher should acquire at least a cursory knowledge. (Amemiya, 1981: 1483–4)

Qualitative response models, also known as categorical, quantal or discrete models, are statistical models in which the endogenous variables take only discrete values. Examples include female labour force participation, occupation choice, consumer brand choice, customer satisfaction, bank loan approval, audit concern, commuter mode choice, tourist destination choice, household residential and location choice, and any dependent variable recorded on a Likert scale (Amemiya, 1981; Maddala, 1983; Ben-Akiva and Lerman, 1985; Greene, 1993). One can see that many problems dealt with by economic and business researchers are either inherently discrete or recorded in a discrete manner. Although simple QR models have been used extensively in biometrics for a much longer time, the more complex discrete models, used in economics and business, have been developed only during the last two decades (Amemiya, 1981), a trend that parallels the development of advanced computer technology.

Besides the advances in computing techniques and equipment that facilitated their estimation, several other factors also contributed significantly to the upsurge in the application of discrete models in economics. Most economically relevant behaviour is necessarily at the level of the individual decision-making unit. Therefore, data at the individual, household or firm level are increasingly being collected through surveys or automated technologies such as scanners. Many of these data, such as the J.D. Powers Survey of Car Buyers and the Information Resources, Inc. (IRI) scanner panel data, are now readily available to researchers in portable electronic storage devices. Since aggregation of these data prior to estimation will result in the loss of precision of the estimated parameters if the aggregated groups are not homogeneous with respect to the independent variables, there has been a shift towards the analysis of data in their disaggregated form, particularly in discrete choice methods (Train, 1986). With individual-level data, more precise estimates of behavioural parameters can be obtained because of the higher variation in each factor and lower covariation among factors. When the underlying behaviour patterns of individuals are analysed, the outcomes are often not continuous and standard regression techniques are not appropriate. Discrete choice models, based upon the economic theory of consumer choice are hence increasingly being used for analysing these data.

Discrete choice models and economics

A major impetus behind the proliferation of discrete choice models in economics and marketing is the theoretical linkage made between the economic theory of consumer choice and discrete statistical models. Many important decisions made by economic agents involve choices among discrete alternatives, and economic analysis using the neoclassical or marginalist approach is quite cumbersome. Discrete choice models therefore rely more on the concept of random utility introduced first in mathematical psychology and formalized later in econometrics by Manski (1977) and McFadden (1974, 1981).

Consider a consumer n who faces a choice among a finite set of the J_n alternatives that is mutually exclusive and collectively exhaustive. The consumer will thus choose one and only one alternative from his or her choice set. Classical economic theory postulates that the consumer will choose an alternative i if it yields the highest utility among all alternatives. Although the consumer is assumed to make his or her choice consistently with a deterministic utility function, the analyst is unable to observe or accurately account for all influences that affect his or her choice. These discrepancies, which lead to deviations from expected outcomes, are captured in the random utility model (RUM) by introducing a random component ε_{in} into the consumer's indirect utility function, in addition to the systematic component V_{in} that is specified by the analyst. The researcher can thus assign a probability that the consumer will select any one of the J_n alternatives given the observable influences and assumptions about the distribution of the random component.

The probability that consumer n will choose an alternative i is equal to the probability that the utility derived (U_{in}) is greater than the utility (U_{jn}) associated with selecting any other alternatives in the choice set.

$$P_{in} = P(U_{in} \geq U_{jn})$$
$$P_{in} = P(V_{in} + \varepsilon_{in} \geq U_{jn} + \varepsilon_{jn})$$
$$P_{in} = P(V_{in} - V_{jn} \geq \varepsilon_{jn} - \varepsilon_{in}).$$

In this formulation, we have assumed that the utility of any alternative depends only on the characteristics of the alternative and the consumer but not of other alternatives. However, the attributes of other alternatives are important in determining choice because it is the differences between utilities that determine choice. Any factor that does not vary between alternatives will therefore not affect the consumer's choice. For example, although income is an important consideration in consumer purchase decisions, it does not vary across the alternatives. Hence it will have no impact on consumer choice, unless it is incorporated as a set of alternative specific constants or interacted with another variable, such as price, which does vary across choices.

In addition, adding a constant to or multiplying the utility by a constant will also not affect choice. This implies that the mean and scale parameter of the distribution can, in general, be set arbitrarily. For convenience, the mean is often set to zero, particularly when a constant term is included in the model, and the scale is chosen to be consistent with that of the indirect utility.

For simplicity, we begin by analysing a dichotomous choice situation in which the choice set of consumer n contains only two alternatives. For example, Ghazali, Ghosh and Tay (1995) estimated a model of the career choice of graduates in Singapore between self-employment (i) and salaried employment (j) with indirect utilities given by U_{in} and U_{jn}, respectively. As in most simple dichotomous choice models, we can reformulate the graduate's choice problem and define his or her choice y_n to equal one if he or she chooses to be self-employed and to equal zero if otherwise.

To operationalize the model, we need to specify the distribution for the random term and the most widely used distribution is the normal distribution which gives rise to the binary probit model. Another common model, the binary logit model, is obtained by assuming instead that the disturbances are Gumbel (Type I Extreme Value) distributed, or equivalently, by assuming that the differences in the random terms are logistically distributed. It is difficult to choose between the logit and probit model in practice because of the similarity between the normal and the logistic distributions, although the latter has slightly heavier tails. Amemiya (1981) suggested that, as a quick comparison, the logit estimates should approximately be equal to 1.6 times the estimates obtained in a corresponding probit model.

Because y_n is either equal to 1 or 0, the residuals can take only two values, which violates an important condition required to use standard regression. Therefore, like most discrete choice models, the binary logit and probit models are usually estimated using the maximum likelihood estimation (MLE) technique which yield estimates with the usual desirable properties.

When more than two alternatives are available to the consumer, we have to model the consumer's problem using a multinomial framework and the most common distributional assumption made is that the error terms are independent and identically distributed Extreme Value Type I which give rise to the multinomial logit (MNL) model. Tay and McCarthy (1991), for example, estimated an MNL model of household vehicle purchase using data from the US. The consumer in the sample is assumed to select from a set of 141 alternatives, the make-model that maximizes his or her utility. To estimate the model, we again let $y_{in} = 1$ if alternative i is chosen by consumer n and $y_{in} = 0$ if otherwise, and apply the maximum likelihood method.

A major constraint in estimating a multinomial model is that the size of the database increases very quickly with the number of alternatives available in the choice set. Unlike in standard regression, we need J_n lines of data for each observation in a discrete choice model because we need information on all alternatives available to the consumer and not just on the chosen alternative. If the number of alternatives is the same for all consumers then the number of records is equal to the number of observations times the number of alternatives for each consumer. In addition, if we need to include attributes, such as demographic variables, that do not vary across alternatives, we need to incorporate them as alternative specific constants. This will expand the number of independent variables by a factor of $(J - 1)$ for each of these attributes. Fortunately, consistent estimates can be obtained by using only a subset of the alternatives. Ben-Akiva and Lerman (1985) provide an excellent summary of the various methods and the correction factor required for sampling the alternatives.

As in most regression models, we have assumed that the disturbances are independent and identically distributed. The assumption of independence of the random terms will result in the MNL model having the independent from irrelevant alternatives (IIA) property which, in some cases, may create a problem. The IIA property holds that for an individual, the ratio of the choice probabilities of any two alternatives is entirely unaffected by the systematic utilities of any other alternatives. Ben-Akiva and Lerman (1985) show that this constraint will lead to the overprediction of the probabilities of alternatives that are closely related. The core of the problem lies in the assumption that disturbances, which capture the unobserved influences, are mutually independent and any model based on this assumption will produce counterintuitive results.

A common misinterpretation of the IIA property is that it holds for the entire population. The IIA property applies only to an individual and not to the population as a whole. Therefore, the ratio of the shares of the population choosing any two alternatives can be affected by other alternatives. As a practical consequence, MNL models that reasonably account for population heterogeneities, by including many socioeconomic characteristics, should perform better than those that do not (Ben-Akiva and Lerman, 1985).

When the IIA property is a serious restriction, we can assume instead that the disturbances have a multivariate normal distribution which will allow for the unobserved influences to be correlated. However, as in the binary probit models, the resulting polychotomous probit model does not have a closed-form solution. Instead it requires the solution of a $J - 1$ dimensional integral to evaluate the choice probabilities. The multinomial probit model is, for all practical purposes, computationally feasible only for a small number of alternatives, which seriously limits its application.

Another way to relax the IIA assumption is to group together into a nest alternatives that are closely related, and allow for their unobserved attributes to be correlated in some systematic way while maintaining independence across nests. For example, when modelling household vehicle purchase, McCarthy and Tay (1998) divide the choice set into three nests containing only low, medium or high fuel efficiency vehicles in each nest. Although the nested logit (NMNL) model is derived from the assumptions about how the unobserved attributes are the correlated, it is often interpreted as a sequential or hierarchical choice model.

One common problem that arises in developing a nested structure is that there are potentially many different ways in which the alternatives can be grouped or nested. The choice of nests often depends on the policy issues that the analyst is concerned with and some statistical or theoretical criteria. For example, McCarthy and Tay (1998) grouped vehicles by their fuel efficiency because they were interested in drawing implications about fuel efficiency and consumption. The actual fuel efficiency ratings used to divide the vehicles into their respective nests were chosen based on the Akaike information criterion, which is a statistic that provides information on the relative performance of various models in explaining the variations in the observed data. In addition, the coefficient of the inclusive value, which can be interpreted as the expected maximum utility associated with each group or nest, has to lie between 0 and 1 for the nested structure to be consistent with random utility maximization.

As mentioned previously, the NMNL model can be interpreted as a sequential decision structure and is often used to estimate choice models involving multiple decisions. For example, Tay (1990) estimated a recreational decision model in which the consumer selected the number of trips per year and the destinations of the trips conditional upon the number of trips. One common problem that arises with this type of model is that there can be several different, or no sequence of, decisions that are consistent with random utility maximization. For example, for a model involving three decisions, there may be anywhere between zero and six models that are consistent with random utility maximization. In addition, if the model is estimated sequentially, the estimation errors will cumulate with each decision, which severely limits the number of decisions that can be modelled.

One way to avoid these problems is to estimate a portfolio choice model. For example, Tay, McCarthy and Fletcher (1996) estimated a portfolio choice model of the demand for recreational trips in which the consumer is assumed to select the portfolio of trips that yields the highest utility. A portfolio is defined to consist of a particular combination of the number of trips of different durations to different destinations. The model can then be estimated using the multinomial logit framework. This approach, however, involves some fairly complex processes to construct an appropriate choice set for each consumer.

Most of the polychotomous choice models discussed above involve choices among alternatives that are unordered. When alternatives are ordered, the analyst

160

should use either the ordered logit or the ordered probit model. Tay (1998), for example, developed and estimated a model of entrepeneurial career choice in which consumers could select either salaried employment, self-employment (full or part-owner of an existing business) or starting a new business, depending on their level of entrepreneurship.

Interpretation of estimation results

As in most nonlinear models, there is no measure that serves the same function as the R^2 in standard regression which indicates how well the model fits the data collected. The most widely used indicator in discrete choice models is the likelihood ratio index which is the ratio of the log-likelihood of the estimated model and the corresponding value when no explanatory variable is used. It is clear that the index will be bounded between 0 and 1 but unlike the R^2, this measure has no natural interpretation for values between 0 and 1. Furthermore, the upper bound is less than one and is generally dependent on the model, making comparison between models difficult. It is most useful, nevertheless, for comparing two specifications of the same model using the same sample and choice alternatives but with different specifications of the indirect utility function.

The likelihood ratio test serves the same function in discrete choice models as the *F*-test in standard regression. The model is said to be useful or have substantial explanatory power if twice the difference between the log-likelihoods is found be significantly different from zero. The likelihood ratio test can also be used to test for any linear restriction imposed on the model by simply replacing likelihood without explanatory variables with the value of the log-likelihood for the restricted model. Finally, the significance of any explanatory variable can be examined using the standard *t*-test.

Table 1: Prediction table example

	$y_n = 0$	$y_n = 1$	Total
$\ddot{y}_n = 0$	145	5	150
$\ddot{y}_n = 1$	25	25	50
Total	170	30	200

Another measure often used to gauge the 'goodness-of-fit' of discrete choice models is the 'percent predicted correctly' which is the proportion of the sample observations having the same predicted choice as the actual choice. Ben-Akiva and Lerman (1985), however, recommend against its use because of its potential for misleading results and its insensitivity to the values of the predicted probabilities. The first problem can be overcome, when the choice set is small, by presenting instead a prediction table similar to the one shown in Table 1. Readers can easily infer that this model is clearly better than a naive model which predicts all observations to be equal to zero although both have the same 'percent predicted correctly' statistic of 85 per cent. This approach, however, cannot address the second concern because the table treats a correct prediction with a choice probability of 51 per cent the same as one predicted with a choice probability of 95 per cent.

A common mistake made by some researchers and readers who are not familiar with these models is in the interpretation of the estimated coefficients. Unlike standard regression, the coefficient estimates do not represent the marginal effects of the independent variables on the dependent variable. Instead, the coefficients represent the estimated marginal effects on the indirect utility of a unit increase in the explanatory variable. For example, if price is one of the attributes used in the choice of mode, then its coefficient can be interpreted as the marginal utility of income. This measure of the marginal utility of income is consistent with Roy's identity.

To compute the marginal effect on the choice probability of a change in any explanatory variable, one has to obtain the derivative of the choice probability with respect to the attribute. Unlike standard regression, the marginal effects of discrete choice models will depend on the values of independent variables, and as in most nonlinear models, it is usually computed using their mean or median values. It is clear that this computation assumes that the attribute of interest is continuous and differentiable. However, if the attribute is a dummy variable, then it is more informative to compute the change in probabilities when the indirect utility function includes and excludes the attribute.

Besides the marginal effects, another commonly reported measure for comparative static or sensitivity analysis is the choice elasticity. Although there is no ambiguity about the scale of the probability itself, some economists prefer choice elasticity because it is not dependent on the unit of measurement of the independent variables. This can easily be accomplished by multiplying the marginal effect by the ratio of the attribute to choice probability. In addition to the own-choice elasticity, the cross-choice elasticity of alternative i with respect to a change in attribute k of another alternative j is also frequently reported.

In business and economics, an analyst often has to impute a monetary measure for the cost or benefit of a policy change which is reflected by a change in one of the explanatory variables. In discrete choice models, this is accomplished using two common measures. Suppose the indirect utility is a function of the price and another attribute such as waiting time. Holding the indirect utility constant, the tradeoff between price and waiting time will give a measure of the consumers' willingness to pay (WTP) for a reduction in waiting time, and is given by the negative of the ratio of their respective coefficients.

To get a more theoretically consistent measure of the value of an attribute, one should estimate the compensating variation. The most widely used welfare measure is the one developed by Small and Rosen (1981). This measure is obtained by dividing the difference in the expected maximum utility due to the policy change by the marginal utility of income.

Concluding remarks

Despite their increasing importance and use in economics and business over the last two decades, many researchers and readers have yet to acquire a working knowledge of discrete choice models. This entry presents an introduction to these models by beginning with a simple formulation of the consumer choice problem under the random utility framework, and developing several of the widely used discrete choice models. In addition, the differences between these models and the standard regression technique are highlighted, and several common misunderstandings on the empirical issues peculiar to these models are discussed. It avoids, however, the more technical aspects that a reader would likely encounter in standard econometric theory. In particular, the various specification tests are deliberately omitted, even though they are important in many applied works. Readers are advised to familiarize themselves with these tests from the references provided.

RICHARD S. TAY

Bibliography

Amemiya, T. (1981) 'Qualitative Response Models: A Survey', *Journal of Economic Literature*, **19**: 1483–536.

Ben-Akiva, M. and Lerman, S. (1985) *Discrete Choice Analysis: Theory and Application to Travel Demand*, Cambridge, MA, MIT Press.

Ghazali, A., Ghosh, B. and Tay, R.S. (1995) 'The Determinants of Entrepreneurial Career Among University Graduates in Singapore', *International Journal of Management*, **12**: 26–35.

Greene, W. (1993) *Econometric Analysis*, New York, MacMillan.

Maddala, G.S. (1983) *Limited Dependent and Qualitative Response Models*, Cambridge, Cambridge University Press.

Manski, C. (1977) 'The Structure of Random Utility Models', *Theory and Decision*, **8**: 229–54.

McCarthy, P. and Tay, R.S. (1998) 'New Vehicle Consumption and Fuel Efficiency: A Nested Logit Approach', *Transportation Research: Logistics and Transportation Review*, **34**: 39–51.

McFadden, D. (1974) 'Conditional Logit Analysis of Qualitative Choice Behavior', in Zarembka, P. (ed.) *Frontiers in Econometrics*, New York, Academic Press: 105–42.

McFadden, D. (1981) 'Econometric Models of Probabilistic Choice', in Manski, C. and McFadden, D. (eds) *Structural Analysis of Discrete Data*, Cambridge, MA, MIT Press: 198–272.

Small, K. and Rosen, H. (1981) 'Applied Welfare Economics with Discrete Choice Models', *Econometrica*, **49**: 105–30.

Tay, R.S. (1990) 'Modelling Recreational Demand Using Discrete Choice Frameworks', Doctoral Dessertation, Department of Economics, Purdue University.

Tay, R.S. (1998) 'Degree of Entrepreneurship: An Ordinal Probit Model of Career Choice', *Journal of Small Business and Entrepreneurship*, **15**: 83–99.

Tay, R.S. and McCarthy, P. (1991) 'Demand Oreinted Policy for Improving Market Share in the US Automobile Market', *International Journal of Transport Eonomics*, **18**: 151–66.

Tay, R., McCarthy, P. and Fletcher, J. (1996) 'Portfolio Choice Model of the Demand for Recreational Trips', *Transportation Research: Methodology*, **30**B(5): 325–37.

Train, K. (1986) *Qualitative Choice Models*, Cambridge, MA, MIT Press.

Dual Self

The nature of the dual self

The concept emanates from humanistic psychology, particularly from Abraham Maslow's later writings. He pointed to the fact that humans have a *twofold* (lower and higher) nature: they are characterized by both creatureliness and god-likeness, with a gap between what they are (actuality) and what they would like to be (potentiality). He also stressed the difference between ego-centered *deficiency motivation* and personal *growth motivation* based on *ego-transcendence* (1968: 11–12, Ch. 3). In a sense, Maslow echoed the philosophical idea expressed already in the fifteenth century by Giovanni Pico della Mirandola who depicted Man as a creature neither of heaven nor of earth, but endowed with a capacity to *freely* shape his own being by either descending to the lower, brutish forms of life or ascending to the superior orders of life (1956: 7–8, emphasis added). Since Pico, this view of human duality has been rearticulated in the philosophical anthropology of Immanuel Kant and his followers. It is implicitly embedded in both Western and Eastern culture, most clearly, perhaps, in Hindu spirituality. In all these views of the person there is a recognition of some level of reality that *transcends* the individual and the social and which is potentially accessible to every human being. This also bears a correspondence to Erich Fromm's (1976) distinction of the perennial human tension of being and having.

The dual self can be taken as self-evident, in the same way that Lionel Robbins saw the postulate of an individual's preference order: 'It is so much the stuff of everyday experience that [it has] only to be stated to be recognized as obvious' (1984: 79). The dual-self perspective faults Robbins not for what he said but for what he left out.

To appreciate this, we need only look at the following everyday statements of aspiration of an individual who likes to watch TV all the time, but at the same time hopes that he or she will not become addicted to watching television. When I say, 'I want to watch TV', there is the *I* and the watching of TV, and they are referred to as subject and object. However, when I say something like, 'I wish I could give up TV watching', we note that there are two *I*s here, which are contained in the phrase 'I wish I* could give up TV watching'. The I*, the subject of the first statement, becomes the object for I in the second statement — thus the *dual* self.

The idea of aspiration, again the stuff of everyday experience, is the key to seeing both the pervasiveness and the relevance of the conception of the self as not single but dual. To aspire means to seek an ideal, whether of overcoming garden variety addictions like watching too much TV, or to be a better person in some complete sense.

To recognize this phenomenon is also to affirm real choice which must mean free will, and this was stated above when we paraphrased Pico about the nature of the human being. Thus the conception of the dual self lifts economics, or a social science that adopts it, out of the realm of deterministic or mechanistic science. Utility maximization economics can be seen as an instance *par excellence* of a conception of human beings and of science rooted in nineteenth-century materialism. In that conception, rationality is instrumental or single-end determined, and this end is 'given'. According to the conventional canons of such rationality, there is one 'overarching' utility function by which all wants or preferences are made commensurable. This is generally referred to as self-interest. The single end of self-interest, by making all preferences, or means, commensurable, reduces choice to an algorithmic process. This involves the assigning of a preference ranking or weights to the array of preferences, so that the calculation is seen as what determines the behavioural outcome. There is simply no room for free will.

The notion of a dual self, on the other hand, is the human condition, and it comes about precisely because the self is dual. In the words of Isaiah Berlin: 'To assume that all values can be graded on a scale, so that it is a mere matter of inspection to determine the highest, seems to me to falsify our knowledge that men are free agents, to represent moral decisions as an operation which a slide rule, in principle, could perform' (1969: 171).

The duality of the self consists in what can be called a higher and a lower nature, or higher or lower self. The higher self, being the self that is aspired to, concerns innermost values or personal principles such as truth, fairness, integrity, honesty, love and so forth. The lower self, taken by itself, is much closer to the self of standard economics and involves urges, inclinations, pleasure, self-aggrandizement, vanity and other expressions of self-interest. Such distinction is mirrored in the differentiation between first-order preferences (actual preferences) and second-order preferences (preferences about preferences) (Frankfurt, 1971). Amartya Sen (1987) developed a somewhat similar structuring of preferences and introduced the idea of a *meta-preference ordering*. Either way, we have a logic of two kinds of preferences, where one set is lower, and the other is higher or deeper.

Another issue must be resolved if the concept of the dual self is to be properly understood and not obscured in a merely linguistic confusion. The word self can be and is used in ordinary language to refer to what from a dual-self conception is one of three possible things: the lower self, the higher self, or the place of interaction between the two. Probably the latter meaning is the most common use of ego or self (for example, self-determination), with its use as more or less equivalent to the lower self (e.g., self-renunciation) next most common, with the least commonly being identified with the higher self, (for example, self-fulfilment defined as 'fulfillment of one's aspirations') (*Webster's Dictionary*: 1322).

From the dual-self perspective, when self or ego is used singly, it is being equated to the place of interaction or intersection of the higher and lower self. As already mentioned, this is the realm of freedom. In other words, human free choice does not lie either in the lower self or in the higher self alone. The former situation represents the 'animal nature' of the human being, left over from the evolutionary journey consisting of sensory impulses and passions. Taken by itself, it is pure urge and inclination. The higher self alone is the realm of truth and thus pure freedom. In this transcendental state of perfection, choice no longer has a meaning. This is traditionally referred to as finding freedom in the truth, (that is, 'the truth will make you free'). Therefore, it is only when both exist as a choice before the human being that we have the required conditions for human free will or free choice.

The dual-self notion of the person has sharply contrasting features to other models in standard economics that are seeking to represent self-control in formal terms. In an often cited model, Thaler and Shefrin (1981), for example, propose a '*two-self economic man*' that features the individual as an organization with a far-sighted *planner self* trying to maximize lifetime utility and an (infinite number of) *doer selves* eager to maximize utility and consumption, one doer self for each moment. It is a model of intertemporal conflict of preferences, not of a conflict between self-interested and moral behaviour at any point in time. Nowhere is there any departure from the standard assumptions of instrumental rationality and self-interest.

166

Manifestation and relevance of the dual self

The claim of a dual interest or a dual self is most clearly recognized in the legal concept of *conflict of interest*: 'a term used to describe the situation in which a public or fiduciary of the public, contrary to the obligation and absolute duty to act for the benefit of the public or a designated individual, exploits the relationship for personal benefit, typically pecuniary' (*Guide to American Law*, 1983: 143). This doctrine clearly implies an image of the person that is twofold, something which is denied by the mono self–self perspective where there is only *one* interest to be maximized in action, and the whole 'choice' reduces to an algorithmic calculation of the best means. In economics, this problem finds some recognition with the conundrum of the 'agency problem'. More generally, we encounter the conflict of interests in many other spheres imbued with public interest, in journalism, in politics, even in the making of science (Wible, 1991). Finally, there is the well-known phenomenon that most people, when given a chance, prefer to cooperate rather than to 'free ride', to honour 'implicit contracts' even where noncompliance is virtually impossible to monitor. In the process we often are faced with what Sen has called 'counter-preferential choice' behaviour, as also manifested in consumer boycotts, or the refusal to cross union picket lines (Sen, 1982: 54–60; Sen, 1977).

The dual-self conception is important to economic thinking on two basic levels: a reconsideration of the notion of economic rationality, as well as a better understanding of human motivation and socioeconomic institutions.

The dual-self image of the person reveals the limitations of economic, or *instrumental* rationality. According to the conventional canons of such rationality, reason operates only to evaluate different *means* to best satisfy a *single* and 'given' end. As soon as we, in accordance with the dual self, allow for two ends of action, the economist's algorithmic choice breaks down. Agents now have to rank their preferences nonalgorithmically by appeal to their intuitions. As a result, the preference ordering will typically lack completeness and determinateness. With plural goals, there may be no compelling reason to follow either, or there may be compelling but conflicting reasons for each of the goals. In one case we have 'incompleteness', in the other 'overcompleteness' or 'indeterminacy' (Sen, 1987: 65–8; Seung and Bonevac, 1992). Similarly, two incommensurable and conflicting ends cannot be resolved through a calculus employing an 'overarching utility' function. That again would presume a single overarching or ultimate end, a criterion of self-interest by which utility and morality are made commensurable (Hamlin, 1986: 40).

In place of instrumental rationality, the dual-self conception demands also a rationality of ends, Sen's *reflection rationality* (1987: 13–14), Elizabeth Anderson's *expressive rationality* (1993: Chs 2-4), or Alan Hamlin's *extended rationality*: 'The fundamental points in any version of extended rationality are that own utility is not the sole motivator of individual action, and that there exists an internal tension between self-interest and other rational goals' (1986: 22). It allows us to recognize real altruism and the motivations inherent in moral commitment and obligation. Extending rationality beyond self-interest also will provide for a potential escape from the prisoner's dilemma, offer a solution to the free-rider problem, and provide for a more satisfactory model of choice under uncertainty (1986: 35–52). Furthermore, it recommends a richer picture of work which would also include intrinsic work motivation and the importance of the workplace culture.

More generally, going beyond the 'all-is-self-interest' dogma of modern economics allows us to make sense of the interpersonal phenomenon of *trust* which can be defined as 'a firm belief in the honesty, reliability of another' (*Webster's Dictionary*). Self-interest here will not do. We do not 'trust' that somebody will indeed follow his or her own advantage or behave opportunistically. Quite to the contrary, we have trust in the possibility of the other identifying with his or her higher self, and *not* with his or her self-interest. Moreover, the fact that trust is both an important resource in an economy, and an indicator of quality of life of some consequence, suggests the significance of having this word in the economic vocabulary.

The dual-self conception will also radically change the nature of welfare economics. It will put more emphasis on qualitatively desirable preferences rather than on maximum preference satisfaction. Similarly, we can no longer suppress the social costs of enticing people to indulge in preference satisfactions that are not sanctioned by their higher ('deeper' and more rational) self. Internalization of such human cost would, for example, entail the taxing of suggestive advertising.

The dual self can also shed light on the related phenomena of *addiction* and *consumerism*. Both refer to compulsive behaviour in which the will has surrendered to the lower self. Such behaviour is seen from the dual self perspective as the essence of irrational behaviour, since it defeats the goal of ego-transcendence. This gives a deeper meaning to the concept of self-destructive behaviour, since that now can be understood as destructive to the higher self.

Last, but not least, there are social structures and institutions that can serve as catalysts (not incentives!) to promote growth in personal values and the likelihood of higher self-identification. In this respect, a dual-self-based *humanistic perspective* attempts to enumerate a number of such catalysts (for example, economic security, perceptions of fairness, fulfilling work) that can be expected to encourage more altruistic and moral behaviour in economic conduct (Lutz and Lux, 1988: 121–5; Lutz, 1998: Ch. 7). Conversely, excessive competitive pressures are seen to invite unrestrained maximization of a selfish character thereby exerting a corrupting force that would tend to inhibit personality growth.

KENNETH LUX AND MARK A. LUTZ

Bibliography

Anderson, E. (1993) *Value in Ethics and Economics*, Cambridge, MA, Harvard University Press.

Berlin, I. (1969) *Four Essays on Liberty*, Oxford, Oxford University Press.

Frankfurt, H.G. (1971) 'Freedom of the Will and the Concept of the Person', *Journal of Philosophy*, **68**: 5–20.

Fromm, E. (1976) *To Have or To Be*, New York, NY, Harper & Row.

Guide to American Law (1983) New York, West Publishing Company.

Hamlin, A.P. (1986) *Ethics, Economics and the State*, New York, St. Martin's Press.

Lutz, M.A. (1998) *Economics for the Common Good,* London, Routledge.

Lutz, M.A. and Lux, K. (1988) *Humanistic Economics*, New York, Bootstrap Press.

Maslow, A.H. (1968) *Towards a Psychology of Being* (2nd edn), New York, NY, Van Nostrand Reinhold Co.

Pico della Mirandola, G. (1956) *Oration on the Dignity of Man*, Chicago, IL, Henry Regnery Co.

Robbins, L. (1984) *An Essay on the Nature and Significance of Economic Science* (3rd edn), London, Macmillan.

Sen, A. (1977) 'Rational Fools: A Critique of the Behavioral Foundations of Economic Theory', *Philosophy and Public Affairs*, **6**: 317–44.

Sen, A. (1982) *Choice Welfare and Measurement*, Oxford, Basil Blackwell.

Sen, A. (1987) *On Ethics and Economics*, New York, Basil Blackwell.

Seung, T.K. and Bonevac, D. (1992) 'Plural Values and Indeterminate Rankings', *Ethics*, **102**: 799–813.

Thaler, R.H. and Shefrin, H.M. (1981) 'An Economy of Self-Control', *Journal of Political Economy*, **89**: 392–406.

Wible, J. (1991) 'Maximization, Replication and Economic Rationality of Positive Economic Science', *Review of Political Economy*, **3**: 164–86.

Ecology and Consumption

For more than three decades, ecological degradation and its consequences for human quality of life have furthered a growing public and scientific concern. As a result, they have received much of the attention of citizens, politicians, scientists and marketers discussing the need for global changes to ensure ecological sustainability. What is commonly called the environmental crisis is in fact mainly a crisis of the modern consumption society, or, put slightly differently, *Homo oeconomicus* has become the greatest danger to the survival of *Homo sapiens*. In particular, the consumption patterns of Western societies pose a significant threat to the natural environment as products and services are often created in response to expected consumer demand for convenience, greater availability and low prices (Durning, 1992). Such production and demand have fostered product proliferation, excessive packaging, pollution of the environment, and overexploitation of natural resources. It is estimated that 30 to 40 per cent of the strain on the natural environment is directly related to the consumption patterns of private households. However, as less affluent societies strive for increasing economic growth, they too become more susceptible to environmental degradation.

It seems evident, therefore, that a major factor in tackling the ecological/consumption crisis consists of promoting the ideas of qualitative consumption and sustainable development (the latter term was coined by the *Brundtland Report* in 1987). This entails informing relevant publics about corresponding behavioural patterns with the objective of changing existing production and consumption patterns into more environmentally responsible ones. Thus it seems necessary to address all individuals and groups present in the marketplace, that is, producers, distributors, retailers and consumers. Many governmental and intergovernmental programmes, such as Agenda 21 of the Rio Conference in 1992, designate consumers as one important target group and outline various means to decrease the influence of consumption patterns on the natural environment.

The current state of public and scientific debate is the reaction to more than three decades of environmentalism which can be traced back to *Silent Spring*, Rachel Carson's (1962) book about the pesticide industry. The early 1970s witnessed a growing distrust of industry and technology, the Club of Rome's warnings against unlimited growth, and the oil crisis which demonstrated that belief in limitless nonrenewable energy resources was illusory. While more and more evidence of the survival-threatening consequences of human consumption patterns was accumulated in the seventies, the 1980s witnessed increasing disinterest on the institutional side and resignation on the citizens' side. This was partly due to renewed economic prosperity in the industrialized nations.

However, the increasing incidence of manmade catastrophes — linked to names such as Seveso, Bhopal, Chernobyl, Sandoz and Exxon Valdez — led to a reawakening in the late 1980s and early 1990s. The 1990s have thus far evidenced a growing environmental concern by citizen-consumers that is reflected in attempts by the business community to respond to the ecological challenge.

The focus of social scientists in the consumer behaviour and marketing research area has, to a great extent, paralleled the public debate in the last two decades. One stream of studies that aimed at profiling sociodemographic and psychological characteristics of the 'green' consumer has led to their being described as relatively young, with rather high income and social status. They are well educated, politically less conservative, socially less alienated, personally more autonomous, display internal locus of control, are self-confident, goal-orientated, and the like. Although the findings regarding demographic variables often turned out to be inconclusive, sometimes even contradictory, this marketing-orientated research claimed to have identified a 'green consumer' segment, thus leading to the development of 'green' products and services and inspiring the publication of several textbooks on environmental marketing management in the past few years.

Another stream of studies, focusing more on methodological aspects, has attempted to describe, define and operationalize concepts such as 'social consciousness' and 'environmental concern'. Numerous indicators of environmental concern were developed, often specifying concern as a general attitude following the tripartite attitude model with cognitive, affective and conative components. The environmentally concerned consumer was then defined as a person who knows that the production, distribution, use and disposal of products leads to external costs. He or she further evaluates such external costs negatively trying to minimize them in his or her own behaviour (Balderjahn, 1988). However, this 'ideal' — or idealistic? — person rarely exists. And behaviour can take on various forms, among others those of conspicuous 'green' consumption when owning a Body Shop bag, putting a Greenpeace sticker on the car's rear bumper, proclaiming World Wildlife Fund membership, or wearing T-shirts with nature-related slogans are suggestive of environmental responsibility.

Moreover, environmental concern was shown to be a rather weak predictor of (mostly self-reported) environmentally responsible behaviour, and gradually other concepts were added to the models. The concepts most commonly introduced were values, social and personal norms, personality traits, motivations and knowledge. In addition, the set also included concepts such as cost–benefit evaluations, financial incentives and peer influence (for an overview see, for example, Hines, Hungerford and Tomera, 1987; Ölander and Thøgersen, 1995).

The two general approaches briefly described above were often combined to study such areas as energy conservation, product information, recycling behaviour, and reactions to legislative/regulatory means. Their overall goal was to suggest strategies that would promote consumer-citizens' commitment to environmentally responsible behaviour. The emphasis shifted from acquisition of products to their use and then to disposal issues, although only rarely was a decrease in overall consumption as a possible approach considered. Based on the various findings, especially in the energy conservation area, three different strategies for promoting environmentally responsible behaviour were proposed: maintenance, curtailment and investment (Ritchie and McDougall, 1985). Maintenance refers to appliances being in good working order to avoid waste of resources, curtailment involves modifying present usage behaviour such as driving less, and investment relates to structural changes in household equipment by acquiring resource-efficient technology. Firms also began incorporating the same ideas in their own operations. The Body Shop, 3M and Dow Chemical are examples of firms that have attempted to develop more ecologically benign methods and technologies. Many firms have also begun to 'green' their processes and products both within and beyond legal mandates, for example by adopting certification standards such as ISO 14001 and EMAS (the Environmental Management and Eco-Audit System), or by signing voluntary declaration such as the declaration for sustainability of the International Chamber of Commerce (ICC).

The merits of all these attempts notwithstanding, two major issues remain unsolved to date. These are the weak, or virtually nonexistent, relationship between citizen-consumers' behaviour and their declared proenvironmental attitudes or environmental concern, and the failure to consider abstainable rather than sustainable consumption. These considerations are left mainly to the environmental literature and grassroots organizations.

In the past decade, two approaches for tackling these issues have evolved. The first approach is still based on the general assumption of an attitude–behaviour relationship and aims at deepening its understanding by including possible mediating, moderating, and co-determining variables that condition or shape the influence of attitudes on behaviour (Stern et al., 1995). This research focuses on refining the traditional approach to understanding what environmental concern is about and, therefore, emphasizes a micro-level perspective.

The other approach frames the problem from a macro-level perspective pointing out that environmental concern (read: attitudes) refers to a collectivist goal while daily consumption behaviour relates to individual need fulfilment and utility maximization. With the 'tragedy of the commons' (Hardin, 1968) as starting-point, the management of limited resources to protect the environment has been identified as a social dilemma that describes the difficult choice of whether to act in self-interest or in the public interest. In this scenario, the destruction of environmental amenities is virtually assured under the particular regimes of property rights that characterize many Western societies. In individualistic, market societies, public goods or environmental amenities will be underproduced and private goods destructive of the environment will be over-produced. This is the familiar 'public goods problem'. Cooperation is required to circumvent these problems, but four main barriers to this cooperation have been identified: the wish to maintain one's freedom, the desire to avoid being a sucker, self-interest and mistrust of others (Wiener and Doescher, 1991). Strategies to solve social dilemmas consist of either behavioural or structural solutions, where behavioural solutions refers to inducing individuals to cooperate for the sake of cooperation, and structural solutions attempt to change the characteristics of a given situation so that it no longer represents a social dilemma. Still, both strategies call for cooperation and do not necessarily remove any of the four barriers.

More recently, the conflict between individualistic and collectivist goals has been reinterpreted by suggesting that it is the overall cultural context which serves as a blueprint for individual motivations and beliefs, thus determining the degree to which concern can be transformed into action. Hence, it may be the failure to assess citizen-consumers' general frames of reference rather than deficiencies in attitude and behaviour measurement that is responsible for limited understanding of the contradiction between individuals' expressed beliefs and their behaviour in the environmental arena. This overall context — the culture we live in, that influences us, and that we shape in a constant interplay — is referred to as the dominant social paradigm (Kilbourne, McDonagh and Prothero, 1997). It is the context out of which individuals develop and continuously modify value systems that play a central role as antecedents, consequences and correlates of human action and experience. It is thus argued that neither a satisfactory explanation of seemingly contradictory behaviour nor successful policy strategies for a change towards sustainable development can be derived if the role of the various dimensions of the dominant social paradigm — beliefs about the interplay among politics, economy and technology — and their shaping of value systems are not understood.

Here we must also consider the level of environmental knowledge that consumers possess even when they are seriously concerned and desire to be environmentally responsible. Since ecological processes and human effects on them are extremely complex, it is unlikely that most consumers have a full understanding of their relationship to the environment. In examining US consumers for example, Kempton, Boster and Hartley (1995) demonstrate that many consumer beliefs about such relationships are erroneous. The brighter side of this result is that, while environmentally concerned consumers may misperceive the relationship, their behaviours frequently are supportive of the environment.

The mixture of inconclusive results from more than two decades of research into the relationship between consumption and ecology thus seems to be to a large extent the result of the failure to examine the underlying structure motivating environmental concern and the behavioural manifestations it engenders in both consumption and production. Most of the more traditional research approaches have focused on the later stages of a multistage process, often neglecting findings from disciplines outside of marketing and consumer behaviour. The different stages, from the more general to the more specific, to be examined are (i) institutional structures in society as overall cultural context, that is, the dominant social paradigm, (ii) value systems as motivations, (iii) general beliefs about the relationship between humans and nature, (iv) specific ecological beliefs and attitudes, (v) behavioural commitments, and (vi) behaviour (compare Beckmann and Kilbourne, 1997). Studies aiming at understanding the factors leading to environmentally (ir)responsible behaviour need to integrate all levels of the hierarchy. This might ultimately lead to a better understanding of the sequence through which institutional structures motivate and inform values leading to environmentally responsible behaviours. The implication of such an expanded approach to the study of the environment is that, for enduring behavioural change on the part of consumer-citizens to take place, changes in the institutional structures of a culture are necessary. Focusing only on the lower stages of the sequence and trying to change levels of concern, as has been the case in much consumer research, can leave individuals with contradictory signals regarding the environment and their impact on it. Without examining the environmentally related cultural institutions that mould value systems, individuals may well be asked to become frugal in a society that subtly demands profligacy.

SUZANNE C. BECKMANN

Bibliography

Balderjahn, I. (1988) 'Personality Variables and Environmental Attitudes as Predictors of Ecologically Responsible Consumption Patterns', *Journal of Business Research*, **17**: 51–6.

Beckmann, S.C. and Kilbourne, W.E. (1997) 'The Interplay Between the Dominant Social Paradigm and Value Systems: Influences on Danish Business Students' Environmental Concern', Working Paper no. 4 /CEC Working Paper no. 1 (July) Copenhagen, Copenhagen Business School, Department of Marketing.

Carson, R. (1962) *Silent Spring*, Boston, Houghton-Mifflin.

Durning, A. (1992) *How Much is Enough? The Consumer Society and the Future of the Earth*, New York, W.W. Norton.

Hardin, G. (1968) 'The Tragedy of the Commons', *Science*, **162**: 1243–8.

Hines, J.M., Hungerford, H.R. and Tomera, A.N. (1987) 'Analysis and Synthesis of Research on Responsible Environmental Behavior: A Meta-Analysis,' *Journal of Environmental Education*, **13**: 1–8.

Kempton, W., Boster, J.S. and Hartley, J.A. (1995) *Environmental Values in American Culture*, Cambridge, MA, MIT Press.

Kilbourne, W.E., McDonagh, P. and Prothero, A. (1997) 'Can Macromarketing Replace the Dominant Social Paradigm of Consumption? Sustainable Consumption and the Quality of Life,' *Journal of Macromarketing*, **17**: 4–24.

Ölander, F. and Thøgersen, J. (1995) 'Understanding of Consumer Behaviour as a Prerequisite for Environmental Protection', *Journal of Consumer Policy*, **18**: 345–85.

Ritchie, J.R.B. and McDougall, G.H.G. (1985) 'Designing and Marketing Consumer Energy Conservation Policies and Programs: Implications from a Decade of Research', *Journal of Public Policy and Marketing*, **4**: 14–32.

Stern, P.C., Dietz, T., Kalof, L. and Guagnano, G.A. (1995) 'Values, Beliefs, and Proenvironmental Action: Attitude Formation Toward Emergent Attitude Objects', *Journal of Applied Social Psychology*, **25**: 1611–36.

Wiener, J.L. and Doescher, T.A. (1991) 'A Framework for Promoting Cooperation', *Journal of Marketing*, **55**: 38–47.

World Council on Environment and Development (1987) *Our Common Future. The Brundtland Report*, New York, Oxford University Press.

Economic Socialization

Economic socialization is a specific concept referring to the whole process by which a child will develop an understanding of the economic world. It is related to 'naive economics', the economics of nonspecialists. Even though children, as well as many adults, are 'naive subjects', they are familiar with parts of the economic world and possess some knowledge and understanding of how it works. Economic socialization concerns the acquisition of the knowledge, skills, behaviour, opinions, attitudes and representations, which are relevant to the economic world. The concept refers to the maturing child who is learning how to apprehend the world of adults. Furthermore it refers to the adult who is changing roles and evolving through life with various economic events — such as getting his or her first job, being unemployed or retiring — since these changes will have an effect on his or her ways of thinking about economy. In the past ten years, there has been an array of research concerning the influence, decision power and buying power of children. In order to understand economic socialization, different authors use a variety of methods and techniques which will be described later in this entry.

Different theoretical orientations

Economic socialization is, as Zigler and Child wrote in 1968, 'a broad term for the whole process by which an individual develops, through transactions with other people, specific patterns of socially relevant behaviour and experience'. Although the literature proposes various definitions, their main conceptual contents are the same: socialization refers to the problem of general education in any society, implying a process of interaction between the subjects and their environment. In fact, two main theories dominate the field: the Piagetian developmental–cognitive approach and the environmentalistic learning theory. Jean Piaget proposed a transactional process which links children's cognitive stages to their experience of the world, emphasizing the primacy of children's actions in their development and maturation, while learning theory (behaviourism) stresses the effects of the environment on children's behaviour. According to this theory, a functional behaviour will be imitated because it appeared previously to be rewarding. As Youniss (1978) indicates, there is nothing really incompatible between these two models. The cognitive model is applied to the development of thinking processes while learning theory explains behaviour. Piaget's approach deals with the framework, and the behaviourists supply the information regarding the content of socialization. The first model stresses intraindividual differences as the child grows up, while the second describes interindividual variations at the same age. Both theories assume that contacts with social reality are necessary for the buildup of a predictable pattern of behaviour.

An example of the use of the Piagetian developmental–cognitive approach dealing with economic socialization is Berti and Bombi's research (1988); by testing children of ages corresponding to the stages defined by Piaget, they investigate the effects of the Piagetian developmental stages on economic socialization. This type of study speculates that adults have a fully developed knowledge and understanding of the economic world; it is therefore incompatible with theories suggesting that there is a constant evolution of economic socialization, evolving as the person is modified by different experiences and phases of life, such as, for example, unemployment or buying a new house.

Two fundamental theoretical orientations constitute the basis of research in the field of economic socialization: problematics are either centred on the understanding of the economic world of the grown-ups, or on the analysis of how children solve the economic problems of their own world. Depending on the orientation chosen by the authors, the methods and techniques used are often different. Webley and Lea (1991) argue that current research in economic socialization is unsatisfactory when it adopts an adult-centred view of the economic world; these authors believe that researchers should be more concerned with the real economic world of childhood and suggest several lines of investigation based on how children solve the economic problems they are faced with.

Methods and techniques

It is important to note the diverse research methods in the field and the great originality of the techniques used. We shall first give examples of different types of surveys, including studies using observations and/or projective tests, and then provide descriptions of laboratory studies with experimental tasks.

Surveys with interviews and questionnaires

Investigations with surveys are frequently carried out with different kinds of semi-structured interviews. This technique has been used in an international research project conducted in 14 different countries and dealing with major domains of the economic world (Leiser, Roland-Lévy and Sevòn, 1990). A great variety of questionnaires are used in the field of economic socialization. Vergès (1992) focused on social representations of the economic world; he used word association tests to investigate the spontaneous representation of an economic domain, for example money, others (for example, Roland-Lévy, 1991) have studied credit and debt in the same way. Subjects often have to classify items, to rank or to group phenomena or to match notions; this provides very rich information about how children and teenagers organize economic ideas. Burris (1981) investigated the child's understanding of buying and selling with a list of items which were presented to 4–5-, 7–8- and 10–12-year-old children. They were asked to classify the items, making one pile of 'those which can be sold or bought' and the other of 'all the others'. In another study the same author explored children's concepts of economic value by presenting to them a pair of objects and asking them to indicate 'Which of the two would cost more?' and to explain why. Other authors have used scales for measuring opinions and attitudes; Cumming and Taebel (1978) used scales to measure American children's opinions about private property, government, unions and so on. Researchers have studied the definitions of situations, concepts or phenomena. Important insight into children's understanding of unemployment was provided by Webley and Wrigley (1983) who asked children to define unemployment and to explain how unemployed people differ from others. In studying children's understanding of the economic world, most surveys use attractive visual material such as pictures, drawings, films or objects, giving the child the possibility of manipulating a complex phenomenon; this is especially appropriate for young children or for the investigation of abstract topics such as insurance or employment. Pictures of situations were used in a study, based on semi-structured interviews, concerning insurance and 'what could be insured' (Lassarre and Roland-Lévy, 1989). Other authors have used pictures of situations in order to obtain descriptions of an abstract notion such as unemployment. Despierre and Sorel (1979) showed pictures depicting various degrees of unemployment to 11–12- and 15–16-year-old children; the children were asked to describe the images, and their interpretations were collected through semi-structured interviews.

Interviews are also linked to observation. This can be participant observation as described in Willis (1977), or the observation of a child's behaviour in a particular environment. For example, Watiez (1987) observed children visiting small supermarkets, in order to study the behaviour of children in a store. The observations were based on 'behaviour episodes' as a combination of acts or speech; at the end of their shopping, children were interviewed about 'the different things that they found interesting in the supermarket'. It is interesting to note that gender differences appear in economic knowledge, and one possible explanation comes from these observations of behaviour: girls seem to be more 'at home' in stores than boys, and girls adopt behaviour which is very similar to that which adults tend to do when shopping. Another innovative study using observation should be mentioned, which was conducted in a school playground and involved observing children's games of marbles (Webley and Webley, 1990). In this study, Webley and Webley show that children, via a game, reproduce the same economic behaviour as adults; in the playground, children appear to have excellent economic thinking.

Occasionally a projective approach has been utilised. Pictures have been used in a projective test concerning economic situations as part of a longer interview by Lassarre (Lassarre and Roland-Lévy, 1989), who studied the short stories of four hundred 11–12-year-old children. The stories were evoked by four pictures: two of potential consumerism (in one case a woman is looking at a shop window and in another at a view of an open-air market) and two of employment with two possible professional situations. This projective approach allows children to demonstrate their ability to describe complex situations extracted from the economic world of adults

Laboratory studies with experimental tasks
The second major theoretical orientation — behaviourism — leads to the second method used in the field of economic socialization. Studies of how children solve the economic problems they are faced with tend to use experimental tasks. In an attempt to examine the real economic behaviour of childhood, experimenters have organized a variety of creative and ingenious laboratory studies. Experimentation, appearing frequently in terms of a play economy, is used to explore the understanding of concepts.

In 1991, Abramovitch, Freedman and Pliner organized a laboratory experiment with children aged 6, 8 and 10; this study dealt with differences in children's behaviour towards money, especially credit versus cash. The children received $4 either in cash or in the form of a credit card to spend in an experimental toy store; what they did not spend in the store could be taken home. The observers noted what they did, how much they spent, how they did it, what for, and so on. The results showed that the children who did not ordinarily receive pocket money spent more in credit than those who did get a regular allowance.

Webley, Levine and Lewis (1993) studied children in another play economy. Subjects received money (tokens) and were put in a setting which consisted of different rooms in which they could either save their money in a bank, or spend some (as little or as much as they wanted) on various activities. Some of the activities were free, while others were not. Over a period of time, the children had to find ways of spending as little money as possible and of saving some in order to buy a toy which they wanted.

These examples demonstrate how experiments may be constructed to study processes of children's economic socialization in an original way, especially when orientated to how children solve the kind of economic problem they are faced with in their everyday lives.

Conclusion

Furnham and Lunt's (1996) edited volume provides a general overview of research in the field of economic socialization. To conclude let us review of the main findings in the field of economic socialization. Many studies tend to present their results in terms of differentiating factors, such as those related to age, gender, social class or educational environments. Most studies founded in Piaget's theory remain descriptive and demonstrate that conformity and consistency increase as children get older (DeFleur and DeFleur, 1967). Studies of economic thinking have found no real differences between boys and girls, whereas gender differences appear when dealing with economic knowledge; this may be explained by the fact that girls take a larger part in activities related to consumption, such as shopping (Lassarre and Roland-Lévy, 1988).

Social class is the most frequently investigated factor in studies of economic knowledge. These studies reveal that upper-class children are more familiar with banking vocabulary and prestige of occupations, while those who come from the working class seem to understand more about industrial relations. Lautrey (1980) showed that parents' cognitive structures and educational styles directly influence the quantity, type and diversity of economic information, and that they determine informal socialization through discussions; this leads to differences in the family's consumption habits.

The last finding is related to cross-cultural studies. It appears clearly that children from different countries have more or less the same knowledge and understanding of economic phenomena at approximately the same age. Where there are differences, the social, economic and political situation of the countries should be taken into account. For example, French and Algerian children produce different answers to questions which clearly relate with their culture: in order to increase the amount of money they have, French children would 'invest the amount in a bank' whereas Algerian children, deeply influenced by the words of the Koran forbidding the practice of usury and interest, say that 'they should work more' (Roland-Lévy, 1990). Such findings illustrate the importance of collective representation in the construction of knowledge and practices related to the economy. The field of economic socialization is currently taking a new turn with more studies focusing on the influence of parent's lay conceptions of the economy, and on the links between social representations of economic phenomena and economic behaviour (Roland-Lévy, 1994; Walter, 1994).

CHRISTINE ROLAND-LÉVY

Bibliography

Abramovitch, R., Freedman, J.L. and Pliner, P. (1991) 'Children and Money: Getting an Allowance, Credit Versus Cash, and Knowledge of Pricing', *Journal of Economic Psychology*, **12**: 27–45.

Berti, A.E. and Bombi, A.S. (1988) *The Child's Construction of Economics*, Cambridge, Cambridge University Press.

Burris, V. (1981) 'The Child's Conception of Economic Relations: A Study of Cognitive Socialization', Paper presented at the Annual Meeting of the American Sociological Association, Toronto, and described in Lea, S.E.G., Webley, P. and Tarpy, R.M. (1987) *The Individual in the Economy*, Cambridge, Cambridge University Press.

Cumming, S. and Taebel, D. (1978) 'The Economic Socialization of Children: A Neo-Marxist Analysis', *Social Problems*, **26**: 198–210.

DeFleur, M.L. and DeFleur, L.B. (1967) 'The Relative Contribution of Television as a Learning Source for Children's Occupational Knowledge', *American Sociological Review*, **32**: 777–89.

Despierre, J. and Sorel, N. (1979) 'Approche de la Représentation du Chômage Chez les Jeunes' (Teenagers' Representation of Unemployment), *L'Orientation Scolaire et Professionnelle*, **8**: 347–64.

Furnham, A. and Lunt, P. (eds) (1996) *Economic Socialization*, Cheltenham, Edward Elgar.

Lassarre, D. and Roland-Lévy, C. (1989) 'Understanding Children's Economic Socialization', in Grunert, K.G. and Olander, F. (eds) *Understanding Economic Behavior*, Dordrecht, Kluwer: 347–68.

Lautrey, J. (1980) *Classe Sociale, Milieu Familial et Intelligence* (Social Class, Family, and Intelligence), Paris, PUF.

Leiser D., Roland-Lévy, C. and Sevòn, G. (eds) (1990) 'Economic Socialization', *Journal of Economic Psychology*, **11**: No. 4 (special issue).

Roland-Lévy, C. (1990) 'A Cross-National Comparison of Algerian and French

Children's Economic Socialization', *Journal of Economic Psychology*, **11**: 567–81.

Roland-Lévy, C. (1991) 'Les Jeunes et le Crédit à la Consommation' (Young People, Credit, and Consumption), *Connaître les Modes de Viee et de Consommation des Jeunes*, Paris, Colloque Européen: 393–408.

Roland-Lévy, C. (1994) 'Savings and Debts. The Impact of the Family Structure on the Processes of Money Management', in Antonides, G. and van Raaij, W.F. (eds) *Integrating Views on Economic Behavior* (Proceedings of the 1994 IAREP/SABE Conference), Rotterdam, The Netherlands.

Vergès, P. (1992) 'L'Évocation de l'Argent: Une Méthode pour la Définition du Noyau Central d'une Représentation' (Associations Around Money: A Method to Define the Central Nucleus of a Representation), *Bulletin de Psychologie*, **405**: 203–16.

Walter, C. (1994) 'Economic Man's Missing Teenage Years: Adolescents' View About Money, Credit and Debt', in Antonides, G. and van Raaij, W.F. (eds) *Integrating Views on Economic Behavior* (Proceedings of the 1994 IAREP/SABE Conference), Rotterdam, The Netherlands: 581–96.

Watiez, M. (1987) 'Comportements Économiques sur les Lieux de Vente: Observations et Questionnaires dans les Supermarchés' (Economic Behaviour in Shops; Observations and Questionnaires in Supermarkets), in Lassarre, D. et al. (eds) *Education du Jeune Consommateur. Les Sources d'Information Économiques des Enfants de 11-12 Ans*, Paris, University of Paris V: 57–88.

Webley, P. and Lea, S.E.G. (1991) 'Vers une Psychologie plus Réelle de la Socialisation Économique' (Towards a More Realist Psychology of Pconomic Socialisation), *Connaître les Modes de Vie et de Consommation des Jeunes*, Paris, Colloque Européen.

Webley, P., Levine, M. and Lewis, A. (1993) 'A Study in Economic Psychology: Children's Saving in a Play Economy', in Sonuga-Barke, E.J.S. and Webley, P. (eds) *Children's Saving: A Study in the Development of Economic Behaviour*, Hove, Erlbaum: 127–46.

Webley, P. and Webley, E. (1990) 'The Playground Economy', in Lea, S.E.G., Webley, P. and Young, B. (eds) *Applied Economic Psychology in the 1990s*, Exeter, Washington Singer Press: 1082–7.

Webley, P. and Wrigley, V. (1983) 'The Development of Conceptions of Unemployment among Adolescents', *Journal of Adolescence*, **6**: 317–28.

Willis, P. (1977) *Learning to Labour: How Working Class Kids Get Working CLass Jobs*, London, Saxon House.

Youniss, J. (1978) 'The Nature of Social Development: A Conceptual Discussion of Cognition', in McGurk, H. (ed.), *Issues in Childhood Social Development*, London, Methuen: 203–27.

Zigler, B. and Child, I. (1968) 'Socialization', in Lindzey, G. and Aronson, E. (eds) *Handbook of Social Psychology*, Vol. 3, Reading, MA, Addison-Wesley: 450–555.

Emotions and Consumer Behaviour

The last two decades have witnessed a growing interest in models of consumer behaviour that emphasize situational influences, such as emotions and feelings, in order to understand economic behaviours. These behaviours are often difficult, if not impossible, to explain with the neoclassical economic approach which suggests that people are 'reasonable' and try to maximize some utility function. This approach could also be observed in psychology, where the so-called 'cognitive turn' dominated for several decades, using an analogy of the individual as an information-processing mechanism. Emotions, feelings and affect were then regarded as being irrational, even dysfunctional. It became, however, more and more obvious that many consumer behaviours cannot be sufficiently explained within the information processing paradigm: gambling for high stakes, watching fear-arousing movies, collecting teddy bears, engaging in risky sports like skydiving, buying from impulse, or browsing leisurely through shopping malls. As Scitovsky (1986) has pointed out, when applying optimal arousal theory in an economic context, the tremendous increase in security and safety due to social, economic and technological progress seems to have triggered the need for finding sources of excitement in consumption-related areas.

Within economics, Scitovsky's pioneering work was complemented by Earl (1983) with the aid of personal construct psychology, whose perspective on emotions he integrated with an information-processing perspective to provide an alternative to neoclassical theory. Put simply, the idea was that certain kinds of situation can have an emotional dimension because the way they are seen has potentially damaging implications for the chooser's information-processing system. These implications might be mitigated by sticking to a particular course of action, avoiding particular opportunities and so on, often regardless of matters concerning relative price, unless marketers could diffuse the consumer's anxiety, guilt or hostility by providing a different perspective.

The work of Scitovsky and Earl on these themes had little impact on their fellow economists' ways of looking at the world, even though it has become increasingly common for financial journalists to discuss household financial behaviour with reference to not merely consumer confidence but also the idea of a sometimes euphoric 'feel-good' factor or caution associated with employment anxieties. However, consumer behaviour research outside of economics departments has reflected psychology's so-called 'rediscovery of affect' and increasingly acknowledged the influence of emotional states in evaluating such situations as service encounters, responding to point-of-purchase stimuli, high versus low involvement in products, attitudes towards advertising, extent of perceived risk, or processing of marketing communications. On the other hand, it is also recognized that any encounter with the world of goods can trigger various emotions during the consumption experience, either actively sought out by the consumer or involuntarily evoked by dis/satisfaction with products and services.

The term emotion will be used here as an umbrella term for feelings, moods and affect-based personality characteristics. Feelings are high in intensity, mainly of short duration and highly specific, while moods are less intense, last longer, and are of intermediate specificity. Affective personality characteristics refer to the pleasure, arousal, dominance (PAD) paradigm that assumes that individual temperament differences can be described by differences in preferred pleasure, arousal and dominance levels. They are low in intensity, long in duration, and low in specificity.

Functions of emotions

Emotions serve at least four functions in human behaviour. These functions are important for the understanding of the role of emotions as antecedents, correlates and consequences of consumer actions (compare Pieters and van Raaij, 1988):

1. interpretation and organization of information and knowledge about one's own somatic and psychic functioning as well as about one's physical and social environment;
2. mobilization and allocation of resources. Emotions change people's states of readiness for action through arousal or performance enhancement (for example, fear or anger), motivation (for example, pleasure), or interrupting an ongoing task;
3. sensation seeking and avoiding in order to pursue an optimum level of arousal between the extremes of boredom and stress, reflected in a need for stimulation;
4. interpersonal communication via facial expressions and body language revealing to and sharing one's feelings and preferences with others.

Interplay between emotions and cognition

The relationship between cognition and emotion — or logic and reason versus sensuality and irrationality — has been debated for centuries. While the behaviouristic paradigm of the 1950s focused on studying experiences and behaviour solely in their externally observable and measurable appearance, the cognitive 'revolution' of the 1960s called for recognizing the cognitive processes that individuals perform when dealing with their environment. This culminated in the view of the individual as an information processor who logically analyses and evaluates environmental stimuli leading to cost–benefit-based decisions about actions. The 'emotional turn' emphasized by Zajonc (1980) initiated the well-known Zajonc–Lazarus exchange over whether feelings needed thinking or

183

not. In Zajonc's stream of research, the relationship between cognitive and affective reactions was such that affect could occur before or in the absence of cognitive processing. The results are inconclusive on this count as empirical support from research findings is mixed in such contexts as advertising, packaging and brand names. Today it seems that many research efforts either ignore the paradigmatic stances preferring to concentrate on the research question at hand, or focus on the interactions with emotions and cognitions by developing integrative models (for example, Grunert, 1993).

Other researchers have concentrated mostly on the effects of emotions on various aspects of consumer behaviour arguing that the consumption experience embraces 'fantasies, feelings, and fun' (Holbrook and Hirschman, 1982). Gardner (1985) examined the mediating role of mood states and their implications for consumer behaviour in the areas of service encounters, point-of-purchase stimuli, and context and content of communications. This review of the psychological literature linked the findings to the potential feasibility and viability of mood-related approaches to marketing strategies.

Empirical evidence

Multiple studies have investigated the interaction of emotions with concepts such as impulse buying, self-gifts, gift-exchange processes, recreational shopping, self-regulatory (eating) behaviour, need for stimulation, perceived risk and satisfaction.

Using the PAD-paradigm, Rook and Gardner (1993) found that impulsive buying is most likely in the case of low arousal mood states such as boredom, low pleasure/high arousal mood states such as anxiety, and low to mid-range dominance mood states such as frustration. This indicates that impulsive shoppers are prone to act impulsively under many different circumstances or that they may have developed behavioural heuristics for coping with their moods that nonimpulsive shoppers have not. Here, the above-mentioned functions (1) and (3) of emotions seem to apply.

Somewhat related to impulse buying is the notion of self-gift behaviours. Mick and DeMoss (1990) suggest that self-gifts are a complex class of personal acquisition that are premeditated and context bound. They are a form of personally symbolic self-communication, and for women they are precipitated by personal situations such as significant life transitions, work situations and disrupted interpersonal relations (Mick, DeMoss and Faber, 1992). The factors in the retail setting that affect self-gift giving include novelty of the brand, price, and the salesperson's empathy for the buyer's personal situation. Functions (2) and (3) of emotions are here the most prominent.

Not only self-gifts, but also gift-exchange processes involve emotions: the types of events and situations that lead to the expression of certain emotions through gift-giving on the one hand, and the types of emotions that are experienced by givers and recipients under various conditions of gift exchange. It was found in various studies that both givers and recipients are quite specific about the type of emotions (to be) expressed at various gift giving occasions (Ruth, 1996). For instance, joy was associated with birthdays and weddings, pride with graduation and awards, hope with house-warming and retirement, gratitude with hostess/host gifts, and affection with anniversary, courtship, and funerals. These examples illustrate functions (1) and (4) of emotions.

Recreational shopping, that is, browsing in shopping malls or department stores as leisure activity, is another area of consumer behaviour in which emotions play an important role to ensure an enjoyable use of time in a sensually stimulating environment. Within a Finnish setting and based on the PAD-paradigm, it was found that the recreational shopping tendency is a manifestation of a more general exploratory tendency and that it is dependent on an individual's preferred emotional state, particularly on the preferred arousal level (Boedeker, 1997). In other words, recreational shopping is a consumer activity aimed at satisfying a need for stimulation, thus being a case in point for function (3) of emotions.

Engaging in consuming has also been described as a means to regulate one's emotions, both pleasant and unpleasant. Grunert (1993) presented a schema-theoretical model of the cognitive representation of emotions in which encounters with objects, persons or events evoke emotions that the individual strives to regulate. In the case of positive emotions, schemas containing procedural knowledge of how to maintain or enhance the pleasant state are activated. In the case of negative emotions, conversion schemas are initiated that include guidelines for action on how to alter the unpleasant state. This model offers an explanation for emotion-related consumer activities such as self-gifts, emotional eating, going out with friends, watching movies, or relaxing with music. Hence, it covers functions (1), (2) and (3).

There have been a number of studies dealing with the emotional content of advertising, based on the assumption that in a world where material needs are satisfied, the need for informational content becomes less important. But there seem to be individual differences in preferred level of stimulation. In an exploratory study using a series of fear-appeal advertisements, it was shown that 'need for stimulation' (NST) is a key moderating variable between the arousal potential of a stimulus and the evaluation of that stimulus. Further, the effect of arousal potential on arousal was stronger for individuals with higher NSTs, and the level of arousal at which stimulus evaluation reaches a maximum is higher for individuals with higher NSTs (Steenkamp, Baumgartner and van der Wulp, 1996). This result is an example of function (3).

It has been suggested that emotions in the consumption experience are linked to perceived risk, with negative emotions being positively related and positive emotions being negatively related (Chaudhuri, 1997). Studies with both products and services as units of observation revealed that emotional dimensions such as joy, affection, sadness, anger and anxiety in conjunction with product involvement and perceived differences between alternatives account for a substantial amount of perceived risk. Perceived risk was also shown to mediate the effect of negative emotion and perceived differences on brand loyalty and information search while positive emotions were not related to any of these variables. Function (2) seems to be represented in these findings.

Another way of looking at perceived risk is to assess product satisfaction in the post-consumption experience. A study in which respondents evaluated both high- and low-involvement products in current use reported affective responses. Their assessment of their levels of satisfaction did reveal that two primary dimensions of product evaluation, namely utilitarian and hedonic judgement, are causal antecedents to the affect dimensions of pleasantness and arousal and to product satisfaction (Mano and Oliver, 1993). This covers especially function (1).

These contributions represent only a limited sample of the manifold studies on the role of emotions in consumer behaviour: it covers a broad range of areas in which consumers' emotions are shown to be important antecedents, correlates or consequences of shopping behaviour. The findings provide further evidence that the understanding, explanation and prediction of human action is enriched by accepting emotions as an integral part of cognitive processing.

SUZANNE C. BECKMANN

Bibliography

Boedeker, M. (1997) 'Recreational Shopping. The Role of Basic Emotional Dimensions of Personality', Turku, Finland: Turku School of Economics and Business Administration, Series A-9:1997 (http:www.tukkk.fi).

Chaudhuri, A. (1997) 'Consumption Emotion and Perceived Risk: A Macro-analytic Approach', *Journal of Business Research*, **39**: 81–92.

Earl, P.E. (1983) *The Economic Imagination*, Brighton, Wheatsheaf.

Gardner, M.P. (1985) 'Mood States and Consumer Behavior: A Critical Review', *Journal of Consumer Research*, **12**: 281–300.

Grunert, S.C. (1993) *Essen und Emotionen* (Eating and Emotions), Weinheim, Psychologie Verlags Union.

Holbrook, M.B. and Hirschman, E.C. (1982) 'The Experiential Aspects of Consumption: Consumer Fantasies, Feelings, and Fun', *Journal of Consumer Research*, **9**: 132–40.

Mano, H. and Oliver, R.L. (1993) 'Assessing the Dimensionality and Structure of the Consumption Experience: Evaluation, Feeling, and Satisfaction', *Journal of Consumer Research*, **20**: 451–66.

Mick, D.G. and DeMoss, M. (1990) 'Self-Gifts: Phenomenological Insights from Four

Contexts', *Journal of Consumer Research*, **17**: 322–3.

Mick, D.G., DeMoss, M. and Faber, R. (1992) 'A Projective Study of Motivations and Meanings of Self-Gifts: Implications for Retail Management', *Journal of Retailing*, **68**: 122–44.

Pieters, R. and van Raaij, F. (1988) 'Functions and Management of Affect: Applications to Economic Behavior', *Journal of Economic Psychology*, **9**: 251–82.

Rook, D.W. and Gardner, M.P. (1993) 'In the Mood: Impulse Buying's Affective Antecedents', *Research in Consumer Behavior*, **6**: 1–28.

Ruth, J.A. (1996) 'It's the Feeling that Counts: Toward an Understanding of Emotion and its Influence on Gift-Exchange Processes', in Otnes, C. and Beltramini, R.F. (eds) *Gift Giving: A Research Anthology*, Bowling Green, OH, Bowling Green State University Popular Press: 195–214.

Scitovsky, T. (1986) *Human Desire and Economic Satisfaction: Essays on the Frontiers of Economics*, Brighton, Wheatsheaf.

Steenkamp, J.-B.E.M., Baumgartner, H. and van der Wulp, E. (1996) 'The Relationships Among Arousal Potential, Arousal and Stimulus Evaluation, and the Moderating Role of Need for Stimulation', *International Journal of Research in Marketing*, **13**: 319–30.

Zajonc, R.B. (1980) 'Feeling and Thinking: Preferences Need No Inferences', *American Psychologist*, **35**: 151–75.

Entrepreneurship and Innovation

During the last decade particularly, there has been increasing interest on the part of academics, business leaders and government officials in the role of entrepreneurs and innovation in economic development. During this time, the importance of entrepreneurs and innovation to the creation of new products and services and employment and the resulting economic growth has become increasingly evident. Despite this increase in interest and understanding, there has been very limited research on the roles of innovation and the entrepreneur and their impact. Yet the two are intertwined — innovation involves ingenuity and imagination in creating and putting the new idea into practice and entrepreneurship involves understanding the individual who is initiating and managing this process resulting in the creation of a new venture. This act of creating new ideas can involve recombining existing ideas; it can occur by analogy and intuition, by misadventure, or by inspiration (Koestler, 1964). Some feel that the creative act is the unearthing of hidden analogies resulting in an innovation that is then further developed.

The entrepreneur

The concept of the entrepreneur has been developed from principles and concepts from a business, economic and psychological perspective. The psychological perspective can be viewed in terms of: cognitive variables (factors affecting the individual's alertness to opportunities); motivational variables (factors affecting the cost of taking advantage of opportunities); and social variables (factors affecting both of the above) (Gilad, 1986). The aspect of alertness to opportunities has been explored by focusing on entrepreneurs being more alert than the general populace, particularly in being able to see unexploited market opportunities that others do not notice (Kirzner, 1973). In terms of motivational variables, several entrepreneurial characteristics have been identified, such as the need for independence and achievement, high energy level, persistence, self-confidence, moderate risk taking, visionary leading and support for employees (Hisrich and Peters, 1998). Cognitive variables relevant to entrepreneurs include the locus of control and power. Entrepreneurs have significantly more internal locus of control than the general populace, and have a sense of control over their lives. They also are very sensitive to power and the changes in power, particularly as it affects them. Several social variables have been identified as impacting on the entrepreneur: family (particularly the encouragement of independence, and the careers of the father and mother); role-model availability; and networks. In this context, the importance of the business culture setting has been identified (Casson, 1982; 1995). Of particular importance are the norms and boundaries affecting behaviour and ethical decision making.

These concepts and principles have led to a variety of definitions containing such notions as newness, organizing, creativity, wealth creation, managing and risk taking. Most definitions are somewhat restrictive since entrepreneurs are found in all professions — education, medicine, research, law, architecture, government, engineering, social work — not only for profit areas and business. To include all types of entrepreneurial behaviour as it relates to innovation the following definition is useful:

> *Entrepreneurship* is the process of creating something different with value by devoting the necessary time and effort, assuming the accompanying financial, psychic, and social risks, and receiving the resulting rewards of monetary and personal satisfaction and independence. (Hisrich and Peters, 1998: 9)

This entrepreneur, who most often has a large amount of technical expertise, is the key in terms of the eventual success of the innovation process. There is really no such thing as a true entrepreneurial profile, as entrepreneurs are individuals with significant differences. They come from a variety of educational backgrounds, family situations and work experience. The next entrepreneur may presently be a nurse, secretary, truck driver, assembly line worker, salesperson, mechanic, homemaker, manager or engineer. A potential entrepreneur can be male or female, majority or minority, or from any nationality.

Regardless of the background or characteristics, entrepreneurs shift resources from areas of low productivity and yield to areas of higher productivity and yield, experiencing enthusiasm, frustration, anxiety and hard work. There is a high degree of emotional and financial risk and a high failure rate due to such things as poor sales, intense competition, lack of capital, lack of management ability, and lack of understanding the appropriate business strategy and skills. This is particularly true for high-tech entrepreneurs who are bringing unique innovations to the market.

How do these entrepreneurs get their ideas? One way is recognizing an unexplored market opportunity. This ability of the entrepreneur has been related to personal construct psychology in terms of certain individuals having in their repertoires the constructs necessary to notice particular things (Earl, 1984). This often involves recombining existing ideas or products into new ones, such as using paper and soap to develop wash-and-dry travel towelettes or antiseptics added to the wash and dry travel towelettes to develop Germ Away, an antiseptic wipe. This requires that the entrepreneur be open to change and deal with new ideas in an effective manner (Nolan, 1981). Finding and dealing with ideas often involves employing any one of various problem-solving techniques such as: brainstorming, reverse brainstorming, synectics, the Gordon method, the checklist method, free association, forced relationships, collective notebook methods, the heuristics, scientific method, the Kepner–Tregoe method, value analysis, attribute listing, morphological analysis, matrix charting, a sequence attribute/modification matrix, the inspired big dream approach, or parameter analysis (Hisrich and Peters, 1998).

Using creative problem-solving techniques or being alert to unexploited market opportunities requires focusing on the paradigms and norms involved in the entrepreneur's problem situation. Within the structural uncertainty of the entrepreneur's environment, problem solving occurs in real time by testing in the market a hypothesis about the value of an innovative product or service. By such experiments, entrepreneurs accumulate knowledge of human wants, actions and productivity in the context of the market environment (Harper, 1996).

The innovation
In addressing the area of innovation, it is important to have a definition that illuminates the innovation process and the role of entrepreneurship in that process. Given this criteria, a useful definition is: the overall innovation process encompasses a spectrum of activities from basic research to commercial application and marketing. For the innovation process to be productive, the generation of new knowledge and the translation of that knowledge into commercial products and services must be linked (Prager and Omenn, 1980).

From this definition, innovation is bounded by the invention on one side and by commercialization and the adoption or diffusion that follows the initial commercialization success on the other. There are differences in the risks in both the invention and the innovation process. In terms of the invention, the key risk is that the process or product will not perform its intended function. The risk in the innovation process is that the process or product cannot be priced, distributed and serviced in a way that is acceptable to the potential market.

The idea that large organizations do not and cannot innovate is a myth more than a reality. There are numerous instances of large organizations such as IBM, 3M, Johnson and Johnson, and Citibank developing and engineering innovative products and processes and doing exceptionally well. In fact, large organizations tend to be more successful than startup ventures in process innovations and product innovations that are essentially improvements. This reflects the size, capital, intensity, internal structure and product expertise of the large organization. How can innovation process risks be reduced? By exploiting change through systematic innovation as change usually provides the opportunity for successfully developing something new and different. What is this systematic innovation? It consists of the purposeful and organized search for change, and the systematic analysis of the opportunities such changes might offer for economic or social innovation (Drucker, 1986: 35).

The intersection
The entrepreneurs and the innovation, regardless of the degree of uniqueness or the technology of the innovation, are closely related as entrepreneurs are a means by which each innovation evolves and develops. This is particularly true at the high technology end of the spectrum. To be successful, high-tech entrepreneurship must be systematic, well managed, and based on an innovation that has a purpose and creates a resource that is desired by a group of users. Sometimes problems arise when the entrepreneur focuses too much on the aspect of innovation and does not undertake appropriate managerial and business activities. This has implications both for the success of the initial innovation as well as the successful continuation of the venture created.

For the successful integration of innovation and entrepreneurship, several factors must be operant.

First, there must be a clearly identified market, and an openness on the part of the entrepreneur that the initial focus may have to be redirected to another market not originally identified. Although the entrepreneur needs to fully understand what the innovation can do, he/she must also be open to new customers or uses not originally envisaged. This is particularly true for new high-technology innovations as anything new usually creates markets hard to imagine at the incipiency of the innovation. The tendency of entrepreneurs to be comfortable in familiar areas can produce tunnel vision and exclude possible market areas.

Second, the successful intersection requires obtaining the appropriate amount of capital and then carefully managing the cash flow. All too often entrepreneurs do not put into place the needed controls and policies to ensure that the cash is well spent and capital is available when needed. It is a rare venture that does not quickly outgrow its capital structure.

Finally, a strong management team must be carefully developed. This requires that the entrepreneur determine his/her strengths and weaknesses and role in the company as well as anticipate management needs and bring on appropriate managers accordingly. The most critical issue is the balance between cash outflow and the venture's need for management. Ideally, the management team needs to be built before the venture actually reaches the point of critically needing one. Since it takes time to locate and build a good team, the process must be started before the need becomes critical. This requires that the entrepreneur and other key managers in the company define the key activities of the firm, decide the activities each company team member can do effectively, determine the activities needing attention, and find the appropriate person for these identified activities. Sometimes this process needs independent, objective outside advice. Without a strong management team the intersection will not be successful.

The future

The future of entrepreneurship and innovation is very bright. Today is the age of the entrepreneur with entrepreneurship being endorsed by governmental units, society, business and even educational institutions to some extent. Innovation and entrepreneurship offer possibilities for the successful creation and growth of the companies that will produce the next generation of new products and services and create the wealth and jobs of the future. Entrepreneurship and innovation add to the vitality and flexibility of an economy, serving as the new source of competition in an internationally hypercompetitive world.

Small high-technology firms will continue to be an important part of each growing economy. These firms depend on flexible specialization and derive their technological dynamism from their ability to innovate. While competing vigorously in their market, they often exhibit significant amounts of cooperation in research and development, marketing and technology transfer. By employing a flexible strategy in their high-technology firms, the entrepreneur is able to identify, develop and market the innovation, successfully bridging the gap between science and the marketplace while positively on impacting the economy.

ROBERT D. HISRICH

191

Bibliography

Acs, Z.J. (1996) 'Innovation of Entrepreneurial Firms', *Small Business Economics*, **8**: 203–18.

Casson, M.C. (1982) *The Entrepreneur*, Oxford, Martin Robertson.

Casson, M.C. (1995) *Entrepreneurship and Business Culture*, Aldershot, Edward Elgar.

Daghfous, A. (1994) 'Information and Innovation: A Comprehensive Representation', *Research Policy*, **23**: 267–80.

Drucker, P.F. (1986) *Innovation and Entrepreneurship*, New York: Harper & Row.

Earl, P.E. (1984) *The Corporate Imagination: How Big Companies Make Mistakes*, Brighton, Wheatsheaf Books.

Elton, R. (1996) 'Making Innovation Fly', *Business Quarterly*, **61**: 59–64.

Gilad, B. (1986) 'Entrepreneurial Decision Making: Some Behavioral Considerations', in Gilad, B. and Kaish, S. (eds) *Handbook of Behavioral Economics*, Vol. A, Greenwich, JAI Press: 189–208.

Harper, D. (1996) *Entrepreneurship and the Market Process*, London, Routledge.

Hisrich, R.D. and Peters, M.P. (1998) *Entrepreneurship: Stating, Developing and Managing a New Venture* (4th edn), Chicago, IL, Irwin–McGraw-Hill.

Jones-Evans, D. (1996) 'Technical Entrepreneurship Strategy and Experience', *International Small Business Journal*, **14**: 15–39.

Kirzner, I.M. (1973) *Competition and Entrepreneurship*, Chicago, IL, University of Chicago Press.

Koestler, A. (1964) *The Act of Creation*, New York, NY, MacMillan.

Livesay, H.C. (1996) 'Human Factors and the Innovation Process', *Technovation*, **16**: 173–86.

Nolan, V. (1981) 'Open to Change — How to Initiate, Cope With and Benefit From Change of Work', *Management Decision*, **19**: 3–96.

Prager, D.J. and Omenn, D.S. (1980) 'Research, Innovation, and University — Industry Linkages', *Science*, **207**: 2–23.

Escalation of Commitment

The phrase 'escalation of commitment' suggests irrationality and conflict; but this must be distinguished from a broader escalation of commitment paradigm (ECP) in psychology, which is a wide-ranging investigation into decision making with sunk costs. In the ECP literature, the term 'sunk costs' refers specifically to past monetary outlays on a project or a product (note: an alternative usage of 'past outlay — the current net realizable value'). The ECP is unusually wide in scope: strategic signalling; capital investment and project abandonment decisions; the motive to justify past decisions, the desire to avoid waste and the social norm of consistency; cognitive biases, heuristics, frames, mental-accounts and the empirical variants of subjective expected utility models; the economic value of waiting and capital fixities; and the place of economic rationality within the general theory of rationality. In addition, the ECP literature also offers various suggestions for preventing dysfunctional escalation, or the tendency to throw good money after bad, in personal and managerial life.

The ECP has a unifying theme: decision-making episodes must contain some explicit description of past outlays or expenditures. It therefore spans several economic contexts, including reinvestment (for example, continuation of a project), post-purchase consumption (for example, theatre attendance), as well as the post-acquisition deployment of revenue generating assets (for example, fielding players in a professional team sport).

The dollar auction

The ECP really 'kicked off' almost 30 years ago, with Shubik's (1971) 'dollar auction'. In this game, members of an audience bid openly for a one dollar prize; an opening bid might be ten cents. The rules are that the highest bidder pays the amount bid and gets the dollar, but the second-highest bidder (the runner-up) must also pay the amount of his or her second-highest bid, getting nothing in return. When bidding reaches about 90 cents, the second-highest bidder (say, 80 cents) typically realizes that he or she can improve his or her position by bidding, say, $1.10, thereby standing to lose a net 10 cents, not 80 cents. This often triggers a series of escalating bids, well beyond the one dollar mark, in which motives become varied.

The game demonstrates aspects of political conflict similar to those in an arms race. It particularly shows that a simple economic preference (that is, paying 80 cents for one dollar) can quickly give way both to strategic behaviour (that is, signalling an intention to beat the opponent), and to psychological motives, such as a desire to appear less foolish than another bidder, or to punish, or exact revenge from him or her (at a high dollar cost).

Laboratory studies of project-completion decisions

In the psychology literature, the ECP dates from a series of laboratory studies on project completion (Staw, 1976). Subjects were presented with short written scenarios and asked to allocate funds (in two stages) to one of two alternative research and development (R&D) projects. Those who chose an R&D project that underperformed, subsequently invested (relatively) more in an apparent attempt to turn things around. This 'escalation' effect was mediated by the level of perceived responsibility for the original allocation decision.

The result has been difficult to replicate (Singer and Singer, 1986; Garland 1990), yet the original study remains most noteworthy for the proposed conceptual framework, which included (i) the motive to justify the past decision, to self and to others, since if a responsible decision maker abandons an ongoing project, he or she will often be asked why he or she started it; (ii) the social norm of consistency (that is, the 'hero effect'); and (iii) optimistic bias in forecasting (the returns from any further investment). Thus, from its inception, the ECP in psychology has invoked many explanations.

Subsequent laboratory research on project completion has involved rather simple tests, with diverse interpretations. Arkes and Blumer (1985) and Conlon and Garland (1993) found that the monetary amount of past investment had little effect on a decision to invest more, but written information on the 'percentage completed' did have a strong effect (for example, more than 85 per cent of subjects chose to fund a venture when it was described as '90 per cent completed').

Such research is open to a variety of interpretations. More than a quarter of a century ago, Wolf (1970: 789) postulated a psychological 'mechanism' whereby 'present action is influenced by a desire to protect or preserve a present benefit whose magnitude is indicated by the scale of prior costs'. More recently, Staw and Hoang (1995) have offered a rather similar interpretion of the accumulated experimental evidence on project completion, as follows: 'In natural settings, decision-makers may regularly confound the amount they have expended with progress on a project'.

However, an economist or a practising project manager would find much to criticize in this sort of statement. Consider, for example, the above proposition about 'confounding' one's estimate of progress on a project: in 'natural' settings: one is faced with obvious (concrete) facts, such as a partly-completed dam or tunnel (for example, look out the site-office window!). It is simply implausible that practitioners could 'regularly confound' such facts with documented reports of the historical monetary expenditures to date. Furthermore, any ambiguities within written managerial reports (like those present in the experimental stimulus materials!) would, in practice, be quickly identified and clarified — unless, of course, managers were playing political games such as creative accounting. Viewed in this critical light, it is not surprising that Garland, Sandefur and Rogers (1990) found in an experiment that a group of actual practitioners tended not to escalate.

This gap between theory and practice, in the project-completion context, appears to be explicable in terms of subjects' interpretations of the experimental stimulus materials. For example, the natural language phrase 'a project is 90 per cent completed', when used in a proper or natural context, often entails an unspoken 'according to plan', or 'nicely on-budget'. With this reading, subjects could then reason, correctly, that cost overruns on the remaining 10 per cent are unlikely. This, in turn, would imply that further investment would probably secure the full originally estimated benefit stream from the project. (Moreover, if we replace '10 per cent' with, say, 50 per cent, the economic case weakens, in line with the experimental results obtained.)

This viewpoint, that subjects in project completion experiments are being quite sophisticated and economically rational rather than resorting to an imperfect cognitive habit, is also consistent with several other experimental findings in which the stimulus texts were rather less ambiguous but no escalation effect was obtained (Garland et al., 1990). Yet, in the ECP project-completion literature, such considerations of text interpretations are nowhere to be found. The reason, as Staw and Hoang (1995: 490) suggest, is that 'this is not the way in which laboratory research is carried out'. In empirical psychology, one makes only those statements that can be backed up by pointing to the result of an experiment — however questionable the methodology. Certainly, in analysing project-completion decisions, this epistemology has some serious weaknesses.

Laboratory studies of post-purchase consumption decisions
Experiments on the post-purchase consumption context have been much cleaner and far more useful. Here, subjects respond to questions, such as:

> You have tickets for a basketball game in a city 60 miles from your home. The day of the game there is a major snowstorm. Holding constant the value you place on going to the game, are you more likely to go to the game (a) if you paid $20 each for the tickets, or (b) if you got the tickets for free? (Thaler, 1985)

> Which pre-paid ski trip would you choose: a trip likely to be more enjoyable, or a trip that cost the most? (Arkes and Blumer, 1985)

In these (and similar) cases, a majority of subjects say that they would 'consume' the product or service for which they had 'paid' the most. Put differently, preferences are influenced by the sunk-cost episodes.

Here, it appears that subjects might be misapplying a rule of thumb such as 'price paid is a guide to quality' (also known as the Chivas–Regal effect), even though the text guards against this. Alternatively, it could be that subjects reflect upon the likely determinants of their own psychic utility, seeing that it would be greater if they were to consume the more expensive alternative. The reasons could then include dissonance reduction, avoidance of regret, or the feeling of frustration that one has wasted money.

The theatre-ticket phenomenon uncovered by Tversky and Kahneman (1981), provides further insight into post-purchase sunk-cost effects. A majority of subjects will choose to pay $10 for a theatre ticket, following discovery of a loss of a $10 bill from their wallet; but not following the loss of a $10 ticket they had already purchased. There is a 'topical mental account', triggered by the transaction (the ticket purchase), in which the monetary total (money already spent plus money to pay now) is mentally compared with the psychic utility of consumption. Therefore, in the lost-ticket condition, the decision frame is $20 versus the psychic utility (no deal); but with the loss of cash, the frame is $10 versus the psychic utility. In this case, the sunk-cost episode has the effect of doubling the framed price, but there is no consequent effect on the subjects' preference for consuming the higher 'priced' good (in other words, there is no Chivas–Regal effect).

Many other studies have used hypothetical (quantitative) gambles or risky propects in order to explore further the phenomena of cognitive framing, editing and mental-accounting effects related to sunk costs. Some of the results (that is, majority responses) have been accommodated into a class of formal models known as the hybrids, or behavioural decision theories, or empirical variants of subjective expected utility models (also known as behavioural decision theories). Examples are Prospect Theory (Tversky and Kahneman, 1981) and Transaction Utility Theory (Thaler, 1985).

Field studies on sunk costs

In an attempt to increase the real-world validity of the ECP experiments, there have been some controlled field studies. In a study of post-purchase consumption, Arkes and Blumer (1985) arranged to have real theatre tickets sold at different prices. They then recorded the actual level of attendance, or consumption. Those who had paid more for their ticket were indeed more likely to attend.

In a recent sophsticated study of post-purchase asset deployment in the National Basketball Association, Staw and Hoang (1995) found that 'teams granted more playing time and longer periods of retention to their most highly drafted players' (that is, the ones they had paid most for); but this occurred to a greater extent than could be justified by the actual (post-purchase) measured performance of these players. Put differently, this study controlled for direct sunk cost factors (see section the section on the generic sunk cost problem, below) such as the fact that highly-drafted players continue to have high fan appeal, hence greater revenue-generating power. After allowing for such factors, experienced professional managers and recruiters still appeared to be unduly influenced by sunk costs (that is, 'this guy cost us a lot, so we'll play him and retain him').

Examples of cost overruns in capital projects

There have been no field studies of project-completion; but anecdotes and case studies abound. For example:

1. In aerospace: A consortium persisted from 1959–69 with the development of the Concorde supersonic aircraft, which finally came in at ten times the original budget to completion. For many years, the annually updated 'budget to completion' stayed roughly the same (at £3 million!).

2. In power-generation schemes: A grand plan to dam the Danube river system in Central Europe, which dated back to 1951, was being reconsidered in the early 1990s amid a host of unforeseen political and ecological problems. Another nuclear power scheme in the US, originally budgeted at $70 million, eventually cost $5.5 billion over 20 years, but was never completed. Yet another plant came on stream at 16 times the original budget.

In these 'natural settings', political and institutional factors usually dominate, but many of these lie outside the scope of the ECP in psychology. A typical sequence of events is: (i) there is high-level political backing for a project, for strategic reasons such as 'industry development'; (ii) entities (for example, consortia) put in their lowest feasible bids to win a contract, plus the political connections that go with it; (iii) 'concrete' actions are taken, after which it becomes politically costly to abandon the project (the norm of consistency and the justification motive); then, as time goes by, (iv) reports become manipulated (for example, creative accounting) and cost-plus deals start to creep in to the supply chain; and (v), as a final twist, further cost overruns are excused with reference to the alleged but as yet unquantified likely future spinoffs for other projects (for example, microchips from the Apollo program and so forth). The project has become a gravy train.

The generic sunk-cost problem

The complex mixture of political, institutional and psychological factors raises the question of whether these can all be captured within a framework of foward-looking economic rationality (for example, in decision tree form). To this end, a generic sunk-cost problem (GSCP) has been defined (Singer, 1993) as follows. A project or plan P is being reconsidered, by an entity, at some time, tn. Part of P (that is, $P-$) has already been implemented. Continuation with the next part of P (that is, $P+$) is being reconsidered. Thus, the entity will either continue with P (in other words, chose $P+$) or else abandon P, thereby choosing an alternative (not $P+$ with $Palt$).

The GSCP covers all the ECP cases: project completion, post-purchase asset deployment and consumption. It quickly points to directions for further research and inquiry, such as:

1. The decision-making entity: Experiments and field studies have been on individuals (with a few on groups, or teams). Yet interpretations and discussions of behavioral escalation have extended to a larger entity-set, including nation-states, consortia and even insects (Dawkins and Brockmann, 1980).
2. Abandonment: The meaning of non-escalation ('not $P+$ and $Palt$') is often

glossed over in the ECP studies. In project completion it often means investing in a scaled-down version. It can also mean delayed reinvestment (such as an individual's decision to upgrade a PC, but to wait for a price drop; or a national strategic decision to persist with capital-intensive steel manufacturing, but to skip a generation of technology). In asset-deployment, it can mean spinning off or breaking up a productive asset. Finally, in post-purchase consumption, it simply means not consuming (wasting, or perhaps giving away) a good.

3. Forecastability: Although 'economists universally caution against the use of sunk costs' (Staw and Hoang, 1995: 475), normative economic theory does in fact explicitly recognise the impact (on $P+$ and $Palt$) of such historical factors as reputation, learning and contractual obligations.

In the GSCP decision-tree analysis there are two classes of factor which explicitly refer to the entity's past actions and past expenditures (but not the actual dollar amount of sunk costs). They are:

1. Direct sunk-cost factors: identifiable events or conditions caused by the entity's past behaviour, in $P-$, but now affecting the forecast benefits from $P+$ (for example, reputation, learning, motivation; or NBA player fan appeal, arising from a high draft and so on);

2. Opportunity sunk-cost factors: similar to (1) but now affecting the evaluation of the alternative (for example, contractual obligations arising from $P-$).

In addition, there are any number of other factors that must also affect the forecast returns, but that are not caused by the entity's own past behaviour (for example, macroenvironmental trends, the uses by competitors of project assets that are sold off, possible spinoffs of the project technology and so forth). In practice (and most certainly in laboratory studies of project completion) many of these 'sunk-cost factors' have been unjustifiably ignored.

Plural rationality
The general theory of rationality also informs the GSCP and ECP. In the Staw (1976) framework, prospective rationality (forecasting) was contrasted with the retrospective form (that is, justification and norm of consistency). There are several other distinctive backward-looking forms of rationality not mentioned to date in the ECP psychology literature. These include the posterior, ratchet and constrained forms — respectively, the emergence of goals from past actions; the benefits from coordination with other status-quo biased entities; the folly of abandoning a longstanding personal plan for the sake of a possibly fleeting

preference and so on)

The various meta-rational arguments that link backward-looking with foward-looking forms then swing on such considerations as: (i) the richness of the descriptions of the objects of choice; (ii) strategic signalling; (iv) self-knowledge (for example, persistence may be a worthwhile habit or character trait to develop, when viewed over an entity's whole life); and (v) evolutionary stability: utility maximization is not necessarily an evolutionarily stable strategy, whenever resources are squandered in big fights for prizes widely perceived as valuable (Dawkins and Brockmann, 1980).

Preventing escalation in practice

The ECP and management literatures have identified many policies and techniques that could work to prevent dysfunctional escalation, wasteful combat, or the throwing of good money after bad, in practice. Curiously, most apply to the least-well-researched context: that of cost overruns in capital projects. They include:

1. From the start, define exit criteria and design multiple possible exits. This keeps options open and maintains flexibility.
2. Different decision makers should be used at each of the pre-planned exitpoints of a large project. Also, the responsibilities of all parties should be made clear.
3. For small projects, a superior gives tacit approval only, that is, no comment, so that he or she can more easily turn around later and stop it (Singer, 1986).
4. Seek out detailed information at every stage of a project (for example, cashflows to date). Search out possible ambiguities and have them clarified. (for example, multiple projects should be reported seperately, accounting practices should be explained, especially 'deferred' reporting of development-expenditures).
5. Decision makers should consciously try to compensate for optimistic biases in forecasts, or the effects of framing on judgements of utility and risk.
6. Cost-plus contracts should be avoided.

Conclusion

The notion that sunk costs create tension in economic, political and psychological life is one with a very long intellectual history. In a commentary on an ancient Sanskrit text, it is written: 'Any work begun in the material plane has to be completed, otherwise the whole attempt becomes a failure. But any work begun in (the spiritual plane) has a permanent effect, even though not finished' (Prabhupada, 1986). In Homer's *Iliad*, an account was given of how the brave Agamemnon persuaded the Greeks to persist and persevere with their fight against the Trojans, 'by pointing out that withdrawal would cause dishonour to those whose lives had already been lost' (cited in Wolf, 1970: 789). In the last few decades, another (fragmented) chapter of this history has been written; but the element of mystery surely remains. Such issues as the prevention of waste, for example, are not only economic challenges, they are also moral imperatives. Moreover, to a craftsperson whose primary goals are aesthetic and expressive, an unfinished work can cause a high level of psychic disutility, even profound spiritual suffering. Curiously and perhaps sadly, the ECP in psychology has remained quite silent on these matters. It seems that considerations of spirituality and honour, aesthetics and morality, not to mention many other important dimensions of the GSCP, remain substantially beyond the reach of the experimental method.

ALAN E. SINGER

Bibliography

Arkes, H.R. and Blumer, C. (1985) 'The Psychology of Sunk Costs', *Organisational Behavior and Human Decision Processes*, **35**: 124–40.

Conlon, D.E. and Garland, H. (1993) 'The Role of Project Completion Information in Resource Allocation Decisions', *Academy of Management Journal*, **36**: 402–13.

Dawkins, R. and Brockmann, H.J. (1980) 'Do Digger Wasps Commit the Concorde Fallacy?', *Animal Behaviour*, **28**: 892–6.

Garland, H. (1990) 'Thowing Good Money after Bad: The Effect of Sunk Costs on the Decision to Escalate Commitment to an Ongoing Project', *Journal of Applied Psychology*, **75**: 728–31.

Garland, H., Sandefur, C.A. and Rogers, A. (1990) 'Deescalation of Commitment in Oil Exploration: When Sunk Costs and Negative Feedback Coincide', *Journal of Applied Psychology*, **75**: 921–7.

Prabhupada (His Divine Grace A.C. Bhaktivedanta Swami) (1986) *The Bhagavad Gita As It Is*, Borehamwood, Bhaktivedanta Book Trust.

Shubik, M. (1971) 'The Auction Game: A Paradox in Noncooperative Behavior and Escalation', *Journal of Conflict Resolution*, **15**: 109–11.

Singer, A.E. (1986) 'When the Stakes are High', *Accountancy*, November, 92–3.

Singer, A.E. (1993) 'Strategy with Sunk Costs', *Human Systems Management*, **12**: 97–113.

Singer, M.S. and Singer, A.E. (1986) 'Individual Differences in the Escalation of Commitment Paradigm', *Journal of Social Psychology*, **126**: 197–204.

Staw, B.M. (1976) 'Knee-Deep in the Big Muddy: Study of Escalating Commitment to a Chosen Course of Action', *Organizational Behavior and Human Performance*, **16**: 27–44.

Staw, B.M. (1981) The Escalation of Commitment to a Course of Action', *Academy of Management Review*, **6**: 577-87.

Staw, B.M. and Hoang, H. (1995) 'Sunk Costs in the NBA', *Administrative Science Quarterly*, 40: 474–94.

Thaler, R. (1985) 'Mental Accounting and Consumer Choice', *Marketing Science*, **4**: 199–214.

Tversky, A. and Kahneman, D. (1981) 'The Framing of Decisions and the Psychology of Choice', *Science*, **211**: 453–8.

Wolf, C. (1970) 'The Present Value of the Past', *Journal of Political Economy*, **78**: 783–92.

Expectancy Value Models

Expectancy value models, developed independently from a variety of disciplines, have enjoyed a longstanding acceptance in psychology, marketing, and economics (Feather, 1982a), and have found application in various facets of consumer research, such as motivation, cognitions, decision making and attitudes. At the same time, the application of these models has been surrounded by controversy arising from a number of different issues. In an attempt to address these issues, researchers have attempted to modify expectancy value models and/or have described them within contingency frameworks. Yet, some issues remain unresolved and opportunities exist for future research in consumer behaviour to address them.

Researchers in a number of disciplines are concerned with how cognitions influence action. Consequently, expectancy value models have been conceived (in somewhat different forms) in several disciplines to explain this complex process, and represent a leap from stimulus-response explanations for behaviour. Based largely on a study of animal behaviour, Tolman (1932) hypothesized that (higher-level) animals and people tend to process information based on a $\sum E_i V_i$ process where E_i is the expectation that an action will lead to outcome i with a value of V_i. Although recognized for his seminal work in cognitive psychology, Tolman was criticized for not making a more explicit link between cognitive representations and behaviour; in response, Tolman later suggested that in addition to forming cognitions based on the $\sum E_i V_i$ process, there is an attempt to maximize behaviour based on this process. Other instances of expectancy value models in subdisciplines of psychology abound.

Motivational psychology has given rise to a model of risk-taking behaviour that was an early example of an expectancy value model. Cognitive models of motivation based on an analysis of the situation, possible outcomes, consequences of outcomes, and action taken, are closely tied to expectancy value models. Organizational psychology has developed an expectancy approach for job choice and job satisfaction. Social learning literature has incorporated the concept of locus of control in its expectancy approach, wherein an internal locus of control results in higher expectancies. (All of these early models are referenced in Feather, 1982a.)

Edwards (1954) developed the subjective expected utility (SEU) model drawing mainly from economics and mathematics, but integrating discussions from psychology and philosophy. The model proposes that in making decisions, individuals gauge the subjective probabilities P_i and subjective utilities U_i associated with various actions i and choose the alternative that maximizes SEU, that is, $\sum P_i U_i$. Based on a challenge of the traditional economic model by other economists in the late 1940s and early 1950s, Edwards took the riskless, completely informed, economic man model, and converted it to a form that incorporates incomplete knowledge and risky behaviour. Although the SEU model draws on a variety of disciplines and is used to explain past behaviour as well as predict future behaviour, it is clearly an expectancy approach like the models developed by psychologists. As Feather (1982a: 2) writes, 'common to all (expectancy value models) is the recognition that action and consequences are embedded in a complex means–end structure that involves beliefs about the implications of events'.

The expectancy value model most widely adopted in consumer behaviour is Fishbein and Ajzen's (1975) theory of reasoned action, which is drawn from attitudinal research, and also viewed as a multiattribute model. Unlike other attitude models, however, it also accounts for social influences on an individual's intentions and behaviour. The theory states that attitude and subjective norms (towards a given behaviour) have a direct effect on intentions to engage in that behaviour, and, in turn, intentions have a direct effect on behaviour. The expectancy value approach is embedded in the model through the conception of both attitudes and subjective norms. Specifically, this model proposes that attitude towards a behaviour is determined by $\sum b_i e_i$ where b_i represents cognitive beliefs about consequences i (of the behaviour) and e_i represents evaluations about consequences i and that subjective norms are determined by $\sum (NB)_i MC$ where $(NB)_i$ represents normative beliefs about consequences i and MC represents motivation to comply. Although this model has received wide empirical support and is intuitively appealing (because it incorporates the influence of the individual's own judgement as well as social influences on behaviour), it has also met with much criticism; the issues common to expectancy value models in general are discussed below.

Despite their wide application, expectancy value models raise several issues, some of which have been addressed through discussion and modification. The models have been criticized for not encompassing actual probabilities of occurrence and thereby resulting in inaccurate information processing. For consumer research, however, subjective probabilities are not a problem; instead, we expect that consumer expectations and estimates of probabilities will be subjective and wish to capture them exactly in that form. The same view applies to the formation of (subjective) beliefs in the Fishbein and Ajzen model. The subjective framework used in consumer behaviour suggests that individuals have their own experiences and perceptions, and attach their own values to a set of consequences. This framework fits well with the underlying premise of expectancy value models.

A second criticism is that not every decision is likely to use a proactive evaluation process. Impulsive buying or hedonic consumption certainly do not fit these models when they are applied to the case of consumer behaviour. (A reverse argument could be made based on a longstanding debate in consumer behaviour that even in seemingly mindless actions, there may be complex cognitions occurring at a subconscious level.) Other situations call for reactive action largely guided by past behaviour. It may be noted, though, that some authors of expectancy value models have accounted for past behaviour. For example, in discussing sources of expectations, Tolman included memories of past behaviour and inferences drawn from related experiences. Similarly, Fishbein and Ajzen propose that past experiences are incorporated into the formation of beliefs and evaluations which in turn influence attitudes. At the same time, it is possible that past behaviour influences intentions or behaviour directly and not through cognitions as proposed by all expectancy value models. In other words, each decision/action is not necessarily a separate instance as proposed by expectancy value models, but rather a part of ongoing behaviour based on previous experiences.

Yet another criticism is that the mathematical process underlying these models is quite complex and it is unlikely that individuals use such an intricate calculation in selecting a particular alternative from a set of alternatives. Some expectancy value models do recognize the complexity issue and limit the number of values summed to between five and nine, following Miller's Rule about the practical limitations of what human decision makers can typically keep in mind. Even so, in real life, people are unlikely to make decisions based on complex calculations involving an evaluation of every viable alternative. In defence of the models, it may be said that they are not meant to imply actual thought processes but simply to simulate them. In other words, the models should be viewed as paramorphic (see Hoffman, 1960) whereby they serve as good predictors of behaviour but do not necessarily represent the conscious cognitive process. Interestingly, economic theorists have suggested that people learn to use multiattribute utility models in a conscious way to make better decisions.

A related problem of expectancy value models is that a large number of beliefs (or values) and their associated evaluations (or expectations or probabilities) are incorporated; it is implied that individuals will carry out all these multiplications separately and then add the products in their minds. This assumption is an unrealistic description of conscious information processing and some researchers have suggested modifications of expectancy value models to make them closer to the way people think. For example, Bagozzi (1981) suggested that rather than a unidimensional attitude made up of $\sum b_i e_i$, people think in terms of expectancy value components where information about attributes is grouped by schema and, as a result, the attitude formed is multidimensional. Other researchers (such as Dabholkar, 1994) have proposed that because evaluating all possible information is mathematically tedious and costly, and at the other extreme, relying only on gut feelings is risky, an optimizing solution is a tradeoff between risk and cost, wherein individuals tend to focus on higher-level, simplifying abstractions rather than concrete attributes; these abstractions are often drawn from similar attributes grouped together and form the basis of expectancy value components.

Another related issue is that expectancy value models assume a compensatory process, whereas many individuals prefer to use heuristics or noncompensatory processes to make decisions. Further, expectancy value models assume that each consequence of a proposed action is independent, whereas in reality different consequences may be tied together and may be either directly or inversely proportional to each other. In this case, expected probabilities would have to account for these relationships, further complicating the presumed cognitive process.

One issue not widely recognized is a scaling problem associated with expectancy value models. As in most social science research, measures of the variables in an expectancy value model tend to be interval rather than ratio scaled, and this fact has serious implications for the product terms in the equation. Bagozzi (1984) suggests that hierarchical regression tests be used in empirical research to ascertain whether interval scaling of measures has invalidated the multiplicative product in an expectancy value model and caused the model to be arbitrary and misleading both in explanation and in prediction. Kuhl (1982) proposes that because interval scale measures are based on several assumptions that cannot be tested directly, we should move to testing expectancy value models through other means, such as 'the logical statement analysis' which places more emphasis on the inductive part of scientific inquiry, and thus avoid this measurement issue. As of yet, neither suggestion has been widely adopted and hence much empirical research on expectancy value models may be suspect.

A major issue related to expectancy value models is to determine the conditions when they are appropriate. In general, expectancy value models are more likely to be used for important or risky decisions, where sufficient time is available to process alternatives, and when the individual is prone to being 'cognitive'. Feather (1982a) writes that expectancy value models are used when there is purposeful planning (that is, for actions where foresight and planning are possible) and when intentions are conscious (i.e., there is volitional control). (It may be noted that this would be true even when there is only perceived control rather than any real control of the circumstances.) He further proposes that expectancy value models are reasonable mainly within a means–end or instrumental framework, when there are a number of possible actions and the outcomes are clear (or it is possible to seek information), and when there is a small time gap between intentions and action. He further suggests that the models may be applicable to some individuals ('planners') over others ('impulsives').

Dabholkar (1994) proposes that expectancy value models are applied in different ways under different conditions: conditions for an extensive (or full) use of expectancy value models include cases with few, highly comparable alternatives, or very few salient beliefs that cannot be grouped naturally into dimensions. Both conditions make it relatively easy to engage in this detailed cognitive process. Also, in highly unfamiliar situations that need careful evaluation, individuals may be forced to go through a detailed, cognitive process. In general, this type of complex decision making is more likely when individuals have a high need for controlling error or a low need for reducing information-processing effort. Under other conditions, individuals may prefer to use expectancy value component models, where related beliefs or attributes are grouped into dimensions (components) to simplify information processing. This approach would be viable when there are few, somewhat comparable alternatives with many salient beliefs that can be grouped naturally into dimensions, or few, noncomparable alternatives where abstract dimensions may be common across alternatives and may be used to simplify the process. It would also apply to somewhat unfamiliar situations, or when individuals are not experts on concrete attributes (or consequences) and therefore would be more comfortable evaluating alternatives at a higher, abstract level. (In very familiar situations, no form of the expectancy approach would likely be used at a conscious level, as individuals would look to their own past behaviour as a guide.)

Other conditions for the use of expectancy value component models, or a simplified expectancy approach, include situations where there is a moderate need for controlling error and a moderate need for reducing information-processing effort. The actual components in these simplified expectancy value models are likely to be different for different segments of people based on schema and levels of abstraction that are natural to them. In terms of methodology, factor analysis is a useful tool to uncover natural schema related to information processing and may reveal different schema groupings by product, individual and situation.

There are some issues related to expectancy value models that are still not addressed. Although researchers have suggested that these models may tend to be used by some individuals over others, more research is needed on this subject.

Future studies could investigate whether individuals with personality traits or demographic attributes linked to cognitive propensity tend to use expectancy value models more frequently or more readily. Such studies would be useful for consumer research as well as various areas in psychology. Similarly, with greater knowledge or experience about a given situation, individuals may be less likely consciously to use expectancy value models and more likely to use past behaviour as a guide. At the same time, with greater experience, they may be more able to think and make decisions in a manner that approximates the outcomes of expectancy value models. Researchers have examined the effect of consumer experience and knowledge on information processing; applying the same variables to expectancy value models would simply be an extension of this research.

The role of affect has received little attention in the treatment of expectancy value models, although at one level, because expectations, values and motives are closely linked to affect, the notion of affect is indirectly incorporated into these treatments (Feather, 1982b). Feather writes (p. 275) that the value systems that individuals hold are not 'affectively neutral' but instead are 'tied to feelings and can function as general motives'. Although much research has been conducted on affect and its links to motivation, its role in the cognitive-behaviour link needs further investigation. Researchers recognize that affective evaluations associated with past behaviour often impel action directly without complex information processing and that anxiety about consequences may influence certain types of information processing, but the precise role of affect within an expectancy value framework is not yet clear.

The fact that empirical evidence for expectancy value (or other cognitive) models is generally gathered through verbal or written responses raises several issues. The main issue is that no one knows what actually goes on in the 'black box' of the individual's mind. Another concern is about social desirability biases that could influence respondents to provide inaccurate and somewhat enhanced self-reports about their information processing. Yet another issue is that respondents themselves may not know how exactly they process information; the study of metacognition has revealed major gaps in people's ability to report on their own cognitive processes. As a result, cognitive psychologists are often sceptical about the value of introspection for higher-order cognitive processes (Nisbett and Wilson, 1977) and place little weight on self-reports in these cases. Even though cognitive models do not claim to be 'conscious thought models', they are proposed as close analogies, verified only through mathematical models. Future studies may be able to use electrophysiological techniques to capture actual cognitive processes and verify whether expectancy value models are a good approximation of conscious thought under certain conditions.

Lastly, by envisaging each belief as a separate cognition, expectancy value models fail to draw on natural links between the cognitions (with the exception of the expectancy value component models discussed earlier). Attitudes are summarized based on a formula and the impact of each individual belief is lost. Yet, there is no doubt that attitudes are based on value systems which are generally arranged in a hierarchical fashion in the individual's mind (Feather, 1982b). Past research has suggested that the way these value systems influence expectancy value models is that some consequences become more attractive (based on the value system) and this guides behaviour. Perhaps future research can investigate the hierarchical structure of these beliefs (values) through a laddering process based on a means–end framework or through network analysis. Such analysis would reveal higher- and lower-order beliefs (values) and the means–end chains that are the most dominant for an individual or for a given segment of individuals. The dominant chains would be most likely to represent the motivating force that guides behaviour. Such in-depth explication of the relationships among cognitive beliefs would offer greater insights into the basis for attitudes and the effect on behaviour, and would find application in consumer research as well as in various subdisciplines in psychology.

PRATIBHA A. DABHOLKAR

Bibliography

Bagozzi, R.P. (1981) 'An Examination of the Validity of Two Models of Attitude', *Multivariate Behavioral Research*, **16**: 323–59.

Bagozzi, R.P. (1984) 'Expectancy-Value Attitude Models: An Analysis of Critical Measurement Issues', *International Journal of Research in Marketing*, **1**: 295–310.

Dabholkar, P.A. (1994) 'Incorporating Choice into an Attitudinal Framework: Analyzing Models of Mental Comparison Processes', *Journal of Consumer Research*, **21**: 100–118.

Edwards, W. (1954) 'The Theory of Decision Making', *Psychological Bulletin*, **51**: 380–417.

Feather, N.T. (1982a) 'Expectancy Value Approaches: Present Status and Future Directions', in Feather, N.T. (ed.) *Expectations and Actions: Expectancy Value Models in Psychology*, Hillsdale, NJ, Lawrence Erlbaum Associates: 395–420.

Feather, N.T. (1982b) 'Human Values and the Prediction of Action: An Expectancy Valence Analysis', in Feather, N.T. (ed.) *Expectations and Actions: Expectancy Value Models in Psychology*, Hillsdale, NJ, Lawrence Erlbaum Associates: 263–89.

Fishbein, M. and Ajzen, I. (1975) *Belief, Attitude, Intention, Behavior: An Introduction to Theory and Research*, Reading, MA, Addison-Wesley.

Hoffman, P.J. (1960) 'The Paramorphic Representation of Clinical Judgment', *Psychological Bulletin*, **57**: 116–31.

Kuhl, J. (1982) 'The Expectancy-Value Approach within the Theory of Social Motivation: Elaborations, Extensions, Critiques', in Feather, N.T. (ed.) *Expectations and Actions: Expectancy Value Models in Psychology*, Hillsdale, NJ, Lawrence Erlbaum

Associates: 125–60.

Nisbett, R.E. and Wilson, T.D. (1977) 'Telling More Than We Can Know: Verbal Reports on Mental Processes', *Psychological Review*, **84**: 231–59.

Tolman, Edward C. (1932) *Purposive Behavior in Animals and Men*, New York, Appleton-Century-Crofts.

Expectations

In the natural order of things, individuals make decisions, consciously or sub-consciously, on numerous occasions throughout their lives. Those decisions, or choices, embrace the whole gamut of human affairs: economic, political and social. To effect a decision, information is required. That information will very often involve the need to formulate expectations about the values that specific factors will assume; and it will determine whether it will turn out to have been the best decision. Individuals (*per* individuals or as households) continually make many 'economic' decisions, for example: as consumers of goods, services, financial products (such as insurance and pensions policies, as well as stocks and shares) and liabilities (loans), and as providers of labour services. Firms similarly have to effect decisions over a range of issues: for example, 'What should be the current level of production?'; 'What should be the level of the stocks of intermediate materials that are required for production?'; 'Should the plant be expanded by the purchase of more machinery?' and a host of other, related questions. Governments, too, have to effect decisions across a spectrum of issues and also require information to enable them to take the best action they believe they can in the given circumstances. For example, in the conduct of monetary policy, the central bank will want to know how (say) the levels of gross domestic product, unemployment and inflation will (or are likely to) move over the near and the long term in response to some policy initiative; perhaps an increase in the growth of the money supply.

Situations vary in the quantity and quality of information they require. They vary also in the ability of decision takers to ascertain that information (through the availability of time, knowledge of where to search, and so on) and in their ability — their software, to borrow from Herbert Simon (1984) and, in these electronic days, in their hardware — to process any information in their possession. Bearing those two last points in mind we can appreciate that what seems a sensible decision for one individual may seem to be no more than a second-best decision when viewed from the perspective of another individual.

Let us focus on the individual as a consumer. In that capacity the individual will be purchasing a variety of goods and services, some continuously, some at discrete intervals. In respect of purchases of consumer goods (perishables and durables) the individual will be concerned about the quality of the goods, and in the case of new products will have to assess their quality per unit of cost. For consumer durables some forecast of the comparative services and the service life of the competing goods will need to be made. Decisions to purchase, for example, insurance cover will depend upon an evaluation of the costs (annual premia) and benefits, which will depend upon the risk of the event being insured against compared with the do-nothing situation (which would, among other things, include investing the premia).

One major decision that a consumer takes is to evaluate the type of financial instruments in which savings should be held and into which further saving should be placed. In what follows we shall focus on that decision since it is an ideal vehicle for illustrating the nature and role of expectations. Imagine, then, that the individual is concerned with determining the best disposition of a current stock of wealth (net assets, which represent the accumulated value of net savings) across a set of assets, from money to near-money (in banks, building societies and so on) to bonds to stocks and shares. Assume, for the ease of exposition, that decisions about changing wealth allocations are made yearly.

In this context, the individual has to form expectations of the (real) returns on the various financial assets that could constitute part of the disposition of wealth. Those returns require forecasts of the capital value of the investments at the end of the year, for it is the anticipated change in the price of the bond or share that, in conjunction with the interest returns or dividend yields over that period, determines the overall yield, and thereby the percentage yield on the amount invested. In addition, there is a need to quantify the rate of inflation over that period, in order to calculate the anticipated real returns; for those returns are relevant to whether or not wealth should continue to be invested in situations of rapid inflation. In such periods, which can give way to hyperinflations of the kind seen in Europe in the 1930s, the faster earned income is spent the greater will be its purchasing power. Investments are undertaken to enhance future wealth perhaps for its own sake, but more frequently to engender a higher level of consumption in the future; so that financial decisions are not independent of consumption decisions.

The monetary and financial world has changed significantly in recent years, due to a concatenation of circumstances, not the least of which are the globalization of markets, deregulation of those markets and the electronic revolution. Share ownership has widened substantially as a result of these trends and the period of rapid economic development they have engendered in almost every corner of the world. Many investors choose not to manage their own portfolios but instead to use unit trusts and other managed funds. This itself can be an optimum decision once the costs of choosing and monitoring individual investments in a portfolio are taken into account, together with the likelihood that the practitioners in the markets will have access to better quality information about the performances of business companies and their impact upon their share prices and dividends. But still the individual consumer of stocks, shares and bonds has to evaluate the comparative performance of unit trusts and managed funds in which he or she might invest. So, for all groups of investors, expectations of future asset prices and their income are required.

The most influential types of expectations-determining mechanisms extant in the literature are: myopic; adaptive; recursive; and what we shall call 'evidential' or 'informational'. The latter type encompasses the variant known as rational expectations — originated in economics by John Muth (1961) and developed by the Nobel Laureate Robert Lucas (1981) — or 'stochastic perfect foresight' which has played such a prominent role in the discussion of the efficacy of government policies and intervention in the economic and political spheres (see, as examples, Lucas, 1981; Sargent, 1986). Evidential expectations also embrace the 'states of the world' approach to expectations formation which is the foundation of almost all models of decision making.

1. *Myopic* In this situation the individual is short-sighted in forming his or her view of the expected values of the relevant variable, here the yields. The current actual values of the yields are taken to be their expected values; this represents inertia. The weak form of myopic expectations maintains that an individual will form the expectation today of the asset yield over the next year by setting this equal to today's yield, but will adjust it upwards (or downwards) by a fraction of the excess (shortfall) of today's yield from the yield a year ago: that is, some allowance will be made for the trend in the yield.

Lord Keynes (1937: 214) contended that individuals are confronted frequently with 'uncertain' knowledge in the sense that probabilities of outcomes just cannot be calculated: but decisions still have to be taken. To effect action he argued that:

(1) We assume that the present is a much more serviceable guide to the future than a candid examination of past experience would show it to have been hitherto. In other words we largely ignore the prospect of future changes about the actual character of which we know nothing.

(2) We assume that the *existing* state of opinion as expressed in prices and the character of existing output is based on a *correct* summing up of future prospects, so that we can accept it as such unless and until something new and relevant comes into the picture.

(3) Knowing that our own individual judgment is worthless, we endeavour to fall back on the judgment of the rest of the world which is perhaps better informed. That is, we endeavour to conform with the behaviour of the majority or the average. The psychology of a society of individuals each of whom is endeavouring to copy the others leads to what we may strictly term a *conventional* judgment.

2. *Adaptive* This mechanism supposes that the individual has somehow in the previous period formed an expectation of a given yield; and it hypothesizes that the individual will only alter that expectation if it should turn out to have been incorrect. If it turns out that the yield was under-predicted its expected value will be increased and vice versa; by how much the changes in the expectations will be adjusted by those errors will depend upon the temperament of the individual.

3. *Recursive* This mechanism is effectively one for altering given expectations, and the recursive method is one means of quantifying those initial expectations which has a long history in economics, psychology and statistical/econometric work. It is based on the view that the time series on the history of the variable itself will predict its likely future value. The future value is assumed to be a weighted average of the past values of the variable; in our example, of the past returns on a given stock. Different past time periods and weighting schemes are used in such time-series analysis. To take the latter first, a weighting scheme is often adopted that attaches smaller importance to more remote time periods and the weights advocated usually decline quickly, often exponentially. Such schemes are commonly referred to as distributed lag specifications of expected values. They permit the calculation of a measure of dispersion, or uncertainty or risk, surrounding the expected value. We can select weights (all less than one) so that they decline to zero after a number of periods and sum to unity. Such weights can be viewed as probabilities and used alongside the set of past values of the asset's yield to ascertain its variance or spread; the closer this lies to zero, the greater is the probability of the expected value's occurring.

4. *Evidential* In (1), (2) and (3) it is contended that past information is needed to predict the future. Furthermore, these schemes are applied to the variable itself without reference to the surrounding circumstances that have generated the pattern of outcome of asset yields. The *rational expectations* view maintains that individuals will seek information on all the variables and factors that affect the asset yields. In the extreme, we can imagine that, like government treasuries or central banks, they will attempt to formulate a set of variables that determine asset yields and the relationship between those yields and the variables. In that way they will arrive at an equation that links the asset yields to particular variables; the equation itself will be a weighted average of the variables, the weights representing the impact that a change in any one of the variables has on each asset's yield. Such 'determining' variables might be the rate of inflation, the central bank discount rate, the foreign exchange rate, the growth of the money supply or the government's budgetary position. Those who hold to the rational expectations view argue that the individual will take the expected value of the equation that determines the yield of each of the assets. The equation might not

be the 'correct' one, but we can assume that it is the best the individual can discover in the time (taking into account search costs). So the individual will find that the expected value of the asset's yield depends, for example, on the expected future values of some other variables, including government and central bank policy variables (such as the expected government deficit or surplus, and the rate of growth of the money supply). Hence, future and past information on other variables will be used; but not necessarily past values of the asset's yield.

The rational expectations notion implies that individuals construct a model of the determination of monetary yields and of inflation and then take the expected value of the equation that they believe determines those variables. There are three points worthy of mention here. The first is that this sort of process cannot realistically be adopted by all investors. It can be by unit trusts and investment fund managers and other professionals, and by some individuals who manage their own financial affairs (perhaps relying upon the help of other agents via the purchase of investment magazines). However, for many, small investors this will not only be impossible (because of limits imposed by hardware and software), but also suboptimal: they should invest, to minimize costs (monetary and psychic), in managed funds. The second point is that such a process produces an expected value for the particular asset's real yield, but if the individual has in mind a range of possible values of the causal variables, such as the money stock, then there will exist in his or her mind a range of feasible values for that yield. In that way a spread of yields around the expected value can be calculated. The third point is that under rational expectations individuals have to anticipate structural breaks; for example, if the central bank changes the way in which it determines the money supply people will have to be aware of this when forming his or her estimate of the future stock of money in the equation that they believe determines the rate of inflation.

We can now move on, naturally, to the notion that the individual maps out a set of possible states of the world and constructs a payoff matrix from investing a unit of currency in each of the assets that could compose a portfolio. These states of the world are various sets of circumstances that the individual imagines could occur; each one could represent a combination of events (such as differing combinations of government policies), and need not be limited to dichotomous events, such as the possibility of war or of peace. The most informative way of seeing this is to transpose the problem: assume the individual has in mind a range of possible real yields from investing a unit of currency in a specific asset. For each possible value the individual may have in mind various states of the economic–political scene that will give rise to them; such as, 'low rates of interest, a balanced government budget'.

When the individual feels certain about the outcome on a specific share, it will have the same value for each state of the world. In general, this will not be the case. It is then necessary for the individual to combine the range of outcomes for each share into an expected value. The orthodox argument is that to each possible outcome (or alternatively, state of the world) the individual will assign some degree of his or her strength of 'belief' in its occurrence. The conventional measure of the latter is the probability assigned to an outcome. The probability of each outcome multiplied by the outcome when summed across all outcomes is the expected value of the share's yield. From that process other characteristics of the probability density function for the share's outcome can be calculated (such as its variance and skewness). Thus there is a connection between the states of nature approach and the rational expectations schema. The events that are felt to cause the given possible share yields are alternative combinations of the determining variables (for example, monetary growth, short- and long-term interest rates) and their probabilities.

This connection brings us close to the logical theory of probability that was popularized by Lord Keynes (1921). But this and related ways developed in the literature of economics and philosophy for measuring 'degree of belief' have come in for criticism from those who hold that the epistemic standing of any feasible outcome in a set of outcomes cannot be represented by probability, subjective or otherwise, logically or frequentist based.

This sceptical view is held because of two claims: (i) the set of possible outcomes is not known, so that the probabilities cannot sum to unity (as required). In the language of statisticians, the universe of discourse is not known; and (ii) individuals frequently have to make decisions that are unique or are at best only partly redeemable. This is the case in the choice of a career; a portfolio investment, for which all capital could be lost. The gist of the argument here is that the probability distribution can only be sampled once; frequentist interpretations of probability, for example, then have no meaning. Such contentions led to the view that expectations are being formed and decisions taken by individuals under conditions of uncertainty and not under conditions of risk.

Instead of probability, it was proposed by G.L.S. Shackle (1949, 1979, and in many of his other works) that the individual would assess uncertainty by the degree of potential surprise. This was originally based upon his concept of degrees of possibility. The idea in a nutshell is that the individual will assign to any yield on a share a degree of surprise which measures the degree of surprise he or she would feel if that outcome were to come true. The degrees of surprise range from a zero value (so that the individual saw no obstacle to the outcome's occurring) to some maximum (which can vary across individuals) which indicates total disbelief in the occurrence of the particular outcome. The concept of belief is largely jettisoned, since an individual cannot believe simultaneously

213

in more than one outcome: in Shackle's schema all outcomes could in principle be assigned a degree of potential surprise of zero. The set of feasible outcomes for an asset's yield in that schematic can be derived in the ways outlined above (as Shackle's work has intimated): however, one of its limitations is that it cannot permit us to determine the individual's expected value of a share's yield. The measure of uncertainty and the set of expectations about any type of outcome are inputs into Shackle's novel theory of decision making under uncertainty.

Expectations, naturally, have no life of their own: they have to be incorporated into a model of decision-making or into a decision rule. Many models of normative or positive decision making are based on the use of probability as the measure of the epistemic standing of feasible outcomes. Shackle's theory and related perspective theory (Ford, 1987) appear to be the only ones that offer a decision rule based on an alternative measure.

There is a large body of experimental work in economics and psychology on the nature of the decision making models and rules that individuals utilize in a variety of situations. This kind of research has been extended to examine the behaviour of individuals acting on markets (such as the stock market) and in bargaining situations. By comparison, little work has investigated the expectations-formation mechanisms used by individuals, to determine whether they are concerned with the realism of their expectations, and how they measure their 'confidence' in them. For exceptions, see Hey (1985) and Ford and Ghose (1998). The paucity of such experiments may reflect the difficulty of framing them so as to force the subjects to reveal their true, underlying, measure of uncertainty. Even in experiments designed to evaluate the decision models that subjects use, and which are easier to construct, and for which an appropriate incentive scheme can be devised, framing effects have been a major problem in the interpretation of the findings ever since the pioneering study by Kahneman and Tversky (1979).

J.L. FORD

Bibliography

Earl, P.E. (1986) *Lifestyle Economics: Consumer Behaviour in a Turbulent World*, Brighton, Wheatsheaf.

Ford, J.L. (1987) *Choice under Uncertainty: A Perspective Theory Approach*, Aldershot, Edward Elgar.

Ford, J.L. and Ghose, S. (1998) 'The Primitive Uncertainty Construct: Possibility, Potential Surprise, Probability and Belief; Some Experimental Evidence', *Metroeconomica*, **49**: 195–220.

Hey, J.D. (1985) 'The Possibility of Possibility', *Journal of Economic Studies*, **12**: 70–88.

Jeffrey, R. (1992) *Probability and the Art of Judgement*, Cambridge, Cambridge University Press.

Kahneman, D. and Tversky, A. (1979) 'Prospect Theory: Analysis of Decision Under Risk', *Econometrica*, **47**: 263–91.

Keynes, J.M. (1921) *Treatise on Probability*, London, Macmillan.

Keynes, J.M. (1937) 'The General Theory of Employment', *Quarterly Journal of Economics*, **57**: 209–23.

Levi, I. (1972) 'On Potential Surprise and Inquiry', in Carter. C.F. and Ford, J.L. (eds) *Uncertainty and Expectations in Economics: Essays in Honour of G.L.S. Shackle*, Oxford, Basil Blackwell.

Lucas, R.E. (1981) *Studies in Business-Cycle Theory*, Oxford, Basil Blackwell.

Muth, J.F. (1961) 'Rational Expectations and the Theory of Price Movements', *Econometrica*, **29**: 315–35.

Ozga, S. (1965) *Expectations and Uncertainty in Economics*, London: Weidenfeld & Nicolson.

Sargent, T.J. (1986) *Rational Expectations and Inflation*, New York, Harper & Row.

Shackle, G.L.S. (1949) *Expectation in Economics*, Cambridge, Cambridge University Press.

Shackle, G.L.S. (1979) *Imagination and the Nature of Choice*, Edinburgh, Edinburgh University Press

Simon, H.A. (1984) *Reason in Human Affairs*, Oxford, Basil Blackwell.

Wright, G. and Ayton, P. (eds) (1994) *Subjective Probability*, London, Wiley.

Experimental Asset Markets

Experimental asset markets offer an important avenue towards understanding financial markets by providing the possibility of changing and isolating factors that may influence price evolution. A typical experiment consists of a number of participants who are initially endowed with some combination of cash and/or a security whose 'value' is described in the instructions — see, for example, the surveys by Smith and Williams (1992) and Davis and Holt (1993: 162–7). The subjects may subsequently trade this security using a computer network through an auction procedure defined by the experimenters.

A laboratory asset market devised by Smith, Suchanek and Williams (1988b) established a number of trading periods in order to examine the time evolution of the trading prices and volume. A series of experiments that has been replicated under many different conditions demonstrated the boom and subsequent bust endogenous to trading — see Porter and Smith (1994) and references therein. Similar asset markets have also been used to study the role of asymmetric information and insider trading — see Güth, Krahnen and Rieck (1997) and reference therein. A standard 'bubbles' experiment involves nine participants who are given some distribution of cash and shares of an asset or security which will pay a dividend, with expected dividend of 24 cents, at the end of each of the 15 periods. Thus the realistic or 'fundamental' value of the asset is clearly $3.60 at the outset of the experiment and declines stepwise by $0.24 each period until it becomes worthless after the 15th period. Classical theories of economics or finance, such as the rational expectations, would predict a time evolution of the trading price that is similar to this fundamental value with some fluctuations due to randomness of trading.

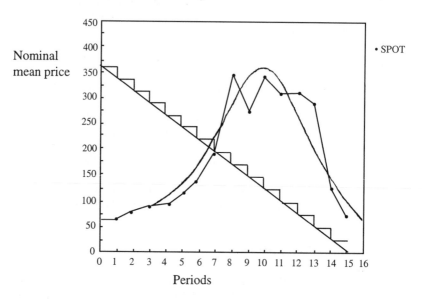

Prediction: An experiment of Porter and Smith involves trading an asset whose fundamental value is given by the stepwise decreasing line. The connected dots show the trading prices for each period. The smooth curve is an out-of-sample prediction generated by the differential equation (Caginalp and Balenovich, 1994) using only the first-period trading price, the fundamental value and the two parameters calibrated from another experiment. The presence of a futures market in this experiment does change the nature of the bubble significantly so that a good prediction is possible even with parameters calibrated from an experiment with only a spot market.

Figure 1: A 'bubbles' experiment and differential equations

In the experiments, however, one usually observes an initial period trading price that is well below the realistic value of $3.60, followed by rising prices that overshoot the fundamental value in the intermediate periods, creating a characteristic 'bubble' and a dramatic 'crash' of prices near the end of the experiment (see Figure 1). The large number of variations on this experiment have included the use of short selling and margin buying, the imposition of trading costs, the removal of any uncertainty of expected dividends, the use of equal initial endowment to traders, the addition of futures markets, the imposition of price change limitations and the use of corporate executives or small business persons as the subject pool. None of these factors were found to eliminate the boom and bust; as Porter and Smith (1994) concluded: 'In replicable laboratory experiments, experience, particularly common group experience, together with common information is sufficient to yield trading near fundamental value'.

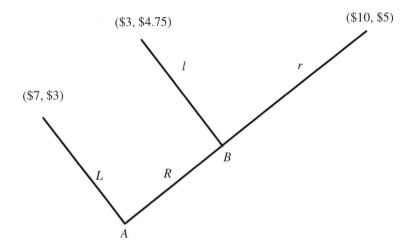

Note: Player *A* can choose between *L* and *R*. If he chooses *L* the game terminates. If he or chooses *R* then the outcome depends upon the choice (*l* or *r*) of Player *B*. The payout for Player *A* and *B*, respectively, is given by (*X*, *Y*) in each case. In this example, in which Player *A* can choose between $10 contingent upon Player *B*'s self-interested maximization (choice *R*) or a 'secure' $7, 20 per cent of the subjects chose the secure payout. In other experiments featuring a smaller difference for Player *A*, the secure choice was made by up to 85 per cent of the participants.

Figure 2: Design of Beard and Beil experimental games

The experiments with no uncertainty about the expected dividends, in particular, draw attention to the idea, expressed above, that the actions and strategies of other traders can provide the only element of uncertainty to participants. This leads to an important distinction between exercising self-optimizing behaviour and the reliance upon the the self-optimizing behaviour of others. In a set of fundamental experiments, Beard and Beil (1994) demonstrated in simple experimental game theory (see Figure 2), that Player *A* would choose the smaller but certain payoff over the larger payoff that was contingent simply upon Player *B* choosing the larger of two payoffs (with no contingencies) for Player *B*. In the Beard and Beil experiments, extensive experience in the role of Player *B* gradually led Player *A* to a greater reliance on others' self-optimizing behaviour, consistent with the asset market conclusions of Porter and Smith (1994). If traders cannot rely absolutely upon the self-optimizing behaviour of others, then the motivation for selling an overvalued security or buying an undervalued security is incomplete in many market situations. In particular, if there is a downtrend while the asset is trading below fundamental value, then traders are explicitly receiving some information as to the unreliability of the congregate self-optimization of the group.

From this perspective, it is difficult to avoid the conclusion that the price trend contains some important information on the strategies and inclinations of the other traders. In attempting to understand the reasons for the evolution of bubbles and their inevitable demise, one must consider the price trend in conjunction with the deviation of price from the fundamental value. A basic economic factor involved in all of the asset market experiments is the balance of cash to shares. The supply of cash is fixed throughout the experiment (except for the influx of dividends), while the total market value of the shares is proportional to the trading price of the shares. Suppose one focuses on the ratio of total cash to total market value of the asset. After a rapid rise in trading price, this ratio is considerably lower, so that even with the same inclination to continue the trend, traders have a relatively lower supply of cash to bid up the shares. This finite size effect thus plays an important part in these experiments, as it undoubtedly does in many market situations.

If price trend and finite size are important complements to valuation in market phenomena, then several questions arise. First, how can one model these effects in terms of mathematics and statistics? Second, can one make accurate forecasts of the experiments? Third, can one use these models to develop quantitative links between experiments and world markets? And finally, what other experiments can one perform to test these models and provide quantitative explanations of other phenomena in markets? Mathematical modelling that addresses these questions has the potential for enhancing the role of experimental asset markets in terms of understanding (particularly quantitatively) a spectrum of market behaviour that is not adequately explained in terms of efficient market theories.

A natural way of performing this modelling is by use of a set of ordinary differential equations, which can also be studied as finite difference equations, as is done in numerical study with a computer. Let $P(t)$ denote price as a function of time, while $B(t)$ is the fraction of total assets that are represented by the asset, and $k(t)$ is the probability that someone with a unit of cash will choose to purchase the asset. Caginalp and Ermentrout (1990) used these variables to model a single asset under the assumptions that the rate of change of price, $\partial P/\partial t$, is given by the excess demand which is naturally related to B and k. The transition rate, k, is composed of two components involving the recent price trend and the difference between $B(t)$ and the fundamental value. The two components are weighted with coefficients F_1 and F_2, which characterize the system. Using a single experiment of Porter and Smith (1994) for example, the values F_1 and F_2 can be calibrated so that a forecast of any other experiment (see Figure 1) is possible by using only the initial period's trading price (Caginalp and Balenovich, 1996). These forecasts were significantly better than those of the efficient market hypothesis. Using these experimentally calibrated values of F_1 and F_2, one can also obtain good agreement with recent market crashes such as that of 1987, under the assumption that the fundamental value of the average stock is unchanged during the week.

In a basic test of this model, Caginalp, Porter and Smith (1998b) conducted 'baseline' experiments to calibrate the parameters F_1 and F_2. In subsequent experiments that restrict the trading prices during (only) the first period, it was possible to make good predictions from the differential equations for the entire price dynamics before the experiment starts.

An alternative approach to describe markets quantitatively is to use a statistical time-series procedure (known as ARIMA) that extracts a model without reference to any economics assumptions. The simplest of these models would just be a random walk, in which the expected value for the next data is the current data. This is a possible model for asset prices once fundamental factors have been extracted from data (for example, in the experiments this would be the trading price minus the expected dividend value). Another possibility would be a 'pure momentum' model in which $y(t + 1) - y(t)$, the expected value of tomorrow's derivative, is today's derivative, $y(t) - y(t - 1)$. Caginalp and Constantine (1995) applied these methods to the ratio of two closed-end funds investing in Germany with essentially identical portfolios, thereby eliminating any changes in fundamental value. They found that the optimal ARIMA model is that which interpolates midway between the two, namely, $y(t + 1) - y(t) = 0.5[y(t) - y(t - 1)]$. This model, which produced good out-of-sample predictions on the market data, was also capable of predicting the price evolution in the Porter and Smith experiments. The success of these predictions provides a strong quantitative link between the experimental and world markets, and an indication that similar market forces underlie both.

The availability of several theories that can be used to make at least short-term predictions suggests the possibility of designing experiments that can be used to gauge the forecasts. A series of experiments was done to compare the relative accuracy of the predictions. One of the forecasting methods involved excess bids (Smith, Suchanek and Williams, 1988a), where the price change in period t is assumed to be proportional to the difference between the number of bids and number of offers submitted in period $t - 1$. The differential equations model was updated with recent price data in order to predict the next period and two periods ahead. Along with the ARIMA model and random walk, it employed human forecasts by a participant who had been among the most successful traders in a similar experiment. The level of success was comparable among the different forecasts, with the excess bids having the edge in the one-period-ahead forecasts while the updated differential equations forecast performed better than the other models in the two-period forecasts.

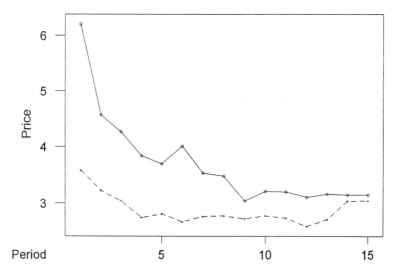

Note: For each period the mean of all of the experiments entailing an initial surplus of cash relative to asset is computed for each period and displayed by the solid line. Similarly the means for the experiments with an initial surplus of asset are displayed by the dashed line. The mean cash-rich values are higher for the duration of the experiment, although the difference is most pronounced at the outset. The solid line represents the mean of cash-rich experiments, and the dashed line the mean of asset-rich experiments.

Figure 3: Mean period prices for initial public offering experiments

Recently, the experimental asset markets have been used to address some other problems that have implications for both fundamental economics and pragmatic finance. A series of asset experiments (Caginalp, Porter and Smith, 1998a) is designed similarly to those described above except that there is only one dividend of expectation value $3.60 at the end of the experiment, so the fundamental value is constant throughout the experiment. In some of the experiments, the total cash endowment at the start of the experiment exceeded the total value of the asset, while the reverse was true in the others. In experiments with the higher proportion in cash, the trading prices were higher than the others in comparable periods (see Figure 3). This is contrary to what would be predicted by classical economics or game theory, and consistent with the predictions of the differential equations. The difference is most significant at the outset and gradually tapers near the end of the experiment. The experiments also suggest that there is a time scale on which an evolution towards fundamental value occurs even though there is no new information about the true value during the experiment. Also, a very significant aspect of this line of experimentation involves the finiteness of cash and security. In particular, the initial price avoids the issue of a prior trend. The traders tend to establish a price of almost twice the fundamental value when there is twice the available cash.

These experiments are a direct analog to initial public offerings (IPOs) in the financial markets. A special case of IPOs involves closed end funds which trade like ordinary stocks independent of their fundamental value consisting of the total value per share of the securities owned. The persistent discount in many of these funds has been a puzzle both theoretically and fundamentally. From the perspective of these experiments, as well as the differential equations theory, the discount can be explained on the basis of a saturated market at the outset. That is, when trading commences, many of those in the game already own the shares and there is inadequate cash on the part of the people who would be likely to purchase the closed end fund.

Laboratory asset markets, coupled with quantitative modelling methods, have the potential to address issues in financial markets such as volatility or inefficient pricing in IPOs discussed above. An important conclusion on the volatility of markets in general is that price limits do not prevent bubbles, and may enhance them (Porter and Smith, 1994: 120). The recent sharp declines in currencies in Southeast Asia raise another question as to whether, and in what proportions, large-scale speculator selling can destabilize a market. Questions such as this can be addressed in appropriately designed laboratory experiments complemented with differential equations modelling that takes into account different groups with distinct interests and levels of capital.

GUNDUZ CAGINALP, DAVID PORTER AND VERNON L. SMITH

Bibliography

Beard, T.R. and Beil, R.A. (1994) 'Do People Rely on the Self-Interested Maximization of Others? An Experimental Test', *Management Science*, **40**: 252–62.

Caginalp, G. and Balenovich, D. (1996) 'Trend-Based Asset Flow in Technical Analysis and Securities Marketing', *Psychology and Marketing*, **13**: 407–44.

Caginalp, G. and Constantine, G. (1995) 'Statistical Inference and Modeling of Momentum in Stock Prices', *Applied Mathematical Finance*, **2**: 225–42.

Caginalp, G. and Ermentrout, G.B. (1990) 'A Kinetic Thermodynamic Approach to the Psychology of Fluctuations in Financial Markets', *Applied Mathematics Letters*, **4**: 17–19.

Caginalp, G., Porter, D. and Smith, V.L. (1998a) 'Initial Cash/Asset Ratio and Asset Prices: An Experimental Study', *Proceedings of the National Academy of Science*, **95**: 756–61.

Caginalp, G., Porter, D. and Smith, V.L. (1998b) 'Momentum and Overreaction in Experimental Asset Markets', preprint, University of Arizona.

Davis, D.D. and Holt, C.A. (1993) *Experimental Economics*, Princeton, NJ, Princeton University Press.

Güth, W., Krahnen, J. and Rieck, C. (1997): 'Financial Markets with Asymmetric Information: A Pilot Study Focusing on Insider Advantages', *Journal of Economic Psychology*, **18**: 235–58.

Porter, D. and Smith, V.L. (1994) 'Stock Market Bubbles in the Laboratory,' *Applied Mathematical Finance*, **1**: 111–28.

Smith, V.L. (1982) 'Microeconomic Systems as an Experimental Science', *American Economic Review*, **72**: 923–55.

Smith, V.L., Suchanek, G.L. and Williams, A.W. (1988a) 'An Experimental Analysis of Stock Market Bubbles: Prices, Expectations and Market Efficiency', *Finanzmarkt und Portfolio Management*, **3**: 19-32.

Smith, V.L., Suchanek, G.L. and Williams, A.W. (1988b) 'Bubbles, Crashes and Endogenous Expectations in Experimental Spot Asset Markets', *Econometrica*, **56**: 1119–51.

Smith, V.L. and Williams, A.W. (1992) 'Experimental Market Economics', *Scientific American*, **267**: 116–21.

Williams, A.W. and Smith, V.L. (1984) 'Cyclical Double-Auction on Markets With and Without Speculators', *Journal of Business*, **57**: 1–33.

Experimental Economics

Although consumer decision making is a highly complex process, laboratory studies of individual decision making have typically been conducted to test a single assumption about behaviour. A study of decision making under uncertainty might, for example, employ a binary lottery choice. The criticism of this approach to researching consumer decision making is that it is, in fact, too basic. While some would argue that this criticism renders this approach to research useless, proponents would claim it as an advantage. If a basic expected result cannot be found in a simple environment, it is unlikely to be found in a more complex environment. When trying to figure out why an expected result was not found, there are fewer other factors to eliminate. This approach allows researchers to isolate a single issue. Results from the basic experiment form a starting-point for studying more complex issues — a single experiment can form the background for many more complicated studies. This type of experimental research in economics took off via the pioneering work of Vernon Smith in the 1960s. Some key articles are reprinted in Smith's (1990) edited volume.

The plan of this entry is as follows. The next four sections offer an outline of selected results in individual decision making. Following this is a discussion of some important methodological considerations regarding this type of laboratory research. Concluding remarks are presented in the final section.

Dealing with risks

Expected Utility Theory (von Neumann and Morgenstern, 1944) is a normative model of choice under uncertainty meant to characterize human behaviour. The theory is based on a set of very basic and plausible-sounding assumptions. One of these, known as the substitution (or independence) axiom states that when presented with two options, one should focus on what is different between the two options, rather than what is the same. Allais (1953) quickly constructed a counter example. Kahneman and Tversky (1979) replicated Allais's result using the following example:

Problem 1. Choose between the following two options:

A.   *$2500 with probability 0.33*
            $2400 with probability 0.66
            $0 with probability 0.01
B.   *$2400 with certainty.*

Problem 2. Choose between the following two options:

A.   *$2500 with probability 0.33*
            $0 with probability 0.67
B.   *$2400 with probability 0.34*
            $0 with probability 0.66.

Since problem 2 is obtained from problem 1 by reducing the chance of earning $2400 by 0.66 for both options *A* and *B*, the substitution axiom would predict that someone who prefers *A* to *B* in problem 1 would also prefer *A* to *B* in problem 2. Kahneman and Tversky found from their experiments that 18 per cent prefer *A* in problem 1 and 83 per cent prefer A in problem 2. They theorize that this behaviour is caused by a form of risk aversion caused by an attraction to certain outcomes, and call this the 'certainty effect'.

Further research suggests that characterizing people as 'risk averse' or 'risk loving' is an oversimplification. Tversky and Kahneman (1986) conducted another series of experiments where choices were identical except that the choices were framed in terms of gains in one case and losses in the other.

> *Problem 3.* *Assume yourself richer by $300 than you are today. Choose between the following:*

A. *A sure gain of $100*
B. *A 50 per cent chance to gain $200 and a 50 per cent chance to gain nothing.*

> *Problem 4.* *Assume yourself richer by $500 than you are today. Choose between the following:*

A. *A sure loss of $100*
B. *A 50 per cent chance to lose $200 and a 50 per cent chance to lose nothing.*

Since 72 per cent of subjects choose *A* in problem 3 but only 36 per cent choose *A* in problem 4, the authors conclude that subjects are risk averse when it comes to gains, but risk seeking when it comes to losses. Their studies of decision making in the presence of risk led Kahneman and Tversky (1979) to offer Prospect Theory as an alternative to Expected Utility Theory.

Understanding risky situations
Consider the following problem:

> *You have the option to bid on an item which is worth between $0 and $100 to its current owner with all values equally likely. There is no way for you to ascertain its value in advance. The item is worth 50 per cent more to you than it is to the current owner which means that if it is worth $50 to the current owner it is worth $75 to you. You may make only one bid. If your bid is higher than or equal to the owner's value they will accept it and you will receive the item and pay the bid price. If your bid is lower than the owner's value then they will reject your bid and you will pay nothing. What is your bid?*

Ball, Bazerman and Caroll (1991) gave MBA students the chance to bid in a similar game 20 times. They found that 93 per cent of the subjects chose to bid on the item, with a mean bid of 53. Subjects arrived at this bid using the following type of logic: 'The value is uncertain but will be $50 on average. That means that the average value to me is $75. So if I make a bid of $50 I can make a reasonable profit and have a good chance of having my bid accepted'.

Their logic is irrational. The 'correct' bid for an individual who is risk neutral or risk averse is zero, a bid made by only 7 per cent of participants. To see this, consider an alternative way of analysing the problem: 'Suppose I bid $60. Since I know that the owner won't sell to me for less than his value, this means that the true value must be between $0 and $60. On average this means the item is worth $30 and that I will have paid $60 for something worth $45'.

Two implications for individual decision making come from this study. First, people make mistakes when thinking about probabilistic situations and overpay — a situation called the 'winner's curse'. The winner's curse is not unique to this study: Kagel and Levin (1986) find further evidence in an experimental auction market for an item of uncertain value. This problem is exacerbated by the fact that people are unable to correct their logical errors despite feedback that they are doing something wrong. In both studies, subjects earned cash rewards which were linked to their decisions. Both found that subjects steadily lost money during the experiment, yet chose neither to stop bidding nor to reduce their bids to avoid losses.

A second implication — that people do not understand uncertain outcomes correctly — comes from protocol analysis conducted by Ball, Bazermand and Caroll (1991). Subjects were asked to say whatever they were thinking during the experiment. Comments were tape recorded and coded. These protocols, and subsequent regression analysis of the data, revealed that most subjects did not treat the values of the 20 items as statistically independent, despite emphasis in the written and verbal instruction and the fact that they had all recently studied the concept during their statistics class. Observations of gambling behaviour are consistent with these findings. Some people will play a number on a roulette wheel which has not occurred because they believe that this makes it more likely to be chosen. Others will choose numbers which have occurred recently because they believe this makes them more likely to be chosen. Assuming that the roulette wheel is, as advertised, calibrated to choose numbers with equal frequencies, both rules for choosing numbers are both incorrect and harmless.

Value formation

Economic theory predicts that people will have a 'reservation value' for goods. At prices above this value they should be willing to sell. At prices below this value they should be willing to buy. Environmental economists suspected that there was a gap between the willingness to pay (WTP) and willingness to accept (WTA). To investigate, Boyce and colleagues (1992) designed four treatments which used small Norfolk Island pine trees (a small tree that is suitable for both a houseplant and an outdoor tree) as the item to be bought and sold. In the first two treatments, subjects (i) were asked to make an offer to buy the tree or (ii) were given a tree and asked to set a price at which they would sell the tree to the experimenters for cash. In the second two treatments, subjects were told that the tree would be killed if (iii) they failed to bid enough to purchase the tree or (iv) they sold the tree back to the experimenter. Subjects in all conditions were given an initial balance of $40 in conditions (i) and (iii) or $30 and a tree in conditions (ii) and (iv). The decision about whether the experimenter would buy or sell the tree was made using a random device which chose a price with which to compare subjects' bids or offers.

In treatments (i) and (ii), WTA was $8, and WTP was $4.81, which meant the gap, as measured by their ratio, was 1.66. In (iii) and (iv) WTA was $18.43 and WTP was $7.81 for a ratio of 2.36. The authors conclude that there is substantial evidence of a WTA/WTP gap. The authors suggest that price differences between treatments (i) and (iii) and between (ii) and (iv) might have something to do with an 'intrinsic value' which subjects placed on the trees. They theorize that the disproportionate size of the offers in treatment (iv) can be explained if subjects felt that since it was their tree, they bore 'the moral responsibility associated with the needless death of a tree' (Boyce et al., 1992: 1367).

Relative payoffs

A different group of studies of economic behaviour have focused on non-pecuniary issues in decision making. One tool which has been used to examine fairness in decision making is the *Ultimatum Bargaining Game*. In these experiments there are two players called a *proposer* and a *respondent* . The proposer determines a split of a fixed amount of money, say $10, and the respondent accepts or rejects the proposal. If the proposal is accepted the money is divided according to the proposal and each bargainer leaves the experiment with cash in hand. If the proposal is rejected then neither negotiator makes any money. While this is a very abstract representation of a negotiation, the relevance of the game may be better understood if the proposer is renamed 'retail seller' and the respondent is renamed 'shopper'.

Economic theory makes a clear prediction about the outcome of this game. This prediction is the subgame perfect equilibrium of the game, where the proposer makes an offer which leaves the respondent with the smallest possible increment of money. If money must be divided in dollars this means $9 for him-herself and $1 for the respondent. The respondent then accepts what he or she is offered, since any amount of money is preferred to no money.

Güth, Schmittberger and Schwarze (1982) show that subjects in this game are motivated by more than just money. Proposers' offers are, on average, much closer to a 50–50 split than the equilibrium prediction suggests. In addition, respondents are likely to reject offers which deviate from a 50–50 split. The authors conclude that respondents consider fairness as well as money in making their acceptance decisions. Anticipating this behaviour on the part of respondents, the proposers keep as much of the pie for themselves as they believe they can, given the fairness considerations of the respondents.

Social status affects which outcomes are considered fair. Ball and Eckel (1996) report on a series of ultimatum bargaining games where subjects are awarded artificial status. Subjects are paired so that all possible combinations of status and role in the bargaining game are tested. Proposers and respondents know the status of their opponents, but their opponent's identity is concealed. Their data suggest that high-status respondents receive higher offers than low-status respondents. If high-status individuals fare better in decision-making environments, it is sensible for people to pay to achieve high status. This result has implications for marketing goods so that they are perceived to confer high status on the purchaser.

Hoffman and Spitzer (1985) study another type of bargaining problem. In their research one subject is assigned the role of *controller* and has the unilateral authority to decide the outcome of the bargaining problem if no agreement can be reached through negotiation. This role is assigned based on either a coin flip or the results of a skill game. The authors find, contrary to predictions of economic theory, that controllers are most likely to exploit their advantage when they are assigned the role based on the skill test and told (a second treatment) that they had earned the right to be the controller. Subjects in this experiment will treat each other more fairly than economic theory predicts unless they believe they are entitled to their position of advantage. This result yields insights into the results of other experiments in this section and suggests that people care about justice as well as money.

Methodology

A brief word is in order about important considerations when evaluating experimental work on decision making. As noted in the introduction, *realism* in experiments for the purpose of replicating all of the detail of the real-world environment may be sacrificed in order to create a clean test of one experimental factor. There is yet another reason for abandoning a search for absolute replication of the real world: *practicality*. It is futile to try to replicate every minute detail of a decision-making situation. Someone will always be able to hypothesize a missed detail which could invalidate the replication. Better to design an experiment which allows us to learn something useful about the most important issues to be studied.

Control is the next consideration in evaluating experimental results. By limiting the differences between treatments in an experiment to those which the experimenter has chosen, results can be attributed to the factors to be tested. If, for example, in the ultimatum game experiments discussed above the proposer is called 'management' and the respondent called 'union', subjects are likely to respond differently from how they will in the context neutral case which is reported. If this were to occur, the data would test a joint hypothesis of behaviour in an ultimatum game and feelings about labour unions. Provided that this is not the intent of the experiment, this would constitute a loss of control. Such losses of control can be eliminated by the experimenter. Other factors, such as learning by the subjects, cannot be eliminated from the experiment, but can be statistically analysed and reported. By changing only one factor of the experiment at a time, results can be correctly attributed.

Finally, subjects should receive payments which are linked to their performance. It must be known how outcomes translate into money, and there must be enough money involved so that the subjects care more about the decisions that they make than any other factor such as 'impressing the experimenter'. Some experiments have been, and continue to be, conducted without these payoffs. While it is entirely likely that some results would not be changed by a lack of payoffs, in other cases unpaid subjects show a higher variance of outcomes or even a different result entirely from paid subjects. (See Ball and Eckel, 1996, for an example.) Concerns about whether or not subjects need to be paid is one of the main issues which sometimes separates psychologists' experiments on economic phenomena from those peformed by economists. Further discussion of these design issues is found in Hey (1992).

Conclusion

Laboratory tests of individual decision making are a necessary partner to theories of behaviour. One should be just as sceptical of accepting an untested social science theory as of taking an untested but 'theoretically sound' drug. On the other hand, it is important to avoid the temptation to ignore a theory just because an experiment produced an anomalous result. A better approach is one where theories are tested and experiments producing unexpected results are carefully analysed and replicated. Theories can then be adjusted to account for the behavioural results and retested. These are the methods which will ultimately produce the strongest and most reliable research results.

SHERYL B. BALL

Bibliography

Allais, M. (1953) 'Le Comportement de l'Homme Rationel Devant le Risque, Critique des Postulates et Exiomes de l'École Americane' (The Behaviour of the Rational Man in the Face of Risk: Critique of the Postulates and Axioms of the American School), *Econometrica*, **21**: 503–46.

Ball, S.B., Bazerman, M.H. and Caroll, J.S. (1991) 'An Evaluation of Learning in the Bilateral Winner's Curse', *Organizational Behavior and Human Decision Processes*, **48**: 1–22.

Ball, S.B. and Eckel, C.C. (1996) 'Buying Status: Experimental Evidence on Status in Negotiation', *Psychology and Marketing*, **13**: 381–405.

Boyce, R.R., Brown, T.C., McClelland, G.H., Peterson, G.L. and Schulze, W.D. (1992) 'An Experimental Examination of Intrinsic Values as a Source of the WTA–WTP Disparity', *American Economic Review*, **82**: 1366–73.

Güth, W., Schmittberger, R. and Schwarze, B. (1982) 'An Experimental Analysis of Ultimatum Bargaining', *Journal of Economic Behavior and Organization*, **3**: 367–88.

Hey, J.D. (1992) 'Experiments in Economics — and Psychology', in Lea, S.E.G., Webley, P. and Young, B.M. (eds) *New Directions in Economic Psychology*, Aldershot, Edward Elgar: 85–98.

Hoffman, E. and Spitzer, M.L. (1985) 'Entitlements, Rights and Fairness: An Experimental Examination of Subjects' Concepts of Distributive Justice', *Journal of Legal Studies*, **14**: 259–97 (reprinted in Smith, V.L. (ed.) (1990) *Experimental Economics*, Aldershot, Edward Elgar: 203–41).

Kagel, J.H. and Levin, D. (1986) 'The Winner's Curse and Public Information in Common Value Auctions', *American Economic Review*, **76**: 894–920.

Kahneman, D. and Tversky, A. (1979) 'Prospect Theory: An Analysis of Decision Under Risk', *Econometrica*, **47**: 263–91.

Smith, V.L. (ed.) (1990) *Experimental Economics*, Aldershot, Edward Elgar.

Tversky, A. and Kahneman, D. (1986) 'Rational Choice and the Framing of Decisions', *Journal of Business*, **59**: S251–76.

von Neumann, J. and Morgenstern, O. (1944) *Theory of Games and Economic Behavior*, Princeton, NJ, Princeton University Press.

Fairness

Following Rawls's definitive writing on justice as fairness, the normative concept of justice has been operationalized in the empirical literature as fairness. Thus an understanding of fairness in any specific context would need to be grounded in its normative foundation. The normative foundation for the fairness of economic behaviour is found in philosophical deliberations on economic justice.

The notion of economic justice in the context of a free-market ideology is seriously constrained, as it is caught in the conflict between the two competing values of contemporary culture: individualism and egalitarianism. While individualism sees a rational economic agent driven by competitions and egoistic self-interest, egalitarianism sees the same agent being motivated by a concern for justice and a sense of the equality of all.

The normative foundation of economic individualism is typically traced back to the utilitarian philosophies. Chief of these are: the Lockian theory of natural rights, the Hobbesian notion of egoistic utilitarianism, Adam Smith's vision of the 'invisible-hand-aided' free market, as well as Spencer's social Darwinian presumption of the 'survival of the fittest' in the progression of economic competitions.

The normative basis for economic egalitarianism has its roots in the deontological philosophies in modernity: the Kantian theory of moral rights and duties and the Rawlsian theory of distributive justice. In contrast to the egoistic focus of the utilitarian tradition, both deontological theories emphasize not only the restraint of self-interest in economic pursuits, but also the importance of the universal rules of procedural justice (for example, equality in treatment) and 'outcome justice' (for example, due rewards) in the affirmation of each individual economic agent's sense of fairness and dignity.

While both individualism and egalitarianism are valued in contemporary culture, it is the ethos of individualism that forms the core of the free-market ideology. And as such, this prevailing economic ideology inevitably comes into conflict with the value of economic egalitarianism. The tension of this fundamental individualism–egalitarianism divide has manifested itself in the persistent 'efficiency versus equality' debate in virtually all domains of economic behaviour.

However, it is believed that there is now 'indisputable' evidence showing that the free-market system's efficiency in the allocation of societal resources 'cannot be surpassed by currently available alternative systems' (for example, Kuenne, 1993: 385). The question of economic justice thus becomes whether the free-market system, having already satisfied the value of efficiency, would also result in a just and fair allocation of existing societal resources. This question has been debated in economic philosophy (from various perspectives including contractarianism and libertarianism), in game theory (for example, decision theoretic models and social choice theory), and in theories of rationality including multiple forms of rationality (for example, utility-maximization Rawlsian deliberative rationality).

In normative economics, several economists have argued that the mutually beneficial exchange process of the free-market system, when aided by conditions specified in the envy-free or superfairness theories (for example, corrections of individual initial endowment, considerations of intergenerational factors, and individual efforts), can ensure that the entire economic system reaches a state of equilibrium whereby no individual agent would envy or prefer another's 'bundle' to his/her own. However, the impracticality of achieving this superfair state is widely recognized (for reviews, see Silver, 1989; Zajac, 1995).

Normative literature aside, there exists a limited empirical literature on fairness in economic behaviour. This literature pertains to both micro issues of individuals as an economic agent and macro issues of the fairness of the allocation of limited societal resources. Several studies in this literature are relevant to two questions which are of fundamental significance to economic justice: 'As economic agents, are individuals primarily motivated by egoistic self-interest?'; and 'In the allocation of limited resources, is the principle of meritocracy, the key to free-market efficiency, compatible with the principle of "equality of treatment"?'.

Regarding the former question concerning the egoistic motive, empirical findings appear to converge in suggesting that individual economic agents are not solely motivated by egoistic self-interest, other prosocial motives in the form of collectivism or altruism may under certain circumstances be in operation to ensure a greater good for a greater number of people (for example, Batson, 1996; Korsgaard, Melino and Lester, 1997).

Concerning the latter question of merit-based allocation, findings also converge in suggesting two somewhat antagonistic trends. On the one hand, a merit-based allocation, while achieving the goal of efficiency, is bound to be in conflict with equality-based allocation. On the other hand, allocations based on merit are typically perceived as fairer and more just than those based on the particularities of the individual such as in diversity-based allocations (that is, preferential or quota hiring based primarily on candidate ethnicity or gender).

Therefore, empirical data, reflecting the normative analysis, have shown that the prevailing free-market ideology based on efficiency is at odds with the goal of social justice as equality for all. However, justice concerns are a fundamental human motive (for example, Lerner, 1982) and that in the literature of social and organizational justice, studies have repeatedly shown that violations of the rights and dignity of individual economic agents can have far-reaching organizational and societal consequences (for a review, see Singer, 1997).

Cognizant of these facts, many scholars have turned to the search for the best tradeoffs between the two goals of economic efficiency and social justice. While some advocate rational means in the search by emphasizing the purposiveness of economic agency or a reasoned consensus of a fundamental ethos for a fair society (for example, Hudson, Miller and Feder, 1994; Kuenne, 1993), others appeal to the notions of compassion, cooperation and trust (for reviews, see Kipnis and Meyers, 1985). Either way, a practical solution would need to involve ongoing social dialogues based on an enhanced moral sensitivity towards opposing points of view.

Regardless of the means to achieve a balanced tradeoff, ultimately there can be only one treadable path for all meaningful economic endeavours: one that fosters economic justice by integrating moral considerations with those of efficiency. In a similar vein, Etzioni (1989) argues for an I/we paradigm of economic decision making that links utility with morality, while Sen (1996: 8) argues for the importance of 'the use of substantive ethical principles and moral sentiments in business and economic behaviour', and suggests that 'we can ignore them only by impoverishing economic analysis and by demeaning the sophistication and breadth of human conduct'.

MING SINGER

Bibliography

Batson, C.D. (1996) 'Do Prosocial Motives Have any Business in Business?' *Social Justice Research*, **9**: 7–26.

Etzioni, A. (1989) *The Moral Dimension: Towards a New Economics*, New York, Free Press.

Hudson, M., Miller, G.J. and Feder, K. (1994) *A Philosophy for a Fair Society*, London, Shepherd-Walwyn.

Kipnis, K. and Meyers, D. (eds) (1985) *Economic Justice: Private Rights and Public Responsibilities*, Totowa, NJ, Rowman & Allanheld.

Korsgaard, M.A., Meglino, B.M. and Lester, S.W. (1997) 'Beyond Helping: Do Other-Oriented Values Have Broader Implications in Organizations?', *Journal of Applied Psychology*, **82**: 160–77.

Kuenne, R.E. (1993) *Economic Justice in American Society*, Princeton, NJ, Princeton University Press.

Lerner, M.J. (1982) 'The Justice Motive in Human Relations and the Economic Model of Man: A Radical Analysis of Facts and Fictions', in Derlega, V. and Grezlak, J. (eds) *Cooperation and Helping Behavior: Theory and Research*, New York, Academic Press: 121–45.

Schmidt, F.L., Ones, D.S. and Hunter, J.E. (1992) 'Personnel Selection', *Annual Review of Psychology*, **43**: 627–70.

Sen, A. (1996) 'Economics, Business Principles and Moral Sentiments', Paper presented at the First World Congress of Business, Economics and Ethics, Japan.

Silver, M. (1989) *Foundations of Economic Justice*, Oxford, Basil Blackwell.

Singer, M. (1997) *Ethics and Justice in Organisations: A Normative–Empirical Dialogue*, Aldershot, Avebury.

Zajac, E.E. (1995) *Political Economy of Fairness*, Cambridge,MA, MIT Press.

Fashion

Within the broad field of collective behaviour, social scientists such as Blumer (1969) have examined contagion and convergence within social systems. The general framework used in collective behaviour is that individuals react to their social systems when making decisions that collectively result in a behavioural norm emerging for the social system. Although not explicitly defined in much of this literature, underlying the collective behaviour framework is the notion of social dynamics. Given that no explicit definitions exist, we define social dynamics as: *The dynamic process of (i) individual decision making (ii) under the reciprocating influence of other individuals (iii) resulting in aggregate social behaviour.* This definition directly addresses the long-established fact that individual consumer decision making may be influenced by other members of the social system. The degree of that influence depends upon the motivations of the individual in the specific situation. However, the above definition explicitly recognizes that the individual's decision outcomes will influence the social system. These bidirectional influence patterns may result in trends in aggregate social behaviour when examined in a dynamic context. In fact, it has been shown in a mathematical model that it is the individual's motivating factors and the exact nature of the sociogram that largely determines the time path of the aggregate social behaviour (Miller, McIntyre and Mantrala, 1993). As such, any social dynamic process must: (i) delineate the individual's motivations; and (ii) establish the type of social interaction; which then can be used to (iii) deduce the dynamics at the aggregate level.

Many definitions of fashion have been proposed in such diverse disciplines as economics, home economics, sociology, psychology, and marketing. These definitions are well summarized by Sproles's (1979) definition of fashion as: 'A way of behaving that is temporarily adopted by a discernible proportion of members of a social group because that chosen behaviour is perceived to be socially appropriate for the time and situation'. In keeping with this definition, we note that the 'fashion process' involves the adoption of symbols primarily to provide the individual with identity relative to others (Reynolds, 1968). The second point that is highlighted by this definition is that social symbolism and trends in that symbolism are typically not due to the functional superiority of one style over another. The functionality of a style is of only incidental relevance to

233

the fashion's life cycle (Robinson, 1975). As such, we now examine the fashion process in terms of the three components of any social dynamic process, the individual's motivations, social interaction and the resulting aggregate level dynamics.

Individual motivations

At the core of the fashion process is the individual who (i) uses information sources to (ii) deduce the symbolic meaning attached to alternative fashion items and (iii) selects the ones that make the desired symbolic statement (see left side of Figure 1).

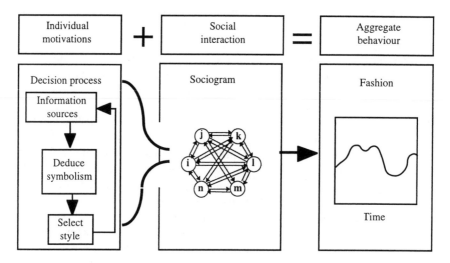

Figure 1: The social dynamic process of fashion

Information sources

There are two primary categories of information sources used by the individual to deduce the symbolic meaning attached to alternative fashion items: (i) other members of the social system, (2) industry sources, including both suppliers (for example, retailers and designers) and the media (for example, TV, magazines).

An individual searches for information from others both verbally and, perhaps more importantly, nonverbally. Nonverbal search is conducted by noting which styles have been adopted by others in recent similar situations. The pattern of information search may be different across situations and across people. For example, a person might be attributed high positive influence as a referent for the symbolic meaning attached to athletic wear, but hold a negative influence when determining the meaning attached to business attire. However, a second person might reverse these assessments. The differences in breadth and depth of interaction, and the differences in referencing, are reflections of a person's individuality.

An individual may also use industry sources for information regarding the symbolic meaning of alternative styles, ranging from media sources (for example, reading fashion magazines) to displays at desirable retail outlets (for example, 'window shopping'). Additionally, the mass media may amplify the influence of some individuals, such as rock stars on MTV. All of these activities allow certain individuals to exert an extremely broad influence within a society (for example, Puff Daddy, editors of fashion magazines, key fashion retailers and designers), although that influence may be indirect and/or nonpersonally communicated. The broad influence of these individuals is due to the sheer number of people that reference them and the high reliance placed on them. This has led some to the mistaken conclusion that fashion is a synthetic creation of the designers, retailer and/or the mass media. However, the observably low batting average of those who would attempt to create fashion clearly refutes this notion (Wasson, 1968). Even extensive mass media coverage and industry support cannot completely homogenize the influence patterns within a society towards a specific individual or group of individuals and, therefore, create individuals with sufficient influence to exclusively dictate fashions trends (Blumer, 1969; Daniels, 1951).

Symbolic meaning
The information collected about the symbolic meaning attached to alternative styles is used by the individual to determine which style(s) is(are) appropriate for a given time and situation. The appropriateness of a style is determined by the symbolic statement the individual desires to make. Although there can be many desired symbolic statements, among the most dominant statements are membership in desired groups, demarcation from undesirable groups, and consistency of self-image.

Humans have a natural tendency to form groups. Individuals esteem the members of some groups and shun the members of others. The adoption of symbolic items communicates the individual's identity to others by adopting the symbols of the esteemed group to communicate membership in that group, while avoiding the symbols of shunned groups communicates distance from them. Considering that different individuals place different reference weights on the other social members, each individual's desired symbolic statement may be unique.

Selecting styles
Group membership and group demarcation do not, however, entirely determine

the individual's preference and selection of particular merchandise. It is widely recognized that people differ on the degree of change that they can tolerate and/or enjoy. Fashion theorists have recognized that some people's self-identity is virtually driven by changing styles and taking fashion risks, while other people have a strong resistance to changing styles and incurring risks (compare Sproles, 1981). Changing adopted styles incurs risk to the individual because a substantial resource investment must be made (for example, replacing existing clothing prior to the end of their functionality) while the future meaning, and therefore symbolic utility, is uncertain. Additionally, extreme changes in adopted styles may place the individual's consistency of self-image at risk. Therefore, the individual must balance the attraction to esteemed groups and the desire to be distant from shunned groups along with a desire to reduce change in selecting an appropriate style.

Social interaction
The individual-level motivations drive all members of the society. Each individual learns the symbolic meaning(s) attached to a style for a given time and situation by referencing others, places a value on the symbolic meaning(s), and selects a style to adopt. The individual's adopted style then communicates information to the other members of the social system. Those members of the social system whom the individual influences may perceive the symbolic meaning of their adopted style as having changed due to this information and they too will adopt new styles. These style changes then influence others to change styles, including the first individual, *ad infinitum*.

As indicated in sociological research, the differences in patterns of interpersonal information search across individuals yields an intricate web of bi-directional interpersonal influence patterns at the societal level. Some individuals may generally be held in high regard across large sections of a society, influencing others towards their adopted styles and are, therefore, considered to be fashion leaders within the society. Other individuals may not be highly concerned with communicating group membership or group demarcation and therefore would be considered fashion independents within the society. It is this web of interpersonal influence that determines the time path of the resulting fashion cycle (for a recent economic perspective on this process, see Cowan, Cowan and Swann, 1997).

Aggregate behaviour
The literature contains descriptions of two main types of aggregate fashion trends within a society. First are fashion trends wherein members of a society adopt styles that tend to be an outgrowth or elaboration representing a relatively small change in an attribute from the immediately preceding styles (compare

Richardson and Kroeber, 1940; Blumer 1969; Sproles, 1981). These incremental changes are progressively more extreme in one direction (for example, shorter skirt lengths), and then, at later points in time, are progressively more extreme in the opposite direction (for example, longer skirt lengths).

In most cases, the cyclical fashion trend shifts direction due to either (i) the particular style, or attribute of a style, becoming so extreme that technological constraints forbid further movement in the same direction, or (ii) the particular style, or attribute, reaches a point where strong functional or cultural barriers limit further changes in styles in that direction. For example, it has been noted that during the middle ages the gothic arch became increasingly pointed until the engineering limitations of the time restricted further movement in that direction. Potential for using catastrophe theory to model such cyclical processes has not gone unnoticed (see Thompson, 1979). However, the cyclical nature of this type of fashion trend is not regular in frequency or amplitude. At times, the 'normal' cycle may be interrupted by a shift in direction prior to reaching an extreme or the progression may speed up or slow down.

These cyclical fashion trends can be explained by individuals attempting to be perceived as members of the same social group tending toward increased conformity in their adopted symbols. However, when imitators begin to copy the social group's fashion symbol, the fashion symbol no longer serves as a line of demarcation for group membership. Faced with a destruction of the uniformity of the group's coherence, the members of the social group turn away from that fashion symbol and adopt a new one, which reestablishes the demarcation between members and imitators. The aggregate social behaviour that results from this elaborate game of tag is a cyclical fashion cycle based on the continual adoption and dismissal of items based on the item's temporary social symbolism, not because of the item's fixed functionality. Yesterday's kitsch products may become today's collectibles (see Thompson, 1979: Ch. 2).

The second type of aggregate fashion trend described in the literature is a trend that does not exhibit any cyclicality except in the very long run. This type of fashion trend, termed a 'classic', is a convergence within a society on the meaning of a symbolic item that is relatively stable over time. For example, the blue pin-striped suit has been a classic style over a fairly long period. The classic fashion trend results from an insufficient threat to group demarcation from imitators to warrant dismissing a symbol and readopting a new symbol.

Although individuals tend to adopt styles in congruence with the aggregate fashion trend, each individual appears to behave somewhat randomly in the vicinity around the underlying trend. Additionally, a few individuals adopt styles that may appear in gross violation of the underlying fashion trend during some time periods. These trends are the result of differences across individuals in the level of concern they hold for group membership and demarcation, resistance to change, differences in the pattern of information sources used to deduce symbolic meaning, as well as what symbolic meaning the individual desires to express.

Summary
Although there are clearly additional influences on the fashion process, the social dynamic representation developed in Figure 1 represents the core of the fashion process. The individual motivations lead consumers to differentially search for information regarding the symbolic meaning attached to fashion objects. The individual then weights this information to determine what style communicates the desired symbolic message within a given time and situation. The adoption and display of that style may change the symbolic meaning deduced by others in the society, causing them to alter styles, and the process continues through time. In essence this sequence can be viewed as the dynamics of the social norm component of the Fishbein expectancy value model under reciprocating influence.

Because of the inherent complexity of social dynamic processes, there has been limited work on empirically validating this approach to understanding the fashion process. Preliminary results of computerized experiments that simulate the social dynamics underlying the fashion process indicate that by changing the pattern of social influence across subjects it is possible to manipulate the type and speed of the resulting fashion cycle. However, these results are speculative at this point and further empirical research is required.

CHRISTOPHER M. MILLER

Bibliography
Blumer, H. (1969) 'Fashion: From Class Differentiation to Collective Selection', *Sociological Quarterly*, **10**: 275–91.

Cowan, R., Cowan, W. and Swann, P. (1997) 'A Model of Demand with Interactions Among Consumers', *International Journal of Industrial Organization*, **15**: 711–32.

Daniels, A.H. (1951) 'Fashion Merchandising', *Harvard Business Review*, **29**: 51–60.

Miller, C.M., McIntyre, S.H. and Mantrala, M.K. (1993), 'Toward Formalizing Fashion Theory', *Journal of Marketing Research*, **30**: 142–57.

Reynolds, W.H. (1968) 'Cars and Clothing: Understanding Fashion Trends', *Journal of Marketing*, **3**: 44–9.

Richardson, J. and Kroeber, A.L. (1940) 'Three Centuries of Women's Dress Fashions, A Quantitative Analysis', *Anthropological Records*, **5**: 111–53.

Robinson, D.E. (1975), 'Style Changes: Cyclical, Inexorable, and Foreseeable', *Harvard Business Review*, **53**: 121-31.

Sproles, G. (1979) *Fashion: Consumer Behavior Toward Dress*, Minneapolis, MN, Burgess Publishing Company.

Sproles, G. (1981) 'Analyzing Fashion Life Cycles — Principles and Perspectives',

Journal of Marketing, **45**: 116–24.

Thompson, M. (1979) *Rubbish Theory: The Creation and Destruction of Value*, Oxford, Oxford University Press.

Wasson, C.R. (1968) 'How Predictable are Fashion and Other Product Life Cycles?', *Journal of Marketing*, **32**: 36–43.

Fear Appeals and Persuasion

Advertising messages that accentuate consumer fears with threats of adverse consequences are called fear appeals. Over the last four decades, several theories have been proposed to explain the persuasive impact of these fear appeals. The effect of fear on consumers' attitudes and behaviours, however, is still uncertain. We are still in need of a unifying fear–persuasion paradigm that accommodates extant data and is capable of providing specific guidelines for using fear as a persuasive advertising strategy. The following sections explain and critique the fundamental models proposed to explain the relationship between fear and persuasion, and provide specific suggestions for further investigation.

Theories of fear and persuasion

Several theories attempt to explain the relationship between fear and persuasion. These theories can be grouped according to whether they predict a negative monotonic (Janis and Feshbach, 1953; Miller, 1963), an inverted-U (Janis and Leventhal, 1968), or a positive monotonic (Sutton, 1982; Boster and Mongeau, 1985) relationship between fear and persuasion.

Negative monotonic model

The fear-resistance explanation predicts a negative correlation between the amount of fear in a persuasive message and compliance with the message's recommendations. According to the fear-resistance model, high levels of perceived fear initiate defensive processing of the message. At a high level of fear, the message recipient begins to avoid or deny the importance of the threat. Conversely, at a low level of fear, the message recipient does not engage in defensive avoidance and pays attention to the recommendations. Thus, message persuasion increases as perceived fear decreases.

Although a number of studies demonstrate empirically that low fear is more effective than high fear, two recent meta-analytic reviews of the fear literature by Sutton (1982) and Boster and Mongeau (1985) indicate that the fear–persuasion relationship is positive monotonic. The positive relationship between fear and persuasion is discussed below.

Positive monotonic model

The fear-drive explanation predicts a positive relationship between level of fear and persuasion. According to the fear-drive model, the perceived fear aroused by the message serves as a drive to motivate trial-and-error behaviour. A high level of fear motivates the message recipient to try various behaviours to reduce or alleviate the fear. It is the *reduction* of fear that motivates the learning of new behaviours. For example, a message outlining the link between exercise and the decreased risk of heart attacks may arouse fear in the message audience. If mental rehearsal of the recommendation (for example, imagining oneself exercising) reduces the state of fear, then the recommended behaviour will be reinforced and is more likely to occur. However, if cognitive rehearsal of the recommendation fails to reduce the fear, impulsive responses will be tried out until one reduces the tension (for example, eating or working). Often, this defensive reaction is to deny the threat or avoid the message.

There are a number of conceptual and methodological problems with the fear-drive model (see Sutton, 1982, for a detailed exposition of the weaknesses associated with the fear-drive model). From a theoretical perspective, the fear-drive model fails to distinguish whether persuasion is proportional to the *amount* of fear reduction (for example, a reduction from high fear to low fear versus a reduction from high fear to moderate fear) or dependent on the *completeness* of fear reduction (for example, a reduction from high fear to no fear). Additionally, if mental rehearsal is sufficient to reduce the fear state, then an acceptable end-goal would be thinking about the behaviour rather than actually performing it.

From a methodological perspective, an adequate test of the fear-drive model would entail a before–after test of fear level to determine the relationship between reduction of fear arousal and acceptance of the recommendation. Thus, the timing of the fear measurement (how soon after the message is seen, fear is measured) and the speed of fear reduction (how quickly the fear reduction occurs) are critical information before one can draw conclusions of message acceptance. In the typical study, fear is measured only once after initially seeing the message (Sutton, 1982).

There is considerable empirical support for a positive monotonic relationship between fear and persuasion. In a meta-analysis of 21 previous studies on fear appeals, Sutton (1982) demonstrated a main effect of fear such that an increase in fear arousal leads to an increase in acceptance of the communication. Similarly, Boster and Mongeau (1985) integrated the results of 25 fear studies and found that subjects are more persuaded when they are exposed to a high (versus low) fear message. The finding that higher levels of fear are more effective than low or moderate levels of fear has since been supported in numerous applications (King and Reid, 1990).

Nonmonotonic models

Empirical support for the negative monotonic and positive monotonic models can be reconciled with an inverted-U perspective (Janis, 1967; McGuire, 1968; see Berlyne, 1971 for the more general optimum arousal theory). The inverted-U model suggests persuasion is minimal when the level of fear is low because the message is viewed as inconsequential. In other words, the level of fear evoked is not sufficient to motivate the message recipient to attend to and/or comply with the message recommendations. Similarly, acceptance of the recommendations should be minimal when the level of fear is high because recipients engage in defensive mechanisms, rather than follow the message recommendations. Compliance with the recommendation is predicted to be strongest when the level of fear is moderate; at this level a balance is reached whereby recipients are sufficiently aroused to attend to the message and interfering effects, such as defensive tendencies, are minimal.

The inverted-U model is popular because it can accommodate almost any pattern of results; however, this flexibility can be criticized as being little more than a *post hoc* descriptive schema (Leventhal, 1970). Additionally, most studies of fear and persuasion include only two levels of fear and so it is impossible to assess the inverted-U perspective. Thus, although the nonmonotonic model is superior to the fear-drive model in that it has testable predictions, the main problem with this model is the operational difficulty of testing three or more levels of fear.

Sternthal and Craig (1974) provide an alternative explanation for the curvilinear effects by extending Leventhal's parallel response model to predict an inverted-U effect of fear on acceptance of the recommendations. The parallel response model asserts that any fear communication activates two processes: fear control and danger control. Danger control is a problem-solving process, during which behaviours that avert the threat or prevent the danger are activated. Fear control is an emotional coping process, during which recipients of the message focus on internal emotional responses that reduce their perceived fear rather than responses that decrease the danger. The fear control responses may interfere with message acceptance. Sternthal and Craig suggest that at low levels of fear, both danger- and fear-control processes are relatively weak since the threat is not serious. At moderate levels of fear, the danger control process is stronger than the fear-control process, and message acceptance is optimal. Although at high levels of fear both processes are strong, the tendency of emotional responses (fear control) to interfere with danger control reduces the acceptance of the recommendation to avoid danger.

Rogers (1975) argues that the major inadequacy of the parallel response explanation is that it is untestable. In particular, the model fails to specify the stimulus variables that determine the extent to which fear and danger control processes operate. Thus, like the inverted-U model, the parallel response model can account for almost any fear–persuasion relationship without specifying the conditions under which different outcomes are expected to occur.

Rogers (1975) originally developed protection motivation theory to explain the inconsistencies in the research on fear appeals and specify variables that determine persuasion, however, protection motivation theory has primarily been used to model health decision making and behaviour (Maddux, 1993). According to protection motivation theory, viewing a health-related message provides the impetus for an individual to assess the severity of an event, probability of the event's occurrence, and belief in the efficacy of the recommendations provided in the message. Perceptions about these three factors arouse 'protection motivation' (as indexed by behavioural intentions) which in turn provides the incentive to seek a healthier behaviour (Rogers, 1975, 1983).

These three variables do seem to be predictive in that intentions to comply are generally greater when the threat is severe, the person feels vulnerable, and following the recommendations is perceived as an efficacious way to reduce the threat — see Eagly and Chaiken (1993) for a review of protection motivation theory findings. Despite overall acknowledgement of the importance of each of these variables, empirical studies of protection motivation theory fail to support Rogers's premise that the three components are equally important in determining behavioural intentions. The presence of main effects (or interaction effects) of perceived vulnerability, severity and efficacy vary from one study to the next (Eagly and Chaiken, 1993). To address the inconsistent empirical support for protection motivation theory, Block and Keller (in press) suggest that people at different stages of readiness to change are differentially affected by levels of these predictor variables. Block and Keller find that the relative importance of vulnerability, severity, response and self-efficacy vary from precontemplation to contemplation to action, three of the stages of change identified by the transtheoretical model (Prochaska, Norcross and DiClemente, 1994).

The most recent explanation of how fear arousal affects persuasion focuses on the extent of the viewer's elaboration on the fearful message. The typical fear appeal contains two distinct parts: the consequences of the threat (for example, lung cancer) and the recommendations to avoid the negative outcome (for example, stop smoking). This arousal-elaboration model (Keller and Block, 1996) suggests that when a low level of fear is ineffective, it is because there is insufficient elaboration of the harmful *consequences* of engaging in the destructive behaviour. Therefore, for a low fear appeal, an increase in elaboration on the consequences increases elaboration on the recommendations, and thus increases persuasion. By contrast, when appeals arousing high levels of fear are ineffective, it is because too much elaboration on the harmful consequences leads to defensive tendencies such as message avoidance, and decreases persuasion.

Rather, for a high fear appeal, a reduction in elaboration on the consequences increases elaboration on the solution, and thus increases persuasion.

The arousal-elaboration model addresses inadequacies of the earlier non-monotonic models in that it does specify elaboration as the process that affects the facilitating and interfering effects of fear on message acceptance, and specifies the conditions under which different outcomes are expected to occur. Furthermore, the Keller and Block (1996) model offers easily implementable ways to increase the persuasiveness of fear appeals; use elaboration enhancing mechanisms (for example, self-referencing or imagery processing) to increase the persuasiveness of a low fear appeal, and use elaboration suppressing mechanisms (for exmaple, other referencing or objective processing) to increase the persuasiveness of a high fear appeal. Earl (1986) presents related theorizing on the cognitive implications of threat and anxiety on self-image. If the threat is perceived as a challenge to the core construct of one's self-image, an individual may choose to engage in behaviour that restores the desired self-image rather than reduces the undesirable consequences. This theorizing is consistent with the arousal-elaboration explanation. Support for the arousal-elaboration model was obtained in the context of a communication advocating that people stop smoking, however, further replications of the model across multiple contexts are needed to substantiate the model's generalizability.

Emerging themes in fear research

Although the positive monotonic, negative monotonic and nonmonotonic models described above provide a promising start to understanding the nature of the fear and persuasion relationship, the limitations of the models and inconsistent empirical results suggest the need for theorizing on the factors that moderate the effect of fear on persuasion. Two review papers, Sternthal and Craig (1974) and Sutton (1982) provide a comprehensive discussion of the studies prior to 1974 and 1982, respectively, that examine the role of several moderating factors, such as source credibility, on persuasion. As is evident in these review papers, although many moderator variables have been explored, few general conclusions can be drawn from these studies. For example, Sutton (1982) discusses a few personality factors that moderate the effect of fear on persuasion: coping style, self-esteem, chronic anxiety, extroversion and locus of control. Because the results from these studies of personality styles and fear appeals are inconsistent and complex, Sutton concludes that no summary conclusions may be drawn from this literature. More recently, several researchers have explored the informational components of the message, such as positive versus negative framing (Block and Keller, 1995) and the vividness of the information (Sherer and Rogers, 1984; Block and Keller, 1997), as moderators of fear on persuasion.

Further investigation of the interaction of fear and various personality and message variables will help us better understand the nature of the fear–persuasion relationship. Additionally, there are several fundamental areas for future research that would greatly contribute to fear research. A standard scale to measure fear would help in the comparison of levels of fear across studies. A comprehensive temporal study of fear could provide direction for the uniform timing of fear measurement. Suggestions for operationalizing fear within the message to disentangle the confounds of fear and severity, or fear and vividness, would enable clearer interpretation and generalizability of results.

One emerging perspective in the study of fear and persuasion is that since health behaviours differ in fundamental ways, a more segmented approach to understanding the impact of advocacy communications is needed. As a starting-point to segmentation, a few researchers have identified three different categories of health behaviours: prevention, promotion and detection (Maddux, 1993; Rothman and Salovey, 1997). Prevention behaviours are those behaviours that people engage in, or cease to engage in, because of their belief that by performing (or ceasing to perform) this behaviour, they can prevent illness or other harmful consequences. For example, some people exercise to prevent heart disease, others quit smoking in order to prevent lung cancer. Promotion behaviours, on the other hand, are behaviours that people engage in to maintain a healthy state of being, rather than to prevent a serious consequence. For some, exercise is a promotion behaviour: many people exercise to achieve a desired state of fitness or to maintain their current weight. Thus, the distinction between prevention behaviours and promotion behaviours is blurred. The person's goals rather than the nature of the behaviour itself determine whether the behaviour is preventive or enhancing. Additionally, what begins as a prevention behaviour often turns into health promotion, as in the case of exercise. Detection behaviours provide information about the presence or absence of an unhealthy condition. These behaviours may be performed by the individual (for example, breast self-examination) or by a physician (for example, mammography). Because these behaviours are undertaken only to detect the presence of a potentially serious illness, detection behaviours are perceived to be more threatening and more risky than prevention behaviours (Rothman and Salovey, 1997). Of course, the knowledge resulting from detection might spur preventive behaviour; for example, a woman who detected breast cancer might opt for surgery to remove the tumour. Given the differences in nature among prevention, promotion and detection behaviours, future research is needed that examines the effects of fear, personality variables and message variables across these types of behaviour.

LAUREN G. BLOCK

Bibliography
Berlyne, D.E. (1971) *Aesthetics and Psychobiology*, New York, Appleton-Century-Crofts.

Block, L.G. and Keller, P.A. (1995) 'When to Accentuate the Negative: The Effects of Perceived Efficacy and Message Framing on Intentions to Perform a Health Related Behavior', *Journal of Marketing Research*, **32**: 192–203.

Block, L.G. and Keller, P.A. (1997) 'The Effects of Self-Efficacy and Vividness on the Persuasiveness of Health Communications', *Journal of Consumer Psychology*, **6**: 31–54.

Block, L.G. and Keller, P.A. (in press) 'Beyond Protection Motivation: An Integrative Theory of Health Appeals', *Journal of Applied Social Psychology.*

Boster, F.J. and Mongeau, P. (1985) 'Fear-Arousing Persuasive Messages', *Communication Yearbook*, **8**: 330–75.

Eagly, A. and Chaiken, S. (1993) *The Psychology of Attitudes*, Fort Worth, TX, Harcourt Brace Jovanovich.

Earl, P.E. (1986) *Lifestyle Economics: Consumer Behaviour in a Turbulent World*, New York, St. Martin's Press.

Janis, I.L. (1967) 'Effects of Fear Arousal on Attitude Change: Recent Developments in Theory and Research', in Berkowitz, L. (ed.), *Advances in Experimental Social Psychology*, **3**, New York: Academic Press.

Janis, I.L. and Feshbach, S. (1953) 'Effects of Fear-Arousing Communications', *Journal of Abnormal and Social Psychology*, **48**: 78–92.

Janis, I.L. and Leventhal, H. (1968) 'Human Reactions to Stress', in Borgatta, E. and Lambert, W. (eds), *Handbook of Personality Theory and Research*, Chicago: Rand McNally.

Keller, P.A. and Block, L.G. (1996) 'Increasing The Persuasiveness of Fear Appeals: The Effect of Arousal and Elaboration', *Journal of Consumer Research,* **22**: 448–59.

King, K.W. and Reid, L. N. (1990) 'Fear Arousing Anti-Drinking and Driving PSAs: Do Physical Injury Threats Influence Young Adults?', *Journal of Current Research and Issues in Advertising*, **12**: 155–75.

Leventhal, H. (1970) 'Findings and Theory in the Study of Fear Communications', in Berkowitz, L. (ed.), *Advances in Experimental Social Psychology*, **5**: New York: Academic Press.

Maddux, J.E. (1993), 'Social Cognitive Models of Health and Exercise Behavior: An Introduction and Review of Conceptual Issues', *Journal of Applied Sport Psychology*, **5**: 116–40.

McGuire, W.J. (1968) 'Personality and Susceptibility to Social Influence', in Borgatta, E. and Lambert, W. (eds) *Handbook of Personality Theory and Research*, Chicago, IL, Rand McNally: 1130–88.

Miller, G.R. (1963) 'Studies on the Use of Fear Appeals: A Summary and Analysis', *Central States Speech Journal*, **14**: 117–25.

Prochaska, J.O., Norcross, J.C. and DiClemente C.C. (1994) *Changing For Good*, New York, William Morrow & Company.

Rogers, R.W. (1975) 'A Protection Motivation Theory of Fear Appeals and Attitude Change', *Journal of Psychology*, **91**: 93–114.

Rogers, R.W. (1983) 'Cognitive and Physiological Processes in Fear Appeals and Attitude Change: A Revised Theory of Protection Motivation', in Cacioppo, J.T. and Petty, R.E. (eds.) *Social Psychophysiology*, New York, Guilford Press: 153-76.

Rothman, A.J. and Salovey, P. (1997) 'Shaping Perceptions to Motivate Healthy Behavior: The Role of Message Framing', *Psychological Bulletin*, **121**: 3–19.

Sherer, M. and Rogers, R.W. (1984) 'The Role of Vivid Information in Fear Appeals and Attitude Change', *Journal of Research in Personality*, **18**: 321–34.

Sternthal, B. and Craig, C.S. (1974) 'Fear Appeals: Revisited and Revised', *Journal of Consumer Research*, **1**: 22–34.

Sutton, S. R. (1982) 'Fear-Arousing Communications: A Critical Examination of Theory and Research', in Eiser, J.R. (ed.) *Social Psychology and Behavioral Medicine*. New York: John Wiley & Sons: 303–37.

Gambling

Gambling has a long history with references to dice games and the drawing of lots dating back more than 2000 years. Furthermore, in most countries, where gambling is legal, the majority of individuals within a society have gambled at some time in their lives and are likely to gamble in any given year. These claims refer to institutionalized gambling. When it is recognized that individuals may gamble informally, and that the notion of gambling can be widened to embrace all activities involving risk, it can be seen that gambling is an important and common part of life in every society. Thus, the word 'gambling' can be used in a broad sense referring to all actions involving risk, or in a more restricted sense of risking money on the outcome of a gambling event. The more restricted usage is also the more common. From this perspective, gambling is the activity of staking money on the uncertain outcome of an event within a game. The game may range from number games such as lotteries and slot machines, through casino games, to horse and dog racing. In this context, not all gambling is legal in any given society.

History of gambling

Gambling has been a part of human society for many thousands of years. Dice and gaming equipment have been found dating back to 2000 BC in archaeological excavations in Egypt, China and India. It is believed that gambling in China is even older. Although gambling has been present at one time or another among all races, the meaning of gambling varies widely according to its historical and social context (McMillen, 1996). Early gambling is likely to have occurred in the context of religious festivals. Gambling in preindustrial Britain was common and an accepted part of the leisure activities of the masses. From time to time, gambling was also used by British and French monarchs to finance armies and to pay public servants, a concept which has modern equivalents in the financing of hospitals, sports and other community benefits by lotteries, casinos and the like. Attitudes to gambling among the ruling class in Europe began to change with the advent of the industrial revolution. Increasingly gambling was seen as antithetical to hard work and thus morally wrong. The increasing rejection of gambling as an acceptable activity paralleled the increasing rejection of alcohol, and reached a climax in Victorian England with the passage of legislation forbidding both gambling and drunkenness. The twentieth century — especially the second half of the century — is notable for the liberalisation of attitudes to gambling in government, in religion, and among the general public. Among the societies that have rejected the spread of gambling, Communist and Islamic countries stand as the major ideologies endorsing more conservative doctrines.

Gambling as leisure

In Western societies, where most forms of gambling have been legalized, it is estimated that 80 to 90 per cent of the adult population gamble in some way at some time within a twelve-month period. In these societies gambling is promoted as an appropriate activity for both men and women. Gambling games may be categorized as: gaming (including most of the games available in casinos), sports betting (including horse and dog races), and number games (including lotto and lotteries). However, gambling exists is a wide variety of forms and strict categorization is not possible. Thus, sporting contests may be presented in gaming machines for betting purposes and thus can be regarded as either gaming or sports betting.

The most common form of sports betting involves wagering money on the outcome of horse races. Betting on horses has a long history which has been traced as far back as the Hittites in approximately 4000 BC. This form of gambling was revolutionized by the introduction of *pari-mutuel* betting devised by Pierre Oller in 1872 and the invention of the totalizator several years later in New Zealand. *Pari-mutuel* betting involves setting the odds for each horse according to the proportion of the pool attracted by each horse, and once this principle was mechanized in the totalizator, the totalizator system was adopted throughout the world as a fairer system than bookmakers. The totalizator also increased efficiency in the collection of government taxes.

Casino gambling was legalized in France in 1907, and by 1995 there were more than 45 established casinos. Similar developments have taken place throughout the Western world and the spread of legal casinos has become a world- wide phenomenon. The rapid spread of casinos in the twentieth century reflects the remarkable growth of gambling as an acceptable leisure pursuit. Associated with the spread of casinos has been the increasing technological sophistication of gaming machines. The invention of the first gaming machine is attributed to Charles Le Fey in 1895 in the United States. The original machine was a fruit machine with three reels and fruit symbols on each reel. Since the original machine, slot machines have progressed to different types of games including card games and sports such as horse racing. Modern machines accept multiple coins of varying denominations and pay out according to a large variety of events. Furthermore, groups of machines may be linked to provide large jackpots. It is believed that slot machine gambling is the most popular form of gambling in the world at this time. The recent development of the internet and the World Wide Web has enabled the general public to access *virtual casinos* and thus to gamble while remaining at home. Whether or not internet gambling will become a popular form of gambling remains to be seen.

Characteristics of gamblers

Studies of gambling in modern societies suggest that the extent of involvement varies according to gender, age, socioeconomic class, religion and cultural background of the individual. Furthermore, the patterns of involvement in gambling appear to be changing as gambling becomes more common. Gender differences in gambling involvement provide a good example of these changing patterns. For most of the twentieth century, men have been more likely than women to be involved in gambling. This was true especially of gambling on card games and at the race track. This gender difference was reflected in levels of gambling-related problems where, in the 1970s, men were nine times as likely as women to be classified as compulsive gamblers. More recent surveys in the US suggest that gender differences in the frequency, expenditure and leisure time spent on gambling are becoming smaller (Volberg and Steadman, 1992). Nevertheless, gender differences remain in the types of gambling preferred with men more likely to bet on horse racing, women more likely to play bingo, and both sexes equally likely to play gaming machines.

Although many countries have age restrictions in relation to gambling, it often begins before the age of 15 years with cards, lotteries and gaming machines being the main forms used. In most countries throughout the world, children are prohibited from playing slot machines. This is not the case in Britain where gaming machines are found side by side with video amusement machines in arcades. Among adults, the average age of gamblers depends on the type of gambling involved. In general, gamblers who prefer gaming and betting are younger than those who prefer number games. Where gambling becomes excessive, the evidence suggests that the individual began gambling at an earlier age and in the context of a family that encouraged gambling (Walker, 1992).

Socioeconomic class is also linked to gambling, with higher percentages of the working-class population than the middle class gambling regularly. This result is especially true for number games and slot machines. Examples of class differences in gambling may be culture specific. Thus, there is evidence that casino gambling in Britain is a more middle-class activity than playing the pools. Similar trends have not been demonstrated in Australia and New Zealand. Interestingly, there is some evidence that religion is associated with gambling involvement. Catholics have been reported to gamble more frequently and with greater expenditure than Protestants (Grichting, 1986), and in self-help groups for compulsive gambling, Jewish people are overrepresented. These religious differences may well be linked to cultural differences.

Psychology of gambling

Why people gamble is a psychological question rather than an economic one. All gambling games are constructed so that the expected payoff to the gambler is less than the initial bet. The percentage taken by the gambling provider ranges from less than 1 per cent in casino blackjack to more than 40 per cent in some lottery games. If gamblers were rational and motivated to maximize their assets, then gambling would not be expected to be a popular leisure activity. For this reason a range of psychological explanations have been suggested. Behavioural explanations focus on the fact that gambling behaviour is rewarded from time to time by payouts and assume that it is the expectation of further payouts that maintains the behaviour. More purposive explanations have centred on the fact that gambling is exciting and thus can be used to manipulate mood and alleviate anxiety or depression, in much the same way as chemical substances are used. Cognitive explanations take a different point of view. It is assumed that gamblers are attempting to increase their assets but are mistaken about the likelihood that they will do so. Such explanations focus on erroneous beliefs and superstitious thinking that lies behind gambling. Psychodynamic explanations state that the propensity to gamble has much earlier origins and fulfils hidden needs. For example, gambling has been explained in terms of an oral fixation where the important psychological principle is 'something for nothing'. Such explanations suggest that broader personality factors such as impulsiveness may have a role.

Whether or not gambling is rational behaviour is a contentious issue. Much of the argument concerns what is meant by the term 'rational'. If rational refers to the optimum set of decisions to reach a specified goal, then gamblers are irrational when they gamble in order to increase their assets. However, if rational refers to the optimum set of decisions within the subjective reality of the individual, then gambling may be rational. According to prospect theory (Kahneman and Tversky, 1979), the subjective value of money varies according to whether it is perceived as money won or money lost: money lost carries the greater weight. It follows that individuals are motivated to take more risks when losing than when winning. From this perspective, gambling is a consequence of the cognitive makeup of human beings. Another defence of gambling as rational, points out that for the majority of individuals, the only way in which a million dollars will be obtained is by entering a lottery. A small outlay of money ensures that chance, whereas saving the money takes away the chance. Finally, gambling may be defended as rational by including the observation that increasing one's assets is not the only goal, or even the major goal, of many gamblers. In response to survey questions, individuals frequently report that they gamble for social reasons such as having fun with friends. Thus gambling losses are treated as the cost of having fun.

It is clear that no one explanation of gambling is complete in itself, and that the full explanation of gambling may involve a range of cognitive, emotional and behavioural factors. Furthermore, the explanation of regular and heavy gambling may involve quite different explanations from occasional gambling for low stakes. At this time, there is no agreed explanation for why people gamble.

Gambling problems

The majority of gamblers maintain their financial losses within acceptable limits. This may occur because the gambling is infrequent and for small sums only, or because the gambler maintains control over the extent to which losses can accrue to a disruptive level. Many regular gamblers experience occasional problems where larger losses occur than anticipated. Nevertheless, these problems are solved sufficiently satisfactorily for the gambling to continue. However, for a small minority of gamblers, estimated at between 1 and 2 per cent of the adult population in societies where gambling outlets are readily available, the gambling is excessive and causes a range of problems in the gambler's life. The causes of excessive gambling are not agreed and may involve loss of control over the gambling, persistence with inappropriate gambling strategies, or simply avoidance of other unpleasant aspects of the gambler's life. Perhaps the most common cause of excessive gambling involves increasing the stakes in order to win back losses. If the losses are too great for the gambler to sustain, then he or she may be tempted to risk more money to recoup those losses. In the event of further bad luck, as is likely, the losses increase. Further funds must be invested to recoup the increased losses, and the cycle is repeated. This process is called *chasing* and has been identified as a strong indicator of gambling-related problems (Lesieur, 1984).

The problems caused by excessive gambling involve different areas of the gambler's life: financial, personal, social, employment and legal. The level of financial loss is a major factor in the problems caused by excessive gambling. A likely consequence of these financially-based stresses is a range of personal problems including both psychological aspects, such as severe anxiety and depression, and physiological aspects, such as sleeplessness and gastric problems. Where the gambler lives with family or friends, the problems are highly likely to include relationship issues. Spouses of gamblers report deceitfulness, secrecy and anger in their relationships with gamblers, and the sexual intimacy and caring aspects of the relationships are disrupted. Excessive gambling is associated with employment problems and high rates of unemployment. Gamblers frequently commit crimes in order to finance their activities. It has been estimated that between half and two-thirds of gamblers seeking treatment have committed non-violent property crimes to finance their gambling activities. In some cases these legal problems lead to incarceration (Blaszczynski and Silove, 1995).

Pathological gambling and its treatment

'Pathological gambling' is the term preferred by the American Psychiatric

Association for persistent and recurrent maladaptive gambling. The term 'pathological' is contentious since it implies that the gambling is best explained in terms of illness rather than normal psychological processes. At various times and in different countries the labels pathological gambling, compulsive gambling, excessive gambling, problem gambling and gambling addiction have all been applied to individuals with similar gambling-related problems. Each term implies a different focus for both explanation and treatment. Individuals seek help from psychiatrists, clinical psychologists, counsellors and self-help groups. Furthermore, self help manuals are increasingly available.

In general, interventions with pathological gamblers do not appear to be highly effective, with relapse rates two years after treatment being relatively high (Walker, 1992). One likely explanation for the high relapse rates is that many gamblers seeking treatment for gambling-related problems may not realize that their excessive gambling is the cause of their problems. Many gamblers believe that they can control and cut back their gambling at will despite numerous failures when they have attempted to do so. The current view of treatment procedures is that they are unlikely to be effective until the gambler recognizes gambling as the cause of the problems and becomes committed to curbing and stopping the gambling itself. Although there is relatively little evidence concerning the effectiveness of different treatment procedures, especially in controlled trials where the gambler is assigned randomly to alternative approaches, both behavioural and cognitive therapies have shown positive effects. The best results appear to have been achieved by procedures aimed at extinguishing the excitement associated with gambling, and by procedures which alter the beliefs and attitudes of gamblers towards gambling. However, despite these efforts, the majority of gamblers with severe gambling-related problems seek help from a self-help organization called 'Gamblers Anonymous'. Most treatment agencies urge their clients to attend Gamblers Anonymous in addition to receiving specific treatment and counselling concerning the effects of excessive gambling.

MICHAEL WALKER

Bibliography

Blaszczynski, A. and Silove, D. (1995) 'Cognitive Behavioural Therapies for Pathological Gambling', *Journal of Gambling Studies*, **11**: 195–220.

Eadington, W.R. (1987) 'Economic Perceptions of Gambling Behavior', *Journal of Gambling Behavior*, **3**: 264–73.

Grichting, W.L. (1986) 'The Impact of Religion on Gambling in Australia', *Australian Journal of Psychology*, **38**, 45–58.

Kahneman, D. and Tversky, A. (1979) 'Prospect Theory: An Analysis of Decision Under Risk', *Econometrica*, **47**: 263–91.

Lesieur, H.R. (1984) *The Chase: Career of the Compulsive Gambler*, Cambridge, MA, Schenkman.

McMillen, J. (1996) 'Understanding Gambling: History, Concepts and Theories', in McMillen, J. (ed.) *Gambling Cultures: Studies in History and Interpretation*, London, Routledge: 6–42.

Spanier, D. (1987) *Inside the Gambler's Mind*, London, Secker & Warburg.

Volberg, R.A. and Steadman, H.J. (1992) 'Accurately Depicting Pathological Gamblers: Policy and Treatment Implications', *Journal of Gambling Studies*, **8**: 401–12.

Walker, M.B. (1992) *The Psychology of Gambling*, Oxford, Pergamon.

Game Theory

Game theory studies strategic interaction among players. Usually this requires social situations, but one can also model intrapersonal decision conflicts as games, for example the conflict between passion and reason suggested by Plato (see Frank, 1996, and the comment by Güth and Kliemt, 1996). The tasks of game theory are to represent strategic conflicts formally by *game forms* and to provide *solution concepts*.

The main game forms are extensive or stage games, which allow for sequential decision processes and complex information conditions. The static normal form describes noncooperative or strategic games, and the characteristic function for cooperative games focuses on the possible payoff constellations.

The solution concept depends on the game form. It can define a unique result or a subset of possible results. Traditionally game theory has assumed perfect rationality in decision making. Compared to this normative theory, behavioural game theory is far less developed (see Kagel and Roth, 1995). But even in behavioural approaches one often relies on the game theoretic solution for a standard of comparison.

Game forms

Extensive games (in which plays and strategy sets are finite; no simultaneous moves are possible) and *stage games* describe dynamic interactive decision processes and their information conditions. For example, in *ultimatum bargaining* (Güth, 1995), only the proposer may know whether the cake is large or small, a condition that can be formalized as an initial chance move whose probabilities reflect the responder's beliefs. Knowing the cake size, the proposer decides on an offer to the responder who then, knowing the offer but not the cake size, can only either accept or reject it.

The *normal form* of this game simply describes the strategies and the payoffs for both players. Since a strategy is a complete behavioural plan, the proposer strategy specifies two offers, one for the small and one for the large cake. The responder strategy prescribes for all possible offers whether they are to be accepted or not. The payoff function assigns numbers that represent the utilities to both the proposer and the responder for all the possible strategy constellations.

In applications one often assumes that payoffs are simply monetary rewards. But game theory then turns out to have little predictive power (for example, Güth, Schmittberger and Schwarze, 1982). Untroubled believers in human rationality react to such results by adding nonmonetary costs and rewards into the payoff function (Bolton, 1991) or by incorporating other repairs (for example, the 'psychological' games of Geneakoplos, Pearce and Stacchetti, 1989).

In cooperative games only the possible payoffs matter. The *characteristic function* describes the outcome possibilities for all subgroups of players. Where *side payments* are allowed, players can arbitrarily redistribute their rewards, and the redistribution is represented by 'money' transfers which enter their payoffs/utilities as an additive linear term. If in ultimatum bargaining the responder, too, knows the cake size, c, both players can achieve all payoff/utility vectors whose sum does not exceed c. Furthermore, no individual player can make sure of obtaining more than 0. Without side payments no redistribution is possible.

Solution concepts

For games in extensive, stage or normal form, the solution requires the equilibrium property (Cournot, 1838; Nash, 1951). An *equilibrium* is a vector of individual strategies from which no single player can profitably deviate. The stronger requirement that no subgroup of players can gain by deviating collectively cannot be generally satisfied: for example in the prisoner's dilemma game, cooperation is mutually advantageous but not an equilibrium. Only equilibria induce behavioural expectations that will self-enforce. In addition to optimality, equilibria assume rational expectations or (converse) consistency. When some players have already chosen their solution strategies, a *consistent* solution also defines the solution behaviour of the remaining players in the reduced game. Recently there have been attempts to justify equilibria as the stable results of learning or evolutionary processes (Weibull, 1995).

All reasonable games have equilibria (Nash, 1951), but more than one equilibrium may exist. To resolve this troublesome ambiguity, one can refine the equilibrium concept (van Damme, 1987, provides a survey) or select among equilibria (Harsanyi and Selten, 1988).

The main refinements of equilibrium include *subgame perfect equilibria* (if a game has proper subgames, a strategy vector must induce equilibria for each of them), *perfect equilibria* (an equilibrium must be robust against small perturbations, implying that players must choose every strategy with a small positive minimum probability) or the generically equivalent *sequential equilibria* (every move has supporting beliefs which must be consistent with the actual behaviour). Many games have more than one refined equilibrium.

In *evolutionary game theory* the main idea is that of an *evolutionarily stable strategy* (ESS). This implies a symmetric equilibrium of a symmetric game with the additional property that when confronting any alternative best reply to the ESS the ESS is better than that alternative.

In cooperative or characteristic function games the main set-value concepts are the *core* (a payoff vector is in the core if no coalition or subgroup of players can improve upon it), the *von Neumann and Morgenstern (1944) solutions* requiring internal and external stability, and the *bargaining set*.

Unique payoff vectors are selected by value concepts such as the *Shapley (1953) value* or the *nucleolus* (Schmeidler, 1969). These can be viewed as attempts to distribute rewards according to what all coalitions of players can guarantee themselves. In *equity theory* (Homans, 1961) such threat possibilities are neglected.

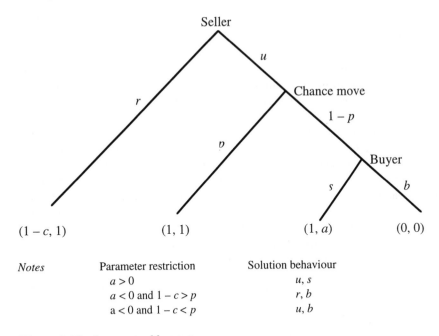

Notes	Parameter restriction	Solution behaviour
	$a > 0$	u, s
	$a < 0$ and $1 - c > p$	r, b
	$a < 0$ and $a < 0$ and $1 - c < p$	u, b

Figure 1: The lemons and boycotts game

On lemons markets and consumer boycotts

This section describes an application to provide insight into the development of lemons markets (where the goods offered are characteristically unreliable), and the effect that consumer boycotts have on this development.

A seller may choose to offer either r (reliable) or u (unreliable) goods. The reliability of r is certain, but the reliability of u only has probability p where $0 < p < 1$. The buyer has a choice between b (boycott) and s (stay), but the boycott option is only ever exercised if the product has been unreliable. The seller receives utility of 1 from selling the low-quality good, and the additional cost of the higher-quality good is c, with $0 < c < 1$. The buyer receives utility of 1 from the reliable good, utility of a from the unreliable one.

The extensive game and its obvious solution are given in Figure 1. To interpret the figure, start at the top. Different choices appear as one progresses down and the figure concludes at the bottom with the utility outcomes (seller's left, buyer's right) resulting from the sequence of choices followed. The constellations $a > 0$ and $a < 0$ with $1 - c < p$ can be described as lemons markets where only low-quality products are available (Akerlof, 1970). In the case where $a < 0$ and $1 - c > p$, the threat of a consumer boycott guarantees high product quality.

Some remarks

Game forms and solution concepts are usually mathematically defined and discussed. Game theory is partly applied mathematics. Its outrageous assumptions regarding rationality (chess strategies, for instance, are far too complex for human brains) allow only a normative interpretation of its prescriptions.

Nevertheless it is often claimed that game theory predicts well. It does so in special situations or if one redefines the game after observing behaviour (Güth, 1995, writes of neoclassical repairs). In evolutionary game theory one gives up rationality completely. However, in this theory the baby is poured out with the bath water, since no allowance at all is made for cognition. A (social) psychological perspective would prescribe a behavioural theory of game playing. But for this it is not enough merely to weaken the rationality assumptions slightly. Such repairs produce theories which are neither normatively convincing nor good predictors of actual decision behaviour.

WERNER GÜTH

Bibliography

Akerlof, G. (1970) 'The Market for Lemons: Quality Uncertainty and the Market Mechanism', *Quarterly Journal of Economics*, **84**: 488–500.

Bolton, G.E. (1991) 'A Comparative Model of Bargaining: Theory and Evidence', *American Economic Review*, **81**: 1096–136.

Cournot, A. (1838) *Recherches sur les Principes Mathématiques de la Théorie des*

Richesses (Researches into the Mathematical Principles of the Theory of Wealth), Paris, L. Hachette.

Frank, B. (1996) 'The Use of Internal Games: The Case of Addiction', *Journal of Economic Psychology*, **17**: 651–60

Geneakoplos, J., Pearce, D. and Stacchetti, E. (1989) 'Psychological Games and Sequential Rationality', *Games and Economic Behavior*, **1**: 60–79.

Güth, W. (1995) 'On Ultimatum Bargaining — A Personal Review', *Journal of Economic Behavior and Organization*, **27**: 329–44.

Güth, W. and Kliemt, H. (1996) 'One Person — Many Players? On Björn Frank's "The Use of Internal Games: The Case of Addiction"', *Journal of Economic Psychology*, **17**: 661–68.

Güth, W., Schmittberger, R. and Schwarze, B. (1982) 'An Experimental Analysis of Ultimatum Bargaining, *Journal of Economic Behavior and Organization*, **3**: 367–88.

Harsanyi, J.C. and Selten, R. (1988) *A General Theory of Equilibrium Selection in Games*, Cambridge, MA, MIT Press.

Homans, G.C. (1961) *Social Behaviour: Hs. Elementary Forms*, London, Routledge & Kegan Paul.

Kagel, J. H. and Roth, A.E. (1995) *The Handbook of Experimental Economics*, Princeton, NJ, Princeton University Press.

Nash, J.F. (1951), 'Noncooperative Games', *Annals of Mathematics*, **54**: 289–95.

Schmeidler, D. (1969) 'The Nucleolus of a Characteristic Function Game', *SIAM Journal of Applied Mathematics*, **17**: 1163–70.

Shapley, L.S. (1953) 'A Value for *N*-person Games', in Kuhn, H.W. and Tucker, A.W. (eds) *Contributions to the Theory of Games II*, Princeton, NJ, Princeton University Press: 307–17.

van Damme, E.E.C. (1987) *Stability and Perfection of Nash Equilibria*, Berlin, Springer-Verlag.

von Neumann, J. and Morgenstern, O. (1944) *Theory of Games and Economic Behavior*, Princeton, NJ, Princeton University Press.

Weibull, J.W. (1995) *Evolutionary Game Theory*, Cambridge, MA, MIT Press.

Gifts

Many social occasions are marked by gifts, and these can provide a useful 'window' on some of the more covert processes of social interaction. Gift giving is linked to both the economic and social domains of exchange and is subject to some of the tensions that characterise this dichotomy. This means that gifts can be defined in a number of ways. For example, they have been described as goods or services 'voluntarily provided to another person or a group ... through some sort of ritual prestation' (Belk and Coon, 1993: 394). On the other hand, Cheal (1988: 87) has defined gifts as 'investments in human and social capital'. Although there is a considerable literature on gift exchange in pre-industrial cultures (for example, Mauss, 1925/54), it is only since the late 1970s that this behaviour has attracted much attention in modern industrial societies. However, research can now draw upon the insights of a range of disciplines including psychology, economics, sociology and anthropology.

There is a great diversity of gifts and gift-giving occasions, but most investigators in Western societies have concentrated their efforts upon ritual occasions, such as Christmas and birthdays. We now know a great deal more about the unwritten 'rules' that govern these events, such as the cost of gifts, what kinds of things can be given to whom, and when. Caplow's study of Christmas in a midwestern American town revealed striking regularities in the kinds of gifts that were exchanged, with most gifts 'scaled' to reflect the formal relationship between donor and recipient (Caplow, 1982, in Caplow, 1984). Norms also influence the type and cost of gifts in dating relationships in order to signal different levels of commitment (Belk and Coon, 1993). Money is often unacceptable as a gift (Webley and Wilson, 1989), but more acceptable when it passes down a status hierarchy, such as from older to younger members of a family (Burgoyne and Routh, 1991). However, research to date has looked only at a small number of gift-giving contexts, and much of the current literature is confined to Western societies. At present, this area lacks a degree of theoretical integration, although a number of conceptual approaches have proved useful, most notably those based on theories of exchange and symbolic communication. These will be discussed below. First, we examine some of the important features that distinguish gifts and commodities.

Gifts and commodities
In capitalist societies, gift exchange can be regarded as a parallel economy to that of the market, and there exists a certain tension between the two. This is because the gift economy draws upon market resources in order to function, yet at the same time has to maintain a distance from it. The vast majority of gifts take the form of commodities bought with money, and may sometimes be in the form of money itself — the most potent symbol of the market and economic exchange. But this does not mean that gift exchange is merely an exchange of commodities. If this were the case, then money, with the flexibility and freedom of choice that it offers the recipient, would be much more popular as a gift than it currently is. Commodity exchange is primarily an exchange of goods, with little importance attached to the nature of the relationship between the people involved in the exchange. However, in gift exchange, it is the relationship between the people that is of primary importance, even when there is a simultaneous exchange of gifts. Of course, market exchange often contains elements of social exchange (such as trust), and the economic value of a gift may sometimes be as important, if not more so, as the relationship between donor and recipient. There may be few 'pure' cases of economic and social exchange, but there are clearly

important differences of emphasis. So how are ordinary commodities detached from the commercial world and turned into gifts? In many cases this is done by ceremonial wrapping. If a present is impossible to wrap, then it will usually be given some form of symbolic wrapping, such as a ribbon or decorative label. This ensures that, at least for the few seconds it takes to give and receive a gift, the item loses its identity and much of its material significance and attention is focused upon the *act* of giving. Carrier (1995) argues that Christmas shopping also plays a part in this process of gift 'appropriation'. By characterizing the shopping as an arduous task, the efforts of the shopper are combined with the mundane reality of the commodity, which then becomes a 'possession', worthy to be used as a gift.

Social and economic exchange

As the foregoing discussion indicates, the dominant paradigm in this area is that of social and economic exchange, and this provides a useful conceptual tool for many types of gift giving (see Sherry, 1983, for some examples). From this perspective, life can be viewed as a series of reciprocal transactions, based upon a rational calculus of utilities given and received. According to the economic model, exchange focuses upon the market value of a gift, with balanced (or sometimes, negative) reciprocity as the goal (Belk and Coon, 1993). In the social exchange model, utility is derived from the more symbolic value associated with the relationship between the giver and receiver, which also determines whether or not the goods themselves should be of equivalent value. In both types of exchange, the giving of the first gift can be regarded as the transmission of a debt, since it demands some form of reciprocation. However, in contrast to the norms of commodity exchange, the debt imposed by a gift is not typically *discharged* by a return gift. Nothing can quite make up for the unsolicited nature of a first gift, so the debt is never wholly discharged (Schwartz, 1967). Instead, the return gift imposes its own, separate debt upon the recipient. These impositions of debt and counter-debt help to bind people together in a series of mutually beneficial transactions. Since it is women who tend to be seen as the 'kin-keepers', this notion of gift exchange as a kind of 'cement' in the maintenance of important relationships helps to explain why it is mainly women who have the primary responsibility in the running of the gift economy (Cheal, 1988).

Given the centrality of reciprocation in theories of exchange, it might seem paradoxical that the need for it in gift giving is often vigorously denied. There may be some diffuse sense of obligation, but it is important that this remains somewhat nebulous, and it would be highly insulting to make it too explicit. People do not like to admit that their close or intimate relationships may even be based partly on exchange, and of course, the instrumental nature of gifts is not the whole story — gifts also have an expressive function. Despite the undoubted success of the exchange paradigm, therefore, it does not account for all gift behaviour. It may not be entirely appropriate for the phenomenon of 'self-gifts', although it may be possible in some cases to see a self-gift in terms of rewarding oneself for past achievements, or as a consolation for undeserved misfortunes (Mick and DeMoss, 1990). However, the main problem for the exchange approach is altruistic giving. Even in the context of social exchange, some gifts may be purely expressive, such as those motivated by unselfish love or *agape* (Belk and Coon, 1993). Thus, there may be gifts which are given with no expectation of reciprocation (such as romantic or brotherly love), and others where direct reciprocity is explicitly ruled out, such as anonymous donations to charity. There may also be unreciprocated gifts of a different kind — agonistic gifts — that aim to achieve dominance over another, or to cause harm (Schwartz, 1967).

This reminds us that giving also has its darker side. Gifts can threaten social ties as well as reaffirm them (Sherry, McGrath and Levy, 1992). The onerous task of getting the 'right' present can mean that gift giving is fraught with a high level of psychosocial anxiety. Skill is required in order to handle gift exchange successfully, especially when there is any degree of insincerity (such as ambivalent or hostile relationships within the family). Sherry et al. suggest that unsuccessful gifts provoke highly negative emotions in the recipient, and the task of returning unsatisfactory gifts to the shop is experienced as an unpleasant extension of the gift exchange ritual.

Although gifts may often be given for benevolent reasons, they may also provide an opportunity for the giver to impose their view of the recipient's identity and of the relationship (Schwartz, 1967). If this is unacceptable to the receiver, then both the gift and the giver may be rejected. For example, a very expensive gift given too early in a dating relationship may signal a greater level of intimacy than is assumed — or wanted — by the recipient. If this is so, then steps may be taken to cool or end the relationship (Belk and Coon, 1993). Of course, giving can also say something about the character and standing of the giver, which may account for some of the more public acts of philanthropy, and certain forms of conspicuous consumption (Veblen, 1979), such as lavish dinner parties. These carry echoes of the *potlatch* in which the donor's status is elevated if the receiver cannot reciprocate with an even greater display of wealth (Mauss, 1925/54).

Gifts as communication

Another perspective on gift giving that takes account of these expressive functions is that of gifts as symbolic communication. Gifts can be used to shape or reflect aspects of social identity, such as membership in specific groups, or to indicate social distance or relative intimacy; boundaries may be established and maintained via gift exchange, since those to whom we give differ from those to whom we do not (Sherry, 1983). One way that relationships grow and develop is through the transmission of shared meanings. Thus, Caplow (1984) sees gift exchange in terms of a language, or a system of meanings, which contributes to the *construction* of particular social realities. Conversely, the *absence* of a gift is also a lexical sign — signifying the absence of a close relationship, or the desire to disengage from an existing one. One cannot choose to ignore or misunderstand a language having once learned it, because to do so would be to send messages of hostility or indifference. However, gifts are not perfect as channels of communication, and there is the risk that messages will be misinterpreted. As mentioned earlier, several different kinds of message may be incorporated in a single gift, including the importance of the relationship, the level of perceived intimacy, and the giver's perceptions of self and other.

The first task for the recipient is to decode these messages, and to identify and evaluate the motivations of the giver. This may be a private act, or it may involve the reactions of others present at the exchange. If the gift occasion involves a simultaneous exchange, then the gift may be evaluated in the light of the gift given. Is this a 'true' gift, or a disguised payment for past favours, or perhaps a bribe (a payment for future favours)? Are there any implications in terms of either a business or interpersonal relationship? Does it represent a spontaneous, altruistic act, or one that is rule governed and routine? In other words, a process of attribution takes place, and the recipient's response is framed accordingly. Of course, many of these questions may not arise if the context is sufficiently transparent. The meaning of a gift that is wrapped and presented on the occasion of a birthday is clear enough, unless it comes from an anomalous source, or violates some relevant rule, such as a highly personal gift from an acquaintance. However, not all gifts are so easy to 'decode' and there is plenty of scope for misattribution. The nature of the gift and its cost are also useful (although not infallible) sources of inference about the intentions of the giver. Sherry (1983) refers to this stage in the process as 'reformulation' in which the relationship may be reinforced, weakened or even terminated. If the question of reciprocation arises, then a decision has to be made about the type and timing of the return gift. At this stage, the cycle is completed, and the recipient may take over the role of donor.

Despite an increasing literature on gifts, much of the research to date has been somewhat individualistic and static. Little is known about changes in gift giving over time in particular relationships, or how the dyadic relationship fits into the wider networks of exchange. Given the importance of context, more work needs to be done in other cultures. Much therefore remains to be understood before we can build a comprehensive account of this type of behaviour.

CAROLE B. BURGOYNE

Bibliography

Belk, R.W. and Coon, G.S. (1993) 'Gift Giving as Agapic Love: An Alternative to the Exchange Paradigm Based on Dating Experiences', *Journal of Consumer Research*, **20**: 393–417.

Burgoyne, C.B. and Routh, D.A. (1991) 'Constraints on the Use of Money as a Gift at Christmas: The Role of Status and Intimacy', *Journal of Economic Psychology*, **12**: 47–69.

Caplow, T. (1984) 'Rule Enforcement without Visible Means: Christmas Gift Giving in Middletown', *American Journal of Sociology*, **89**: 1306–23.

Carrier, J.G. (1995) *Gifts and Commodities: Exchange and Western Capitalism since 1700*, London, Routledge.

Cheal, D. (1988) *The Gift Economy*, London, Routledge.

Mauss, M. (1925/54) *The Gift*, Aberdeen, Aberdeen University Press (Translation by I. Cunnison).

Mick, D.G. and DeMoss, M. (1990) 'Self-Gifts: Phenomenological Insights from Four Contexts', *Journal of Consumer Research*, **17**: 322–32.

Schwartz, B. (1967) 'The Social Psychology of the Gift', *American Journal of Sociology*, **73**: 1–11.

Sherry, J.F. (1983) 'Gift Giving in Anthropological Perspective', *Journal of Consumer Research*, **10**: 157–68.

Sherry, J.F., McGrath, M.A. and Levy, S.J. (1992) 'The Disposition of the Gift and Many Unhappy Returns', *Journal of Retailing*, **68**: 40–65.

Veblen, T. (1979) *The Theory of the Leisure Class*, Harmondsworth, Penguin (Original work published 1899).

Webley, P. and Wilson, R. (1989) 'Social Relationships and the Unacceptability of Money as a Gift', *Journal of Social Psychology*, **129**: 85–91.

Growing Old

This entry reviews individual and societal aspects of growing old. It is based on the research literature dealing with ageing, retirement, the economic status of older people, their incomes, possessions and consumption, and the economics of ageing. The emphasis is upon research that involves the direct study of people growing old. To begin, retirement and some of its consequences are examined.

Retirement is one of the major transitions of later life (Aiken, 1995; Moen, 1996). It is associated with growing old and becoming aged. The retired population is coextensive with the old population, although many people retire voluntarily or involuntarily before age 60. Government policies are highly influential in establishing societal expectations about retirement. Government is fully or partly in control of the age pension, unemployment benefits for older people, and the financial-taxation circumstances of occupational pension, superannuation and private pension schemes. It uses retirement partly to manipulate unemployment.

Where choice is available, an individual's decision about retirement is complex, reflecting personal, family, financial, job satisfaction and employment factors. People who retire voluntarily usually welcome retirement and adjust readily to the changes it entails. Those who are coerced into retirement, who retire because of illness or injury, retire on low income, or who have a troublesome marriage, are more likely to experience difficulties. People in high-paid, high-status employment tend to be relatively resistant to retirement. None the less, retirement is becoming an active life stage for most people. It is a do-it-yourself stage which offers freedom from the constraints of the labour market. Retirement lifestyles have become exceedingly varied.

Patterns of employment, unemployment and retirement in later life have been changing over the past generation, with the average retirement age going down. Early permanent retirement, and diverse retirement moves in and out of full- and part-time jobs, have become pronounced features of national labour markets. For many people, these developments, in association with widespread falls in real incomes and the progressive casualization of national labour markets, have been reducing not only their returns from income-earning employment but also their returns from income-related retirement benefits. The time people spend in income-earning employment has been contracting, and the time spent in retirement expanding, while life expectancy has been increasing. The outcome is a need for resources to be generated, during a much shorter more insecure period of paid employment, to support a longer more expensive retirement period of life.

At retirement most people experience a large fall in money income. However, the income situation of older people has tended to improve in the latter half of this century. The incidence of abject poverty has been reduced, but many older people are located in the near-poverty zone. At the same time, there are massive inequalities in incomes among older people, with a tiny minority having huge incomes. These inequalities are very much a continuation of inequalities of earlier years. Moreover, the highly skewed distribution of wealth among older people parallels that for incomes. Income and wealth inequalities are associated with inequalities in consumption and economic security. Income, wealth, consumption and security differ greatly among older people; their economic heterogeneity is a key characteristic (Smeeding, 1996).

Retired women average lower incomes than retired men because they average lower incomes when employed, average fewer years in employment, and benefit far less from occupational pension schemes, superannuation and the perks of employment packages at the upper end of the labour market (Aiken, 1995; Hutton, 1996; Shaver, 1996). Having an employed spouse gives married women (and some married men) greater freedom of choice about retirement. When married women who have a husband receiving an occupational pension become widows, usually they lose much or all of their husband's occupational pension income as well as his portion of any government pension. Older people who live alone, usually single women or widows, are highly vulnerable economically, and frequently exist in or near poverty.

Although the money incomes of older people are typically well below average money incomes among the employed, older people are often described as well-to-do, woopies, greedy, affluent, even rich. This has come about partly because of the fashion among the followers of current orthodox economics to impute large 'income' to older people from ownership of their own housing, material goods and appliances, and from goods in kind they receive including public health and transport services. If generous 'rental incomes' are imputed to their possessions, and goods in kind are treated as the equivalent of money income, then the 'incomes' of older people are apparently sizeable. This can have bizarre results. For example, if an older person receives serious injuries in a traffic accident that require much expensive surgical and therapeutic treatment, then the person may move into the top 1 per cent of income earners (and become instantly rich) because the cost of medical treatment is imputed as income. To define serious illness and injury requiring expensive treatment among older people (or the young) as income is worse than specious. To lump their goods and services together and treat them as if they were an annuity of income equivalents is contentious. Moreover, if all the costs incurred by older people in acquiring and maintaining possessions prone to deterioration were taken into account, then any imputed income would be massively reduced, and maybe become negative income.

The life-cycle hypothesis (LCH) is an argument that people borrow when young adults, save in middle age, and spend their assets or dissave in retirement so as to maintain more or less a pre-retirement standard of living. It follows that lifetime income approximately matches lifetime consumption. The proponents of the LCH assume individuals arrive at an optimal life-course strategy, and follow it relentlessly through life. This influential economic hypothesis has been criticized as an explanation of life-course saving and consumption for three significant reasons. First, yearly consumption rates are too highly correlated with income to be consistent with the LCH; the age-consumption pattern is influenced strongly by income. Second, people have much too low a tendency to consume home equity or pension wealth for this behaviour to be consistent with the LCH. Third, the fungibility assumption of the LCH, which allows all assets to be treated as equivalent to a money sum for consumption purposes, is not valid because people do not treat assets as nearly perfect substitutes.

From the perspective of the LCH, older people appear to consume too little and to dissave too slowly. The people with resources generally use them up steadily during retirement, and hold on to housing equity. In retirement, people tend to be relatively well off when they first retire, particularly when they are living in pensioner couples. Typically, financial assets and possessions are expended during the retirement years; more rapidly by singles than couples, by older than younger people. In addition, there is continuing government 'reform' pressure to reduce the value of the age pension and to increase the age of eligibility. This means that for most people, during older adulthood, there is an ongoing decline in income towards the basic age pension, which is intensified with widowhood.

Poverty rates among the old increase with age. Poverty or near-poverty in older adulthood is more likely to be long-term or permanent than in earlier life. Every year relatively older and relatively poorer old people tend to die, and they are replaced by younger, better-off, new entrants to the ranks of the retired. New arrivals average higher incomes and assets than those departing at death. This is a major process in sustaining the economic status of older people as a segment of the population (Smeeding, 1996).

The percentage of gross national product that is spent on public pensions in the wealthier nations varies considerably, from less than 6 per cent to more than 12 per cent (Smeeding, 1990, 1996). Australia, Canada, and the US spend meagrely in contrast with many nations. International comparisons present Australia, Canada and the US in a poor light with reference to governmental treatment of older people who are not rich. In Australia, entitlement to an old-age pension is subject to means-testing of both income and assets, which results in many older people being in difficult circumstances. Means-testing is used in some nations to withhold retirement benefits from those who are not in or not very close to poverty. This creates a trap for those who have too little to be financiallly secure, but have enough to be penalized by means-testing. Smeeding (1990) has called these marginal and insecure people 'tweeners'.

For people of all ages, money is the universal medium of exchange and store of cash worth. Monetary values, attitudes and behaviour are not transformed by retirement. Rather they are a continuation of earlier values, attitudes and behaviour that, with the passing years, are adjusted progressively to the changing realities of life. People who have worked to make money are deprived of their working life's purpose on retirement, which requires a reordering of their life. Those who have used money as a way of dealing with feelings of inadequacy or other negatives in their earlier life, may have to resort to changed self-defences after losing income on retirement. Money and possessions can become entangled in severe emotional problems and neuroses among older adults, as they do among younger adults. Older people who age to a period of serious deterioration, including advanced dementia, suffer declining cognitive and behavioural powers in managing their affairs which may end with a complete loss of ability to deal with them.

Money and useful material possessions are empowering resources. In sufficient quantity they permit personal independence, freedom of choice, autonomy, self-regard, dignity and self-expression. They enable older people to control life independently of others, and may cushion any financial shocks that occur. These resources are positively associated with education, health, activity and residential neighbourhood quality in old age. Prolonged financial strain is detrimental to health and well-being. Early retirement and increased longevity heighten the financial uncertainties of later life.

Money, financial assets and material possessions contribute to status among older as well as younger people. These resources are significant factors in marriages and re-marriages for older people, including the more affluent. Among them, there may be concerns about who inherits each partner's estate after marriage, with pre-nuptial agreements possibly being used to arrange transfer of each spouse's property to their own descendants.

Money can be used as a resource to control, manipulate or punish others; to buy companionship, friendship or love. This applies to marital, family and other relationships. One expression of this is in the writing and rewriting of wills. Another expression is gift giving to relatives and friends, which may promote unpleasant family politics. Older people may have to cope with the behaviour of greedy relatives who desire to benefit from their income and possessions. Money can be used as aid when older people attempt to overcome whatever stands in their way of accomplishing something.

Although economic resources typically decline during later life, older people are usually more satisfied with their income and resources than younger adults. Financial satisfaction tends to be unexpectedly high among older people, while income tends to be relatively low. Older people view their financial circumstances differently from younger people, and are satisfied with less. They tend to compare themselves with other older people who average low incomes, not with adults in paid employment. Older people are often too unrealistically satisfied with inadequately low levels of income, which render them vulnerable to financial strain, insecurity and other problems. Yet more frequently than their juniors they have learned when enough is enough.

In later life, the subjective aspects of financial affairs are by no means all rosy. Commonly, older people worry about their financial resources meeting expenses and being adequate for the future. Further, they worry specifically about any future illness, accidents, care requirements and widowhood, and their monetary costs. Older people face a future uncertain in terms of life duration, health, financial needs and ability to maintain an independent household, in which there exists a visible possibility of catastrophe. Many of their material resources do not provide money income, they cannot spend imputed income. They are far less satisfied with future prospects than with present circumstances. It has been argued that the potential catastrophes of later life are sufficient to strip the sense of control over life, which is illusory in earlier years, away from many older people.

Consumer expenditure varies by age, income and responsibility for relatives, especially children (Cook and Settersten, 1995; Wilkes, 1995). Largely because of the fall in income on retirement, older people spend much less on consumer goods and services than middle-aged and younger adults. On average, older people have far less purchasing power, but there exist huge income-based differentials among them. However, declining health, injuries and increasing medical treatment expenses, mean that this health and personal care category of expenditure is a partial exception to the general downward trend. From a consumer perspective, most people do not accumulate the resources to maintain the same standard of living in retirement as in their period of full-time employment. But affluent older people who have health, money and free time are attractive to business (Cole and Castellano, 1996).

Compared with younger adults, older people spend a higher proportion of their income on essentials such as food, health care, and household utilities; they spend a lower proportion on transport, clothing, life insurance, pensions, and entertainment. The cash cost of maintaining housing, material goods and appliances may become difficult, burdensome or impossible as real income declines further with advancing years. None the less, older people are an expanding segment of the consumer market because of the drop in the birth rate and increase in life expectancy. This segment is further divided into submarkets, with education and income being important demarcation factors. High-income older households are part of the market in luxury goods and services.

Given that the specialist literature asserts that older consumers are different to their juniors, interest in explaining age differences in consumer behaviour is growing. Research to date has been influenced obviously by ageist stereotypes. There has been an emphasis on cognitive decline (especially with reference to memory and speed of information processing), brand loyalty, resistance to new products and services, the advancing obsolescence of growing old, and disengagement from social life. In practice, business incompetence and ineffectiveness in manufacturing, marketing and advertising causes problems for older as for younger consumers. In addition, there is a good deal of ageist prejudice directed against older people in marketing, advertising and the mass media in general. Further, older adults are frequently the target not only for sharp business practices but also business crime, and confidence tricks. Age-related changes in consumer behaviour are extremely variable. As indicated by Cole and Castellano (1996), the existing literature raises a host of questions about the consumer behaviour of older people. Among other things, answers to questions about consumer behaviour will come partly from taking account of older people's knowledge, experience, maturity and survival skills.

Possessions, including home and staple goods, contribute to the preservation of a sense of control of life among older people (Dittmar, 1992). They can also provide security, satisfaction, status, enjoyment, nostalgia, solace and symbolic significance. They may act as a buffer when people are experiencing losses in some areas of their lives, including loss of home with a move into an institutional setting. Older people attach instrumental and symbolic values to their homes. Home is a place to live, an emotional refuge, a source of biographical memories, a focal point for relatives and friends, a possibility for self-expression in decor and garden, and a place offering opportunity to maintain self-esteem. Remaining independent and active in daily living in one's own home is important to older people.

Possessions as symbols of self and others, including people important to them who have died, can be highly valued or treasured. Heirlooms, photographs, family memorabilia, gifts, souvenirs, and collections (such as dolls, silver, china, stamps, jewellery) may well become more valued by their owner as time passes. They are object reminders of the past, of relationships with others, and of enjoyable times; they play a role in preservation of self-identity. Personal possessions may function as objects of reminiscence and life review.

Finally, people can make a mark on the future after their death by gifts and will provisions. They can accomplish some objectives after their inevitable death. Money, property, financial assets and possessions can be passed to relatives and others in such a way as to express feelings, as reminders of the dead benefactor, as heirlooms, for intergenerational continuity of some sort, or to maintain family reputation and worth. Heirlooms and family memorabilia have special, maybe unique, value across generations. A concern with posterity can help older people resolve the challenges of late life and in approaching death.

BARRIE G. STACEY

Bibliography
Aiken, L.R. (1995) *Aging*, Thousand Oaks, CA, Sage.
Cole, C.A. and Castellano, N.N. (1996) 'Consumer Behavor', in Birren, J.E. (ed.) *Encyclopedia of Gerontology*, San Diego, CA, Academic Press.
Cook, F.L. and Settersten, R.A. (1995) 'Expenditure Patterns by Age and Income: Does Age Matter?', *The Gerontologist*, **35**: 10–23.
Dittmar, H. (1992) *The Social Psychology of Material Possessions*, Hemel Hempstead, Harvester Wheatsheaf.

Hutton, S. (1996) 'Current and Future Incomes for Older People', *Ageing and Society*, **16**: 775–87.

Moen, P. (1996) 'Gender, Age and the Life Course', in Binstock, R.H. and George, L.K. (eds) *Handbook of Aging and the Social Sciences* (4th edn), San Diego, CA, Academic Press.

Shaver, S. (1996) 'Universality and Selectivity in Aged Income Support' in Minichiello, V., Chappell, N., Kendig, H. and Walker, A. (eds), *Sociology of Aging: International Perspectives*, Melbourne, International Sociological Association.

Smeeding, T. (1990) 'Economic Status of the Elderly', in Binstock, R.H. and George, L.K. (eds) *Handbook of Aging and the Social Sciences* (3rd edn), San Diego, CA, Academic Press.

Smeeding, T. (1996), 'Economics: Individual', in Birren, J.E. (ed.) *Encyclopedia of Gerontology*, San Diego, CA: Academic Press.

Wilkes, R.E. (1995) 'Household Life-Cycle Stages, Transitions, and Product Expenditures', *Journal of Consumer Research*, **22**: 27–42.

Habit

The concept of habit is a relatively neglected topic in economic psychology and consumer research despite being one of the more obvious areas of application of the concept. This neglect, in part, reflects a lack of interest in habit by the social sciences in general (Camic, 1986). For example, orthodox economic theory with its 'rational economic man' and interpretative sociological theory with its conscious, reflective actor grant little theoretical status to habit, instinct and emotion as other possible components or modes of behaviour. The psychological sciences have also tended to emphasize the deliberative character of individual decision making (for example, the theory of reasoned action). Thus despite the call by George Katona (1951) for the inclusion of habit in economic analysis and empirical research such as Houthakker and Taylor (1970) indicating the pervasiveness of habit in consumption, habit is usually treated in textbooks on consumer behaviour as a side issue to more complex models of decision making. However, this may change as cognitive science provide further insights into — and raises the prominence of — the unconscious, automatic and embodied nature of cognition.

The role of habit

Habit is usefully defined as 'a more or less self-actuating disposition or tendency to engage in a previously adopted or acquired form of action' (Camic, 1986: 1044). A habit may be consciously invoked as part of a goal-directed activity, but once instigated it proceeds automatically with little deliberation or consideration of informational cues. Koestler (1967) uses the example of driving a car as illustrative of the nature of habit. When first learning to drive a car a lot of concentration is required, but with practice driving becomes a partially unconscious, programmed behaviour. While driving we may be forced to switch to more conscious processing if something unusual happens (for example, someone cuts in front of you) however, some other habits are not so easily accessible or overridden (especially some habits of thought).

The concept of habit was once a staple theoretical tool in the social sciences and was acknowledged, often prominently, in the writings of Aristotle, David Hume, Emile Durkheim and Max Weber. But perhaps the most comprehensive treatment of habit appeared in the works of the American pragmatists — Charles Sanders Peirce, William James and John Dewey .

According to the pragmatists, the main function of habit is to economize and simplify our actions. Human behaviour is not rigidly determined by instinct and much of our behaviour is learned. But, at the same time, we cannot be actively conscious of all we have learned. In William James's famous chapter on habit in *The Principles of Psychology* (1890) he points out that if there were no such mechanism as habit to economize the effort required for learned performance, humans would 'be in a sorry plight'. Fortunately, people store the fruits of past experience so as to economize effort and simplify action: habit reduces the need for conscious supervision and leaves consciousness free to deal with the more problematic situations we encounter in life. So, for example, when driving to work the programmed habits of driving along a standard route allow us to concentrate on other tasks such as planning the day ahead, rather than wasting all our cognitive energy on the somewhat tedious task of driving and selecting the best route.

It was further understood by the pragmatists that many of our habits are of a social nature and provide a crucial role in sustaining social cohesion by providing predictability and a sense of 'normalness' to the social world. More recently, Ronald Heiner (1983) has examined how habits make our social life more predictable than would be the case if our actions were custom tailored to the peculiarities of individual contexts. The predictability and routineness that habit injects into everyday life also provides a sense of 'ontological security' to counteract the anxiety associated with a contingent and otherwise uncertain world.

The social dimension of habit became one of the cornerstones of the economic thought of Thorstein Veblen (1948), the father of institutional economics. Veblen, in fact, defined institutions as 'settled habits of thought common to the generality of men'. His discussion of conspicuous consumption treats consumption as essentially habitual, being shaped by cultural norms and status relations rather than by rational considerations.

The pragmatists also gave habit a fundamental role in the creation of meaning and our ability to make sense of the world. Peirce's (1931–58) famous pragmatic criterion equates the meaning of a concept with the habits of action that it involves. Dewey (1910) also highlighted how our habits of action are intimately intermeshed with the environment and that cognition is part of a wider process that reaches beyond the skin and bone of the individual's head. Only very recently have these themes of 'embodied' and 'situated' cognition reemerged as prominent themes in cognitive science.

Habit in consumer behaviour
Habit mainly disappeared from the social sciences after the 1930s as a casualty of the social sciences trying to establish autonomy from psychology and biology (Camic, 1986). Some economic psychologists and marketing scientists, however, have kept contact with the concept, particularly in its role of economizing cognitive effort. Thus, for example, in contrast to neoclassical economics, there is a recognition that buying a car involves a different level of cognitive effort from buying toothpaste.

Early research used behaviourist theories to identify the type of learning that was involved in establishing a habit (Assael, 1992: Ch. 3). Instrumental conditioning was used to describe the establishment of 'brand loyalty' in which repeated satisfaction of some types of high involvement product leads to commitment to a particular brand. Classical conditioning was used to describe 'consumer inertia' in which the consumer buys the same brand, not because of brand loyalty, but because it is not worth the time and trouble to search for an alternative. While these two types of consumption habits may differ in how they are formed (and how they may be broken) they share the characteristic of minimal information search and cognitive evaluation once they are established.

Marketing scientists were well aware of the implications of minimal cognitive effort of some purchasing behaviour in their design of distribution, advertising and pricing policies. For example, advertising for habitual products is more likely to be used for reminder purposes and, as such, frequent advertising is important. By contrast, products characterized by complex decision making are more likely to use advertising selectively to convey information to specific audiences (Assael, 1992).

With the decline of behaviourism from the 1950s, interest in habit as stimulus–response behaviour declined as attention was turned to the various processes that occurred in the mind of the individual. However, with the rise of cognitivist theories came the recognition that even with complex decision making, habits-of-mind or heuristics are an integral part of this process. Herbert Simon's (1957) development of the concept of 'bounded rationality' was an important contribution in recognizing the limited informational capabilities of the decision maker. The work of Kahneman and Tversky (1982) also demonstrated that not only are these heuristics often biased but they are also often not available to conscious inspection (that is, heuristics are not always consciously employed rules of thumb but often operate automatically and unconsciously in the true sense of a habit). More recently, Payne, Bettman and Johnson (1993) have tried to show how the adaptive decision maker, with limited information-processing capabilities, employs different cognitive strategies as a compromise between the desire to make the most accurate decision and the desire to minimize cognitive effort.

However, while cognitive psychology does not deny the unconscious nature of much of our thinking processes, there has been a tendency, at least in the applications to consumer behaviour, to overemphasize the conscious, deliberative nature of cognition. That is, there is a lack of recognition that even though conscious, 'rational' considerations (including rules of thumb) may have been involved in the original choice decision once the behaviour becomes repetitive a habit can become established that no longer ensures sensitivity to new information or potential choice strategies and hence may no longer be optimal (even in terms of the accuracy–effort tradeoff). Furthermore, the usual methodology of setting decision-making problems in laboratory conditions, and often demanding accountability of these decisions, may bias the participants to engage in more active thinking than would otherwise be the case. Verplanken, Aarts and Van Knippenberg (1997) is one study that has tried to measure the level of information use with habitual behaviours as well as the effects that attention and accountability may have on these habits. Using an independent measure of habit, they have found that habit does indeed reduce the elaborateness of information use in judgements of travel mode use. If a generalized travel habit has developed, the habitually used travel mode (for example, bicycle) is capable of being immediately activated upon instigation of a specific goal to travel (for example, having to go university) without reflecting on any aspects of the trip (for example, weather considerations, time of day and so forth). By manipulating attention and accountability, habit can, to some extent, be temporally overridden, resulting in increased information acquisition and choice evaluation. However the chronic effects of habit tend to reemerge after a few trials.

New directions from cognitive science
Cognitive science — the interdisciplinary scientific study of the mind — is providing new perspectives on the mind from a number of directions which may be relevant for the study of habit. Cognitive psychology has seen a renewed interest in the cognitive unconscious including such phenomena as subliminal perception, priming, blindsight, implicit learning and procedural memory. Cohen and Bacdayan (1994) is one example of a recent study which has drawn upon work that locates habits and skills in procedural memory in order to understand routines in the organization. They claim that this new work in psychology may help explain how routines arise, stabilize and change, as well as offer insight on why routines may 'misfire' in inappropriate circumstances.

Psychologists have also begun to create explicit models of automatic (habitual) and strategic (reflective) thinking that capture some of the key distinctions, as well as links, between these two modes of thinking. Grunert (1996) has applied this research to advertising effects, which, he argues, has been dominated by cognitive models of information processing, in which information processing is largely equated with strategic, conscious thought processes. Grunert lists a number of differential effects that these two processes have for issues such as learning, attention, brand evaluation and attitude. For example, the attention problem, often discussed in advertising literature, is relevant only for strategic processes. Connectionist (or neural network) modelling also offers a new tool for modelling habit. While connectionist models need not necessarily be equated with habitual behaviour, there do seem to be a number of features of connectionist systems which are similar to habit: learning through repetition, durability, slow degradation and generalization capabilities.

The study of embodied cognition, in the tradition of Peirce and Dewey, is also becoming a major topic in cognitive science and may open new avenues for understanding automatic behaviour. Put crudely, this approach views memory not so much as a store of preferences and beliefs but rather as a repository of habits or 'encoded patterns of action'. Malter (1996) has argued that, from this perspective, quick decision making and impulse buying should be viewed as a natural mode of cognition. When the projectable properties of the environment (for example, the packaging of a product) mesh perfectly with the patterns of action from memory, the effect can dominate thoughts of alternatives and evoke in the consumer a feeling of 'rightness' — as if sufficient information or evaluation has been made to make a rational decision. In contrast, in order to evaluate the product deliberatively, effortful conscious suppression of these feelings is necessary to permit the construction of counterarguments regarding such factors as affordability and practicality of the product and so on.

In many ways, much of this work can be linked to the growing 'knowledge' literature in economics which draws on research from psychology, such as personal construct theory, as well as the literature on Kuhnian paradigms and Lakatosian research programmes from the philosophy of science. This work continues from Peirce's critique of the Cartesian conception of the mind in which complete doubt and 'pure' reasoning are seen as possible, free from any prejudices and preconceptions. Such a mind is not possible according to Peirce and the more recent literature. Our minds inevitably create and organize knowledge and although we may have some ability to alter this framework reflexively we can never step outside it. The study of habit can contribute to this examination of the way we perceive and conceive the world, and thus broaden the analysis beyond the reasoning/inference procedures based on these perceptions.

Conclusions

Because habits are essentially unconscious and automatic we are not fully aware of how much of our daily life is governed by them. This is one reason why the greater part of social science research has tended to neglect habit and focus on the less frequent activity of reflective deliberation. While psychology has not ignored or denied that much cognitive activity occurs below the level of conscious awareness, the application of psychology to consumer behaviour has also tended to emphasize the conscious, strategic nature of cognition. Thus, in general, when habit is considered in theoretical work there is still a tendency to try to subsume habit within a rational or boundedly rational framework. This approach tends to miss some of the most distinctive features of habit. However, as cognitive science begins to take a closer interest in issues such as the cognitive unconscious, automatic processing, connectionist (neural-network) modelling and embodied cognition, the foundations may be set for a deeper understanding of habit. From this new perspective, behaviours such as consumer inertia, impulse buying, brand loyalty and ritual behaviour may not be seen as problematic or unusual but rather as expressions of a natural mode of cognition. This new work may become an important complement to the traditional information-processing paradigm of modelling consumer behaviour.

PAUL J. TWOMEY

Bibliography

Assael, H. (1992) *Consumer Behavior and Marketing Action*, Boston, MA, PWS–KENT.
Camic, C. (1986) 'The Matter of Habit', *American Journal of Sociology*, **91**: 1039–87.
Cohen, M.D. and Bacdayan, P. (1994) 'Organizational Routines Are Stored as Procedural Memory — Evidence from a Laboratory Study', *Organization Science*, **5**: 554–68.
Dewey, J. (1910) *How We Think*, New York, Heath.
Grunert, K. (1996) 'Automatic and Strategic Processes in Advertising Effects', *Journal of Marketing*, **60**: 88–101.
Katona, G. (1951) *Psychological Analysis of Economic Behaviour*, New York, McGraw-Hill.
Koestler, A. (1967) *The Ghost in the Machine*, London, Hutchinson.
Heiner, R.A. (1983) 'The Origins of Predictable Behavior', *Amercian Economic Review*, **73**: 560–95.
Houthakker, H.S. and Taylor, L.D. (1970) *Consumer Demand in the United States: Analysis and Projections* (2nd edn), Cambridge, MA, Harvard University Press.
James. W. (1890) *The Principles of Psychology*, New York, Henry Holt & Company.
Kahneman, D. and Tversky, A. (1982) 'Judgement Under Uncertainty: Heuristics and Biases', in Kahneman, D., Slovic, P. and Tversky, A. (eds) *Judgement Under Uncertainty: Heuristics and Biases*, Cambridge, Cambridge University Press.
Malter, A. (1996) 'An Introduction to Embodied Cognition: Implications for Consumer Research', *Advances in Consumer Research*, **23**: 272–6.
Payne, J.W., Bettman, J.R. and Johnson, E.J. (1993) *The Adaptive Decision Maker*, Cambridge, Cambridge University Press.
Peirce, C.S. (1931–58) *collected Papers of Charles Sanders Peirce*, 8 vols, edited by C. Hartshorne, P. Weiss and A. Burks, Cambridge, MA, Harvard University Press.
Simon, H.A. (1957) *Models of Man*, New York, Wiley.
Veblen, T. (1948) *The Portable Veblen*, ed. M. Lerner, with an introductory essay, New York, Viking Press.
Verplanken, B., Aarts, H., and Van Knippenberg, A. (1997) 'Habit, Information Acquisition, and the Process of Making Travel Mode Choices', *European Journal of Social Psychology*, **27**: 539–60.

Hedonic Consumption

In 1982, two papers appeared which encouraged consumer researchers to explore the experiential boundaries of consumption beyond the narrow confines of cognitive psychology and utilitarian economics (Hirschman and Holbrook, 1982; Holbrook and Hirschman, 1982). As the authors noted (Holbrook and Hirschman, 1982: 136),

> Some experientially relevant personality constructs include:
> * *Sensation Seeking*, a variable likely to affect a consumer's tendency to enjoy more complex entertainment, to be fashion conscious, to prefer spicy and crunchy foods, to play games, and to use drugs
> * Creativity and related variables tied to variety-, novelty-, or arousal-seeking.

Holbrook and Hirschman (1982: 137) further proposed that

> [The] relevant emotions [for consumer research] include such diverse feelings as love, hate, fear, joy, boredom, anxiety, pride, anger, disgust, sadness, sympathy, lust, ecstasy, greed, guilt, elation, shame, and awe. This sphere of human experience has long been neglected by psychologists, who are just beginning to expand early work on arousal in order to develop systematic and coherent models of emotion.

Following this, several studies were conducted exploring various aspects of hedonic and experiential consumption; we shall review five representative examples here.

First, Havlena and Holbrook (1986) compared two classification systems for emotion: Mehrabian and Russell's (1974) paradigm and Plutchik's eight emotional categories (1980). Using an elaborate series of multivariate procedures they determined that the three-dimensional model — pleasure, arousal, dominance — proposed by Mehrabian and Russell was superior in representing emotion during actual consumption experiences.

Second, in a study of emotions resulting from consumer purchasing experiences, Westbrook and Oliver (1991) examined the assumption of unidimensionality (that is, favourable to unfavourable) for satisfaction judgements. Because of the lack of prior work on emotions in the area of consumer behaviour, researchers were forced to improvise, using scales drawn from psychology. For this reason, Westbrook and Oliver used Izard's (1977) measure of emotion, which contains '10 subscales representing the frequency with which subjects experience each of 10 fundamental emotions: the positive affects of interest and joy; the negative affects of anger, contempt, disgust, shame, guilt, sadness, fear, and surprise' (Westbrook and Oliver, 1991: 87).

However, the present author questions whether 'interest' and 'surprise' actually constitute *emotions*, as that term was intended by Holbrook and Hirschman (1982). Rather, interest would seem to describe a state of *cognitive curiosity*, a desire to learn about something. Similarly, surprise would seem to represent a cognitive state of *disconfirmed expectations*, that is, an event turned out differently than one expected. And sure enough, these two scales did not behave as predicted in the Westbrook and Oliver study (1991: 87) which reported that

> Generally, respondents experienced interest and joy more effectively than the negative affects, with the affect of surprise located between the extremes. Although the negative emotions tend to be highly correlated, of note here is the fact that interest and joy are not. Surprise is moderately correlated with all of the emotions except interest.

Third, Allen, Machleit and Klein (1992) examined whether recollected emotions regarding an emotionally-mixed consumption experience (blood donation) could serve as incremental predictors (beyond attitudes) of behaviour. They argue that emotion extends beyond attitude and encompasses 'a richer and more diverse domain of phenomenological experience' (p. 494). They further propose that much emotional experience is likely stored in *episodic memory*, whereas attitudinal judgements are likely found in *semantic memory*. In this case, by using Izard's (1977) emotional taxonomy, the researchers found that 'emotion can have a direct influence on behavior that is *not* captured or summed up by attitude judgements' (Allen et al., 1992: 50).

Towards the end of their article, Allen et al. (1992: 502) write evocatively of the measurement problems inherent in using emotion measurement scales and recollected events:

> While defending our selection of measures, we do not mean to suggest that 'conventional' measures of emotion cannot be improved on for consumer research. Measures such as Izard's are essentially aided-recall tasks in which individuals are asked to recollect past episodes and report frequency of occurrence. Little is known about how best to direct individuals to recollect emotive experience. For example, would detailed descriptions of a particular consumption context yield more predictive and diagnostic emotional reports than just a general reference to the context would? Might the actual presence of artifacts from the context enrich the nature of the reports? Could mood-induction techniques be adapted to encourage respondents to re-create their feelings prior to measurement? If we are to do a better job of integrating emotive experience into consumer research, there are important improvements needed in the measurement area.

What was needed was not merely novel approaches to *measurement, per se*, but rather novel approaches in the *methodology* used to comprehend emotion within the consumption experience. The following year, two revolutionary efforts, by Arnould and Price (1993) and Celsi, Rose and Leigh (1993), did just this.

Fourth, the context of Arnould and Price's research was whitewater rafting on the Colorado River — a consumption experience that usually evokes the gamut of emotions for most participants. In contrast to prior studies, the Arnould and Price article used a combination of *ethnography*   and *survey-scaling* methodologies, creating a very rich and detailed data base from which to construct interpretations. The consumers of the river rafting experience typically have emotional responses which are longlasting and profound:

> The experience is extraordinary, offering absorption, personal control, joy and valuing, a spontaneous letting-be of the process, and a newness of perception and process. It is recalled easily for years after, but because of its considerable emotional content, it is difficult to describe. People sometimes report that it changed them forever. It is magical. As such, satisfaction with river rafting, a hedonic encounter between customer, guide, and 'nature,' does not seem to be embodied in attributes of the experience such as amount of time spent freezing in wet clothes, uncomfortable toilet facilities, bad food, or any summary index of specific attributes of the trip. Rather, satisfaction is embodied in the success of the narrative, an interactive gestalt orchestrated by the guide over several days' journey into the unknown. (Arnould and Price, 1993: 25)

Because of the nature of their methodology, Arnould and Price were able to trace sociological/anthropological aspects of the emotional experience which traditional measurement devices would have missed. Among these were the perception by several consumers of the experience as a pilgrimage/rite of passage and the growth of bonding among participants and between the participants and their guide over the course of the journey. The research project also shed light on rarely investigated emotions such as transcendence and ecstasy, which lie at the extremes of the positive emotional spectrum. Notably, many consumers did not want to translate their experience into cognitive material: 'Participants do not appear to want to engage in very much *cognitive* recall of the experience. It is as if river magic is best preserved if the associated *feelings* and *sensations* are not examined too closely' (Arnould and Price, 1993: 37, italics added in second and third cases). This finding is consistent with Holbrook and Hirschman's (1982) early proposition that hedonic experiences are evaluated emotionally, rather than within a utilitarian/rational framework.

Fifth, similar findings resulted from the investigation of skydiving by Celsi, et al. (1993), who proposed that high-risk consumer behaviours are 'motivated by a dramatic worldview' (p. 2) having a distinct beginning, middle and end over which the experience occurs (this could also readily be labelled as *romantic adventure* or *heroic quest*). The researchers discovered that participants' motives

278

varied from thrill seeking to social compliance (for example, to accompany a friend or spouse) and that all participants saw it as involving some degree of risk acceptance, although the risk was viewed as directly controllable through sound training and quality equipment. As with Arnould and Price's consumers, these also cited personal mastery (that is, 'I can do it'), transcendence/ ecstasy and identity construction/renewal as significant outcomes of the behaviour. And, as before, the participants felt a sense of *communitas* or bonding with other participants (that is, 'we've been through this together').

Finally, these researchers introduced another aspect of consumer desire for such high-risk experiences — the addictive high resulting from the adrenaline rush they provide:

> [L]ike heroin addicts who grow to enjoy the actual act of self-injection (though initially unpleasant), skydivers grow to love leaping from planes because they learn to associate the subsequent thrill with the initially frightening act itself. . . . Moreover, they crave skydiving when they are away from the sport. 'It's like an addiction, I suffer withdrawal when I haven't jumped in a while'. 'I love it, man. I just can't get enough of it [free-fall]. (Celsi et al., 1993: 15)

As those researchers note, while the addiction model does not fully account for all aspects of the high-risk consumption experience, it does serve as a phenomenological explanation for much of it.

In the 15 years since the publication of the original articles on hedonic (Hirschman and Holbrook, 1982) and experiential consumption (Holbrook and Hirschman, 1982) the intellectual realm of consumer research has broadened substantially. In particular, increased emphasis upon the emotional aspects of consumer interactions with products has provided a much deeper grasp of satisfaction. Further, ethnographic and other interpretative methods have granted us a much fuller and more authentic knowledge of the consuming experience.

ELIZABETH C. HIRSCHMAN

Bibliography

Allen, C.T., Machleit, K. and Klein, S.S. (1992) 'A Comparison of Attitudes and Emotions as Predictors of Behavior at Diverse Levels of Behavioral Experience', *Journal of Consumer Research*, **18**: 493–504.

Arnould, E.J. and Price, L.L. (1993) 'River Magic; Extraordinary Experience and the Extended Service Encounter', *Journal of Consumer Research*, **20**: 24–45.

Celsi, R.L., Rose, R.L. and Leigh, T.W. (1993) 'An Exploration of High Risk Leisure Consumption through Skydiving', *Journal of Consumer Research*, **20**: 1–23.

Havlena, W.J. and Holbrook, M.B (1986) 'The Varieties of Consumption Experience: Comparing Two Typologies of Emotion in Consumer Behavior', *Journal of Consumer Research*, **13**: 394–404.

Hirschman, E.C. and Holbrook, M.B. (1982) 'Hedonic Consumption: Emerging Concepts, Methods and Propositions', *Journal of Marketing*, **46**: 92–101.

Holbrook, M.B. and Hirschman, E.C. (1982) 'The Experiential Aspects of Consumption: Consumer Fantasies, Feelings, and Fun', *Journal of Consumer Research*, **9**: 132–40.

Izard, C.E. (1977) *Human Emotions*, New York, Plenum.

Mehrabian, A. and Russell, J.A. (1974) *An Approach to Environmental Psychology*, Cambridge, MA, MIT Press.

Plutchik, R. (1980) *Emotion: A Psychoevolutionary Synthesis*, New York, Harper and Row.

Westbrook, R.A. (1987) 'Product/Consumption-based Affective Responses and Potpurchase Process', *Journal of Marketing Research*, **24**: 258–70.

Westbrook, R.A. and Oliver, R.L. (1991) 'The Dimensionality of Consumption Emotion Patterns and Consumer Satisfaction', *Journal of Consumer Research*, **18**: 84–91.

Hermeneutics

Our field generally values the objectivity of researchers and seeks to generate empirical findings that are free from the biases of any individual. Thus, individuals' experiences are believed to affect their apprehension of reality and this influence must somehow be removed or minimized. In fact, many researchers believe that methodological rigour acts as an insurance policy against damage to the field's body of knowledge from any one individual's perceptions and biases. Methodological rigour is achieved, in part, when individual researchers are separated from their research findings (for example, the controlled laboratory experiment). Nevertheless, in recent years, some researchers in the field are taking an 'interpretative turn' (Hudson and Ozanne, 1988) and exploring alternative ways of seeking knowledge about consumers from diverse paradigms such as feminism, existential phenomenology and literary criticism (for a review, see Sherry, 1990). In contrast to traditional approaches that attempt to minimize the role of the individual in the research process, these approaches assume that the individuals' goals and perceptions are essential to the act of interpretation. Thus, those things that make us human — our hopes, biases and experiences — make interpretation possible whether we are consumers, social scientists or natural scientists.

It is against this backdrop that the field of hermeneutics is relevant for all of science (Arnold and Fischer, 1994; Thompson, Pollio and Locander, 1994). Hermeneutics is devoted to the study of understanding and seeks to know how we can take the utterances of others and give them meaning based on our own understanding of the world (Bleicher, 1980). In Greek mythology, it was the god Hermes' responsibility to transform knowledge that was beyond human comprehension into an intelligible form. In fact, the original meaning of hermeneutics is the act of 'bringing to understanding' (Palmer, 1969: 13).

Hermeneutics is probably most often associated with biblical exegesis or interpretation. It is generally applied to the interpretation of religious, literary and legal texts and hermeneutics has been viewed as a subdiscipline in theology, literary criticism and history. Only in the nineteenth century did hermeneutics achieve the status of an actual discipline (Bleicher, 1980). In contemporary hermeneutics, the notion of a text is broadly conceived to include written texts, verbal utterances and behaviour. Thus, within our field, texts may include such far-ranging 'utterances' as advertisements and packaging, focus group transcripts, personal product histories, or purchase behaviour in a retail store. (For a relevant application, see Thompson et al., 1994.)

Confusion surrounds hermeneutics since the term is used in three distinctive ways as a theory, philosophy and critique (Bleicher, 1980). Friedrich Schleiermacher and Wilhelm Dilthey sought to develop a hermeneutical theory in which the original authors' intended meaning could be recaptured. Thus, the goal of interpretation was to be able to hear again and re-experience the original meaning of the text (Howard, 1982). In contrast, philosophical hermeneutics, as practised by contemporary theorists such as Gadamer (1989), assumes that it is impossible to reclaim the original meaning of a text. Texts cannot be objectified into fixed and static objects for they are ongoing, unfinished projects and understanding is continually being revised (Weinsheimer, 1985). Finally, critical hermeneutics seeks to explore language as a form of domination and suggests that underlying political interests must be revealed and critiqued. And, recently, the phenomenological hermeneutics of Ricoeur seeks to bridge these three movements (Arnold and Fischer, 1994).

While no single version of hermeneutics exists and clear differences can be found among various approaches, three concepts are employed by most contemporary theorists and provide a useful starting-point for gaining a general understanding of hermeneutics: pre-understanding, understanding and hermeneutic circle (Arnold and Fischer, 1994). Each of these elements is discussed next.

Pre-understanding
No clear starting-point exists for the act of interpretation. Prior to the act of interpreting a text, we anticipate a meaning for the text based on language, history, culture, tradition and so on. While much of modern science seeks to remove this pre-understanding or 'prejudice' (Gadamer, 1989), this anticipation of meaning makes conscious thought possible and shapes it. No act of self-control or carefully devised method can eradicate this prejudice. Prejudice is a prerequisite of conscious thought that enables us to make sense of the world (Weinsheimer, 1985). Thus, objectivity as a removal of prejudice is impossible, but this does not mean that we are entangled by our own prejudice. Hermeneutics

suggests that if we are cognizant of these anticipated meanings, then we can be open to the text and its own meanings. The text can talk back. This pre-understanding, therefore, is not fixed but it is continually being revised (Riser, 1997).

Understanding
Within logical empiricism, understanding means that a specific event can be subsumed under a general law (Hudson and Ozanne, 1988). An event is understood if it fits within a nomological network. Hermeneutics assumes that the world can only be apprehended through language. Language shapes our experience of the world (Gadamer, 1989). Understanding is then inescapably linguistic (Arnold and Fischer, 1992). Hermeneutical understanding of a text involves a projection of possibility, a potential meaning, or a whole on to a text. For example, if a researcher seeks to understand a consumer's experiences with a product, this researcher may begin with his or her expectations regarding the possible meaning of the consumer's text. Thus, in many ways, this act of projection means that understanding always involves self-understanding. But this self-understanding does not dictate the process of understanding. Our misunderstandings may be challenged by the text and revised. Hermeneutics involves an active challenge and questioning of the text (Weinsheimer, 1985). Understanding not only requires self-understanding and reflection, but is also self-development. When a text is interpreted, possibilities are projected and evolve for the self: 'We appropriate for ourselves new alternatives and project into our own lives their potential' (Arnold and Fischer 1994: 59).

Hermeneutic circle
The term 'hermeneutical circle' is often used to describe the iterative and cyclical methodological process for interpreting text (Hudson and Ozanne, 1988; Thompson et al., 1994). It is a never-ending process in which the total understanding of the whole text is not possible without an understanding of the individual parts. But the parts alone are meaningless unless taken in the context of the whole. Thus, knowledge from a reading of a text flows through a hermeneutical circle back and forth between the parts and the whole. Over multiple readings the circle spirals towards an increasingly consistent and inclusive account. No single objective interpretation of a text exists, however. As a community, we may judge and prefer one interpretation over another based on coherence, but because understanding is always perspectival there is not one true story (Arnold and Fischer, 1994).

An application
Hermeneutics can be applied to understanding the way consumers interpret

advertisements. When viewed from the perspective of hermeneutics, (i) the interpretation would be made possible by the pre-understanding or prejudice (that is, experiences) of the consumer, (ii) the consumer would project a total meaning onto the advertisement, (iii) the consumer would seek to verify this meaning by iterating back and forth between the projected possibility of the whole and the individual parts of the advertisement, and then (iv) he or she would revise the anticipated meaning based on inconsistencies. For example, consider an advertisement composed of a picture, a headline and a subheading. The consumer first sees the large heading: 'Sometimes it's okay to suck up to the boss'. The initial projected meaning given by the consumer may be that sycophantic and toady behaviour to a supervisor is offensive and this may generate images of brown-nosing, apple-polishing or bootlicking. When the consumer's gaze moves to the picture of a mother breast-feeding a new born infant, the projected possible meaning is revised. Perhaps now the consumer makes sense of the advertisement as an appeal to mothers to breast-feed their children, and upon reading the subheading ('You've got what it takes to make a healthy baby. And it doesn't cost a thing') finds that it is consistent with this understanding. Moreover, an expectant mother, a father of three children, and a mother bottle-feeding would interpret this advertisement differently. No single true interpretation exists because the understanding changes, based on perspective. (This example is derived from an actual advertisement from the Infant Feeding Action Coalition.)

JULIE L. OZANNE

Bibliography

Arnold, S.J. and Fischer, E. (1994) 'Hermeneutics and Consumer Research', *Journal of Consumer Research*, **21**: 55–70.

Bleicher, J. (1980) *Contemporary Hermeneutics: Hermeneutics as Method, Philosophy and Critique*, London and New York, Routledge & Kegan Paul.

Howard, R.J. (1982) *Three Faces of Hermeneutics*, Berkeley, CA, University of California Press.

Hudson, L.A. and Ozanne, J.L. (1988) 'Alternative Ways of Seeking Knowledge in Consumer Research', *Journal of Consumer Research*, **14**: 508–21.

Gadamer, H.G. (1989) *Truth and Method*, New York, Crossroad.

Palmer, R.E. (1969) *Hermeneutics; Interpretation Theory in Schleiermacher, Dilthey, Heidegger, and Gadamer*, Evanston, IL, Northwestern University Press.

Riser, J. (1997), *Hermeneutics and the Voice of the Other*, Albany, NY, State University of New York Press.

Sherry, J. (1990) 'Postmodern Alternatives: The Interpretive Turn in Consumer Research', in Robertson, T.S. and Kassarjian, H.H. (eds) *Handbook of Consumer Research*, Englewood Cliffs, NJ, Prentice-Hall.

Thompson, C.J., Pollio, H.R. and Locander, W.B. (1994) 'The Spoken and the Unspoken:

A Hermeneutic Approach to Understanding the Cultural Viewpoints That Underlie Consumers' Expressed Meanings', *Journal of Consumer Research*, **21**: 432–51.

Weinsheimer, J.C. (1985) *Gadamer's Hermeneutics: A Reading of Truth and Method*, New Haven, CT, and London, Yale University Press.

Heuristics and Biases

People frequently make judgements under uncertainty. Among other things, they need to estimate quantities, forecast events, and assign probabilities to hypotheses, which then form the bases for belief and action. People vote for candidates who seem honest and effective, buy stock that appears promising, and avoid risky areas of town. The required judgements are often explicitly numerical: real estate brokers assess the price at which a house will sell, negotiators estimate the other side's anticipated offer, and sports fans assign likelihoods to their favourite team or their favourite horse winning the event. In fact, subjective confidence is itself often expressed in percentages ('I am 90 per cent sure that . . .').

A particular approach to the study of judgement under uncertainty has been labelled 'heuristics and biases'. It originated in a series of experiments reported by Amos Tversky and Daniel Kahneman in the early 1970s. The term judgemental heuristic refers in this context to a relatively simple or intuitive mental computation, which is used to provide an answer to a question that ideally calls for a more sophisticated computation. For example, the question, 'What is the probability that this high school student will become a lawyer?', may be approached by tacitly answering a much simpler question, 'How similar is this student to a stereotypical lawyer?', and then mapping the answer to the latter question on to the probability scale. The heuristic involved in this example is called *representativeness*. In judgements by representativeness, the likelihood that object *A* belongs to class *B*, or that event *A* originates from process *B* is evaluated by the degree to which *A* resembles *B*.

Another major heuristic that Tversky and Kahneman studied in this vein is the *availability* heuristic, wherein the frequency or the probability of an event is assessed by the ease with which instances of the event come to mind, through retrieval, visualization or mental simulation. For example, the question 'Which is a more frequent cause of death in the US today, homicide or diabetes?', may be approached by tacitly evaluating a much simpler question, 'How easy is it for me to think of known instances of death by homicide versus death from diabetes?', and then mapping the answer to the latter question on to the probability scale.

The role of heuristics in judgement can be demonstrated in multiple ways, sometimes quite directly. For example, participants were presented with character descriptions of fictitious graduate students, together with a long list of possible areas of specialization. Participants in one condition ranked these characters by representativeness, that is, by the degree to which the description of the individual matched the stereotype in that area of specialization. Other participants ranked the same possibilities by the probability that the individual was actually engaged in each of the specializations. The rankings were essentially identical, providing direct support for the link between representativeness and likelihood judgement.

Some direct validation was also provided for the availability heuristic by showing a correlation between judgements of frequency and the number of instances that experimental participants were able to retrieve. Compelling demonstration was also provided regarding the specific role of ease of recall in judgement. In a typical experiment, some participants were asked to recall four instances in which they were assertive. Other participants were asked to retrieve twelve such instances. All participants were then asked to assess their own assertiveness. Although the subjects who were instructed to recall twelve retrieved more instances than those who were asked to recall only four, they experienced considerable difficulty in bringing the last few instances to mind. As expected from the definition of availability in terms of ease of recall, self-ratings of assertiveness were higher in the four-instances condition, where retrieval was easy, than in the twelve-instances condition, where it was hard.

Other, less general, heuristics have since been documented in the literature, among them the 'how-do-I-feel?' heuristic, in which people refer to their affective state at the time of judgement as an indicator of their well-being in general. Some judgements, moreover, can be made by *ad hoc* and quite specific heuristics. One study, for example, examined the correlation between overall self-reported happiness and the number of dates that a sample of college students reported having had in the previous month. The correlation was 0.12 when the happiness question came first, but 0.66 when it came second. The respondents in the second condition evidently applied a 'dating heuristic' to answer the relatively difficult question of how happy they were. In the context of the preceding question about dates, the evaluation of happiness appears to have changed, with greater emphasis placed on the salient dating dimension.

A frequently used procedure for studying heuristics, and the one that gave the general approach its name, is the study of biases. Heuristics can often be effective, but are bound to lead to bias. A judgemental bias is a systematic discrepancy between intuitive judgement and a relevant normative standard. The standard can be factual accuracy, or conformity with the principles of probability theory, the rules of logic, or the statistical rules of hypothesis testing, estimation and prediction. judgemental heuristics are necessarily associated with biases, because any heuristic is sensitive to some factors that are normatively irrelevant to the obtained judgement, and insensitive to other factors which are essential to

285

correct computation.

The availability heuristic, for example, can be quite useful (for example, when estimating whether there are more Fords or Rolls–Royces in the streets of New York), but it is bound to be misleading whenever the availability of instances is imperfectly correlated with their frequency. Thus, people estimate (incorrectly) that homicides are a more frequent cause of death in the US than diabetes, because instances of the former are more vivid, more frequently reported by the media and thus more readily available to most respondents. Along similar lines, partners in many types of situations, from professional collaborations to marriages, perceive themselves as exerting most of the effort, because one's own efforts are more frequently observed and more readily available than those of others.

The role of representativeness has often been studied by examining inadequate sensitivity to normatively relevant variables that are not included in the computation of representativeness or similarity. The following example illustrates the logic of such studies. Consider an individual named John about whom three items of information are provided: (i) John has been sampled randomly from a specified population; (ii) John has been described by a casual acquaintance as 'xxxxx'; (iii) John is either an accountant or an airline pilot. The task is to assess the probabilities of the two outcomes. The representativeness hypothesis, which has been confirmed in numerous studies, is that the probabilities will reflect the relative similarity of John's description to the stereotypes of the two professions. This heuristic is insufficiently sensitive to variables that are normatively relevant to the assessment of probability in this situation, including the reliability and informativeness of the acquaintance's description and the relative base rates of accountants and pilots in the relevant population. As predicted, experimental variations of these factors have been shown to have little impact on judgements.

In a well-known study, people were presented with a description of a 31-year-old woman, Linda, who had been a philosophy major and a political activist concerned with issues of social justice. On average, people rated Linda more likely to be a 'feminist bank-teller' than a 'bank-teller' (feminist or not), thus violating the conjunction rule of probability, according to which the likelihood of a conjunction cannot exceed that of its conjuncts. The representativeness heuristic produces bias whenever features that influence the likelihood of an observation do not have a corresponding effect on its representativeness. Sample sizes and prior odds do not impinge on how representative an observation appears and thus tend to be relatively neglected.

Reliance on representativeness forms part of a general tendency to focus on the strength of evidence (for example, the warmth of a letter of reference) with insufficient regard for its weight (for example, how well the writer knows the candidate). This tendency predicts systematic biases in probabilistic judgement, including the failure to appreciate regression phenomena, and the fact that people are generally overconfident (when evidence is remarkable but its weight is low), and occasionally underconfident (when the evidence is unremarkable but its reliability high). For example, the expectation that local sequences be representative of a general process yields specific biases due to the representativeness heuristic. Thus, even when there are only a few observations to rely on, people tend to expect future observations of uncertain processes to resemble past observations. In documenting the inadequate sensitivity to sample size, Tversky and Kahneman noted that people appear to believe that the law of large numbers applies to small numbers as well. Scientists with considerable sophistication in statistics were found to overestimate the probability that a true hypothesis would be confirmed by the results of a sample. These scientists understood the relevant concepts, but when they followed their intuitions in deciding on an appropriate sample size, they designed studies of surprisingly low statistical power.

The expectation that the essential characteristics of a population will be manifest in small samples has diverse implications. One familiar instance of this tendency is the 'gambler's fallacy', wherein people expect a coin to show, say, 'heads' after four tails, because the process of a fair coin toss creates the expectation that even short sequences should be roughly constituted of an equal heads–tails distribution. Another well-known example is the misperception of the 'hot hand' in basketball. Because people expect fewer streaks than a chance process in fact yields, they are prone to perceive players as intermittently 'hot' or 'cold'.

Whereas heuristics are typically associated with bias, many biases in human judgement are not necessarily the result of a simple heuristic. A number of self-serving biases are motivational in nature, such as the common tendency to attribute success to ability or effort, but failure to bad lack or unfairness. In addition, people exhibit unrealistic optimism about their traits, abilities and chances. Most people (even those who have been hospitalized for serious automobile accidents) believe that they are 'better than average' drivers; workers believe they are 'better than average' at work; and people think they are less prejudiced, more moral, less likely to have an unwanted pregnancy, and more likely to have a gifted child, than the average.

Two other common biases are those of *hindsight* and *anchoring and insufficient adjustment*. The hindsight bias refers to two common observations: people believe that events that are known to have occurred were probable before the fact; they also distort their memories of their own earlier beliefs about these events. An anchoring effect is observed in tasks of estimation of quantities when people are led to focus their attention on a particular candidate value, prior to making an estimate. Typically, people adjust too little, leaving them unduly influenced by the initial 'anchor', even when arbitrarily selected. In a classic illustration of this heuristic, people observed a (rigged) spinning wheel land on the numbers '10' or '65'. They were then asked whether they thought the percentage of African countries in the United Nations was smaller or greater than that number, and were asked to give their best estimate. Median estimates of the percentage of African countries were 25 and 45 for the groups that anchored on the two numbers, respectively. For another example, subjects in an experiment were asked to add 400 to a number formed by the last three digits of their social security number. They were then asked whether Attila the Hun invaded Europe before or after the data corresponding to this number. Finally, they were asked to estimate the date of the invasion. A pronounced correlation was observed between respondents' estimates and their social security number. Merely considering a value as a candidate answer to a question appears to enhance its plausibility.

Evidence of heuristics and biases has been experimentally documented among professional analysts, expert auditors and real estate brokers. Also, studies suggest that increased financial incentives neither eliminate bias nor lead people, even experts, to abandon heuristic judgement. The research has generated some debate about the normative status and interpretation of the biases. Intuitive probability judgements often violate basic normative rules. At the same time, people can exhibit sensitivity to and appreciation for the normative principles. The coexistence of fallible intuitions along with an underlying appreciation for normative judgement yield a subtle picture of probabilistic reasoning.

ELDAR SHAFIR AND DANIEL KAHNEMAN

Bibliography

Arkes, H.R. and Hammond, K.R. (1986) *Judgment and Decision Making: An Interdisciplinary Reader*, Cambridge, Cambridge University Press.

Bazerman, M.H. (1994) *Judgment in Managerial Decision Making*, New York, Wiley.

Camerer, C. (1995) 'Individual Decision Making', in Kagel, J. and Roth, A. (eds) *The Handbook of Experimental Economics*, Princeton, NJ, Princeton University Press.

Goldstein, W.M. and Hogarth, R.M. (1997) *Research on Judgment and Decision Making: Currents, Connections, and Controversies*, Cambridge, Cambridge University Press.

Griffin, D. and Tversky, A. (1992) 'The Weighing of Evidence and the Determinants of Confidence', *Cognitive Psychology*, **24**: 411–35.

Kahneman, D., Slovic, P. and Tversky, A. (eds) (1982) *Judgment Under Uncertainty: Heuristics and Biases*, New York, Cambridge University Press.

Kahneman, D. and Tversky, A. (1996) 'On the Reality of Cognitive Illusions', *Psychological Review*, **103**: 582–91.

Lord, C. (1997) *Social Psychology*, Orlando, FL, Harcourt Brace & Co.

Nisbett, R. and Ross, L. (1980) *Human Inference: Strategies and Shortcomings of Social Judgment*, Englewood Cliffs, NJ, Prentice–Hall.

Strack, F., Argyle, M. and Schwarz, N. (eds) (1991) *Subjective Well-Being*, Oxford, Pergamon.

History of Economic Psychology

Early authors

Although there were attempts to combine economics and psychology during the nineteenth century, the concept of 'economic psychology' was probably used for the first time in 1881 by the French social scientist Gabriel Tarde (1843–1904). In 1902, Tarde wrote a two-volume book *La Psychologie Economique*. For Tarde, economic psychology is not a separate science, but concerned with the fundamental assumptions of economics. Man is a social being and interaction between people should be the basis for economics. Tarde became well known for his book *The Laws of Imitation* (1890), in which he describes the social reference influence, also in consumption and lifestyle (Hughes, 1960).

Another social scientist, born in Norway and living in the US, Thorstein Veblen (1857–1929), published *The Theory of the Leisure Class* in 1899. In this book, he criticized the conspicuous lifestyle of wealthy American tycoons such as J. Pierpont Morgan and Cornelius Vanderbilt. This book is an essay on the conspicuous spending behaviour of the wealthy 'nouveaux riches' which is an economic–psychological topic. Tarde's and Veblen's work could be called the 'first wave' of economic psychology.

Veblen versus Knight

Thorstein Veblen could also be called a 'second-wave' economic psychologist. He and others tried to introduce behavioural sciences into mainstream economics in the 1920s (Veblen, 1919). Psychology had developed to a respectable science, and they tried to introduce a better psychological foundation for economics. Economists were generally unwilling to do so. They preferred to start with a priori assumptions of human behaviour, such as rationality, stable preferences, complete knowledge and utility maximization. This for many economists was not a dogma, but rather a starting-point for theorizing. If predictions from the theory based on these assumptions were refuted, these assumptions could be relaxed (Coats, 1976; Van Raaij, 1985). In this manner, economic theory could be based on a simplification of human behaviour. This was certainly not descriptive of real-life behaviour, but as long as it provided feasible predictions, it was acceptable for the time being. The model of human behaviour should be made more complex only if necessary. This progress from simple to more complex models is similar to the approach in physics and other sciences.

Knight (1921), as Veblen's opponent, argued that economics is not about human behaviour, but about universal relationships between concepts. The Slutzky–Hicks–Allen indifference curve analysis and the development of econometrics marked the failure to introduce psychology into economics during this period. Lakatos (1968) argued that the defenders of the neoclassical paradigm in economics survived this attack and came out of it even stronger than before.

George Katona
A 'third wave' of economic psychology occurred in the late 1930s and 1940s. George Katona (1901–81) was its main proponent (Wärneryd, 1982). A summary of his major work can be found in Katona (1975); see also the entry on Katona elsewhere in this book. Katona's successors at the Survey Research Center of the University of Michigan were Burkhard Strümpel (1935–90) (Van Raaij, 1991) and Richard Curtin.

Economic psychology in Europe
A 'fourth wave' of economic psychology developed in Europe in 1960s and 1970s. At the Louis Pasteur University in Strasbourg, France, Pierre-Louis Reynaud (1908–81) (Albou, 1982) held a chair in political economics from 1946. He was interested in the psychoeconomic aspects of economic development, especially in the Mediterranean area. He wrote textbooks on economic psychology (Reynaud, 1954, 1974/81). Reynaud's successor in France was Paul Albou at the University René Descartes in Paris (Albou, 1984).

In 1957, Karl-Erik Wärneryd was appointed as associate professor of economic psychology at the Stockholm School of Economics, Sweden. His research focuses on consumer behaviour, with special foci on saving, mass communication and experimental studies on consumer reactions to prices and mass communication. He published the first Swedish textbook on economic psychology in 1958 and brought out a revised edition in 1967. One of his co-workers was Folke Ölander, who became professor of economic psychology at the Aarhus School of Business, Denmark, in 1974. His research focuses on consumer policy and environmental concern.

In the Netherlands, economic psychology started in 1972 at the psychology department of Tilburg University, where Gery Van Veldhoven became the professor of economic psychology. Research topics were saving behaviour, personality and consumer behaviour. One of his co-workers was Fred Van Raaij, who became professor of economic psychology at Erasmus University, Rotterdam, in 1979. His main research topics were consumer behaviour, consumer confidence, mass communication and environmental concern.

Other European universities followed, and chairs in economic psychology

Table 1: Past and future conference sites and conveners of IAREP colloquia

	Year	City and country	Conveners (in association with):
1	1976	Tilburg, The Netherlands	Gery Van Veldhoven
2	1977	Strasbourg, France	Pierre-Louis Reynaud
3	1978	Augsburg, Germany	Walter Molt, Peter Stringer
4	1979	Stockholm, Sweden	Karl-Erik Wärneryd
5	1980	Leuven-Brussels, Belgium	Piet Vanden Abeele
6	1981	Paris, France	Paul Albou
7	1982	Edinburgh, Scotland	Hilde Behrend, Stephen Lea
8	1983	Bologna, Italy	Enzo Spaltro
9	1984	Tilburg, The Netherlands	Gery Van Veldhoven, Theo Poiesz
10	1985	Linz-Zell an der Pram, Austria	Hermann Brandstätter
11	1986	Haifa-Kibbutz Shefayim, Israel	Shlomo Maital (SABE)
12	1987	Aarhus-Æbeltoft, Denmark	Folke Ölander
13	1988	Leuven-Brussels, Belgium	Piet Vanden Abeele
14	1989	Warsaw-Kazimierz Dolny, Poland	Tadeusz Tyszka, Joanna Sokolowska
15	1990	Exeter, England	Stephen Lea, Paul Webley
16	1991	Stockholm, Sweden	Karl-Erik Wärneryd (SASE)
17	1992	Frankfurt, Germany	Werner Güth (DFE)
18	1993	Moscow, Russia	Sergei Malakhov, Elena Tougariova
19	1994	Rotterdam, The Netherlands	Gerrit Antonides, Fred Van Raaij (SABE)
20	1995	Bergen, Norway	Sigurd Tröye, Ingeborg Kleppe
21	1996	Paris, France	Christine Roland-Lévy
22	1997	Valencia, Spain	Ismael Quintanilla Pardo
23	1998	San Francisco, USA	Monroe Friedman (IAAP)
24	1999	Turin, Italy	Francesco Scacciati
25	2000	Vienna, Austria	Erich Kirchler
26	2001	Bath, England	Alan Lewis

were established at the University of Exeter, UK (Stephen Lea; chair in psychology with emphasis on economic psychology) and the Johannes Kepler University of Linz, Austria (Hermann Brandstätter; research on household decision making). Economic psychology is now also taught in, for example, Bath

(UK), Bergen (Norway), Brussels (Belgium), Reims (France), Valencia (Spain), Vienna (Austria) and Warsaw (Poland).

In 1976, the first colloquium on economic psychology was held in Tilburg, The Netherlands. This meeting was attended by twelve people. The international 'society' was called 'European Research in Economic Psychology'. Later this organization became the International Association for Research in Economic Psychology (IAREP). Although researchers from outside Europe attend the IAREP colloquia, IAREP is still largely a European organization with conferences held in Europe, with the exception of an excursion to Israel in 1986. Some colloquia have been held in conjunction with other organizations such as SABE (Society for the Advancement of Behavioral Economics) and SASE (Society for the Advancement of Socio-economics). In 1998, the IAREP meeting was in San Francisco, in conjunction with IAAP, the International Association for Applied Psychology. This was the first time an IAREP colloquium had been held in North America.

A number of European textbooks and readers on economic psychology have been written or edited by Lewis (1982), Furnham and Lewis (1986), Lea, Tarpy and Webley (1987), Van Raaij, Van Veldhoven and Wärneryd (1988), Lea, Webley and Young (1992), Antonides, Van Raaij and Maital (1997), and Furnham and Argyle (1998).

Journal and summer school
A significant activity was the establishment of the *Journal of Economic Psychology* (JoEP) in 1981. JoEP editors to date have been Fred Van Raaij (1981–90) and Stephen Lea (1991–95). The present editor is Alan Lewis. JoEP, as a scientific journal, has a broader scope than IAREP, and at least 50 per cent of the papers published in the journal originate outside Europe from North America, Australia or New Zealand. JoEP began in 1981 with four issues in an annual volume of 320 pages. In 1998, JoEP had grown to six issues in an annual volume of more than 800 pages.

In order to increase interest in economic psychology, including that in Eastern Europe, summer schools were held in Linz (Austria) in 1993 and 1995, organized by Hermann Brandstätter. These summer schools were successful in attracting young people to economic–psychological research. Many of the summer school students later researched in economic psychology.

Beyond Europe
In the US interesting economic-psychological research has been carried out by Herbert Simon (1963), Richard Thaler (1985), Jack Knetsch, Daniel Kahneman, Amos Tversky (see Kahneman and Knetsch, 1992; Kahneman, Slovic and Tversky, 1982; Van Raaij, 1998), David Alhadeff (1982), Harvey Leibenstein

(1976), Thomas Schelling (1978) and others, although they did not call themselves economic psychologists. Other significant contributions were made by Scitovsky (1976), MacFadyen and MacFadyen (1986), Albanese (1988) and Earl (1988, 1990). Tibor Scitovksy brought economics and (physiological) psychology together in his book *The Joyless Economy*. The MacFadyens brought together a number of papers on the theory and applications of economic psychology. Paul Albanese's book grew out of an international conference held in the autumn of 1985 at Middlebury College, Vermont. Peter Earl (1988), at that time in Tasmania, edited a book entitled *Psychological Economics* emphasizing the use of psychology in economic models of decision making. Work on prospect theory, heuristics in decision making, the money illusion and probabilistic insurance are also relevant for economic psychology.

SABE and SASE are also American initiatives. SABE ('behavioural economics') is an organization of economists introducing behavioural factors in economics and economic models. SASE ('socioeconomics') is an organization to include mainly sociological and political-science factors in economics and economic models. In contrast to IAREP, these initiatives were started mainly by economists and sociologists. Books that should be mentioned in this context are Gilad and Kaish (1986), Maital (1982), and Maital and Maital (1984).

Research domains
The research domains of economic psychology are on the interface of economics and psychology. In principle, all behaviours related to scarce resources, such as money, time and effort, are part of economic psychology. Economic psychology can be conceptualized as both the effect of the economy on individuals and the aggregated effect of individuals on the economy, and can be modelled as a cycle of influencing and being influenced (Van Raaij, 1981). It includes organizational, entrepreneurial and many other 'economic behaviours'. It does not include behaviours covered by organizational psychology, although a clear distinction between organizational and economic psychology is lacking.

Economic psychology includes the study of consumer behaviour. Consumer research focuses on how people choose products, services and brands and spend their money and satisfy their desires (Antonides and Van Raaij, 1998).

Own methodology?
Economic psychology is characterized mainly by its domain of economic behaviours. The methodology of economic psychology is largely similar to social psychology: survey research, experimentation and observation. Panel research and analysis of secondary data are typical of, but not unique to, economic psychology. Panels are used to measure consumer expenditure and consumer confidence. Analysis of secondary data on consumer expenditure, consumer

confidence, opinions and attitudes is common in economic psychology.

Economic–psychological variables are often included in economic models as intervening or supplementary variables. For example, if unemployment affects confidence and confidence affects spending, the standard economic approach is to leave out confidence and examine the direct effect of unemployment on consumption. Another approach is to have psychological variables explain variance additional to that explained by economic variables. If income affects spending, what is the extra explained variance if we use both income and confidence to explain consumption? The methodology is thus sometimes an economic approach, or an economic approach with intervening or supplementary psychological variables.

Goals and objectives

The goals and objectives of the early economic psychologists were to completely restructure the foundations of economics. Veblen's (1919) satirical portrayal of the hedonistic conception of man who passively responds to external stimuli was persuasive, when contrasted with the actively intelligent model of Man in psychology. This ambitious goal failed. Obviously, the economic paradigm was not that easy to refute.

A second ('fall-back') option is to include behavioural and psychological factors in economic models (Earl, 1988). If the psychological variables prove to be useful additions to the economic model, some recognition of an economic–psychological contribution is ensured.

The present goals and objectives of economic psychologists are more modest. The goal is to establish a separate domain of economic psychology, adjacent to and distinct from economics. The two areas will have a separate development, but, hopefully, influence each other in a fruitful manner.

A fourth option is to regard economic psychology is a field of applied social and cognitive psychology. This option has some validity, but does not recognize the special relationship of economic psychology to economics.

As a concluding observation, economic psychology has succesful relations with and impact on consumer research, marketing, advertising, consumer policy, finance and experimental economics.

W. FRED VAN RAAIJ

Bibliography

Albanese, P.J. (1988) *Psychological Foundations of Economic Behavior*, New York, Praeger.

Albou, P. (1982) 'Pierre-Louis Reynaud (1908–1981)', *Journal of Economic Psychology*, 2: 33–8.

Albou, P. (1984) *La Psychologie Economique*, Paris, Presses Universitaires de France.

Alhadeff, D.A. (1982) *Microeconomics and Human Behavior: Toward a New Synthesis of Economics and Psychology*, Berkeley, CA, University of California Press.

Antonides, G. and Van Raaij, W.F. (1998) *Consumer Behaviour: A European Perspective*, Chichester, John Wiley.

Antonides, G., Van Raaij, W.F. and Maital, S. (1997) *Advances in Economic Psychology*, Chichester, John Wiley.

Coats, A.W. (1976) 'Economics and Psychology: The Death and Resurrection of a Research Programme' in Latsis, S.J. (ed.) *Method and Appraisal in Economics*, Cambridge, Cambridge University Press: 149–80.

Earl, P.E. (ed.) (1988) *Psychological Economics*, Boston, MA, Kluwer Academic.

Earl, P.E. (1990) 'Economics and Psychology: A Survey', *Economic Journal*, **100**: 718–55.

Furnham, A. and Argyle, M. (1998) *The Psychology of Money*, London, Routledge.

Furnham, A. and Lewis, A. (1986) *The Economic Mind: The Social Psychology of Economic Behaviour*, Brighton, Wheatsheaf.

Gilad, B. and Kaish, S. (1986) *Handbook of Behavioral Economics*, Greenwich, CT, JAI Press.

Hughes, E.C. (1960) 'Tarde's *Psychologie Economique*: An Unknown Classic by a Forgotten Sociologist', *American Journal of Sociology*, **66**: 553–9.

Kahneman, D, and Knetsch, J.L. (1992) 'Valuing Public Goods: The Purchase of Moral Satisfaction', *Journal of Environmental Economics and Management*, **22**: 57–70.

Kahneman, D., Slovic, P. and Tversky, A. (eds) (1982) *Judgement Under Uncertainty: Heuristics and Biases*, Cambridge, Cambridge University Press.

Knight, F.H. (1921) *Risk, Uncertainty and Profit*, New York, Harper & Row.

Katona, G. (1975) *Psychological Economics*, New York, Elsevier.

Lakatos, I. (1968) 'Criticism and the Methodology of Scientific Research Programmes', *Proceedings of the Aristotelian Society*, **69**: 149–86.

Lea, S.E.G., Tarpy, R.M. and Webley, P. (1987) *The Individual in the Economy: A Survey of Economic Psychology*, Cambridge, Cambridge University Press.

Lea, S.E.G., Webley, P. and Young, B.M. (1992) *New Directions in Economic Psychology. Theory, Experiment and Application*, Aldershot, Edward Elgar.

Leibenstein, H. (1976) *Beyond Economic Man*, Cambridge, MA, Harvard University Press.

Lewis, A. (1982) *The Psychology of Taxation*, Oxford, Martin Robertson.

MacFadyen, A.J. and MacFadyen, H.W. (eds) (1986) *Economic Psychology: Intersections in Theory and Application*, Amsterdam, North-Holland.

Maital, S. (1982) *Minds, Markets, and Money*, New York, Basic Books.

Maital, S. and Maital, S.L. (1984) *Economic Games People Play*, New York, Basic Books.

Reynaud, P.-L. (1954) *La Psychologie Economique*, Paris, Rivière.

Reynaud, P.-L. (1981) *Economic Pychology*, New York, Praeger (Translation of *Précis de Psychologie Economique* (1974)).

Schelling, T.C. (1978) *Micromotives and Macrobehavior*, New York, W. W. Norton.

Scitovsky, T. (1976) *The Joyless Economy*, New York, Oxford University Press.

Simon, H.A. (1963) 'Economics and Psychology', in Koch, S. (ed.) *Psychology: A Study of a Science*, New York, McGraw-Hill.

Tarde, G. (1890) *Les Lois de l'Imitation*, Paris, Alcan (two volumes) (in French).

Tarde, G. (1902) *La Psychologie Economique*, Paris, Alcan (in French).

Thaler, R. (1985) 'Mental Accounting and Consumer Choice', *Marketing Science*, **4**: 199–214. Van Raaij, W.F. (1981) 'Economic Psychology', *Journal of Economic Psychology*, **1**: 1–24.

Van Raaij, W.F. (1985) 'The Psychological Foundation of Economics: The History of Consumer Theory', in Tan, C.T. and Sheth, J.N. (eds) *Historical Perspective in Consumer Research: National and International Perspectives*, Singapore, National University of Singapore: 8–13.

Van Raaij, W.F. (1991) 'The Life and Work of Burkhard Strümpel', *Journal of Economic Psychology*, **12**: 13–26.

Van Raaij, W.F. (1998) 'The Life and Work of Amos Tversky', *Journal of Economic Psychology*, **19**: in press.

Van Raaij, W.F., Van Veldhoven, G.M. and Wärneryd, K.-E. (1988) *Handbook of Economic Psychology*, Dordrecht, Kluwer Academic.

Veblen, T.B. (1899) *The Theory of the Leisure Class*, New York, Macmillan.

Veblen, T.B. (1919) *The Place of Science in Modern Civilisation*, New York: B.W. Huebsch.

Wärneryd, K.-E. (1958/67) *Ekonomisk Psykologi*, Stockholm (in Swedish).

Wärneryd, K.-E. (1982) 'The Life and Work of George Katona', *Journal of Economic Psychology*, **2**: 1–31.

Household Decision Making

Private households

Private households consist of one or more persons occupying a housing unit. Families, in contrast, are defined by the Census Bureau of the United States as groups of two or more persons, related by blood, marriage or adoption, and residing together. While households are constituted by a single person or by a group of people of the same or opposite sex who are not necessarily intimately related, families consist of more than one member — traditionally of married spouses with children. Radical transformations have led to various forms of families: in 1991, married couples living together with one or more children represented only 26 per cent of all American families (Milardo, 1991). Single-parent families, childless couples, lesbian or gay male couples with or without children have become more frequent. Studies on economic and noneconomic decisions within the private household and family most frequently focus on a dyad or a group of more than two adults and children living in the same housing unit. The terms household and family, respectively, are used here with reference to two or more closely related persons living under a common roof.

Everyday life within private households

Economic and noneconomic decision-making processes represent day-to-day events in households. Normative models assume that decisions can be marked by a precisely definable beginning and a clearly detectable end. Decision makers move through several specific stages, such as desire, information collection and evaluation, to end the process by selecting the best alternative among those available.

Weick (1971) leaves little doubt that decision making in everyday situations deviates markedly from the images found in normative models: people in a household solve their problems when they are all still tired in the morning, or tired again in the evening after work. Decisions are embedded in everyday family life, which in turn is interlaced with a variety of different problems. These problems often do not occur in neat sequential order, but must be solved concurrently. Household members jump from one problem to the next, often without first solving the previous one.

Economic and noneconomic decisions in private households must be considered within their overall context. Decisions are not isolated actions by partners which can be plucked out of everyday events and analysed separately. The dynamics of decisions can only be adequately understood if studied within the flow of a variety of simultaneously occurring activities.

Kirchler (1989) set up a framework for analysing decision-making processes in everyday life situations: first, interaction processes among household members are conceptualized; second, various types of decisions are distinguished, and finally, processes of decision making are designated.

A decision-making model

Interaction principles

Depending on the structural characteristics of the partnership, that is, the nature of the relationship and the relative dominance of the spouses, partners' mutual interaction ranges from businesslike bartering to spontaneous altruism. The interactive behaviour can be described by four principles: love, credit, exchange, and the egoism principle.

Partners in harmonious relationships act in accordance with the 'love principle' and do so regardless of whether or not one has power advantages over the other. The more harmonious a relationship:

1. the more closely interwoven will be the feelings, thoughts and actions of the two partners;
2. the more likely it will be that the results of the decision will be optimized for the mutual good instead of being a mere cost/benefit proposition;

3. the more diverse the resources will be that the partners offer to each other;
4. the more likely the partners will be to feel responsible for satisfying each other's needs; and
5. the less they will consider and make demands on the other.

The weaker the emotional tie between the spouses and the less satisfying the relationship, the more the love principle mutates into a 'credit principle'. The partners may still make an effort to do each other favours and may show consideration towards each other; however, they always wait for a response to their efforts and favours, granting the other partner long-term 'credit'.

If the quality of the relationship falls further, the interaction starts to be guided by the 'equity principle'. The partners act more and more like two business partners. Exchange theories aptly describe interactions in partnerships of average to poor quality.

If the quality of the relationship becomes poor, power differences between the partners become more important and interaction is guided by the 'egoism principle'. The person who holds the greater power in a relationship which has 'cooled off' is the one who manipulates the exchange transactions with the other to his/her own advantage. The greater that person's power becomes, the more he/she insists on getting his/her own way.

Types of decisions
Economic decisions — which include money management, expenditures, saving, asset management — can be described according to (i) uniqueness or frequency of repetition of a decision, (ii) costs involved, (iii) symbolic significance in society at large of the decision alternatives, and (iv) effect of the decision on one or all members of the household. For decisions that have to be made frequently, the decision makers will have cognitive scripts which automate the dynamics of decision making. If purchase decisions relate to goods that are not particularly expensive, have little social prestige and scarcely affect the members of the household, differences of opinion between the partners can be resolved without a great deal of effort. Rather than decide jointly, a spouse may take decisions out of habit, decide spontaneously, or autonomously after some reflection. The more expensive, socially prestigious and relevant a good is for all, the more likely it is that all members of the household will participate in the decision.

Decisions which involve two or more persons can be categorized according to whether or not the partners have differing opinions on the decision. Depending on the type of disagreement, one can speak of probability, value and distributional conflicts.

Value conflicts arise when there are fundamental differences in the goals of the partners. The decision then becomes not so much a matter of solving an objective problem, but of what one considers to be of value. Probability conflicts centre on assessments about the actual facts and options involved in a solution. A probability assessment is necessary when the partners agree on the value and the importance of an alternative, but arrive at different preferences because they have either received different information or evaluated the information in different ways. The partners are interested in analysing the situation objectively in order to determine the best alternative. A distributional conflict occurs when a decision is a matter of distributing profit and costs.

The decision-making process
In Figure 1, a process model of decision making is presented which refers to the purchase decisions of two adults. The model can easily be generalized to economic and noneconomic decisions and extended to a group of more than two people.

When one or more people feel certain needs, information is sought out on the goods and services available to satisfy these needs. The desire for a given good can sometimes be satisfied immediately (spontaneous purchase). In the case of frequently purchased products, a habitual purchase is made according to the cognitive programme available. If the desire arises to purchase a rarely bought good, a genuine decision-making process begins. The partner with the desire for a good can inform the other of the desire either immediately, or only after information on various product alternatives has been gathered and a preselection has been made. The active partner — the one who wants to make the purchase — can gather information about alternatives and either inform the other of his/her purchase intention or make an autonomous decision without discussing the matter with the other first. Unlike individual decisions, autonomous decisions are not made completely independently of the passive partner — the one without any particular desire to make the purchase. The active partner will assess how the good might benefit the other and try to ascertain whether the other would consent to the purchase and then consider these factors in the final decision.

If the good is not bought on impulse, as a habitual purchase or as the result of an autonomous decision, a decision-making process between the partners begins. After one or both partners have collected information on possible alternatives and assessed them to determine how suitable each would be to meet the need at hand, the degree of satisfaction with the alternatives is estimated and a choice is made. The partners may differ in their interests and in the amount of information they have, so that disagreement arises.

Within disagreement situations, there are always two goals existing side by side. It can be assumed, on the one hand, that individuals want to satisfy their egoistic needs and on the other, that they do not want the relationship to suffer as a result.

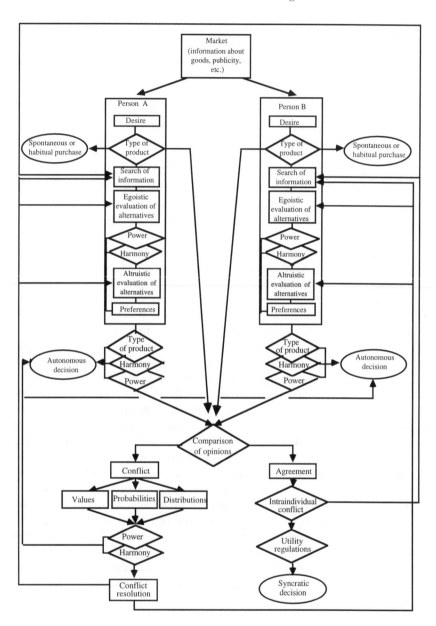

Source: Based on Kirchler (1989: 14).

Figure 1: Descriptive model of purchase decisions within private households

The more satisfied the partners are with their relationship, the more likely their interaction processes will be guided by the love principle and that each will weight the other's anticipated satisfaction with the product as equally important to or more important than his/her own satisfaction. In credit or exchange relationships, weight is given either to one's own satisfaction or to that of the partner, depending on whether the partner is owed something or owes something. In egoistic relationships, only one's own satisfaction is considered.

For partners to know what each other's preferences are, they have to discuss the matter. In arduous, sometimes stubborn, discussions an attempt is made to influence the divergent viewpoints of the other side and thus arrive at a joint decision. The influence tactics for swaying another's preferences vary according to whether the conflict involves an assessment of probabilities, value issues, or the distribution of amenities. They can entail objective or normative techniques, attempting to persuade the partner through promises or intimidating the partner through threats. Kirchler (1993) identified 18 influence tactics (Table 1). Spouses were found to use different tactics depending on the type of conflict and the quality of their relationship.

Tactics are applied to influence the other. Influence, spouses' roles and determinants in economic decisions have been the main focus of marketing and consumer research on household issues (Engel, Blackwell and Miniard, 1995). A brief review on roles and sources of influence is presented in this section.

If the partners manage to resolve the conflict and reach agreement, the decision-making process is still not over. First a check is made to see if the purchase of a good is in any way asymmetrical in terms of the utility it brings. If one partner benefits substantially more from the purchase than the other, 'utility debts' are created. For example, if one partner wishes to buy an expensive article of clothing, he/she will seek the consent of the other partner. If the choice of the one partner coincides with the taste of the other and the latter agrees to the purchase, the purchase is made. Although both partners have opted for the same article in the range of clothing offered, the partner who will wear the article has still incurred utility debts in making the purchase. The next time the other partner desires to make a purchase, he/she can expect to receive the other's consent, depending of course on the internal rules regarding overall utility differences within the relationship.

Once agreement has been reached on the utility debts, nothing more stands in the way of a final decision and the decision-making process is over, except for the post-purchase phase.

Marital roles
Which partner has most say in economic decisions and how does influence vary with product categories? What are the determinants of influence? These

301

questions have been addressed most frequently by marketing scholars who have asked spouses who in the household initiates a decision, who collects information about alternatives, who takes the final decisions, and who uses a certain good. As concerns purchase decisions, it is reasonably established that spouses' roles differ considerably among decision topics, decision stages and relationship characteristics.

Table 1: Influence tactics

Persuasion tactics
 1. Positive emotion (manipulation, humour)
 2. Negative emotion (threats, cynicism, ridicule)
 3. Helplessness (acting helpless or ill, crying)
 4. Aggression (constraints, hurt, violence)
 5. Rewards (offering services)
 6. Punishments (withdrawing resources)
 7. Insisting (insisting, discussing until the other yields)
 8. Leaving the scene (resigning, yielding, leaving the scene)
 9. Overt information (talking openly about one's interest)
10. Distorted information (lying)
11. Indirect coalition (reminding the other of children's needs)
12. Direct coalition (talking in the presence of others)

Conflict avoiding tactics
13. Deciding autonomously (taking a decision without talking to the partner)
14. Deciding according to roles (deciding autonomously according to role segregation)
15. Yielding according to roles (the partner decides according to role segregation)

Bargaining
16. Tradeoffs (bookkeeping, reminding others of past favours)
17. Integrative bargaining (searching for an optimal solution which satisfies both partners)

Reasoned argumentation
18. Reason (talking in an emotionally neutral and objective way, logical argumentation)

Empirical studies dispel some of the conventional wisdom that views the world of supermarket purchase as women's domain. Husbands are aware of many brands in many product categories and are also involved in actual purchasing, although wives clearly predominate. Purchases of food, cleaning products and kitchenware were found to be wife-dominated. The husband's influence is greater with technically complex items (for example, cars, television and VCRs) and joint decisions are most likely if expensive, socially visible goods are at stake, such as vacations, housing or children's education (Davis, 1976; Engel et al., 1995).

One of the most important sources of influence is gender norms. Societal norms prescribe which decisions a spouse should make: in the past, the husband was accorded legitimate power to make decisions concerning extrafamilial matters and working life, whereas the wife was supposed to govern household activities and childrearing. Changing societal norms in Western industrialized countries have led to a more symmetrical or egalitarian role structure which might result in higher interdependence rather than autonomy of the spouses in decision situations.

Besides societal norms, explanations of influence have been derived from relative resource contributions theory. Blood and Wolfe (1960) suggested that the spouse who contributes most to the common budget exercises the greatest power in economic decisions. This suggestion has stimulated extensive research both supporting and contradicting the theory. In the 1950s and 1960s, relative resource contributions were frequently found to determine spouses' influence. Today this seems no longer to be the case: the main determinants of influence are partners' interest in the decision outcome and knowledge. Evidence indicating that a spouse's relative preference intensity for a good and relative expertise make the strongest contributions to relative influence comes from Corfman (1985) and Kirchler (1989). Recently, also, decision history has been addressed as an explanation for influence. Obtaining one's own way can be conceived to be a highly appreciated outcome accredited by the submissive spouse to the other. Winning a decision not only leads to a valuable outcome, namely the fulfilment of a purchase desire, but also may be thought of as a highly attractive resource in itself. Having one's way in decisions is an intangible resource which needs to be balanced between the partners. According to reciprocity rules, the partner who had the say in the past decision or who took the highest profit has accumulated debt and needs to pay back to the other by yielding to the other's desire in a later decision.

ERICH KIRCHLER

Bibliography
Blood, R.O. and Wolfe, D.W. (1960) *Husbands and Wives: The Dynamics of Married*

Living, Glencoe, Free Press.

Corfman, K.P. (1985) 'Effects of the Cooperative Group Decision-Making Context on the Test–Retest Reliability of Preference Ratings', *Advances in Consumer Research*, **13**: 554–7.

Davis, H.L. (1976) 'Decision Making within the Household', *Journal of Consumer Research*, **2**: 241–60.

Engel, J.F., Blackwell, R.D. and Miniard, P.W. (1995) *Consumer Behavior* (8th edn), Hillsdale, NJ, Dryden Press.

Kirchler, E. (1989) *Kaufentscheidungen im privaten Haushalt* (Decision Making in Private Households), Göttingen, Hogrefe.

Kirchler, E. (1993) 'Spouses' Joint Purchase Decisions: Determinants of Influence Tactics for Muddling through the Process', *Journal of Economic Psychology*, **14**: 405–38.

Milardo, R.M. (1991) 'Family Relations', in Manstead, A.S.R. and Hewstone, M. (eds) *The Blackwell Encyclopedia of Social Psychology*, Oxford: Blackwell: 244–9.

Weick, K. (1971) 'Group Processes, Family Processes, and Problem Solving', in Aldous, J., Condon, T., Hill, R., Straus, M. and Tallman, I. (eds) *Family Problem Solving: A Symposium on Theoretical, Methodological and Substantive Concerns*, Hillsdale, NJ, Dryden Press: 711–34.

Household Life Cycle

Individuals and families undergo certain life status changes, for example, marriage, dissolution of marriage, death of spouse, birth of first child, that often significantly alter relationships. Historically referred to as the family life cycle, this concept has been guided mainly by the developmental perspective in both the sociological and consumer behaviour literature. These transitions are thought to be associated with distinctive changes in expenditures for goods and services. For example, newly married couples with no children have been reported to be particularly likely to purchase cars and sensible furniture; arrival of a child, especially the first child, is said to stimulate purchases of washing machines, dryers, plus the assortment of baby-orientated products.

In their pioneering work, Wells and Gubar (1966) proposed that most households pass through an expected and orderly progression of stages: bachelor, newly married couples, newly married couples with dependent children, older married couples with dependent children, older married couples with no dependent children at home, and solitary survivors. However, this traditional conceptualization has been criticized for being overly reliant on the developmental approach and for being estranged from contemporary societal makeup. Regarding the first point, the 'normal' progression from single to married to married with children is seen as neither normal nor desirable by a substantial number of people who opt instead for alternative household arrangements, spending long periods — sometimes their entire lives — as singles or as couples in either opposite sex or same sex relationships without formal marital status. With respect to the second criticism, the traditional life-cycle model fails to incorporate the significant effects on family composition of recent demographic shifts. For example, the delay of time at first marriage in the US and other developed countries has increased the amount of time that both men and women spend in the single stage. High divorce rates in many industrialized nations similarly have prolonged the time spent in some type of singles household, thus directing attention to nontraditional categories not recognized in the traditional life-cycle model. Moreover, changing marital status in industrial societies creates pressure for a household life cycle model that accommodates recycling as families are created through marriage, dissolved through divorce, and recreated through remarriage. These and other reservations about traditional life cycle models prompted Murphy and Staples (1979) to propose the 'modernized' life cycle model shown in Figure 1. This revised model accounts for a higher number of people than did the traditional model and more appropriately reflects changing demographic trends.

The shift away from a strongly developmental approach has also prompted calls for a more appropriate name and the concept is now more commonly referred to as the household life cycle. Whether the concept involves 'stages' (implying a type of flow) or categories is also a subject of debate. The term 'stage' is adopted here for discussion purposes only.

The principal question of interest from a consumer behaviour perspective is whether purchasing behaviour in the household can be systematically related to specified transitions in family situations, even after considering the effects of other potentially influencing variables such as income. Work by Modigliani and Brumberg (1954) sought to relate expenditures to a life cycle of income which incorporates current income as well as longer-term considerations of wealth. Lansing and Morgan (1955) documented changes in the use of credit over the life cycle.

Efforts to confirm that systematic changes in expenditures can be linked to the household life cycle are greatly facilitated through the use of large data sets not typically found in academic research. As a consequence, studies of this concept are often restricted to small samples, investigate only a few products or services, and/or focus on individual stages or categories of the life cycle. These limitations notwithstanding, there is empirical support for the notion that household spending is significantly influenced by the transitions embodied in the household life cycle. For example, housing consumption decisions have been found to be especially influenced by two stages: the formation of families through marriage and the entry of children into school. Until recently, the most comprehensive research in this area was Wells and Gubar's identification of four groups of products for which life cycle discriminated better than age. The

Household Life Cycle

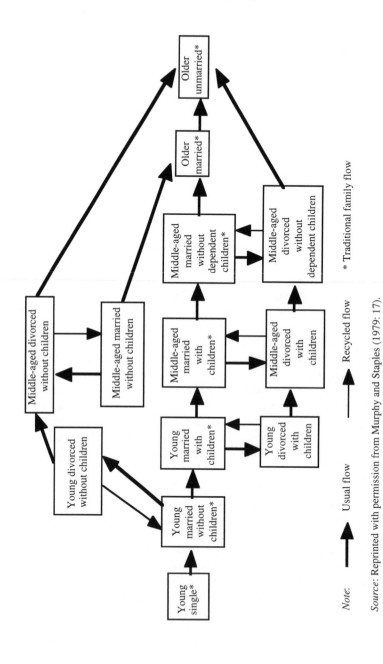

Note:

    →   Usual flow   →   Recycled flow   →   Traditional family flow

    * Traditional family flow

Source: Reprinted with permission from Murphy and Staples (1979: 17).

Figure 1: Modernized household life cycle

presence and activities of children were reported to be the major influence on the spending variations manifested. As previously indicated, however, nontraditional families — for example, divorced single parents — were not included by Wells and Gubar in their analysis.

The most comprehensive exploration to date of the household life cycle comes from Wilkes (1995). Utilizing data from the large-scale survey of consumer expenditures by the United States government, this study analysed the annual expenditures of 7337 respondents across 21 product categories. Although household life cycle is itself a multidimensional concept incorporating age, marital status, presence of a child under age six, and labour force participation, a major objective of the study was to establish life cycle effects apart from other influencing variables. Consequently, expenditures were adjusted for the effects of certain factors suggested by prior research to be influential, namely, total spending (as a proxy for income), wife's education, and family size. While total expenditures were significant for almost every product examined, the discussion here focuses on the independent effects of life cycle on expenditures. As specific assessment was not made of the use of debt or the role of savings, results obtained in this study undoubtedly reflect the effects suggested in the Modigliani–Brumberg theory.

This may be reflected initially in the burst of spending over many product categories that occurs as households shift from being young singles to being young marrieds. In fact, except for products that specifically target children (for which spending is essentially unchanged) and alcohol (for which spending declines), couples increase their spending sharply on products associated with establishing new households, such as automobiles, furniture, tools, home improvement and insurance. Both male and female clothing also show substantially higher expenditures among these newly established households. However, as these households expand their numbers through the birth of children and enter the stage long referred to as 'full nest I', they behave as though children and consumer products or services are interchangeable, that is, spending is reduced in some areas in order to meet increased demand for spending in other areas. This dramatic reallocation of spending is consistent with the notion of fertility as consumption (Bagozzi and Van Loo, 1978). As would be expected of households with children under age six, infant clothing and child care show bursts in spending, accompanied by substantially higher insurance and medical expenditures. And while it may be intuitively appealing to think that the arrival of infants would stimulate higher spending on furniture, this is not the case. Confirming expectations, spending on major appliances rises sharply with the transition to this life-cycle stage. Contrary to expectations, however, expenditures on major appliances do not fall off after this stage, but actually accelerate during the follow-on stages of the traditional life cycle, up to but not

307

including middle-age married without children at home (empty nest). It would appear that the tradeoff in higher spending for certain products during the life-cycle stage with children under age six comes partly from sharply lower expenditures on services (travel, entertainment, eating out), both women's and men's apparel, and alcohol. The effects of credit, to the extent that they are influential during this period, are apparently not sufficient to offset this reallocation in spending.

Although less dramatic for 'delayed full-nest' households (that is, husbands are 35 or older), the spending effects of having a child under age six in the household are similar to the 'full nest I' stage involving fathers under age 35. An important exception to this similarity is produced by the significantly higher spending on furniture, possibly for the new arrival, among delayed full-nest households. The altered impact of infants in this life-cycle stage suggests that income moderates the substitution effects of young children on household spending.

Having young children in the household also has substantial effects on expenditures in nontraditional households. As divorce shifts young married couples with young children to divorced single parents, the effects are increased spending on furniture and child care but decreased spending on eating out, stereo equipment, alcohol and women's clothing. For other types of single households, dramatic shifts in spending are evident, but the specific influence varies substantially by type of product involved. Thus it appears that a simple age-based classification does not satisfactorily capture the spending patterns of one-adult households. Rather, spending rises sharply for certain products with the shift from young single to divorced single household status, but increases for other products. Substantial differences in spending are evident across one-adult households without children. Consequently, there does not exist a monolithic 'singles market'. Spending allocation is greatly influenced by the particular life-cycle category in which the household is classified at the particular time. Just as is the case in more traditional households, different types of singles households manifest substantially varied expenditures as household composition changes from young single to divorced single to single parent to older single, and so on.

Several distinctive spending patterns are manifested as households make the transition between categories or stages of the household life cycle. A common pattern is a generalized inverted U-shaped pattern in which expenditures rise dramatically from young single to young married, then decline with the presence of children in the household, and then rebound — generally to a level higher than prior to the arrival of children — as families grow and mature; finally, spending falls off, often sharply, during the last one or two stages or categories of the traditional life cycle, that is, older (age 65 or more) married couples and older solitary survivors. This pattern is particularly evident for expenditures targeting children, such as apparel. Also fitting this particular pattern of spending are tools, large appliances, small appliances, furniture, entertainment, eating out, travel, sports equipment, automobiles, men's clothing and women's clothing.

A less frequent pattern has generally increasing expenditures across the traditional life-cycle stages and declining spending in the last one or two stages (older married couples and older solitary survivor). Products that fit this spending pattern are home improvement, insurance and medical equipment/services. Medical spending increases over the life cycle until the last stage ('solitary survivors') with one exception — spending falls sharply in 'full-nest II' households in which all children are between 7 and 17 years old.

In summary, empirical evidence documents that changes in household and family situations can be meaningfully related to systematic spending behaviour. These effects are attributable to the change in life cycle as households make the transition from one category (or stage) of the life cycle to another and can be distinguished from other influencing factors such as income and family size. Household resources appear to undergo a reallocation to accommodate these changed circumstances. An especially strong influence in this reallocation is the presence of young children in the household. This is true for both traditional and nontraditional households. The addition of household life cycle to a model of expenditures increases R^2 values by an average of approximately 25 per cent for the products and services studied by Wilkes.

Existing research does not document the effects on spending of households that are recycling through previous categories, such as re-marriage versus first marriage. Length of time spent in the previous category might also be an influencing variable on expenditures during the follow-on category. In addition, only limited evidence exists with respect to the issue of whether this concept influences acquisition (that is, purchases) or inventory or both. It would probably prove helpful for future research of the household life cycle to incorporate the effects of savings, credit and the anticipation of future income on expenditures. Finally, evidence from an even wider range of products and services would further clarify the relative contribution of the household life-cycle concept to marketing theory and practice.

ROBERT E. WILKES

Bibliography

Bagozzi, R.P. and Van Loo, M.F. (1978) 'Fertility as Consumption: Theories from the Behavioral Sciences', *Journal of Consumer Research*, **4**: 199–228.

Lansing, J.B. and Morgan, J.N. (1955) 'Consumer Finances Over the Life Cycle', in Clark, L.H. (ed.) *Consumer Behavior, Vol. II: The Life Cycle and Consumer Behavior*, New York, Harper.

Modigliani, F. and Brumberg, R. (1954) 'Utility Analysis and the Consumption Function:

An Interpretation of Cross-section Data', in Kurihara, K.K. (ed.) *Post-Keynesian Economics*, New Brunswick, NJ, Rutgers University Press.

Murphy, P. and Staples, W. (1979) 'A Modernized Family Life Cycle', *Journal of Consumer Research*, **6**: 12–22.

Wells, W. and Gubar, G. (1966) 'Life-Cycle Concept in Marketing', *Journal of Marketing Research*, **3**: 355–63.

Wilkes, R.E. (1995) 'Household Life-Cycle Stages, Transitions, and Product Expenditures', *Journal of Consumer Research*, **22**: 27–42.

Howard, John A.

During the middle part of the twentieth century, a great change occurred in the way the discipline of marketing regarded itself and defined its role in the contemporary business world. Specifically, under the influence of thinkers such as Peter Drucker and Ted Levitt, marketers began to recognize the importance of satisfying customer needs and wants as the key to business success. Clearly, from this customer-orientated perspective, the critical significance of studying and understanding buyer behaviour follows immediately.

Prior to this period, studies of the consumer had focused primarily at the aggregate level of markets as a whole via the perspective of macroeconomics; at the highly abstracted level of the individual firm or buyer via the utility-maximizing precepts of microeconomics; or at the level of specific individuals examined in great depth via the clinical methods of motivation research. However, macroeconomics failed to examine the dynamics of everyday consumption; microeconomics left the determinants of preferences in doubt; and motivation research was aggressively attacked as both unscientific and unethical. Hence, with the new emphasis on a customer-orientated marketing perspective, the neglected area of buyer-behaviour studies awaited the emergence of intellectual leadership.

In moving to fill this gap, many scholars contributed to the development of consumer research. For example, the trend towards studies of consumption gained momentum when a group of prominent marketing scholars — including Ray Bauer (Harvard), Paul Green (Wharton), Al Kuehn (Carnegie), Sid Levy (Northwestern), Bill Massy (Stanford), Charles Ramond (Columbia), Gary Steiner (Chicago) and Bill Wells (Rutgers) — gathered at Stanford University in October 1964 for a Symposium on Consumer Behavior (see Newman, 1966). Collectively, this work represented a wide range of methodological and theoretical perspectives, each focused on some aspect of 'Knowing the Consumer'. However, despite the heroic summary chapter provided by Newman, an integrated viewpoint capable of inspiring and coordinating the efforts of followers and disciples was still missing. The formulation of such a vision required the contributions of an integrative thinker with a framework suited to organizing the efforts of other consumer researchers. In retrospect, although he did not attend the Stanford Symposium, such a leader had already begun to emerge. Indeed, by any reasonable standards, if any one person deserves recognition as the 'Father of Buyer-Behaviour Theory', that person would be John A. Howard.

Born and raised in rural Illinois, Howard graduated from Blackburn College, earned his doctorate in economics at Harvard under Joseph Schumpeter, taught briefly at the University of Chicago, and then settled for a time during the late 1950s and early 1960s at the University of Pittsburgh. As elucidated by a recent videotaped interview done as part of the American Marketing Association's Oral History Project (Holbrook, 1989), Howard used his position at the University of Pittsburgh to draw on the influence of Herbert Simon at the nearby Carnegie Institute of Technology (now Carnegie–Mellon). Simon had introduced models of human behaviour based on computer-orientated logical flow diagrams — a boxes-and-arrows style of representation that modelled human behaviour as a causal network of paths in which antecedent variables influence consequent variables via highly complex patterns of mutually interacting relationships. Howard's initial innovations in the theory of buyer behaviour drew strongly on this approach and appeared originally in a watershed revision of his earlier textbook on *Marketing Management* containing a chapter that presented what turned out to be the first formal model of consumer behaviour (Howard, 1963). Those innovations were followed rapidly and in some cases almost simultaneously by competing versions created by Nicosia (1966), Engel, Kollat and Blackwell (1968), and others.

Among other insights, these emerging perspectives suggested the need for a multidisciplinary approach to the study of customers — that is, organizational buyers as well as consumers. Under the influence of Howard and the other members of the new subdiscipline that rapidly coalesced, buyer-behaviour researchers began to borrow heavily from the social sciences (defined broadly to include psychology, sociology, anthropology, communication theory, public opinion research, statistics, economics, home economics, management science and so on). By the end of the 1960s, such borrowings from other disciplines were commonplace and definitive in turning consumer research into a truly interdisciplinary area of inquiry.

During this critical period, Howard moved from Pittsburgh to Columbia University, where he and his colleagues delved ever more deeply into the systematic development of buyer-behaviour theory while building an academic centre for the study thereof. Specifically, he brought Jagdish Sheth, John Farley, Don Morrison, Don Lehmann and others to Columbia and established a vibrant intellectual climate that fostered the growth of the fledgling subdiscipline of consumer research.

Having adapted Simon's boxes-and-arrows flow charts to the task of describing consumer behaviour, Howard dedicated the next thirty years of his life to the task of developing and refining these boxes-and-arrows models. Thus, after he had arrived at Columbia University in the mid-1960s, Howard's colleagues witnessed the almost feverish unfolding of the creative adventure in which he and Jagdish Sheth produced their masterpiece on *The Theory of Buyer Behavior* (Howard and Sheth, 1969). Wandering into class with stacks of freshly mimeographed copies of their latest chapter, Howard would press his students to find flaws in the text until its wrinkles had been ironed out to perfection. Thus, *The Theory* achieved a kind of magisterial authority that immediately registered the leadership of its authors in the field of consumer research, exerting an impactful influence that has continued to the present day.

From the beginning, Howard has adopted and adapted an old paradigm whose use extends all the way back to Plato: cognitions —> affect —> behaviour. This framework appeared in the aforementioned revised text on marketing management (Howard, 1963), where Howard traced the flow of effects from 'information seeking' (cognitions) to 'predispositions' (affect) to 'purchase' (behaviour). It thereby provided the original springboard for subsequent elaborations of the theory. Thus, pursuing the same cognitions–affect–behaviour or C–A–B theme, Howard and Sheth (1969) accomplished a major extension in their theory of buyer behaviour by focusing on the linkages from 'brand comprehension' (C) to 'attitude' (A) to 'intention' (B). Later, Howard (1977) retained this terminology in a further reformulation aimed at encouraging contributions to making the theory more testable empirically.

Some had criticized the boxes-and-arrows style of model building as inherently untestable (Tuck, 1976). However, Howard (1977) drew upon Farley and Ring's (1970) groundbreaking representation of the model as a system of simultaneous equations. Such causal models — further pursued by several of Howard's doctoral students, junior colleagues and others — have provided empirically testable structural models on the familiar C–A–B theme, as in recent attempts by many consumer researchers (for example, Batra, Holbrook, Lutz, MacKenzie, Mitchell, Olney, Olson, Ray, Shimp and so on) to add an epicycle to the model by incorporating the mediating effects of 'attitude-towards-the-ad'. Further, even those who have attempted to break free from the decision-orientated C–A–B scheme have often started with that formulation as a basic foundation. Indeed, when Holbrook and Hirschman (1982) wrote a piece suggesting the need for certain departures from the traditional information-processing formulation, they couched their advocacy of the 'experiential view' stressing 'fantasies, feelings, and fun' as a series of comparisons based on the structure of the Howardian C–A–B paradigm.

Meanwhile, Howard has continued to tinker with his C–A–B model, reducing it to the streamlined version that appeared in the *Journal of Marketing* (Howard 1983) and in the more recent text on *Consumer Behaviour in Marketing Strategy* (Howard, 1989). The new, more compact theory (1989) includes only 'information/identification' (1983) or 'information/recognition' (C) plus 'attitude/confidence' (A) and 'intention/purchase' (B) as key variables.

Even more recently, although retired from his official teaching duties, Howard has worked tirelessly on a second edition of the consumer text (Howard, 1993). This revision retains the earlier focus on information, recognition, attitude, confidence, intention, and purchase, but provides a more extensive treatment of the stages in problem solving and how they change over the course of the product life cycle (including the decline phase in which nostalgia seems to play a role). These stages encourage distinctions between extensive problem solving or EPS (at the introductory phase of the product life cycle); limited problem solving or LPS (at the rapid growth phase of the PLC); routinized problem solving or RPS (at the mature phase); and what the present author would call 'nostalgic problem solving' or NPS (at the decline phase).

In working out these issues, Howard has pursued the task of further refining his theory with ceaseless dedication. With his typical curiosity, eclecticism and multidisciplinary zeal, he has reached out for advice from scholars in diverse fields of inquiry scattered all around the world. Indeed, in the videotaped interview mentioned earlier, Howard refers to this conversational style of gathering insights as his preferred mode of scholarly investigation. In other words, unlike those of us who tend to bury ourselves in the library, searching for relevant books and periodicals, Howard habitually does something straightforward but amazingly effective. He talks to people. This flair for meaningful conversation has put Howard in close touch with such influential thinkers as Herbert Simon, Bill McGuire and Paul Lazarsfeld. Such communications have enabled him to share their ideas and have kept his thinking fresh for several decades.

Both this propensity towars meaningful interpersonal contacts and his generous mentoring role with students and junior colleagues identify Howard as a person who has thrived and prospered intellectually by virtue of his ability to elicit and synthesize valuable insights gained from working collectively. On this theme, it seems fitting to finish by quoting the conclusion of the aforementioned videotape subtitled *A Life in Learning* (Holbrook, 1989). As the interview reaches its end, the camera freezes on Howard's sensitive face in what may have been a rather emotional moment for him — as it certainly was for the interviewer, who had just asked Howard what aspects of his distinguished career have brought him the most satisfaction. John Howard replies: 'The greatest satisfaction that I have gotten is from interaction with people ... talking together, putting ideas together, and ending up with a creative structure. It is very satisfying and almost a spiritual kind of satisfaction'.

MORRIS B. HOLBROOK

Bibliography

Engel, J.F., Kollat, D.T. and Blackwell, R.D. (1968) *Consumer Behavior*, New York, Holt, Rinehart & Winston.

Farley, J.U. and Ring, L.W. (1970) 'An Empirical Test of the Howard–Sheth Model of Buyer Behavior', *Journal of Marketing Research*, **7**: 427–38.

Holbrook, M.B. (ed.) (1989) *John A. Howard: A Life in Learning*, Chicago, IL, American Marketing Association (videotape).

Holbrook, M.B. and Hirschman, E.C. (1982) 'The Experiential Aspects of Consumption: Consumer Fantasies, Feelings, and Fun', *Journal of Consumer Research*, **9**: 132–40.

Howard, J.A. (1963) *Marketing Management*, Homewood, IL, Richard D. Irwin.

Howard, J.A. (1977) *Consumer Behavior: Application of Theory*, New York, McGraw-Hill.

Howard, J.A. (1983) 'Marketing Theory of the Firm', *Journal of Marketing*, **47**: 90–100.

Howard, J.A. (1989) *Consumer Behavior in Marketing Strategy*, Englewood Cliffs, NJ, Prentice-Hall.

Howard, J.A. (1993) *Buyer Behavior in Marketing Strategy* (2nd edn), Englewood Cliffs, NJ, Prentice-Hall.

Howard, J.A. and Sheth, J.N. (1969) *The Theory of Buyer Behavior*, New York, John Wiley & Sons.

Newman, J.W. (ed.) (1966) *On Knowing the Consumer*, New York, John Wiley & Sons.

Nicosia, F.M. (1966) *Consumer Decision Processes*, Englewood Cliffs, NJ, Prentice-Hall.

Tuck, M. (1976) *How Do We Choose?*, London, Methuen.

Humanistic Perspective

The humanistic perspective in psychology emanated from the work of the late Abraham Maslow. It was conceived in opposition to the orthodox conception of science which to Maslow both mechanized and dehumanized the person. He rejected reductionism and mathematical atomism as methods that are ill-suited in psychology (Maslow, 1966: Ch. 1). He felt that the first obligation of any meaningful science was to confront all of reality as experienced by men and women, rather than to confine research only to phenomena that are tractable to the conventional scientific method. Science was to be 'problem centred' rather than 'method centred'. In his earlier career the available methodological tools served him well as Maslow worked with dogs and monkeys, but it failed miserably when he started to ask questions about the so-called 'higher life' of human beings. It was at this stage that he saw a need for a *humanistic* psychology quite different from the prevailing behaviourism centred on research involving pigeons and rats. In short, the term 'humanistic' must be understood in contrast to 'animalistic'. There cannot be any meaningful knowledge about human nature unless we come to grips with the distinctly human needs that are not shared with animals; they include the higher needs for self-respect, truth, justice, self-actualization and self-transcendence. Such emphasis characterizes the humanistic research agenda. It explicitly recognizes motivations that are moral or social, thereby transcending self-interest and allowing for so-called 'disinterested behaviour', intrinsic motivation, genuine altruism and moral conduct. Maslow's theory has generated mixed empirical results, but even critics accept its powerful impressionistic appeal, particularly when it is investigated across societies at different stages of development (see Lea, Tarpy and Webley, 1987: 145–8, 498–500).

In economics, the humanistic perspective asserted itself in more rudimentary form almost two centuries ago in the writings of J.C.L. Simonde de Sismondi, a Swiss economist, who criticized the early preoccupation with accumulation of wealth and the neglect of how this wealth should be distributed in order to alleviate human suffering and maximize human well-being. Later on, it was the Englishman John Ruskin and his follower John Hobson who criticized economics for neglecting the human element, especially the economist's emerging inclination to focus almost exclusively on consumer satisfaction and the efficiency of competition often at the cost of meaningless and degrading work. E.F. Schumacher continued this tradition, but focused on the process of economic development and the use of a more personal 'human-scale' technology, even adding a chapter on 'Buddhist economics'. In other words, the keynotes of a humanistic economics have always been an analysis of the effect of economic processes and institutions on *human* welfare, *including* the higher needs of personality and moral integrity.

Focusing on basic needs
Ever since Sismondi, the person has been described as a being with various basic needs — material, social and moral. As conventional economists were drawn increasingly to the use of mathematics — in the process attempting to reduce needs to a set of commensurable wants — it was the mathematical economist Nicholas Georgescu-Roegen who reminded his colleagues that the treatment of qualitatively different, or hierarchical, needs 'is a lexicographic ordering that cannot be reduced to a single ranking index' (Georgescu-Roegen, 1968: 264). Such an alternative procedure was subsequently applied in various settings, particularly the effects of new commodities on consumer behaviour (Ironmonger, 1972).

Maslow's famous hierarchy of basic human needs running from material to social to self-actualization needs can be very helpful in reconsidering economics (Lutz and Lux, 1979). One of its special features is the singling out of the security need as a basic gateway to the development of the higher social and moral needs. In other words, Rational Economic Man may be seen as an individual who, in competitive society, cannot find the necessary security to outgrow his materialist and instrumentalist mentality. In this context, it is especially heart- warming that John Hobson, already in the late 1920s, anticipated much of the Maslowian hierarchy of basic needs and explicitly recognized the catalyst role security can play in human development. He stipulated:

> When moralists talk of altering human nature they are often misunderstood to mean that instincts and desires deeply implanted in our inherited animal outfit can be eradicated and grafted on. Now no such miracles are possible or needed. . . . For example by alterations in the organization and government of businesses and industries, so as to give security of employment and of livelihood to workers . . . it seems reasonably possible to modify the stress of personal gainseeking and to educate a clearer sense of social solidarity in the discontent of modern workers. . . . Security is, therefore, the first essential in any shift of the relative appeal to personal and social motives. (Hobson, 1929: 234)

The Hobson/Maslow emphasis on security has long been recognized by enlightened common sense and has found application in the institutions of lifetime security granted to American judges to shield them against the influence of politics and other irrelevant considerations that might affect their judgments. Another example is the provision of tenure for university professors to promote the pursuit of truth.

Hobson also pioneered in applying his holistic approach to the theory of the consumer by repeatedly criticizing Marshallian marginal utility theory (Hobson, 1914: 332; 1926: 128). Georgescu-Roegen, too, attacked the equimarginal principle as being incompatible with the notion of irreducible and hierarchical human needs. At one point he offers the following illustration:

> If all wants were reducible we could not explain why in any American household water is consumed to the satiety of thirst — and therefore should have zero 'intensity' of utility at that point — while, since water is not used to satiety in sprinkling the lawn, it must have a positive 'final degree of utility'. Yet, no household would go thirsty — no matter how little — in order to water a flower pot. In other words, if a commodity satisfies several wants, it may very well happen that its 'marginal utility' with respect to some wants may be zero; (because these wants are completely satisfied) and yet the 'utility' of the last unit be not null (Georgescu-Roegen, 1954: 515).

In all these cases the problem arises from the same difficulty: qualitatively different needs cannot be treated as if they were merely different wants serving the same type of interest. Economic theory suppresses the basic fact that two basic needs may be comparable but never commensurable, thereby committing what Georgescu-Roegen called the 'ordinalist fallacy'.

Focusing on higher values

If we turn to philosophical anthropology for the image of the person, another critical limitation to economic analysis becomes evident. In a seminal paper, Harry Frankfurt pointed to the phenomenon of self-awareness as the distinguishing human attribute. It allows for a critical self-examination of one's preferences and thereby ushers in second-order preferences, that is, preferences about preferences of the kind 'I wish I did not like to smoke'. Economics, by ignoring these higher-order preferences, treats every agent as what Frankfurt calls a 'wanton', which he describes as follows:

> What distinguishes the rational wanton from the rational agent is that he is not concerned with the desirability of his desires themselves. He ignores the question of what his will is to be. Not only does he pursue whatever course of action he is most strongly inclined to pursue but he does not care which of his inclinations is the strongest. (Frankfurt, 1971: 11)

Amartya Sen (1977) chose to label this infrahuman creature, parading as Rational Economic Man, a 'rational fool', and proposed a *meta-preference ordering* to capture a person with any social and moral aspirations. Both Frankfurt's and Sen's insights provide the foundation for the humanistic reformulation of rationality grounded in the conception of a *dual self* (see separate entry). It demonstrates the limits of self-regarding instrumental rationality and seeks to establish the need for some kind of ends rationality that is sensitive to altruistic and moral concerns. Economic choices often are bedevilled by a tension between individual expediency and personal integrity, two incommensurable goals that can only be resolved through *intuitive* balancing or judgement, not through calculation or the algorithmic 'choice' underlying both marginal utility and indifference curve analysis (Lutz, 1998).

Choice that is algorithmic is no choice in the sense of the term. As G.L.S. Shackle noted, 'Conventional economics is not about choice, but about acting according to necessity . . . choice [here] is empty, and conventional economists should abandon the word' (Shackle, 1961: 272). For an example of 'intuitive balancing', consider the decision making of an admissions committee selecting college applicants. Here we have to take into account test scores, grade performance, civic qualities and a host of other considerations. The solution ends up being a qualitative judgement (see Seung and Bonevac, 1992).

The human capacity for freedom of the will also serves as ground for *human dignity* shared by all persons from any culture. The very meaning of human dignity is intrinsic worth, a value which establishes a claim to have others and the state respect every member in society as an end in itself. It is also the basis of moral philosopher Immanuel Kant's categorical imperative never to treat others merely as means but always also as an end. Compare this with Lionel Robbins's injunction concerning the Rational Economic Man assumption: a trader can never regard his or her partners in exchange as ends; instead the theory demands that 'they are regarded merely as means' (Robbins, 1984: 97).

In other contexts as well, the explicit recognition of intrinsic human dignity will be quite incompatible with the instrumental temper exhibited by much of economics (Lutz, 1995). Mention of three examples will have to suffice. First, the well-being of future generations must count equally as much as our own; it cannot be discounted or otherwise curbed by the way we exploit nonrenewable resources. Second, labour should not be treated as a commodity on a par with machines or other capital and a strong argument has been made suggesting that the wage system, or the practice of renting oneself to an employer, may not be consistent with the imperative of human dignity (Ellerman, 1992: 91–176). Third, much of commercial advertising is clearly designed to manipulate consumer behaviour and therefore must also be seen as an affront on human dignity. Moreover, to the extent that it effectively lowers internal resistance to addictive and harmful consumption, it would also inflict human costs that go unheeded in the commercial marketplace. A substantial tax on advertising may be necessary to internalize such an externality — although an opposing view has been expressed by Littlechild (1982) in the light of Gestalt psychology and psychoanalysis.

More generally, through the lens of both humanistic psychology and philosophical anthropology, *consumerism* emerges as problematic, if not pathological. Psychologically, a preoccupation with materialist values can be explained in Maslowian terms as the result of stunted growth brought about by a blocked security need. So, for example, the new phenomenon of widespread job insecurity can also be blamed for a greater susceptibility of consumers to the lures of commercial advertising. What ultimately matters in terms of human well-being is not so much the optimal satisfaction of our desires to consume, but the development of a meaningful life embedded in human community and the natural environment. Maslow had long stressed that the higher human needs of social esteem and self-respect cannot be satisfied through market purchases. Moreover, it certainly stands to reason that an ever-expanding consumption, or the quest for *having*, might interfere with the building of self-esteem and with it, the search for *being*. In the present perspective, consumerism looms as a deplorable aberration in the progress of humanity. Given environmental considerations, it may even be a fatal mistake.

MARK A. LUTZ

Bibliography

Ellerman, D. (1992) *Property and Contract*, Oxford, Blackwell.

Frankfurt, H. (1971) 'Freedom of the Will and the Concept of the Person', *Journal of Philosophy*, **68**: 5–20.

Georgescu-Roegen, N. (1954) 'Choice, Expectations and Measurability', *Quarterly Journal of Economics*, **68**: 503–53.

Georgescu-Roegen, N. (1968) 'Utility', *International Encyclopedia of the Social Sciences*, New York, NY, Macmillan and the Free Press, **16**: 236–67.

Hobson, J.A. (1914) *Work and Wealth*, New York, Macmillan.

Hobson, J.A. (1926) *Free Thought in the Social Sciences*, London, George Allen & Unwin.

Hobson, J.A. (1929) *Economics and Ethics*, London, D.C. Heath.

Ironmonger, D.S. (1972) *New Commodities and Consumer Behavior*, Cambridge, Cambridge University Press.

Lea, S.E.G., Tarpy, R.M. and Webley, P. (1987) *The Individual in the Economy: A Textbook of Economic Psychology*, Cambridge, Cambridge University Press.

Littlechild, S.C. (1982) 'Controls on Advertising: An Examination of Some Economic Arguments', *Journal of Advertising*, **1**: 25–37.

Lutz, M.A. (1995) 'Centering Social Economics on Human Dignity', *Review of Social Economy*, **53**: 171–94.

Lutz. M.A. (1998) *Economics for the Common Good*, London, Routledge.

Lutz, M.A. and Lux, K. (1979) *The Challenge of Humanistic Economics*, Menlo Park, CA, Benjamin Cummings.

Maslow, A.H. (1966) *The Psychology of Science*, Chicago, IL, Henry Regnery.

Maslow, A.H. (1968) *Toward a Psychology of Being* (2nd edn), New York, Van Nostrand Reinhold.

Robbins, L. (1984) *An Essay on the Nature and Significance of Economic Science* (3rd edn), London, Macmillan.

Sen, A. (1977) 'Rational Fools: A Critique of the Behavioral Foundations of Economic Theory', *Philosophy and Public Affairs*, **6**: 317–44.

Seung, T.K. and Bonevac, D. (1992) 'Plural Values and Indeterminate Rankings', *Ethics*, **102**: 799–813.

Shackle, G.L.S. (1962) *Decision, Order and Time in Human Affairs*, Cambridge, Cambridge University Press.

Illusion of Control

When an individual has an expectancy of a personal success probability greater than the objective probability would warrant, his or her confidence is attributed to a phenomenon called the illusion of control (Langer, 1975). In a classic demonstration of the illusion of control, a research participant overestimates his or her chances of a success for an outcome that is determined by pure chance (for example, by lottery). As the name suggests, this overconfidence results from the individual's objectively false belief that he or she can influence the outcome. Why would a rational individual subscribe to an illusion of control — in other words, why would a rational person treat a chance event as controllable? Consider four reasons (Langer, 1983): (i) we are motivated to master our environment; (ii) we seek to avoid the negative consequences of thinking we have no control (for example, depression); (iii) we confuse elements of skill and chance; and (iv) we are strategically better off if we treat events as controllable (because we are more likely to take action).

Research
Several lines of social psychological research support Langer's analysis. That people are motivated to feel they have control over their environment is demonstrated by a tendency to make causal attributions or perceive contingency between two nominally unrelated events that happen to occur in sequence (example: crossing one's fingers and scratching a winning lottery ticket). Studies of people's belief in the contingency of events typically fall into two groups. In one, research participants shown pairs of unrelated events (clouds being seeded or not being seeded; rainfall or no rainfall) overestimate the correlation between events. In the other, research participants asked to use a response (for example, pressing a button) to determine whether they can affect an outcome (for example, turning on a light) overestimate the contingency between their response and the outcome. A high response rate or a high rate of successful outcomes increase the likelihood that the person will develop an illusion of control. People are even willing to believe that some people have more control than others over picking a card out of a deck, as evidenced by a greater willingness to bet against those who seem to have less control, or to bet with those who seem to be in control (Langer, 1975).

Conversely, researchers have shown that the right instructions can prevent an illusion of control. Matute (1996) noticed that in naturalistic settings, people use a high response rate strategy to effect a desirable outcome (you have no doubt noticed people pressing elevator buttons repeatedly in an attempt to speed the elevator's arrival). In such settings, the event (the elevator arrives speedily) always occurs in the presence of a response (multiple button presses), and this facilitates the illusion of control. When placed in an analytical setting, that is, when instructed to try not responding on half the trials, Matute's research participants were able to determine accurately the contingency between their response and the outcome. Gollwitzer and Kinney (1989) found that people who are in a deliberative mind-set (mindfully making a decision about the outcome) are less likely to develop illusion of control than people who are in an implemental mindset (mindlessly trying to act out a decision).

Thompson, Armstrong and Thomas (1988) propose a *control heuristic* (a quick, unconscious judgement of control) to explain these findings. The control heuristic relies on two cues: whether one wishes to control the outcome, and whether one perceives a connection between one's actions and the desired outcome. These cues trigger the control heuristic, facilitating the illusion of control. For example, when we select a stock for purchase, we hope that our selection will result in a future increase in value (control). If the market is steadily rising, the value of our purchase will increase, and these cues will trigger the control heuristic. When the task is to judge probability, we are less likely to use the control heuristic and more likely to make an accurate judgement.

Uses

Consumers may be misled by illusions of control to believe that their choices predict the future. Perhaps an insurance company can predict the probability of any new car being in an accident but, as Shackle (1979) points out, the individual purchaser cannot predict whether his or her own vehicle will be hit. Yet the purchaser may believe that the car — or even the colour — chosen will enhance safety. State lotteries deftly take advantage of illusion of control when they allow bettors to choose the numbers they play rather than play random numbers; when they offer multiple games that allow bettors to exercise choice between lotteries; when they increase bettors' participation (for example, scratching a ticket); when they make gambling familiar; and when they suggest control (for example, advertising that 'you can't win if you don't play'). Especially important, in the light of analysis by Thompson et al. (1988), is the opportunity to win small amounts with some frequency. The experience of success facilitates the illusion of control. In situations where failure is expected (for example, competition for a prestigious grant or award) one is unlikely to have an illusion of control.

Is illusion of control healthy?

The feeling of not having control is aversive and can lead to feelings of helplessness and ultimately to depression. In seminal work, Seligman (1975) showed that perceived loss of control leads to learned helplessness, the belief that nothing a person does can influence an aversive outcome. Even perceived low control on the job has been linked to negative health outcomes. Conversely, increased perceived control has health benefits (Langer, 1983). Illusion of control, on the other hand, has been narrowly defined to mean unwarranted belief in one's control over a given outcome. The debate over whether the illusion of control is a healthy adaptation, leading to better performance (Taylor and Brown, 1988) or a cognitive distortion, leading ultimately to suboptimal performance (Colvin and Block, 1994) may be the wrong issue. Before the debate can be resolved, we must understand that what we have called the 'illusion of control' is behaviour as seen from the perspective of the observer (for example, the experimenter). The mental health benefits of perceived control are legion. From the actor's perspective, the belief is not false. There is no illusion unless we are privy to some absolute reality.

A new look at the illusion of control

The illusion of control is an observer's phenomenon. To the actor, the perceived control is not illusory. The research described above is often cited to show that people are poor at discriminating between controllable and uncontrollable events. Langer's (1992) more recent analysis is that researchers do not discriminate between uncontrollable and indeterminate events. More specifically, an uncontrollable event is uncontrollable from the perspective of the observer — namely, the researcher, who has rigged that light to come on independently of the button. But the participant does not know this so, to the participant, the relationship between the button and the light is indeterminate. Is it uncontrollable? If the participant has no control, the researcher surely does. It is the researcher who has defined the outcome in terms of probability, and hence defined controllability. Langer's analysis is in agreement with Shackle's (1979) warning to economists that whatever its use to insurance actuaries, probability is not a good way to view future outcomes in respect of individual choices. Indeed, in life, all seemingly uncontrollable events should be treated as indeterminate. An indeterminate event is susceptible to becoming determined, and once it is determined, the factors related to its outcome are explicable. At the point of purchase, a consumer may have no control over his or her vehicle being in a future accident. Once an accident has occurred, however, we may deduce what factors — including the colour of the car — played a role in the outcome. Because the future is unknown, all we can say about an event that has not yet been controlled is that one day that which now seems uncontrollable may be both explained and controlled.

ELLEN J. LANGER AND JUDITH B. WHITE

Bibliography
Colvin, C.R. and Block, J. (1994) 'Do Positive Illusions Foster Mental Health? An Examination of the Taylor and Brown Formulation', *Psychological Bulletin*, **116**:

3–20.

Gollwitzer, P.M. and Kinney, R.F. (1989) 'Effects of Deliberative and Implemental Mind-sets on Illusion of Control', *Journal of Personality and Social Psychology*, **56**: 531–42.

Langer, E.J. (1975) 'The Illusion of Control', *Journal of Personality and Social Psychology*, **32**: 311–28.

Langer, E.J. (1983) *The Psychology of Control*. Beverly Hills, CA, Sage.

Langer, E.J. (1992) 'Control from the Actor's Perspective', *Canadian Journal of Behavioral Science*, **24**: 267–75.

Matute, H. (1996) 'Detecting Response-Outcome Independence in Analytic But Not in Naturalistic Conditions', *Psychological Science*, **7**: 289–93.

Seligman, M.E.P. (1975) *Helplessness: On Depression, Development and Death*, San Francisco, CA,Freeman.

Shackle, G.L.S. (1979) *Imagination and the Nature of Choice*, Edinburgh, Edinburgh University Press.

Taylor, S.E. and Brown, J.D. (1988) 'Illusion and Well-Being: A Social Psychological Perspective on Mental Health', *Psychological Bulletin*, **103**: 193–210.

Thompson, S.C., Armstrong, W. and Thomas, C. (1998) 'Illusions of Control, Underestimation, and Accuracy: A Control Heuristic Explanation', *Psychological Bulletin*, **123**: 143–61.

Images in Advertising

The images that appear in advertising draw a great deal of popular and professional interest, as well as criticism from many quarters. In the academic literature, there are both empirical investigations of consumer response to imagery, most of which appears in the marketing or consumer behaviour journals, and theoretical treatises on the role of advertising in contemporary society, most of which appears in venues orientated towards the humanities. Within marketing and consumer behaviour, three streams of research have investigated audience response to images in advertisements. The first is social science orientated in that primarily it uses survey instruments. The second takes its inspiration from psychology and uses experimental methods. While both the social science and psychological research streams use quantitative methods to investigate their questions, the third research stream is interpretative or qualitative in nature and draws upon various cultural theories. Recently, proposals to combine aspects of psychological and interpretative approaches have had some popularity under the rubric of what is being called a 'rhetorical approach'. However, empirical investigations of this idea are still in their early stages.

Marketing and consumer behaviour

The first investigations of consumer response to imagery were descriptive studies that took large samples of advertisements, broke them down into various graphic components (type size, colour, illustration versus photography, and so on), exposed large groups of consumers to the same selection of advertisements, and then analysed the relationships between consumer response to them and the presence or absence of particular formal components. In most cases, the method was analysis of variance, with the dependent variable being recall. The earliest of these studies was conducted in the late 1960s, with others appearing intermittently through the 1980s. Collectively, the results were spotty and inconsistent, thus ultimately contributing very little to knowledge about consumer response to visual advertising elements. Perhaps because of these disappointing results, no studies of this sort have been published in the marketing literature since 1987.

Interest in large-scale studies of advertising components was superseded in the late 1970s by experimental studies of consumer response to stimuli that were contrived to test various elements thought to determine the effectiveness of advertisements. Several psychological theories were proposed and tested under this rubric; however, the approaches can be grouped according to the underlying theory of visual response. In one theory, the visual stimulus is thought to act upon consumer response in an unconscious or automatic fashion via either classical conditioning or direct impact upon the emotions (without cognitive engagement). In this research, images were understood to point in a straightforward fashion to objects in the empirical world and to have a simple positive or negative value, based on the positive or negative associations with the objects pictured. Images typical of advertising — highly stylized, metaphorical, fictive images — were not studied. Given the frequency with which trade characters like the Jolly Green Giant appear as well as the range of visual styles found in advertisments (from cartoons to mimicry of high art to surrealistic photographs), this omission is puzzling. This body of work essentially proposed that images worked on consumer consciousness in a manner independent of cultural mediation, cognitive activity or judgement. Although such a notion of 'how advertising works' is consistent with widely-held folk theories, this research, thus far, does not support the idea that consumers respond to images in this way. Instead, empirical investigators have begun to move towards more sophisticated theories. In the second stream of psychological experiments, the consumer is seen as a processor of information and is studied according to the principles of cognitive psychology. However, the visual elements are seldom treated as information in this paradigm, but are usually treated as peripheral cues or noncognitive stimuli instead. Thus, most studies of visual elements, even in the domain of cognitive psychology, treat images as if they were, essentially, unconditioned stimuli.

The classical conditioning or affective response research appears to be fading from favour, probably due once again to a paucity of generalizable results. The information-processing or cognitive approach seems likely to be more successful, particularly since some researchers working in the mid-1990s were beginning to treat visual elements in a more sophisticated manner by testing for the impact of style and the surrounding text, as well as by recognizing the potential for more language-like communication through pictures and the impact of enculturation upon response. The empirical literature on images is reviewed in MacInnis and Price (1987), Percy (1983), Rossiter and Percy (1983) and Scott (1994).

Beginning in the mid-1980s, an 'interpretative turn' in consumer behaviour resulted in several essays and studies that attempted to deal with advertising images in a less reductive manner than was typical of the experimental work being done at that time. The primary theoretical orientations have been semiotics and rhetoric (for a review, see Scott, 1994). Methods employed have included interpretative analysis, as well as more ethnographic tools for studying consumer response to imagery. In contradiction to what both folk theory and empirical research (at that time) would have suggested, the initial ethnographic work on advertising images revealed an alarming degree of variation in the messages that consumers derived from advertising images. Rather than being direct impressions of unmediated stimuli, consumer responses to advertising images seemed discouragingly idiosyncratic, representing a range of factors from culture to individual life story. In the interpretative essays, the ability for advertising images to carry connotation, to interplay with headlines, and to create tropes was noted, suggesting that empirical investigation would need to be grounded in a wider view of the visual stimulus than the simple representational formula that was then prevalent.

Today, research on advertising images seems to be converging towards a combined interpretative/experimental approach that treats the visual as something more akin to language than has been the case in the past (McQuarrie and Mick, 1996; Phillips, 1997). In addition, graphic elements are being studied as meaningful message elements, as opposed to the nonsemantic approach taken by the earliest descriptive studies. Interestingly, while the theoretical approach has been shifting, so has methodology: often, 'qualitative' methods such as focus groups and depth interviews are combined with experiments and surveys in the current research milieu. While a few initial studies have been promising, it remains to be seen whether this new direction will be more fruitful than earlier approaches.

While the research in marketing and consumer behaviour on the response to advertising images has not yet produced firm findings in the scientific sense, the narrative and direction of investigation suggests that a few qualified observations may be made. For instance, the failure of simple effects models to explain consumer response in empirical studies suggests that the way people 'process' or 'read' images is considerably more complex than is commonly thought. Certainly, the kind of 'mindless' absorption of images that is often asserted to be characteristic of consumer society is not supported by this research experience. Further, the individual response appears to be highly situated, not only in that person's own consumption context, but also in the particular aspects of the message at hand. For instance, Linda Scott (1994) discusses a Clinique advertisment showing a tall glass of club soda with ice and a twist of lime, in which a lipstick and a tube of blush are submerged. Scott argues that this advertisement communicates that the new colours are 'as refreshing as a tall glass of soda', even though there is no copy. This reading is dependent upon prior cultural knowledge, however, so a consumer who did not have this knowledge might read the message quite differently. For instance, a child might take this image to mean that the product tastes like lime. An older viewer would know that blushers do not come in flavours and so would eliminate that possible reading. Prior knowledge of the brand would also affect the reading. Some lipsticks do come flavoured, for instance, but such a benefit would be inconsistent with the positioning of Clinique, which uses austere, almost clinical imagery to present itself as a high-end form of everyday hygiene. Flavoured lipsticks, in contrast, are normally impulse items that are pictured and positioned more like toys or candy. So, prior knowledge about what benefits a product might be likely to offer, as well as previous familiarity with a particular brand, inform the interpretation. Variations in the knowledge and experience of the reader, as well as differences in picturing and positioning in the advertisement would, therefore, affect the message derived. Thus, the claims for widespread and uniform effects often heard in critical and policy contexts appear less valid in the light of the variability of outcomes. Visual elements seem to interact with text, music and other formal cues in ways that are difficult to isolate and challenging to theorize. Thus, research will probably ultimately have to deal with the advertisement on a more integrative basis instead of focusing on images as such.

Humanistic literature

Work on advertising images that appears in the humanistic literature is highly critical (Leiss, Kline and Jhally, 1990, provide a review). Often, the evils of capitalist society are specifically located in advertising images themselves. Advertising imagery is charged with creating false expectations, encouraging materialism, reinforcing stereotypes and restraining political action. This body of literature generally takes its theoretical orientation either from some variation of political analysis (such as Marxism or feminism), or from language theory (such as structuralism/semiotics or poststructuralism), or from psychoanalysis (either Freudian, Jungian or Lacanian). Overall, the key differences between discussions of advertising images in the humanistic tradition and the marketing/consumer behaviour literature are (i) the more critical attitude taken by humanist critics (although consumer behaviour is not without its critical speakers) and (ii) the lesser concern with empirical validation of theoretical constructs. There are a few content analyses of advertising images (appearing mostly in the mass communications literature but also in marketing) which attempt to validate critical charges that advertising images underrepresent or misrepresent minorities, stereotype women, overemphasize luxury consumption and the like. Studies undertaken in the early 1970s, for instance, did tend to support claims that advertisements showed few persons of colour and stereotyped both women and minorities. However, in the intervening years, surprisingly few efforts have been made to update these analyses. Consequently, continued charges that advertising images degrade or ignore minorities or that they represent women only as housewives and sex objects rely on data collected more than twenty years ago for empirical support.

A few historical works use advertisements as evidence for more subtle historical and social claims, such as Roland Marchand's *Advertising the American Dream* and Jennifer Wicke's *Advertising Fictions*. As Marchand points out, however, the use of advertisements as historical evidence must be done carefully, since the tendency to glamorize and otherwise distort circumstances and products for rhetorical impact makes these images less than accurate as mirrors of historical reality. While both of these works make sophisticated use of advertisments to discuss the emerging role of advertising in modern life, as well as the role of advertisers and their agencies, it is important to note that neither make the kinds of sweeping claims for the effects of advertising on consumers that characterizes most of the literature in the humanities.

More theoretical works, such as interpretative essays, are seldom concerned with empirical validation of consumer response. Such articles, drawing as they do upon traditions like literary criticism, are not really directed at exploring actual reader behaviour and so should probably not be judged on that basis. However, these essays typically use interpretations informed only by critical theory and a handful of advertisements to make generalizations about the effects of advertising on consumers' perceptions, beliefs and behaviours — and thus upon the society at large. While it seems reasonable to suggest, for example, that stereotypical images of women in the advertisements of a sexist society are not unrelated to gender politics in that society, these claims for broad, but direct causal effects nearly always imply a consumer response that is not only uniform, but automatic, unconscious and unproblematic. In other words, this criticism

327

relies heavily on a notion of advertising effects that has already been abandoned in empirical research. Furthermore, the tight association between cultural studies and language theory seems to produce a strong bias in favour of words versus images, such that this discourse is noticeably iconophobic, attributing powers to images that are nearly demonic. This rather Calvinistic attitude towards images is, again, dependent upon a magical notion of image-processing that excludes judgement, mediation or contingency. Finally, the critical literature in the humanities, like the early marketing surveys, overlooks the range of forms commercial imagery takes and its communicative, imaginative capabilities. Thus, ironically, both the rudimentary concept of image processing and the impoverished understanding of visual communication that impeded empirical research for so long, continue to have an undeserved currency in the humanities. Perhaps the future will bring a cross-fertilization to this discourse that will be as productive as the influence of the humanities was upon marketing and consumer behaviour research on advertising images.

LINDA M. SCOTT

Bibliography
Leiss, W., Kline, S. and Jhally, S. (1990) *Social Communication in Advertising*, Scarborough, Nelson Canada.

MacInnis, D.J. and Price, L.L. (1987) 'The Role of Imagery in Information Processing: Review and Extensions', *Journal of Consumer Research*, **13**: 473–91.

McQuarrie, E.F. and Mick, D.G. (1996) 'Figures of Rhetoric in Advertising Language', *Journal of Consumer Research*, **22**: 424–38.

Percy, L. (1983) 'A Review of the Effect of Specific Advertising Elements upon Overall Communication Responses', in Leigh, J.H. and Martin, C., Jr (eds) *Current Issues and Research in Advertising*, Vol. 6, Ann Arbor, MI, University of Michigan Press.

Phillips, B.J. (1997) 'Thinking Into It: Consumer Interpretation of Complex Advertising Images', *Journal of Advertising*, **26**: 77–87.

Rossiter, J.R. and Percy, L. (1983) 'Visual Communication in Advertising', in Harris, R.J. (ed.) *Information Processing Research in Advertising*, Hillsdale, NJ: Erlbaum.

Scott, L.M. (1994) 'Images in Advertising: The Need for a Theory of Visual Rhetoric', *Journal of Consumer Research*, **21**: 252–73.

Impulse Buying

Impulsive behaviour has attracted the interests of philosophers, theologians, economists, psychologists, medical researchers and criminologists for many years. Marketing researchers have also demonstrated an enduring interest in impulsive consumer behaviour, a focus which dates back at least to DuPont's 'Consumer Buying Habit Studies' of 1945. Today, the Point-of-purchase

Advertising Institute fields an extensive annual survey that classifies grocery store products according to the degree to which their purchase is impulsive or planned. And many marketing managers design strategies and allocate resources to encourage impulsive buying of their products and brands.

Arguably, the world has never been more congenial to impulsive consumption than it is today in mature and developing economies. Twenty-four-hour retailing, telemarketing, direct mail, ATMs, credit cards, sophisticated retail merchandising, scientifically designed store layouts and managed environmental atmospherics provide an infrastructure that motivates and facilitates unprecedented levels of impulsive purchase behaviour. Despite the marketplace significance of impulse buying, and consumer researchers' enduring interest in it, published findings have not yet resolved several persistent puzzles. The most basic of these centres around the very nature and definition of impulse buying. The following discusion addresses this and other key questions.

An impulse-buying continuum

Historically, 'impulse buying' was defined as an 'unplanned' purchase, and operationalized as any purchase that was not on consumers' shopping lists. To a considerable degree, this orientation still prevails today, particularly in commercial studies. This notwithstanding, equating impulsive with unplanned buying has serious conceptual and empirical consequences. Almost 40 years ago, Nesbitt (1959) noted that housewives constructively add to and modify their shopping lists as they shop, and in ways that are hardly impulsive. Yet, because the ensuing purchases were not on shoppers' initial lists, they would be classified as impulsive, a practice which clearly exaggerates the amount of impulse buying, and masks shoppers' levels of in-store planning. In a landmark *Journal of Marketing* article, Kollat and Willett (1969) expanded this criticism, and questioned the very utility of the impulse-buying construct.

Subsequently, academic research of impulse buying retreated into a 15-year hibernation. In the 1980s, Rook (1987; Rook and Hoch, 1985) suggested that the conceptualization of impulse buying might be improved by considering its behavioural contents more explicitly. Rather than depicting impulse buying simply as 'unplanned' purchase behaviour, Rook (1987: 191) offered a definition that identifies its cognitive, affective, temporal, and kinetic qualities:

> Impulse buying occurs when a consumer experiences a sudden, often powerful and persistent urge to buy something immediately. The impulse to buy is hedonically complex and may stimulate emotional conflict. Also, impulse buying is prone to occur with diminished regard for its consequences.

While this interpretation provides more behavioural content than prior approaches, it still does not address or answer the longstanding question of

329

Kollat and Willett (1969) about the utility of a single construct.

In 1962, Hawkins Stern proposed that a range of buying behaviour exists between the perfectly planned and the entirely impulsive. More recently, Hoch and Lowenstein reiterated the idea that the single term 'impulse buying' has been used to refer to a wide range of processes, which likely 'obscures more than it illuminates' (1991: 504). In the spirit of this thinking, the following discussion proposes that impulse buying has three distinctive behavioural manifestations: casual, prototypic and compelling. As summarized in Figure 1, these behaviours are nested in a larger continuum whose anchor points are rational choice at one end, and impulse disordered behaviour at the other. Obviously, situations often occur in which consumers make a shopping plan and execute it without any variation, particularly when a purchase is single-minded. Going out to get a McDonald's 'Happy' meal, rent the 'Braveheart' video, buy a copy of *People*, or purchase some Rolling Stones tickets, are examples of behaviours that likely represent *perfect planning*. Another type of shopping involves behaviour that has elements of both preplanning and spontaneity. Consumers' depart from their planned shopping agenda for quite rational reasons, as when they substitute a sale item for what they originally had in mind. Such behaviour is generally practical, *contingent buying*, which has little in common with impulsive buying behaviour.

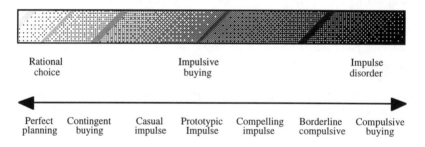

Figure 1: A fuzzy set impulse buying continuum

What differentiates impulsive from rational buying behaviour is an increasing presence of emotional factors, an urgency to consume, and a psychophysical proclivity to make an immediate purchase. These elements are least intense in *casual impulse buying*. This type of behaviour involves a spontaneous product cathexis, when a consumer spots something interesting, new, different, pretty, sexy or tasty, and becomes suddenly motivated to buy it. Casual impulse buying likely involves the purchase of relatively low-priced 'little somethings' that make consumers feel good, smart, special or creative. On the other hand, consumers' varying economic circumstances make the definition of 'little' quite elastic.

A second type of impulse buying is the *prototypic*. This label draws upon cognitive psychological 'fuzzy set' theory, which argues that many behavioural categories include highly variable behaviours. Certain behavioural instances, however, are more ideal examplars of the category than others, and these episodes represent the behaviour's prototypic expression. Compared to casual impulse buying, prototypic impulse buying is more arousing and urgent. The stakes are often higher, involving more money, more purchases and more personal meaning. Such an episode might begin with a spontaneous encounter with a jacket, followed by subsequent impulsive purchases to create a new 'outfit'. Prototypic impulse buying is generally more emotional than rational purchase behaviour (Piron, 1993; Rook and Gardner, 1993).

Much psychological and sociopsychological thought concludes that some impulses are almost irresistible. Analogously, in some impulse-buying instances, consumers' experience a sense of diminishing self-control, accompanied by an increasingly *compelling* urge to buy something. The initial, spontaneous arousal gives way to strong feelings of 'having to have', and a growing, even reckless disregard of consequences. At some clinically-defined threshold, a qualitative shift occurs in which consumers feel substantially out of control. In *borderline* compulsive-buying episodes, consumers may engage in binge buying, serial shopping until they drop, satisfying obsessive needs and heading for trouble. At the end of this continuum is *compulsive* buying, which is conceived as a consumer pathology involving impulse control disorders (O'Guinn and Faber, 1989). There has been a tendency in the literature to exaggerate the more compelling instances of impulse buying, perhaps because of its dramatic psychosocial content, or because consumers recall these episodes best. Logically, however, casual impulse buying occurs at least as frequently, and merits more attention from researchers than it has thus far received.

Buying impulsiveness and other research priorities

Other aspects of impulse buying remain largely unexplored, and invite discovery-orientated research. Psychological research has long viewed impulsiveness as a basic personality trait, and parallel thinking conceptualizes buying impulsiveness as an aspect of consumers' personalities. Rook and Fisher (1995) developed and validated a nine-item measure of buying impulsiveness, and demonstrated how this trait affected consumers' buying behaviour in different purchase situations. With a working trait measure, researchers might broadly explore the consumption behaviour of segments that differ in their buying impulsivity. Trait-orientated research might also inform the long-running debate about the utility of classifying products as 'impulse' items. Better understanding its trait aspects should inform efforts to discover relationships between different types of impulse buying and consumers' decision criteria in casual, prototypic and more compelling impulsive purchases.

Most published impulse-buying research has been fielded in the United States, with notable exceptions conducted in Germany, the UK and Southeast Asia. This raises questions about the generalizability of existing theory and findings. Economic analyses support the view that the world is moving towards an impulse-buying infrastructure similar to the American model. This implies that growing income, consumer credit, telecommunications and retailing innovations will transform marketplaces into ones that are hot-wired for impulse buying. Incorporating cultural factors into the analysis suggests caution in generalizing from the American experience. Many US consumers have considerable economic autonomy and personal freedom at an early age. They typically leave home at eighteen, for work or college, and while living in generationally extended families occurs, it is not the norm. Also, regional migration of married and single adult children is commonplace. Thus, kinship spending and buying norms and practices are likely weakened by distance, and individual consumers feel more freedom to act on impulse. Obviously, other cultures have kinship patterns and systems that place individual behaviour under greater scrutiny. Varying the cultural setting of impulse-buying research will provide valuable information about how diverse social structures and prescriptions affect impulsive consumption behaviour.

DENNIS W. ROOK

Bibliography

Hoch, S.J. and Lowenstein, G. (1991) 'Time-Inconsistent Preferences and Consumer Self-Control', *Journal of Consumer Research*, **17**: 492–507.

Kollat, D.T. and Willett, R.P. (1969) 'Is Impulse Buying Really a Useful Concept in Marketing Decisions?', *Journal of Marketing*, **33**: 79–83.

Nesbitt, S. (1959) 'Today's Housewives Plan Menus as They Shop', *Nesbitt Associates Release*, 2–3.

O'Guinn, T.C. and Faber, R.J. (1989), 'Compulsive Buying: A Phenomenological Exploration', *Journal of Consumer Research*, **16**: 147–57.

Piron, F. (1993) 'A Comparison of Emotional Reactions Experienced by Planned, Unplanned and Impulse Purchasers', in McAlister, L. and Rothschild, M.L. (eds) *Advances in Consumer Research*, Provo, UT, Association for Consumer Research, **20**: 341–4.

Rook, D.W. (1987) 'The Buying Impulse', *Journal of Consumer Research*, **14**: 189–99.

Rook, D.W. and Fisher, R.J. (1995) 'Normative Influences on Impulsive Buying Behavior,' *Journal of Consumer Research*, **22**: 305–13.

Rook, D.W. and Gardner, M.P. (1993) 'In the Mood: Affective Elements in Impulse Buying', in Arnold-Costa, J. and Belk, R.W. (eds) *Research in Consumer Behavior*, Greenwich, CT: JAI Press, **6**: 1–28.

Rook, D.W. and Hoch, S.J. (1985) 'Consuming Impulses', in Hirschman, E.C. and Holbrook, M.B. (eds) *Advances in Consumer Research*, Provo, UT: Association for Consumer Research, **12**: 23–7.

Stern, H. (1962) 'The Significance of Impulse Buying Today', *Journal of Marketing*, **26**: 59–62.

Inflation

The inflation experienced in Western economies in the 1970s and 1980s evoked considerable concern in the general public and gave rise to governmental efforts to reduce it. Naturally enough, another product of the concern was heightened research interest in the subject, and, although much of the ensuing research was purely economic, psychological factors in inflation were not neglected.

Public perception of inflation

In theory, inflation, defined as a rise in the overall level of prices, need not affect people adversely. If, for example, prices went up 10 per cent in a given time period and wages, social welfare benefits and other payments were indexed so that they all went up 10 per cent to compensate, then there need be no effect on people's material well-being. In practice, of course, no economy is or was completely indexed, and inflation affects different groups to different extents and at different times (for example, Leijonhufvud, 1977). Nevertheless, it is still true that inflation produces both winners and losers (Fischer, 1986), and — leaving aside possible effects on eventual economic growth — no average effect on spending power.

Such reasoning suggests that the average person living in an inflationary economy might be little concerned by it. On the other hand, there are also grounds for believing the opposite. For example, the existence of money illusion, in which people accept money at its nominal rather than its real value, suggests that they would not remain indifferent to inflation. Inflation may also lead to changes in the rewards obtained from different activities or strategies: for example, it might become more important for workers to belong to a strong union than to receive productivity bonuses (Leijonhufvud, 1977). Then again, if inflation acts so as to blur price differentials, an issue outlined below, it will have a detrimental effect on people's economic behaviour, particularly as consumers.

While the theories may not be decisive on this point, the research evidence is solidly in favour of people finding inflation aversive. A number of studies replicate the finding from opinion polling in many countries that most people in inflationary economies are both concerned about inflation as a serious societal problem and see themselves as adversely affected by it. Thus, for example, Fischer (1986: 371) conceived of the inflation problem less as one of price rise than as 'a perceived decrease in economic well-being'; Epstein and Bahad (1982), who investigated reactions to inflation in the US and Israel, concluded that the effects of inflation were better explained in terms of psychological stress than as changes to real income.

Perception of inflation and price memory

When people have been asked to estimate the current rate of inflation, their estimates, if somewhat variable, are accurate on average. On the other hand, studies from a number of different countries which have asked people to estimate past prices either generally or of specific items (for example, 'How much did 500 gm of butter cost 10 years ago?') have found the average prices remembered to be subject to consistent bias. Prices from the previous year or two are remembered as lower on average than they actually were; prices from longer ago are remembered as higher on average than they really were. Put another way, the impact of inflation over the past year or so is overestimated while that over longer periods is underestimated (for example, Bates and Gabor, 1986; Kemp, 1987; Kemp and Willetts, 1996).

A number of other factors have been shown to influence people's memory for past prices. Consumers tend to recall prices that are in line with their expectations (Helgeson and Beatty, 1987). Moreover, while prices of different items actually do not rise at the same rate during inflation, these differences are not well remembered, so that people tend to recall a general trend rather than the deviations from it and to remember all commodities as having experienced similar price rises (Kemp, 1987; Kemp and Willetts, 1996).

Inflation blurs price information

Prices play a crucial role as signals in both economic theory and the reality of consumer behaviour. Higher prices are supposed to be regarded by producers as a signal to produce more and by consumers as a signal to shift demand to other products. It is clearly conceivable that inflation could act so as to confuse the price signals of particular items. In Shamir's (1985: 383) words, 'Higher variance in the general inflation level may blur the information a price conveys . . . as inflation increases so does its variance'.

The evidence suggests that individual price differences are in fact blurred by inflation. As noted above, differences in the past price trends of different items do become homogenized in memory, an effect found for producer as well as for consumer goods (Kemp and Willetts, 1996).

The strongest evidence for blurring comes from economies with high inflation. In a study conducted in Israel at a time when inflation exceeded 100 per cent per annum, Shamir (1985) found that Israeli respondents often claimed not to know the present prices of relatively common items, and in comparison with respondents in countries with lower inflation rates were much more inaccurate at estimating them. During the Argentine hyperinflation in 1989 and 1990, some shopkeepers displayed signs stating that they were 'Closed for lack of prices' (Heyman and Leijonhufvud, 1995: 105).

Inflationary expectations

Many economists have thought that inflation is caused at least in part by expectations about inflation which are, in turn, a product of people's past experience with inflation. Research done on inflationary expectations suggests that these tend to be the product of people's perceptions of inflation rather than of the actual inflation that has occurred (for example, Behrend, 1966; Blomqvist, 1983). People who underestimate the past impact of inflation tend to have lower inflationary expectations than those who overestimate the past impact (Kemp, 1987).

Inflationary expectations are influenced not only by real or perceived inflationary experiences but also by such variables as political attitudes and expectations (Webley and Spears, 1986), and, consistent with the distorting effect that inflation has on price information, inflationary expectations themselves are held with little certainty by respondents (Jonung, 1986).

This phenomenon ties in with another. In times of high inflation, wage negotiations are conducted at more frequent intervals (Heyman and Leijonhufvud, 1995). The greater frequency of these negotiations are a natural consequence of the greater uncertainty and stress that accompany inflation: workers cannot afford to wait months for pay rises and employers cannot afford to make settlements in advance. This is also a good example of how inflation brings about changes in the way business is done.

SIMON KEMP

Bibliography

Bates, J.M. and Gabor, A. (1986) 'Price Perception in Creeping Inflation', *Journal of Economic Psychology*, 7: 291–314.

Behrend, H. (1966) 'Price Images, Inflation and National Incomes Policy', *Scottish Journal of Political Economy*, 13: 273–96.

Blomqvist, H.C. (1983) 'On the Formation of Inflationary Expectations: Some Empirical Evidence from Finland', *Journal of Economic Psychology*, 4: 319–41.

Epstein, Y.M. and Bahad, E.Y. (1982) 'Economic Stress: Notes on the Psychology of Inflation', *Journal of Applied Social Psychology*, 12: 85–99.

Fischer, C.C. (1986) 'The Differential Impact of Inflation on Key Societal Interest Groups and Public Policy Implications', *Journal of Economic Psychology*, 7: 371–86.

Helgeson, J.G. and Beatty, S.E. (1987) 'Price Expectation and Price Recall Error', *Journal of Consumer Research*, 14: 379–86.

Heyman, D. and Leijonhufvud, A. (1995) *High Inflation: The Arne Ryde Memorial*

Introspective Research

Lectures, Oxford, Clarendon.

Jonung, L. (1986) 'Uncertainty about Inflationary Perceptions and Expectations', *Journal of Economic Psychology*, **7**: 315–25.

Kemp, S. (1987) 'Estimation of Past Prices', *Journal of Economic Psychology*, **8**: 181–9.

Kemp, S. and Willetts, K. (1996) 'Remembering the Price of Wool', *Journal of Economic Psychology*, **17**: 115–25.

Leijonhufvud, A. (1977) 'Costs and Consequences of Inflation', in Harcourt, G.C. (ed.) *The Microeconomic Foundations of Macroeconomics*, London, Macmillan: 265–98.

Shamir, J. (1985) 'Consumers' Subjective Perception of Price in Times of Inflation', *Journal of Economic Psychology*, **6**: 383–98.

Webley, P. and Spears, R. (1986) 'Economic Preferences and Inflationary Expectations', *Journal of Economic Psychology*, **7**: 359–69.

Introspective Research

Introspection has a long history in social science fields such as psychology (for example, Wundt, 1897) and the a priorist tradition in economics in which theorists observe phenomena within themselves, as well as externally (Hutchison, 1977: 159). It is a valuable research tool for investigating consumer behaviour because it goes to the heart of that behaviour, that is, inner lived experience and the mind as consuming organ (Gould, 1993; Schelling, 1986). In this perspective, consumers use goods to satisfy needs which ultimately manifest in inner psychological space. Thus, all research methods which explore cognitive or affective processes (for example, surveys, phenomenological interviews) rely in the final analysis on consumers doing the work of introspection, i.e. searching their own minds for their own thoughts and feelings. Introspection as a technique also informs the analytic processes of consumer researchers, themselves, who whether they acknowledge it or not face issues of reflexive subjectivity in designing, executing and interpreting empirical studies. In fact, whether the investigator seeks to exclude subjectivity as traditional research obliges or whether he or she acknowledges the presence of subjectivity as an inextricable part of the process as suggested by poststructuralism, he or she can explore these issues through introspection. Thus, by seeking self-understanding, the researcher can not only develop parallel insights about others but also refine the process by which those insights emerge.

What is introspection?

Researchers have tended to label introspection in various ways: introspection (Gould, 1991), subjective personal introspection (Holbrook, 1988) and researcher introspection (Wallendorf and Brucks, 1993). These labels and their application suggest that introspection by a researcher is a special type within the larger category of introspection which anyone may do. Thus, in defining introspection, we need to consider first its broad definition and application and then its narrower use by consumer researchers engaged in self-investigation.

Introspection is a process by which one observes one's own thoughts, feelings and states. Generally, we also think of it as a conscious process in which how and what one observes is a matter of context and motivation. Thus, consumers may choose to focus on particular inner phenomena, both during consumption and also during self-report concerning it. However, what they observe may emerge unconsciously, as well as consciously (Gould, 1993). For example, a consumer may be instructed to follow his or her reactions while watching a movie but may not perceive all of them, may forget them, or may (un)consciously repress them. Thus, introspection is a product of the holistic conscious–unconscious continuum of the individual and may vary in degree and depth across individuals, situations and even cultures. While such degree and depth has been a subject of controversy (for example, Nisbett and Wilson, 1977), one can train in and develop introspection. For example, various processes ranging from psychoanalysis to meditation serve to enhance one's introspective abilities (Gould, 1991, 1993; Holbrook, 1988). Parallel to mere exposure effects, the very act of adopting an introspective stance and exposing oneself to one's own mind can enhance introspection.

While introspection focuses on inner states, consumer researchers have also included behaviour as an aspect. This is appropriate provided the researcher considers an introspective–extrospective perspective (Gould, 1993). Introspection is a focus on the inner world while extrospection is a focus on the external world. Most research is externally focused. However, the observation of one's own behaviour can also be seen as an introspective activity since it involves inner watching of that behaviour. One is a participant observer in, and constructs a *self-ethnography* of, one's own life. Moreover, introspection as a process is strengthened if one triangulates between one's external behaviour and one's inner thoughts and feelings. To illustrate, follow a consumer behaviour that you engage in regularly or study. Watch the behaviour and how you think and feel during it. If it involves many behaviours within the larger behaviour, observe them (for example, eating a meal in which many behaviours of choosing food to eat, eating first a bite of this and then a bite of that). What is the relationship between your inner states and outer actions? Are they nondual (that is, energetically, cognitively and/or affectively experienced through similar perceptual processes) as some Asian theories suggest (Gould, 1991)? Can you discern patterns? Do your observations vary across meals and if so, how? Finally, does cognitive dissonance cause you to overlook some thoughts or feelings?

The researcher as introspector

The researcher as introspector is a special category of consumer research which I largely focus on in this entry because of prior emphasis on it in consumer research. This method simply involves the researcher applying introspection to him- or herself, nothing more and nothing less. While some think this is limiting, anecdotal, narcissistic and not very generalizable (Wallendorf and Brucks, 1993), it none the less can be very helpful. First, it is a useful tool for discovery. Since one cannot escape oneself, one is surrounded by the richness of one's own life and consumption. Why not draw on this wealth? Instinctively and without acknowledging it many researchers do this anyway. Second, the training of new researchers can be enhanced by their engaging in introspection. This application, however, may raise privacy issues (that is, students writing up introspective studies for their teachers may be sacrificing privacy). Perhaps students can be instructed to do this for themselves. Third, researcher introspection may help to develop empathy with other consumers in ways that no other technique could. For example, exploring one's own limitations introspectively might help one to better understand consumers who are challenged in their health, economic or some other status. Fourth, researcher introspection can be used as a technique for confirmation of other research (Gould, 1995). The researcher would ask, 'Do these results make sense to me? Do I experience things this way?'. This not only applies to other studies but is a good way to triangulate one's own research which examines other consumers through other methods. Indeed, introspection has been joined with a number of techniques including participant observation, 'auto-autodriving', psychoanalysis and meditative techniques (Gould, 1993, 1995; Holbrook, 1995). Finally, such researcher investigation will inform our understanding of introspection in general and therefore the great range of all consumer research which engages the consumer in self-report.

Insights to-date from introspection in consumer research

While it is impossible to review here all the introspective insight gained in consumer research (see Gould 1993 and Holbrook 1995 for reviews), several themes emerge. First, researchers using introspection tend to draw on their own personal experience to develop new perspectives. For example, I based my introspective energy research on the idea that 'Much of consumer research has failed to describe many experiential aspects of my own consumer behaviour, especially the everyday dynamics of my pervasive, self-perceived vital energy' (Gould, 1991: 194). Second, introspective researchers have tended to be highly revelatory in the self-material they write about. Reporting one's own psychoanalytic or sexual experiences as they have done is a quite unusual approach to consumer research. They also take all sorts of personal risks, while simultaneously gaining a new freedom of expression and discovery.

338

Third, introspective styles vary quite a bit. Holbrook tends to be highly personal, lyrical and poetic. For example, he describes himself by name as 'Morris the Epicurean'. I tend to use introspection in a more impersonal way. I do cite illustrations from my own life as theoretical exemplars, but I also have come to ask the reader to confirm on the same introspective basis whether these results relate to his or her own life. Still, both of us have shared the goals of using and advancing introspection. In contrast, many more others have used introspection more obliquely without calling it that.

Fourth, while introspection in consumer research is relatively new, it has provided an anchor point for how researchers perceive the field. The work applying it is cited for pushing the field's limits, is read in doctoral programmes, and remains of interest to researchers engaged in it.

Finally, despite a running debate in which Wallendorf and Brucks (1993) and I (Gould, 1991, 1995) have spelled out the controversies over introspection, the fact remains that it can be done, is insightful, and may provide understanding not only of the contents of consumption (for example, thinking about shopping) but also the processes of thinking about it (for example, one's reasoning processes involved in shopping). As I (Gould, 1995) suggested, any consumer researcher can investigate the limits of introspection within oneself, can learn to improve such introspection through training and experience, and could conceivably discover new consumer behaviour phenomena.

The future of introspection

The future for introspection appears bright on an interdisciplinary basis. Consciousness studies and cognitive science are expanding our understanding of mind. In particular, real-time introspection concurrent with actual consumer behaviour is likely to become more accessible and of interest. On a post-structuralist level, the introspective stories people, especially researchers, tell should become more accepted in consumer research just as they are in such respected journals as *Qualitative Inquiry*.

Currently, I am developing two new forms of introspection: *meditative introspection* and *experimental introspection*. Meditative introspection draws on the rich meditative experience of Asia to suggest better ways to induce, sustain and interpret introspection. It involves focusing attention through following one's thoughts and feelings. While a lengthy description of it is beyond our scope here, I would suggest that interested readers seek to experience various meditative practices as Asians and others have applied them in such rituals as the Japanese tea ceremony or in using various material things such as meditative gardens or ritual objects. What effect do they have on you? Can you describe these effects? Can you apply them in developing your understanding of everyday consumer behaviour? For example, how do such activities as wine tasting and movie viewing compare?

Experimental introspection involves intentionally changing one's behaviour and/or inner states to test the effects on one's consciousness. To illustrate how this works in consumer behaviour, try the following exercise. Imagine experiencing a minor pain. Sometimes, you take a pain killer and sometimes you try to get by without taking anything. When you get such a pain, try a feeling and thought-experiment. See what happens if you do not take the painkiller versus if you do (ideally at two different times). How do you feel and what do you think about? As a separate exercise, try working with a consumption object that brings you pleasure. Can you induce that pleasure in your mind without using the actual object? Experiment with different objects, both physically and in your imagination, and see what happens.

The promise of future developments places us on the threshold of a new introspective era. As consumer behaviour increasingly becomes an activity which explores inner space and even blurs outer and inner experience (for example, virtual reality), research which is introspectively informed will be required. The mind as consuming organ cannot be engaged in any other way.

STEPHEN J. GOULD

Bibliography

Gould, S.J. (1991) 'The Self-Manipulation of My Pervasive, Perceived Vital Energy through Product Use: An Introspective–Praxis Approach', *Journal of Consumer Research*, **18**: 194-207.

Gould, S.J. (1993) 'The Circle of Projection and Introjection: An Introspective Investigation of a Proposed Paradigm Involving the Mind as "Consuming Organ"', in Costa, J.A. and Belk, R.W. (eds) *Research in Consumer Behavior*, Volume 11, Greenwich, CT, JAI Press: 195–230.

Gould, S.J. (1995) 'Researcher Introspection as a Method in Consumer Research: Applications, Issues and Implications', *Journal of Consumer Research*, **21**: 719–22.

Holbrook, M.B. (1988) 'The Psychoanalytic Interpretation of Consumer Behavior: I Am an Animal', in Hirschman, E.C. and Sheth, J.N. (eds) *Research in Consumer Behavior*, Volume 3, Greenwich, CT, JAI Press: 149–179.

Holbrook, M.B. (1995) *Consumer Research: Introspective Essays on the Study of Consumption*, Thousand Oaks, CA, Sage.

Hutchison, T.W. (1977) *Knowledge and Ignorance in Economics*, Chicago, University of Chicago Press.

Nisbett, R. and Wilson, T.D. (1977), 'Telling More than We Can Know: Verbal Reports on Mental Processes', *Psychological Review*, **84**: 231–59.

Schelling, T.C. (1986) 'The Mind as Consuming Organ', in Elster, J. (ed.) *The Multiple Self*, Cambridge, Cambridge University Press.

Wallendorf, M. and Brucks, M. (1993) 'Introspection in Consumer Research: Implementation and Implications', *Journal of Consumer Research*, **20**: 339–59.

Wundt, W. (1897) *Outlines of Psychology*, London, Williams & Norgate.

Involvement

In the context of consumer research, the concept of involvement can be said to refer to the perceived personal importance of an object to an individual. More precisely, involvement is seen to refer to the psychological linkage between an individual and an object (Laaksonen, 1994: 96). In simple terms, when consumers are highly involved with a particular activity, it is the sort of thing about which they can get passionate or defensive — as the saying goes 'hot under the collar' — because it matters to them a lot; their personalities are in some important sense entangled with it. High involvement with a particular consumption activity need not entail spending a lot of time on the activity, although it may do so: for example, one may play a lot of social tennis as a low-involvement form of relaxation, or one may be highly involved with tennis having set one's heart on becoming club president or reaching a particular performance league. In the latter case, the person takes the activity seriously: it 'matters' to them.

The concept was introduced to consumer behaviour literature with great vigour at the end of the 1970s. The motivator behind involvement research was a new understanding of the nature of consumer behaviour. It was recognized that much of the behaviour of consumers could be characterized by a limited degree of information processing, evaluative activity and physical efforts (Olshavsky and Granbois, 1979). This was contradictory to the dominating view which assumed consumers to behave as internally-directed, active information seekers and extensive problem solvers. Consumer researchers were challenged to renew their theoretical thinking and empirical research to additionally account for the behaviour described by limited cognitive and physical efforts.

This kind of behaviour was termed 'low-involvement behaviour'. The cognitive information processing behaviour, on the other hand, was relabelled 'high-involvement behaviour'. Thus, the concept of involvement was assumed to be central in explaining the nature of consumer behaviour. Consequently, involvement was studied in relation to products, brands, advertising, media, consumers, situations, learning, information processing and so on. During the 1980s, involvement was among the most researched topics in consumer behaviour (for example, Laurent and Kapferer, 1985; Park and Mittal, 1985; Vaughn, 1986; and Zaichkowsky, 1985).

At the present there seems to prevail a general agreement that involvement has a central role in explaining consumer behaviour. However, while most consumer theory texts now discuss the topic, my opening definition should not be taken to imply the existence of consensus on the concept of involvement itself. The determination and measurement of the concept has varied. There have been attempts to handle the diversity by specifying different types of involvement such as enduring involvement, appeal involvement, stake involvement, situational involvement, purchase involvement, response involvement and so on. The question then arises whether there is a common concept behind all these involvement definitions or whether they should be regarded as distinct concepts in themselves.

The treatments of involvement can broadly be classified into three distinct yet related conceptualizations. For the sake of clarity these are here termed as 'response involvement', 'situational involvement' and 'personal involvement'.

Response involvement

Consumer researchers often talk about low-involvement versus high-involvement decision making and information processing, thus connecting involvement with a specific type of response. There are also several definitions that describe the level of involvement in terms of differences in the nature and/or extent of information processing or brand-choice development. The assumption here is that under low-involvement conditions the level of information processing is superficial whereas highly involving communications receive more attention and cognitive efforts. In a similar manner it has been suggested that low involvement is present when a person devotes limited time and limited efforts to brand choice and decision making.

Processing dynamism has also been found to be affected by the level of involvement. In particular, the level of involvement has appeared to influence the order of cognitive, affective and conative development of information processing. It has been assumed that whereas low involvement characterizes processing where affective development follows conative development (growth of desire to perform an action), the opposite holds true for high involvement. For example, Ray (1973) suggested that, when a consumer's involvement is low, the information-processing hierarchy is characterized by the sequence: (i) cognitive development, (ii) conative development, (iii) affective development. It follows that advertisements should focus more on inducing consumers to try a product (to behave) rather than on creating positive brand attitudes (affects). This is because low-involved consumers form attitudes only after using the product. However, highly involved consumers are assumed to behave according to their pre-established attitudes and this is why advertisements that create positive brand images are needed in these situations.

The response involvement literature determines the level of involvement by describing different static or dynamic responses of an individual when he or she faces an information-processing or a choice task. However, this analysis is problematic. For example, it should be noted that the limited amount of cognitive and physical efforts can stem from a variety of reasons: the object or activity might have little personal relevance but it may also be the case that the emotional or habitual nature of the processing or the situational pressure can enable or induce a consumer to limit the degree of processing. These response scenarios have thus been criticized and it has been suggested that they should be viewed more as assumed response effects of involvement rather than as involvement itself (Laaksonen, 1994).

Situational involvement

This second category comprises those approaches to involvement that describe it as the extent of motivation a person experiences in a given situation. This term refers to the amount of arousal, activation, (emotional) attachment, interest and/or motivation. When understood in this manner, involvement varies across consumers, products and points in space and time.

Situational involvement is reactive in nature, that is, it has a behaviour-inducing capacity. For example, if people have low involvement with wine, their typical wine choice problem is presumably characterized by limited efforts. However if they are going to buy a bottle of wine as a present, a heightened level of involvement occurs and it follows that they are likely to devote more cognitive and physical efforts to brand choice (Clarke and Belk, 1979). Situational involvement has been assumed particularly to affect the extent and type of processing, searching and decision making the consumer undertakes. Hence the number of attributes used in comparing brands, degree of attention devoted to brand purchase, and amount of time spent in searching among different brands, are assumed to be influenced by the level of involvement. It follows that the assumed response effects are similar to those described under the term 'response involvement', above.

Situational involvement has commonly been applied in consumer research, probably because much of the research is focused on understanding time- and situation-specific processes such as information processing and brand-choice behaviour. The situation-specific conceptualization of involvement has been applied to account for the motivation of an individual to participate in the temporal process at hand. Increased motivation may or may not be realized in an actual processing situation. For example, a consumer may be highly involved in making an optimal brand choice, but due to time limitation he or she has to be content with the first satisfying alternative. Another consumer may be only slightly involved when purchasing a particular product, but the unavailability of the product may force the consumer into extensive efforts in order to obtain the product. These examples shed light on the basic distinction between the response and situational definitions of involvement (see also Laaksonen, 1994).

The situational definitions of involvement have been accepted most commonly within the communication context. Involvement has referred to the extent to which a consumer is motivated to process an advertisement. It has been shown that under low-involvement conditions the level of information processing is superficial whereas high-involving communications receive more attention and cognitive effort. However, the level of involvement affects not only the extent of information processing but also the processes of persuasion.

The elaboration likelihood model (ELM) of persuasion suggests that the processes underlying attitude formation and change are different under the conditions of low versus high involvement (Petty and Cacioppo, 1986). Given their ability to process information, consumers under high involvement are predicted to engage in higher levels of elaboration, evoke more cognitive responses and emphasize central cues in attitude formation. On the other hand, less-involved consumers are more likely to look for background cues in the advertisement, which opens up a peripheral route to persuasion.

In communication studies the most common way to proceed has been through manipulating the level of involvement. The research has focused on the assumed effects of involvement rather than on the concept of involvement itself. The opposite holds true in other areas of involvement research, where the main focus has been first on defining the concept of involvement and afterwards on developing reliable and valid measurement scales.

Personal involvement

Those definitions which we here term 'personal involvement' give a more stable and ongoing nature to involvement which is not affected by situational variations. It refers to the perceived personal importance of an object (usually a product) to an individual. Involvement increases as the strength of the psychological linkage between the product and an individual tightens. The greater the number and the closer the linkages people make between the object and their personal values the more involved they are seen to be. More specifically, involvement is seen to increase as the strength, number and centrality of the personal consequences or implications associated with a product increases.

What then are the potential consequences that develop linkages between a person and a product? It has been suggested that the basis for involvement can be found in utilitarian, hedonic, personal and/or social importance of the product. These dimensions can be seen to act as the cognitive ground for involvement. The number of dimensions included may vary from consumer to consumer and also from product to product. Cultural differences may also exist in the bases for evaluating the meaning of a product.

The personal involvement conceptualization stresses the role of involvement as an interactive variable which is determined by the characteristics of a person and those of an object. Because of this interactional base it is possible that involvement can account for differences in selected aspects of consumer behaviour both across products and across consumers. To illustrate: detergents are often mentioned as examples of low-involvement product and cars as examples of a high-involvement product. Generally speaking this may hold true, but it should be noted that there are individuals who are highly involved with detergents (for example, because of environmental or health reasons) and also those whose involvement with cars is low. Involvement is supposed to be positively correlated with activities such as the extent of ongoing information search (such as paying attention to product-related magazines and advertisements and visiting dealers without an immediate intention to buy), money spent on that type of product category and frequency of product/service usage. It should be noted that the assumed response effects of involvement are, from this standpoint, more related to the use and ownership of a product. The brand choice, on the other hand, is affected not only by the perceived personal involvement but also by several marketing- and consumer-determined situational factors as well as by past experience in coping with similar situations.

Measurement of involvement
Although involvement has been analysed from a variety of perspectives, it seems that the perceived personal importance view is gaining growing acceptance. Two types of attempts to measure personal involvement have been undertaken. First, there are scales that directly focus on the intensity of perceived importance itself. A unidimensional scale capturing the intensity of perceived personal importance has been sought (see Mittal, 1995). Second, there are scales that focus on the underlying sources that produce the perception of personal importance. The studies (for example, Strazzieri and Hajdukowicz-Brisson, 1995) suggest from two to four dimensions stressing utilitarian, hedonic, social and/or personal aspects of product evaluation should be included in an involvement scale. The intensity of involvement is obtained by summing up the different dimensions or it is viewed as a profile reaching across these dimensions.

In consumer decision-making research the differences in responses under low and high involvement have received only limited attention. As the studies have concentrated on defining and/or measuring involvement, the assumed response effects have often been included only in order to evaluate validity. Most of the researchers assume that decreasing involvement reduces the amount of cognitive and behavioural efforts devoted to brand choice. However, as stated above, these kinds of responses may be seen as the outcomes of the situational involvement and as only resulting indirectly from the personal involvement .

It can be argued that behaviours related to owning, using and consuming

8

88

products are more readily related to personal involvement than are the temporal characteristics of the choice process. But this question has not been researched. The personal involvement conceptualization challenges us to broaden the scope of involvement research to the investigation of more consumption-related issues beyond the act of purchasing. In particular, the objects of consumption should not be viewed solely in terms of product attributes (such as price and quality) relevant in a choice situation, but also in terms of symbolic and cultural meanings connected to product ownership and consumption. For this purpose new kinds of research frameworks and instruments are needed: for example, the means–end chain theory of product knowledge has assisted us to reveal a richer and deeper picture of the meanings of products (Reynolds and Gutman, 1988). It assumes product attributes as instrumental in receiving personal value fulfilment. It develops a mental ladder between product attributes and individual values. This theory can assist us also in determining the level of involvement (Laaksonen 1994).

The initial ideas that activated involvement research demanded a different paradigm and different frameworks to research the low-involvement consumer. It was a clear challenge for the (then) dominant cognitive information-processing paradigm. However, the paradigm captured the concept. Involvement has been studied within the cognitive information-processing paradigm as an important mediating variable, but so far only part of the potential of the concept has been released. In order to release the full potential we need to broaden our viewpoint to study the consumer. The hedonistic paradigm has done this by providing tools to understand behaviour under high-feeling-based involvement. What remains questionable is our ability to understand the processes underlying low-involvement behaviour. Is this behaviour similar to high-involvement behaviour except for requiring minimal efforts or are the processes underlying behaviour under varying involvement levels different in themselves?

It may be that under low involvement, consumers rely more on external situational sources instead of acting in internally-directed ways as assumed by the cognitive information-processing paradigm. Increased involvement could increase the influence of intraindividual product-related cognitions on brand choice. It follows that involvement may determine not only the extent but also the nature of consumer-purchasing behaviour. More research into this area might enable involvement to release its potential as a useful theoretical as well as a practical concept for product marketers.

PIRJO LAAKSONEN

Bibliography
Clarke, K. and Belk, R.W. (1979) 'The Effects of Product Involvement and Task Definition on Anticipated Consumer Effort', in Wilkie, W.L. (ed.) *Advances in*

Consumer Research, **6**: 313–18, Ann Arbor, MI, Association for Consumer Research.

Laaksonen, P. (1994) *Consumer Involvement: Concepts and Research*, London, Routledge.

Laurent, G. and Kapferer, J.-N. (1985) 'Measuring Consumer Involvement Profiles', *Journal of Marketing Research*, **22**: 41–53.

Mittal, B. (1995) 'A Comparative Analysis of Four Scales of Consumer Involvement', *Psychology and Marketing*, **12**: 663–82.

Olshavsky, R.W. and and Granbois, D.H. (1979) 'Consumer Decision Making — Fact or Fiction?', *Journal of Consumer Research*, **6**: 93–100.

Park, C.W. and Mittal, B. (1985) 'A Theory of Involvement in Consumer Behavior: Problems and Issues', in Sheth, J.N (ed.) *Research in Consumer Behavior 1*, Greenwich, CT, JAI Press: 201–31.

Petty, R.E. and Cacioppo, J.T. (1986) *Communication and Persuasion: Central and Peripheral Routes to Attitude Change*, New York, Springer.

Ray, M.K. (1973) 'Marketing Communication and the Hierarchy-of-Effects', in Clarke, P. (ed.) *New Models of Mass Communication Research*,, Beverly Hills, CA, Sage: 147–76.

Reynolds, T.J. and Gutman, J. (1988) 'Laddering Theory, Method, Analysis and Interpretation', *Journal of Advertising Research*, **28**: 11–31.

Strazzieri, A. and Hajdukowicz-Brisson, E. (1995) 'Clearing up Ambiguity about Enduring Involvement by Opposing Appeal-Involvement to Stake-Involvement', in Jolibert, A., Peterson, R.A. and Strazzieri, A. (eds) *Proceedings of the First International Research Seminar on Marketing Communications and Consumer Behavior*, Institut d'Administration des Enterprises d'Aix-en-Provence, Université d'aix-Marseille: 471–89.

Vaughn, R. (1986) 'How Advertising Works: A Planning Model Revisited', *Journal of Advertising Research*, **26**: 57–66.

Zaichkowsky, J.L. (1985) 'Measuring Involvement Construct', *Journal of Consumer Research*, **12**: 341–52.

Katona, George

George Katona, who was born in Hungary in 1901, first trained as a psychologist and later studied economics. He received the doctor's degree in experimental psychology at the University of Göttingen in 1921. As the employment situation for psychologists was poor he had to take a job in a bank where he came face to face with the economic problems after World War I. After a later career as an economic journalist in Germany and as an investment adviser in the US, he fell ill and had to change to something quieter so he again started to do psychological research. His speciality was to utilize Gestalt theory in the study of learning and problem solving. Katona's *Organizing and Memorizing* (1940) is a classic in the field and still widely cited.

When World War II broke out, Katona used some of his psychological knowledge to warn against uncontrolled inflation of the kind that he had experienced in Germany. His book *War without Inflation* (1942) aroused interest among some leading economists. He accepted a job with the Cowles Commission and made a study of businessmen's reactions to price control, based on interviews. Katona next became a cofounder of the Survey Research Center at the University of Michigan, where he directed the Economic Behavior Program from 1946 to 1972. In 1950 he was appointed professor of economics and psychology at the University of Michigan. He died in Berlin in 1981 shortly after receiving his third honorary doctor's degree.

Let me begin the review of Katona's work with a personal memory. In 1953, George Katona visited the University of Chicago where I was a graduate student of psychology. He gave a lecture to psychology students and the next day a lecture to economics students. He began his lecture in front of the psychology students: 'I am a psychologist, but now I am going to put on my other hat and talk like an economist'. To the economics students he said: 'I am an economist, but now I am going to put on my other hat and talk like a psychologist'. Surprisingly enough, the lectures were almost identical, but the answers to questions were differently phrased with due consideration to the background of the audience.

In his lecture, Katona described among other things how economists at the end of 1948 and in early 1949 predicted a serious recession and his research group presented survey data showing that consumers were planning to spend as much on consumer durables in 1949 as they had in 1948. If Katona's report was right there would be no recession. The prediction was right, 1949 was a prosperous year and the economists' interest in consumer plans and subjective expectations was aroused. This meant a breakthrough for the use of answers from survey interviews to make short-run predictions of business-cycle development.

In the mid-1940s, Katona had started a research programme that involved asking consumers and businessmen about their expectations of their own financial status and the national economy. The consumer expectations were summarized as the Index of Consumer Sentiment (ICS). Similar indices were later developed in many other countries in the 1950s. The original ICS is computed as the 'balance' for each question, i.e. the difference between the percentage of those who report improvement and the percentage of those who report deterioration, averaging over the five questions. The ICS is a predictor of turning-points in business cycles and expresses changes in optimism–pessimism about the financial future, in mass media contexts called 'consumer confidence'. The interpretation is that the population is becoming more optimistic or more pessimistic rather than that the majority is optimistic or pessimistic. The measure used is a pure macro measure of change. The measure is computed for the aggregate and there is no exact equivalent at the individual/household level. Since 1989, the ICS has been included in the US Index of Leading Economic Indicators for the Commerce Department's Bureau of Economic Analysis.

The ICS has been used in many economic and econometric studies. It has been found to be a significant predictor of total consumption and savings. It should be noted that Katona himself did not think of the use of ICS in econometric models as a proper test of its usefulness, since he viewed the ICS as only one step in the forecasting procedure. The interviews comprised follow-up questions and the answers to those contributed significantly to the interpretation of the index.

While economists were still preoccupied with the idea that expectations were determined solely by earlier events, Katona declared that in some cases consumers formed new expectations that could be completely different from earlier experience. While expectations could remain the same over long periods of time when little happened, they could change dramatically when there were good reasons for expectations to change. Katona's studies of expectations in surveys made him suggest 'There is hardly any limit to the factors that may serve to change expectations; income or price expectations may be influenced by taxes, interest rates, political and international developments, the urban crisis etc.' (Katona, 1972: 555). He took this to mean that the only way to assess expectations in situations where changes in the economy were imminent was to ask consumers about their expectations. He strongly rejected the fundamental assumption of rational expectations theory that decision-makers use the same information and make the same inferences from it as expert economists do.

George Katona gave outstanding contributions to behavioural economics in many areas in addition to the theory and measurement of expectations. He based his research on a simple theory of consumption/saving. He assumed that economic behaviour could be explained by variables intervening between economic stimuli and consumer reactions. The effect, for example, of an income change depends on the state of one or more intervening variables. Katona's micro model was useful primarily at the macro level: saving/consumption is dependent on *ability* to save/consume and *willingness* to save/consume. Consumer ability to save/consume is defined as disposable income and willingness is assessed through interview data on consumer expectations, attitudes and other personality characteristics such as motives. After Keynes, economists had focused their study of consumption growth and savings on income (ability) and had disregarded the role of willingness to consume which Malthus had previously emphasized. While Keynes had spent considerable time on the role of businessmen's expectations for the business cycle, he had completely neglected consumer expectations. Katona was highly critical of this neglect and demonstrated that consumer expectations had an influence on the national economy.

While ability and willingness to save were simple concepts in Katona's model of saving, they were carefully spelled out as detailed questions in the surveys he and his co-workers carried out. He distinguished three types of saving, based on reasons or motives for saving: (i) contractual saving, (ii) discretionary saving and (iii) residual saving.

Contractual saving is similar to the precommitment ideas brought forth by Strotz and some later economists. Regular saving is self-imposed or imposed by others. For example, buying on instalment necessitates later regular saving since the debt must be paid off; buying life insurance or a retirement pension scheme involves a contract to save regularly and usually for long periods of time.

Discretionary saving is an original concept and along with discretionary consumption is one of Katona's main theoretical contributions to behavioural economics. It relates to the scope for genuine decisions that many people have in affluent societies. They can choose between attractive alternatives since there is money left after the basic needs have been satisfied. People may decide to save for many reasons, such as wanting to purchase an expensive durable, to go on a long vacation or just desiring to have money available if opportunities for attractive spending arise. Katona (1975) declared (as did the economist Irving Fisher) that most of saving was 'for a rainy day'. Katona's critique of Keynes's psychological law, which stipulated that consumption was in the long run tied to current income, was based on the idea of discretionary consumption. The consumer's freedom to save or to spend some of the current income made it difficult to find stable relationships between income and consumption or saving.

Residual saving refers to money that has not yet been spent. It is saved by default rather than planning and may involve a need for cash management, a temporary repository for money, for example, in a bank account.

The effects of macroeconomic changes, say, the effects of a tax cut on savings, are assumed to depend on such intervening variables as the attitudes and expectations of the taxpayers. Since the pertinent future attitudes and expectations can rarely be predicted on the basis of easily available objective data, the consequence is that new data on the state of the intervening variables will almost always have to be collected before the effects can be explained or predicted.

Katona was highly critical of abstract economic theory and asked for better descriptive theory. He was concerned mainly with macroeconomic issues such as the sales rates of durable goods, saving, and inflation. He complained that economic theory made completely wrong assumptions about behaviour at the micro level so that aggregate predictions were mostly wrong. He seems to have become more and more convinced that it was necessary to build up a special field of study. He advocated an economic–psychological theory that was descriptive and low level, that is, close to empirical observations. This theory would be a valuable complement to, or even replacement for, the abstract economic theory and the empirical research based on it. Similar ideas about the role of psychology as provider of rich descriptive data on actual economic behaviour have later been propounded by other authors, among them Herbert Simon.

In a Festschrift in honour of George Katona, James Tobin appraised Katona's contributions to economics in the following terms: 'Katona was the great entrepreneur of survey data collection, and for this alone the economics profession owes him an immense debt'. Through panel studies, Katona and his research group provided an invaluable data base for consumption and saving studies. Tobin (1972: 37–9) continues:

> Katona's other major enterprise in survey data collection has been the continuous monitoring of consumer attitudes, expectations, and intentions. . . . Katona saw two major developments in America and, with a lag, in other economies as well which make consumption a less and less predictable function of cash income. One is general affluence; as consumption spending becomes further and further removed from basic subsistence, both its direction and its timing become more discretionary. The other is the improvement of credit markets, the appearance and growth of institutions enabling consumers to borrow against houses, other durable goods, or simply their names and earning prospects.

Have the US and other economies changed so much that Katona's ideas are no longer valid and interesting? In 1980, Katona himself made the following sober statement: 'Behavioral economics, developed in an era of spreading affluence and optimism, is confronted with new tasks in an era of limited growth and uncertainty' (Katona, 1980: 16). While the ICS gets more attention than ever both in the mass media and in its increasing use in empirical economic research on consumption growth, it seems to have had little influence on macroeconomic theory and Katona's name is rarely cited in such contexts. The basic model for consumption, stating that consumption is a function of ability and willingness to consume, is still valid if both ability and willingness are interpreted in a broad sense and modern cognitive and social psychology is used. Close reading of some of Katona's works reveals many ideas that are still applicable and testable on consumption and saving.

KARL-ERIK WÄRNERYD

Bibliography
Katona, G. (1940) *Organizing and Memorizing: Studies in the Psychology of Learning and Teaching*, New York, Columbia University Press.
Katona, G. (1942) *War Without Inflation:The Psychological Approach to Problems of War Economy*, New York, Columbia University Press.
Katona, G. (1951) *Psychological Analysis of Economic Behavior*, New York, McGraw–Hill.
Katona, G. (1953) 'Rational Behavior and Economic Behavior', *Psychological Review*, **60**: 307–18.
Katona, G. (1954) 'Economic Psychology', *Scientific American*, **191**(4): 31–5.
Katona, G. (1960) *The Powerful Consumer*, New York, McGraw–Hill.
Katona, G. (1972) 'Theory of Expectations', in Strumpel, B., Morgan, J.N. and Zahn, E. (eds) *Human Behavior in Economic Affairs. Essays in Honor of George Katona*, Amsterdam, Elsevier Scientific Publishing Company: 549–82.
Katona, G. (1975) *Psychological Economics*, New York, Elsevier.
Katona, G. (1979) 'Toward a Macropsychology', *American Psychologist*, **34**: 118–26.
Katona, G. (1980) *Essays on Behavioral Economics*, Ann Arbor, MI, Institute for Social Research, University of Michigan.
Tobin, J. (1972) 'Wealth, Liquidity, and the Propensity to Consume', in Strumpel, B., Morgan, J.N. and Zahn, E. (eds) *Human Behavior in Economic Affairs. Essays in Honor of George Katona*, Amsterdam, Elsevier Scientific Publishing Company: 37–56.

Labour Supply

The labour market has a number of unique characteristics. Unlike the product market in which commodities have entities separate from their provider and can therefore be fully exchanged, labour services can only be supplied when the person selling his or her labour is present during work! As a result, social and psychological factors influencing the individual are bound to influence labour market decisions. Although a degree of attachment to the commodity may exist in the case of the market for houses or other previously owned durable goods such as automobiles, the labour market obviously possesses distinct features due to this inseparability of labour from its provider.

Neoclassical economic theory concerns itself with several features of the labour market: prominent in the labour economics literature are analyses of labour supply, including labour force participation, the decisions regarding hours of work, choice of the job package and job mobility. This review highlights major features of labour supply analysis in neoclassical theory and developments in the areas of labour supply of women and youth, the job package and labour mobility — areas in which social and psychological factors can play a major role.

Social and psychological factors

Monetary rewards to economic activity play a significant role in explaining observed labour supply decisions. However, when individuals are asked why they work, a number of other factors are also noted with prominence. These include a sense of contribution or doing something worthwhile, a chance to meet others, learning skills, responding to the social expectations of having a job and the avoidance of boredom. To the extent that personal needs for these factors are variable across individuals, different labour supply responses would be observed even if the economic factors were perfectly controlled for.

In an international setting, for example, to the extent that different cultural values can generate different psychological responses to economic incentives in the labour market, different labour supply behaviour is likely to result. While expectations of work by males of primary working age are generally consistent internationally, cultural differences are much more prominent in relation to labour supply of married women and teenagers.

The fact that female labour force participation rates are significantly different at an international level, or the observation that similar local labour market conditions often lead to very different labour market responses by different immigrant or ethnic groups, highlights interesting interactions between economic, social and psychological factors. In this regard, it is useful to think of economic decision making discussed in the next sections as operating *under an umbrella of cultural–social–ethical values* (Leibenstein, 1976; Etzioni, 1988). This can explain, for example, why very high earnings due to illegal activities are not acceptable to most people despite the usual work/leisure effects, even if the probability of getting caught is zero.

The idea that economic factors affect individual behaviour *after passing through personal filters* in interpreting economic stimuli is prominent in the work of Leibenstein (1976). This framework can be applied to cultural values to explain why a wage rise, for example, could fail to generate a large enough labour supply response if cultural values generated a sense of guilt or great concern (for example, for work by mothers) or shame (for work that may be considered culturally beneath a specific socioeconomic group). Other factors, however, such as the existence of extended families and childcare by members of the extended family such as grandparents, can further facilitate the participation of mothers of young children in the labour force, by reducing the feelings of guilt or concern.

The need to understand why individuals have different preferences may not be very pressing in a culturally homogeneous society since tastes or personality traits may be assumed to be normally distributed. In many multicultural societies, however, labour market responses of different groups may be quite different and here the analysis of social and psychological values can help towards more accurate predictions of the labour supply behaviour of subgroups. This indicates that the elasticity of labour supply could be usefully estimated for cultural subgroups within a labour market. This has implications, for example, in the area of responses to economic incentives for leaving unemployment or a welfare dependence status.

In a dynamic framework which incorporates social and psychological responses, cultural factors can influence labour supply decisions at any time, while economic factors may, in turn, change cultural values when they persist over time and when a critical mass of individuals within the relevant social group responds to economic factors (Jones, 1984). For example, Western countries during the past four decades have experienced increased labour force participation and labour supply of women, decreased fertility rates and increased years of investment in education by women. This provides a wide literature and supporting evidence for the dynamic nature of the inter-relationship between economic factors and social and psychological responses due to tradition. In turn, this evidence demonstrates how traditions themselves can change over time partly due to economic stimuli.

Neoclassical theory of labour supply

The analysis of labour supply is a well-established area of neoclassical economics. It encompasses the decision to enter the labour force, the choice of

354

hours of work, the years of work over the life cycle and occupational choices (for analytical reviews, see, for example, Mincer 1962, Cain, 1966, and Killingsworth, 1983). These decisions are generally analysed as the outcome of a process of constrained maximization, where individual or household utility is derived from *leisure* and *goods* consumed, subject to time and income constraints. Goods can be bought by giving up leisure for earnings.

Neoclassical analysis of the labour market makes a number of simplifying assumptions, which allow labour to be treated as a factor of production. The model in its simplest form focuses mainly on the earnings/leisure choice. Among other simplifying assumptions are the 'independence' of utility maximization and productivity of individuals or households, 'full information' and 'perfect mobility' in the labour market.

The simple model is undoubtedly useful in explaining and predicting the labour supply behaviour of primary workers and overall changes in labour supply due to wage changes, income, or time constraints. A number of assumptions of the simple model, however, proved to be too restrictive in analysing the inter-relationships of labour supply within the household where substitution and complementarities in household production exist, especially in relation to the labour supply behaviour of married women and secondary workers such as youth.

A second generation of labour supply models (Becker, 1965, 1981) addressed this shortcoming by extending the analysis of labour supply to models of household utility maximization in which individual household members faced potentially different market wage rates and time constraints. This extension allowed a more realistic modelling approach in which household members may have different productivity levels and relative comparative advantages in home and market production. The analysis now incorporated the significance of the *relative wage* of household members in determining the labour force participation and tl.e hours of work of household members. This further explained why, for example, a partner may specialize fully in home production, due to his or her relative productivity level. It also allowed the incorporation of the decision to bear children within a long-term labour supply framework.

These improvements in the neoclassical theory of labour supply have significantly extended the framework for the analysis of both home and labour market activities. However, the fact that empirical studies of labour supply can generally explain less than fifty per cent of cross-section variations in labour supply due to the wage, relative incomes and the number of children is consistent with the observation that individual personal differences and preferences also influence labour supply decisions (for example, see Killingsworth, 1983, and Baxter, 1988).

In particular, the task of parenting is one for which actual 'household production' activities are expected to entail far more complexity than most mainstream theories of household production have attempted to incorporate. Examples are parents' feelings of duty, attachment to one's child or concern in leaving young children in the care of others. This could also mean that perfect substitutability of time of either parent may not be meaningful for childcare requirements. Thompson (1995), for example, has examined the labour supply of women over the lifecycle in what he refers to as the 'juggling lifestyles' of career women. He finds that these make more sense if one thinks in terms of systems and complementarities of household members rather than simple substitutability of members for household tasks.

The job package
The idea that individuals are different in their personal tastes and preferences, and that jobs are different in their pecuniary and non-pecuniary characteristics, goes back to Adam Smith (1776). As Smith pointed out, some jobs are less pleasant, or others are more prestigious. Therefore, controlling for other factors, unpleasant jobs should offer a higher premium to attract workers. Since workers have different tastes and preferences (for example, some might prefer outdoor work, while others may dislike it), particular jobs will be taken by those workers who have a lower marginal disutility of accepting the job characteristics in question. This theory of 'compensating wage differentials' was developed further by Thaler and Rosen (1975) in showing how personal characteristics such as risk aversion can allocate workers to more or alternatively less risky jobs through self selection.

Although risk aversion or a desire for job safety may be expected to be normally distributed, this development in neoclassical theory showed that individuals from low-income families are more likely to allocate themselves to jobs that impose a risk to health or physical safety, since at lower income levels the marginal utility of other goods (and income) relative to job safety is expected to be higher. This indicated that at lower income levels individuals may take jobs whose safety levels fall short of what is socially optimal and hence that legislating minimum health and safety standards would be desirable in some circumstances. In addition, the importance of the assumption of 'full information' about all job characteristics and its relaxation in these analyses proved to be important (for example, see Viscusi and Magat, 1987, and Kask and Maani, 1992).

The theory of compensating wage differentials was further extended to show how other systematic factors such as 'time constraints' faced by mothers of young children can lead to women accepting jobs that pay less. Personal preferences by mothers for working in the proximity of their home or according to flexible shorter hours can explain why some women allocate themselves to jobs with those characteristics, but with lower pay, as this limits the set of job options available to them.

Job mobility
Social and psychological factors play an important role in determining job mobility, both in physical terms and regarding social mobility through jobs. To the extent that job characteristics other than the wage rate (such as the work environment, friendships, convenience, the geographic locality of the job and so on) are important to different individuals, mobility from one job to another in response to wage opportunities is influenced to different degrees. This makes the concept of job mobility more complicated than its portrayal in the simple versions of the neoclassical model in which individuals respond only to wage differences and move to other jobs with similar conditions and higher pay. For example, a more realistic mobility model would include the individual's current job, which possesses a known combination of pecuniary and non-pecuniary characteristics, compared with alternative jobs with somewhat unknown characteristics. In this framework, risk averse individuals are obviously less likely to change their jobs due to the anxiety of working in a new environment, while adventurous individuals are more likely to change employment or occupation. Given an extended framework which includes social and psychological factors, alternative job opportunities and wage gains are expected to influence job mobility if they are greater than some threshold level. Likewise, unsatisfactory job conditions are not likely to induce quit behaviour unless they reach a level above a threshold of dissatisfaction.

The theory of 'non-competing groups' has, in turn, addressed long-term immobility in the labour market due to different degrees of education or human capital. 'Dual' and 'segmented labour market' theories (Doeringer and Piore, 1971) have, in turn, addressed the importance of access to information, existence of role models and job feedback effects on worker productivity in creating barriers to labour market mobility. Further extensions of neoclassical models by Borjas (1994) have incorporated the effect of socioeconomic factors on long-term or inter-generational economic mobility. In this analysis, 'ethnic capital' — that is, a common source of information shared by various social groups — is incorporated in the formal modelling of long-term job mobility by a socioeconomic or ethnic group through the knowledge of the labour market, job aspirations, investment in human capital, and the resulting access to economic mobility though jobs. This analysis explains why certain socioeconomic or ethnic groups may show relative socioeconomic immobility through jobs over time due to both group social norms and information effects.

SHOLEH A. MAANI

Bibliography:

Baxter, J.L. (1988) *Social and Psychological Foundations of Economic analysis*, Hemel Hempstead, Harvester-Wheatsheaf.

Becker, G.S. (1965) 'A Theory of Allocation of Time', *Economic Journal*, **75**: 493–517.

Becker, G.S. (1981) *A Treatise on the Family*, Cambridge, MA, Harvard University Press.

Borjas, G.J. (1994) 'Immigrant Skills and Ethnic Spillovers', *Journal of Population Economics*, **7**: 99–118.

Cain, G.G. (1966) *Married Women in the Labour Force*, Chicago, IL, University of Chicago Press.

Doeringer, P.B. and Piore, M.J. (1971) *Internal Labor Markets and Manpower Analysis*, Lexington, MA, D.C. Heath & Co.

Etzioni, A. (1988) *The Moral Dimension: Toward A New Economics*, New York, Free Press.

Jones, S.R.G. (1984) *The Economics of Conformism*, Oxford, Basil Blackwell.

Kask, S.B. and Maani, S.A. (1992) 'Uncertainty, Information, and Hedonic Pricing', *Land Economics*, **68** : 170–84.

Killingsworth, M.R. (1983) *Labour Supply*, Cambridge, Cambridge University Press.

Leibenstein, H. (1976) *Beyond Economic Man: A New Foundation for Microeconomics*, Cambridge, MA, Harvard University Press.

Mincer, J. (1962) 'Labor Force Participation of married Women', in Lewis, H.G. (ed.) *Aspects of Labor Economics*, Princeton, NJ, Princeton University Press.

Smith, A. (1776) *The Wealth of Nations* (reprinted 1974), Harmondsworth, Penguin.

Thaler, R. and Rosen, S. (1975) 'The Value of Saving a Life: Evidence from the Labour Market', in Terlekyi, N. (ed.) *Household Production and Consumption*, New York, NBER.

Thompson, C. (1995) 'Gendered Consumption Meanings and the Juggling Lifestyles', *Journal of Consumer Research*, **22**: 388–407.

Viscusi, W.K. and Magat, W.A. (1987) *Learning about Risk: Consumer and Worker Responses to Hazard Information*, Cambridge, MA, Harvard University Press.

Lay Economic Beliefs

Up until now, the phrase 'lay economic beliefs' has perhaps had its greatest currency in the recent textbook by Lewis, Webley and Furnham (1995). Indeed, the first and last of these authors have made extensive contributions to the extant literature (compare Furnham, 1988). As Lewis et al. explain (p.13), such beliefs comprise the views of 'ordinary' people as opposed to members of various elites, that is they are 'popular' or everyday beliefs. Already, investigators have explored people's beliefs in a great many economic domains: debt, gambling and spending; poverty, wealth and saving (Lewis et al., 1995) equity, equality and need (Swift, Marshall, Burgoyne and Routh, 1995).

What are beliefs?

For present purposes, it is probably helpful to adopt a fairly broad working definition of the term 'belief'. Thus, following Kluegel and Smith (1981), let us suppose that it refers to any information (whether veridical or not) which people may think or feel they possess about some phenomenon. Obviously, such usage includes many other psychological concepts such as perceptions, values, norms, attitudes and so on, which can be a basis for many different kinds of thoughts, feelings and actions involving beliefs.

This may seem to be a little overinclusive. But, it is consistent with what may be found by means of a Thesaurus, or, a more specialized psycholinguistic tool, such as the World Wide Web version of WordNet 1.6, developed by George Miller's team at Princeton University (see Fellbaum, 1998). The latter reveals that there are at least three primary senses of belief: (i) some mental or cognitive content held to be true; (ii) some dogma or tenet asserted to be true (without proof); and (iii) some kind of vague feeling, impression or notion attracting a degree of confidence. The first sense is the most important for present purposes, and, as WordNet shows, it is associated with a myriad of subordinate meanings (hyponyms) including the following: (strong) conviction; doctrine or 'ism'; expectation, outlook or prospect; faith or trust; (public) opinion; superstition; theory; and values. On the other hand, investigators in this area appear to have been fairly profligate in the types of questions which they have used to probe respondents' beliefs. Thus, one finds questions ranging over perceptions of fairness (in allocating wealth and income), reasons for poverty or wealth, the desirability of government policies (for example, ownership of industries or utilities), satisfaction with life, and even estimates of the income of different occupational groups (for example, see Kluegel, Mason and Wegener, 1995). In fact it must be surprising for the newcomer to discover just how rarely people seem to have been asked any direct questions about their beliefs, such as 'What do you believe about *X*?'.

Types of beliefs

A further important distinction is that beliefs can range from 'is' or existential beliefs through to 'ought' or normative beliefs (Kluegel et al., 1995). Thus, sometimes it has been suggested that popular perceptions of the way things are should have an influence on people's perceptions about the way things should be, as indexed by popular support for a government policy. However, the issue of causality is particularly problematic here, since once a person subscribes to an 'ought belief', this may well have a reciprocal influence on any associated existential view they may have (Burgoyne, Routh and Sydorenko, 1998).

We should also note the existence of dominant, ideological beliefs comprising a set of widespread or core beliefs which may be held to justify economic inequalities in a society. An example would be the so-called 'just world belief' that people get what they deserve (Lewis et al., 1995; Burgoyne et al., 1998). Such beliefs may be acquired and strengthened in a succession of institutional contexts (educational, political, occupational and religious). Contrasting with dominant ideological beliefs, there can also be experientially-based beliefs which are derived from a person's own present economic circumstances (chances of getting ahead; fairness of income and so on). An interesting possibility here is that people can and do maintain a degree of psychological separation between their core and experiential beliefs, even in the face of contradictions and inconsistencies. This 'split-consciousness' hypothesis is supported by the fact that despite injustices and adversities associated with economic problems, people none the less frequently appear to maintain their support for the core beliefs (Kluegel, 1988).

Finally, because of space limitations, we can do no more than mention the existence of relevant work in cognitive science concerning comparisons of belief and knowledge systems. Also work on beliefs is implicitly involved in studies of the relation between attitudes, intentions and behaviour. Here structural equation modelling and multiple indicators involving beliefs have been employed to test the theories of reasoned action and of planned behaviour, among others.

Theoretical and methodological pluralism

Any student or scholar attempting to understand the scope of this topic for the first time is liable to encounter an almost bewildering degree of complexity. While it probably does not rival the *Tower of Babel*, it may none the less pose difficulties for someone trying to track down the extant literature using, say, PsycLIT on CD-ROM: an attempt to use the phrase 'lay economic beliefs' to search the book and journal literature in psychology from 1974 through to December 1997 yielded zero hits, while 'economic beliefs' gave 20, and 'lay beliefs' 27. If we step outside the 'economic' domain for the moment, we may say that this kind of difficulty arises because various investigators have subscribed to a fairly wide range of theoretical and methodological approaches, involving different definitions and terminologies.

Theoretical pluralism has meant that much of the relevant work on lay beliefs has been framed in accordance with subtle differences in the preoccupations of different investigators. Thus we can find the following sorts of foci: lay explanations, everyday accounts, commonsense theories, causal attributions, intuitive understanding, implicit knowledge, lay epistemics and folk psychology ('reading' other people's minds and behaviour), among others (Furnham, 1988; Lewis et al., 1995).

The field also exhibits a considerable degree of methodological pluralism, where of course a multimethod approach can be a strength. Perhaps the commonest approach has involved the use of questionnaires (administered by face-to-face or telephone interviews, or even self-administered by computer). However, one can find imaginative departures from the norm. In the context of a larger multimethod project, Lunt and Livingstone (1991) explored ordinary people's views about the importance of various factors as causes of debt. Using such data, they derived a cause x cause proximity matrix, which they submitted to multidimensional scaling and cluster analysis. Their analyses led to a subset of representative factors held to be causes of debt. By studying the extent to which one cause was held to influence another, and by using causal network analysis, they were able to elucidate a system of 'knock-on' effects progressively moving from distal, societal causes through to more proximal, personal causes (Lunt and Livingstone, 1991: 320). Another germane approach is exemplified by work which attempts to compare laypeople's beliefs with those of professionals, a topic which is particularly relevant for any area which needs to employ public persuasion, for example, advertising or social policy (see Friestad and Wright, 1995).

Kinds of research questions

The sorts of research goals needed in this area were well articulated by Kluegel and Smith (1981). We need to understand what sorts of things are believed, what principles govern the organization of people's beliefs in various domains, what factors determine what is believed, and what social and political consequences may follow from the beliefs. Apart from giving proper prominence to social stratification (for example, class) they also stressed the desirability of both comparative (cross-national) and longitudinal studies. In this context, there is evidence that theories of folk psychology differ across cultures (Lillard, 1998), and so it is not surprising that there should be differences in lay economic beliefs pertaining to distributive justice (Kluegel et al., 1995).

Research findings

Much of the research on lay economic beliefs has been descriptive, attempting to elucidate what popular beliefs are held by people. It is a sad but ineluctable fact that not all the research has made use of representative probability sampling. As statisticians and survey experts would emphasize, studies based upon nonprobability, convenience and snowball samples, which sometimes masquerade as 'surveys', are fairly useless for inferences about populations: their representativeness cannot be known.

In many ways, the sorts of answers which were sketched out by Kluegel and Smith (1981) have stood the test of time (compare Lewis et al., 1995). There is a burgeoning literature covering many interesting domains. As an example, consider recent studies of beliefs about the poor which still suggest they are wholly or partially to blame for their poverty, and lacking in appropriate motivation, ability and morals (Kluegel et al., 1995; Lewis et al., 1995). Also, in the domain of distributive justice, people's judgements of fairness still reflect support for principles based upon functional (justified) inequality, need and equality of outcome, although this is conditioned by factors such as sex, education, class, class identity and political allegiance (Swift et al., 1995). Finally, it should be noted that the work of the International Social Justice Project (Kluegel et al., 1995) has yielded interesting comparative data for 13 nations, and a partial replication study has now been completed.

DAVID A. ROUTH

Bibliography

Burgoyne, C.B., Routh, D.A. and Sydorenko, S. (1998) 'Perceptions, Attributions, and Policy in the Economic Domain: A Theoretical and Comparative Analysis', *International Journal of Comparative Sociology*, in press.

Fellbaum, C. (ed.) (1998) *WordNet: An Electronic Lexical Database*, Cambridge, Massachusetts, MIT Press.

Friestad, M. and Wright, P. (1995) 'Persuasion Knowledge: Lay People's and Researchers' Beliefs about the Psychology of Advertising', *Journal of Consumer Research*, **22**: 62–74.

Furnham, A.F. (1988) *Lay Theories: Everyday Understanding of Problems in the Social Sciences*, Oxford, Pergamon Press.

Kluegel, J.R. (1988) 'Economic Problems and Socioeconomic Beliefs and Attitudes', *Research in Social Stratification and Mobility*, 7: 273–302.

Kluegel, J.R., Mason, D.S. and Wegener, B. (eds) (1995) *Social Justice and Political Change: Public Opinion in Capitalist and Post-Communist States*, New York, Aldine De Gruyter.

Kluegel, J.R. and Smith, E.R. (1981) 'Beliefs About Stratification', *Annual Review of Sociology*, **7**: 29–56.

Lewis, A., Webley, P. and Furnham, A. (1995) *The New Economic Mind: The Social Psychology of Economic Behaviour*, London, Harvester Wheatsheaf.

Lillard, A. (1998) 'Ethnopsychologies: Cultural Variations in Theories of Mind', *Psychological Bulletin*, 123: 3–32.

Lunt, P. K. and Livingstone, S.M. (1991) 'Everyday Explanations for Personal Debt: A Network Approach', *British Journal of Social Psychology*, 30: 309–23.

Swift, A., Marshall, G., Burgoyne, C. and Routh, D.A. (1995). 'Distributive Justice: Does It Matter What the People Think?', in Kluegel, J.R., Mason, D.S. and Wegener, B. (eds) (1995) *Social Justice and Political Change: Public Opinion in Capitalist and Post-Communist States*, New York, Aldine De Gruyter.

Leisure, Psychology of

It has been 24 years since John Neulinger's (1974) *The Psychology of Leisure* was published. Since then an outline of the area and the subject matter has begun to emerge. Inevitably there are more gaps than knowledge and a myriad of questions remain unanswered, even unasked. Yet, despite the latter, the influence of the psychological approach within the study of leisure is undoubted. Crucially, it has influenced the definition and conception of leisure itself.

Previously, leisure had, in various ways, been understood as a companion concept to that of work. For example, a standard sociological definition of leisure considered it to be equivalent to that proportion of time left uncommitted after deducting time for work and maintenance activities (for example, washing, cooking). In contrast, Neulinger strongly argued in his book that the essential defining criteria for leisure are psychological and, as a consequence, subjective. Whether called the 'subjective', 'psychological' or 'state of mind' definition of leisure, his proposal quickly gained support and has affected the shape of the leisure research agenda. The nature of the leisure experience and motivations for leisure, for example, have received increasing attention.

Interestingly, however, and in keeping with the multidisciplinary nature of leisure research, there has also been a distinctly social psychological and even broadly social scientific cast to psychological research on leisure. In fact, as will be discussed, there are close connections to be found between the psychology of leisure and economic psychology, not only in terms of overlapping subject matter but in theoretical approaches as well.

Neulinger (1974) notes that the term 'psychology of leisure' can be understood either broadly as the application of psychological theories and methods to the understanding of leisure, or, more narrowly, as the particular psychological features involved in leisure (similarly, one could speak of the psychology of the criminal 'mind'). Inevitably, the following will deal with both meanings since the particular theories and methods of psychology used in the study of leisure will influence conceptions of the psychological nature of leisure.

According to Neulinger, there are two criteria that must be met if people are to experience leisure: *perceived freedom* and *intrinsic motivation*. For persons to be at leisure they must first consider that their present activity has been freely chosen. In other words, the activity has been undertaken without the influence of any perceived coercive force. Importantly, this freedom only needs to be *perceived*. Even the 'illusion' of freedom, according to Neulinger, can have the important consequence of leisure.

Intrinsic motivation, the second requirement for leisure, refers to motivation which is derived from some internal property of an activity as opposed to that principally produced by (perceived) external consequences. Leisure, from

Neulinger's point of view, is motivated principally by the experiences directly associated with an activity (for example, joy, pleasure, excitement, interest and so on). Unfortunately, the research has not supported this second criterion to the same extent as it has perceived freedom (Mannell and Iso-Ahola, 1987). Intrinsic motivation is, nevertheless, still seen to be very significant in many, even most, leisure experiences.

Importantly, from this perspective activities such as paid work, previously considered to be antithetical to leisure, could provide opportunities for leisure. As long as the work is perceived to involve a reasonable amount of freedom and autonomy and the tasks are intrinsically motivating to some extent (despite the presence of supposed external motivators such as money and status), then there is no reason not to call such activity 'leisure'. In fact, pushed to the extreme, even situations of apparently undeniable constraint and lack of freedom — such as slavery — do not completely prevent the experience of leisure as long as these elements are present (or perceived to be present). Not surprisingly, it is this theoretically possible lack of concern for the role of objective circumstances in defining leisure that has produced most criticism.

As pointed out above, a major task in the psychology of leisure is the description and explanation of the leisure experience. There is, of course, not one leisure experience, but many. Tinsley and Tinsley (1986) have suggested, however, that these experiences principally vary along a quantitative dimension (such as intensity, duration and so on). In contrast, the quality of a leisure experience should usually be at the positive end of the dimension. They assume, that is, that the vast majority of leisure activities, since they are freely chosen, will tend to result in positive experiences as opposed to negative ones. The type of leisure experience that is highly positive and very intense (at the extreme of both dimensions) they call the 'leisure state'. It is this type of leisure experience that has received the most theoretical and empirical attention in the literature since it is assumed, perhaps simplistically, to be the key to explaining the motivations of many forms of leisure activity.

One of the most widely discussed concepts in this context is Csikszentmihalyi's (1975, 1990) notion of 'flow'. Csikszentmihalyi is concerned principally with human happiness rather than leisure and developed the concept of 'flow' after interviewing a broad range of people about their most enjoyable experiences. Flow is similar but not identical to Abraham Maslow's famous 'peak experiences' and describes a general psychological state characterized by such qualities as total absorption, focused concentration, loss of self-consciousness, time distortion (typically it is perceived to go faster, at least in retrospect), enjoyment and a sense of control over outcomes. (The word 'flow' was used by several of his interviewees — his more technical term is 'psychic negentropy'.)

Flow is most reliably produced, according to Csikszentmihalyi, in situations where challenges are closely matched to skill levels, clear goals exist and there is fast and accurate feedback on performance. Dancers, musicians, rock climbers, surgeons and even parents in interaction with their children report these optimal experiences in very similar terms. Interestingly, passive — and very popular — forms of leisure such as television watching are associated with high levels of relaxation but relatively low levels of enjoyment and flow (in fact, according to Csikszentmihalyi, mood seems to be negatively correlated with length of time watching television). This finding is presumably because such activities involve little in the way of goals, challenges or skills — although there are instances such as watching certain kinds of quiz shows or predicting plots in soap operas where it could be argued that these factors exist. Certainly in certain forms of literature, drama and music people often speak of the challenges involved in fully appreciating a work and experiencing the imagined world represented, despite the appearance of passive entertainment.

Dissenting voices have suggested that the notion of flow may be applicable only to 'active' forms of leisure as opposed to, for example, meditative and relaxing forms of leisure (see Ajzen, 1992 for a concise and critical review of Csikszentmihalyi, 1990). The latter are frequently claimed to induce various types of heightened experience that do not rely on such things as challenges and skills. It may, however, be surprisingly difficult to distinguish 'active' from 'passive' forms of leisure, especially given the comments just made in relation to television watching. Some techniques of meditation, for example, could be said to require skills and to present challenges and, at a stretch, even relaxing on a beach at least has the 'goal' of relaxation.

It could, nevertheless, still be argued that flow is culturally skewed (although Csikszentmihalyi claims that these experiences are reported in all cultures and social groups) in so far as the 'healthiest' and most enjoyable experiences happen to be the ones that support the values of order, activity and productivity. Csikszentmihalyi's (1990) theory of mind and self certainly claims that without the structuring provided by these enjoyable, flow-inducing activities, minds and selves succumb to 'psychic entropy', a natural tendency towards psychic disorder and dissolution which results in the experience of negative affect (such as anger, hate, frustration, confusion and so on). As Ajzen (1992) points out, no reasons are given as to why the mind should have this tendency.

The psychology of leisure is, however, not just about subjective experiences. Seppo Iso-Ahola (1980, 1989) has developed a social psychology of leisure that draws on optimal arousal theory (the idea that individuals seek out levels of arousal from the environment that will push current levels towards the individual's optimal level, measured in terms of such factors as performance or enjoyment). The concept of optimal arousal is, of coure, also used in accounts of stress and its effect on performance. This provides a further link to the notion of 'flow' since optimal levels of arousal allow for optimum performance, which should be reflected in a perceived balance between competence (skill) levels and task demands.

As well as optimizing arousal it is also possible to optimize what Iso-Ahola terms 'incongruity'. That is, humans are often motivated by opposing, incongruous forces such as needs for change and stability. Once again, leisure allows individuals to 'fine tune' their current levels of incongruity towards a desired optimum. Iso-Ahola (1980) encapsulates his perspective in terms of a leisure needs 'pyramid' ranging from deep-level and unconscious biological dispositions and needs for optimal arousal and incongruity to more conscious needs for perceived freedom and competence and, finally, expressed leisure needs. This approach provides a simple but flexible model that helps explain such situations as: the same individual choosing a relaxing beach holiday at one time and an arduous and challenging adventure holiday at another; a novice chess player who, in time, seeks out more and more experienced opponents as greater mastery of the game is achieved (requiring more-skilful opponents to provide the same optimal levels of intellectual 'arousal'); the reclusive hobbyist who escapes the perceived excess of social stimulation while simultaneously introducing the stimulation of a challenging hobby.

The optimization assumption is, of course, used extensively in economic theory which, in itself, should suggest numerous connections between the two areas. Similar ideas to those just discussed can be found, for example, in the work of Tibor Scitovsky (1976, 1981). In *The Joyless Economy* Scitovsky suggests that Western (American) life has become so safe and emphasizes the values of production over consumption to such an extent that, in a variety of ways, opportunities for arousal that previously existed are no longer available. Thus, people are driven to any number of activities — when at leisure, for example — which provide them with the appropriate levels of arousal that are now lacking. In turn, this clearly links to the work on hedonic consumption (see entry above). Unfortunately, however, Scitovsky seems to limit the notion of arousal to physiological arousal — as discussed in the early work of Berlyne (1960). Psychology, and especially social psychology, has moved on significantly since the earlier studies on optimal arousal to the point where there is far greater acknowledgement of the cognitive, social and cultural factors which bear on the concept of arousal. Scitovsky's (1981) provocative concluding speculation that protesting citizens in dictatorships may well be seeking a kind of collective raising of arousal levels (from the excitement of the protest, apparently) because their government has provided too safe and secure an environment, could well be made more reasonable if these other factors were included in the speculation. Scitovsky's work does demonstrate, nevertheless, that there are significant areas of overlap in both subject matter and theory between the psychology of leisure and economic psychology.

Leisure is often naively promoted as a sphere of freedom within modern life. While this may be too simplistic a view, the study of human behaviour in an area of life that at least promises sheer freedom must be of interest to all psychologists. If for no other reason than this, the psychology of leisure deserves increased attention.

KEVIN MOORE

Bibliography
Ajzen, I. (1992) 'Review of *Flow: The Psychology of Optimal Experience* by M. Csikszentmihalyi', *Leisure Sciences*, **14**: 165–6.
Berlyne, D. (1960) *Confluct, Arousal and Curiosity*, New York, McGraw-Hill.
Csikszentmihalyi, M. (1975) *Beyond Boredom and Anxiety: The Experience of Play in Work and Games*, San Francisco, CA, Jossey-Bass.
Csikszentmihalyi, M. (1990) *Flow: The Psychology of Optimal Experience*, New York, NY, Harper & Row.
Ingham, R. (1986) 'Psychological Contributions to the Study of Leisure — Part One', *Leisure Studies*, **5**: 255–79.
Ingham, R. (1987) 'Psychological Contributions to the Study of Leisure — Part Two', *Leisure Studies*, **6**: 1–14.
Iso-Ahola, S.E. (1980) *The Social Psychology of Leisure and Recreation*, Dubuque, IA, W.C. Brown & Co..
Iso-Ahola, S.E. (1989) 'Motivation for Leisure', in Jackson, E.L. and Burton, T.L. (eds) *Understanding Leisure and Recreation: Mapping the Past, Charting the Future*, State College, PA, Venture Publishing.
Mannell, R.C. and Iso-Ahola, S.E. (1987) 'Psychological Nature of the Leisure and Tourism Experience', *Annals of Tourism Research*, **14**: 314–31.
Neulinger, J. (1974) *The Psychology of Leisure*, Springfield, IL, Charles C. Thomas.
Scitovsky, T. (1976) *The Joyless Economy*, New York, Oxford University Press.
Scitovsky, T. (1981) 'The Desire for Excitement in Modern Society', *Kyklos*, **34**: 3–13.
Tinsley, H.E.A. and Tinsley, D.J. (1986) 'A Theory of the Attributes, Benefits, and Causes of Leisure Experience', *Leisure Sciences*, **8**: 1–45.

Literary Explication and Deconstruction

Literary explication and deconstruction are text-orientated methods of analysis applicable to advertising text, consumer-generated prose and research accounts. They have been applied to a wide range of contexts, ranging from 1920s soap flakes to a variety of contemporary products (for some examples, see the articles by Stern listed in the bibliography at the end of this entry).

Explication

Explication contributes to stimulus-side research on advertising by providing a method for analysing all textual attributes that may influence consumer responses. The method was popularized by the New Critics in the 1960s and applied to advertising/marketing text in the 1980s in Stern's works. It is a structured and orderly methodology (Brooks and Warren, 1960) based on close reading of a text.

Systematization was the aim of the New Critics — John Crowe Ransom, I.A. Richards, Cleanth Brooks, Robert Penn Warren and others — who considered themselves spiritual descendants of Aristotle. They followed his empirical bent, aiming at scientific definition and classification of the elements in poetry by close observation of what was 'in' a text. The New Critics focused on inherent and formal qualities of the text, which they construed as a complete, coherent, self-contained and stable entity (Lentricchia, 1980).

They set forth a stepwise analytical procedure to facilitate attention to individual textual elements. The rationale is practical, for although numerous elements can be perceived simultaneously, they cannot be described at the same time. Close reading permits examination of individual elements such as grammar, syntax, diction, imagery, prosody and tone, which can then be interpreted as a synergistic whole. The *gestalt* is said to be the work's 'meaning'. Close reading of advertisements leads to more sophisticated information about the attributes of a stimulus, which in turn allows for more accurate testing of the effects on consumers.

For example, explication of a cents-off coupon for snacks for dogs (Quaker Oats' 'Snausages' and 'Pup-Peroni') reveals a poem: 'Spring has sprung,/The flowers have too./Snausages for me,/Pup-Peroni for you' (Stern, 1996a: 65). Identification of the attributes of rhythm, rhyme, sound effects, metaphor, humanized animals and comedic plot enables the researcher to perceive the resemblance of the advertisement to animal allegories, a classical literary form used to teach children and naive audiences lessons about behaviour. The coupon aims at persuading dog owners that their pets will enjoy special snacks bestowed as a reward for good behaviour. Explication illuminates the connection between modern persuasive messages and their antecedents, which strengthens the researcher's capacity to derive hypotheses that are not only historically validated but also demonstrably linked to a text's attributes.

Deconstruction

Deconstruction picks up where explication leaves off, for although the focus is on the text, attention is paid not to what is 'in' the text, but to what is left out. That is, although deconstructive criticism begins with explication, its ultimate goal is not to bolster the notion of 'meaning', but to shatter it. Unlike its modernist antecedents, deconstruction is a postmodern paradigm, originated by Jacques Derrida, the French philosopher responsible for its framework and vocabulary (1967a, 1967b). Derrida challenged the hegemony of determinate meaning (a single finite reality resident in any text), replacing it with that of indeterminacy (a shifting and contradictory clash of voices). His distinctive strategy of reading and writing exposes the undecidability of play in language and undermines Western faith in convergence. His works argue against the likelihood of discovering 'true' meaning, proposing instead continual divergence.

In the 1970s and 1980s, Derrida's ideas were disseminated in the United States by the 'Yale School' of literary critics — Paul de Man, Geoffrey Hartman, J. Hillis Miller and Harold Bloom. By the 1990s, second-generation researchers modified the concepts for other disciplines. The Yale School's applications-orientated criticism is just beginning to make an impact on consumer research (Stern, 1996). To locate deconstruction in postmodern criticism, let us begin with a brief historical overview.

Defining deconstruction

A typically playful Derridean comment (one of many) challenges the research convention of beginning with construct definition. Derrida's mock-definition — 'What deconstruction is not? everything of course! What is deconstruction? nothing of course!' (1983: 275) — signals his subversive intent. Definition is always a work in progress, for any deconstructive reading *deconstructs itself*, unravelling as it proceeds. The problem extends beyond language, in so far as text is considered the locus of reality. Derrida's most famous aphorism states that 'there is nothing outside the text [there is no outside-text]; il n'y a pas de hors-texte]' (1967a: 158). Nothing is not text, and the realities of social institutions such as marketing, consumption and advertising are inseparable from their discursive practices.

Challenging structuralism

When consumer researchers began to study consumption as text (Hirschman and Holbrook, 1992), structural analysis rather than deconstructive reading became the method of choice. The methodological procedure begins with an identification of binaries, then examines those which are most important, and finally reconciles the conflicts. This approach posits reconciliation as an outcome of the processes of transformation (each binary moves towards its opposite) and of mediation (the opposites are incorporated into a gestalt entity). The goal is always convergence, and differences between binary terms are presumed reconcilable.

Ironically, at the same time as structuralist analysis was finding favour in consumer research, Derrida was arguing against Claude Lévi-Strauss's

369

elaboration of self-enclosed language systems derived from Ferdinand de Saussure's linguistics. Derrida set out to undermine structuralism by displacing the concept of resolvable oppositions. He claims that no sign can evade the play of opposites, insisting that deconstruction alone can address the paradox of language play, rooted in the multiple and contradictory meanings of words. He aims at unravelling moments in a text that reveal a space between what is articulated (the signifier) and what is mentally constructed (the signified), undermining the Western preference for presence, unity and certainty.

In this way, deconstructive readings shatter the structuralist system of self-enclosed language that presupposes agreed-upon meaning, rendering futile not only the possibility of unity as the end of critical inquiry, but also its value as a goal. They treat text as unfixed, unstable and indeterminate, ultimately unable to account for itself fully. Following this strategy, consumer researchers can actualize deconstructive strategy by beginning with close reading, moving through structuralist analysis, and then undoing the readings in a deconstructive act.

Différance: a suitcase word

The strategy is encapsulated in a suitcase word — *différance* (1968) — that must be unpacked to expose Derrida's challenge to Western thought. The term refers to the playing movement that signifies both the presences and absences 'in' words. Derrida's invented word plays grammatical and acoustical games by simultaneously functioning as both pun and homonym. As a pun, it conflates two senses of the verb *différer* — to differ and to defer — compressing the spatial sense of difference among words in contiguity and the temporal sense of deference of words in time. As a homonym, it compresses the active and passive voice in the '-ance' ending. The ending allows the verb to function as a noun, thereby creating a new grammatical entity that fuses the passive nominal designation of a state of being with the active participles of 'differing' and 'deferring'.

Derrida displaces this cultural imperative. He denounces the Western philosophical acceptance of constructed meanings as evidence of ideological favouritism, claiming that meaning is equally embodied in the absent terms repressed to 'prove' linguistic stability. Thus, he elevates absence as coequal with presence by inventing the term *différance* to express what *is not*, cannot exist, is not present in the present form (1968). *Différance* deprivileges language's stability, permanence and finiteness by fusing presences and absences of meaning.

The automatic privileging of presence is expressed when the dominant terms in a binary suppress cultural awareness of their submerged opposites by forcing the latter to defer to the former. Exposure of *différance* is Derrida's recommended strategy for disassembling hierarchies of submission (for example, 'male/female', 'monosexual/bisexual' and 'presence/absence') that permeate all texts, including those pertinent to consumer research.

In our example, the simplistic message is deconstructed by pulling apart the binary oppositions and the hierarchical superiority/inferiority in paired terms such as human/animal, society/nature and feeder/fed. This reveals the cultural imperative that situates humans as rightful masters of the animal world, empowered to impose behavioural criteria on animals and reward them for compliance. Western assumptions such as the infantilization of pets and the propriety of taming aggressive animals, are shown to be aspects of a society affluent enough to provide snacks for animals, as opposed to one so poor that dogs must be eaten. Dismantling the hierarchy reveals that the presumption of cultural 'rightness' in cherishing dogs as surrogate children is chauvinistic, implying that wealthy countries are superior to impoverished ones.

Thus, reading for *différance* forces readers to abandon the dualistic mindset that buries unexpressed ideas under expressed ones and to acknowledge evidence of pluridimensional symbolic thought. Deconstructive assumptions are designed to undermine deferential relationships, pull apart binary hierarchies and force awareness of contradictions.

Phallogocentrism

The aim of disrupting binary relationships is most relevant to arguments against 'phallogocentrism', the opposition between man and woman so deeply inscribed in Western logocentric thought that it is one and the same system: the paternal logos. Phallogocentrism empowers the pattern of dominance/suppression expressed by the male/female binary, which treats the first term as superior and the second as the negative, corrupt, undesirable 'other'. Derrida argues against all binary thinking, for instead of accepting the structuralist notion that 'X is the opposite of Y', he proposes a doubled elaboration in which 'X is added to Y' and 'X replaces Y'. In this way, each term penetrates the other by 'invagination', displacing the power relationship in fixed structures of primary/ secondary. Derrida's anti-hierarchical rereading of the gender binary has led to the rethinking of femininity not as the opposite of masculinity, but as that which both includes and subverts the opposition.

Implications for consumer research

Does this revolutionary strategy have anything to contribute to consumer research? Advocates of deconstruction claim that focusing on the power structure embodied in language enables revelation of the extent to which the interpretative community's discourse elevates some voices and drowns out others. One critical consequence of subversive reading is to puncture the taken-for-granted relationship between the discipline's texts and the ideological worlds they inhabit. Denying the universality of 'universal' assumptions opens the discourse to a sceptical rereading of institutional structures that politicize what has erroneously been thought of as neutral. By breaking up the structural categories that render binary hierarchies oppositional, 'natural' oppositions are shown to be neither natural nor opposed.

One such opposition is 'marketer/consumer', taken for granted rather than carefully analysed. Yet the implications of the binary spin out a chain of significations — mating/nonmating, human/animal, desire/inhibition, satisfaction/annihilation, life/death, madness/sanity and subject/object — that have barely been discussed. By subverting definitions, researchers can air repressed *différance* to revitalize stale discourse and turn it in new directions.

A much-needed new direction is the inclusion of silenced voices — African–American, nonheterosexual, Asian–American — in our discourse. Most consumer behaviour research prior to the mid-1980s was assumed to represent the universal and normal scientific perspective: Western-educated, male, white and middle class. However, closer examinations of the play of textualization (creating a written code) and intertextualization (reading one text in the light of others) shows that this ostensibly neutral discourse is dominated by the patriarchal voice of the 'Dwems': dead, white, European males. Deconstructive strategy forces one to attend to the 'other' voices suppressed by the one officially established as universal. The strategy demonstrates that all thought is shaped by the binary system encoded in the primal male/female one. In displacing hierarchical male privileging, it also displaces the concomitants of maleness — whiteness, heterosexuality, middle-class capitalism — that dominate treatment of most topics in consumer research. If the domain of consumer research is to represent consumption in all of its variety, the panoply of otherness must be brought into the open.

To do so, we must read against the grain, looking for gaps not only in research themes, but also in research processes. These processes sum up to a set of discursive practices that empower the research establishment to control discourse. The politics of consumer research are inscribed in hierarchies such as researcher/subject, reviewer/researcher, editor/reviewer and editor/researcher, even less well-examined than the marketer/consumer binary. Sceptical probing of these and other givens keeps the field vibrant by allowing unforeseen and unpredictable types of discourse to pop up and generate controversy.

Perhaps the most exciting contribution that deconstruction can make to consumer research is as an *agent provocateur*, a force for making the field revisit itself. The scepticism that ensues when everything is called into question breathes life into a research discourse often stultified by the practical urge to forgo uncomfortable questions. At its best, deconstructive criticism is playful, optimistic, and forward-looking. It is the only postmodern 'ism' that does not end in rage or despair, but instead looks ahead to a fruitful clash of alternative points of view. Derrida clears the way for reinvigoration, doing so generously, without acrimony, and with respect for his peers and predecessors — yet another instance of constructive provocation.

BARBARA B. STERN

Bibliography

Brooks, C. and Warren, R.P. (1960) *Understanding Poetry:* (3rd edn), New York, Holt, Rinehart, & Winston.

Ciardi, J, and Williams, M. (1975) *How Does a Poem Mean?* (2nd edn), Boston, MA: Houghton Mifflin.

Derrida, J. ([1967a] 1976) *Of Grammatology*, translated by G.C. Spivak, Baltimore, MD, Johns Hopkins University Press.

Derrida, J. ([1967b] 1991) *Speech and Phenomena, and Other Essays on Husserl's Theory of Signs*, translated by D.B. Allison, in Kamuf, P. (ed.) *A Derrida Reader: Between the Blinds,* New York, NY, Columbia University Press: 6–30.

Derrida, J. ([1968] 1982) 'Différance', in *Margins of Philosophy*, translated by A. Bass, Chicago, IL, University of Chicago Press: 1–27.

Derrida, J. ([1983] 1991) 'Letter to a Japanese Friend' in Kamuf, P. (ed.) *A Derrida Reader: Between the Blinds*, New York, NY, Columbia University Press: 269–76.

Hirschman, E.C. and Holbrook, M.B. (1992) *Postmodern Consumer Research:The Study of Consumption as Text*, Newbury Park, CA, Sage.

Lentricchia, F. (1980) *After the New Criticism*, Chicago, IL, University of Chicago Press.

Stern, B.B. (1988a) 'How Does an Ad Mean? Language in Services Advertising', *Journal of Advertising*, **17**: 3–14.

Stern, B.B. (1988b) 'Medieval Allegory: Roots of Advertising Strategy for the Mass Market', *Journal of Marketing*, **52**: 84–94.

Stern, B.B. (1989a) 'Literary Criticism and Consumer Research: Overview and Illustrative Analysis', *Journal of Consumer Research*, **16**: 322–34.

Stern, B.B. (1989b) 'Literary Explication: A Methodology for Consumer Research', in Hisrchman, E.C. (ed.) *Interpretive Consumer Research*, Provo, UT, Association for Consumer Research: 48–59

Stern, B.B. (1993) 'Feminist Literary Criticism and the Deconstruction of Advertisements: A Postmodern view of Advertising and Consumer Responses', *Journal of Consumer Research*, **19**: 556–66.

Stern, B.B. (1996a) 'Textual Analysis in Advertising Research: Construction and Deconstruction of Meanings', *Journal of Advertising*, **25**: 61–73.

Stern, B.B. (1996b) 'Deconstructive Strategy and Consumer Research: Concepts and Illustrative Exemplar', *Journal of Consumer Research*, **23**: 136–47.

Stern, B.B. (1998) 'Deconstructing Consumption Text: A Strategy for Reading the (Re)constructed Consumer', *Consumption, Markets and Culture: A Journal of Critical Perspectives*, **1**: 361–92.

Material Values

There are noticeable differences among people in the way they interact with *things*. Some people take great pride in their possessions and are pleased when people compliment them on these things; others could not seem to care less about what kind of car they drive, how nice their house is, or their other personal possessions. Some people work hard, perhaps taking two jobs, so that they can buy more things for themselves and their families; others are happy to simply get by with the more basic necessities. These individuals differ in their material values, that is, their personal beliefs about the importance material goods should (and do) play in their lives.

Material values are closely allied with the concept of 'materialism'. The term materialism has been used to refer to a variety of behaviours or orientations. In common usage, materialism is viewed as a pattern of behaviours involving greed and conspicuous consumption. Scholars often have been only slightly more precise in their usage of the term, sometimes separating conspicuous or status-orientated consumption from the acquisitiveness associated with materialism. Writings on materialism frequently involve judgements about the morality of materialistic behaviour or about its (presumably negative) impacts on social relationships and psychological well-being. The environmental impact of consumer societies, in which large segments of the population embrace materialism, has been another topic of concern (Durning, 1992).

The study of materialism was revitalized in the mid-1980s by Russell Belk (for example, Belk, 1985). His work, based on the view that materialism is reflected in the personality traits of envy, possessiveness and nongenerosity, stimulated a continuing stream of materialism research in the field of consumer behaviour. One interesting area of inquiry has been the relationship between material goods and social identity (for example, Dittmar, 1992).

The review presented here is narrower in scope and is limited to the examination of material values — people's personal beliefs about the importance that material goods should play in their lives. This review takes a primarily Western, secular orientation to material values and does not cover Eastern perspectives or the extensive religious literature on material values.

Values are prescriptive beliefs about desirable goals in life and modes of being and may be the most important beliefs that a person holds. Hence, *material values* relate to the importance ascribed to material goods and wealth in achieving major life goals or states. Because the pursuit of one goal often requires the neglect of some other goal (for example, working more hours to increase income reduces the time one can spend with friends or family), critical writings frequently view material values as inimical to spiritual or interpersonal values.

Two bodies of work that have addressed material values are the focus of this review. The most sustained analysis of material values has been carried out by Ronald Inglehart, a political scientist. Stimulated by social upheavals that he observed in Europe in the late 1960s, he began documenting Europeans' values in 1970 and has continued with periodic reassessments. His most recent analysis is presented in Abramson and Inglehart (1995). In Inglehart's view, material values are represented by the importance one places on economic and physical security.

A more recent approach, which appears in the consumer behaviour literature, defines material values as centrally held beliefs about the importance of possessions in one's life. In this literature, material values have been measured by a series of Likert-scaled questions that assess the extent to which respondents view the acquisition of possessions as central to their lives, as an important route to happiness, and as necessary to living a successful life (see, for example, Richins and Dawson, 1992).

These two approaches differ in more than their definitions. Inglehart's work has been directed primarily towards studying material values at a societal level and towards understanding the causes and effects of cultural shifts in these values. The consumer behaviour literature has been primarily (although not exclusively) concerned with individual differences in material values, or intracultural variation. Writings addressing material values at the societal and at the individual levels are discussed separately below.

Cultural material values
Researchers in a variety of disciplines have been interested in the material values held by a society at large and in the factors that cause these values to change. Although beyond the scope of the present review, historical analyses have examined in detail some of the major social shifts in people's relationships to the material world. For example, Mukerji (1983) examined the development of hedonistic consumption in Europe between the fifteenth and eighteenth centuries, and McKendrick, Brewer and Plumb (1982) described the consumer revolution in England in the eighteenth century. Historical analyses have suggested a number of factors responsible for shifts in consumption and material values, including religious factors, technology changes, income fluctuations, the introduction of the fashion system and changes in production and distribution practices. Although historical relationships such as these are sometimes difficult to test empirically, this literature suggests hypotheses that might be tested cross-culturally and provides useful perspectives for students of material values, regardless of their discipline.

Trends

In the more limited time frame of the twentieth century, critics have suggested that materialism is mounting relentlessly worldwide and that a global consumer culture is about to emrege or has already done so. A number of observers have expressed concern about the impact of this emergent consumerism on the environment, depletion of natural resources and social discontent as desire for goods outstrips supply or consumers' buying power.

Most analysts have concluded that in recent decades the importance placed on material goods has increased and that societies are becoming more materialistic. Some of these studies have used content analysis of a country's literature or advertisements to trace this trend (for example, Belk and Pollay, 1985). These studies show an increasing emphasis over time on luxury goods and materialism themes in advertising and an increasing presence of brand names in a country's literature and other representations of culture. Others have used time-series surveys of attitudes to infer changes in material values (for example, Easterlin and Crimmins, 1991). For example, over time, American youth have increased the importance they place on such life goals as 'being very well-off financially'. In addition, a number of scholars have observed that as the economies of lesser-developed countries begin to advance and the general level of affluence to increase, consumerism and the emphasis on material goods rise along with (and in advance of) the level of affluence.

Inglehart, however, has concluded that materialist values are declining. He offers an impressive body of evidence suggesting that in countries with developed economies, concern about economic issues is gradually being displaced by a greater concern about freedom, self-expression and quality of life, a value orientation which he labels 'postmaterialism'.

A reconciliation

The conflicting conclusions offered by these two sets of literature may be due more to differences in their conceptualization and measurement of material values than to conflicts in fact. Inglehart typically measures material values by listing four goals and asking respondents to identify which two of the four should be their country's top two goals. Respondents who place highest priority on 'maintaining order in the nation' and 'fighting inflation' are classed as materialists; those who place highest priority on 'giving the people more say in important government decisions' and 'protecting freedom of speech' are classed as postmaterialist.

Inglehart believes that materialism is a unidimensional construct, that an individual is either a materialist, a postmaterialist, or somewhere in between. Accordingly, Inglehart's method forces unidimensionality, but there is evidence that materialism and postmaterialism form two separate dimensions, and that a single citizen might strongly hold values that are both materialist and postmaterialist (Bean and Papadakis, 1994).

Further, it is likely that consumers who would be scored as postmaterialist using Inglehart's method (that is, people who want more say in government decisions and who value freedom of speech) might also have strong material values, as that term is defined by other scholars (that is, they place high importance on getting and having things). As societies progress and economies develop, there is usually an accompanying increase in social stability and a rising standard of living. Because citizens' needs for physical and economic security are now being met, they are less likely to mention these needs as most important when surveyed. Instead, their thoughts are focused on unmet needs that are troubling them, and, when asked, they are more likely to request that their government place as a priority those values that Inglehart calls postmaterialist. This is not to say, however, that these same citizens have forsaken their desire for increasing their wealth and having more possessions, the hallmarks of material values in the view of many scholars and social observers. Instead, these citizens are asking for something more, for voice and freedom in addition to prosperity.

From this analysis, it is evident that the finding of some researchers that materialism is increasing and Inglehart's findings that postmaterialism is increasing are not necessarily in conflict. However, Inglehart's hypothesis that increasing affluence and economic security in a culture lead to a decrease in materialism may be incorrect. As a society becomes more affluent, citizens will be exposed more frequently to evidence of affluence of others and to luxury images in media, raising their own expectations about the quantity of possessions they ought to have. These increased reminders of material affluence and expressions of materialistic behaviour are likely to increase the value that individuals and society at large place on material goods (Belk, 1988; Richins, 1995).

Personal material values
The second literature concerned with material values examines individual differences in materialism *within* a culture or society. Such research has generally examined either the factors that encourage people to hold strong material values or has looked at the likely consequences (usually negative) of placing a high importance on material things. Due to space limitations, the literatures in religion, philosophy and psychoanalytic theory are excluded from the discussion that follows.

Influences: childhood circumstances
Because core values are formed early in life, researchers have studied the childhood circumstances of individuals to assess their relationship with material

values held as an adult. Family structure is one element that appears to influence material values. Rindfleisch, Burroughs and Denton (1997) found that young adults who had grown up in disrupted (divorced) households were more likely to be materialistic than their counterparts raised in intact families. This effect was independent of the economic consequences that frequently accompany family disruption. Kasser, Ryan and Zax (1995) found that 18-year-olds who espoused more materialistic values had less nurturing mothers than their less materialistic counterparts.

The family's economic status during childhood may also influence material values. Inglehart has proposed that material values will be given high priority by those who experienced economic insecurity as children; more economically secure children will grow up to espouse postmaterialist values. Although this argument has some intuitive appeal, the hypothesis has not been directly tested in the published literature, and indirect evidence for this is subject to alternative explanations.

Influences: media

Media, particularly advertising, are most frequently singled out as the cause of an inappropriate preoccupation with material goods, although empirical tests of this idea are difficult to carry out. Moschis and Moore (1982) conducted a longitudinal study of American children in middle and high school and found significant effects for exposure to television advertising on material values. The effect of advertising exposure was greatest for those children who were initially low in materialism. That is, among those children who were low in materialism at t_1, those who watched more television were significantly higher in materialism 14 months later than were those who had watched less television.

Consequences

There are numerous possible outcomes when a person places a high value on material goods. Material aspirations may encourage young people to continue their education, presumably improving their quality of life on several dimensions and enabling them to make a higher-quality contribution to society. Another possible outcome is that materialistic consumers might work harder to earn more so that they can obtain the things they desire. At the individual level, this hard work enables people to provide greater financial security for their families and a richer array of social and cultural experiences for their children. At a societal level, when many citizens are materialistic and work hard to fulfil their material desires, the results would be a higher standard of living for the society as a whole and enhanced economic productivity.

However, little research has examined these potential positive outcomes of materialism at either a societal or individual level. Instead, most authors have emphasized the negative consequences of materialism. Research has shown that materialistic people tend to be more self-centred and place a lower importance on interpersonal relationships than their low materialism counterparts (for example, Richins and Dawson, 1992). Studies have also demonstrated that those with strong material values tend to be less happy than other people.

Although scholarly attention to material values has increased in recent years, research for the most part has been fragmented and lacks a unifying theoretical framework. Such a framework would provide useful research impetus and direction.

MARSHA L. RICHINS

Bibliography

Abramson, P.R. and Inglehart, R. (1995) *Value Change in Global Perspective*, Ann Arbor, MI, University of Michigan Press.

Bean, C. and Papadakis, E. (1994) 'Polarized Priorities or Flexible Alternatives? Dimensionality in Inglehart's Materialism–Postmaterialism Scale', *International Journal of Public Opinion Research*, **6**: 264–88.

Belk, R.W. (1985) 'Materialism: Trait Aspects of Living in the Material World', *Journal of Consumer Research*, **12**: 265–80.

Belk, R.W. (1988) 'Third World Consumer Culture', in Kumcu, E. and Firat, A.F. (eds) *Marketing and Development: Toward Broader Dimensions*, Greenwich, CT, JAI Press.

Belk, R.W. and Pollay, R.W. (1985) 'Images of Ourselves: The Good Life in Twentieth Century Advertising', *Journal of Consumer Research*, **11**: 887–97.

Dittmar, H. (1992) *The Social Psychology of Material Possessions: To Have Is To Be*, New York, St. Martin's Press.

Durning, A.T. (1992) *How Much is Enough? The Consumer Society and the Future of the Earth*, New York, W.W. Norton.

Easterlin, R.A. and Crimmins, E.M. (1991) 'Private Materialism, Personal Self-Fulfillment, Family Life, and Public Interest: The Nature, Effects, and Causes of Recent Changes in the Values of American Youth', *Public Opinion Quarterly*, **55**: 499–533.

Kasser, T., Ryan, R.M. and Zax, M. (1995) 'The Relations of Maternal and Social Environments to Late Adolescents' Materialistic and Prosocial Values', *Developmental Psychology*, **31**: 907–14.

McKendrick, N., Brewer, J. and Plumb, J.H. (1982) *The Birth of a Consumer Society: The Commercialization of Eighteenth-Century England*, Bloomington, IN, Indiana University Press.

Moschis, G.P. and Moore, R.L. (1982) 'A Longitudinal Study of Television Advertising Effects', *Journal of Consumer Research*, **9**: 279–86.

Mukerji, C. (1983) *From Graven Images: Patterns of Modern Materialism*, New York, Columbia University Press.

Richins, M.L. (1995), 'Social Comparison, Advertising, and Consumer Discontent',

American Behavioral Scientist, **38**: 593–607.

Richins, M.L. and Dawson, S. (1992) 'A Consumer Values Orientation for Materialism and Its Measurement: Scale Development and Validation', *Journal of Consumer Research*, **19**: 303–16.

Rindfleisch, A., Burroughs, J.E. and Denton, F. (1997) 'Family Structure, Materialism, and Compulsive Consumption', *Journal of Consumer Research*, **23**: 312–25.

McClelland Hypothesis

McClelland argued that a nation's economic growth depends upon the level among its population of a psychological motive, which he called 'need for achievement' or '*n*-Ach'. Need for achievement (*n*-Ach) was conceptualized by McClelland as an essential feature of human motivation, developing in middle childhood to become a stable feature of adult personality, albeit one that is not subject to direct measurement. *N*-Ach is a motivational rather than an attitudinal variable, reflecting an inner preoccupation with improving one's social and material circumstances. In his seminal book, *The Achieving Society*, McClelland presented a wide range of often ingenious empirical studies whose aim was to demonstrate the causal relationship between national economic growth and indices of national 'achievement motivation' or '*n*-Ach' (McClelland, 1961).

McClelland was by no means the first to argue that psychological traits and attitudes could account for economic development. Indeed, it may seem a truism to state that the drive and entrepreneurial activity of individual human beings contribute to economic growth. McClelland's particular innovation was to develop methods of assessing the motivation to achieve — both at an individual and at a societal level — by which this hypothesis could be empirically tested.

The key studies described in his book involved correlating rates of national economic growth with measures of national achievement motivation. The latter measures were based upon a content analysis of stories in primary school books obtained from two samples of 23 and 41 nations, respectively. The first set of national *n*-Ach scores was based upon the average rating of a large number of stories taken from school primers written in the 1920s, while the latter were drawn from an equally large number of school primers written in the late 1940s and early 1950s. For his indices of economic development, McClelland used data on national electricity production per capita and national income. To measure rates of growth, he compared actual with predicted growth in electricity production for the periods 1929–51 and 1952–58. In his first study, he correlated the 1920s textbook measures of *n*-Ach of the 23 countries with two measures of their economic growth from the 1920s to the early 1950s. The correlations were both positive and significant. His second study was based upon a much shorter time period — measuring growth from 1952 to 1958 — using only the rate of growth in electricity production in 40 countries during this period. Despite the shorter time period, the results were equally positive and significant.

McClelland was keen to establish the psychological determinism embodied within his hypothesis. He demonstrated that while there was a predictive causal relationship between his motivational measures and subsequent economic growth, nAch levels in 1950 were *unrelated* to previous rates of growth. In short, he claimed to have demonstrated that motivational factors act upon the economic sphere rather than being merely the psychosocial product of economic change.

Since the publication of his book, there have been numerous attempts to subject his hypothesis to further tests. Most of the cross-national studies have re-examined McClelland's hypothesis using improved measures of economic growth, principally in the period since 1950. While the economic growth indicators in these studies have become much more sophisticated, the indices of nAch that McClelland derived from his 40-nation sample of school primers of the 1950s have not been revamped in any way. The results of these international studies have been at best equivocal, with studies showing either a much weaker effect (compare Tekiner, 1980; Frey, 1984), or none at all (compare Finison, 1976; Mazur and Rosa, 1977). Studies that have attempted to correlate individual variations in nAch with variations in such economic indicators as productivity and social mobility within a single country have tended to be more supportive of the hypothesis (for example Singh, 1970; Rosen, 1971). Unfortunately, there are problems in extrapolating a relationship based upon individual co-variation between a psychological characteristic and external measures of success within a single society. Moreover, several such studies are retrospective — for example, observing a correlation between current measures of *n*-Ach and past social mobility. It is not possible to derive much empirical support from these findings to a theory that attempts primarily to account for international variations in economic growth. Indeed the whole chain of inference from schoolbook contents to national motivational levels to international league tables of economic growth can be thought of as too tenuous to bear testing.

Looking back from the perspective of the last years of the twentieth century, McClelland's hypothesis can be seen as an interesting cultural product of that postwar period of optimism when the West, and America in particular, exhibited an almost naive faith in the prospects for world development. Writers such as McClelland, Hagan (1962) and Kunkel (1970) were all advocates of an 'individualist' perspective in explaining economic development. While McClelland's original hypothesis emphasized the childhood origins of *n*-Ach, he sought later to demonstrate that it was possible to increase levels of *n*-Ach in adults using a training programme for potential entrepreneurs in India (McClelland and Winter, 1969). Since the financial crises of the mid-1970s, economic growth has been less predictable and more volatile than in those first two postwar decades. It seems unlikely that we shall see again any grand psychological theory designed to explain, predict and later to create economic development. While psychological traits may still be used to fit the right people into the right posts to secure a firm's maximum efficiency and effectiveness, there seems little prospect of any large-scale investment in a psychological training programme designed to boost national GDP. Nevertheless, McClelland's work retains an importance in its determination to consider the role of the psychological in the development of social and economic change, and its imaginative use of social products as markers of psychological processes which are not susceptible to direct measurement.

CHRISTOPHER GILLEARD

Bibliography
Finison, L.J. (1976) 'The Application of McClelland's National Development Model to Recent Data', *Journal of Social Psychology*, **98**: 55–9.

Frey, R.S. (1984) 'Does *n*-Achievement Cause Economic Development? A Cross-Lagged Panel Analysis of the McClelland Thesis', *Journal of Social Psychology*, **122**: 67–70.

Hagan, E.E. (1962) *On the Theory of Social Change*, Homewood, IL, Dorsey Press.

Kunkel, J.H. (1970) *Society and Economic Growth: A Behavioral Perspective of Social Change*, New York, Oxford University Press.

Mazur, A. and Rosa, E. (1977) 'An Empirical Test of McClelland's "Achieving Society" Theory', *Social Forces*, **55**: 769–74.

McClelland, D.C. (1961) *The Achieving Society*, New York, Free Press.

McClelland, D.C. and Winter, D.G. (1969) *Motivating Economic Development*, New York, Free Press.

Rosen, B.C. (1971) 'Industrialization, Personality and Social Mobility in Brazil', *Human Organisation*, **30**: 137–48.

Singh, N.P. (1970) '*n*-Ach Among Agricultural and Business Entrepreneurs of Delhi', *Journal of Social Psychology*, **81**: 145–9.

Tekiner, A. (1980) 'Need Achievement and International Differences in Income Growth: 1950–1960', *Economic Development and Cultural Change*, **28**: 293–320.

Money

Yes! ready money *is* Alladin's Lamp. (Lord Byron)

Money doesn't talk, it swears. (Bob Dylan)

Money is like fire, an element as little troubled by moralizing as earth, air and water. Men can employ it as a tool or they can dance around it as if it were the incarnation of a god. (Lewis H. Lapham)

The meanings of money

If we were prohibited from talking of money and the uses to which we might apply it, we would be as impoverished of words for daily conversations as the poor are impoverished of money for daily expenditures. As this contention and the epigraphs suggest, the metaphors by which we refer to money may tell us much about our regard for money. In English as well as in a number of other languages, one set of money metaphors involves liquids: we speak of liquid assets, cash flows, floating a loan, taking a bath, solvency, slush funds, our life's blood, income streams, greasing the palm, priming the pump, and lubricating the economic system. These terms imply that we see money as moving and as slippery — our incomes come and go, our fortunes rise and fall, money rains down and slips away down the drain, and money greases the rails of transaction while its absence can create friction. A second set of money metaphors refers to money as food: it is dough, bread, gravy, lettuce, chicken feed or peanuts. These metaphors imply that we regard money as nourishing us; it is a necessity, a staple, a fact of life. Without it we grow lean and perish. If we have it in abundance we are fat cats. In a third set of metaphors money is sexual. We long for smackers, receive an ample or meagre endowment, prefer hard cash or hard currency, regard money as the measure of a man, shoot our wad of money, and spend until we are drained dry. As this largely masculine set of metaphors suggests, to have money is to be potent, virile, vigorous and powerful, while to lack money is to be infantile, impotent, spent or wasted. Money is fertile with possibilities and can generate more money. It can inflame our desires. Just as Sigmund Freud equated money with faeces, each of these alternative metaphors are revealing.

These metaphors also help get us away from the narrower functionalist view of economics that money is a medium of exchange, a store of value, a unit of account and a standard of deferred payment. Money does play all these roles. But it has other, more symbolic, meanings that offer deeper insights into how money affects our lives. We have known since William James that money is a part of our extended self and that as our bank account waxes and wanes, so symbolically do we. Money extends the self because it has the potential to acquire for us objects and services, to command others to do our bidding, and to demand respect or at least deference. We not only associate having money with being powerful, but with being talented, skilled, beautiful, healthy and intelligent. In a capitalist society, poverty is regarded as a personal inadequacy, a failing, an evidence of sloth, stupidity or lack of character. Money is seen as a sign of success, freedom, independence, security, cleverness, blessedness, deserving-ness, status and well-being. The tendency to hold or save money can also be seen as an attempt to reduce feelings of insecurity about the future, as both John Maynard Keynes and George Katona have theorized. In this sense money means comfort. There are exceptions to these positive associations, but they derive more from the sources and uses of money (considered below) rather than to the simple fact of having money.

Money also evokes negative emotional meanings. Our financial status relative to others can induce anxiety, envy, guilt, depression, panic, fear and insecurity. Social comparison theory suggests that we compare ourselves to others with a bit more or a bit less. Deprivation or privilege is relative. We also attend to cultural norms for spending, saving and displaying wealth. Because of fear of self-disclosure of our true financial status, as well as the masking effects of credit and spending styles, we are seldom certain whether we have more or less than others. We therefore judge wealth based on the imperfect index of spending patterns and if we cannot keep up with referent others we lose prestige. Veblenian conspicuous consumption and conspicuous waste are not just things of the past. Status can also depend on what Pierre Bourdieu calls the cultural capital of taste, knowledge and connections, but these are also linked to wealth and the things it buys. While spending money on ourselves and our families can be a source of pleasure, it can also be a source of anxiety. Should we be saving or investing rather than spending? Have we bought wisely? Are we becoming too heavily indebted? Are we being too selfish? Questions such as these are sources of further anxiety and negative emotions. Our culture helps construct what are the socially acceptable answers to such questions.

Sources of money
In part our evaluations of money relate to how it is acquired. Blood money, inheritances, gifts, windfall income, borrowed money, salaries and wages are all regarded differently; as more or less honourable, more or less fungible, more or less suited to be used for necessities, luxuries, savings, or investment. In part, as Zelizer (1994) demonstrates, this is because money is differentially linked to other people whom it represents. In part, too, these different moneys are seen as more or less deserved and more or less earned. Treasure tales around the world warn that unearned and undeserved wealth is evil (Belk and Wallendorf, 1990). For some people, credit cards also carry hints of sin and evil because this money

is too easily come by and not yet earned. Money obtained from crime and especially through murder, is often seen as cursed. The expression in English, 'Easy come, easy go' implies that we are not as attached to money we did not earn, unless of course it has interpersonal meanings such an inheritance from a deceased parent. Notions of earned and unearned wealth also relate to pre-capitalist religious prohibitions against usury.

In the general economy, sources of money and attributions of why some people have it and others do not are often quite mysterious. Like the alchemists of old, brokers, financiers, bankers and other 'high priests' of finance are sometimes seen as performing a kind of magic that creates money. It is not just that their actions are opaque and not well understood, there also appear to be ritualistic aspects of money that have overtones of religion. Belief, whether in gods or currencies, is largely a matter of faith. The slogan on American currency, 'In God we Trust' should probably be amended to refer to the Federal Reserve System. For Third World countries, it is the World Bank and International Monetary Fund that are seen to wield these magical powers. Our faith in paper and electronic money is likely put to the test most in times of economic depression and rapid inflation. Contemporary moneys depend upon an institutional structure that consumers understand quite imperfectly.

Nevertheless, our faith in money is greater when it is from our own nation. Foreign currency seems too much like 'play money', and therefore may be more easily spent. Alternatively, it is conceptualized only in terms of a sometimes crude mental conversion into the traveller's national currency. This naturalization of our own national currencies presents a challenge to introducing new moneys such as the Euro. Given the strong symbolic meanings of national moneys (bolstered by the heroic national themes they commonly depict), changing currencies may be perceived as tantamount to changing national flags or national anthems.

Uses of money

We can do many things with money. We can spend it on diverse things. We can save it, give it as a gift, bequest, tip, donation or charitable contribution. We can save it, lend it, invest it or wager it in a gamble. Although economists idealize universally exchangeable money and cynics suggest that everyone and everything has its price, there are a number of things that we commonly deem to be above price. These may include love, children, people generally, life, death, human bodies and body parts, and reputations. While sex can be bought and sold, we have unflattering names for those who do so. Less opprobrium may attach to those who sell blood, human organs, sperm, embryos and children, but most people feel distinctly uneasy about such transactions. This has not dissuaded economists such as Gary Becker and legal theorists such as Richard Posner from characterizing virtually all human interactions as exchanges that reveal the monetary value that presumably underlies our regard for all objects, services, persons, rights, governments, environmental conditions and so forth. As Radin (1996) has argued, such 'commodification' rightly horrifies and dismays many people. Nevertheless, some scholars seem mystified as to why anyone would object to characterizing life as a series of 'trades' revealing monetary equivalences between all things.

Anthropologists and sociologists generally suggest that the gift economy and the commodity economy are separate and opposing spheres. The former binds us to each other, while in the latter we can walk away without further obligations. To introduce money into the gift economy is problematic. Thus, if a friend has us over for dinner, to attempt to pay for the meal is regarded as a profane insertion of commodity norms into the gift economy. However, bringing the hostess flowers or wine is generally seen as a nonequivalent counter-gift rather than a form of barter payment for the meal. On the other hand, tipping service providers is, at least in cultures where it is common, an act regarded as much closer to a monetary exchange and one where a nonmonetary gift would seem too personal and out of place. However in cultures like those of Australia and New Zealand where tipping is less common, a service provider may resist tips and resent them as debasing the intrinsic motivation for providing good service.

Anthropologists have also described 'special moneys' that can only be used for certain purposes. While we like to think that the general purpose moneys of national currencies are devoid of such restrictions, Zelizer (1994) finds many instances in which money is not fungible and is seen as appropriate for certain uses only. Money received as an inheritance, a gift, or in a rite of passage such as a wedding or funeral, generally falls in this special money category. Using such moneys for frivolous purposes is profane, as is using windfall income such as lottery winnings for serious purposes.

The uses to which we put money and the ways in which we do so has also led to spending typologies, many categories of which are regarded as pathological. Spender types include misers, hoarders, spendthrifts, compulsive givers, compulsive buyers, impulsive buyers, bargain hunters, gamblers, capitalists, bulls, bears, *nouveaux riches*, martyrs, security junkies, power junkies, anal retentives, anal expulsives, Shylocks and debtors. While some of these types have clinical or psychometric evidence behind them, it is well to remember that, like categorizations of luxuries and necessities, these spender types are all social constructions that vary with cultural and temporal contexts.

Effects of money
While money may not literally make the world go round, it has undeniably important effects on us as individuals, groups, and nations. It affects our sense of

386

self, including self-esteem, feelings of control or dependency, security, indebtedness, and even, in some accounts, our sexual potency. Traditionally bankruptcy has been traumatic to self-image, but the stigma appears to be lessening as bankruptcy becomes more common and money more abstract. Money is not the only or even the most important motivator of work and initiative, but surely it is a significant incentive. Many forms of crime appear to be motivated by money as well. But while many of us believe that more money will enhance our happiness and well-being, this is true only up to a point and also depends on gain relative to others. Since money is a social construction, children must learn about money and what it means as well how it can and should be pursued and used within our culture and subcultures. Besides their role as models, parents use money to reward, punish and teach children lessons about its value and proper uses.

Interpersonally, money is related to differences in age, gender, class and political power. It affects which people we are likely to date and marry. While traditionally men have sought beauty in a mate and women have sought money, with more women working around the world, there is evidence that both sexes increasingly value a potential mate's financial resources and earning power. The realm of gift giving in this and other contexts is one way in which money power is used. The more removed from money a gift is, the more it is seen to be removed from potential exercises of power, indebtedness and ingratiation. It is normally assumed that the family operates primarily within the gift economy rather than the commodity economy, but there are opportunities for manipulation within the family as well, through gifts, allowances, promised bequests and allocations of funds within the household. As we come to rely on having money as a source of (financial) security we generally remove ourselves from reliance on others as a source of (social) security, both in youth and old age.

Among strangers rather than kin and friends, considerations in the distribution of money move from underlying notions of morality, love and justice to considerations of law. Different cultures and political systems enact different monetary welfare systems, based in part on beliefs about deservingness, helplessness and societal obligations. Religions offer various ethical principles to account for differences in wealth, including a promise that life's ultimate rewards and punishments come after death. Nations are affected by the degree to which people spend, save and borrow wealth, which in turn depends upon cultural norms and levels of optimism. Nations also measure their own status according to wealth, debt and obligations. Banks, stock markets, currency exchanges and other monetary institutions are increasingly globally interdependent. The general uses of wealth to produce and consume have important environmental consequences that are also increasingly global. Even tourism is increasingly global and may (but may not) bring environmentally friendly sources of foreign currency to impoverished portions of the world, at the potential cost of neocolonial dependency. And the monetary and materialistic attitudes of consumers also spread globally as the world shrinks and wealth and consumption patterns in one part of the world become increasingly visible to other parts of the world. Thus, even if money does not make the world go round, it surely shapes what goes on around the world.

RUSSELL W. BELK

Bibliography

Belk, R.W. and Wallendorf, M. (1990) 'The Sacred Meanings of Money', *Journal of Economic Psychology*, **11**: 35–67.

Burgoyne, C.B. (1990) 'Money in Marriage: How Patterns of Allocation Both Reflect and Conceal Power', *Sociological Review*, **38**: 634–65.

Crawford, T. (1994) *The Secret Life of Money: Teaching Tales of Spending, Receiving, Saving, and Owing*, New York, G.P. Putnam's Sons.

Doyle, K.O. (ed.) (1992) 'The Meanings of Money', special issue, *American Behavioral Scientist*, **35** (6).

Jackson, K. (ed.) (1995) *The Oxford Book of Money*, Oxford, Oxford University Press.

Klebanow, S. and Lowenkopf, E.L. (eds) (1991) *Money and Mind*, New York, Plenum Press.

Lewis, A., Webley, P. and Furnham, A. (1995) 'The Psychology of Money', in *The New Economic Mind: The Social Psychology of Economic Behaviour*, New York, Harvester-Wheatsheaf: 53–76.

Lunt, P.K. and Livingstone, S.M. (1992) *Mass Consumption and Personal Identity: Everyday Economic Experience*, Buckingham, Open University Press.

Radin, M.J. (1996) *Contested Commodities*, Cambridge, MA, Harvard University Press.

Zelizer, V.A. (1994) *The Social Meanings of Money: Pin Money, Paychecks, Poor Relief, and Other Currencies*, New York, Basic Books.

Morals, Markets and Green Investing

Most people will be familiar with Adam Smith's (1776/1937: 423) 'invisible hand' whereby an individual who 'intends only his own gain' is

> led by an invisible hand to promote an end which was no part of his intention. Nor is it always the worse for society that it was no part of it. By pursuing his own interest, he frequently promotes that of the society more effectively than when he really intends to promote it.

This appears to legitimize 'selfishness' as no bad thing although others may prefer terms like 'wealth creation'. Certainly this quotation has been seized upon by the political right as have the more contemporary views of Milton Friedman (1962: 133) that the corporation's only responsibility is to 'use its resources and engage in activities designed to increase its profits as long as it stays within the rules of the game — which is to say, engages in open and free competition, without deception or fraud'. So the Enlightenment still shines bright; an unfettered economy is to the benefit of us all. But those holding such views do not have it all their own way. As the millennium approaches it is clear that the 'consumer movement' is growing ever stronger; it is difficult to envisage a decline. Consumer protection is everywhere and litigation common almost to the point where *caveat venditor* has taken over from *caveat emptor*. Perhaps it is timely to take heed of Herbert Spencer's (1891) warning that 'the ultimate result of shielding men from the effects of folly is to fill the world with fools!'.

The modern history of the consumer movement is not the only evidence we have that not all is rosy on the market applecart; the presence of Business Ethics on the curriculum of most of the major business schools is another. Any large company worth its salt employs experts on consumer law, showing perhaps that businesses are keen to put their own houses in order before the government or some organized group of consumers does it for them: it makes good commercial sense. Recalling Friedman, it seems that the size of the profit alone is no longer enough: consumers, shareholders and businesspeople, are concerned with how that profit was accrued; whether it be by fair means or foul.

Psychologists, sociologists, even some economists, have become aware that reductionist modelling of market mechanisms may be elegant but miss vital aspects of how markets 'really' work. The 'invisible handshake' may be a superior metaphor to the 'invisible hand'. Commercial understandings are based on social rules, which are frequently implicit; economic life is part of social life and is influenced by attitudes, preferences, notions of fairness and appropriate behaviour, in much the same way as other aspects of social behaviour. These largely tacit understandings become more apparent when the 'rules' are broken, for example, when shopkeepers raise the prices of snow-shovels after heavy falls of snow or where employers reduce the wages of their current employees as unemployment rates rise. It is difficult, even impossible, to produce data which substantiate a psychological or sociological explanation in preference to an economic one. In the example above a social scientist would argue, 'here is evidence that social understandings predominate; look, the shopkeeper does not raise the price of his snow-shovels because it would be unfair, similarly the employer does not reduce the wages of his employees because it would be unfair'. Alternatively an economic commentator might say: 'The shopkeeper does not raise the price of his snow-shovels because although his short-term profits will rise, he knows that his customers would view this as profiteering and he would lose custom in the long run'. Therefore not raising the price is the economically rational thing to do, not necessarily the fair thing to do. The economic commentator might continue: 'The employer does not reduce the wages of his staff as this might cause unrest and loss of efficiency because the employees would see this as unfair. Even if these recalcitrant workers were sacked, new employees would be unknown quantities and would need to be trained'.

What becomes clear from these cases is that even if you prefer the 'economic' explanation, the entrepreneur concerned (whether selling snow-shovels or whatever) gains through both his or her economic *and* his or her social knowledge. The problem here is that this regresses to some form of explanation such that an economic actor only needs to know that amount about people and social rules that will make a profit. What I prefer to believe is that people have mixed motives and are not calculating utility maximizers, but are instead individuals holding internal dialogues with the voice of social motives and morals pulling them in one direction and the voice of 'straightforward' wealth maximization the other (similar points have been made by Steedman and Krause,1986).

Mixed motives

It is my view that it is productive to get away from the either/or argument between rational economic models and the 'softer' ones. This in itself is not in turn a 'soft option' as it becomes important to investigate markets qualitatively and in more depth; to appreciate how people resolve these dilemmas as an aspect of social (and economic) skill and competence. It has become important to find out from participating economic actors what they think they are doing: relying on judgements from the general public about hypothetical instances, although valuable, is not enough. Returning to the snow-shovel example, the majority of the general public say they view the raising of prices as unfair, but if you ask, instead, small shopkeepers, they say they *would* raise prices, although still not to the extent of risking the wrath of their customers.

Ethical/green investing

Recent work by myself and my colleagues has concentrated on ethical and green investing. These investments (called 'social investments' in the US) are typified by ' exclusions' where investors (usually through independent financial advisers) decide they are not prepared to invest in companies which pollute, manufacture weapons, cigarettes, alcohol and whatever they prefer not to be their or other peoples' poison. In the UK, for example, there are now over thirty ethical/green unit trusts which reflect these preferences. Surely this is an explicit example where people are putting their money where there morals are. If this is the case are they prepared to take a loss? How do they manage their portfolios? Why are they doing what they do and do they believe it makes a difference? This was variously investigated using questionnaires, interviews and focus groups, and, most importantly, the participants were real investors.

In the UK at present, ethical/green unit trusts are performing little (if at all) worse than unit trusts which are not so 'clean'; the acid test would be when profits fall: how soon would investors pull out? There is some evidence that ethical investors persist, but most (if not everyone) has a price they are not prepared to pay. We have become convinced that the majority of ethical investors invest in other parts of the market as well and are actively engaged in moral and economic compromises; there is no simple division between saint and sinner. When asked, these investors are happy to say that, at least for some of the time, they are salving their consciences and they have to invest 'unethically' for thoroughly sound moral reasons, for example, in order to bequeath to sons and daughters. This decision to invest ethically is part of a lifestyle package; these investors are frequently members of organizations such as Friends of the Earth, Greenpeace, Oxfam and other charities, are active in religious groups and are very unlikely to vote Conservative. These people are far from being eccentric; people from the health and education sectors are overrepresented compared to the usual demographic characteristics of investors. These people freely admit to salving their consciences and making moral compromises; they also believe that their actions *do* make a difference to markets, rather like water dripping on stones (similes and metaphors of this type came up regularly). There is also the belief that ethical investment is a growing movement; enough drips make a more troublesome body of water.

Economists that I have spoken to are keen to dismiss these 'movements' as mere fads and fashions, but environmental problems will not go away quite as easily. Investors would prefer ethical unit trusts themselves to take action by lobbying for change rather than ignoring the 'bad' companies altogether (or in Hirschman's (1970) terms a preference for 'Voice' over 'Exit'). The economists' view is that this form of 'boycotting' (like other examples in the marketplace) is unlikely to have an influence on share values directly but it certainly makes ethical issues more visible and businesses are becoming aware that short-sightedness can lead to a tumble.

Speculations
There is now a growing body of evidence that markets have moral and social characteristics and that these aspects, because they are relatively enduring, can stabilize markets. It would be in no one's interest to behave like self-interested utility maximizers, in the narrow sense, because the system would soon break down as retailers lost trust in wholesalers and consumers lost trust in retailers (compare Etzioni, 1988). It has become apparent that, at the very least,

enlightened self-interest has to incorporate social knowledge and competency and that economic actions, at varying levels and to varying degrees, are driven by mixed motives. More qualitative and in-depth studies of markets are needed. These kinds of studies are not uncommon in social anthropology and sociology but they have largely not been successful in combining generalizations based on descriptive depth and inductive insights with deductive modelling. This should be the aim of economic psychology in the future.

ALAN LEWIS

Bibliography
Etzioni, A. (1988) *The Moral Dimension*, New York, Free Press.
Friedman, M. (1962) *Capitalism and Freedom*, Chicago, IL, University of Chicago Press.
Hirschman, A. (1970) *Exit, Voice and Loyalty*, Cambridge, MA, Harvard University Press.
Kahneman, D., Knetsch, D. and Thaler, R. (1986) 'Fairness as a Constraint on Profit Seeking', *American Economic Review*, **76**: 728–41.
Kaufmann. P., Ortmeyer, G. and Smith, N.C. (1991) 'Fairness in Consumer Pricing', *Journal of Consumer Policy*, **14**: 117–40.
Lewis, A. and Warneryd K.-E. (eds) (1994) *Ethics and Economics Affairs*, New York and London, Routledge.
Lewis, A., Mackenzie, C., Webley. P. and Winnett, A. (1998) 'Morals and Markets: Some Theoretical and Policy Implications of Ethical Investment', in Taylor-Gooby, P. (ed.) *Choice and Public Policy*, London, Macmillan.
Lewis, A., Webley, P. and Furnham, A. (1995) *The New Economic Mind: The Social Psychology of Economic Behaviour*, New York and London, Harvester-Wheatsheaf.
Smith, A. (1776/1937) *An Inquiry into the Nature and Causes of the Wealth of Nations*, New York, The Modern Library.
Smith, N.C. (1990) *Moralty and the Market*, London and New York, Routledge.
Spencer, H. (1891) *Essays*, Volume III, London, Macmillan.
Steedman, I. and Krause, U. (1986) 'Goethe's *Faust* , Arrow's Possibility Theorem and the Individual Decision Taker', in Elster, J. (ed.) *The Multiple Self*, Cambridge, Cambridge University Press.

Multiattribute Utility Models

Multiattribute utility models can be traced back to the pioneering work of Kelvin Lancaster (1966). Their development arises from questions that are not satisfactorily addressed by traditional economic theory. For example: (i) Why do some consumers consume Pepsi and others Coke? (ii) Why are Coke and Pepsi closer substitutes than Coke and Canada Dry Ginger Ale? (iii) Why do we see the current set of soft drink offerings rather than some other? (iv) Why does the demand curve for Pepsi look as it does? A related set of questions interest marketing managers. (i) What should be the characteristics of a new brand? (ii) How can our brand be changed to increase profit? (iii) Can we group consumers with similar tastes, and, if so, which groupings should our marketing efforts target? (iv) What should our advertisements to these segments focus on? Multiattribute utility modelling offers insights into each of these questions.

This entry presents an overview of multiattribute utility models. It begins by looking at multiattribute models in general. Next, alternative multiattribute utility concepts are discussed. Estimation issues are then addressed. Lastly, some issues ripe for further research are raised.

Multiattribute models of consumer behaviour

There are three broad types of multiattribute models. Unlike traditional economic theory, each hypothesizes that the consumer does not judge a brand in and of itself. Rather, the consumer's preference for or choice of a particular brand depends on the levels of the relevant physical and psychological factors (attributes) inherent in the brand as well as its price. The three types differ in how they deal implicitly with the fact that it is costly for consumers to collect and process information about brands. Information may be actively searched for (for example, by reading labels or consumer magazines or talking with friends) or retrieved from memory. Regardless of how much or what information is collected, mental, time and monetary costs are incurred. Rarely is it worthwhile to collect complete information on all the relevant brands since the cost of doing so exceeds the benefit. Consequently, consumers assess the purchase situation and chooses the brand evaluation process they feel will lead to the best choice given the cost of using the process and its related information collection costs. The different types of multiattribute models correspond to different evaluation processes. A limitation of the three model types is that none explicitly incorporates the tradeoff between the additional cost of more information search and its expected benefit.

The simplest type of model borrows heavily from the psychology and behavioural economics literatures. Reasonable heuristics or 'rules of thumb' dictate choice. Many of these rules can be seen as variants of Simon's (1959) idea of satisficing, where the consumer chooses the first brand they encounter that is 'satisfactory'. Some 'rules', such as buy the first car you find that provides more than 30 miles per gallon and costs less that $10 000, involve multiattribute brand evaluations. Many do not. One such heuristic is to purchase the brand of laundry detergent your mother used. Another is to buy the line of clothing most fashionable to your social set. Very little information is collected and its processing is reduced to a minimum. Hence, these 'rules' are associated with low-involvement purchase situations. The rationale is that for routine choices or choices among brands that all generate little benefit or difference in benefits, there is little incentive to invest much in collecting and processing information, so following a simple rule is most cost-beneficial. See Earl (1995) for a more detailed discussion.

Noncompensatory preference and choice models constitute the second set of multiattribute models. These models also arise from the psychology literature and explicitly involve multiattribute brand evaluation. They earn the noncompensatory title because tradeoffs among the attributes are not allowed — the effect of an unfavourable level of one attribute on the preference for a brand cannot be compensated for by a highly favourable level of another attribute. Two common examples of this type are the conjunctive and the priority-based models. They both depict the consumer as setting cutoff levels for each attribute. The conjunctive model assumes the consumer has a checklist of requirements and dismisses from consideration any brand having *any* attribute level below its cutoff. A consumer acting according to a set of priorities first rejects brands that fail to meet the top priority target, tests the remainder against the second priority and so on, and keeps working down the priority list until only one brand is left. Thus, noncompensatory models utilize a simple evaluation process that typically requires a limited amount of brand information. An economic rationale for these models is offered by Shugan (1980) who argues that the cost of collecting and processing brand information makes it optimal, in an expected benefit versus cost sense, to ignore some available information, in this case through the use of a noncompensatory model. Representation of these models functionally (that is, as a multiattribute utility function) is possible if extremely nonlinear functions are allowed. Earl (1995) again provides a thorough overview of these models.

Multiattribute utility models — the focus of this entry — form the third broad of multiattribute model. These models are compensatory — tradeoffs among the attributes are modelled — and require the greatest amount of information collection and processing (referred to as brand decision costs, hereafter). The utility of brand i to consumer m is depicted as a function of the levels of the attributes it provides. That is, $U_{im} = f(z_{i1m}, z_{i2m}, \ldots, z_{iJm})$ where there are J attributes relevant to the consumer (price being one of these) and z_{ijm} is the level of attribute j perceived to be derived from product i. A similarity to Becker's (1965) household production function idea, mapping goods into consumption activities, is clear. Brand decision costs are incorporated implicitly through the consideration set. Before forming their preferences in any particular product class (set of competitive brands), the consumer collects information about the brands' attribute levels. Because this search is costly, the consumer must trade off between the amount and quality of information to collect about each brand and the number of brands to collect information on. Compensatory models assume that the consumer leans more towards the former (while noncompensatory models tilt more towards the latter). Consequently, the consumer develops a consideration set of brands for possible purchase that is unlikely to include all the brands in the product class. For each brand in this consideration set, data concerning each relevant attribute is collected. Imperfect and incomplete collection of information typically results in inaccurate perceptions of the attribute levels inherent in the brands. Information processing amounts to a utility assessment of each brand and the choice of the one that maximizes perceived utility.

Multiattribute utility
Insights into the questions raised in the introduction depend intimately on understanding the tradeoffs individual consumers make among the attributes when assessing brand utilities and the heterogeneity in these tastes across individuals. Two streams of research have developed to model these tradeoffs theoretically and to assess them empirically. Economists developed mathematical models to better understand the consumer's decision process (Lancaster, 1966) and firms' brand choices (Rosen 1974). These models utilize objective attributes, such as horsepower and miles per gallon, and empirical work uses aggregate level sales data and logit analysis to assess the utility function of a 'representative' consumer. Marketers' use of multiattribute models is much more prevalent and has its origin in the use of regression analysis to understand empirically which attributes are most strongly related to a particular individual's preferences over a set of brands. The attributes evaluated are often subjective in nature (for example, comfort and style). Besides a better understanding of consumer behaviour, many papers in this stream are interested in predicting choice behaviour under simulated 'what if' scenarios. Gradually the two streams have merged. For example, utility-based modelling is now common in marketing and the industrial organization literature shows a strong interest in generating managerially relevant multiattribute insights based on less-aggregated data.

Two functional forms for multiattribute utility generally are used. The linear model assumes constant marginal utility for each unit of an attribute. That is, the utility that consumer m has for brand i is:

$$U_{im} = \sum_{j=1}^{J} w_{jm} z_{ijm}. \tag{1}$$

The w_{jm} term reflects the relative importance of attribute j to consumer m's preference formation and is referred to as an attribute weight. The relative magnitudes of the attribute weights reveal the tradeoffs the consumer makes among the attributes when assessing brand utilities.

The part worths model does not impose any a priori structure other than additivity. Marginal attribute utilities need not be constant and more of each attribute need not be preferred to less. However, estimation concerns restrict the researcher to a limited number of levels (generally two to four) for each attribute. The resulting utility formulation is:

$$U_{im} = \sum_{j=1}^{J} \sum_{k=1}^{K_j} u_{jkm} D_{ijkm} \tag{2}$$

where each attribute has K_j levels. The D_{ijkm} variables constitute the attribute level information and are represented as dummy variables equal to one if brand i has a perceived level k of attribute j, and zero otherwise. The u_{jkm} terms represent the utility (attribute weight) consumer m associates with level k of attribute j.

The use of multiattribute utility models is typically associated with high involvement choice settings (for example, middle- to high-priced or infrequently purchased products). However, since they also depict behaviour well for inexpensive and frequently purchased products (Johnson and Meyer, 1984), and are easy to estimate, they are commonly used in place of noncompensatory models.

Given that consumers have inaccurate and incomplete information about the brands' attribute levels or prices, expected utility rather than utility modelling is actually more appropriate (Horsky and Nelson, 1992). Functionally, after some simplifying assumptions mostly concerning risk attitude, expected utility boils down to adding an additional overall uncertainty 'attribute' to the multiattribute utility function. The uncertainty arises from the consumers' knowledge that their attribute level and price perceptions may be inaccurate. The overall uncertainty attribute (risk premium) is generally statistically significant and models including it provide better prediction than models assuming consumer certainty (Hauser and Urban, 1979). Despite these findings, consumer uncertainty and, hence, expected utility, is rarely modelled.

Estimation

Multiattribute studies typically involve individual consumer level estimation of equations (1) or (2) based on survey data. Regardless of the eventual managerial or academic objective behind the study, estimation of each individual's attribute weights (the w_{jm}'s in equation (1) or the u_{jkm}'s in equation (2)) is desired. Average weights pertaining to a 'representative' consumer do not reflect the distribution (heterogeneity) of consumer tastes very well. Thus, individual-level analysis allows more accurate prediction of both individual and aggregate behaviour, better representation of individual behaviour, and an opportunity to group the population into 'benefit segments' which are needed for cost-effective targeting of the firm's marketing efforts. Typically, fewer than eight attributes are modelled.

Before attribute weight estimation can take place, the attributes relevant to consumers must be identified. Often a list of brands likely to be considered must also be identified. Personal interviews, focus groups and past experience are typically used to identify preliminary lists. Further personal interviews are used to condense these lists. Two statistical techniques, nonmetric multidimensional scaling and factor analysis, are often used to help identify the final attributes. These techniques usually result in a limited number of subjective (psychological) attributes and explain behaviour fairly well (Wilkie and Pessemier, 1973).

Once the attribute list has been decided upon, a large representative sample of consumers is surveyed. Two types of preference responses are utilized to estimate each sample consumer's personal attribute weights (the w_{jm}'s or u_{jkm}'s). The respondents may simply be asked to reveal the relative preference they have for each attribute or attribute level by, say, dividing 100 points up between the attributes. Edwards (1977) provides a nice overview of this direct elicitation or self-explicated weights technique. Because of predictive validity concerns, more often respondents are asked instead to provide their stated preferences over a set of real or hypothetical brands (Wilkie and Pessemier, 1973). The relationship between these preferences, which serve as a proxy for utility, and the brands' attribute levels is used to estimate the individual's attribute weights. When hypothetical brands are used this procedure is referred to as conjoint analysis.

When collecting stated brand preferences the consumers are asked to rate how much they like (prefer, intend to buy, or are willing to pay for) a brand on a scale of, say, 0 to 100 with a value of 0 meaning strongly dislike and 100 meaning strongly like. Alternatively, the respondent may simply provide a ranking of the brands or perform comparisons among various brand pairs. Regression analysis is the most popular estimation technique with one of the stated preference measures as the dependent variable and the attribute as the independent variables. The parameter estimates are the attribute weights (the w_{jm}'s or u_{jkm}'s). Other estimation techniques include MONANOVA, logit and linear programming. See Green and Srinivasan (1990) for further details.

Attribute-level data are often not collected from the consumer. Individual-specific perceived attribute levels (the z_{ijm}'s) are collected in many studies utilizing stated preferences for real brands to estimate the consumer's utility function. However, conjoint analysis is more prevalent since it does not require the respondent to answer the many questions needed to acquire attribute perception data. The descriptions of the hypothetical brands contain their attribute levels (thus, $z_{ijm} = z_{ij}$ for all consumers m), so only preference data is collected. In either case, the attributes may be objective, such as miles per gallon, price and engine size, or subjective, such as comfort, image and style (typically measured on a 1–7 scale).

Recently, a desire to reduce the number and complexity of the questions asked the consumer has led researchers to use both self-explicated weights data and stated brand preferences to estimate individual-level attribute weights. These hybrid techniques use self-explicated weights as priors and then ask brand preference questions (often simply 'How much do you prefer Brand A to Brand B?') which are used to update these weights (Green, 1984). A popular commercial example is adaptive conjoint analysis by Sawtooth Software. Similarities to Bayesian updating in statistics and belief change in philosophy are clear.

Future research areas

Four promising areas for additional research in multiattribute utility are the relationship between subjective and objective attributes, context effects, revealed versus stated preferences and choice, and the modelling of hierarchical multiattribute evaluations.

There is a trend to define utility as a function of a long list of objective attributes rather than a limited number of subjective attributes. The rationale behind this is as follows. Brand design engineers must choose particular levels of objective attributes when designing a brand. The mapping of objective to subjective attributes is many to one and, furthermore, not exactly defined. So, to avoid these mapping problems, why not just define utility with respect to the objective attributes? Two pitfalls arise, however. First, consumers do not directly evaluate the objective attribute levels of the brands. Hence, the utility function is misspecified. This may hurt predictive ability but more importantly may generate misleading attribute weight estimates. Second, a statistical problem arises since the number of independent variables (attributes) in the regression equation increases dramatically while the number of observations (brands) cannot since the number of real brands is limited, as is the number of hypothetical brands which the respondent can credibly assess. This degrees of freedom problem requires that utility function estimation be done at the segment or aggregate level and we have already mentioned the problems associated with such estimation. It may be more fruitful to make a better assessment of the subjective–objective attribute mapping, often referred to as quality function deployment or the house of quality (Horsky and Nelson, 1992).

Multiattribute utility modellers have largely ignored the idea that the consumers' preferences, and, hence, their utility functions, may be context dependent. A vast literature in psychology and marketing provides anecdotal evidence that stated preferences are dependent on among other things, the situation and type of question asked. This has led to numerous theories that explain these 'deviations from rationality', the most generic and well known of which are prospect theory (Kahneman and Tversky, 1979) and transaction utility or reference price modelling (Thaler, 1985). This issue poses an alarming problem both to utility theorists and managers. To theorists these deviations from rationality question the assumptions behind expected utility theory. To managers, the quality of all multiattribute study results is questionable because of concerns about whether the context in which the data were collected matches the contexts under which managers will implement their marketing decisions.

A particular context effect gaining interest with multiattribute modellers is the relationship between stated preferences, stated choices and actual choices (revealed preferences). Marketers have found that, for example, price sensitivity is often underestimated when consumer utility functions are estimated using stated preferences for a set of real or hypothetical brands. Consequently, there has been a movement towards estimation based on stated choices (Carroll and Green 1995). This involves consumers looking at different sets of hypothetical brands and choosing their favourite in each set. Logit analysis is then used to generate maximum likelihood estimates of the attribute weights. Unfortunately, once again there is usually a degrees of freedom problem, which causes estimation to be done at the segment or aggregate level. In addition, stated choices among hypothetical, or even real, brands may not reflect actual behaviour. For example, Horsky and Nelson (1992) show that consumers' stated first choices do not match perfectly with their actual choices.

Hierarchical choice models have become fairly standard in the analysis of grocery store scanner data. That is, consumers are first modelled as choosing between, say, powdered and liquid laundry detergents and then choosing among the various brands within the product type chosen. However, this type of modelling has not found its way into the multiattribute utility literature in more than a qualitative manner. For example, because of brand decision costs the consumer may first decide what price range to consider and then use a compensatory model to assess the brands in that price range. Alternatively, the consumer may first disregard all cars providing less than 20 miles per gallon fuel economy, then use a compensatory model to compare among broad types of cars such as compact, utility, sport and luxury, and finally perform a final compensatory analysis (with different attribute weights) of the brands within the chosen product type.

PAUL NELSON

Bibliography

Becker, G.S. (1965) 'A Theory of the Allocation of Time', *Economic Journal*, **75**: 493–517.

Carroll, J. and Green, P. (1995) 'Psychometric Methods in Marketing Research: Part 1, Conjoint Analysis', *Journal of Marketing Research*, **32**: 385–91.

Earl, P.E. (1995) *Microeconomics for Business and Marketing*, Aldershot, Edward Elgar.

Edwards, W. (1977) 'How to Use Multiattribute Utility Measurement for Social Decision Making', *IEEE Transactions on Systems, Man, and Cybernetics*, SMC–7: 326–40.

Green, P. (1984), 'Hybrid Models for Conjoint Analysis: An Expository Review', *Journal of Marketing Research*, **21**: 155–69.

Green, P. and Srinivasan, V. (1990) 'Conjoint Analysis in Marketing: New Developments with Implications for Research and Practice', *Journal of Marketing*, **54**: 3–19.

Hauser, J. and Urban, G. (1979) 'Assessment of Attribute Importances and Consumer Utility Functions: Von Neumann–Morgenstern Theory Applied to Consumer Behavior', *Journal of Consumer Research*, **5**: 251–62.

Horsky, D. and Nelson, P. (1992) 'New Brand Positioning and Pricing in an Oligopolistic Market', *Marketing Science*, **11**: 133–53.

Johnson, E. and Meyer, R. (1984) 'Compensatory Choice Models of Noncompensatory Processes: The Effect of Varying Context', *Journal of Consumer Research*, **11**: 528–41.

Kahneman, D. and Tversky, A. (1979) 'Prospect Theory: An Analysis of Decisions Under Risk', *Econometrica*, **47**: 263–91.

Lancaster, K. (1966) 'A New Approach to Consumer Theory', *Journal of Political Economy*, **74**: 132–57.

Rosen, S. (1974) 'Hedonic Prices and Implicit Markets: Product Differentiation in Pure Competition', *Journal of Political Economy*, **82**: 34–55.

Shugan, S. (1980) 'The Cost of Thinking', *Journal of Consumer Research*, **7**: 99–111.

Simon, H.A. (1959) 'Theories of Decision-Making in Economics and Behavioral Science', *American Economic Review*, **49**: 253–83.

Thaler, R. (1985) 'Mental Accounting and Consumer Choice', *Marketing Science*, **4**: 199–214.

Wilkie, W. and Pessemier, E. (1973) 'Issues in Marketing's Use of Multiattribute Attitude Models', *Journal of Marketing Research*, **10**: 425–41.

Wittink, D. and Cattin, P. (1989) 'Commercial Use of Conjoint Analysis: An Update', *Journal of Marketing*, **53**: 91–6.

Needs and Wants

'Need' and 'want' are often used interchangeably. Nor is this a quirk of English since both *besoin* and *Bedürfnis*, for example, can be translated by either term. When unreflective usage distinguishes between them it is normally to attribute greater emphasis to 'need'. To need something is to suggest that in some way that it is necessary, while to want something is to indicate the presence of a desire or aspiration.

Philosophers have taken this usage and argued that there is in fact a conceptual and not merely a semantic difference between the two. The crucial distinction (because other differences flow from it) is that 'need' refers to an objective state of affairs, while 'want' depends on a subjective state of mind or belief. Because these are different then it is conceptually possible to need what you do not want and to need what you do not know you need (heart surgery) and, conversely, it is conceptually possible to want what you don't need and impossible that you can want something without knowing that you want it (the version of your car in metallic paint). Wants, it follows, are privileged, because I can have my own personal reasons, which no one can contradict, for wanting my car painted metallically (it pleases me aesthetically). Needs, by contrast, are not privileged, my doctor, because he or she possesses publicly accessible knowledge about cardiac functions, can say what I need.

That a distinction betweeen needs and wants can be made in this way is commonly accepted but its wider significance is less clear. Much hinges on the interpretation given to 'needs'. There is a dispute whether it is meaningful to discriminate between types of need, in particular whether there are some needs that are so basic as to constitute a distinct category, where 'basic' signals normative or moral seriousness. This disagreeement bears significantly on economic and political arguments.

Those who make no discrimination argue that *all* need-statements have a similar triadic structure. In White's (1975) version this is expressed abstractly as: A needs V in order to F. That White expresses his point formulaicly is symptomatic of his argument that the triad applies regardless of subject matter: of *any* need it can be asked, what is it for? On this view any normativity resides in the final leg (F) rather than in what is needed (V): I can need a sharp instrument equally to carry out a life-saving operation, to cut my pizza or to slash an Old Master painting.

This view is criticized for depriving needs of their special normative force. In particular, it cannot account for the presence of needs that are 'basic' (or 'fundamental' or 'absolute'). These are needs which are not 'for' anything; they are just needs that need to be possessed. In their case, the triadic formula is unnecessary. The crux of this case is that

> [i]n normal circumstances the questions 'Do you need to survive?' and 'Do you need to avoid serious harm?' are logically inappropriate, because they involve a category mistake akin to the category mistake involved in questions 'Is death fatal?' and 'Is harm harmful?'. (Thomson,1987: 21)

Basic needs are practically necessary and indispensable; there is no alternative, on pain of suffering serious harm, but to obtain what we need fundamentally. Standard examples, which are frequently broken into subsets, are the need to be healthy and the need to be able to function effectively within society. Whether these are all on a par or can themselves be prioritized (as in Maslow's (1943) fivefold hierarchy) is less important than the 'fact' that they can genuinely be said to be objective. More than this they are universal; we all have these needs, they are properties of us generically *qua* humans not *qua* individuals. Whereas we only have some needs because we have some prior want (I need a brush because I want to clean my shoes), basic needs are what we have whether we want them or not.

Seemingly I can do nothing about my basic needs (I just have them) but *my* wants are amenable to my control. My desire for a pint of beer can be amended upon learning that it is flat or upon perceiving cider or upon recalling my resolution to forgo alcohol and so on. More significantly, my sense of who I am is given concrete expression in the realization of my wants — laying down claret, investing for my grandchildren, buying tickets for the 'big match' or the opera, *ad infinitum*. These realizations are not trivial matters; seeing a favourite opera, supporting 'my team' can be important constituents in an individual's 'good life'. Moreover because there is a seemingly infinite variety of such wants, then their realization establishes within society a variety of goods. Wants in this way can be seen to carry normative weight and their recognition underwrites a basic social pluralism.

Although needs and wants can thus both be seen to carry moral weight, the 'principle of precedence' (Braybrooke, 1987) claims that it is morally preferable to meet needs before satisfying wants. For example, food should be given to a starving person before provision is made for clean footwear or public money can properly be disbursed on relieving poverty but not on luxuries. But the force of this 'principle' is contentious. Those who accept the triadic formula can plausibly ask even of the putative basic needs, what are they for? Furthermore once the triadic formula is accepted it follows that all needs are instrumental or conditional — if you (*A*) want *F* then you need *V* — so that, understood in this manner, there is no difference in principle between my need for a brush to clean my shoes and for food to eat. This instrumental quality assimilates this discussion to the notion in marketing theory of a means–end chain (Gutman, 1982). And the conditionality chimes in with the work of economists of the 'Austrian School' such as Menger (1950), as it does also with the related approach of neoclassicists such as Marshall (1961), for whom recourse to objective properties like 'needs' is superfluous since all human actions are effectively explained in terms of meeting 'wants'. Indeed, mainstream 'positive' economics adopts a purely technical approach, such that the difference between a 'necessity' and a 'luxury' lies in their relative elasticity.

The contentiousness of the principle of precedence intimates how this philosophical debate moves into the realm of economics and politics. It is a supposed virtue of markets that they enable me to realize my wants (or preferences) without having to get the permission or approval of others. Money in a market system is an instrumental need to that end but sufficient funds are required to effect this realization. Critics fasten upon this contingency and point out the consequence that in the market system, money is equally an instrumental need to meeting basic nonoptional needs. Accordingly it is a central argument of socialism that these morally significant needs should be exempted from the contingency of market forces and that they should be met, in some manner, by agencies of the State.

This is made prima facie justifiable by trading on the 'objectivity' of needs. It is just some such assumption that is made when food, for example, is exempted from a sales tax. However, this 'use' made of the notion of 'needs' can be criticized for opening the door to paternalism and foreclosing a morally desirable pluralism. Paternalism seems invited because the objectivism of needs can give 'experts' a key role. Experts (doctors, teachers, social workers, inspectors and so on) speak with authority. This authoritativeness attached to the language of need can be used to discount preferences. While the child with a preference for truancy can be compelled to attend school because the need for education is deemed (by the State) more important than honouring (immature) wants, it is less obvious that I as a mature adult should be compelled to undergo the heart surgery that I have been told I need. It is possible that I will have a different order of priorities; I may decide to postpone the operation (in knowledge of the risks involved) in order to realize my desire for a round-the-world cruise. That desire, moreover, as a constituent of my conception of a good life is in its own right morally compelling.

This suggests that while indeed needs and wants may be conceptually separate it does not of itself underwrite the principle of precedence; wants on occasion may legitimately take priority over needs. While food is indeed a basic need (for without it we die), and this is true whatever we might happen to believe, it can, in line with the triadic formula, always be asked of an individual how indispensable it is. 'Food' indeed is not so much quantum of calories as a 'cultural good': a Jew (say) does not just need food, but kosher food and bacon may well be unacceptable even if it is all that is available (even conceivably on pain of starvation).

403

Once even a putatively basic need like food is seen as open to interpretation then the authoritativeness of needs-language is thrown into question. Some take this to mean that it plays a propaganda role in economic or political discourse (Minogue, 1963), while others maintain that needs indeed cannot be divorced from their social setting. This latter view is closely associated with the idea that poverty is relative. According to Townsend, needs are 'the conditions of life which ordinarily define membership of society' (1979: 195) so that it is possible to find more poverty in a wealthy than in a less wealthy country. This conclusion is not paradoxical since Townsend also holds (consistent with a belief in the objectivism of needs) that people may be in poverty when they believe they are not. Attempts have been made to salvage the appropriateness of needs while simultaneously recognizing their cultural form and denying their relativity (see Doyal and Gough, 1991).

But if needs cannot be given automatic priority, and if the realization of wants is itself a source of value, then how the State should act becomes the contended stuff of politics. Liberalism tends to emphasize indirect State action because of its willingness to accept wants as the authentic voice of individual preference as well as because of its inclination to be distrustful of the paternalism of much needs-talk. Liberals thus favour the market as a principle of allocation since resources will (tend to) go where people actually want them to go and certainly will go there with greater efficiency and accuracy than if some expert decides where they need to go. Conversely, socialism tends to emphasize direct State action (identifies more 'merit goods') because of its willingness to assess wants for any self-deception or lack of authenticity as well as because of its inclination to use needs as a basic distributive principle. Socialists thus think that health (a basic need, possessed by everybody) is best provided through a Welfare State, where treatment is free at the point of need and is financed compulsorily out of taxation.

That there is a conceptual difference between needs and wants is clear but that it can used to resolve social questions is less certain.

CHRISTOPHER J. BERRY

Bibliography
Braybrooke, D. (1987) *Meeting Needs*, Princeton, NJ, Princeton University Press.
Doyal, L. and Gough, I. (1991) *A Theory of Human Need*, London, Macmillan.
Gutman, J. (1982) 'A Means–End Chain Model Based on Consumer Categorization Processes', *Journal of Marketing*, **46**: 60–72.
Marshall, A. (1961) *Principles of Economics* (9th edn), London, Macmillan.
Maslow, A. (1943) 'A Theory of Human Motivation', *Psychological Review*, **50**: 370–96.
Menger, C. (1950) *Principles of Economics* (traaslated by J. Dingwall and B.F. Hoselitz,), New York, Free Press (first published in 1871).

Minogue, K. (1963) *The Liberal Mind*, London, Methuen.
Thomson, G. (1987) *Needs*, London, Routledge.
Townsend, P. (1979) *Poverty in the United Kingdom*, Harmondsworth, Penguin Books.
White, A. (1975) *Modal Thinking*, Oxford, Blackwell.

Negotiation

Negotiation is one means for resolving conflicts of interest. The principal goal in negotiations is for two or more individuals (or groups) to determine how resources will be divided between them. The situation has several defining characteristics: (i) the parties are interdependent, that is, the outcome cannot be determined by either party acting alone; (ii) communication between the parties is possible, so that offers and counter-offers are traded; and (iii) the conflict is not ended until both parties agree to a specific settlement. Readily recognizable examples of negotiation include buyer–seller and union–management interactions.

Payoffs and outcomes in negotiation

In its consideration of negotiators' outcomes, negotiation theory draws heavily on game theory, especially in identifying the different payoff structures that are found in negotiations. Paralleling the distinction between zero- and nonzero-sum games, negotiation outcomes are described as either distributive or integrative. *Distributive* (zero-sum) payoffs represent win–lose outcomes. They create situations in which one negotiator can gain only if an opponent loses. A simple example of such a negotiation would be a decision about how to divide $10.00 between two people. As one person's share increases, the other's must decrease. When negotiators face distributive payoffs, their key strategic task is to influence the other person's willingness to give up resources. *Integrative* (nonzero-sum) payoffs create the potential for win–win outcomes. Such outcomes reflect occasions on which it is possible to maximize outcomes for both negotiators. Although negotiators may encounter distributive payoffs, they are far more likely to encounter situations that offer integrative potential. More detailed descriptions of outcome types and the negotiators' dilemma may be found in Lewicki and Litterer (1981) and Lax and Sebenius (1986).

Negotiation basics

Early negotiation research was dominated by a concern for linking readily observable components of the negotiation process to negotiators' outcomes. In particular, this research focused on how the level of initial demands and concession rates influenced negotiators' outcomes. Carnevale and Pruitt (1992), in summarizing this early research, suggest that there is a curvilinear relationship between demands, concessions and outcomes: poor outcomes are obtained either when negotiators are excessively 'soft' (make low initial demands and rapid concessions) or when they are excessively 'hard'. Negotiators whose strategies lie between these extremes obtain better outcomes.

Multiple issues, multiple motives

Typically, negotiations involve multiple issues that are valued differently by the parties to the negotiation. When negotiations hold integrative potential, the situation becomes considerably more complex because negotiators then face two competing pressures. The first dilemma for negotiators is that, to the extent that negotiators value issues differently, they offer integrative potential; to the extent that, at some stage, resources must be divided, they have a distributive component. Consequently, negotiations are frequently described as *mixed motive*: negotiators must choose between competing for the goal of maximizing individual gains and cooperating for the goal of maximizing joint gains. The second dilemma is that either choice has associated risks. Negotiators who choose to cooperate and work for joint gain face the possibility that an uncooperative partner will exploit them; negotiators who choose to compete for individual gain face the possibility that a like-minded partner will create an escalating cycle of conflict that ends in stalemate (Pruitt, 1981). Underlying this dilemma is the classic prisoner's dilemma (see entry on Game Theory).

Negotiating scripts as determinants of strategy

Extending this dilemma to negotiations focuses us on one of the key issues in negotiation research: the need to understand why, when faced with tasks that offer the possibility of maximizing joint gains, individuals frequently behave competitively and work towards maximizing individual gains. In looking for answers, researchers have focused on a sequence in which (i) situational and dispositional variables predispose individuals to either cooperate or compete; (ii) this predisposition influences the strategies that individuals select; and (iii) the choice of either a more competitive or cooperative style of bargaining influences whether individual or joint outcomes are maximized.

Research in this area draws heavily on the concept of scripts (Carroll and Payne, 1991): the idea that negotiators hold specific goals for a negotiation, as well as a set of beliefs about appropriate and inappropriate behaviours. Drawing on the seminal work of Walton and McKersie (1965), negotiation scripts have been categorized as either integrative or distributive. Integrative scripts are associated with a preference for high joint gain, a focus on information exchange, and problem solving. Trust, rather than power, characterizes such relationships and negotiations emphasize affinity and equality. Research has demonstrated clear links between high joint gain when negotiations characterized by more proposals and counterproposals, more agreement with proposals and problem solving. Problem solving is associated with higher levels of priority information exchange and a greater focus on needs, as well as more systematic concessions.

Conversely, distributive scripts are typically associated with a preference for high individual gain, positional arguing, threats and minimal information exchange. Power provides the dominant negotiating dynamic and negotiations emphasize power differences and equity. A key concern of distributive negotiators is to shift the minimum outcome an opponent is prepared to accept, while simultaneously misrepresenting their own bottom line. Tactics such as positional arguing, personal attacks, threats, rejections, and false information, high initial demands with increased pressure to concede, low information exchange and positional commitment have all been shown to lead to distributive outcomes. An excellent summary of the relationship between strategies and negotiated outcomes may be found in Carnevale and Pruitt (1992).

Structural and cognitive influences on strategy selection

Several factors influence whether negotiators hold a competitive or cooperative orientation. Neale and Bazerman (1991) provide an excellent overview of the many situational factors influencing strategy selection.

Foremost among these situational variables is negotiator power. Power is determined by the number of alternatives available to an individual, should a particular negotiation break down: the more available alternatives, the greater the negotiator's power. A well-known example of this type of power is reflected in the description of markets as either buyers' markets or sellers' markets. Power rests with the individual or group that holds the greatest range of alternatives. Contentiousness further increases when negotiators are accountable to others for their outcomes, when there is no expectation of future interactions, and when negotiators are explicitly encouraged to compete.

Three cognitive biases are also known to affect the behaviour of negotiators. The most extensively researched of these is negotiator frame. Negotiators may focus on what they stand to lose (adopt a loss frame) or on what they stand to gain (adopt a gain frame). When they adopt a loss frame, negotiators set a higher bottom line, making higher initial offers and smaller concessions, all suggesting that loss frames support distributive scripts. A gain frame, conversely, leads to more collaborative behaviours and supports an integrative script. Two further beliefs — the fixed-pie error and the incompatibility error — are also more likely to invoke a distributive script. The fixed-pie error describes the commonly held belief that what is most important to me in a negotiation is also most important to you. Because integrative behaviour and the possibility of making tradeoffs relies on negotiators' recognition that the value placed in issues may vary from one negotiator to another, this error, by ruling out the possibility of making trade-

407

offs, results in distributive bargaining. Finally, the incompatibility error blocks recognition of the possibility that both negotiators want the same outcome.

Compared to the research attention given to situational influences on negotiators' strategies, relatively little attention has been paid to dispositional influences. Generally, attempts to link personality variables to negotiating styles and outcomes have been unsuccessful. However, recently a small, but growing, body of research has been focusing on the role of social value orientations and individualism–collectivism in predicting strategy selection and negotiation outcomes. This research uses personality measures to classify individuals on the basis of their preference for maximizing individual or joint outcomes, and on the extent to which they view power and status as key factors in social relationships. Although a new area, this research already indicates that personality is also a powerful influence on the strategies adopted by negotiators and, consequently their outcomes. Extensions of this research take us into the field of cross-cultural negotiation, since several well-known classificatory schemes (Hofstede,1991; Triandis, 1995) also distinguish cultures along these dimensions.

Negotiation from a communication perspective
Parallel to the research described above, a second stream of research has examined in more detail the role of communication in the negotiation process (Putnam, 1990). Two key themes emerge in this research.

The first, focused on phases in the negotiation process, tests the assumption that different behaviours are critical to different stages in the negotiation. Phase models of negotiation separate the negotiation process into three phases. These are *initiation*, during which individuals explore the problem, establish their relationship and define the negotiating range; *problem solving*, in which they adopt a variety of strategies to further define and strengthen their position, to better understand the opponent's position, and to identify a range of possible solutions; and, *resolution*, in which settlement is reached (Holmes, 1992). These models all imply that there will be systematic changes in the tactics that individuals employ as they move through a negotiation. Tactics that represent information exchange, identify and define priorities and limits should dominate the initiation stage, and decrease thereafter. Distributive tactics, aimed at determining how resources will be divided, should show an increase over time and peak in the final resolution phase. Tactics that specifically challenge an opponent's position and support a negotiator's position should be highest in the middle, problem-solving phase.

A second theme deals with how communication sequences define and alter the negotiating context, at the same time as the negotiating context influences the interpretation of ambiguous strategies. According to theorists in this area, negotiating strategies cannot necessarily be classified as either distributive or integrative. Rather, their meaning evolves as a consequence of how and when they are used. Central to this line of thinking is the importance of strategic reciprocity; that is, the extent to which like is met with like. When negotiations are characterized by high levels of distributive reciprocity, a competitive script is invoked; when they are characterized by high levels of integrative reciprocity, a collaborative script is invoked. These scripts, in turn, serve to guide the interpretation of polysemous strategies. Included in this second group are: threats, which may serve to escalate conflict or be interpreted as signalling firmness; information exchange, which may be an attempt to gain a unilateral advantage or a means for discovering underlying needs and values; procedural suggestions, which may be a means for gaining process control or a means to a more collaborative style of bargaining; and concessions, which may signal yielding to another's demands or a willingness to collaborate. Research in this area has linked not only strategic reciprocity but also specific strategic sequences to the quality of negotiated outcomes.

Principled negotiations
In 1981, Fisher and Ury introduced the notion of principled bargaining. Their idea captures the essence of integrative negotiation and provides a series of steps for maximizing joint gain. The thrust of their recommendations is based on the assumption that negotiations go wrong when negotiators invest energy in managing their opponent rather than explicitly tackling the conflict. Their recommendations suggest that negotiators should start by ensuring that they are focused on the problem or conflict. Negotiators should then look beneath the presenting positions of their opponents to understand the needs that have led to specific claims. One way of achieving this is to offer an explanation of why a particular solution seems desirable to you. When both negotiators offer such explanations, their understanding of underlying needs increases. It then becomes possible to tailor make a solution to meet both parties' needs.

Summary
Negotiation theory has moved from a consideration of the 'mechanics' of negotiating — such factors as initial demands and concession rates — to a consideration of the broader context in which negotiation occurs. The next step, reflecting dominant concerns in psychology, was to consider how a range of cognitive and structural variables influenced the negotiating process and outcomes. This resulted in the identification of two negotiating styles, one competitive or distributive; the other cooperative or integrative. More recently, attention has turned to the role of communication in shaping interpretations of an opponent's behaviour. The communication perspective has been influential in identifying the multiple meanings conveyed by strategies, and the role of timing

and sequencing in unscrambling that meaning.

MARA OLEKALNS

Bibliography

Carnevale, P.J. and Pruitt, D.G. (1992) 'Negotiation and Mediation', *Annual Review of Psychology*, **43**: 531–82.

Carroll, J.S. and Payne, J.W. (1991) 'An Information Processing Approach to Two-Party Negotiations', *Research on Negotiation in Organizations*, **3**.

Fisher, R. and Ury, W. (1981) *Getting to Yes: Negotiating Agreement Without Giving In*, London, Arrow Press.

Hofstede, G. (1991) *Culture and Organizations: Software of the Mind*, London, McGraw-Hill.

Holmes, M.E. (1992) 'Phase Structures in Negotiation', in Putnam, L.L. and Roloff, M.E. (eds) *Communication and Negotiation*, Newbury Park, CA, Sage.

Lax, D. and Sebenius, J. (1986) *The Manager as Negotiator*, New York, Free Press.

Lewicki, R.J. and Litterer, J.A. (1985) *Negotiation*, Homewood, IL, Irwin.

Neale, M.A. and Bazerman, M.H. (1991) *Cognition and Rationality in Negotiation*, New York, Free Press.

Pruitt, D.G. (1981) *Negotiation Behavior*, New York, Academic Press.

Putnam, L.L. (1990) 'Reframing Integrative and Distributive Bargaining: A Process Perspective', *Research on Negotiation in Organizations*, **2**: 3–30

Triandis, H.C. (1995) *Individualism and Collectivism*, Boulder, CO, Westview Press.

Walton, R.E. and McKersie, R.B. (1965) *A Behavioral Theory of Labor Negotiations: An Analysis of a Social Interaction System*, Ithaca, NY, ILR Press.

Organizational Culture and Profitability

Is organizational culture one of the keys to financial performance? Many organizations invest in culture development with an expectation of a return on their investment. Resources are allocated to, for example, induction programmes for new employees, and the development of symbols and rituals aimed at creating a collective feeling of belonging. Behaviours and attitudes viewed as appropriate are 'shaped' by formal and informal processes with the aim of strengthening the cultural identity of the workforce and the organization. Often the assumption driving such expenditure is that an appropriate or strong organizational culture will increase morale, commitment, cooperation and coordination, which will ultimately improve goal achievement and financial performance. This entry examines research and debate on this functionalist perspective of organizational culture.

Organizational culture can be defined by way of the mechanisms through which it is expressed. For example, material symbols — the gleaming office tower, the chauffeur-driven limousines for executives, and the corporate jet — symbolize perhaps success and quality. Similarly, annual rituals, such as the Mary Kay Cosmetics annual award meeting, can convey the organization's values, in this case achievement. Less obvious means of transmitting culture are the stories that are passed from employee to employee, the use of organization specific language, and the written and unwritten rules which guide employee behaviour.

Underlying these expressions of culture are attitudes and values. The degree to which an organization's members can be defined by a prescribed set of attitudes and values, and the degree to which their behaviour expresses these attitudes and values is viewed by some as a measure of the strength of its culture. Given the conformity implied by these definitional components it is not difficult to see why managers assume that culture must be linked in some way to performance.

Organizational culture can also be expressed and defined by management's approach to key processes, such as labour division, control, coordination, conflict, careers and so on. This approach has tended to lead to the classification and labelling of culture types. For example, Poupart and Hobbs (1989) describe the characteristics of the 'father-founder', 'bureaucratic', 'participative', 'professional' and 'managerial-entrepreneurial' cultures. Along similar lines, Jeffrey Sonnenfold of Emory University has developed a labelling schema which uses the terms 'academy', 'club', 'baseball team' and 'fortress' (Hymowitz, 1989).

One example of a cultural classification which has received considerable attention is the Japanese management style. Often the contrast between the

Japanese style and organizational culture (management practices) in Western countries focuses on the considerable influence which the Japanese culture (that is, a society characterized by racial homogeneity, uniform education, team orientation and a spirit of cooperation) has on management styles. The Japanese approach has led to many innovative developments (for example, just-in-time production, and continuous training) which reflect key values, and which arguably have produced economic benefits. Based on Japan's apparent success, should every organization seek gains through the development of its culture?

Siehl and Martin (1990) provide a useful review of empirical studies which have examined the link between culture and organizational performance. Their review classifies the empirical work into one of three perspectives which might be termed the strong-culture thesis (Alvesson, 1993), the culture effect model, and the contingency perspective. Studies that have investigated the strong-culture thesis predict that having the appropriate type of strong culture, as indicated by commitment of employees and managers to the same set of values, beliefs and norms, will be causally linked with profitability (see Denison, 1984). Siehl and Martin conclude that little empirical support has been found for the strong-culture thesis.

Research adopting the culture-effect model also assumes a direct link between culture components and performance, but the direction of causality is reversed. It is predicted that an organization's performance level in part influences its culture. For example, a period of excellent performance can provide excess resources, which can be directed towards developing a particular cultural attribute (for example, humanistic values). Furthermore, in some industries improved performance may be associated with image problems (for example, erosion from deforestation, air pollution, exploitation of labour) and resources may be directed into publications (for example, annual reports) in an attempt to portray themes which improve public perception. Again, evidence supporting these types of relationships is scarce.

The remaining empirical work takes a contingency view where it is argued that the culture must be appropriate to the business strategy for performance to benefit. Specifically, an organization is suggested to have poor performance prospects if its culture is in conflict with its management strategies. Again, conclusive evidence supporting this view is hard to find, although it should be noted that few studies have examined the link between culture and performance from this perspective. Thus Siehl and Martin (1990) conclude that there is little empirical support for any form of relationship between organizational culture and performance. This is also the general conclusion of a review by Calori and Sarnin (1991).

Lack of empirical support for some form of link between culture and performance does not necessarily mean that such links do not exist.

Methodological problems with past research efforts and the difficulties of researching in this area, which all studies must overcome, may explain the plethora of nil results. An inference which can be drawn from definitions of organizational culture is that it is not easily measured. The complexity of organizational culture necessitates research measures which give representation to a large number of varied components. Also important is the issue of how each culture component is weighted in a measurement system. For example, should an organization which does not have a readily recognizable symbol be viewed as having a weak culture? Or can other culture-related factors compensate for the lack of a corporate symbol? From this reasoning it is obvious that equitable measurement of culture across organizations which might be measured as performing at different levels can be difficult. Furthermore, reduction in breadth of a culture measure in order to facilitate sampling may reduce the richness of the data to the point where the value of the results must be questioned. Of course if one subscribes to the contingency model, comparable measures across organizations may not be appropriate. Measures of financial parameters also pose problems and rarely take account of variables such as organization size, market competitiveness and the economy.

Saffold (1988) identifies methodological problems as but one of the possible reasons why the intuitively appealing link between organizational culture and performance is not routinely identified. Other reasons offered by Saffold include: (i) that the focus has been on measurement of a single strong culture, whereas multiple subcultures may be operating within any one organization; (ii) culture strength is difficult to measure and a broad classification of cultural strength may not be capturing the important variance; and (iii) there are numerous ways in which culture and performance can be linked and generally only a subset is examined. Saffold also discusses how future research efforts might be improved.

Alvesson (1993) offers a somewhat different classification system for the literature on organizational culture and performance. His classification is based on the emphasis that theoretical accounts of organizational culture place on instrumental values. The extreme perspective views culture as providing meaning, focus, force, direction, and energy to an employee's work efforts. In other words, culture is directly instrumental in the determination of work behaviour and its effectiveness. This view can be criticized for its generality and failure to incorporate research on the many other variables which can determine work performance.

The second perspective outlined by Alvesson views culture as a management tool, which can be manipulated to enhance and maintain a favourable situation. Many factors, including external environmental forces, are assumed to have a significant influence on work behaviour and culture functions to solidify and stabilize this behaviour. For example, the development of a highly skilled team is partly determined by selection predictor validity, and coordination between team members may be enhanced through a team-building workshop, whereas focused application of skills and coordinated effort towards an organizational goal may be achieved through culture management.

The third perspective discussed by Alvesson views culture as being somewhat rigid and resistant to manipulation. However, its existence needs to be acknowledged and its parameters understood in order to identify how it does and will restrict management efforts. Here considerable emphasis is placed on how external factors, such as local culture and traditions, determine organizational culture and the importance of understanding these. Such customs and traditions may define certain management initiatives as appropriate and others as inappropriate. From this an understanding of culture-appropriate action may lead to better performance. For example, a Western company seeking to develop a business in Japan would be well advised to consider carefully how its management style could be adapted to suit the Japanese culture.

In conclusion, it would be harsh indeed to suggest that past failures should be used to justify a reduction of research on the links between organizational culture and performance. It may, however, be timely to caution against large investments in cultural engineering. Despite the lack of empirical support for a strong link between culture and performance, the literature contains a number of papers describing how performance advantages might be gained from 'culture engineering'. For example, Barney (1986; also see Poupart and Hobbs, 1989; Schneider, 1995) suggests that to be a source of sustained competitive advantage, an organization's culture must be valuable in that it generally improves outputs and/or reduces inputs, is rare or relatively unique, and imperfectly imitable such that other organizations cannot easily and quickly imitate its characteristics. Perhaps it might be judicious to invest energy and resources into management activities with careful consideration of their impact on culture, rather than assuming that investment in culture development will enhance management performance.

CHRISTOPHER D.B. BURT

Bibliography

Alvesson, M. (1993) *Cultural Perspectives on Organizations*, Cambridge, Cambridge University Press.

Barney, J.B. (1986) 'Organizational Culture: Can It Be a Source of Sustained Competitive Advantage?', *Academy of Management Review*, **11**: 656–65.

Calori, R. and Sarnin, P. (1991) 'Corporate Culture and Economic Performance', *Organization Studies*, **12**: 49–74.

Denison, D. (1984) 'Bringing Corporate Culture to the Bottom Line', *Organizational Dynamics*, **13**: 4–22.

Denison, D. (1990) *Corporate Culture and Organizational Effectiveness*, New York, John Wiley & Sons.

Hymowitz, C. (1989) 'Which Culture Fits You?', *Wall Street Journal*, 17 July: B1.

Kotter, J. and Heskett, J. (1992) *Corporate Culture and Performance*, New York, Free Press.

Poupart, R. and Hobbs, B. (1989) 'Changing the Corporate Culture to Ensure Success: A Practical Guide', *Nation Productivity Review*, **8**: 223–38.

Saffold, G.S. (1988) 'Culture Traits, Strength, and Organizational Performance: Moving Beyond "Strong" Culture', *Academy of Management Review*, **13**: 546–58.

Schneider, W.E. (1995) 'Productivity Improvement Through Cultural Focus, *Consulting Psychology Journal: Practice and Research*, **47**: 3–27.

Siehl, C. and Martin, J. (1990) 'Organizational Culture: A Key to Financial Performance?', in Schneider, B. (ed.) *Organizational Climate and Culture*, San Francisco, CA, Jossey-Bass: 241–81.

Perceived Quality

How do consumers decide what a product or service is worth? Consumer researchers address this question under the banner of 'perceived quality', by which they mean a global assessment of a product's superiority on dimensions that the consumer considers important. Perceived quality is different from 'objective' or 'actual' quality in that perceptions of quality are subjective judgements whereas actual quality is based on an objective standard of measurable, verifiable superiority. In practice, there appears to be little correlation between perceived and objective product quality (Lichtenstein and Burton, 1989). However, there may be differences in the extent of correlation depending on whether the product is a search good (one for which quality can be determined during search, for example, clothing), an experience good (one for which quality is only discernible through consumption, for example, movies or restaurants), or a credence good (one for which quality is not discernible even after consumption, for example, automobile repairs or surgery). If perceived quality does not reflect actual quality, on what is it based?

Consumers' perceptions of quality are based on intrinsic and extrinsic quality cues (Olson, 1977). Intrinsic cues are inherent to the product composition. They cannot be altered without changing the nature of the product. For example, the body styling of an automobile, its fuel economy and engine size are intrinsic cues. On the other hand, extrinsic cues are part of the augmented product and can be changed without altering the nature of the product. Advertising, price, brand name, reputation of the retailer carrying the product, and warranties, are all examples of extrinsic cues.

Consumers often rely on extrinsic cues to assess quality when they are unable or unwilling to determine product quality through an examination of the intrinsic cues. The complexity of products, and consumers' lack of technical knowledge or other resources contribute to an inability to assess product quality based on intrinsic features. Low perceived risk, lack of time, or low price may contribute to a lack of motivation to engage in an examination of intrinsic quality cues. As a result, consumers often rely on heuristics involving extrinsic cues to determine product quality. For example, the use of the 'you get what you pay for' heuristic uses a presumed positive correlation between price and quality as a means of assessing product quality.

Similarly, large advertising expenditures, high warranty levels and a good retailer reputation, have all been shown to operate as indicators of product quality (Bearden and Shimp, 1982; Boulding and Kirmani, 1993; Kirmani and Wright, 1989). The literature has suggested a hierarchy of extrinsic cue use (Dawar and Parker, 1994). Effect size for brand name tends to be larger than that for price which in turn is larger than other cues. Nevertheless, when presented together in an experimental environment, the various cues tend to cumulate rather than suppress each other when they are consistent (Rao and Monroe, 1989). For example, price-perceived quality effects are larger in the presence of brand information. However, when cues are not consistent, they may lead to lower-quality perceptions than simple additivity might suggest. For example, a high warranty offered by an unknown brand with low credibility might not be believed and lead to a 'too-good-to-be-true' effect, resulting in extremely low perceived quality (Boulding and Kirmani, 1993).

Individual differences in the use of different types of cues have also been identified. Findings suggest that consumers' prior knowledge plays a determining role in both the extent to which extrinsic versus intrinsic cues are used, as well as the accuracy of cue use (Rao and Monroe, 1988). Specifically, consumers who are moderately familiar with the product category or at the early stages of learning the covariation between the cue and quality, tend to use cues accurately, while those unfamiliar or highly familiar are less accurate. It appears that consumers develop schemas about the relationship or covariation between a cue and product quality (Peterson and Wilson, 1985). The extent to which the schema is used to interpret a cue may depend on prior knowledge or familiarity with the product category. For example, consumers unfamiliar with a product category may not have a schema within which to interpret cues. Highly familiar consumers, on the other hand, may neglect available information and rely entirely on their schema to assess product quality, despite the fact that highly familiar consumers are the ones most able to rely on intrinsic cues to assess quality. Familiarity with products allows consumers to focus on the appropriate intrinsic attributes and interpret them correctly, while less familiar consumers are unable to do so for lack of knowledge (Rao and Monroe, 1988). For example, when purchasing a computer, an expert is able to interpret the meaning and benefits of attributes such as CPU speed and memory size, while a novice is unable to rely on these intrinsic attributes for lack of knowledge about them, and may instead use extrinsic cues.

Understanding of consumers' perceptions of quality has more recently been supplemented by empirical examinations of economic signaling theory assumptions and predictions in experimental studies (Boulding and Kirmani, 1993; Kirmani and Wright, 1989; Dawar and Sarvary, 1997). Like previous consumer research, economic signaling theory suggests that consumers use extrinsic cues in arriving at perceptions of quality. For example, warranties have been shown to operate as an effective signal of quality for both firms and consumers. However, economic signalling theory describes signal use as part of an elaborate integration with other market-related information which consumers undertake in order to infer the veracity and credibility of the signal from which product quality is inferred. For example, a long warranty may be interpreted by consumers to indicate high quality because the firm would suffer financially if warranty claims were to be redeemed. However, this straightforward signal may or may not be credible depending on the extent to which consumers believe that the firm will be in existence when its warranties may need to be redeemed: a long warranty offered by a firm that looks as though it might be a fly-by-night operator may appear 'too good to be true' and may, therefore, be discounted, in contrast to one offered by a firm that has been in business for many years (Boulding and Kirmani, 1993). This elaborate inferencing which is assumed on the part of players in a signalling game (including consumers) is in sharp contrast with the simplifying, heuristic role which quality cues are assumed to play in consumer research. Empirical findings from consumer behaviour experiments testing signalling theory assumptions have not been universally consistent, with some studies supporting economic signalling theory, and others suggesting boundary conditions.

While the focus of research has traditionally been on consumers' use of quality cues, there is a growing literature on the consequences of perceived quality. This echoes, at least implicitly, the seminal work on price-quality judgements by Scitovsky (1945). Among other thing, he raised the possibility that rich shoppers might be too busy to engage in extensive search and hence be more prone to rely on price as an indicator of quality. This could enable firms to engage in price discrimination and, in ignorance, the rich could end up paying more than necessary in order to obtain goods of a particular level of objective quality. Hence there might be a smaller difference between the standards of living of rich and poor consumers than would be assessable based simply on their income differences. Much the same might be said nowadays in respect of consequences of spending by affluent consumers on expensive 'designer' brands, where reliance is placed on the label for a quick and peer-acceptable judgement of quality. Recent work recognizes, more generally, that perceptions of quality have consequences in terms of consumers' willingness to pay a premium, customer loyalty, and at the firm level, higher returns on investment, as well as greater shareholder wealth (for example, Aaker and Jacobson, 1994; see also the entry on Brand Equity in the present volume). This approach to perceived quality takes a macro rather than micro focus, in which aggregate data on perceptions of quality are correlated with profitablity or stock returns.

An understanding of the antecedents, formation processes and consequences of perceived quality is central to consumer research because these phenomena address how consumers assess what a product or service is worth. Perceived quality lies at the heart of consumer choice processes.

NIRAJ DAWAR

Bibliography
Aaker, D.A. and Jacobson, R. (1994) 'The Financial Information Content of Perceived Quality', *Journal of Marketing Research*, **31**: 191–201.
Bearden, W.O. and Shimp, T.A. (1982) 'The Use of Extrinsic Cues to Facilitate Product Adoption', *Journal of Marketing Research*, **19**: 229–39.
Boulding, W. and Kirmani, A. (1993) 'A Consumer-Side Experimental Examination of Signaling Theory: Do Consumers Perceive Warranties as Signals of Quality?', *Journal of Consumer Research*, **20**: 111–23.
Dawar, N. and Parker, P. (1994) 'Marketing Universals: Consumers' Use of Brand Name, Price, Physical Appearance, and Retailer Reputation as Signals of Product Quality', *Journal of Marketing*, **58**: 81–95.
Dawar, N. and Sarvary, M. (1997) 'The Signaling Impact of Low Introductory Price on Perceived Quality and Trial', *Marketing Letters*, **8** (3): 251–60.
Kirmani, A. and Wright, P. (1989) 'Money Talks: Perceived Advertising Expense and Expected Product Quality', *Journal of Consumer Research*, **16**: 344–53.
Lichtenstein, D.R. and Burton, S. (1989) 'The Relationship Between Perceived and Objective Price–Quality', *Journal of Marketing Research*, **26**: 429–43.
Olson, J.C. (1977) 'Price as an Informational Cue: Effects on Product Evaluations', in Woodside, A.G., Sheth, J.N. and Bennett, P.D. (eds) *Consumer and Industrial Buying Behavior*, New York, North Holland Publishing Company: 267–86.
Peterson, R.A. and Wilson, W.R. (1985) 'Perceived Risk andPrice-Reliance Schema as Price-Perceived-Quality Mediators', in Jacoby, J. and Olson, J.C. (eds) *Perceived Quality: How Consumers View Stores and Merchandise*, Lexington, MA. Lexington Books: 247–68.
Rao, A.R. and Monroe, K.B. (1988) 'The Moderating Effect of Prior Knowledge on Cue Utilization in Product Evaluations', *Journal of Consumer Research*, **15**: 253–64.
Rao, A.R. and Monroe, K.B. (1989) 'The Effect of Price, Brand Name, and Store Name on Buyers' Perceptions of Product Quality: An Integrative Review', *Journal of Marketing Research*, **26**: 351–7.
Scitovsky, T. (1945) 'Some Consequences of the Habit of Judging Quality by Price', *Review of Economics Studies*, **12**: 100–105.

Perceived Risk

The concept of risk is one of the most pervasive in theories of human choice. Economists, decision theorists and psychologists often include risk as a fundamental element of their normative and descriptive theories. Not surprisingly, researchers and practitioners interested in consumer decision making have also studied how consumers perceive the risk of different products and services, and the strategies which they use to handle such perceived risk. Across these four areas of inquiry, there have been thousands of studies conducted which provide insight into how this construct effects consumer decision making.

An overview of such a rich and complex area of inquiry must be highly selective. Here, the focus is on risk perception and handling within the context of how consumers evaluate and choose products and services. To ground the discussion in its broader theoretical context, I first briefly describe the approach to studying risk in decision theory and some of the reasons why consumer researchers have adopted a different approach to measuring perceived risk. Then a model of risk perception and handling is presented which is used to integrate various streams of consumer research.

Alternative research traditions
Traditionally, decision theorists classify decision making as occurring in one of three types of situations: certainty, risk or uncertainty. The critical aspect which distinguishes these three situations is the decision maker's degree of knowledge about the outcome of a particular course of action. If the outcome is known, the decision is said to take place under certainty. Risky decisions occur when more than one outcome is possible from a particular course of action and the probability of each outcome is known, or can be computed actuarially. Uncertain decisions are characterized by multiple outcomes for each alternative action (some of which may be unknown to the decision maker), and the probabilities of these outcomes are not known. It is the characteristics of this type of decision situation which define most consumer purchase decisions — incomplete information, personal preferences and subjective perceptions.

Consumer researchers use the concept of perceived risk in uncertain decision-making situations — a somewhat confusing use of the term for people schooled in decision theory. The reason for this usage however, can be traced to researchers at Harvard University in the 1960s (Cox, 1967). This group (loosely) defined perceived risk in terms of the uncertainty of the possible adverse consequences which a person thinks will attach to buying or using a product. No specific guidelines were provided about how the construct should be measured. Consequently, consumer researchers who were unaware of, or who chose to ignore, the work in decision theory have measured risk perception in a variety of ways. (For a review, see Dowling, 1986.)

This conceptual fuzziness had a positive and a negative outcome. On the positive side, a new group of researchers experimented with a variety of new measures which were more sympathetic to the way consumer research was, and still is conducted, namely, through short, self-completed or interviewer-administered questionnaires. The traditional way in which decision theorists and psychologists measured a person's disposition to risk was very cumbersome in such applied research settings (for example, see Keeney and Raiffa, 1976; Payne, 1973). On the negative side, many researchers in decision theory and consumer behaviour ignore each other's research. Hence, findings in these two streams of research often go unnoticed in the other research tradition.

The concept of risk

Dictionaries typically define risk in terms of 'the exposure to the chance of injury or loss'. These three components are found in most studies of consumers' risk perception. Exposure is via the purchase or use of a product or service. The chance element is captured by the consumer's subjective assessment of the outcomes of the purchase. For fresh innovations, these assessments can be poorly calibrated because there is little information available, and/or it is of poor quality. Outcomes are typically losses rather than losses and gains. A variety of these losses (and gains) have traditionally been measured: financial, social, performance, psychological, physical and convenience (for example, Peter and Tarpey, 1975). In order to be able to compare losses across people with different levels of monetary wealth (for financial losses) and self-confidence (for other types of loss), most consumer researchers ask the respondent how important such a loss would be.

A fundamental issue in this research tradition is how much of the level of perceived risk is intrinsic to the person and how much is driven by other factors. Traditionally there has been a widespread assumption in many social sciences that most people are risk averse most of the time. Exceptions occur, the most notable being when gambling, especially when playing with 'house money' (that is, just after a win). In consumer-purchase situations we also see that people often exhibit risk-seeking behaviour when buying inexpensive new products. While both these examples can be interpreted as instances of low perceived risk (because the relative amount of the loss is small), they can just as easily be interpreted as deliberate attempts to accept higher than necessary levels of risk. There has been little work by consumer researchers to determine which is the better explanation.

Psychologists have also observed that people may be more risk averse in order to secure a potential gain and more risk seeking to avoid a potential loss (for example, Kahneman and Tversky, 1979). A popular explanation for this effect is that of framing, that is, presenting the same information as a loss or a gain can affect its interpretation. In addition to this decision-making bias, consumer researchers argue that people's perception of different levels of risk for the same product is due to (i) the different levels of wealth, and thus the importance of the loss across respondents, (ii) characteristics of the product (for example, cost, degree of newness and so on), (iii) involvement of the person with the product and/or the purchase, (iv) the knowledge and experience of the person with this type of product (an uncertainty effect), (v) the reason for purchase (for example, personal use or as a gift), (vi) the situation in which the purchase takes place (for example, a flea market versus a retailer with a liberal returns policy),

(vii) the social visibility of the product and the motivation to comply with social norms (for example, fashion clothing), (viii) the ability of the person to reduce initial levels of perceived risk (for example, by acquiring more information), and (ix) the inherent disposition to accept risk by the person (that is, a trait effect). Hence, perceived risk is best modelled within a contingency framework. The relative contribution of each source of variance, however, is still unclear.

Figure 1 integrates the determinants of risk perception identified above (namely, personal and situational factors) with the assessment of risk ('Is the overall level of perceived risk acceptable?') and the major consequences of different levels of risk (attempts to reduce perceived risk and (non)consideration of the product). Dowling and Staelin (1994) provide support for part of this process model of risk perception and handling.

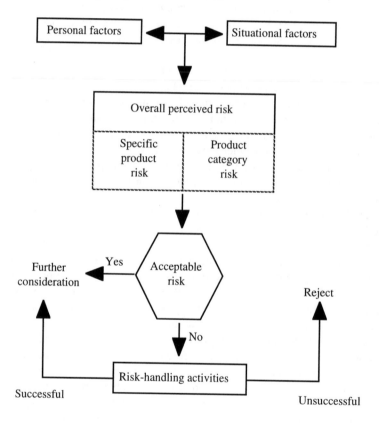

Figure 1: Risk perception and handling

Figure 1 is initialized when the consumer first decides to evaluate a product. The basic premise is that the various personal and situational factors identified earlier combine to produce an overall level of risk perception. Consumer researchers have yet to articulate how these factors combine to form this overall level of perceived risk, although it is possible to manipulate some of them to vary levels of perceived risk (for example, Dowling and Staelin, 1994). The overall level of perceived risk can be decomposed into two parts — one which is specific to the product being evaluated and the other which emanates from the characteristics of the product category (for example, Bettman, 1973). The reason for this is that some brands in a product category are riskier than others and some product categories with products of a similar value are riskier than others (personal computers versus televisions).

The overall level of perceived risk is compared against the individual's threshold risk tolerance. If it is acceptable, then the product will be considered further (for example, via a cost–benefit analysis). If the risk level is too high, then the consumer may activate one or more risk-handling activities. Some of these will be aimed at reducing the risk of the product category (for example, take a knowledgeable friend when buying a new model PC) and some the specific brand (for example, look for an independent quality certification). Again, the use of these risk-handling strategies will be subject to personal cost–benefit considerations. In effect, the risk threshold defines a noncompensatory choice heuristic.

After an initial flurry of research activity which lasted until the mid-1980s, interest by consumer researchers in the study of risk perception has waned. One possible reason for this is that the accurate measurement of perceived risk and risk–reduction activities is a difficult task. Another reason is that the two variables interact. For example, as consumers shop they update their store of information and thus their perception of risk. The measurement of the effects of perceived risk on product choice is also difficult. Here, the key issue is how to conceptualize and measure the threshold level of risk which triggers consumer action. Measurement issues aside, this is an area which can still provide useful insights into consumer behaviour.

GRAHAME R. DOWLING

Bibliography

Bettman, J.R. (1973) 'Perceived Risk and Its Components: A Model and Empirical Test', *Journal of Marketing Research*, **10**: 184–90.

Cox, D.E. (ed.) (1967) *Risk Taking and Information Handling in Consumer Behavior*, Boston, MA, Harvard University Press.

Dowling, G.R. (1986) 'Perceived Risk: The Concept and Its Measurement', *Psychology and Marketing*, **3**: 193–210.

Dowling, G.R. and Staelin, R. (1994) 'A Model of Perceived Risk and Intended Risk-Handling Activity', *Journal of Consumer Research*, **21**: 119–34.

Kahneman, D. and Tversky, A. (1979) 'Prospect Theory: An Analysis of Decision Under Risk', *Econometrica*, **47**: 263–91.

Keeney, R.L. and Raiffa, H. (1976) *Decisions with Multiple Objectives: Preferences and Value Tradeoffs*, New York, Wiley.

Payne, J.W. (1973) 'Alternative Approaches to Decision Making Under Risk: Moments Versus Risk Dimensions', *Psychological Bulletin*, **80**: 439–53.

Peter, J.P. and Tarpey, L.X. (1975) 'A Comparative Analysis of Three Consumer Decision Strategies', *Journal of Consumer Research*, **2**: 29–37.

Personal Construct Theory

Personal construct theory (PCT) was developed during the early 1950s by George Kelly, a clinician and professor of psychology at Ohio State University. His dual role was vital in the development of his view of the nature of the human condition. In an 'afternoon with the obvious' (recalled in Kelly, 1969: 60–1), he had been alternating between advising postgraduates about their studies and counselling patients. He suddenly realized that the two roles were not particularly different: the students were trying to cope as scientists and the patients were trying to find a better way of coping with life. In both cases, his role seemed to be to find out how they were construing their situations — either their goals or their means towards reaching them — and then suggest an alternative way of looking at things that might be more appropriate. Both groups were troubled by their limited capacities for predicting and controlling events, although the 'events' in question ranged diversely from the progress of their dissertations to their own conduct and interactions with others. From this comparison, Kelly made the creative leap of suggesting that people in general should be seen 'as if they are scientists', formulating and testing hypotheses in particular parts of the broad laboratory of life.

This perspective has much in common with attribution theory and the literature on lay economic beliefs. What is different is the thoroughness with which Kelly (1955) developed it: he produced a massive two-volume work that included both an elaborate yet rigorously stated theory-in-words (subsequently republished separately as Kelly, 1963) and a novel approach to investigating how people see the world — known as repertory grid technique — which has subsequently been used very widely in social and business research (compare Stewart and Stewart, 1981). Central to PCT is the idea that the universe does not tell us how to interpret it; the world is what we make it and our individuality arises from differences in our methodological perspectives. Barriers to changing these perspectives lend durability to our personalities and make social life predictable in some degree. Overlaps between individuals in their (sometimes dysfunctional) ways of construing events enable clinicians both to work with each other professionally and to reach diagnoses about their patients. When applied to marketing problems, the presence of broad similarities in worldviews enables psychographic researchers to segment markets into manageable stereotypical lifestyle groupings.

Kelly's theory begins with the notion that although the universe is really an evolving, tangled web of great complexity, people normally cope with it adequately by treating it 'as if' it is a decomposable system and constructing mental models of parts abstracted from the whole. The template-like constructs are then tested for their fit with events as the latter unfold. PCT consists of a fundamental postulate — 'A person's processes are psychologically channelized by the ways in which he anticipates events' (Kelly, 1963: 46) — which is elaborated with the aid of eleven corollaries. In essence, people are seen as constantly seeking to pigeonhole or stereotype things appropriately on a 'compare and contrast' basis to determine what they 'are like': from the standpoint of PCT, the act of diagnosing a personality disorder in a clinical setting has much in common with the act of sizing up untried consumer durables or holiday experiences. Construing is done in terms of limited numbers of bipolar construct axes, although in some areas of their lives people may develop an ability to view events in terms of surprisingly large numbers of constructs. People organize these constructs in complex hierarchical structures that assign directions of causality: for example, 'We'll need to move to a bigger house *if* grandma has to move in, *but* we'll have trouble selling the present one *unless* we renovate it first'. These structures may be open to revision as evidence is gathered, but they may also inhibit learning since some peripheral constructs may be constrained to match 'core constructs' — such as ways of construing one's self — which are used as building blocks for many of one's expectations. The possibility that resistance to changes of mind depends on how people organize their constructs was investigated by Kelly's student Hinkle (1965) in an unpublished PhD thesis that is widely discussed in the major secondary sources such as Adams-Webber (1979) and Bannister and Fransella (1986). Some things may simply be impossible to believe in terms of a given construct system — including even the suggestion that there might be a less dysfunctional way of looking at the world.

Although Kelly's work was concerned with the growth of knowledge, he preferred to speak of people 'reconstructing their experiences' rather than 'learning'. He emphasized that how much we discover depends on how demanding are the questions we ask of the situations we encounter, how brittle we dare to make our hypotheses. Particular methodological rules for coping with life may be arrived at from different starting positions: for example, one may come to see merits in vegetarianism for ethical or health reasons, or both. For successful social interactions to occur — whether in households, in politics (Theodoulou, 1996), or in marketing — people may need to have similar ways of construing the situation at hand.

Scope for seeing where the other person 'is coming from' is limited by difficulties in inferring the underlying structures of his or her construct system; indeed, even in the context of research, Kelly's repertory grid technique and Hinkle's extensions of it, although illuminating, are very time-consuming to implement. Adherents to PCT tend to follow the maxim, 'If you want to understand the basis for someone's actions, ask them' — unlike behaviourists and positivists who are prone to construe direct inquiry as inferior to observation because they construe subjects as possibly having good reason to conceal their true thought processes. However, Kellians construe the open-ended research methods of PCT as well-suited to reducing risks that relevant data will fail to be gathered; observations are limited by not merely by what can be observed but also by preconceptions about what subjects see as significant.

PCT was introduced to economics by Brian Loasby (1983) and Peter Earl (1983a), then both of Stirling University, at the 1981 conference of the British Association for the Advancement of Science, as part of a bid to reestablish subjectivism in economics. They had discovered Kelly's thinking via Charles Suckling, a senior executive at ICI and visiting professor at Stirling, who had found PCT useful for thinking about practical problem solving. Loasby's paper concentrated on the application of PCT to understanding limits to learning within firms. He particularly focused on Kelly's notion of 'construct permeability': an organization needs a durable set of core ways of looking at the world if it is to endure as a coordinating agency — standardized, 'conventional' ways of pigeonholing things can result in rapid processing of information, rather than each piece of news leading decision makers back to first principles — but these blinkers may prevent it from seeing some opportunities or threats to its existence. Management consultants and new staff hired from outside provide fresh perspectives that may facilitate change, in so far as the new ideas can be packaged in ways that permeate existing modes of thought.

While Earl (1984) followed Loasby in using PCT to understand problems of change in firms, his early work focused primarily on constructing a Kellian perspective on consumer behaviour (Earl, 1983b, 1986). Kelly's repertory grid research methods had already been widely used for understanding how consumers and managers think, but the opportunity to look at consumption as if it is an experimental, knowledge-enhancing activity had not been picked up. Many leisure activities entail gathering information and making sense of it, whether in relation to prior hypotheses — such that one may experience delight or disappointment as data are gathered — or by trying to frame experiences, either 'on the run' or reflectively. Often these activities enable us to test ourselves in terms of our capabilities at prediction and control. Many household gadgets can be seen as devices for stopping the forces of entropy from taking over: if someone expects his or her house to look like a show-home, there are plenty of products that can be used to prevent it from looking like a tip. Convenience products basically make life easier to manage: they reduce the skill one needs (and the time needed away from other pressing activities) to produce, say, a particular meal. Clothing and cosmetics products assist those seeking to create particular images of themselves in the eyes of others. In trying, as conspicuous or withdrawing consumers, to create such images we test the robustness of our theories of what kinds of people we are, and possibly increase at the same time our control over some situations (for example, people take us seriously because of how we look, or find us interesting as potential partners).

To make sense of directions of choice, Earl drew both on Kelly's suggestions about the nature of choice and on his relatively untapped analysis of emotions. PCT suggests that when choosing between rival possibilities, people select the activity that seems to open up the most scope for experimentation to increase the *range* or *clarity* of their views of the world. In some situations, such choices will entail selecting activities that keep particular situations under control and thereby facilitate particularly appealing kinds of experimentation; in other cases, choice is focused directly on finding out what certain things 'are like'. However, people will hold back from experimenting in particular areas in so far as they suffer from *anxiety*, which PCT sees as the awareness that one is facing events that one is poorly able to predict and control. (The word 'awareness' is very important here: people who do not see the limitations of their predictive skills may confidently plunge into activities that others, who might even be better able to deal with them, are afraid to carry out.) Like students, consumers will not choose new 'courses' in life if they expect to end up failing them, or passing in them only at the cost of letting other areas, where they could have achieved control, crumble into chaos. An uncertain prospect will only represent a welcome challenge to consumers if they do not see it as too risky. But they will also avoid devoting their time to familiar activities that offer no challenge (which are 'boring') unless everything else is too terrifying or the abandonment of rituals will make their lives appear to have major holes in them. Like corporations, consumers will be torn between investing in areas that they know but where there is little further prospect for growth, and diversification into hazardous new territories.

Some things consumers will be loath to try out because this would make them feel excessively guilty. In PCT, *guilt* is defined as 'the awareness of the dislodgement of the self from one's core role structure' (Kelly, 1955: 502). Such a dislodgement is psychologically unsettling in so far as it implies that the person's own theory of him- or herself is not a reliable predictor. Certain activities may therefore be resisted because they are not seen as the sort of things done by the sort of person the consumer had imagined him- or herself to be like: for example, tax evasion may seem problematic or not depending on whether it is seen as the norm for people like oneself. The classic case of consumers preferring egg-less cake mixes to egg-included ones that were more convenient — because the latter choice seemed to imply that they were too lazy — should remind researchers not to underplay the significance of self-image even for low-value purchases. So, too, should the case of the disposable mousetrap that was thrown away with the mouse inside, enabling users to avoid the messy task of clearing up the remains of mice: people resisted this not because they felt guilty about killing mice (after all, most people think this is the normal way to dispose of the pest) but because they had 'hang-ups' about throwing away mousetraps rather than reusing them.

In terms of PCT, consumers will feel *threatened* when they see significant changes coming up in the position of themselves relative to others (who might include the sales personnel with whom they are dealing, members of their reference groups or other groups in society). By changing their patterns of choice, they can seek to restore their relative positions. However, if this change involves an act of conspicuous consumption, they will be securing their own positions for the moment while threatening someone else's.

Subsequent work by Earl (1986) integrated these ideas with Hinkle-inspired research in clinical psychology on resistance to change and links between cognitive structures and extreme patterns of behaviour. Hinkle's work seemed to imply that, instead of taking demand inelasticities mainly as something to be measured, the economist might be able to anticipate elasticity patterns with reference to patterns of expectations that consumers build up: changing consumption patterns in a seemingly minor way may be strongly resisted if the change seems to have all manner of knock-on implications for the person's cognitive structures. Hence, for example, traffic congestion problems might be better approached with an eye to the psychology of vehicle ownership in terms of freedom and control and addressed in terms of the flexibility and reliability of public transport, rather than as an issue to be tackled by sharp increases in petrol levies or road-user charges, or public transport subsidies.

Similar lines of thinking began to be explored simultaneously in the US by Jonathan Gutman (1982) and his associates, under the heading of 'means–end chain analysis'. Many of the contributions to the marketing literature made by this group present quite complex cognitive mappings obtained via Hinkle's 'construct laddering' technique (for a compendium of theoretical and applied work in this area, see Reynolds and Olson, forthcoming). This enables analysts to begin by eliciting seemingly innocuous constructs pertaining to surface-level product attributes and then go on to reveal their underlying psychological implications. For example, the researcher might say 'You say you prefer a smaller car to a big one; why is this?' and the subject might reply 'I would have trouble parking a big car'. Laddering up to the next level might reveal that the person (i) finds it humiliating to suffer jibes from his or her family as he or she parks well clear of his or her destination in order to get an easy berth; (ii) is worried about looking like a fool as he or she attempted repeatedly to get a big car into a small parking space; and (iii) is not at all sure how he or she would handle a situation in which he or she damaged someone else's car while trying to park. Such an example points towards the need for researchers to use this technique with sensitivity. Often, within no more than four or five steps, they can arrive at a potentially explosive situation in which it could be unwise to try to uncover another layer of constructs by asking 'But why do you prefer X rather than Y?' yet again: the consumer, having reached his or her core constructs, will feel cornered and be likely to reply, in a hostile tone, 'I prefer it because I do, period'.

Means–end chain analysis was gradually developed to provide a basis for theorizing on involvement (see the separate entry by Pirjo Laaksonen, who has been a key contributor). Related studies have also been conducted in the context of farm management, linking laddering methods to ethnographic decision tree analysis (for example, Murray-Prior, 1994). However empirical work has yet to follow up Earl's attempts (in the light of clinical research on obsessive and schizophrenic disorders reported in Adams-Webber, 1979) to suggest parallels between patterns of cognitive linkages in individuals' construct systems and mappings of corporate diversification strategies on the basis of synergy links or shared capabilities between activities. A highly developed and strongly interlinked set of constructs may provide a person or a firm with penetrating insights into a particular field, although at the cost of vulnerability in the event of loss of a key construct on which the architecture of the construct system depends (in common parlance: 'around which it revolves'). By contrast, thinking in terms of highly permeable constructs that are loosely linked together may permit constructs to be discarded easily without troubling knock-on effects, but may not provide much depth of insight. This perspective may be useful in terms of understanding, for example, collecting behaviour (a missing item jeopardizes the integrity of the collection as a whole, but expertise related to part of the collection makes it easy to get the most out of its other parts) or impulsiveness (an item may be purchased without the choice being based on any firm foundation because the person's view of the world is so simplistic that almost anything may fit into it). It also may help answer the broader question of how consumers develop contrasting patterns in the diversity of their activities and interests. The same thinking could be applied to studying the intellectual development and research strategies of academic scientists, who differ in the extent to which their work is highly focused or opportunity driven.

There appears to be considerable scope for designing marketing campaigns to exploit consumer emotions and desires to predict and control events. Firms can, and do, try to show consumers that if they do not buy a particular products, they will find life less easy to control. The texts of many advertisements can be construed in these terms: those for financial service products such as American Express and Mastercard are particularly obvious examples. Firms can also try to improve sales by offering no-quibble guarantees, user-friendly designs and images of friendly staff. But there is great scope for getting things wrong, too. Telling the consumer, in effect, that he or she is an idiot not to have tried the product in the past is very different from telling the consumer that even the experts have now admitted that they had underestimated the product. Threatened consumers *might* purchase a product to prove themselves relative to a sales person (or to avoid embarrassment). But they might instead try to remove the threat by getting out of the selling situation altogether — just as mainstream economists tend to shrink the extent of their fields of inquiry when challenged in ways that cut straight to their core propositions (for example, in respect of ethical issues). Anxieties of entirely the wrong kind may inadvertently be created, with disastrous results. For example, consider what is said to have happened many decades ago when the Raleigh Cycle company was marketing its products in India and its sales staff used advertisements that they construed as showing Indians successfully pedalling at great speed away from pursuing tigers. The target market saw things differently: buy a Raleigh bike and you will get chased by tigers!

PETER E. EARL

Bibliography

Adams-Webber, J.R. (1979) *Personal Construct Theory: Concepts and Applications*, Chichester, Wiley.

Bannister, D. and Fransella, F. (1986) *Inquiring Man* (3rd edn), Harmondsworth, Penguin.

Earl, P.E. (1983a) 'The Consumer in His/Her Social Setting: A Subjectivist View', in Wiseman, J. (ed.) *Beyond Positive Economics?*, London, Macmillan: 176–91.

Earl, P.E. (1983b) *The Economic Imagination*, Brighton, Wheatsheaf.

Earl, P.E. (1984) *The Corporate Imagination*, Brighton, Wheatsheaf.

Earl, P.E. (1986) *Lifestyle Economics*, Brighton, Wheatsheaf.

Gutman, J. (1982) 'A Means–End Chain Model Based on Consumer Categorization Processes', *Journal of Marketing*, **46**: 60–72.

Hinkle, D.N. (1965) 'The Change of Personal Constructs from the Viewpoint of a Theory of Implications', Unpublished PhD thesis, Ohio State University.

Kelly, G.A. (1955) *The Psychology of Personal Constructs*, New York, Norton (reprinted 1991, London, Routledge).

Kelly, G.A. (1963) *A Theory of Personality*, New York, Norton.

Kelly, G.A. (1969) 'The Autobiography of a Theory', in Maher, B. (ed.) *Clinical Psychology and Personality: The Collected Papers of G.A. Kelly*, New York, Wiley.

Loasby, B.J. (1983) 'Knowledge, Learning and Enterprise', in Wiseman, J. (ed.) *Beyond Positive Economics?*, London, Macmillan: 104–21.

Murray-Prior, R.B. (1994) 'Modelling Decisions of Woolproducers: Hierarchical Decision Tree Models and Personal Construct Theory', Unpublished PhD thesis, University of New England, Armidale, NSW, Australia.

Reynolds, T.J. and Olson, J.C. (eds) (forthcoming) *The Means–End Approach to Understanding Consumer Decision Making: Applications to Marketing and Advertising Strategy*, Hillsdale, NJ, Lawrence Erlbaum Associates.

Stewart, A. and Stewart, N. (1981) *Business Applications of Repertory Grid Technique*, New York, McGraw-Hill.

Theodoulou, S. (1996) 'Construing Economic and Political Behaviour', *Journal of Economic Psychology*, **17**: 499–516.

Persuasion

Persuasion permeates everyday life. Some people practise persuasion professionally (for example, advertisers, salespeople, managers, politicians, lawyers), others build careers trying to understand this knowledge domain (for example, university professors), and all of us regularly act as both agents of influence and targets of others' influence attempts. Thus, given the centrality of persuasion, it should not be surprising to find a large body of research that addresses this topic. The focus of this brief review will be the work of persuasion researchers.

Most Western persuasion researchers trace their roots back to Aristotle and his identification of the three elements of effective rhetoric: ethos, logos and pathos. This categorization of the fundamental elements of successful persuasion has been carried forward all these years later in the identification of the source (credibility of the speaker), message (arguments), and receiver (an audience's thoughts and feelings) as critical elements in the persuasion process. Much of the current research identified as being related to persuasion focuses on at least one of these three elements.

However, more recent developments have moved beyond a linear model of influence (from the source through the channel to the receiver) towards an examination of the reciprocal nature of influence and an understanding of the perspectives of both the agent who produces the persuasive message and the target of that message. This approach can be found most directly in research on interpersonal influence processes (Berger and Burgoon, 1995). Another recent development is based on propositions about the interactions between scientific knowledge and everyday understandings (variously labelled as lay theories, subjective theories, folk knowledge, naive psychology or common sense) of a particular phenomenon (for example, Friestad and Wright, 1994; Semin and Gergen, 1990). These latter two types of research are providing some of the freshest, although less tested, insights into how persuasion works outside the controlled environment of the laboratory.

Persuasion is defined as an intentional activity that has the ultimate goal of affecting the behaviour(s) of an identified 'other' (that is, target). However, within the domain of consumer research the largest body of research on persuasion focuses on various precursors to behaviour such as attitudes, beliefs, and preferences.

Attitudes and attitude change: the traditional approach

The attitude construct has been the most central variable in consumer research focused on persuasion. It has also been a core concept for researchers from many other fields. Eagly and Chaiken (1993) have given students and scholars of attitude research an overview of this literature that is invaluable. They cover the fundamentals (definitions and measurement), as well as provide thorough descriptions and reviews of research carried out under all of the major theoretical perspectives (for example, social judgement theory, the expectancy-value model, balance theory, theory of reasoned action, information integration, cognitive response, elaboration likelihood model, heuristic-systematic model, attribution theory, classical conditioning, mere exposure, self-perception theory, inoculation theory). There is no more thorough treatment of this topic available today. However, for the purposes of this review, it is the authors' summary of what they term 'systematic knowledge about attitudes', and their identification of 'serious omissions and limitations' that are of particular interest.

In terms of what is 'known' about attitudes, Eagly and Chaiken (1993) take the position that evaluation is at the core of the attitude concept. They go on to say that the cognitive, affective and behavioural components of attitudes should be seen as 'merely three types of evaluative responses that may underlie attitudes' (p. 666), rather than as independent elements which can be shown to demonstrate discriminant validity with any reasonable level of consistency.

The authors also acknowledge that the issue of identifying when (under what circumstances) attitudes will predict behaviour has been a primary focus of attitude research. In hopes of improving the attitude–behaviour connection, they have proposed in their fourth chapter a model that incorporates variables found in other models (for example, theory of reasoned action, theory of goal pursuit) and other programmes of research (for example, attitude accessibility, activation, relevance). Their 'Composite Model of the Attitude–Behaviour Relation' (p. 209) explicitly incorporates 'habits' as well as attitudes towards the attitude object, and three types of anticipated outcomes (utilitarian, normative, and self-identify), all of which have specific relationships with an individual's attitude towards a particular behaviour, the intention to engage in that behaviour, and actual behaviour.

When discussing what is missing in attitude and attitude change research, Eagly and Chaiken identify the following topics: a lack of attention to how attitudes are formed and become strong; insufficient consideration of social influences (interpersonal, group, social norms); an overreliance on laboratory settings; and the absence of a 'strongly cumulative research tradition' (p. 687).

Petty, Wegener and Fabrigar (1997) bring coverage of the attitude and attitude change literature up to date in their review of the empirical and conceptual progress that occurred between 1992 and 1995. This review gave the most attention to the structural and functional bases of attitudes and the attitude change processes (focusing primarily on the elaboration likelihood model and the heuristic systematic model), and to the consequences of attitudes, in particular the factors that affect the attitude–behaviour relationship. They briefly discuss the impact of attitudes on information processing and social judgements (for example, nonconscious effects of attitudes on social judgements). Furthermore, these authors feel, as do Eagly and Chaiken, that the area of attitude research remains robust, with some very interesting findings coming from the areas examining attitude accessibility and structural consistency. They also identify two research trends as being particularly important. One is represented by an interest in the way in which variables can bias information processing, and how people may attempt to cope with their awareness of that bias by engaging in bias correction. Another trend is one in which there is a move away from seeing variables as absolutes (for example, a central cue or a peripheral cue) and towards a more contingent or conditional approach in which we ask when (under what conditions) will a variable trigger particular processes (for example, message elaboration, affect transfer, heuristic processing).

Interpersonal persuasion and compliance gaining

Communication research on persuasion is an underutilized source of theory and data for most consumer behaviour researchers. This may be, in part, because historically communication research has dealt predominantly with either interpersonal (dyadic or small group) contexts, or mass communication contexts in which the influence attempts involved issues related to the public good (for example, voting, health campaigns) rather than for-profit activities associated with marketing and advertising.

One subset of communication research that should be of interest to consumer behaviour researchers is identified as 'compliance-gaining' research (Berger and Burgoon, 1995; O'Keefe, 1990). This body of work has direct applications to the contexts of personal selling and service delivery. Also, insights may be gained for use in direct marketing, relationship marketing, and in the 'interactive' contexts provided by technological developments (for example, Internet). Thus, any communication situation in which (i) establishing a continuing relationship between the parties is a goal, (ii) there is direct interaction between the parties (providing the possibility of adapting messages), or (iii) there are sequences of exchanges over time, is ripe for insights from compliance-gaining research.

An overview of both the problems and opportunities associated with compliance-gaining research can be found in O'Keefe (1990: Ch. 12) and Boster (1995). Although there are some serious limitations identified (for example, the absence of a unifying theoretical framework) the value for consumer researchers may be that this research examines how the relationship between the two parties (current or desired) affects the choice of compliance-gaining tactics, and the sequential nature of tactical behaviour given that the first persuasion attempt may not be successful, as well as providing a systematic examination of the decision process by which agents strategically produce persuasion attempts. This last point leads to a discussion of another aspect of interpersonal persuasion research.

The systematic analyses of the day-to-day practice of influence and persuasion by salespeople in naturalistic settings has been done only infrequently by academic researchers. One notable exception is the extensive programme of research undertaken by Robert Cialdini (1993), in which he has both immersed himself in the actual culture of persuasion agents (for example, training as a salesman and fund-raiser) and carried out extensive experimental research (laboratory and field) focused on a variety of influence tactics.

For example, Cialdini discusses the commonly experienced context of an automobile salesperson, and illustrates the use of four different categories of influence tactics: *commitment* (getting a customer to decide to actually buy a car by offering a low price that the salesperson never intends to honour), *contrast* (adding the extra $100 option after the $15 000 price has already been agreed to), *liking* (the salesperson who argues with his/her boss, ostensibly in the customer's favour), and *scarcity* (another interested buyer). Other researchers have explored specific influence tactics in non-laboratory settings. In the context of energy conservation, Katzev and Johnson (1983) demonstrated that by making an initial request that required 'minimal justification', it was easier to get consumers to participate in a programme aimed at bringing about major changes in their behaviour: having succumbed to the initial 'foot in the door' request that they would keep a diary of the electricity consumption (and often having been horrified to see when and how they actually used electricity), subjects were easy to take on to the next stage of changing their consumption. In related work, Pardini and Katzev (1986) obtained higher levels of compliance using the tactic of 'defusing potential objections', while Gonzales, Aronson and Costanzo (1988) using a vivid analogy, increased compliance fourfold over an argument based solely on a financial incentive to reduce energy consumption.

The above discussion is not meant to imply that researchers have not 'tested' a wide range of influence tactics in varied persuasion contexts. However, I would argue that the total number of studies focused on the 'messy' context of face-to-face interpersonal persuasion as it actually unfolds in a natural setting is dwarfed by the number of mass media studies and/or experiments that take place in the classrooms and laboratories of college campuses. Further, systematic examinations of the theories and practices of experienced persuasion professionals is only rarely found in the existing literature.

Finally, some more recent work in the area of compliance gaining has begun to examine targets' perceptions of and responses to interpersonal influence attempts (see O'Keefe, 1990: 220). This view of interpersonal persuasion leads directly to the next topic, which examines targets' socially constructed knowledge of persuasion.

Folk knowledge and persuasion

Targets of persuasion (for example, consumers) participate actively in the reception, interpretation, and response to influence attempts. In fact, the development of strategies both to generate and to cope with influence attempts begins early in life and grows more complex with time and experience (Friestad and Wright, 1994). People who do not successfully develop and use 'persuasion knowledge' will be unable to obtain what they need from others, and may be unable to manage (for their own best interest) their responses to the influence attempts of others. Friestad and Wright contend that the role of laypeople's persuasion knowledge has not been explored or incorporated in prior models of the persuasion process. The importance of doing so is consistent with the position expressed by Semin and Gergen (1990), when they state, 'It is essential for the scientist to assay the everyday understandings of the lay person, for knowledge of these understandings is the key to predicting human conduct' (p. 5). Thus, unless and until our research on persuasion explicitly includes consideration of targets' persuasion knowledge, we shall not be able adequately to predict their behavioural responses to our influence attempts.

Research into lay understandings have included common beliefs about intelligence, love and personal relationships, sexuality, psychoanalysis and mental illness (Semin and Gergen, 1990). The contention that there is also a body of common knowledge related to the ubiquitous activity of persuasion is difficult to refute. Some of the specific implications of this perspective are the following. First, that persuasion knowledge is culturally and temporally bound. What is believed to be true by an individual (or the majority of people) in a culture depends on their own experience, their observations of others, and the information that is disseminated from experts (scientists) through formal training and popular writings. Thus, a belief at one point in time (for example, that women are more persuadable than men) will change as research findings are reported.

A second implication for persuasion researchers is that the activation of individuals' persuasion knowledge may change the way they process a persuasion attempt, the meaning they give to it, and ultimately their behavioural responses. In past experimental research, it was considered 'good practice' to eliminate subjects who had become suspicious of the persuasive intent of a particular message (or some element within that message). The result of that practice may contribute to the problem of not being able to replicate laboratory findings in natural settings (for example, where people are completely aware that the message or individual is trying to influence them).

And third, consumers' persuasion knowledge is likely to affect their judgements and evaluations of the source of the persuasive message (for example, company, brand, candidate) so that issues of fairness, manipulativeness, appropriateness and 'poor taste' will determine both their acceptance of the position being advocated by the message itself as well as their evaluations of the agent.

Conclusions

The study of persuasion and social influence crosses a number of disciplinary boundaries (for example, psychology, sociology, communication, marketing). We can approach this area of research from the perspective of the agent or the target. But because both agents and targets are players in the game of influence, research that considers both roles should provide better prediction and a deeper sense of understanding. Because the area of persuasion and social influence is so large, this brief review could not begin to do it justice. Interested readers will find excellent overviews of both basic and applied research in Cialdini (1993) and Zimbardo and Leippe (1991).

MARIAN FRIESTAD

Bibliography

Berger, C.R. and Burgoon, M. (eds) (1995) *Communication and Social Influence Processes*, East Lansing, MI, Michigan State University Press.

Boster, F. (1995) 'Commentary on Compliance-Gaining Message Behavior Research', in Berger, C.R. and Burgoon, M. (eds) *Communication and Social Influence Processes*, East Lansing, MI, Michigan State University Press: 91–113.

Cialdini, R.B. (1993) *Influence: Science and Practice* (3rd edn), New York. Harper Collins College Publishers.

Eagly, A.H. and Chaiken, S. (1993) *The Psychology of Attitudes*, Fort Worth, TX, Harcourt Brace Jovanovich.

Friestad, M. and Wright, P. (1994) 'The Persuasion Knowledge Model: How People Cope with Persuasion Attempts', *Journal of Consumer Research*, **21**: 1–31.

Gonzales, M.H., Aronson, E. and Costanzo, M. (1988) 'Increasing the Effectiveness of Energy Auditors: A Field Experiment', *Journal of Applied Social Psychology*, **18**: 1049–66.

Katzev, R.D. and Johnson, T.R. (1983) 'A Social Psychological Analysis of Residential Electricity Consumption: The Impact of Minimal Justification Techniques', *Journal of Economic Psychology*, **3**: 267–84.

O'Keefe, J. (1990) *Persuasion: Theory and Research*, Newbury Park, CA, Sage.

Pardini, A. and Katzev, R.D. (1986), 'Applying Full-Cycle Social Psychology to Consumer Marketing: The Defusing Objections Technique', *Journal of Economic Psychology*, **7**: 87–94.

Petty, R.E., Wegener, D.T. and Fabrigar, L.R. (1997) 'Attitudes and Attitude Change', *Annual Review of Psychology*, **48**: 609–47.

Semin, G.R. and Gergen, K.J. (1990) *Everyday Understanding: Social and Scientific Implications*, Newbury Park, CA, Sage.

Zimbardo, P.G. and Leippe, M.R. (1991) *The Psychology of Attitude Change and Social Influence*, New York, McGraw-Hill.

Philosophical–Methodological Foundations

All disciplines have philosophical foundations. For over two thousand years philosophers have been developing different 'isms' to serve as foundations for the process of generating knowledge. These 'isms' include: logical positivism, relativism and scientific realism (among others). The various 'isms' address the many 'ologies' of science, including: methodology (the study of procedures in inquiry), ontology (the study of *being*), epistemology (the study of how we *know*), and axiology (the study of what we *value*).

Consumer research has witnessed a spirited debate on its philosophical and methodological foundations. Writers advocating naturalistic inquiry, ethnographic methods, historical methods, critical theory, semiotics, literary explication, existential phenomenology, relativism, constructionism and postmodernism have attacked the philosophical and methodological foundations of consumer research. A common argument of critics can be summarized in three assertions:

1. Logical positivism dominates consumer research.
2. The philosophy of science has abandoned positivism and, therefore, the dominant paradigm in consumer research is discredited or passé.
3. Therefore, consumer research should adopt an alternate 'way of knowing' (for example, relativism, postmodernism and so on).

Unfortunately, the debate, characterized by many as filled with mis-representations, misconceptions, and mischaracterizations, has been philosophically uninformed. The objective here is to illuminate and clarify certain aspects of the debate by briefly examining arguments in favour and against some of the debate's 'isms'. We begin with logical positivism.

Logical positivism

Science in the nineteenth century was characterized not only by the quest for absolutely certain scientific knowledge, but also by the general belief that science had indeed achieved that ambitious goal. Scientific discoveries multiplied exponentially based upon the (presumed) absolutely secure bedrock of Newtonian mechanics. However, Einstein's Special Theory of Relativity in 1905 and his General Theory of Relativity in 1916, when combined with quantum mechanics, struck the foundations of physics like a lightning bolt. Newtonian mechanics was not absolute; it just did not seem to apply at the subatomic level. The 'Newtonian débâcle,' as it has come to be known, triggered renewed inquiry into science's philosophical and methodological foundations.

In the 1920s and 1930s, a group of German philosophers in Vienna (hence, the Vienna Circle) developed a philosophy — later given the label 'logical positivism' — that relied heavily on Machian neopositivism, Humean scepticism, Ludwig Wittgenstein's *Tractatus Logico-Philosophicus,* and Bertrand Russell's *Principia Mathematica.* Heeding the (presumed) lessons of the Newtonian débâcle, the positivists: (i) adopted formal logic as a methodology for studying science, (ii) rejected the view that unobservable concepts should be considered real, (iii) believed that science should avoid metaphysical concepts and rely exclusively on observables, (iv) viewed 'cause' as an unobservable, metaphysical concept that is at best superfluous to science and at worst a source of great mischief, and (v) believed that, since science should restrict itself to 'knowledge with certainty', inductive reasoning is therefore highly suspect (that is, they adopted Humean scepticism).

The objectives of the logical positivists were (i) to help science make sense of the indeterministic nature of quantum mechanics, (ii) to help science avoid another Newtonian débâcle, (iii) to help draw together or 'unify' the various scientific disciplines, and (iv) to effect a rapprochement between science and the discipline of philosophy. (Under Hegelian idealism in the preceding half-century, philosophy had been, at best, irrelevant to modern science and, at worst, openly hostile to it.) The positivists were successful in effecting a rapprochement between large portions of the philosophical and scientific communities, and they did explicate and emphasize the commonalities of apparently diverse scientific disciplines. They did, indeed, develop a philosophy that could accommodate a major interpretation of quantum mechanics (the 'Copenhagen view') and, at least to the present, there has been nothing in science comparable to the Newtonian débâcle.

Uninformed statements about logical positivism abound in the current consumer research literature. Here, we shall focus on two major ones: causality and the nature of reality.

Some authors in the debate claim that the search for causal relations or causal explanations figure prominently in the 'positivistic social science' they are attacking. However, it is historically false that research guided by a positivistic philosophy would seek causal explanations, causal linkages, or assume that *real* causes exist (let alone assume that a *single* causal reality exists). Any research guided by positivism would necessarily *avoid* both the assumption of causality and the search for *real* causes. The positivists rejected causality because they viewed 'cause' as an unobservable, metaphysical concept that violated their Humean scepticism. For the positivists, if a scientist observes that phenomena A and B occur with uniform regularity, then there is no way to show *deductively* anything other than a regularity relationship. In particular, one cannot (and should not) conclude that A *causes B*.

How the positivists viewed the nature of reality (their ontology) is another confused area in the debate. Many authors attacking contemporary social science contend that the positivists were realists. However, according to how 'realism' is most commonly used today in the philosophy of science (that is, unobservables can exist and are appropriate for theory construction), the positivists were, most definitely, not realists. Although they believed that tangible objects, such as what we call 'trees' and 'rocks', exist independently of our perception, they were not willing to generalize this belief to entities that could not be observed (for example, causes, attitudes and beliefs). Indeed, many philosophers of science view positivism's opposition to scientific realism as its major defining characteristic.

The preceding enables us to reexamine the premise underlying the entire debate, namely, that positivism dominates contemporary social science and consumer research. Advocates of naturalistic inquiry, humanistic inquiry, historical methods and postmodernism (among others) claim that consumer research is dominated by the search for *cause*, and by the belief that a single, objective reality exists, which they claim are defining features of positivistic research. However, any research programme following a positivistic philosophy (i) would not search for *cause* (a metaphysical concept), and (ii) would not adopt a realist view with respect to scientific theories. Alas, the entire debate has had a demonstrably false underlying premise. Contemporary social science and consumer research are not dominated by logical positivism.

As to premise two in the debate, it is true that positivism has been discredited in philosophy of science. Positivism suffered from a number of fatal flaws, most of which, ironically, were identified by the logical positivists themselves. Here, we focus on the positivists' 'verifiability principle'.

The positivists had given high status to the importance of science discovering and justifying laws and law-like generalizations. Such laws were generally construed to be universal conditionals relating observable phenomena to other observable phenomena: 'Every time phenomenon "X" occurs, then phenomenon "Y" will occur'. However, in their search for knowledge with certainty, the positivists required that in order for a statement to be meaningful it must be shown conclusively to be either true or false (their 'verifiability principle'). This line of reasoning resulted in an embarrassing dilemma. Since the verifiability principle implied that all cognitively meaningful statements must be shown conclusively to be true or false, then all scientific laws must be cognitively meaningless. This is because all statements having the form of a universal conditional cannot be verified conclusively. (Although observations in the past may have been consistent with a universal conditional, it is always possible that some disconfirming observation might occur in the future.) Therefore, the logical positivists were forced to give up the verifiability principle. Because of such deficiencies of positivism as, for example, their verifiability principle, many researchers in the 1960s and 1970s turned towards *relativism*.

Relativism

Relativism is a term of art from philosophy. All genuine forms of relativism have two theses: the relativity thesis, that is, something is relative to something else, and the nonevaluation thesis, that is, there are no objective standards for evaluating *across* the various kinds of 'something else'. Five forms of relativism are especially significant: (i) *Cultural* relativism holds that (a) the elements embodied in a culture are relative to the norms of that culture, and (b) there are no objective, neutral, or nonarbitrary criteria to evaluate cultural elements across different cultures. (ii) *Ethical* relativism holds that (a) what is ethical can only be evaluated relative to some moral code held by an individual, group, society, or culture; and (b) there are no objective, impartial or nonarbitrary criteria for evaluating different moral codes across individuals, groups, societies or cultures. (iii) *Rationality* relativism holds that (a) the canons of correct or rational reasoning are relative to individual cultures, and (b) there are no objective, neutral or nonarbitrary criteria to evaluate what is called 'rational' across different cultures. (iv) *Conceptual framework* relativism (or 'Kuhnian' relativism) holds that (a) knowledge claims are relative to conceptual frameworks (theories, paradigms, worldviews or *Weltanschauungen*), and (b) knowledge claims cannot be evaluated objectively, impartially, or non-arbitrarily across competing conceptual frameworks. (v) *Reality* relativism, also referred to as constructionism (alternatively spelled 'constructivism'), holds that (a) what comes to be known as 'reality' in science is constructed by individuals relative to their language (or group, social class, theory, paradigm, culture, world view, or *Weltanschauungen*), and (b) what comes to count as 'reality' cannot be evaluated objectively, impartially or nonarbitrarily across different languages (or groups and so on).

One attraction of relativism is that it appears to advocate pluralism and an enlightened tolerance towards other cultures. However, does relativism actually lead to an 'enlightened' viewpoint towards other cultures? Consider the fact that in the late 1970s the Khmer Rouge slaughtered between one and two million of their fellow Cambodians (out of a population of about seven million). Or consider that the Western estimates of 'only' twenty million Soviet citizens being murdered during Stalin's purges have been revised upwards by the Soviet historian Bestuzhevlada to 38–50 million. Or consider that there are still several societies in the world today where the practice of slavery continues unabated. Is it *enlightened* not to condemn these atrocities? Most of us would claim 'no'. Yet cultural/moral relativism implies that none of these three heinous actions and practices could be condemned by non-Cambodians, non-Soviets, or by those in non-slave cultures. Unfortunately, although individual relativists may advocate pluralism and enlightened tolerance, the *philosophy* of relativism does not imply these attributes.

Does relativism imply a tolerant pluralism? Suppose we have two societies, *A* and *B*, both of which are firmly committed to relativism, but which have different religions. Suppose further that society *A* has a norm that states that it has a moral obligation to impose, by force if necessary, its religion on other societies. Such a norm, since it is consistent with the rest of its culture, is 'right' and given relativism, the norm cannot be challenged by outside cultures (for relativism maintains that all cultures are equally good, equally bad, equally right and equally wrong). What logically follows is that society *A* will be morally 'correct' in invading society *B* to impose on *B* the religion of *A*. Not only can other countries (for example, *C* and *D*) not morally condemn society *A* (since it is only following the norm of its culture), but — most ironically — society *B* cannot even condemn *A* (since *B* is firmly committed to relativism). In short, not only does relativism not imply tolerance, but also, relativism can easily be used to defend the most atrociously intolerant actions.

How does relativism view scientific knowledge? Relativists maintain that there are no fundamental differences between sciences and nonsciences. Science is simply what society *chooses* to call 'science'. In particular, there is no such thing as the scientific method. Therefore, the knowledge claims of the nonsciences must have (and should have) as much epistemological warrant as the sciences.

The 'no fundamental differences' argument implies that we have no good reasons to believe and act on the knowledge claims of the sciences in preference to those of the nonsciences when such claims conflict, for if they were then such reasons would constitute fundamental differences between science and nonscience. Therefore, for sincere relativists, if a palmist should diagnose a person as *not* having bone cancer (an example of a nonscience knowledge claim), such a diagnosis must have equal warrant as the diagnosis of a medical doctor that the person *did* have bone cancer (an example of a scientific knowledge claim). Then why do most people act upon the advice of doctors, not palmists? The reason is that palmistry has not adopted the verification system of open empirical testing, and, therefore, its knowledge claims are not intersubjectively certifiable. In short, it is the method of medical science that makes it *science*.

What role does truth play in the philosophy of relativism? First, for relativists to be consistent, they would have to admit that it is only relatively true that all truths are relative; otherwise they would hold the view that all truths are relative, except theirs. If all truths are relative, including relativistic philosophy, then there cannot be good reasons to believe in the tenets of relativism. Thus, relativism is self-refuting. Second, suppose a serious advocate of relativism, who claimed 'truth is relative', were asked: 'Is it true that the earth revolves around the sun?'. The only possible reply would be, 'You must tell me if you accept the paradigm (or theory) of Ptolemy or Copernicus', because truth is a subjective evaluation that cannot be properly inferred outside the context provided by the theory. Taken *seriously*, relativism degenerates to nihilism; it cannot do otherwise.

Scientific realism

Understanding the problems of logical positivism (for example, its verifiability principle) and relativism (for example, it is self-refuting and degenerates to nihilism) many have turned to *scientific realism*, arguably the dominant position in philosophy of science today. After the repudiation of relativism in the 1970s, the philosophy of science turned sharply to a realist orientation (that is, the world exists independently of being perceived). Although there are many views of *scientific* realism, the following is seen as a consensus fundamental tenet: scientific realism maintains that the long-term success of a scientific theory gives reason to believe that something exists like the entities (observable or unobservable) and structure (causal or noncausal) postulated by the theory.

There are three important concepts built into this statement. First, a theory must be successful over a significant period of time in order to give good reason for believing in the entities and structure implied by the theory. Second, the success of a theory gives *reason* to believe, not conclusive warrant to believe, in the entities and structure implied by the theory. Third, the success of a theory

442

provides good reason to believe that 'something like', not 'exactly like', the entities and structure postulated by the theory actually exists. The thesis of scientific realism is at odds with the Humean scepticism of the logical positivists and *anathema* to relativists.

The advantages of scientific realism are that it is open without being anarchistic: it is open to all techniques and procedures that honestly adopt the pursuit of truth as an objective, while denying the anarchistic 'anything goes' view that all procedures are either viable or equally likely to warrant our trust. Furthermore, scientific realism is also critical, without being nihilistic. All knowledge claims are to be subjected to critical scrutiny, but the nihilistic view that knowledge and truth are impossible to achieve is rejected. Therefore, scientific realism makes 'sense' of science and gives due regard to the obvious success of science over the last 400 years.

Critics of scientific realism argue that any philosophy of science that is guided by the search for truth is misguided. They argue that there are no absolutely certain standards for assessing truth or approximate truth. Indeed, they point out that theories once thought to be true have since been shown to be false, for example, the phlogiston theory of fire. As a result, scientists who embrace scientific realism would never know when their theories were true or even when their theories were approximately true. Therefore, critics argue, scientific realism is an inappropriate philosophy for consumer research.

In response, advocates of scientific realism maintain that to claim that a scientific proposition is true is not to claim that it is certain. Rather, it is to claim that the world is as the proposition says it is. Because the very essence of science is that all knowledge claims are subject to revision upon future evidence, no scientific assertion claimed to be true is claimed to be certain. Truth-with-certainty belongs in theology, not in science. Furthermore, it is incoherent to argue that truth and approximate truth must be abandoned because a particular theory of science (that is, the scientific realist theory of science) is false. The claim that some of the assertions contained in the theory of scientific realism are false necessarily implies that they *could* have been true. Therefore, the claim by opponents of scientific realism that truth is an inappropriate goal for science is self-refuting, because critics use 'truth' and 'falsity' in their own critique of scientific realism. Coherent, intelligible, meaningful or substantive discourse about science (and in science) seems to require the use of locutions similar to those normally associated with the concepts 'true' and 'false'.

Finally, the many successes of science give scientists (and the public) reasons to believe that something like the entities postulated by the theories actually exist. For example, the 'germ theory' of disease warranted researchers to search for other entities that may cause other diseases. The warranted belief that entities exist prompted researchers to explore (and find) the virus resulting in

443

AIDS (acquired immunity deficiency syndrome). If one does not have good reason to believe that the entities in one's theory exist, if all such entities are just social constructions, then why engage in a search for them? To work towards *better* descriptions and *better* measures of nonexistent entities is irrational. For example, would it make sense for a researcher attempting to explore the nature of viruses to state: 'Even though viruses do not exist, I shall attempt to explore precisely how large these nonentities are'?

Consider the intangible, unobservable entities found in consumer research. To the extent that theories in consumer research incorporating latent constructs, such as 'attitude', 'intentions', 'beliefs', 'values', 'involvement', 'brand loyalty', 'satisfaction', 'emotions', 'expertise', 'salience', 'personality' and 'cognition', have been successful in explaining, predicting and solving pragmatic problems, such evidence provides warrant for believing that these psychological states of consumers exist independently of researchers' labelling them, that is, they are *real*. Indeed, why would consumer researchers attempt to develop better measures for these entities if they do not exist? For the preceding reasons, scientific realism appears to many in consumer research to provide a reasoned (and reasonable) foundation for the pursuit of scientific knowledge.

Conclusion

The purpose of this entry has been to examine some of the 'isms' that have been offered as foundations for the process of generating knowledge in consumer research. Logical positivism and relativism, we suggest, do not provide adequate foundations for research. An appropriate foundation must be able to explain the successes of science without making them into miracles. Therefore, an appropriate philosophical foundation for science would seem to incorporate some basic concepts: (i) the world exists independently of being perceived; (ii) the job of science is to develop genuine knowledge about the world, even though such knowledge may never be known with certainty; (iii) all knowledge claims must be critically evaluated and tested to determine the extent to which they do, or do not, truly represent, correspond, or are in accord with the world; and (iv) the long-term success of any scientific theory gives us reason to believe that something like the entities and structure postulated by that theory actually exist. All disciplines need philosophical foundations. Scientific realism seems to be a reasonable choice.

SHELBY D. HUNT AND DENNIS B. ARNETT

Bibliography

Anderson, P.F. (1983) 'Marketing, Scientific Progress and Scientific Method', *Journal of Marketing*, **47**: 18–31.

Anderson, P.F. (1986) 'On Method in Consumer Research: A Critical Relativist

Perspective', *Journal of Consumer Research*, **13**: 155–73.

Hunt, S.D. (1990) 'Truth in Marketing Theory and Research', *Journal of Marketing*, **54**: 1–15.

Hunt, S.D. (1991a) *Modern Marketing Theory: Critical Issues in the Philosophy of Marketing Science*, Cincinnati, OH, South-Western.

Hunt, S.D. (1991b) 'Positivism and Paradigm Dominance in Consumer Research: Toward Critical Pluralism and Rapprochement', *Journal of Consumer Research*, **18**: 32–44.

Hunt, S.D. (1993) 'Objectivity in Marketing Theory and Research,' *Journal of Marketing*, **57**: 76–91.

Kuhn, T.S. (1970) *The Structure of Scientific Revolutions* (2nd. edn), Chicago, IL, University of Chicago Press.

Leplin, J. (1984) *Scientific Realism*, Berkeley, University of California Press.

Manicas, P.T. (1987) *A History and Philosophy of the Social Sciences*, New York, Basil Blackwell.

Peter, J.P. and Olson, J.C. (1983) 'Is Science Marketing?', *Journal of Marketing*, **47**: 111–25.

Siegel, H. (1987) *Relativism Refuted*, Dordrecht, D. Reidel.

Suppe, F. (1977) *The Structure of Scientific Theories* (2nd edn), Chicago, IL, University of Illinois Press.

Positioning

Each month hundreds of press articles deal with the positioning or repositioning of brands. P&G introduces new improved Cheer for whiter whites. Montgomery Ward changes its motto to 'Shop smart, live well'. Cadillac turns its eye to a younger market. 'When it absolutely, positively has to be there overnight' defines Federal Express. The Gallo brothers' grandchildren star in commercials as part of an ongoing image shift from mass to class. So what is positioning? A succinct definition geared towards the academic audience is: 'how a brand is perceived relative to its competition on the physical and psychological factors relevant to the consumer'. People with a more managerial viewpoint typically expand on this definition by adding 'and the marketing efforts carried out to inform the desired market'. This entry provides a brief overview of both the academic and the managerial views of positioning.

Academic view

Central to both the basic (academic) and extended (managerial) view of positioning is the multiattribute model of consumer behaviour. Academic articles and commercial research studies rely heavily on a particular type of multiattribute model — the multiattribute utility concept — which depicts the utility of a brand i to consumer m as a function of the levels of the relevant physical and psychological factors it is perceived to provide (Lancaster, 1966).

445

These factors are referred to as attributes. That is, $U_{im} = f(z_{i1m}, z_{i2m}, \ldots, z_{iJm})$ where there are J attributes relevant to the consumer (price being one of these) and z_{ijm} is the level of attribute j perceived to be derived from product i. The consumer uses this function to evaluate all of the brands in his or her consideration set and chooses the brand providing the highest utility. For an overview of multiattribute utility models and their estimation see the separate entry in this volume.

Positioning studies typically are interested in understanding two things, the first of which is how much of each relevant attribute is inherent in each brand in the product class. This is often represented graphically by plotting the brands on a 'perceptual map', the axes of which are the levels of each attribute. These brand positions are determined through expert knowledge, direct elicitation for consumers, and the analysis of consumer perceptions of brand similarities through multidimensional scaling. The second question of interest — what are the relative importances of the attributes to the individual's brand utility assessments — is crucial to understanding why the brands are positioned as they are, whether a profit opportunity exists for a new or repositioned brand, and which consumers marketing efforts should be focused upon.

In order to gain insight into this second question, individual-level multiattribute utility functions are modelled and estimated. The compensatory tradeoffs between the attributes generally are modelled using either a linear or part worths function. The linear model assumes constant marginal utility for each unit of an attribute. Hence, the utility consumer m has for brand i is:

$$U_{im} = \sum_{j=1}^{J} w_{jm} z_{ijm}. \tag{1}$$

The wjm term reflects the relative importance of attribute j to consumer m's preference formation. It is referred to as an attribute weight. Typically, stated preferences for the considered brands are regressed against the attribute levels of these brands with the attribute weights resulting as the estimated parameters.

The part worths model does not impose any a priori structure other than additivity. Marginal attribute utilities need not be constant and more of each attribute need not be preferred to less. However, estimation concerns restrict the model to a limited number of levels (generally two to four) for each attribute. The resulting utility formulation is:

$$U_{im} = \sum_{j=1}^{J} \sum_{k=1}^{K_j} u_{jkm} D_{ijkm} \tag{2}$$

where each attribute has K_j levels. The D_{ijkm} variables constitute the attribute-level information and are represented as dummy variables: one if brand i has a perceived level k of attribute j and zero otherwise. The u_{jkm} terms represent the utility (attribute weight) consumer m associates with level k of attribute j. Dummy variable regression or MONANOVA is used to estimate these weights. The part worths model is appropriate when the marginal utilities of the attributes are not expected to be constant, finite levels of some attributes are most preferred and the attribute levels are nominal in nature (for example, blue, green and red coloured cars).

The utility the consumer derives from any particular existing brand, potentially altered (repositioned) brand or new brand concept is estimated by simply plugging the brand's attribute levels and the consumer's estimated attribute weights into the relevant utility function (equation (1) or (2)). These utility values can then be used to predict consumer choice in simulated 'what if' scenarios involving, say, the entry of a proposed new brand. The heterogeneity across consumers in their attribute weights (tastes) determines predicted total sales for a proposed new or repositioned brand. This heterogeneity in tastes is also the basis for market segmentation and targeting (discussed later).

Two different assumptions are used that detail how estimated brand utilities are transformed into estimated choice behaviour. For infrequently purchased, durable goods, a deterministic choice rule is used in which the consumer is assumed to purchase the brand providing the greatest estimated utility. For more frequently purchased, less expensive brands, measurement errors are felt to be larger relative to the brands' utilities so a probabilistic transformation is used. This 'random choice' transformation mimics the empirically prevalent switching behaviour of consumers and also makes the later optimization analysis easier by making consumer demand continuous in the attributes. A logit transformation is most common. This depicts consumer m's probability of purchase for a considered brand i as depending on the relative utilities of all A brands considered (McFadden 1974). That is

$$P_m(i) = \frac{e^{u_{am}}}{\sum_{a=1}^{A} e^{u_{am}}} \tag{3}$$

Due to differences in attribute weights, attribute level perceptions or consideration sets, $Pm(i)$ differs across individuals. Therefore, assuming the sample of M consumers surveyed is representative, the average probability of choice or the estimated market share for brand i is

$$E[MS_i] = \frac{1}{M} \sum_{m=1}^{M} P_m(i). \qquad (4)$$

Estimated sales, $E[S_i]$, equals industry sales times this expected market share. Sales for an altered (repositioned) product are estimated as follows. The brand's attribute levels are altered as desired and then for each consumer the brand's revised utility calculated. Using this new value in equation (3) a revised choice probability for the brand is estimated for each individual. These probabilities are then summed to arrive at a sales estimate as discussed above. A hypothetical new brand's sales are estimated similarly with each individual's consideration set assumed to include the new brand with some probability. Profit analysis may then be done. Urban and Hauser (1993) provide a detailed textbook review of these ideas. Two examples of brands designed using this methodology are the Courtyard by Marriott hotel chain (Goldberg, Green and Wind, 1984) and Sunbeam's food-processor line (Page and Rosenbaum, 1987).

New brand positioning articles either evaluate a prespecified set of price and attribute-level combinations (new brand concepts) or utilize a computer search algorithm to search over all feasible concepts to find the optimal new brand. The optimal repositioning of an existing brand has not been analysed. Most commercial software used to estimate multiattribute utility models includes a 'choice simulator'. These simulators ask the researcher for a new brand description (attribute levels and price) and produce a sales estimate using the procedure described above. Academic articles are less tied to this simple 'plug and chug' method and tend to use algorithmic search procedures. Algorithmic procedures identify the 'optimal' positioning and price through the use of gradient search techniques (for example, Green and Carroll, 1981) or mixed integer nonlinear programming (Gavish, Horsky and Srikanth, 1983). Sudharshan, May and Shocker (1987) provide an overview and comparison of the various algorithmic procedures.

Since most firms manufacture multiple brands, a few studies have focused on the more difficult problem of optimal product-line design. An example is the paper by Page and Rosenbaum (1987) dealing with Sunbeam's design of its food-processor line. Relevant academic work includes Dobson and Kalish (1993).

A key limitation of most new brand positioning studies is that they seek the brand concept(s) that maximize sales or market share rather than profit. Data availability is behind this decision. Academics find that it is extremely difficult to convince manufacturers to make cost data available and, if this data is available, to allow its publication. Furthermore, many firms lack a precise notion as to how their production costs relate to their physical inputs and know even less about how their brand's cost relates to its attribute levels. Consequently, until recently, when profit analysis was undertaken, costs were either taken as given (Schmalensee and Thisse, 1986) or estimated from accounting data (Hartman, 1985). Recently, the assumptions that observed prices constitute a price equilibrium and all firms choose prices in an attempt to maximize profit have been used to generate a multiattribute cost function estimation procedure requiring no direct cost information (Horsky and Nelson, 1992).

Another limitation of most new brand studies is the assumption that competitors do not react to the new brand's entry. An exception is Schmalensee and Thisse (1986) who utilize subjective increases in the existing brands' utility values to simulate the effect of competitive reaction. Other exceptions are Horsky and Nelson (1992) and Goldberg (1995). They assume that all of the existing firms wish to maximize their profits and react to entry by changing their prices. For each possible new brand location, a post-entry-price equilibrium ensues through the simultaneous solution of the new and existing firms' profit functions with respect to own prices. The entrant then chooses the brand location and corresponding equilibrium price that maximizes profit. Horsky and Nelson (1992) also show that profit estimates for the new brand are greatly overestimated if competitive price reactions are ignored. Furthermore, the new brand's optimal attribute levels and price also may differ significantly.

Before proceeding to the managerial viewpoint on positioning, a caveat requires illumination. Since optimal brand positioning results depend intimately on the estimated attribute weights, it is necessary for the model estimated to describe behaviour accurately in addition to predicting behaviour well. That is, brand positioning results in many cases are not robust to model misspecification or the use of erroneous attribute weights. A different distribution of consumer tastes may generate an extremely different optimal solution. A similar problem arises with model misspecification. If a noncompensatory choice model is appropriate, it is likely to find an optimal brand position that consists of a combination of extremely high or extremely low attribute levels. Inappropriate use of the linear or part worths model in this case is likely to mislead the researcher into believing that a less extreme solution is optimal.

Managerial viewpoint

While the academic literature has focused on analytical methods to identify the optimal price and attribute configuration for a new brand, the managerial literature has focused on more qualitative positioning strategy incorporating our extended definition of positioning. We first look at some standard marketing terminology and then overview selected popular views of positioning.

The concepts of segmentation and targeting both arise from the fact that consumers have different tastes — which translate into different attribute weights. Segmentation refers to the grouping together of consumers with similar tastes. Cluster analysis is a standard technique used to carry out such groupings. Since consumers in the same segment have similar tastes, they are likely to purchase the same brands. Happily, from a marketer's perspective, they often also tend to watch the same television programmes, read the same magazines and so on. Vendors such as A.C. Nielsen and Arbitron collect and sell data relating TV viewership, radio listenership and so on to demographic and lifestyle variables. This enables a firm that sells a brand with great appeal to a particular segment to identify where these consumers live and shop as well as the programmes and magazines that they watch and read. Cost-effective targeting of the brand's advertising and distribution results. Targeting thus is a happy medium between costly one-to-one marketing and mass marketing which, because of its lack of distinctive appeal (differentiation), makes the brand very vulnerable to competition.

The importance of consumer information search on consumer choice and firm behaviour is also evident. Two consumers with the same tastes may purchase different brands because of either perceptual differences concerning the brands' attribute levels or different consideration sets. This highlights the importance of targeting since the failure to be considered or an erroneously derogatory brand perception are most harmful to sales if they occur with consumers who otherwise would value your brand highly. Consumer perceptions also tend to be 'sticky' in that once a perception of a brand's attribute levels is developed, changing this perception more than marginally is extremely difficult and costly. This explains, for example, why Toyota, which did not have a presence in the luxury car market outside of Japan, opted to sell its new luxury line under the Lexus label overseas but under the Toyota label within Japan.

Ries and Trout in their various bestselling books look at positioning as carving out a profitable 'mindspace' in the consumer's cerebral dictionary of product classes. They state that 'positioning is what you do to the mind of the prospect' (Ries and Trout, 1986: 3). The premise is that thoughts about a particular product class are associated with a 'key word or words' — perhaps a fairly general descriptive term such as 'computer' or a more attribute-orientated combination such as 'overnight delivery'. The consumer forms a short ranking of brands in each product class with the top ranking going to the first brand to make a strong connection to the key words. While the physical brand is important, the use of advertising and the choice of a brand name are paramount in generating a strong (highly ranked) perceptual connection with a desired 'word'. This ranking is what appears as the 'definition' of the 'word' accessed and most consumers fail to read past the first brand mentioned in this 'definition'. Hence, a profitable 'mindspace' is a number one ranking with respect to a desirable 'word'. Advertising can also generate new 'words' for the dictionary — spinoffs from the original key words that essentially partition an existing product class into multiple new classes — and then position (generate a ranking for) a brand with respect to this new 'word'. Two examples of brands that have been well positioned in this sense are 7-Up with the corresponding product class 'uncola' and Michelob with 'premium priced domestic beer'. In academic terms, because of the cost of collecting product information, consumer consideration sets are small and product evaluation focuses on the one or two attributes most important to the consumer. This focus on very few key attributes ties in with noncompensatory multiattribute models (mentioned earlier) which have received considerable theoretical attention and empirical support in the marketing and psychology literatures and the hierarchical choice and market structure literatures in quantitative marketing journals.

The competitive strategy work by Porter (1980) argues that strategy formation and positioning are inseparable concepts. He forwards the idea that there are four generic positioning strategies available to the firm. Each strategy consists of one of two possible strategic targets and one of two possible strategic advantages. The strategic target is either broad or narrow. Narrow refers to the targeting of a particular segment and broad to a mass-marketing approach focused on no consumer segment in particular. A mass-market approach may result from an inability to identify the target segments clearly or the existence of a very large target segment which makes it cost-beneficial to ignore the cost of marketing efforts that reach segments who value your brand relatively little ('wasted exposures'). Porter's two possible strategic advantages are low cost and differentiation. These also follow directly from the multiattribute utility model. For a brand to be purchased it must provide the customer with the most utility. This occurs only if the brand provides superior attribute levels (is different in a way that is preferred on the most important attributes) or has a low price.

Two other areas of strategic concern act as both determinants and outcomes of brand positioning decisions. These are the resource-based view of the firm, which deals with such issues as core competencies and sustainable competitive advantages (Montgomery, 1995), and brand equity (Aaker, 1991). The firm's resources (abilities) strongly influence the choice of a physical brand design as well as the manner in which the brand is marketed. Alternatively, a well-defended, well-known brand provides the firm with a major resource upon which to build future marketing efforts such as line extensions. Brand equity is a prominent firm resource. In such, a desirable position typically generates significant brand equity while brand name recognition greatly enhances a brand's positioning (see above).

The farthest tilt away from the physical brand aspects of positioning occurs in trade articles that refer to product repositionings which actually involve no physical brand changes at all. For example, Intel recently repositioned its computer chips. The chips themselves were not changed but the firm's marketing efforts were altered to institute a change in target segment from computer manufacturers to computer end-users.

Summary

Consumers purchase brands for the desires they fulfil and often show a great disparity in these desires. Understanding what these diverse desires are and who desires what is critical to successful marketing strategy and is the focus of multiattribute utility analysis. Without this information, product design as well as pricing, distribution choices and advertising message and media selection are severely hindered. While the academic and managerial views of positioning have clear differences in focus, both are strongly tied to this underlying multiattribute utility concept. Each, however, can gain by incorporating aspects of the other. More detailed survey and quantitative analysis should allow more micro-level strategy formulation and better-informed decision making. Academic work can benefit from more explicit consideration of the impact of information search costs, consumer perceptions and targeting on consumers' brand evaluations.

PAUL NELSON

Bibliography

Aaker, D. (1991), *Managing Brand Equity: Capitalizing on the Value of a Brand Name*, New York, Free Press.

Dobson, G. and Kalish, S. (1993) 'Heuristics for Pricing and Positioning a Product-line Using Conjoint and Cost Data', *Management Science*, **39**: 160–75.

Gavish, B., Horsky, D. and Srikanth, K. (1983) 'An Approach to the Optimal Positioning of a New Product', *Management Science*, **29**: 1277–97.

Goldberg, P. (1995) 'Product Differentiation and Oligopoly in International Markets: The Case of the U.S. Automobile Industry', *Econometrica*, **63**: 891–951.

Goldberg, S., Green, P. and Wind, Y. (1984) 'Conjoint Analysis of Price Premiums for Hotel Amenities', *Journal of Business*, **57**: S111–S132.

Green, P. and Carroll, J. (1981) 'New Computer Tools for Product Strategy', in Wind, Y. et al. (eds) *New Product Forecasting: Models and Applications*, Lexington, MA, D.C. Heath & Co..

Hartman, R. (1985), 'The Use of Hedonic Analysis in the Formulation of Corporate Strategies for Product Design and Pricing', Working Paper, Boston University, Department of Economics.

Horsky, D. and Nelson, P. (1992) 'New Brand Positioning and Pricing in an Oligopolistic

Market', *Marketing Science*, **11**: 133–53.

Lancaster, K. (1966) 'A New Approach to Consumer Theory,' *Journal of Political Economy*, **74**: 132–57.

McFadden, D. (1974), 'Conditional Logit Analysis of Qualitative Choice Behavior', in Zarembka, P. (ed.) *Frontiers in Econometrics*, New York, Academic Press: 105–42.

Montgomery, C. (1995), *Resource-Based and Evolutionary Theories of the Firm: Towards a Synthesis*, Dordrecht, Kluwer Academic Publishers.

Page, A.L. and Rosenbaum, H.F. (1987), 'Redesigning Product Lines with Conjoint Analysis: How Sunbeam Does It', *Journal of Product Innovation Management*, **4**: 123–37.

Porter, M. (1980) *Competitive Strategy*, New York, Free Press.

Ries, A. and Trout, J. (1986), *Positioning: The Battle for Your Mind*, New York, Warner Books, Inc.

Schmalensee, R. and Thisse, J.-F. (1986) 'Perceptual Maps and the Optimal Location of Products', Technical Working Paper, Marketing Science Institute.

Sudharshan, D., May, J. and Shocker, A. (1987) 'A Simulation Comparison of Methods for New Product Location', *Marketing Science*, **6**: 182–201.

Urban, G.L. and Hauser, J.R. (1993) *Design and Marketing of New Products* (2nd edn), Englewood Cliffs, NJ, Prentice-Hall.

Possessions

Material possessions surround us. Some possessions are necessities; others luxuries. According to the traditional economist's view, we value possessions solely for utilitarian purposes, or as symbols for establishing status in the social order. In contrast, consumer researchers have sought to understand how we use possessions to establish, maintain, or even change who we are. People routinely use material possessions to narrate their life stories. Similar to the picture that is 'worth a thousand words', a single possession can represent events, relationships or other matters of personal significance that would take many words to describe. Such possessions are kept because they stand for something very personal and biographical and are used to define and maintain a sense of personal identity.

Using material goods for identity construction and maintenance appears to be an ordinary, universal human practice. To explain this phenomenon, scholars have identified and applied two basic concepts: the extended self and material possession attachment. Those concepts and their applications are described below.

The extended self
Belk (1988) has identified the extended self concept to explain how people literally incorporate material possessions into their self definitions. We invest ourselves into possessions that define 'who I am', 'who I have been', and 'who I

am becoming'. Objects of the extended self are not only reflections of our identities; they are often used to construct an identity. The possessions of the extended self captures 'who I think I am' (and, possibly, 'who I would *like* to think I am').

Anything a person may identify as 'me' or 'mine' is included in the extended self. People psychologically appropriate many sorts of objects, ranging from personal possessions to collectively owned entities such as 'my neighbourhood', national monuments, natural landmarks, and even sports teams. Thus, material possessions can be a significant part of a person's extended self.

Extended self possessions provide a person with a tangible picture of his or her identity. Moreover, by keeping and caring for such possessions (often for a very long time), a person maintains a biographical record that lends permanence and continuity to an otherwise less stable existence. Thus, not only do we use possessions to extend our physical boundaries, we also use them to extend ourselves across time. Finally, Belk suggests that the more energy and emotion we invest into a particular possession because it is more 'me', the more attached we become to it.

Material possession attachment
Just about everyone can identify at least one material possession that is special, favourite, or cherished, and would be difficult to part with. Belk identified that material possession attachments are formed for self extension, but what are the underlying motives for forming certain kinds of attachments?

In their seminal study, Csikszentmihalyi and Rochberg-Halton (1981) identify the following categories of meanings for special possessions that are *past orientated*: past memories (for example, heirlooms, souvenirs), past associations (for example, ethnic or religious, collections). The authors' *present-* or *future-orientated* classes include: experiences (enjoyed objects, objects for release), intrinsic qualities of the object (for example, unique, handcrafted), object style, utilitarian value or connection with personal values (for example, ideals or accomplishments). Other scholars offer related, but different categorization schemes. For example, Dittmar (1992) uses similar categories to show how people of different social categories (for example, male versus female, or different social classes) value special possessions. Similarly, Kamptner (1991) identified these five categories of object meaning: providing control and mastery, moderating emotions, cultivating the self, symbolizing ties with others and constituting a concrete history of one's past. These scholars developed their categories by combining two kinds of information: what respondents report as their reasons for attachment to various possessions; and the researchers' interpretation of what a particular material good represents to people.

Researchers have shown that people become attached to just about anything from photographs and jewellery, to old clothing or cars. Any material possession that is useful for self-identification or self-cultivation may become an attachment. Ball and Tasaki (1992) developed a measurement scale to identify degree of attachment to specific possession objects.

Most of the research about material possession attachment examines goods that people *currently* possess. However, Ball and Tasaki (1992) found a kind of *anticipatory* attachment to goods not yet possessed. Younger subjects sometimes associated strong feelings of 'me-ness' with particular material goods they did not yet own, but strongly desired. Additionally, research about consumer behaviour and nostalgia seeking shows that we sometimes develop a sort of *retrospective* attachment for possessions we no longer have. We are especially prone to nostalgic reminiscing for departed things (for example, objects, music recordings) from our adolescence and early adulthood (Holak and Havlena, 1992). Moreover, anecdotal evidence suggests that we sometimes acquire new versions of possessions long gone (for example, cars, clothing) in an attempt to recapture the meaning and emotional charge associated with that departed possession.

We bond emotionally with material possessions of attachment. Although often beloved, material possession attachments are not always liked. People often identify certain possessions that they strongly dislike, yet are unable to part with. Possessions received as gifts can fall into this category (for example, 'I really don't like that sweater my grandmother gave me, but I can't get rid of it'). Possessions of attachment can evoke a wide range of (sometimes mixed) feelings ranging from joy and pride to sadness or guilt. Such strong emotional connotations come from the object's association with a person's identity and life history.

There is no such thing as a material good to which everyone becomes attached. Whether a person becomes attached to a specific object depends upon what the object means to that individual. Additionally, material possession attachment is distinct from materialism (a personality trait) or material values (such as possessiveness or acquisitiveness). Even the least possessive and materialistic people can identify objects to which they are strongly attached. Thus, attachment is not inherent in the type of possession or individual in question.

Material possession attachment appears to be universal; it spans cultures, ages, the genders and other structural distinctions among people (Csikszentmihalyi and Rochberg-Halton, 1981; Kamptner 1991; Wallendorf and Arnould 1988). Although the specific objects to which people become attached may vary from one culture to another, one age cohort to another, men to women and so on, the fundamental reasons for becoming attached appear to be universal.

What are those basic reasons?

Taking a step back from the details of the possession categorization schemes described above, Kleine, Kleine and Allen (1995) identified two fundamental themes that appear to motivate possession attachment. These themes are found throughout the social psychological literature about self-development and the forces that drive identity formation and change.

The first theme identifies the complementary yet opposing identity forces of *affiliation* (making connections with others) and *autonomy* (becoming a unique and independent individual). For example, a daughter's ring symbolizes her mother's love, a man's favourite chair reflects family heritage; these are affiliation-orientated possessions. Autonomy is reflected in the following examples: a suit that makes its wearer feel good about him- of herself, an athletic trophy, or any possession that reflects 'me' as a distinct individual. People become attached to possessions that are especially useful for negotiating affiliation seeking or autonomy issues.

The second theme reflects the personal change versus continuity balancing act that is inherent in personal identity development. To remain psychologically healthy, individuals must establish some sense of personal continuity, but also negotiate changes in their lives. Possessions that are especially helpful in keeping alive memories of the past, or negotiating personal change are often identified as favourite possessions. Possessions become *least* favourites (weak attachments) when they represent a period in life from which a person wishes to disconnect (a soured relationship, for example). Also, through possessions of attachment people may negotiate becoming selves (see the entry on Conspicuous Consumption elsewhere in this book). Thus, in this view, special possessions facilitate *self continuity* (by connecting with past self, present or future self) and *self change* (disconnect from past by dispossessing a possession that represents something one wishes to leave behind).

We use material possessions of attachment for defining ourselves, who we are, who we are not, who we are becoming; also who we are connected with and who we are as unique individuals. The way in which a possession object develops this special meaning is because it helps mark a path or trail along which we have travelled in arriving at the current me, placing identity in its historical context. Possessions enter and leave the life narrative as the contents of the biographical record change. In short, we use possessions to help narrate our own personal histories; we become attached to possessions that are especially useful for telling our stories.

Predictors and consequences of attachment

Gender may predict the kind of attachment that a person forms with a material possession. Studies have shown that men more often value possessions that have instrumental value or reflect individuality or accomplishment; women tend to cite as special those objects having more communal meanings and that reflect interpersonal connections (for example, Csikszentmihalyi and Rochberg-Halton, 1981; Dittmar, 1992).

Other findings show that children and very young adults more often value special possessions for what they can do with the objects, or the emotional expressions and activities the objects make possible. As people grow older, attachment objects more often stand for relationships and memories, especially those related to self-extension (Csikszentmihalyi and Rochberg-Halton, 1981; Dittmar, 1992; Kamptner, 1991). Dittmar (1992) discusses the literature that shows variations in attachment meanings at different stages of the life cycle. For example, senior citizens more often focus their special possessions on portraying personal history and self-continuity. Thus, gender, age and life-cycle stage have been shown to predict the specific reasons for attachments.

Gift receipt may predict attachment formation, according to emerging evidence (Kleine et al., 1995). Gifts symbolize a connection between the giver and receiver and are often carefully selected to fit the receiver, setting up the potential for attachment due to interpersonal connections or individual identity reflection.

Scholars have suggested that people probably keep possession attachments longer, and care for them better, than if those objects were not special. Also, it seems reasonable that being attached to a possession may determine how it is disposed of (for example, a favourite piece of clothing given to a friend instead of thrown out) or raise concerns about how a new owner might treat the dispossessed item.

Research has documented the emotional distress experienced by those who have had special possessions stolen or destroyed by fire or other natural disasters. Monetary compensation may permit replacement of such goods, but cannot restore a good's en.otional charge and relieve the distress (Dittmar, 1992). Moreover, researchers have observed that as people anticipate getting rid of or losing a special possession, they experience a cooling-off period during which emotional ties to the good are lessened (Belk, 1988) This suggests that some kind of emotional coping process also may follow *unexpected* material losses.

Concretizing our sometimes fleeting memories, placing them before us in palpable form, material possession attachments aid, rather than circumvent healthy progress through various stages of the life cycle (Csikszentmihalyi and Rochberg-Halton, 1981; Dittmar, 1992; Kamptner, 1991). A familiar example may be a baby blanket that facilitates a young child's detachment from a parent. Likewise, special possessions that maintain memories of family, friends and other enriching aspects of life help successful adaptation to old age, especially as an elderly person's life circumstances change (for example, losing a spouse or friend, moving to an elder-care facility). Thus, the possessions literature suggests that attachment to specific possessions is functional and healthy. Yet, apart from studies about trait materialism or material values (which are not necessarily related to attachment), no one has investigated whether becoming attached to specific material possessions is an *optimal* route to self-identification and development.

Summary

We often use material goods not only for utilitarian purposes, but also to stand for personal meanings. These meanings capture our life histories and are used to narrate our personal biographies, identify who we are, who we have been, with whom and what we are connected. Material possessions that are especially useful for these purposes become objects of attachment and become incorporated into the extended self.

SUSAN SCHULTZ KLEINE

Bibliography

Ball, A.D. and Tasaki, L. (1992) 'The Role and Measurement of Attachment in Consumer Behavior', *Journal of Consumer Psychology*, **1**: 155–72.

Belk, R. (1988) 'Possessions and the Extended Self', *Journal of Consumer Research*, **15**: 139–68.

Csikszentmihalyi, M. and Rochberg-Halton, E. (1981) *The Meaning of Things*, London, Cambridge University Press.

Dittmar, H. (1992) *The Social Psychology of Material Possessions*, New York, St. Martin's Press.

Holak, S.L. and Havlena, W.J. (1992) 'Nostalgia: An Exploratory Study of Themes and Emotions in the Nostalgic Experience', *Advances in Consumer Research*, **19**: 380–87.

Kamptner, N.L. (1991) 'Personal Possessions and Their Meanings: A Life-span Perspective', *Journal of Social Behavior and Personality*, **6**: 209–28.

Kleine, S.S., Kleine, R.E., III and Allen, C.T. (1995), 'How is a Possession "Me" or "Not Me"? Characterizing Types and an Antecedent of Material Possession Attachment', *Journal of Consumer Research*, **22**: 327–43.

Wallendorf, M. and Arnould. E.J. (1988) '"My Favorite Things": A Cross-cultural Inquiry into Object Attachment, Possessiveness, and Social Linkage', *Journal of Consumer Research*, **14**: 531–47.

Postmodernism and Consumption

Introduction to postmodernism

Postmodernist tendencies emerged in different fields at different points in time independently of each other. In architecture, where such tendencies were first noticed, postmodernism grew as a reaction against the modernist definitions of form and style whose primary emphasis was on universalism, functionalism and rationalism. Postmodern architecture considered the modernist approach to be too rigid and argued for greater fluidity of design, mixing of styles and local variability. In literature, postmodernism was a reaction against the entrenched notions of Western canon. It has given rise to a poststructuralist movement away from the signified to the signifier, and towards displacement, difference and dispersal instead of rigid origins. In politics, postmodernism moved away from neoclassical liberalism and triggered intense debates based on gender and ethnic issues. At the global level, it has induced the post-colonial discourse. In philosophy, postmodernism was a rejection of Cartesian duality of mind and matter, and cognitive rationalism. Instead, it embraced the ideas of Friedrich Nietzsche, Sigmund Freud and Martin Heidegger which inspired the writings of Michel Foucault, Jacques Derrida, Nancy Fraser and Julia Kristeva. Over time, these disparate postmodernist tendencies appear to have converged with an interdisciplinary fusion of knowledge. This loosely defined commonality of issues has also given rise to a new field, cultural studies. Once these disparate tendencies united to form a loose collective, postmodernism began to assume the character of a major movement.

While rejecting the notions of modernism as the only guiding principles for defining the social order, postmodernism has attempted to do the following:

1. restored aesthetic approaches in human discourse giving prominence to the linguistic, symbolic aspects of human life;
2. elevated visuality and spectacle to levels of critical discourse;
3. recognized subjective experiences as meaningful part of human practices; and
4. redefined the human subject as both a cognitive and an aesthetic subject.

Postmodernism and consumption
Postmodern tendencies in marketing and consumer behaviour originated in the late 1980s and early 1990s. Some notable writings in this area are: Venkatesh (1989), Firat (1990), Ogilvy (1990), Sherry (1991), Hirschman and Holbrook (1992), Brown (1993, 1995) and Firat and Venkatesh (1993, 1995). In addition, special edited volumes of the *International Journal of Research in Marketing* (1993 and 1994) the *European Journal of Marketing* (1997) have also been published (see bibliography for a more complete list).

Conditions of postmodern consumption
Four important conditions of postmodernism may be mentioned as accounting

for new ways of thinking about consumption — hyperreality, particularism, fragmentation and symbolic behaviours.

Hyperreality is the condition that suggests that as human beings we construct our own realities and these realities are a product of our imagination, ingenuity, fantasies and pragmatic needs. The continental thinker closely associated with the term 'hyperreality' is Baudrillard. He posits that the world is now constructed through simulacra and simulations — a hyperreality or a world of self-referential signs. He discusses four evolutionary phases of reality and experience: the first is that of engaging in direct experience with reality; the second is that of working with experiences and representations of reality; third is that of consuming images of reality; and the fourth stage (hyperreality or the age of simulacra) is that of taking images themselves as reality. It is the latter which is of relevance to this discussion of consumption in postmodernity. According to Baudrillard (1988, 1993), consumption consists of the exchange of signs. Signs and images supersede materiality and use value. This is not to argue that the products that we consume have no functional utility; but that functionality itself is treated as a sign. Thus Baudrillard and other postmodernists would argue that we live in a simulated environment where realities are constantly constructed and consumed. The contemporary consumer culture is replete with hyperreal objects, symbols and spaces. For example, we can see exaggerated forms of hyperreality in theme parks, in shopping centres and in various commercial locations frequented by consumers all over the world. These further illustrate that we live in a visual culture where consumer images are packaged into signs, or more accurately, into an endless chain of signifiers. With the emergence of new technologies of information and communication, the visual is supplanting the textual as the cultural order.

Since human imagination has no natural limits, our social and cultural constructions similarly have no real limits. However, the products of our social and cultural constructions are not uniform across time and space. This leads to the next condition of postmodernism which is *particularism*. Different cultures behave differently in regard to the same set of needs because their worldviews are different. Thus the notion of universalism serves at best a limited role in human affairs. It does not mean that different cultures should not have a shared agreement in conducting mutual transactions or be guided by certain common principles of action. This commonness in understanding tends to be a pragmatic principle rather than an inflexible dogma. Particularism does not mean that mutual exclusivity for the human history is nothing but cultures interacting and colliding with each other, and learning from each other. In matters of consumption, particularism has led to synergistic interactions. This is particularly true in matters of food, clothing, housing and various other daily consumable products and consumption situations where people have interacted with each other without concerning themselves about underlying universal principles of behaviour.

Related to particularism is the third condition, *fragmentation*, but fragmentation in a special sense that concerns individual identity construction. When we say consumers are fragmented, we not only mean that they are fragmented into groups (that is, segmented) but that their individual selves are also fragmented. The self is therefore conceived of as a product of imitative assemblage rather than a unified construction. In redefining the self, the consumer becomes continuously emergent, reformed and redirected through relationships to products and people.

Of all the conditions of postmodern consumption, fragmentation seems to define the contemporary consumer the best. The traditional view of the consumer or consumption follows a modernistic perspective of a unified self and unified meaning. The assumption is that consumers are driven by well-defined needs with a sense of well-integrated purpose. In this derivative view, most consumption practices are orientated towards satisfying consumer needs which are logically organized and transparent to the observer. While this is an appealing scenario, postmodernists argue that this is simply not the case. Consumer behaviours vary across time and space, and by contingencies and changing images. In a world filled with choices, there are no sustaining themes or consumption patterns. The idea of consumption is to live in a perpetual present and to mix form and content as one's whim permits. In a number of domains where consumer culture is most visible or visualized, say, in clothing/fashion, in diet, in recreation and travel, and in art and culture, the consumer sets no discernible patterns and engages in multiple experiences. These experiences become narratives of one sort or another, and since narratives can change and since no narrative has a privileged status, all narratives are permissible. Once we employ the term 'narrative', we enter the world of language, in particular, the language of signs, and move away from objective representational schemes. Language is devoid of boundaries, and is composed of different voices and points of view. It is these kinds of postmodern possibilities that the world of marketing offers to the consumers. The very essence of marketing (if one can use the term at all) is to package change, variation and multiplicity of experiences into a spectacle of paradoxes and juxtapositions. When families in rural India watch American soap opera on television beamed to them via the satellite, they are not trying to incorporate this visual experience into a sublime whole, but letting their identities dissolve into their disjunctive (fragmented) ironies. If this postmodern experience can affect a farmer's family in remote rural India, one can imagine how intensified such experience can be in contemporary urban culture. To fail to acknowledge such fragmentary experiences is to ignore the fluidity of life in the current market economy. This is not to say that the whole world is a theatre of the postmodern, but it is important to recognize that the main themes of contemporary consumer culture are postmodern.

The symbolic nature of consumption processes is another condition of postmodernism. Symbols create meanings and consumers negotiate consumption processes via meanings. These meanings are given to them by the media, by the cultural groups they belong to, or families in which they are raised. Meanings are always in transit and as meanings change, so do consumption practices. This does not mean that meanings change at the same rate in all cultures or across all individuals, but that meanings are constructions determined and negotiated by individuals with their cultural affiliations. To the extent that consumption is a significatory process, what is signified changes when new meanings are ascribed to products and services.

What does this mean for consumer research?
For consumer researchers trained in standard methods of social science (survey research, experimentation), the study of consumption processes that are based on postmodern interpretations presents some special challenges. Standard social science methods limit our ability to study consumer meanings, language systems and other significatory processes. New methods have to be devised which include interpretative methods. Hirschman and Holbrook's (1992) book on postmodern consumer research is a good introduction to a new approach. Venkatesh's (1995) new paradigm for the study of cross-cultural consumer behaviour, which he labelled, 'ethnoconsumerism' is embedded in postmodern thinking. Firat and Shultz (1997) have developed some extensive ideas on fragmentation that must be valuable to consumer researchers who want to pursue these ideas further. Similar approaches have been suggested by other scholars, based on existential phenomenology, hermeneutics, semiotics and other interpretative schemes.

ALLADI VENKATESH

Bibliography
Baudrillard, J. (1988) 'Consumer Society', in Poster, M. (ed.) *Jean Baudrillard: Selected Writings*, Cambridge, Polity Press.
Baudrillard, J. (1993) *Simulations*, New York, Semiotexte.
Brown, S. (1993) 'Postmodern Marketing', *European Journal of Marketing*, **27**: 19–34.
Brown, S. (1995) *Postmodern Marketing*, London, Routledge.
Brown, S. (1998) *Postmodern Marketing II*, London, Thompson.
Cova, B. (1997) 'Community and Consumption', *European Journal of Marketing*, **31**: 297–316.
European Journal of Marketing (1997) 'Special Issues on Postmodern Marketing', **31**: Nos 3 and 4.

Firat, A.F. (1990) 'The Consumer in Postmodernity', in Holman, R.H. and Solomon, M.R. (eds) *Advance in Consumer Research,* **17**, Provo, UT, Association for Consumer Research: 70–76.

Firat, A. F. and Shultz, C.J., II (1997) 'From Segmentation to Fragmentation: Markets and Market Startegy in the Postmodern Era', *European Journal of Marketing*, **31**: 183–207.

Firat, A.F. and Venkatesh, A. (1993) 'Postmodernity: The Age of Marketing', *International Journal of Research in Marketing*, **10**: 227–49.

Firat, A.F. and Venkatesh, A. (1995) 'Liberatory Postmodernism and the Reenchantment of Consumption', *Journal of Consumer Research*, **22**: 239–67.

Hirschman, E.C. and Holbrook, M.B. (1992) *Postmodern Consumer Research: The Study of Consumption as Text*, Newbury Park, CA, Sage.

International Journal of Research in Marketing (1993 and 1994) 'Special Issues on Postmodernism and Marketing', **10**: No. 4; **11**: No. 4.

Ogilvy, J. (1990) 'The Postmodern Business', *Marketing and Research Today*, **18**: 4–20.

Sherry, J. (1991) 'Postmodern Alternatives: The Interpretive Turn in Consumer Research', in Robertson, T.S. and Kassarjian, H. (eds) *Handbook of Consumer Behavior*, Englewood Cliffs, NJ, Prentice-Hall: 548–591.

Venkatesh. A (1989) 'Modernity or Postmodernity: A Synthesis or Antithesis?', in Childers, T. (ed.) *Proceedings, American Marketing Association Winter Educators Conference*, Chicago IL, American Marketing Association: 99–104.

Venkatesh, A. (1995) 'Ethnoconsumerism: A New Paradigm for the Study of Cross-Cultural Consumer Behavior', in Costa, J.A. and Bamossy, G. (eds) *Marketing in a Multicultural World*, Newbury Park, CA, Sage: 26–47.

Poverty, Psychology of

In comparison with other social sciences, the psychological study of poverty has been narrowly focused. The principal concerns have been the psychological characteristics of the poor, how people explain poverty and attitudes towards the poor.

The psychological characteristics of the poor

In a recent review of the international literature, Saraceno and Barbui (1997) conclude that material poverty is a risk factor in both the incidence and prognosis of mental illness. The higher incidence of mental illness among the poor has generally been interpreted from one of two perspectives: social causation or social selection. According to the social causation explanation, the poor suffer greater environmental adversity including inadequate maternal and obstetric care, poor nutrition, a lack of social resources, and a greater number of negative life experiences, all of which increase the incidence of mental illness and maladjustment. From the social selection perspective, on the other hand, the higher incidence of mental illness among the poor is due to mentally ill individuals drifting down to, or failing to rise out of, poverty. The relative contributions that social causation and selection make to the higher incidence of mental illness among the poor is a matter of current debate. Indeed, the extent to which the poor suffer from greater mental illness is also disputed, mostly on the basis that the definitions and diagnoses of mental illness and maladjustment may be biased against the poor.

Not as controversial, although still equivocal, is research showing that compared with more advantaged people, the poor have a shorter time perspective, lack ability or desire to delay gratification, have a lower need for achievement, lower expectations for success, an external locus of control (that is, they believe that 'powerful others' control their lives), have a limited belief in a just world, lower self-esteem and a negative self-concept (see Allen, 1970; Furnham and Lewis, 1986). To some extent, these beliefs and motivations are reflected in consumption practices such as impulse buying and compensatory behaviour in which poorer individuals try to emulate the 'good life' through the purchase of more expensive brands and newer models (see Caplovitz, 1963). Capon and Burke (1980) also suggest that the poor are less-competent information processors and so have a high information-processing cost. As a consequence, poorer individuals show an overreliance on brand-name, ignore some product alternatives altogether, employ a brand processing strategy that is conceptually simple but operationally difficult, use less price and testing agency information, and less information in total. The net result is that the product with the maximum utility is often not chosen.

However, researchers have debated which of these consumption practices and more general beliefs and motivations characterize the poor, and whether they are causes or results of poverty. Burns (1981), for example, suggests that the causes and results of poverty interact through a circular feedback process in which poor people's perceptions of the evaluations held for them by significant others affect their evaluations and expectations for themselves. This in turn affects their self-concepts of ability, which affect their behaviours. Their behaviours then influence reference group authorities' evaluations and expectations. The authorities' expectations are then communicated to the people, whoseperception of the evaluations and expectations held for them is influenced in turn, and so the cycle continues. This model suggests that the predominant method of inquiry into the psychological characteristics of the poor, that is, the simple comparison of the poor with the nonpoor on independent constructs, is inadequate as it masks the complex relations among expectations, abilities and power.

How people explain poverty

Another principal direction of psychological research has been laypeople's explanations for poverty. The foundation to this direction was laid by Feagin (1975), who asked more than 1000 Americans to rate the importance of 11 reasons why poverty may exist. The results showed that the reasons fell into three categories: individualistic, structuralistic and fatalistic. Individualistic attributions, such as 'Lack of thrift and proper money management by poor people' and 'Lack of effort by the poor themselves', place the blame for poverty on the poor people themselves. Structuralistic explanations, such as 'Failure of society to provide good schools for many Americans' and 'Low wages in some businesses and industries', conceive poverty as a consequence of the economic system and other social forces. Fatalistic reasons attribute poverty to bad luck. Feagin found that individualistic explanations were rated most important overall, although the pattern varied with demographic variables. For example, older age, middle income, middle education level, and being white and Protestant or Catholic, tended to accentuate the importance of individualistic attributions, whereas younger age, low income, low education level, and being black and Protestant or Jewish, would accentuate structuralistic explanations.

In contrast to factor analytic approaches, network analysis according to Heaven (1994) has the advantages of uncovering the causal structures of the attributions and does not obscure between-group similarity. Using network analysis, Heaven found that both left- and right-wing supporters believed that poverty was most directly due to prejudice, low wages, the poor being taken advantage of and their disinclination for self-improvement. However, they differed in their beliefs of the root causes of poverty: right-wing supporters believed that these were individualistic and unchangeable (for example, low intelligence and lack of ability), whereas left-wing supporters considered them to be a combination of structuralistic and individualistic factors.

Most recently, Harper (1996) has advanced the attributional approach to the study of poverty in two ways. First, most previous research had only examined people's explanations for domestic poverty, and so Harper explores the attributions people in the 'First World' make for poverty in undeveloped and developing nations. Essentially, the attribution categories resemble those about domestic poverty: individualistic explanations such as the behaviour of poor people, structuralistic reasons such as exploitation and bad government, and fatalistic explanations such as climate and the weather. A second, and perhaps more significant contribution, is Harper's criticism that the attribution approach to the study of poverty is excessively individualistic in assuming that people's accounts are unitary and internally consistent and in disregarding the attributions made by social groups and the media. Furthermore, the attributional approach reduces complex political ideologies to simplistic attributional styles, removes the attributions from their context of more elaborate ideologies, and neglects the attributions' social effects and functions. Thus, Harper maintains that in 'ignoring such difficulties, traditional attribution research on poverty explanations has been essentially conservative in its theory and methodology and has failed to deliver findings which might be of use in acting politically and socially against poverty' (p. 252).

As an alternative or complementary approach, Harper suggests a discursive framework that recognizes people's discursive flexibility in constructing different explanations at different times. A discursive approach would, therefore, consider poverty to be a social construction that reflects, in part, ideological influences in the definition, description and account of poverty. A significant concern to social scientists is whether to define poverty in absolute terms (that is, people whose income is insufficient to maintain their mental and physical needs), as a relative concept (for example, the lowest 10 per cent of income earners), or a subjective one (that is, people who identify themselves as impoverished). Harper suggests that these definitions, as well as their related descriptions and accounts, have different effects, such as increasing or decreasing the number of people believed to be impoverished, acting as an emotional defence, or denying one's responsibility to solve the problem. Harper goes on to analyse, from a discursive framework, the attributions that individuals, the media and charity organizations, make for poverty in undeveloped and developing nations.

Attitudes towards the poor
As might be expected, people's explanations of poverty are associated with their attitudes towards the poor. Individualistic attributers are more negative, and structural attributers are more positive, in their attitudes (Furnham and Lewis, 1986). This association can be interpreted from Lerner's (1980) 'just world hypothesis', which postulates a human need to maintain a stable and orderly information-processing system concerning links between reward and virtue, that people get what they deserve. Expanding on the relations among just world beliefs, attributions for poverty and attitudes towards the poor, Zucker and Weiner's (1993) attribution–emotion–action theory suggests that people's attributions about the controllability of poverty affect their feelings toward the poor, which in turn influences their desire to help the poor. Zucker and Weiner suggest that people with strong just world beliefs (that is, conservative ideology) believe that poverty is controllable and caused by individualistic factors and therefore feel antagonistic towards the poor and have little desire to help them, whereas people with weak just world beliefs (that is, liberal ideology) tend to ascribe poverty to societal forces and in turn feel sympathetic towards the poor and are more inclined to help. The pattern of association among attribution, emotion and action depends on whether the helping behaviour is proximal or

distal. In proximal helping behaviour (that is, personal help), the causal chain is ideology ⇒ attribution ⇒ emotion ⇒ behaviour. In distal helping behaviours (that is, social welfare), ideology and attribution have both direct and indirect (via emotion) influences on action.

Furnham and Lewis (1986) concluded from their literature review that three factors made the psychological study of poverty problematic: inconclusive and contradictory results, difficulty in separating cause from consequence, and the weak explanatory power of individual-level psychological variables relative to structural and contextual variables. None the less, Furnham and Lewis argued that psychologists do have a role to play through addressing questions such as why some poor people improve their status while others do not, why people of the same minimal income differ in their identification as a poor person, how attitudes towards the poor and explanations for poverty can be changed, how the behaviour of the poor can be modified, and so on. Ten years after the review, psychological research has still not addressed these questions satisfactorily. On the other hand, some progress has been made in mental health issues, network analysis, the discursive approach and attribution-emotion-action theory. Unemployment, a research topic on its own right, is relevant to the psychology of poverty but the link between the two remains to be more fully explored. Finally, further research is needed that re-focuses attention on how poverty can be reduced and on how poor people may become more politicised. The psychology of poverty will not be complete without a psychology of anti-poverty.

MICHAEL W. ALLEN AND SIK HUNG NG

Bibliography
Allen, V. (1970) *Psychological Factors in Poverty*, Chicago, IL, Markham.
Burns, R. (1981) *The Self-Concept: Theory, Measurement, Development and Behaviour*, London, Longman.
Caplovitz, D. (1963) *The Poor Pay More: Consumer Practices of Low-Income Families*, London, Free Press of Glencoe.
Capon, N. and Burke, M. (1980) 'Individual, Product Class, and Task-Related Factors in Consumer Information Processing', *Journal of Consumer Research*, 7: 314–26.
Feagin, J. (1975) *Subordinating the Poor*, Englewood Cliffs, NJ, Prentice-Hall.
Furnham, A. and Lewis, A. (1986) *The Economic Mind: The Social Psychology of Economic Behaviour*, Brighton, Wheatsheaf.
Harper, D.J. (1996) 'Accounting for Poverty: From Attribution to Discourse', *Journal of Community and Applied Social Psychology*, 6: 249–65.
Heaven, P.C.L. (1994) 'The Perceived Causal Structure of Poverty: A Network Analysis Approach', *British Journal of Social Psychology*, 33: 259–71.
Lerner, M. (1980) *The Belief in a Just World: A Fundamental Delusion*, New York, Plenum.
Saraceno, B. and Barbui, B. (1997) 'Poverty and Mental Illness', *Canadian Journal of*

Psychiatry, **42**: 285–90.

Zucker, G.S. and Weiner, B. (1993) 'Conservatism and Perceptions of Poverty: An Attributional Analysis', *Journal of Applied Social Psychology*, **23**: 925–43.

Protocol and Cognitive Response Analysis

Protocol analysis is a research technique which involves having people verbalize their thoughts: either concurrently during an ongoing situation, such as while watching a commercial; or retrospectively after the situation has occurred, such as after watching the commercial (Ericsson and Simon, 1984). The technique — also known in its various forms as cognitive response, thought sampling methodology, and thinking aloud — has largely been applied in the study of advertising and the message-evoked thoughts it inspires in consumers (Wright, 1980).

The basic methodology

As stated above, protocol/cognitive response methodology essentially involves having a person state or report thoughts and various aspects of cognitive processing concurrently (also referred to as 'online') or retrospectively. Such questioning may be general (all thoughts) or directive, such as reporting counter arguments to an advertisement (Wright, 1980). Questions can be quite simple. For example, Wright (p. 156) suggested using the following: 'report any and all thoughts you have while listening to this radio transmission'. On the other hand, questions and procedures can also be quite complex. For instance, Earl (1995: 81) suggests that an ideal way to study decision making would be for a researcher to 'accompany a decision maker in the process of reaching a verdict' and have the decision-maker 'verbalize the thoughts that go through his/her head. The analyst writes them down [or tape-records them] and then attempts to see what kinds of thought processes can be inferred from the transcript'. In a slightly different application of protocol analysis but one which was informed by the previously described process, Earl (1995: 81–4) provided material from journalists' evaluations and decisions regarding cars and had student analysts 'explain their reasoning' in their own words.

Depending on the question, time allotted, and nature of the material, responses can range greatly in complexity. Typically, cognitive response applications in reaction to advertising last three minutes (for example, Buchholz and Smith, 1991). Researchers could also specify that one continue providing thoughts until all relevant thoughts are exhausted. On the other hand, in more complex protocol analyses and related interpretative interviewing, the response period may be quite long, on the order of hours, for instance. Analysing the various types of protocol analysis can also proceed in a number of ways and involve either deductive analysis in which the analyst tests some a priori hypotheses about the responses or inductive analysis in which the analyst takes an approach that is more exploratory, interpretative or hermeneutic (cycling between the transcript and analyst) (Thompson, Locander and Pollio, 1990; Waterman and Newell, 1971).

Issues of application

Among the issues of application surrounding protocol/cognitive response analysis, three stand out: (i) timing, (ii) time limits, and (iii) coding and interpretation. The timing issue concerns whether verbalization should be done concurrently or retrospectively. According to Wright (1980), concurrent verbalizations may be incomplete because of a strain on one's information-processing capacity since accounting for one's thoughts may compete with attending to the task at hand. On the other hand, retrospective reporting may risk memory loss. The researcher could use concurrent verbalization when the task is relatively long and retrospection when it is short. He or she could also break up a long task into parts and use retrospection in those parts. Or in line with current thinking about triangulating across methods for greater validation or confirmation of results, the researcher could use both concurrent and retrospective verbalizations in the same study — either with the same people doing both or having some people verbalize concurrently and others retrospectively.

Wright also suggests that the time limits on a person engaging in verbalization can be important. For example, many studies have typically involved expressing one's thoughts for three minutes (Buchholz and Smith 1991). But some thoughts may take a longer time to form or emerge. Researchers might experiment with time span and the quality of the thoughts generated. Quasi-longitudinal studies in which people verbalize at different times might also be considered.

Coding and interpretation problems comprise another issue. Generally, deductively derived data may be subjected to various counts and are often used in experimental and/or content analyses to count how many thoughts of various types emerge in given situations (such as in relation to a commercial). Coding this data involves arranging thoughts into various predetermined categories and is usually done by multiple judges among whom high intercoder reliabilities are sought as a standard of agreement. For example, Buchholz and Smith (1991) divided the cognitive responses to an advertisement into three major categories: (i) type of thought (that is, product, message and source-related along with unrelated), (ii) intent of thought (that is, positive, neutral, negative or curiosity statements), and (iii) presence of personal connections (that is, the thoughts connect the brand or other aspects of the advertisement to the consumer's own life). Judges coded the responses into these categories and the resulting categorized data was then available for further statistical analysis. However, ambiguities and disagreements in such coding processes may occur. Moreover, the determination of categories may be difficult and the suppression of some types of thoughts in favour of others, especially in the case of more general initial questions, may limit the scope of a study, for example, favouring *related* over *apparently unrelated* thoughts even though much of the latter may actually be relevant in some previously overlooked ways.

In this regard, protocol/cognitive response data may also be analysed in less-quantitative, more interpretative and inductive ways. Thus, the various protocol/cognitive response analyses comprise a family of techniques which, if it has not been apparent before in the competition between the quantitative and qualitative paradigms in consumer research, can serve to bridge the two and provides ways by which they may inform each other and in some cases be used together. For example, as Gould (1993) suggested, the categories of related and *apparently unrelated* thoughts which are often used as count data in cognitive response studies may also be examined in more depth for the themes, rich description and possibly deeper connections they provide. Moreover, as indicated by the applications of protocol analysis to the investigation of decision rules (Earl, 1995; Waterman and Newell, 1971) and various problem-solving tasks (Ericsson and Simon, 1984), as well as similar studies of legal proceedings (Bennett and Feldman, 1981), the analysis may involve many steps and be quite complex. For example, Earl considers various readings of students' judgements of journalists' transcribed decision rules and poses one reading or interpretation against other alternatives in ways that resonate with other interpretative methods, such as hermeneutics (Thompson et al., 1990). In many respects, the mode of interpretation will depend on the aim of the researcher (for example, deductive versus inductive, general versus directive). In more focused studies, the researcher may be willing to abandon some *seemingly nonrelevant* responses while in exploratory or interpretative research in particular, he or she needs to be open to the more emergent results that might evolve from such data.

Future of protocol analysis
Protocol analysis and cognitive response may be linked to or used in conjunction with other techniques. For example, there are historical and methodological links between cognitive response and introspection (Ericsson and Simon, 1984; Gould, 1993). In both methods, one follows one's thoughts and an introspector might try verbalizing and recording them in any given situation. Another link may be made between various interviewing techniques, especially those which are phenomenologically orientated, and consumers' everyday life experiences (Thompson et al., 1990). In this regard, the phenomenological technique which

usually involves interviewing might be seen as a type of retrospective protocol/cognitive response analysis. However, protocol analysis would gain from the application of hermeneutic and thematic interpretative methods that are commonly employed in phenomenological analysis (Thompson et al., 1990). At the same time, cognitive response might be used as a form of concurrent phenomenological study in which one verbalizes what one is thinking and feeling during an ongoing consumption situation.

Another interesting issue concerns the form of protocol/cognitive response analysis. While it is generally employed as a verbal technique, one may extend and use it on a written basis. Researchers need to explore the similarities and differences in what these two modes of expression might reveal. At the very least, they might serve to triangulate responses both by the same individual or across individuals using one or the other mode of expression and also by applying various methods. For instance, consumers might be engaged in real-time cognitive response while simultaneously and continuously turning a dial on equipment designed to measure their reactions in terms of favourability–unfavourability or usefulness–uselessness to an advertisement or some other phenomenon which is unfolding in front of them (Hughes, 1990). Developing appropriate ways to link these methods might produce far richer data than either could alone. Similarly, consumers in the process of cognitive response might concurrently be hooked up to psychophysiological equipment that assesses such things as brain waves, eye movements and pupil changes, among others, to look for overlapping patterns of similarities or differences.

Reasoning along these lines also suggests that cognitive response should in many instances be linked to feelings and affect. Thus, instead of asking consumers to report their thoughts, the researcher might ask them to report on their physical or emotional feelings. The change of focus would retain the advantages of protocol analysis but likely yield very different data than might otherwise result. Likewise, projective data such as that derived from word association or role playing might be further investigated by having a person engaging in one of them stop at various points and provide cognitive responses concerning the situation. In addition, data from attitude and personality surveys and studies of marketing stimuli, such as advertising and packaging, might also be used to triangulate protocol/cognitive responses. For instance, researchers could do semiotic, content, linguistic and/or literary critical analyses of advertisements and compare these textual results to the protocol responses of consumers about them.

As the variety of possible applications suggests, protocol/cognitive response analysis may serve as a bridge between experimental and interpretative paradigms in consumer and economic psychological research. Not only may such analyses be applied in a number of ways, both experimental and interpretative, but they also may be enhanced by jointly drawing on the training and skills of researchers from the different paradigms. Thus, protocol analysis and cognitive response comprise, on the one hand, a well developed set of techniques, and on the other, a dynamic, evolving class of them which will advance through continuous interaction with other approaches. How the techniques are applied should be determined largely by the researcher's need (Waterman and Newell, 1971) and the creative and experienced investigator will find that he or she possesses a great deal of latitude and choice in their design and use.

STEPHEN J. GOULD

Bibliography

Bennett, W.L. and Feldman, M.S. (1981) *Reconstructing Reality in the Courtroom*, New Brunswick, NJ, Rutgers University Press.

Buchholz, L.M. and Smith, R.E. (1991) 'The Role of Consumer Involvement in Determining Cognitive Response to Broadcast Advertising', *Journal of Advertising*, **20**: 4–17.

Earl, P.E. (1995) *Microeconomics for Business and Marketing*, Aldershot, Edward Elgar.

Ericsson, K.A. and Simon, H.A. (1984) *Protocol Analysis: Verbal Reports as Data*, Cambridge, MA, MIT Press.

Gould, S.J. (1993) 'The Circle of Projection and Introjection: An Introspective Investigation of a Proposed Paradigm Involving the Mind as "Consuming Organ"', in Costa, J.A. and Belk, R.W. (eds) *Research in Consumer Behavior*, Volume 11, Greenwich, CT, JAI Press: 185–230.

Hughes, G.D. (1990) 'Studies in Imagery, Styles of Processing, and Parallel Processing Need Realtime Response Measures', in Goldberg, M.E., Gorn, G. and Pollay, R.W. (ed.) *Advances in Consumer Research*, Volume 17, Provo, UT, Association for Consumer Research.

Thompson, C.J., Locander, W.B. and Pollio, H.R. (1990) 'The Lived Meaning of Free Choice: An Existential–Phenomenological Description of Everyday Consumer Experiences of Contemporary Married Women', *Journal of Consumer Research*, **17**: 346–61.

Waterman, D.A. and Newell, A. (1971) 'Protocol Analysis as a Task for Artificial Intelligence', *Artificial Intelligence*, **2**: 285–318.

Wright, P. (1980) 'Message-Evoked Thoughts: Persuasion Research Using Thought Verbalizations', *Journal of Consumer Research*, **7**: 151–75.

Psychological Discount Rate

A discount rate is a function by which people devalue future events that are delayed from the moment of choice, and/or that are uncertain to occur if chosen. (For very long delays, this includes uncertainty about the person's lifespan.) The psychological discount rate describes the extent to which individual's personal valuation of delayed events decays with delay or uncertainty. The psychological discount rates of people engaged in finance must obviously play a major role in determining financial discount rates; but there is now substantial evidence that the psychological and financial discount rates are not the same.

Marketplaces establish consensual financial discount rates as future prospects of events are bought and sold. In so far as an individual does not accept the consensual market rates, or would accept even more disadvantageous rates than the market imposes, he or she could be said to have a distinct psychological discount rate. Two kinds of psychological discount rates can be identified: those established by a person's theory of what the rate ought to be, and those that describe a person's actual motivation.

Zero discounting as basic

For most of recorded history the accepted theory was that future events should be discounted only for uncertainty, and thus that most choice patterns that were actually observed contained an element of ignorance or weakness. For instance, Plato quotes Socrates as arguing that weighing delayed events the same as imminent ones would prevent bad judgement:

> Do not the same magnitudes appear larger to your sight when near, and smaller when at a distance? . . . Is not the [power of appearance] that deceiving art which makes us wander up and down and take the things at one time of which we repent at another? (Protagoras 356)

Early in this century economists such as A.C. Pigou were still saying much the same thing:

> Generally speaking, everybody prefers present pleasures or satisfactions of given magnitude to future pleasures or satisfactions of equal magnitude, even when the latter are perfectly certain to occur. But this preference for present pleasures does not — the idea is self-contradictory — imply that a present pleasure of given magnitude is any greater than a future pleasure of the same magnitude. It implies only that our telescopic faculty is defective. (Pigou, 1920: 24–5)

Exponential discounting as basic

Justification of any discounting of future events (a 'positive time preference') is still sometimes seen as necessary. However, in modern times the accepted theory of value has gradually conformed to the behaviour of markets, culminating in the ideal of Economic Man — a choice maker who discounts the future to a greater or lesser extent, but whose choices still remain consistent over time in the absence of new information about his options. This consistency implies one particular discount function, an exponential one:

$$\text{Present value} = (1 - \text{Constant})^{\text{Delay}} \times \text{Value-if-immediate}.$$

This function is necessary if discount curves drawn from various pairs of alternatives as a function of delay are never to cross — that is, if preference is never to reverse simply as a function of elapsing time. For all other concave discount functions, there will be some pairs of alternative events separated by some span of time, Δ, such that the earlier event is preferred when the delay, δ, to its occurrence is short, but not preferred when δ is long. Such reversal of preference would make a person vulnerable to exploitation by an agent whose curves did not cross — someone, for instance, who could repeatedly buy this person's winter coat in the spring and sell it back to him or her in the autumn at a markup greater than a consistent discounter would accept. Therefore, exponential discounting has seemed to be the demonstrably normal rationale for decisions. It has become the basis of orthodox utility theory, not only in economics, but in philosophy and most of psychology as well.

Departures from this curve are thought variously to be irrational — signs of a defect in the person's 'telescopic faculty' — or impossible. The latter kind of theories view exponential discounting to be not only normative but descriptive. Conventional utility theory has become this latter kind, and holds that departures from exponential discounting can only be apparent. For instance, alcoholism and drug addiction often provide examples of temporary preferences for acts of consumption that the person would not choose from the perspective of distance — a pattern that seems to imply discount curves with a greater curvature than exponential ones. Theories that assume exponential discounting to be universal dismiss this instability of choice as the artefact of ignorance or a limited time horizon (for example, Becker and Murphy, 1988).

Hyperbolic discounting as basic

Despite the widespread cultural acceptance of conventional utility theory, it fails to account for important properties of addictions, such as addicts' own reports of being trapped in habits they do not want, or their attempts to forestall future consumption (for example, buying the intoxication blockers, disulfiram or naltrexone). Such knowing irrationality occurs not only in addictions and other short-sighted behaviours, but also in many purely financial situations where people fail to maximize their expected returns (Thaler, 1991). Furthermore, parametric experiments consistently show that normal adults discount the prospect of rewards in curves with a greater curvature than exponential curves. Asked their preferences between pairs of a smaller amount of money at delay δ and a larger amount at delay $\delta + \Delta$, people regularly reverse their preferences between the same pair as a function of δ, and show an overall pattern of choice described by

Value = Value-if-immediate / [1 + (Constant × Delay)]

(Green, Fry and Myerson, 1994). Investigators sometimes report that their data fit still better if the denominator is raised to a power, but this power is often close to 1.0, and in any case does not change the important implication of this formula: that the elementary discount curve is hyperboloid, producing a basic tendency to prefer smaller rewards over larger ones *temporarily* when the smaller reward is imminently available. This temporary preference phenomenon is not specific to money; people show it when choosing between 'gut' rewards such as escape from noxious noise or access to a video game. It is not a product of human culture, as shown by extensive animal experiments (reviewed in Ainslie, 1992: 76–80).

Authors have proposed several discounting models to explain the temporary preference phenomenon without abandoning exponential discounting, such as:

- a step function in which immediate events are valued extraordinarily and events at all delays are discounted exponentially;
- an exponential discount rate whose exponent itself varies as a function of delay;
- the summation of separate exponential discount rates for association and valuation; and
- random variation in discount rate (Ainslie, forthcoming).

However, the data behind each of these are scanty compared to those behind hyperbolic discounting; nor do any of them squarely contradict hyperbolic discounting. The main virtue of these proposals has been to escape the awkward question raised by the hyperbolic model: if the basic psychological discount function is not exponential, how do people come to function in financial marketplaces as if it were?

Adjusting to hyperbolic discounting

The observation that a person can compete more effectively on the basis of exponential curves is not sufficient; people can compete more effectively the less they discount the future, too, but this fact has not broken us of the discounting habit. The missing explanation is some psychological mechanism that can counteract the basic tendency to overvalue impending events.

Exploration of this problem also goes back to classical times; the story of Ulysses sailing past the Sirens characterizes temporary preference precisely. If

Homer's paradigm describes a basic part of human nature, a person will have to act towards his orher own future motivations as if they will turn him or her into separate people, people who share only some interests with her present self. However, physical commitments such as those used by Ulysses — blocking up his crew's ears and having himself tied to the mast — have proved to be of limited (although not negligible) value in controlling urges for immediate gratification. Other authors soon discovered a more potent strategy: making choices between whole categories of events at once, rather than evaluating them individually. Aristotle spoke of recognizing 'universals' as an antidote to 'particular' desires (*Nichomachean Ethics*, 1147a24–b17; see detailed discussion in Charlton, 1988: 34ff.). Galen said that passion was best controlled not by looking at individual opportunities but by following the general principles of reason; he noticed that impulse control was a skill that suffered disproportionately from single failures to use it, and that habitual disuse made it especially hard for a person 'to remove the defilement of the passions from his soul' (1963: 44).

Modern psychology recognizes the same principle. For instance, Gene Heyman says that choices made according to 'global' principles come closer to maximizing objective reward than do those made according to 'local' principles (1996). Similarly, Howard Rachlin (1995) has said that self-control comes from choosing patterns of behaviour over time rather than individual acts. Choosing piecemeal is 'molecular' and myopic, choosing patterns 'molar', that is, global, farsighted, based on a series of elements taken as a whole. Unlike earlier authors, however, these psychologists have experimentally tested the validity of this time-honoured wisdom. Heyman describes having pigeons peck for food on one of the usual contingency schedules that demonstrate hyperbolic valuations, then adding a signal that appears only when the birds' choices move closer to exponential valuation. In effect this signal defines a category of farsighted choices. In so far as a bird pays attention to this signal, it presumably compares the values of responses that produce the signal versus those that do not; by computing this way, the subject comes to choose based on some aggregate within each of the two kinds of responses (signal producing versus nonsignal producing), not just the choice immediately at hand. As predicted, the birds learn to respond so as to keep the exponential discounting signal on. That is, as Heyman interprets it, they have come to make their choices in an overall context instead of a local one. Rachlin also demonstrated his point with a pigeon experiment.

These findings are evidence that some basic property of choosing in whole categories makes the psychological discount curve look more exponential. Significantly, this result makes sense only if the elementary discount curve has a highly bowed shape like a hyperbola: if whole series of exponentially discounted rewards are summed, the aggregate curve of the smaller, earlier rewards keeps the same relationship with the curve of the larger, later alternatives, however many are added. There would be nothing gained by making choices according to whole categories. But when hyperbolically discounted rewards are summed, the disproportionate effect of the first small, early reward in the series is diluted by the contribution of later members of the series; the summed curve of the large rewards is shifted relatively higher. Choice becomes more consistent, and more proportional to the objective sizes of the rewards (see Ainslie, 1992: 142–55).

Limitations of adjustment to hyperbolic discounting

While a pigeon has to have categories of reward constructed by an experimenter, a person can presumably construct them for him- or herself. This may be the mechanism for that uniquely human trait, willpower, and a related ability to sometimes choose as if the psychological discount function were exponential (Ainslie, 1991). It is a mechanism that also predicts the particular properties of our well-known human fallibility.

Whenever someone has named a category of choices that he or she sees as similar — those involving a particular addicting substance, for example, or a diet, or a budget — then each of these choices will be a natural precedent that predicts how he or she will make the other choices in the category. This perception will line up the incentives for all subsequent choices on the side of resisting temptation, just as the incentive of maintaining future trust motivates 'self-enforcing' contracts between frequent trading partners. For instance, abstinent alcoholics cannot be sure whether they will be lured into drinking at some time in the future. The best evidence they have is probably their current behaviour: If they are able to abstain now, they can have some hope that they will go on abstaining, but if they take a drink, knowing that it will set a psychological precedent, they will lose much of that hope. This very perception — that each choice sets a precedent for the category of abstaining or not in general — stakes the value of their hopes against each temptation to drink. Their predictions about their future choices are apt to be self-confirming, a situation that may create the 'will' to abstain in each individual case.

The force of a category of larger, later rewards will be proportional to the expectation of getting them; this expectation is a stake that will be reduced whenever people see themselves take the smaller, earlier reward in one of the member choices. Furthermore, hyperbolic discount curves predict a persistent incentive to distinguish each case at hand from the general category — 'It's okay to drink on New Year's Eve, or my birthday, or Saturday night' and so on. If they see too many of the choices that might represent members of the series as isolated decisions — 'exceptions' that do not count — they will lose much of their expectations of getting the relevant larger, later rewards and thus have too little at stake to motivate reward deferral. If they notice that this process of rationalization has begun to run amok, the fall in their expectations may be sudden and catastrophic. Thus the competition between local and global evaluations of rewards becomes legalistic, a matter of evaluating precedents. Successful global evaluators are apt to pay the price of being rigid and emotionally removed from the immediate moment; failed global evaluators will have categories of behaviour where they seem to have no will, that is, where their history of failure makes it impossible to recruit enough hope to stake against further temptations.

This is a volatile situation, in which how much self-control a person has depends on his or her ongoing prediction of how much self-control he or she will have subsequently, much as bull markets or 'business confidence' feed back on themselves. Such a pattern might be analysed by any number of approaches, from chaos theory to philosophical works on free will (Mele, 1995); but the best hope for actual data is probably experimentation with the repeated bargaining game, prisoner's dilemma, which shares many properties with the intertemporal bargaining situation just described (Ainslie, 1992: 171–3).

Conclusions

There is now substantial evidence for the hyperbolic discounting hypothesis. Its many implications have not been well tested, but they include the likelihood that the exponential discounting that is necessary for a person to survive in financial competition is the tenuous achievement of intertemporal bargaining, attained at the expense of some rigidity and other traits which, in the extreme, amount not to rationality but to compulsiveness (Ainslie, forthcoming). Where exponential discounting has been achieved, it can be described as a simple percentage; but the psychological discounting on which it is probably based cannot be described as a rate, or even as the hyperbolic discount function itself. Rather it is apt to be the product of an iterated bargaining situation that arises in response to the partial separation of a person's interests over time, a separation which is in turn the consequence of an underlying hyperbolic discount function.

GEORGE AINSLIE

Bibliography

Ainslie, G. (1991) 'Derivation of "Rational" Economic Behavior from Hyperbolic Discount Curves', *American Economic Review*, **81**: 334–40.

Ainslie, G. (1992) *Picoeconomics: The Strategic Interaction of Successive Motivational States within the Person*, Cambridge, Cambridge University Press.

Ainslie, G. (forthcoming) *Breakdown of Will*, Cambridge, Cambridge University Press.

Becker, G. and Murphy, K. (1988) 'A Theory of Rational Addiction', *Journal of Political Economy*, **96**: 675–700.

Charlton, W. (1988) *Weakness of the Will*, Oxford, Blackwell.

Galen, C. (1963) *Galen on the Passions and Error of the Soul* (translated by P.W. Harkins), Columbus, OH, Ohio State University Press.

Green, L., Fry, A. and Myerson, J. (1994) 'Discounting of Delayed Rewards: A Life-Span Comparison', *Psychological Science*, **5**: 33–6.

Heyman, G.M. (1996) 'Resolving the Contradictions of Addiction', *Behavioral and Brain Sciences*, **19**: 561–610.

Mele, A.R. (1995) *Autonomous Agents: From Self-Control to Autonomy*, New York, Oxford University Press.

Pigou, A.C. (1920) *The Economics of Welfare*, London, Macmillan.

Rachlin, H. (1995) 'Self-control: Beyond Commitment', *Behavioral and Brain Sciences*, **18**: 109–59.

Thaler, R. (1991) *Quasi Rational Economics*, New York, Russell Sage Foundaiton.

Rationality, General Theory of

In a lecture entitled 'economic behaviour and moral sentiments', Sen (1987) noted that, in modern economics, 'human beings are assumed to behave rationally' and that 'characterising rational behaviour is not, in this approach, ultimately different from describing actual behaviour'. Moreover, in economics the 'two predominant methods of defining rationality' were to see it as (i) internal consistency of choice, and (ii) the maximization of self-interest. Provided that some mathematical conditions are satisfied, rational choices may then be represented as the maximization of a utility function.

Given this special approach, it is rather inevitable that there are several other distinctive (but perhaps less 'predominant') forms of rationality, not only within economics but also within the wider spectrum of the social sciences, including philosophy. In other words, there is a set of economic rationalities which comprises a subset of a much larger rationality set.

From such a transdisciplinary vantage point, one can usefully conceive of a general theory of rationality, the construction of which involves the identification of distinctive elements of the rationality set, together with the specification of the relational structure on that set. According to this general theory, 'rationality' is no longer utility-maximization, described by some as a 'mere convention' (for example, Sugden, 1991); rather, it becomes a fabric of many distinctive and intertwined fundamental behavioural principles. This general theory, in turn, affords a perspective on 'rationality' that is both holistic and cumulative, comfortably spanning the micro and the macro approaches to consumer research. It is also essentially pragmatic and therefore rather appropriate to an era of rapid technological change. Indeed, it is not only the forms of rationality but also the decision-making entities that, in the general theory, can have varied and novel forms.

The rationality set

There are more than 40 distinctive elements of the rationality set. Some of the forms are listed below, together with some of the corresponding theme(s) in consumer research. The list is divided up with reference to some of the classificatory meta-rational criteria (belief orientated; backward looking and so on). In describing the forms, the term 'entity' is used throughout. This can be interpreted at various levels of abstraction (an individual, a firm, a network, or a social system and so on).

Belief-orientated forms

Here, the definition of the form of rationality refers explicitly and primarily to (i) the ways that an entity develops (or is assumed to develop) its beliefs, or its expectations, or (ii) the content of those beliefs. For example:

- *Parametric*: The entity's environment is (seen as) a family of parameters that are inputs to a calculated decision process (as in the rational expectations hypothesis of economic theory).
- *Extensive*: The entity's expectations are formed specifically by extrapolating historical data (as in some economic forecasts).
- *Strategic*: The entity's beliefs and expectations take into account the responsiveness and game-theoretic interactions of other entities (as in buyer–seller negotiations).
- *Natural* (pragmatic belief): The entity's beliefs converge towards validity, or become veridicial, as ongoing experience and inquiry prompts piecemeal revision (as when forming the belief that a product is harmful).
- *Contextual* (discourse centred): Rational entities arrive at their beliefs (and intentions) through processes of conversation and rational interaction, that involve the clashing of meanings. To achieve rationality in this sense, power relations must be held in abeyance (as in discourse-centred investigations of consumer behaviour).

Means-orientated forms

Here, the definition refers primarily to the link between an entity's beliefs and its goals. Put differently (Sen, 1987) it concerns the 'correspondence' of an entity's choice with its aims. The term 'instrumental' rationality is also used in a similar way. Examples of means-orientated forms include:

- *Bounded*: The entity (is assumed to) attend selectively to information, to satisfice with respect to goals (that is, search for solutions that are at least satisfactory) and to use heuristics such as the information-processing rules employed when making consumption choices.
- *Quasi*: The entity makes choices that are consistent with the empirically sustained variants of the SEU models of risky choice, such as prospect theory and transaction utility theory.
- *Adaptive*: The entity uses heuristics and decision rules iteratively over time, as further information becomes available, or as experience accumulates (for example, adaptive expectations in consumer decision making).
- *Minimal*: The entity activates some of its relevant beliefs, detects some inconsistencies and makes some appropriate inferences (as when a consumer realizes, say, that a cheap appliance will cost more to run).
- *Contextual* (cognitive): An entity directs its attention only to particular attributes of a decision problem, as determined by the overall social, historical or cultural context (for example, social interaction effects in the

framing of buying decisions).

Ends-orientated forms
Here, the definitions refer primarily to the nature of the entity's goals, together with the ways in which they might be established. Examples include:

- *Extended*: An entity has goals orientated towards the wider society, or the interests of other entities, in addition to self-interest (for example, social marketing).
- *Sympathy*: The entity can best serve its own interests by taking into account the interest of others (for example, when other stakeholders are viewed as constraints on the achievement of marketing objectives).
- *Commitment*: A rational entity can make genuinely counterpreferential choices, sacrificing utility for the sake of other entities (for example, buying charitably from a needy supplier).
- *Deliberative* (reflective): Here, the entity is assumed to deliberate or reflect in various ways on its own goals. For example, should it value justice (in its various forms) and act in ways that are just, or likely to foster justice.

Action-orientated forms
Here, the definitions give priority to the strategic (interdependent) and processual aspects of rational behaviour, for example:

- *Practical*: Rational action to achieve a desired outcome involves selective attention to decision content and process, within a responsive or reactive environment (for example, logical incrementalism in marketing management).
- *Expressive:* Actions are primarily symbolic, communicating values, rather than instrumental. Moreover, the process of goal formation (as in the deliberative or reflective froms) is itself a source of value to the entity, it involves experimentation with preferences and it thereby confirms autonomy.

Backward-looking forms
In contrast to the foward-looking economic rationalities, these forms are defined with some direct and explicit reference to the past history of the entity (or its environment). Examples include:

- *Systemic*: Knowledge, goals, capabilities and behavioural rules accumulate and must be developed by the entity, over time (for example, cognitive learning).

- *Posterior:* The entity's goals (values, preferences) emerge from reflection on its own past actions (for example, cognitive switching costs and the status quo bias in consumer choice).
- *Open*: The entity searches thoroughly for the cause of all past mistakes and then makes all necessary changes (as in aircrash investigations).
- *Resolute*: A rational entity should persist with longstanding missions or plans, rather than abandon them in favour of a fleeting preference (a tourist who has always wanted to see the Pyramids should, on travelling to Egypt, avoid being tempted by an alternative itinerary).
- *Contextual* (institutional): A rational entity is one that acts in ways orientated towards the creation and maintenance of institutions that symbolize a good life with others (for example, choosing and funding universities).

Ethical forms:
Other distinctive forms of rationality have also been defined in ethics and moral philosophy, including:

- *Utilitarian:* A rational entity chooses the course of action that will bring about the greatest good (variously defined) for the greatest number (for example, consumer purchases from green sources).
- *Contractarian* (deliberative): An entity should act so as to promote fairness and justice (for example, corporate supplier-engagement policies).
- *Kantian:* An entity should behave only according to those maxims (principles or rules) that it considers to be applicable to all other entities.

Meta-rationality
At a higher level, the general theory of rationality is also concerned with the classes, relationships and qualities of the plural forms of rationaity — that is, the specification and development of:

1. Classificatory meta-rational criteria, such as the ones used in the previous section, as well as aggregate versus agent orientated; perfect versus imperfect and so on.
2. Relational meta-rational arguments, expressed in formal or natural language, that place elements (and subsets) of the rationality set relative to each other (for example, belief–ends relations). Many such relations are of the type: 'ri is a form of rj' (for example, sympathy is a form of extended ends rationality), or 'rk has significant common properties with rl' (for example, expressive and strategic-belief forms).
3. Rvaluative meta-rational criteria, indicating that some forms are better, or

perhaps more rational, than others (for example, those displaying universalizability, analytic tractabilty, or rigour and precision of definition).

Meta-rational relationships, criteria and arguments may be expressed in natural or mathematical language (as in formal game theory with its natural language meta-theory) and together these lend a complex and evolving relational structure to the rationality set. The rationality set with its meta-relations then offers consumer research an 'off-the-shelf' meta-theory of consumer-choice (see Meyer and Kahn, 1991). For example, when a consumer compares a green product with a cheaper alternative, he or she could invoke a meta-rational argument linking utility maximization with utilitarianism; in contrast, arguments involving expressive rationality could mediate art purchase decisions. The mapping decision-function rationality makes quite explicit the idea that meta-rational arguments are also meta-modelling principles (Singer, 1996).

Captured versus elusive forms
The meta-criterion of elusiveness versus capture generates an important partition of the rationality set. Forms such as bounded and sympathy are 'captured' by psychological arguments that reduce them to rational utility maximization (RUM), for at least some purposes. In contrast, commitment, which involves counter preferential choices motivated by moral consciousness, is plainly elusive. The quasi and expressive forms also have formal structures that do not reduce to RUM (Hargreaves-Heap, 1989).

In many other cases, most notably the deliberative and contextual forms, meta-rational arguments involving capture are by no means settled. Some economic imperialists regard the elusive forms (for example, Kantian) as rather meaningless, arguing that market competition and learning squeeze them out. Other neo-pragmatists (lately joined by postmodernists) respond that 'meaning' surely depends on one's purposes, or whose interests one chooses to serve. Certainly, many ecologists and missionaries have regarded the elusive forms as quite central to their behavioural and policy prescriptions.

Hybrids
The hybrids forms of rationality are straightforward conjunctions of captured and elusive forms. With these forms, captured and elusive components are seen as complements (both/and) rather than mutually exclusive (either/or). The hybrids include:

1. Interdependent utility: A utility function has two values for each object of choice. One represents the moral component of satisfaction, the other the satisfaction of desires (Etzioni, 1988).

2. Consumer *and* citizen: Self-regarding interests and preferences are joined by another distinct set of preferences that reflect a concern for the public good (Sagoff, 1988).
3. Rationality *and* sociality: Sociality, or responsiveness to social and conversational cues, is a necessary augmentation of RUM (Schick, 1984).
4. Self-anchored *and* society-anchored reason: These forms of practical reason are both acquired by socialization, rather than cognitive unfolding. The latter 'society anchored' form is not only indispensible, it is primary (Baier, 1995).

With these (and other) hybrid forms, captured and elusive elements remain in ongoing tension with one another. Decision making with these forms then involves some sort of settlement, resolution or dissolution through design, or through tradeoffs. The *Zeitgeist* currently seems to favour such 'both–and' hybridization of behavioural theories. For example, in the last couple of decades, dynamic systems theory and game theory have identified 'adaptive' or 'optimal' behaviours that involve stability *and* instability, egoism *and* altruism.

Hyper-rationality
The *Zeitgeist* also favours synergy concepts. There are two current usages of the term hyper-rationality. In economics it means an extreme form of calculated rationality. In sociology it refers to synergies among distinctive forms of rationality, especially the neo-Weberian forms. For example:

1. In an industrial system, the values of groupism and harmony (Weberian-substantive) fostered the development of permanent employment systems (Weberian-formal), which in turn reinforced those values (increasing competitiveness by reducing agency costs).
2. In a corporation, profitable exchange (RUM) was used to reinforce a sense of identity (expressive), which in turn increased competitiveness by brand differentiation.
3. A networked entity with special capabilities (selective) to access and process information (minimal, bounded) was, arguably, 'selected' over others by rules embedded in the market environment. The result of repeated applications of these rules was an altered environment, in which the capability was even more favoured than before.

In general, entities that are hyper-rational in the synergy-seeking sense are able to coordinate their actions and design systems in ways that achieve synergies between market exchange processes and the historical, cultural and institutional contexts.

The entity set

As the above examples suggest, any contemporary account of forms of rationality must also be mindful of the many new types of entity (such as information technology-enabled networks) made possible by technological and social change. These types of 'rational' entity are very much engaged in production and consumption. The entity set also includes: (i) individuals with genetic alterations or microchip implants; (ii) collectivities such as learning communities and knowledge pools; and (iii) abstract entities such as autopoietic, living, biological and social systems. Many of these entities appear qualitatively very different from the original units of analysis or decision-making entities in economics and psychology (individuals, groups, firms). Even the distinction between producer and consumer, once definitive to the field of 'consumer research', is becoming rather blurred, as such notions as 'pro-suming' (simultaneous consumption and production), self-production and self-management all gain currency.

Conclusion

The Rationalist philosophers of the European Enlightenment period were the followers of new knowledge who rejected the more traditional (that is, religious) ways. Their nineteenth century successors put foward a 'coherence theory' of truth, subsequently exemplified by neoclassical economics, with its systematic unity and its micro-rationality postulates. More recently, Weberian sociology successfully exposed the hidden linkages between instrumental (means-orientated) forms of rationality and tendencies towards oppression in social systems. As neo-pragmatists and post-modernists have lately come to join the discourse of consumer research and marketing theory (if not economic psychology) they must now grapple with an extended rationality set, as well as the extended entity set. Ironically, in so doing, they might come to resurrect the distinctive social and ethical concerns of a great many of their philosophical predecessors.

ALAN E. SINGER

Bibliography

Baier, K. (1995) *The Rational and Moral Order: The Social Roots of Reason and Morality*, LaSalle, IL, Open Court.
Etzioni, A. (1988) *The Moral Dimension: Towards a New Economics*, New York, Free Press.
Hargreaves-Heap, S. (1989) *Rationality in Economics*, Oxford, Blackwell.
Meyer, R. and Kahn, B. (1991) 'Choice Models in Consumer Research', in Robertson, T.S. and Kassarjian, H.H. (eds) *Handbook of Consumer Behavior*, Englewood Cliffs, NJ, Prentice-Hall.

Sagoff, M. (1988) *The Economy of the Earth*, Cambridge, Cambridge University Press.

Schick, F. (1984) *Having Reasons. An Essay on Rationality and Sociality*, Princeton, NJ, Princeton University Press.

Sen, A.K. (1987) *On Ethics and Economics*, Oxford, Blackwell.

Sherry J. (1991) 'Postmodern Alternatives: The Interpretive Turn, in Consumer Research', in Robertson T.S. and Kassarjian, H.H. (eds) *Handbook of Consumer Behavior*, Englewood Cliffs, NJ, Prentice-Hall: 548–91.

Simon, H.A. (1987) 'Rationality in Psychology and Economics', in Hogarth, R.M. and Reder, M.W. (eds) *Rational Choice*, Chicago, IL, University of Chicago Press.

Singer, A.E. (1994) 'Strategy as Moral Philosophy', *Strategic Management Journal*, **15**: 191–213.

Singer, A.E. (1996) *Strategy as Rationality: Redirecting Strategic Thought and Action*, Aldershot, Avebury.

Sugden, R. (1991) 'Rational Choice: A Survey of Contributions from Economics and Philosophy', *Economic Journal*, **101**: 751–85.

White, S.K. (1988) *The Recent Work of Jurgen Habermas: Reason, Justice and Modernity*, Cambridge, Cambridge University Press.

Rationality in the Face of Uncertainty

In psychology the notion of rationality tends to be viewed in a similar manner to lay thinking: a choice is rational if it is based on reasoning; impulsive choices might not seem to come into this category, or those 'leap in the dark' acts based on gut feelings ('animal spirits' as Keynes called them). Thus, psychologists tend to focus attention on the *procedure* of choosing an act — and not so much on the consequences generated by the act. This approach to rationality allows one to explore whether or not a particular procedure of choice generates dysfunctional consequences.

In economics, by contrast, the idea is tied to normative notions about what kinds of choice in general will enhance a person's welfare. Consider the following decision problem. A consumer has to choose between two actions, namely, A and B. He or she obtains £10 from action A and £5 from action B. On the assumption that the consumer prefers more money to less money, he or she is said to be rational if he or she chooses action A; a consumer who chooses action B is said to be irrational. In the context of this simple decision problem, the concept of rationality is trivial — partly because there is no uncertainty in this decision problem (that is, in particular, the set of feasible actions and the payoff from each action are known with certainty). However, in the context of decision problems with uncertainty, the concept of rationality is far from trivial. For example, consider the following modification to the decision problem stated above. If the consumer chooses action B, then a fair coin is tossed; if heads turns up then the consumer obtains £15, and if tails turns up then he or she obtains £5.

In this much more complex decision problem, it is far from clear as to whether it is still rational for the consumer to choose action A.

Most economic theories of rational choice (both with and without uncertainty) are based on a number of assumptions (axioms). One key assumption is that a rational person's preferences should satisfy the transitivity axiom: if the person prefers A to B, and B to C, then he or she must prefer A to C. If the person were instead to prefer C to A, he or she is said to violate the transitivity axiom, and in turn, said to be irrational.

Most real-life decision situations involve some uncertainty. The uncertainty can be either of the exogenous variety, in that it is resolved randomly by Mother Nature, or of the endogenous variety, in that it is resolved by the actions chosen by some other decision makers. This distinction is important. The nature of the uncertainty involved will, and ought to, affect the way the decision maker perceives and analyses the decision situation. Indeed, economists do classify decision situations under uncertainty into two categories, namely, single-person decision problems and interactive decision problems. Decision theory, which is concerned with problems in the former category, is about rational decision making when the uncertainty is of the exogenous variety. On the other hand, game theory, which is concerned with problems in the latter category, is about rational decision making when the uncertainty is of the endogenous variety.

Exogenous uncertainty

Consider the following general decision situation. A 'player' (who can, for example, be either a consumer, or a firm, or a country) has to choose a 'strategy' (a plan of action) from some set S of alternative strategies. The 'payoff' — which we assume here to be in units of money — from any strategy is uncertain in an exogenous sense, which can be modelled as follows. Suppose there is a finite set of possible 'states of nature', Ω (a state of nature is a complete description of the relevant features of the world). When deciding on his or her strategy, the player does not know the true state of nature, but he or she knows that the state of nature is determined in a *purely random manner* (by Mother Nature). His or her payoff from any strategy may be influenced by the state of nature. For example, the payoff from walking to office with an umbrella is higher if it rains than if it does not rain. For each strategy s that is a member of the set S and each state of nature ω from the set Ω, we denote his or her payoff by $m(s, \omega)$.

Figure 1 describes an example of a decision situation with exogenous uncertainty — there are two strategies, s_1 and s_2, and two states of nature, ω_1 and ω_2. The numbers in the four cells are the payoffs. If there were no uncertainty about the state of nature, then what constitutes the rational choice is trivial: if the true state of nature is ω_1 then it is rational for him or her to choose strategy s_1, and if the true state of nature is ω_2 then it is rational for him or her to choose strategy s_2. This means that when the player does not know the true state of nature, it is far from clear as to what constitutes the rational choice. It depends on the player's beliefs about which state of nature is the true state and on his or her attitude to risk.

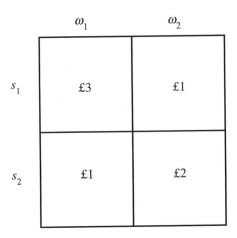

Figure 1: A decision situation with exogenous uncertainty; there are two strategies, s_1 and s_2, and two states of nature, ω_1 and ω_2

There are two basic theories of rational choice in decision situations with exogenous uncertainty: one is due to von Neumann and Morgenstern (1947), and the other is due to Savage (1954) — for an excellent exposition of both theories, see Kreps (1990: Ch. 3) or Marschak and Radner (1972: Ch. 1). Both of these theories generate an *expected utility theorem* (EUT). Before we briefly explain the key difference between these two theories, we describe this celebrated theorem, which lies at the heart of economic theory.

Two new concepts are required to define this theorem: a probability distribution over the states of nature, and a von Neumann–Morgenstern (vN–M) utility function. The former concept is relevant in order to define the rational choice, because it is necessary to assess the relative likelihoods of the states of nature. Thus, we denote by $p(\omega)$ the probability that the true state is ω. Since there is uncertainty in the decision situation, the rational choice depends upon the player's attitude towards risk. The vN–M utility function captures this aspect: we denote by $u(m)$ the utility that the player obtains from £m. The function u is the player's vN–M utility function. If it is concave then the player is averse to risk, while if it is convex then he or she is a risk lover. Furthermore, if it is linear then he or she is neutral to risk.

In the context of the general decision situation with exogenous uncertainty stated above, the expected utility theorem states that strategy s^* from the set S is the rational choice if it maximizes the player's expected utility; the expected utility of any strategy s^* from the set S is the expected value of the player's vN–M utility, where the expectation is taken with respect to the given probability distribution. For example, if in the decision situation described in Figure 1 the states of nature are equally likely (that is, $p(\omega_1) = p(\omega_2) = 0.5$) and the player is risk neutral (that is, $u(m) = m$), then the expected utility of strategy s_1 equals 2, and the expected utility of strategy s_2 equals 1.5. Hence, given these probabilities and this utility function, according to the EUT it is rational to choose strategy s_1. Of course, there exist alternative probabilities and/or utility functions such that the EUT would imply that it is rational to choose s_2. Hence, rationality depends critically upon a player's beliefs and his or her attitude towards risk.

But where do these beliefs come from? Surely the beliefs should be rational? A main difference between vN–M's theory and Savage's theory is to do with this issue. The former theory assumes that the probabilities with which the states occur are known to the player, and hence the player does not have to form beliefs about these states — the probabilities are objective. In contrast, in Savage's theory the probabilities are subjective, in that they are the player's personal beliefs about the relative likelihoods of the states of nature. While vN–M's theory has limited applicability, because it is rare to be given objective probabilities, Savage's theory leaves unanswered the question of where the player's beliefs come from.

A fundamental weakness of these theories is that neither of them actually *describe* what constitutes rational choice in decision situations with exogenous uncertainty. A key assumption in both theories — the 'complete ordering over acts' assumption — implies that the rational choice is (implicitly) known to the player. The theories simply generate a 'representation' theorem — that is, they generate (with the assistance of further assumptions) a convenient and useful *representation* of rational choice — the EUT.

The expected utility representations of preferences (as derived in the vN–M and Savage theories) have been shown to be inconsistent with various experiments, such as the well-known *Allais Paradox*. For a penetrating critique of these expected utility theories, see Machina (1987), who also describes the Allais Paradox and discusses various alternatives to expected, utility theory.

Endogenous uncertainty
A crucial factor in defining rationality in decision situations with exogenous uncertainty are the beliefs of the player about the relative likelihoods of the states of nature, where the true state is determined in a purely random manner by Mother Nature. A main new element in decision situations with endogenous

uncertainty is that the state of nature is now determined 'strategically' by some other player, because the state is actually now a strategy choice of some other player.

Indeed, a game situation is the key type of situation that exhibits endogenous uncertainty. A player is in a game when his or her payoff depends not only on his or her strategy but also on the strategy of some other player. Consider the following 'battle of sexes' game, which involves two players, Romeo and Juliet. It is about 6 pm and they are unable to communicate with each other. However, they must decide where to spend the evening. Each must decide whether to go to the theatre to see the ballet or to the colosseum to see the big fight. If they end up at different performances, then they become rather upset and hence each receives zero utility. However, if they meet at the same venue, then each receives two utils. In addition, Romeo gets another util if they meet at the colosseum, while Juliet gets an additional util if they meet at the theatre. All this information is compactly summarized in Figure 2.

Juliet

	Theatre	Colosseum
Theatre	2, 3	0, 0
Colosseum	0, 0	3, 2

Romeo

Figure 2: A decision situation with endogenous uncertainty — the battle of the sexes game

What constitutes the rational choice for Romeo? It depends on what choice Juliet makes. If she goes to the theatre, then the rational choice for Romeo is to go to the theatre. But if she goes to the colosseum, then the rational choice for Romeo is to go to the colosseum. Hence, the rational choice for Romeo depends on his beliefs about where Juliet will go. The concept of rationality in this interactive decision situation is nontrivial, because Juliet's choice depends on her

491

beliefs about where Romeo will go. Unlike exogenous uncertainty, where the uncertainty is resolved in a purely random manner, endogenous uncertainty is resolved strategically, and makes the concept of rationality pretty complex.

Game theorists have suggested that *if* there exists a rational choice for Romeo and a rational choice for Juliet, then these choices must form a *Nash equilibrium* — which means that neither player has an incentive to deviate unilaterally to an alternative strategy, given the rational choice of the other player. Attention thus focuses on studying the Nash equilibria of the game. For a brief discussion of this and related concepts of game theory, see the entry on Game Theory; and for a more detailed exposition, see Kreps (1990: Chs 11 and 12). The Nash Equilibrium concept, however, fails to identify satisfactorily and persuasively what constitutes rational behaviour in decision situations with endogenous uncertainty. In fact, this is an equilibrium concept, and it simply evades addressing the problems involved in defining the concept of rationality in game situations.

Matters become more complex in the context of *dynamic* interactive decision situations, where the concept of rationality may not be well defined — for example, some (small) degree of irrationality may be required to define and make sense of the concept of rationality. To briefly illustrate this point, consider the following dynamic game with two players, *A* and *B*, which is illustrated in Figure 3. The game begins with player *A* choosing between α and β. If he or she chooses the former, then each player obtains £2; otherwise the game continues with player *B* having to choose between γ and δ. If he or she chooses the former, then player *A* obtains £1 and player *B* obtains £3; otherwise the game continues with player *A* having to choose between η and μ. If he or she chooses the former, then player *A* obtains £5 and player *B* obtains £2; otherwise the game ends with each player obtaining £4.

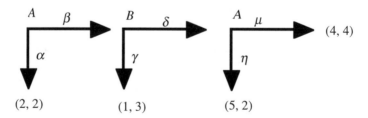

Figure 3: The centipede game

The following, rather persuasive, backward induction argument is meant to identify the rational outcome of this game. Consider *A*'s second decision node, where he or she has to choose between η and μ — which is reached if and only if

A has chosen η at his or her first decision node and B has chosen δ. It seems rational for A to choose η, because he or she then obtains £5 (rather than £4, which is obtained if he or she were to instead choose μ. Proceeding backwards, this implies that it is rational for B to choose γ and obtain £3 (rather than δ, which would give him or her £2, because we have just shown that it is rational for A to choose η). Proceeding backwards, this implies that it is rational for player A to choose α at his or her first decision node. Hence, *backward induction* rationality implies that the game will terminate immediately after A makes his or her first decision. It should be noted that backward induction rationality is the basic concept of rationality in dynamic games.

Backward induction rationality also implies that player B will not be called upon to make the choice between γ and δ. But this conclusion rests on the counterfactual that player A does make the irrational choice of β. How should we interpret this? The standard interpretation is that A has made a mistake, which is uncorrelated with any mistake that A might make at his or her second decision node. Hence, the standard way to get round this fundamental problem with backward induction rationality is to assume that players are prone to some (albeit tiny) mistakes/irrationality. There are, however, some serious problems with such an interpretation; for a detailed discussion of this and related issues, see Reny (1992), who uses this game to discuss the notion that it might be rational to be irrational. It should also be mentioned that most solution concepts in game theory, such as backward induction rationality, implicitly rest on the common knowledge assumption, which includes the assumption that the rules of the game are common knowledge among the players: both players know the rules, both players know that both players know the rules, both players know that both players know that both players know the rules of the game, and so on *ad infinitum*.

Substantive and procedural rationality
Herbert Simon coined the terms *substantive* rationality and *procedural* rationality. He argued that economists have focused attention on the former concept, while psychologists have focused on the latter concept. The issue of defining/discovering *what* constitutes rationality in a decision situation is a matter of substantive rationality, while the issue of defining/discovering the rational *procedure* of choice is a matter of procedural rationality. That is, procedural rationality is about the rationality of the procedure used to reach a decision, while substantive rationality is about the rationality of the decision itself.

The following example illustrates the distinction between procedural and substantive rationality. Consider the situation in which an individual has to buy a television (TV). Suppose that an omniscient observer knows which brand and model of TV the individual should buy to maximize his or her utility — say, it is a Sony 234. Thus, the substantively rational choice is to buy a Sony 234. Now suppose that the individual does not know (for one reason or another) what the substantively rational choice is. He or she would then use some procedure (which is based on his or her information about TVs and so on) in order to arrive at his or her decision as to which TV to buy. The procedure may be considered to be rational if it generates a satisfactory choice, whether or not the choice is the same as the substantively rational choice (which here is a Sony 234). The concept of *satisficing*, which is developed by Herbert Simon and on which there is a separate entry, is intimately connected with the concept of procedural rationality.

In our discussion above, we only addressed the issue of substantive rationality: given a decision situation with exogenous/endogenous uncertainty, we discussed the question of *what* constitutes rationality. We did not address the issue of *how* the player reaches a decision — thus, issues of thought, reasoning and computation were omitted from our discussion. However, such issues are important, especially if we are to understand and develop models of *human* rationality. On this latter point, it should be noted that human rationality might differ to some lesser or greater extent from the concepts of substantive rationality developed by economists, which is linked to the thorny issue of human reasoning/thought processes. Although psychologists have done much research on this latter issue and amassed much data about it, we are far from developing general models of such complex processes.

Procedural rationality has recently been somewhat forced on to the agenda of economic theory, especially because of the recent dissatisfaction with the concepts of substantive rationality and equilibrium developed by economists. Furthermore, the concept of *bounded* rationality, which arises naturally when thinking about procedural rationality and is inextricably linked with the concept of human rationality, has been the subject of much recent investigation in economic theory. This work builds on the ideas developed by Herbert Simon, which are collected together in Simon (1982). A major difficulty involves constructing useful and tractable *formal* models of bounded rationality that take into explicit account the procedural aspects of rationality. For an exposition of some of the recently developed tools and models, and in particular of the difficult modelling issues involved, see Rubinstein (1997).

ABHINAY MUTHOO

Bibliography
Kreps, D. (1990) *A Course in Microeconomic Theory*, Hemel Hempstead, Harvester-Wheatsheaf.
Machina, M.J. (1987) 'Choice Under Uncertainty: Problems Solved and Unsolved', *Journal of Economic Perspectives*, **1**: 121–54.

Marschak, J. and Radner, R. (1972) *Economic Theory of Teams*, New Haven, CT, Yale University Press.

Reny, P. (1992) 'Rationality and Extensive Form Games', *Journal of Economic Literature*, **6**, 103–18.

Rubinstein, A. (1997) *Modeling Bounded Rationality*, Cambridge, MA, MIT Press.

Savage, L. (1954) *The Foundations of Statistics*, New York, John Wiley and Sons.

Simon, H.A. (1982) *Models of Bounded Rationality*, Volume 2, Cambridge, MA, MIT Press.

von Neumann, J. and Morgenstern, O. (1947) *Theory of Games and Economic Behavior* (2nd edn), Princeton, NJ, Princeton University Press.

Reference Price

The topic of reference price is embedded in the construct of perceived value which, in turn, influences purchase intentions and consumer choice. Perceived value is believed to be a function of perceived quality and perceived price (or perceived sacrifice). Rajendran and Hariharan (1996) propose a simple model of value perception and purchase intention. They suggest that perceived quality is a function of objective quality (attributes/levels present) and what consumers want (attributes/levels desired). Likewise, perceived price is a function of objective (actual) price and reference price. Grewal, Monroe and Krishnan (1996) model perceived value in a somewhat complicated manner as 'acquisition' value and 'transactional' value, as suggested by Thaler (1985). They suggest that perceived acquisition value is driven by perceived quality (not defined) and that perceived transactional value is influenced by reference price and the selling price. However, they find that perceived transactional value influences purchase intention only indirectly, that is, by influencing perceived acquisition value. Thus, the simpler model of value perception is provided in Figure 1 as background.

Theoretical basis for reference prices

Reference prices are price standards used by consumers to evaluate prices they encounter in the marketplace. The basic premise is that at least some consumers, when making purchase decisions, compare prices of goods against their reference prices (consciously or not) and, thus, judge them as 'high' or 'low'. Several theories — such as assimilation–contrast theory (Sherif, Taub and Hovland, 1958), adaptation level theory (Helson, 1964), prospect theory (Kahneman and Tversky, 1979) and its extension mental accounting (Thaler, 1985), and price-tier theory (Blattberg and Wisniewski, 1989) — suggest the existence and likely role of reference prices.

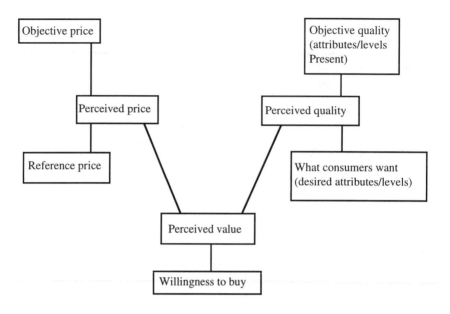

Figure 1: A model of value perception and purchase intention

Assimilation-contrast theory suggests that a new price would be perceived as similar to (and 'assimilated'), or different from (and 'contrasted'), some standard (or reference) price. Presumably this reference price lies somewhere within the consumer's current latitude of indifference, that is, a price zone within which price differences are not perceived by the consumer. Indeed, this theory suggests that the consumer's reference price may in fact be a price range rather than a specific price.

Adaptation level theory suggests that the comparison standard for a new price is the price to which the consumer has become accustomed. Evidently, past prices (past purchase prices, in particular) influence the current reference price for a product. Most empirical studies have, at least in part, modelled reference price as an adaptation level.

Prospect theory suggests that price judgements are relative — that is, consumers respond to changes in prices rather than to absolute prices — and that price evaluations may be influenced by providing different frames of reference. These imply that consumers judge price against a standard that varies with purchase context. In 'Mental Accounting', Thaler explicitly suggests that the reference price is a fair price driven by cost considerations. By implication there is some presumption that consumers have their own theories of likely production costs and profit margins.

Price-tier theory points out that competition among national (manufacturer) brands, store brands (private labels) and generics (that is, those sold without brand names) may be asymmetric. The competition for a national brand is only other national brands, but for a private label the competition may include other private labels as well as a discounted national brand. Likewise, generics may face competition from discounted national brands and discounted private labels. Thus, since the consideration set is different, this theory suggests that the comparison (reference) price depends on the type of brand.

Whether reference prices exist has been empirically examined by several researchers, beginning with Winer (1986). There is now strong evidence that reference prices exist and that they moderate consumer response to price (Gurumurthy and Winer, 1995). However, most of these studies infer the existence of reference prices from econometric analysis of brand choices. They tend to utilize scanner data and evaluate consumer choice models employing binary or multinomial logistic regressions.

Reference price has often been modelled as a function of past prices, a longitudinal approach employing, usually, an exponentially smoothed average of prices paid or observed. This implies that the consumer has a reference price for a brand before the purchase occasion. This type of reference price is usually called the 'internal' or 'temporal' reference price. Rajendran (1988) argued that there may be a cross-sectional component to reference price as well. This implies that consumers form reference prices at the time of purchase also rather than only before. This 'external' or 'contextual' reference price has been variously modelled as average or lowest of other brand prices at the store (Rajendran and Tellis, 1994) or as the 'regular' shelf price of the brand at the time of purchase (Mayhew and Winer, 1992). These later studies demonstrate that incorporating both types of reference prices in the same model greatly improves its explanatory power.

Emerging issues

A key research issue is: what do reference prices mean to consumers? Most studies have assumed that consumers interpret reference price as an expected price based on past prices. However, other interpretations are possible. In an experimental study, Rajendran and Tellis (1991) elicited reference prices from subjects under alternative definitions ('expected price' and 'fair price') and examined their impact on choice behaviour. They found a significant, although small, difference between the 'fair price' and 'expected price' elicited. More importantly, they found that 'fair price' explained choices much better than did 'expected price'. In a later survey-based study Rajendran (1995) attempted to link consumer definitions of value and reference price to their demographic and behavioural correlates. He examined four reference price definitions: 'expected price', 'fair price', 'reservation price' and 'aspiration price' (suggested by Klein and Oglethorpe, 1987). He found that a majority of the respondents interpreted the comparison price they used as a 'fair price', although a substantial number interpreted it as 'reservation price' and an 'expected price'. Few respondents reported interpreting their reference price as an 'aspiration price'. The study suggested that different definitions imply attention to different prices and that consumers may use different definitions for different products.

Most researchers would agree that reference prices are influenced by past prices, current prices and by the purchase context. However, in modelling reference prices researchers have operationalized the purchase context primarily in terms of competitive prices at the point of purchase. Other aspects of the purchase context have so far been ignored. One major issue to be resolved, therefore, is how to incorporate the influence of nonprice situational factors in modelling reference price. Even within competitive prices, there remains the issue of which prices are relevant? Should it be the prices of all competing brands or only some of them? In other words, the composition of the consideration set at the point of purchase is an issue that needs to be addressed. While researchers have assumed that price comparisons are restricted to the store environment, other store prices may be relevant in some purchase situations. So, yet another issue is how other store prices influence reference prices in a given purchase situation.

In this connection, it must be clarified that a number of studies have examined the practice of 'reference pricing', by stores (for example, Biswas and Blair, 1991). Stores explicitly suggest reference prices to consumers (primarily at the point of purchase) in order to influence favourably their evaluation of the selling price of an item. These merchant-supplied reference prices are usually couched in 'was/is' or 'compare at' terms and, presumably, reflect 'normal' prices or prices at a different store. When plausible, these suggested comparison prices may influence the consumer's reference prices. In any case, merchant-supplied reference prices are part of the purchase context and, therefore, are expected to impact consumer price perceptions.

Finally, there is the issue of managerial relevance. Can we segment markets based on whether or not consumers use reference prices, or based on which reference price they use? Are there systematic demographic and behavioural differences among segments to permit and reward use of differential marketing mixes to cater to them? A related issue is how to influence reference prices used by consumers, that is, how to influence the consumer's price perception in a favourable manner?

In sum, we know that reference prices exist and that they influence choices. However, we need to know more about how consumers form, interpret and use reference prices before we can even attempt to address the thorny questions of managerial relevance. We have some ideas and some evidence now, but much work remains to be done.

K.N. RAJENDRAN

Bibliography

Biswas, A. and Blair, E.A. (1991) 'Contextual Effects of Reference Prices in Retail Advertisements', *Journal of Marketing*, **55**: 1–12.

Blattberg, R.C. and Wisniewski, K.J. (1989) 'Price-Induced Patterns of Competition', *Marketing Science*, **8**: 291–309.

Grewal, D., Monroe, K.B. and Krishnan. R. (1996) 'The Effects of Price Comparison on Buyers' Perception of Acquisition Value and Transaction Value', Marketing Science Institute Report No. 96–103, May.

Gurumurthy, K. and Winer, R.S. (1995) 'Empirical Generalizations from Reference Price Research', *Marketing Science*, **14** (3): G161–69.

Helson, H. (1964) *Adaptation Level Theory*, New York, Harper & Row.

Kahneman, D. and Tversky, A. (1979) 'Prospect Theory: An Analysis of Decision Under Risk', *Econometrica*, **47**: 263–91.

Klein, N.M. and Oglethorpe, J.E. (1987) 'Cognitive Reference Points in Consumer Decision Making', in Wallendorf, M. and Anderson, P. (eds) *Advances in Consumer Research*, **14**, Provo, UT, Association of Consumer Research: 183–87.

Mayhew, G.E. and Winer, R.S. (1992) 'An Empirical Analysis of Internal and External Reference Prices Using Scanner Data', *Journal of Consumer Research*, **19**: 62–70.

Rajendran, K.N. (1988) 'A Componential View of Reference Price', TIMS/ORSA Marketing Science Conference, Seattle, WA.

Rajendran, K.N. (1995) 'How Do Consumers Evaluate Price and Value?' INFORMS Marketing Science Conference, Sydney, Australia.

Rajendran, K.N. and Hariharan, H.S. (1996) 'Understanding Value: The Role of Consumer Preferences', *Journal of Marketing Management* (published in the US by the Marketing Management Association — not its namesake, published in the UK by the Academy of Marketing), **6**: 8–19.

Rajendran, K.N. and Tellis, G.J. (1991) 'Is Reference Price a Fair Price or an Expected Price?', TIMS Marketing Science Conference, Wilmington, DE.

Rajendran, K.N. and Tellis, G.J. (1994) 'The Contextual and Temporal Components of Reference Price', *Journal of Marketing*, **58**: 22–34.

Sherif, M., Taub, D. and Hovland, C.I. (1958) 'Assimilation and Contrast Effects of Anchoring Stimuli on Judgments', *Journal of Experimental Psychology*, **55**: 150–55.

Thaler, R. (1985) 'Mental Accounting and Consumer Choice', *Marketing Science*, **4**: 199–214.

Winer, R.S. (1986) 'A Reference Price Model of Brand Choice for Frequently Purchased Products', *Journal of Consumer Research*, **13**: 250–56.

Rewards and the Myth of Performance Decrements

Over the past 25 years, many social psychologists have been critical of the practice of using incentive systems in business, education and other applied settings. The concern is that money, high grades, prizes and even praise may be effective in getting people to perform an activity but performance and interest are maintained only as long as the reward keeps coming. For example, if an artist who enjoys painting is externally rewarded (for example, with money) for painting, the claim is that the artist will come to produce fewer paintings and enjoy painting less once the reward is discontinued. In other words, rewards are said to undermine people's intrinsic motivation. This premise is based on the view that when individuals like what they are doing, they experience feelings of competence and self-determination (Deci and Ryan, 1985). When offered a reward for performance, it is argued that people begin to do the activity for the external reward (Lepper, Greene and Nisbett, 1973), rather than for intrinsic reasons. As a result, perceptions of competence and self-determination are said to decrease and motivation and quality of performance decline. This view is widely accepted and has been enormously influential: it has led people to question the use of rewards and incentive systems in many applied settings.

Those who oppose the use of rewards support their position by citing experimental studies on rewards and intrinsic motivation. Over the past few years, our research team (Cameron and Eisenberger, 1997; Cameron and Pierce, 1994; Eisenberger and Cameron, 1996) has conducted a series of analyses of this literature to determine whether, overall, rewards negatively affect people's intrinsic task interest and to identify the conditions under which rewards produce increments or decrements. Contrary to the belief that rewards are damaging, our meta-analysis of approximately 100 studies indicates that there is no inherent negative property of reward. Instead, our research demonstrates that rewards, when used appropriately, have a much more favourable effect on task interest and performance than is generally supposed. What follows is an outline of the context in which rewards and intrinsic motivation were investigated, a description of the experimental studies we analysed, the meta-analytic procedures and the findings.

Intrinsic and extrinsic motivation
In the standard economic/business view of work, labour is not enjoyed but is completed in exchange for money and perks. This is undoubtedly true for people who labour in smokestack industries, assembly lines, sewage works and so on. Workers in these jobs do not appear to be motivated by the nature of the tasks they perform. Rather, they work for the incentives. A large number of other individuals, however, find their work pleasurable. Notably, artists, academics,

500

professional athletes and others appear to enjoy their work. These differences in reasons for working point to two sources of motivation — extrinsic and intrinsic.

Extrinsic motivation occurs when an activity is rewarded by incentives that are not inherent in the task. That is, extrinsic motivation is external to the individual; rewards such as money are presented for engaging in tasks. A second source of motivation is intrinsic; people may work at a job because it gives them feelings of competence and a sense of personal control, doing the job is fun, the work is a matter of pride, the tasks are challenging, and so on (for example, see Lane, 1991: 337–63). In this situation, the individual is intrinsically motivated to work. Thus, intrinsically motivated behaviours are ones for which there is no apparent reward except the activity itself.

The distinction between intrinsic and extrinsic motivation led psychologists to speculate about the relationship between these two sources. One view was that intrinsic and extrinsic motivation combined in an additive fashion to produce overall motivation. For example, in work settings, organizational psychologists argued that optimal performance would occur when jobs were interesting and challenging and when employees were externally rewarded (for example, with money) for their work (for example, Porter and Lawler, 1968; Vroom, 1964). Other theorists challenged the additive assumption suggesting instead that extrinsic rewards might interfere with intrinsic motivation (for example, deCharms, 1968).

Experiments on rewards and intrinsic motivation

The idea that extrinsic rewards could disrupt an individual's intrinsic motivation instigated a large body of research on the topic. Since the 1970s, dozens of experiments, using a common set of procedures, have been conducted to investigate the effects of reward on people's intrinsic motivation. In a typical experiment, participants are presented with an interesting task (for example, solving puzzles, drawing pictures, playing word games) for which they receive praise, money, candy, gold stars and so forth. A control group performs the activity without receiving a reward. Both groups are then observed during a nonreward period in which they are free to continue performing the task or to engage in some alternative activity. The time participants spend on the target activity during this period, their expressed attitude towards the activity, or both, are used to measure intrinsic motivation. If rewarded participants spend less free time on the activity or express less task interest than nonrewarded participants, reward is said to undermine intrinsic motivation. On the other hand, when interest and performance increase, people are said to experience an increase in intrinsic motivation.

Although experiments using these procedures are frequently cited as evidence that rewards undermine people's intrinsic motivation (for example,

Deci and Ryan, 1985; Kohn, 1993), a cursory examination of the literature reveals a mixed set of findings. That is, in some studies, extrinsic rewards reduce performance or interest; other studies find positive effects of reward; still others show no effect. In order to assess the impact of reward over all the experimental studies, we conducted a meta-analysis of the experimental literature.

A meta-analysis of the effects of rewards on intrinsic motivation

Meta-analysis is a quantitative technique for combining the results from a large number of studies on the same topic (for a detailed technical discussion of meta-analysis, see Hedges and Olkin, 1985). It involves the statistical analysis of a large collection of results from individual studies; the purpose is to integrate the findings. In meta-analysis, each study is the unit of analysis rather than individual participants in a study.

There are several steps to meta-analysis that we used in our research. The first step was to specify the research questions. The questions we addressed were: (i) 'Do rewards overall lead to a decrease in interest and performance (intrinsic motivation)?' and (ii) 'Under what conditions do rewards lead to decreased or increased intrinsic motivation?'. Other steps in the meta-analysis involved specifying the criteria for including and excluding studies, collecting all experiments that met the criteria (approximately 100 studies were included), and reading and coding the studies.

For each experiment, an effect size was calculated to indicate the difference between rewarded and nonrewarded groups on measures of performance and task interest (statistically expressed in standard deviation units). Basically, the larger the effect size, the greater the difference between rewarded and non-rewarded groups. Effect sizes may be positive or negative values. A negative-effect size indicates that the rewarded group spent less time on the task or expressed less task interest than the control group, after rewards were withdrawn. A positive-effect size indicates that rewarded participants spent more free time on the task and reported greater task interest than non-rewarded participants; a zero-effect size means that there is no difference between the groups.

Once effect sizes for each experiment were calculated, they were plotted on a graph to determine the overall pattern of results. Finally, effect sizes were statistically analysed using a computer program, 'Meta' (Schwarzer, 1991).

Overall effects of reward

Figure 1 is a funnel graph of the effect sizes for all of the reward and intrinsic motivation experiments included in the meta-analysis (Cameron and Pierce, 1994). Funnel graphs are used to plot effect sizes (horizontal axis) against sample size (vertical axis) for each study. The advantage of a funnel display is that it capitalizes on a well-known statistical principle (Light and Pillemer, 1984). That

502

is, the larger the sample size, the closer the effect size will come to represent the true effect size. Smaller samples are more prone to sampling error and are likely to deviate considerably about the true effect size. For these reasons, the distribution is expected to take the shape of an inverted funnel; the tip of the funnel will hone in around the true effect size.

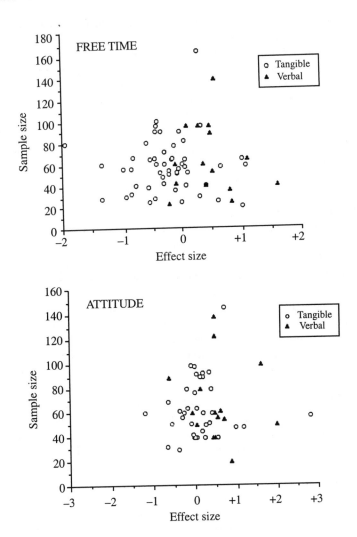

Figure 1: Funnel graph of the effect sizes for all of the reward and intrinsic motivation experiments

Figure 1 presents the pattern of effect sizes for the two measures of intrinsic motivation — performance and interest. As previously indicated, performance was measured as the time spent on the experimental task once reward was withdrawn (referred to as 'free time' on the task). Interest was assessed by questionnaire measures of participants' task interest, enjoyment or satisfaction (referred to as 'attitude' towards the task).

An inspection of the funnel distribution of effect sizes for the free-time measure (regardless of reward type) indicates that overall, the mean effect size (average) concentrates around zero. Our statistical test of this pattern showed that, overall, there was no significant effect of reward on the free-time measure. This finding suggests that there is no evidence to support the claim that rewards have general detrimental effects on performance. In terms of task interest or attitude, Figure 1 shows that rewards have a positive effect. Meta-analysis revealed this positive effect to be statistically reliable. This finding suggests that, generally, people enjoy activities or tasks more when they receive a reward. In summary, the argument that rewards undermine performance and interest is not supported by the experimental data.

A breakdown of reward effects
Although the analysis shows that, overall, rewards do not have generalized negative effects, there may be aspects of reward procedures that result in increments or decrements in performance and interest. The question then is 'when and under what conditions do reward procedures have positive or negative effects on interest and performance?'. One possibility is that different types of rewards may have different effects. To assess this possibility, studies were evaluated that used either verbal or tangible rewards. Verbal rewards involved giving participants praise or positive feedback for their work; tangible rewards were money, tickets to a theatre, gold stars, and so on.

A close inspection of Figure 1 shows that for the free-time measure, the pattern of effect sizes for verbal rewards (closed triangles) is slightly positive and for tangible rewards (open circles) is slightly negative. In other words, verbal rewards (praise and positive feedback) increased performance while tangible rewards reduced time on task. Meta-analysis showed that these effects were statistically significant. On the task interest measure (attitude), Figure 1 indicates a positive effect for verbal reward; tangible rewards leave task interest unchanged.

Although the reduction in performance by tangible rewards appears to support the view that intrinsic motivation is damaged, this finding is not straightforward. It turns out that tangible rewards have different effects depending on how they are administered. Specifically, the results from the meta-analysis indicate that tangible rewards enhance performance and interest when they are offered to people for completing a task, solving a problem, or for attaining or exceeding a specific performance standard (Cameron and Eisenberger, 1997), a circumstance common in applied settings. In fact, the only situation in which tangible rewards were found to decrease intrinsic motivation involved offering a reward to individuals independently of task completion or performance quality. For example, in some studies participants were told that they would receive money for engaging in an activity regardless of how well they performed or whether they completed the task. Under this condition, when the rewards were withdrawn, rewarded participants spent less time on the activity than a nonrewarded group; they did not, however, report less task interest.

Conclusion

A meta-analysis of the effects of rewards on people's intrinsic motivation indicates that the belief that rewards undermine intrinsic task interest is an overgeneralization based on a restricted set of conditions. Importantly, negative effects of reward can be prevented easily. Task interest and performance are enhanced when individuals receive verbal praise, positive feedback, or when tangible rewards are offered for task completion or for attaining or exceeding a performance standard. These findings suggest that in the workplace, in schools and in other institutional settings, rewards can be used effectively to maintain or increase people's intrinsic task interest.

JUDY CAMERON

Bibliography
Cameron, J. and Eisenberger, R. (1997) 'A Meta-analysis of Rewards and Intrinsic Interest', Paper presented at the Society for Research in Child Development (SRCD), Washington, DC.
Cameron, J. and Pierce, W.D. (1994) 'Reinforcement, Reward and Intrinsic Motivation: A Meta-analysis', *Review of Educational Research*, **64**: 363–423.
deCharms, R. (1968) *Personal Causation*, New York, Academic Press.
Deci, E.L. and Ryan, R.M. (1985) *Intrinsic Motivation and Self-determination in Human Behavior*, New York, Plenum Press.
Eisenberger, R. and Cameron, J. (1996) 'The Detrimental Effects of Reward: Myth or Reality?', *American Psychologist*, **51**: 1153–66.
Hedges, L.V. and Olkin, I. (1985) *Statistical Methods for Meta-Analysis*, Orlando, Academic Press.
Kohn, A. (1993) *Punished by Rewards*, Boston, MA, Houghton Mifflin.
Lane, R.E. (1991) *The Market Experience*, CambridgwCambridge University Press.
Lepper, M.R., Greene, D. and Nisbett, R.E. (1973) 'Undermining Children's Intrinsic Interest with Extrinsic Reward: A Test of the "Overjustification" Hypothesis', *Journal of Personality and Social Psychology,* **28**: 129–37.
Light, R.J. and Pillemer, D.B. (1984) *Summing Up: The Science of Reviewing Research,*

Cambridge, MA, Harvard University Press.

Porter, L.W. and Lawler, E.E. (1968) *Managerial Atitudes and Performance*, Homewood, IL, Irwin-Dorsey.

Schwarzer, R. (1991) *Meta: Programs for Secondary Data Analysis*, MS-DOS Version 5.0. Dubuque, IA, Wm. C. Brown.

Vroom, V. (1964) *Work and Motivation*, New York, Wiley.

Ritual

Sociocultural dimensions of consumption

Prior to 1980, consumer research devoted relatively little attention to the socio-cultural aspects of consumption behaviour. Despite groundwork laid by motivational research in the 1950s, and the seminal thinking of prominent scholars such as Sidney Levy, W.T. Tucker and Gerald Zaltman, studies of the social aspects of consumption were relatively rare. Those that appeared in print tended to emerge from one of three research paradigms, in studies of: (i) the effects of social class membership on various consumer behaviours, (ii) the influence of consumer psychographics, or lifestyles, on purchase attitudes and behaviours, or (iii) the relationship between consumers' cultural values and similar dependent measures. This work notwithstanding, the consumer research field 15 years ago was far more interested in studying consumers' mental product purchase machinations than the broader sociocultural milieu in which these activities occur.

This changed quickly and dramatically in the early 1980s. Several forces contributed to what, in retrospect, became a consumer research watershed marking the beginning of vigorous renewed interest in consumption's cultural dimensions. First, a small but significant number of influential marketing scholars abandoned their more conventional research topics and turned towards inquiry into the socially symbolic nature of consumer behaviour. In May 1980, many of these individuals attended the Conference on Consumer Esthetics and Symbolic Consumption, which was held at New York University, and co-chaired by Elizabeth Hirschman and Morris Holbrook. A critical mass of conference participants continued to study consumption symbolism, and they fought successfully for the legitimacy of their research in academic journals.

At the same time, consumer researchers were not only exploring new topics, but they were also beginning to work with new research methods, particularly qualitative ones. Ethnographic field studies, individual depth interviews and projective techniques began to appear in the literature, and provided new insights into the symbolic meanings of not only products and brands, but of shopping, eating, grooming, praying and playing. Third, and concurrent with these developments, anthropologists (Eric Arnold, Grant McCracken and John Sherry,

Jr.), semioticians (David Mick), and literary analysts (Barbara Stern) migrated into marketing departments, and began to publish extensively in marketing and consumer research journals. Collectively, these scholars represent fields in which the study of sociocultural meaning occupies centre stage, and their work helped inspire a more broadly construed consumer research domain. Finally, the steadily growing emphasis on global marketing made cross-cultural consumer understanding not only an academic priority, but a managerial one.

Together, these forces have encouraged what today is a large and diverse research arena. Among the many published studies of consumption's social and symbolic aspects, the topic of consumer rituals and ritualized consumption has attracted early and continuing interest. The following discussion summarizes both the empirical and theoretical contributions of existing ritual research, and it suggests promising areas for future investigations.

Ritual behaviour and research

When it was (re)introduced into the consumer behaviour literature (Rook and Levy, 1983; Sherry, 1983), many scholars declared ritual behaviour an interesting topic, but some were sceptical of its managerial implications and utilities. This ambivalence failed to perceive the cultural pervasiveness of everyday and extraordinary social rituals in consumers' lives; the varying scope of ritual performance, from large-scale societal rituals to more intimate family and personal ones; the profound meaning that consumers extract from their participation in many diverse ritual experiences; and — bottom line — the billions of dollars that consumers spend annually on products and services that function as ritual artefacts. The growing body of research that has studied ritual behaviour over the past 15 years, has targeted an impressive variety of ritual expression. Rook (1985) identified ten ritual types, and subsequent studies have investigated most of these. Perhaps the largest body of research has studied the activities, artefacts and consumer meanings that materialize in large-scale social rituals such as Halloween (Belk, 1990), Thanksgiving (Wallendorf and Arnould, 1991), and professional sports competition (Holt, 1992). Their findings have provided insights into the explicit and more subtle meanings underlying the consumption of, for example, candy and costumes, mashed potatoes and turkey, and baseball's seventh inning stretch, or a stadium 'wave'.

A second stream of ritual research has focused on smaller-scale social rituals, and on their transformational and relational aspects. Rituals that function as social and psychosocial *rites de passage*, and their product artefacts, have been targeted in studies of debutante balls (Escales, 1993), women's business suits (Solomon and Anand, 1985), cosmetic surgery (Schouten, 1991), weddings, and small-group initiation ceremonies. A burgeoning body of gift-giving research has examined the ritual apects of gift exchange and, also, uncovered the

507

considerable ambivalence that often accompanies supposedly joyous and sometimes sacred rituals (Sherry, McGrath and Levy, 1993). Other ritual types have received less attention, for example civic rituals such as elections and trials; family rituals that surround mealtime (Heisley and Levy, 1991), bedtime, and party time; and rituals that are often solitary, such as grooming (Rook, 1985).

Ritual theory

Accompanying this empirical work, some efforts have been directed towards improving conceptualizations of ritual behaviour. Rook (1985: 252) provided a definition of ritual behaviour as:

> a type of expressive, symbolic activity constructed of multiple behaviours that occur in a fixed, episodic sequence, and that tend to be repeated over time. Ritual behaviour is dramatically scripted and acted out, and is performed with formality, seriousness, and inner intensity.

This is an interdisciplinary definition, and scholars working with particular theoretical systems will, inevitably, develop conceptualizations that reflect their varying orientations and purposes. Thus, efforts towards achieving some singular, sanctioned definition of 'ritual' would likely be unproductive and unnecessarily restrictive. On the other hand, opportunity abounds for theoretical refinement and elaboration. 'Ritual' is an umbrella term that encompasses a vast and diverse behavioural domain, and consumer and marketing researchers have barely begun to map it with their own constructs and concerns.

Addressing one key theoretical issue, Rook's interpretation differentiates ritual from habitual behaviour. Although both involve repetitive behaviours, habits *per se* do not typically possess the emotional and symbolic qualities of ritualized expression. In fact, when a ritual's vitality declines, individuals come to view it as merely habitual and devoid of its former meaning. On the other hand, some habits (for example, smoking), evolve into highly ritualized behaviours. This dynamic relationship between ritual and habit is fascinating and uncharted territory that is replete with marketing and public policy implications. Susan Knight's dissertation on habitual consumption, at the University of California, Irvine, promises to contribute to better understanding of both behaviours.

Finally, Rook's definition assumes that 'ritual' is a fuzzy-set construct, and that some ritual expressions will exhibit a majority of these definitional characteristics, while others will be less prototypic. For example, diminution of a ritual's formality may be symptomatic of its deterioration, but not disqualify it as a ritual. On the other hand, as the productive theoretical work by Tetreault and Kleine (1990) correctly suggests, there is a difference between ritualized behaviour and a social ritual. Although most published studies have investigated the latter type of behaviour, ritualized behaviour is, arguably, equally pervasive and significant to consumers.

Unopened doors
In focus and spirit, much ritual research has been descriptive and interpretative, aiming generally to extract the meanings that consumers derive from their participation in various rituals. Relatively little effort has been directed towards studying the structure and nature of rituals *per se*. Two interesting basic issues merit more attention: ritual vitality, and ritual structure and variation. Rook (1985) proposed that a ritual could be deconstructed into artefact, script, role and audience dimensions, and that these provide a basis for assessing a particular ritual's vitality. Graduation ceremonies, for example, are commonly well defined in terms of their script, role and audience aspects. One artefactual element, however — the graduation gift — is less explicitly prescribed, which offers obvious commercial positioning and sales opportunities. Similarly, a decline in a ritual's audience suggests defensive or developmental marketing alternatives for those with particular vested interests. Consideration of a ritual's vitality serves not only managerial interests, as it also helps more broadly orientated behavioural researchers discover how consumer rituals reflect gross and subtle cultural changes.

A second basic issue involves variation in ritual structure and content, and how these changes affect consumers. One of the few studies that has investigated this topic examined the effects of variation in 'ritual syntax' on respondents' brand recall (Kehret-Ward, Johnson and Louie, 1985). McCracken (1986) observed that the meaning of ritual artefacts is constantly changing, and these dynamics merit more vigorous study. A recent promising development in this direction looks at the influence of advertising in influencing or even creating consumer rituals (Otnes and Scott, 1996). For example, Corona beer advertising enhanced its brand positioning by instructing consumers to insert, in quasi-tequilla-ritual fashion, a lime wedge into the neck of the beer bottle. More directly, companies such as Hallmark and the National Football League, have created and defined the consumption content of Mothers' Day and Super Bowl Sunday.

The study of ritual promises to inform two marketplace arenas where it has yet to appear. First, although most ritual research to date falls in the consumer/consumer product domain, specific rituals and much ritualized behaviour occur in business settings; and such behaviour can exert nontrivial influence on the process and outcomes of business meetings, negotiations and ceremonial occasions. Study of these phenomena will help better understand the nature, meaning and potential of ritual performance in organizational settings. Second, the growing diversity of consumer populations in the US, Europe and elsewhere, suggests that ritual forms will migrate across cultures, as we see in the expansion of participation in Chinese New Year and Cinquo de Mayo celebrations. While some rituals may be idiosyncratic and culture-bound, others may have much broader appeal, and enter the burgeoning, global, import–export stream.

Conclusion

Ritual, I believe, is a classically 'interesting' research topic: it is intellectually exciting and endlessly fertile. Although an impressive number of consumer studies have targeted various forms of consumer ritual behaviour in recent years, the field is far from exhausted. As this discussion has noted, several types of ritual behaviour have not yet been examined, and more basic theoretical issues are still at an early stage of development. As sociocultural structures that provide important meanings to consumption behaviour, 'ritual' is likely to be an enduring consumer research topic that encourages continuing multi- and cross-disciplinary investigation.

DENNIS W. ROOK

Bibliography

Belk, R.W. (1990) 'Halloween: An Evolving American Consumption Ritual,' in Goldberg, M.E., Gorn, G. and Pollay, R.W. (eds) *Advances in Consumer Research*, Provo, UT, Association for Consumer Research, **17**: 508–17.

Escales, J.E. (1993) 'The Consumption of Insignificant Rituals: A Look at Debutante Balls', in McAlister, L. and Rothschild, M.L. (eds) *Advances in Consumer Research*, Provo, UT: Association for Consumer Research, **20**: 709–16.

Heisley, D.D. and Levy, S.J. (1991) 'Autodriving: A Photoelicitation Technique', *Journal of Consumer Research*, **18**: 257–72.

Holt, D.B. (1992) 'Examining the Descriptive Value of "Ritual" in Consumer Behavior: A View From the Field', in Sherry, J.F., Jr. and Sternthal, B. (eds) *Advances in Consumer Research*, Provo, UT: Association for Consumer Research, **19**: 213–18.

Kehret-Ward, T., Johnson, M.W. and Louie, T.A. (1985) 'Improving Recall by Manipulating the Syntax of Consumption Rituals', in Hirschman, E.C. and Holbrook, M.B. (eds) *Advances in Consumer Research*, Provo, UT: Association for Consumer Research, **12**: 319–24.

McCracken, G. (1986) 'Culture and Consumption: A Theoretical Account of the Structure and Movement of the Cultural Meaning of Consumer Goods', *Journal of Consumer Research*, **13**: 71–84.

Otnes, C. and Scott, L.M. (1996) 'Something Old, Something New: Exploring the Interaction Between Ritual and Advertising', *Journal of Advertising*, **25**: 33–50.

Rook, D.W. (1985) 'The Ritual Dimension of Consumer Behavior', *Journal of Consumer Research*, **12**: 251–64.

Rook, D.W. and Levy, S.J. (1983) 'Psychosocial Themes in Consumer Grooming

Rituals', in Bagozzi, R. and Tyout, A.M. (eds) *Advances in Consumer Research*, Ann Arbor, MI, Association for Consumer Research, **10**: 329–33.

Schouten, J.W. (1991) 'Selves in Transition: Symbolic Consumption in Personal Rites of Passage and Identity Reconstruction', *Journal of Consumer Research*, **17**: 412–25.

Sherry, J.F., Jr. (1983) 'Gift Giving in Anthropological Perspective', *Journal of Consumer Research*, **10**: 157–68.

Sherry, J.F., Jr., McGrath, M.A. and Levy, S.J. (1993) 'The Dark Side of the Gift', *Journal of Business Research*, **28**: 225–44.

Solomon, M.R. and Anand, P. (1985) 'Ritual Costumes and Status Transitions: The Female Suit as Totemic Emblem', in Hirschman, E.C. and Holbrook, M.B. (eds) *Advances in Consumer Research*, Provo, UT: Association for Consumer Research, **12**: 315–18.

Tetreault, M.A.S. and Kleine, R.E., III (1990) 'Ritual, Ritualized Behavior, and Habit: Refinements and Extensions of the Ritual Construct', in Goldberg, M.E., Gorn, G. and Pollay, R.W. (eds) *Advances in Consumer Research*, Provo, UT, Association for Consumer Research, **17**: 31–8.

Wallendorf, M. and Arnould, E.J. (1991) 'We Gather Together: The Consumption Rituals of Thanksgiving Day', *Journal of Consumer Research*, **18**: 13–31.

Satisficing

The originator of satisficing, Herbert Simon (1982), saw it as an integral component of the bounded rationality approach he developed as an alternative to neoclassical economics. The Nobel Prize committee recognized Simon's work on bounded rationality when it awarded him the 1978 Nobel Prize in Economics 'for his pioneering research into the decision-making process within economic organizations'. Driven by a desire to understand human decision making and problem solving, Simon criticized the following four basic assumptions of neoclassical economics. First, the analysis started from the presupposition that each economic agent had a well-defined utility or profit function. Second, all alternative strategies were assumed to be known to the decision maker. Third, neoclassical economics postulated that all the consequences, no matter how many and how distant, that follow upon each of these strategies could be determined with certainty or in terms of a well-defined probability distribution. Finally, the comparative evaluation of these sets of consequences was assumed to be driven by a universal desire to maximize expected utility or expected profit. Simon believed that these four assumptions illustrated that the neoclassical orthodoxy gave too little attention to institutional constraints on economic behaviour and cognitive constraints on individual decisions.

Instead, Simon sought to include in his bounded rationality approach the entire range of limitations on human knowledge and human computation that prevented economic actors in the real world from behaving in accordance with neoclassical theory. In contrast with the neoclassical postulates outlined above, the following four assumptions characterize Simon's bounded rationality programme. First, it presumed that decision makers had to optimize several, sometimes competing, goals. Second, instead of assuming a fixed set of alternatives among which decision makers chose, Simon's theory of bounded rationality postulated a process for generating alternatives. Furthermore, it argued that under most circumstances it was not reasonable to find 'all the alternatives'. Third, Simon claimed that it was difficult for decision makers to come up with original solutions to problems. Moreover, the presence of uncertainty about the evaluation of the present and future consequences of alternative strategies led Simon to speculate that the mind functions mostly by applying approximate or cookbook solutions to problems. Finally, instead of assuming the maximization of a utility or profit function, Simon's bounded rationality theory postulated a satisficing strategy. It sought to identify, in theory and in actual behaviour, computationally simple procedures for choosing and argued that individuals picked the first choice that met a pre-set acceptance criterion.

For Simon, therefore, satisficing was closely connected with the existence of external, social constraints and internal, cognitive limitations on decision making. Stressing the importance of these constraints, Simon's bounded rationality programme focused on the process rather than the outcome of decision making. This process of selective search, according to Simon, was characterized by procedures such as heuristics for evaluating consequences, and strategies such as satisficing for making choices. Loosely articulated heuristics, or rules of thumb, were used to determine what paths should be taken. In particular, they governed the process of gathering information and choosing alternatives. Furthermore, they were employed generally because they had been proved successful in the past. The search was postulated to halt when a satisfactory solution had been found. This implied that decision makers were searching merely for an adequate solution. That is, they satisficed, they accepted the first solution that was satisfactory according to a set of minimal criteria. In this process, aspiration levels were adapted in response to success or failure.

In Simon's interpretation, then, the search for a satisfactory solution was guided by heuristics and involved choosing an alternative that met the needs of the situation and met or exceeded specified criteria, but that was not guaranteed to be either unique or in any sense the best. The criteria were specified by aspiration levels that were adjusted in response to search outcomes. When the criteria were easily met, aspiration levels were gradually raised. Alternatively, when the criteria could not be met, aspiration levels were gradually lowered. According to Simon, decision makers satisficed when it was impossible to optimize or when the computational cost of doing so could not be overcome. Simon further stressed that satisficing could not be converted into a process of optimizing by taking into account the cost of search, since this would involve informational and computational burdens that could be worse than the original choice, opening up a decision-making black hole of infinite regress. The reason was that decision makers would have to solve the difficult problem of estimating the expected marginal return of search and the opportunity cost. For Simon, satisficing matched what was known empirically regarding the psychological mechanism governing actual choice behaviour. It should be stressed that satisficing is a subjective, procedural notion in that different people will satisfice differently. Furthermore, decision makers may use many different simplifying procedures, and contingent combinations of them, both between and within individual choices.

Although Simon had originally proposed satisficing as a purely hypothetical construct, he later felt that it had been verified as an important component of human decision making by research in information-processing psychology along with computer simulations. Subsequent research has elaborated on satisficing both theoretically and empirically. On the theoretical side, for example, Bianchi (1990) has criticized Simon for not accounting for changes in the rules and routines themselves. Inspired by Joseph Schumpeter, she offered rational innovativeness as an alternative to bounded rationality. In the process, she replaced Simon's psychological framework with a logical one. In particular, she has taken satisficing further by endogenizing change through an emphasis on the active role of search and its innovative character. On the empirical side, some laboratory investigations have found that searchers who are trying to find the lowest price of some good, and initially have essentially no knowledge of the distribution over which they are searching, use rules of thumb that are not optimal, but reasonably good and fairly robust (Hey in Earl (ed.), 1988). They concluded that satisficing is a better explanation of actual search behaviour. Laboratory experiments have also found that optimal behaviour increases with information, decreases with recall but (at least for modest amounts of money) is insensitive to the payment structure. Interestingly enough, this suggests that searchers actually do worse as a consequence of having an extra facility in the form of recall.

Satisficing mechanisms in choice processes have been identified in cognitive psychology, marketing and other areas of business economics. Although satisficing has been used mainly to analyse the behaviour of firms, it can be applied to consumer behaviour as well. For example, driven by a realization of the importance of discovering why people respond (or fail to respond) as they do to various types of persuasion, consumer researchers in general and marketing experts in particular have analysed the role of satisficing in consumers' information processing. However, apart from seminal contributions such as that of Bettman (1979), which references Simon directly and discusses satisficing explicitly, most consumer research mentions Simon indirectly and presumes satisficing implicitly at best (Engel and Blackwell, 1982; Howard, 1977). Since Bettman's work is the subject of a separate entry in this volume, the current entry focuses on the analysis of satisficing in consumer research in general.

Whereas consumer research postulates the consumer as purposeful and goal orientated, it also presumes that consumer behaviour is a process in which the consumer processes information from advertising and selling selectively. Modelling consumer behaviour as a decision cycle structured around phases such as problem recognition, search for information, alternative evaluation, changes in beliefs, attitudes, and intentions, choice and post-choice outcomes, they focus extensive attention on memory organization. Consumers' usage of choice heuristics may be affected by individual and (sub)cultural differences and task and situational factors. For example, a distinction can be made between high-involvement products with high personal relevance and low-involvement products with low personal relevance.

The extent of involvement reflects the extent of personal relevance of the decision to the consumer in terms of his or her basic values, goals and self-concept. In addition, the extent of involvement influences the degree of motivated information search and consequent information processing. Yet, consumers are subject to limitations in computational skills and processing capabilities. For high-involvement products, then, consumers are actively monitoring the environment for relevant information. Since they have higher standards for what is good enough, consumers will tend to engage in more external search. It should be noted that high-involvement decisions may be precisely the ones for which the search process is problematic as a result of the fact that the world may change during the process. However, low-involvement behaviour is more common than high-involvement behaviour. For low-involvement products, consumers do not search for information and the primary effect on cognitive structure comes after purchase and product use rather than before. Since they have lower standards for what is good enough, consumers will tend to engage in less external search. Despite the fact that low involvement characterizes the majority of consumer decisions, it has not been the main research priority. Yet, these decisions are the ones governed mostly by satisficing strategies. Of course, alternative distinctions may be drawn such as that among extensive problem solving, limited problem solving and routinized response behaviour.

Consumers' use of satisficing strategies has important consequences for the effectiveness of marketing strategies. The reason is that consumers' information processing can be influenced by outside sources and, therefore, sets the agenda for the marketing effort. Marketers need to maintain or change consumers' rules to their own advantage. In particular, marketing strategies must be designed such that the consumer perceives a product's features as providing an answer to a perceived problem and felt needs. Hence, marketing strategies need to adapt creatively and strategically to the different decision processes. For instance, firms whose products are not being purchased may want to prove that superior decision procedures would in volve the purchase of their products. For high-involvement products, for example, marketers may want to direct efforts to those who are already neutral or even sympathetic towards the content, develop strategies to overcome the problem of selective organization through controlled exposure, and design additional tools to overcome the problem of miscomprehension. For low-involvement products, in turn, marketers may want to focus on visual representation of the brand name and develop a central character that signifies almost instantly everything that the message is likely to convey.

Other studies concerning satisficing consumer behaviour have represented different groups of consumers by different models that may not be optimal (Bruno and Wildt in Earl (ed.), 1988), relied on personal construct psychology to analyse the influence of satisficing in the sense that consumers resist making changes in their behaviour on demand elasticities (Earl in Earl (ed.), 1988), argued that a significant proportion of purchases may not be preceded by a decision process (Olshavsky and Granbois in Earl (ed.), 1988), discussed the influence of psychological concepts on the nature of the decision-making process for purchasing consumer durables (Pickering in Earl (ed.), 1988), and stressed the connection between risk taking and satisficing (Taylor in Earl (ed.), 1988). Hence, whereas Simon was the originator of the satisficing concept, he was not in complete control of it as others have extended its application.

ESTHER-MIRJAM SENT

Bibliography

Bettman, J.R. (1979) *An Information Processing Theory of Consumer Choice*, Reading, MA, Addison-Wesley.

Bianchi, M. (1990) 'The Unsatisfactoriness of Satisficing: From Bounded Rationality to Innovative Rationality', *Review of Political Economy*, **2**: 149–67.

Earl, P.E. (ed.) (1988) *Behavioural Economics* (Volumes I and II), Aldershot, Edward Elgar.

Engel, J.F. and Blackwell, R.D. (1982) *Consumer Behavior*, Chicago, IL, Dryden Press.

Howard, J.A. (1977) *Consumer Behavior: Application of Theory*, New York, McGraw-Hill.

Radner, R. (1975) 'Satisficing', *Journal of Mathematical Economics*, **2**: 253–62.

Simon, H.A. (1982) *Models of Bounded Rationality* (Volumes 1 and 2), Cambridge, MA, MIT Press.

Winter, S.G. (1971) 'Satisficing, Selection, and the Innovating Remnant', *Quarterly Journal of Economics*, **85**: 237–61.

Saving

Scientific research on saving has been conducted primarily by economists and psychologists. As these disciplines' approaches and points of view differ greatly, reviews and descriptions are presented for each discipline separately. A treatment of methodological developments in the study of saving concludes the present overview.

Economic analysis of saving

The economic point of view is characterized by the assumption that consumers act rationally and that they aim at the maximalization of utility. The principal aim of economic research on saving is to provide a model that accurately describes (saving) behaviour of consumers and households on a macro or aggregate level. Ideally, the model consists of a small number of parameters that, on an aggregate level, consistently and coherently predict changes in consumer behaviour. Given the aforementioned assumptions, individual differences in the behaviour under study cannot easily be explained or predicted. Given their specific purposes, classical economists would reason that there is no need to do so, and they would treat individual differences as error variance. This review will demonstrate, however, that the two research approaches tend to blend: economists tend to incorporate psychological notions into their models, and psychologists may not always be fixated on studying individual differences.

Within the economic tradition, the factor 'income' is considered to be the prime factor in the prediction of saving. Major approaches include the 'relative income' hypothesis (Duesenberry, 1949), the 'permanent income' hypothesis (Friedman, 1957), and the 'life-cycle model' (Modigliani and Brumberg, 1954).

The relative income hypothesis asserts that individuals use their reference groups as a starting-point when deciding on consumption and saving. An individual's reference group is the group of persons an individual compares him- or herself with respect to some matter. In this case, the decision to save (or consume) will depend on the relative income position *vis-à-vis* the incomes of the people in the reference group, and not the absolute income position. Thus, a principle from social psychology is implemented in an economic notion.

The permanent income hypothesis is based on the assumption that individuals have a notion of their 'underlying' income. A certain part of that income is planned to be consumed. These are the primary parameters of the model, its values being fixed or permanent. Actual levels of income and consumption may differ from their permanent counterparts. They are called transitory income and transitory consumption, respectively. Examples of transitory income sources include unexpected bequests and lottery wins. The crux of the theoretical notion is that the amount of saving depends on the discrepancy between the sum of permanent and transitory income on the one hand, and the sum of permanent and transitory consumption on the other hand. Thus, savings are used to keep the level of consumption at a stable optimum during all time periods, while facing future uncertainty with respect to income.

The life-cycle model is the predominant economic theory of saving. This model shares with the permanent income hypothesis the basic notion of maintaining a steady level of consumption from income sources whose levels will vary over a lifetime. Since the life-cycle model has generated a vast amount of research, and has become a focal point in economic studies on saving, this model will be reviewed in more detail.

According to the life-cycle model, individuals' saving behaviour is influenced by the principle of utility maximization. In order to achieve overall maximum utility, the consumption level should be at approximately the same level throughout all phases of one's life cycle. As people's income levels generally fluctuate over time, individuals make adjustments with respect to the amount of money they decide to spend immediately and the amount of money they put aside for later spending. In other words, they engage in the act of saving. Specifically, while the income level may increase steadily over successive life periods, due to work experience and job promotions, consumption needs are pressing even at the start of the life cycle. Consequently, at the start money will be borrowed for housing, furnishing and transportation (car), and the like, resulting in an initial debt position. The debt position will gradually shift to a wealth position, when, over a lifetime, debts are paid back, and wealth is accumulated, due to job promotions and rising salary levels. Of course, expenses will manifest themselves at various stages of the life-cycle. For instance, at a certain point in time, educational fees will have to be paid for the children, while many people, as they grow older, will incur rising levels of health expenditures. In summary: the various saving acts reconcile the life-cycle income profile of an individual, and his or her life cycle consumption profile.

In general, an individual's income level rises with each successive life stage. It is supposed to reach a maximum at the end of the individual's active working life and to drop at the age of retirement. Savings are supposed to be spent from that moment. According to the basic version of the life-cycle model, all savings should be spent at the time of death.

Research on the life-cycle model yields inconsistent results. Whereas some findings offer substantial support for the model, other findings point out serious weaknesses. The strongest criticism derives from studies on the financial behaviour of the elderly. It is now abundantly clear that retirees actually may continue to save rather than spend their savings. As a reaction to these findings, in their so-called 'behavioural life-cycle' hypothesis (BLC) Shefrin and Thaler (1988) proposed three amendments to the life-cycle model. It is interesting to observe that all of these amendments are actually based on concepts emanating from the field of psychology.

The first modification to the model is the addition of the concept of self-control. Although consumers may be inclined to save surplus money, they may experience problems in sticking to their consumption plan. Given that the immediate rewards of spending are higher than the immediate rewards of saving, deciding not to spend all one's money here and now and sticking to that decision requires the investment of mental effort. In other words, it takes willpower to resist the temptation to gratify one's immediate needs and wishes. A closely related concept that also derives from psychology is delay of gratification. Shefrin and Thaler use a metaphor to describe the concept of self-control. In their language, both a planner and a doer coexist within a single individual. The planner develops internal and external rules in order to aid him or her in keeping to his or her original, planned consumption (and saving) plan. As such, the planner needs to counterbalance the potentially detrimental deeds of the doer, who spends it all right away and who thus threatens the maximalization of utility over one's lifetime. This may, for instance, explain the phenomenon of Christmas Club savings accounts: while interest rates are generally lower, as compared to other types of saving accounts, this is compensated for by the diminished accessibility of the money placed in the account.

The second modification is an amendment to the original concept of fungibility. This concept implies that the marginal propensity to consume all types of wealth is equal, assuming that no transaction costs and the like are involved. To put it simply: money is money. Shefrin and Thaler introduced the notion that to a large extent, the source of any given amount of money may affect how easily it is spent. Accordingly, a number of separate 'mental accounts' may be conceived, each with its own, specific marginal propensity to consume or to save. Generally, three accounts are distinguished: current income, future income and current wealth. For example, an individual who earns a bonus at work will spend it more easily than a sum of money from an inheritance.

Finally, and in conjunction with the concept of mental accounting, the concept of framing has been introduced. Framing refers to the process of allocating financial means to various mental accounts. As a consequence of perception processes, the individual 'frames' the money coming in from various sources as belonging to separate mental accounts.

Not surprisingly, the empirical data collected by Shefrin and Thaler disclosed a better fit to the revised model than to the original one. Within this context it is interesting to notice that psychological concepts are included in an economic model and that these concepts provide better insight into the reasons and motivational dynamics of consumer (saving) behaviour. The interrelations between economics and psychology in this respect are elaborated and discussed in an interesting, and highly readable essay by Wärneryd (1989).

Psychological analysis of saving
Surprisingly few attempts have been made to develop overall psychological theories of saving. A review of the literature reveals two major theories. Katona (1975) started from the premise that consumption and saving behaviour depend on two factors, namely, the ability to save and the willingness to save. The first function may be estimated from aggregated data on total disposable income. The second function may be estimated by using information about individuals and households. Katona further introduced the notion of intervening variables. These variables are thought to bridge the gap between an individual's economic, social and cultural environment on the one hand, and the individual's behaviour on the other hand. Examples of intervening variables include personality factors, attitudes, expectations, motives and habits. These variables exert an influence on consumers' perceptions of their environment. In order to capture the effects of these perceptions, Katona developed the Index of Consumer Sentiment (ICS).

This instrument assesses consumer optimism versus pessimism with regard to the (national) economy as well as with regard to one's own household. Although the ICS, as a measurement device, has been subject to methodological criticism, it is still frequently used to predict changes in consumer behaviour at the macro level.

A second example of an overall model of saving is the work of Ölander and Seipel (1970). Their approach may be characterized by its emphasis on decision-theoretical principles. This model depicts saving behaviour as a decision process of an individual consumer. Within this process, several steps may be distinguished. More specifically, the model describes the sequence: perceptions ⇒ evaluation of consequences ⇒ subjective evaluations ⇒ choice and execution. In describing each phase, Ölander and Seipel put a strong emphasis on information processing. Saving is thus considered to be the outcome of a rational, purposeful behavioural sequence. As such, the model is reminiscent of economic models of saving. The psychological nature of the model becomes evident, however, from the subjective way in which individuals are assumed to process information in order to arrive at their saving decisions. Although the model has been developed in sufficient detail to be empirically testable, little research has been based on it thus far.

As almost all studies of saving are aimed at the (saving) behaviour of adults, it is noteworthy that there is a line of research where children's saving behaviour is the focus of interest. Clearly, much can be learned about the dynamics of adult saving behaviour by analysing the ways children develop and expand their saving logic and saving habits, as they grow up and enter maturity. The work of Sonuga-Barke and Webley (1993) describes some of the processes deemed to be relevant in this context; see also Webley's entry on Children's Saving in this book.

Selected psychological concepts
A larger number of studies in the field of saving have been devoted to quite narrow topics and issues. Typically, rather than developing overall models of consumer-saving behaviour, researchers have studied specific aspects of the process. Major topics include the study of saving motives and the effects of subjective timing and planning factors on the act of saving.

Motives
Saving motives have been studied ever since the days of Keynes. Generally, motives refer to a state in which individuals experience a drive to acquire a goal in the (near) future. Predominantly in order to meet the practical goals of specific studies, several motivational categories have been devised. As they all disclose part of the dynamics of individual saving behaviour, it is useful to present some of these approaches here. Within the life-cycle model (discussed earlier),

economists distinguish between the bequest motive, saving for specific commodities, and the precautionary motive. In addition, habitual saving, residual saving (unintended saving as a consequence of lack of spending), and saving as a personal disposition are to be mentioned.

If saving behaviour in itself is taken as the starting-point of the analysis, several 'behavioural motivations' may be distinguished as well. Keynes (1936: 107–8) provides an extensive list of 'motives of a subjective character' that individuals may have for refraining from current consumption, which he sums up as 'Precaution, Foresight, Calculation, Improvement, Independence, Enterprise, Pride and Avarice' (p. 108).

Katona, from a psychological point of view, distinguishes between discretionary saving (saving of freely disposable income), and contractual (institutional) saving. A more recent and hierarchically organized description (Lindqvist, 1981) involves the 'cash management motive' (carrying out cash management), the 'buffer motive' (aimed at being able to face financial disaster), the 'saving goals motive' (aimed at being able to eventually buy durables), and the 'wealth management motive' (managing one's wealth). The hierarchical description of saving motives is an attempt to specify more fully the mental organization and interdependencies of these motives for individuals and, hence, their relative importance.

The study of saving motives suffers from the drawbacks that are logically associated with partial analyses of any given phenomenon. It is unclear, for instance, whether different motives give rise to different kinds of saving behaviour. Similarly, not much has been said about the relative importance of the various motives in predicting the ways or the amounts an individual will save in a fixed period of time.

Time and planning dimensions
From a psychological view of point, uncertainty may well be the crucial concept in models of saving. Uncertainty about future events, and specifically an individual's reflections on it, point to the potential financial risks associated with these events. The thought of not being able to pay the bill when an economic disaster occurs is frightening to almost all individuals. Obviously, uncertainty usually involves a time factor. People are aware of the fact that financial demands need to be met not only here and now, but also in the future. In order to meet these future financial demands, a savings plan has to be developed. This means that the immediate drive to spend money as it comes in must be counteracted. As a result of delaying immediate gratification, a larger gratification may be obtained in the future. As noted earlier, the generic term for this phenomenon in the realm of psychology is delay of gratification.

Within this context, quite a large number of variables have been studied, including uncertainty, foresight, self-regulation, self-efficacy and thriftiness. Although each of these concepts is interesting of its own, it would seem that the development of models of saving behaviour would benefit enormously from an integrated approach which fitted most or all of these concepts into an overall model. At present, the aforementioned concepts have been developed in different contexts, and partially overlap with respect to conceptual meaning and the individual connotations attached to them by consumers.

Methodological developments

Financial management and the saving process

Consumers' saving is an outome of a complex psychological process. However, as demonstrated above, numerous studies have addressed specific and isolated aspects of saving. A specific definition of saving behaviour is typically chosen, and some selected factors that potentially influence this behaviour are then studied. The broader context of household financial management, where consumption actions of other members of the household may block an individual's attempts to save money, generally forms no part of the design. However, this omission may narrow down the scope of the study and thus the generalizibility of its outcomes. In addition, it is largely ignored that saving is a process rather than a state. Most studies assess saving behaviour using one-shot study designs. As a consequence, the value of these studies is necessarily limited to some extent.

Dynamic process tracing approach

A major recent approach to saving behaviour addresses the issue from an overall financial management perspective, incorporating both psychological factors and external influences. This approach, called the dynamic process tracing approach (DPTA) (Groenland, Kuylen and Bloem, 1996) claims methodological refinement by analysing an individual's behavioural trace as he or she decides to engage in the process of saving, dissaving, and choosing specific saving products and services. By closely adhering to actual behaviour sequences it is contended that the ensuing model is characterized by a high level of external validity.

DPTA may be viewed simultaneously as a theory, an interview method and an approach to data analysis. As a theory, it starts from the premise that the target behaviour is complex, dynamically evolving over time and highly idiosyncratic. Furthermore, it is assumed that the sequence of acts that constitute the behaviour under study will, for any time segment, be influenced by both internal, psychological factors and external events. Consequently, the behaviour of interest should be monitored as it develops in time.

For research purposes within a DPTA framework, a qualitative interview method is used. Respondents first describe the major historical events of the household, for example, getting married, buying a house, having children, or changing jobs. Next, the individual decision process related to the behavioural process under study (saving) is tracked from its onset to its end, along with a description, as provided by the respondent in his or her own words, of the internal psychological processes and external events which shaped the saving process over time.

Finally, the behaviour traces thus obtained are analysed with reference to the idiosyncratic step orders used by the respondents to complete the process, the specific (types of) acts of the individuals, and the psychological and contextual influences immanent in each step of the process. The idiosyncratic behaviour traces are thus converted into tree-like descriptors, which finally are subjected to a form of cluster or scaling analysis aimed at finding segments of consumers which can be characterized by a specific style of handling their financial decisions. By postponing the segmentation process to the final stages of analysis and by including step-order information, it is claimed that the idiosyncrasy of individual behaviour traces is preserved in a generalizable model. Given the recent development of DPTA, however, at present no fully-fledged empirical study has been reported which corroborates the theoretical soundness of the approach.

Conclusion

Classical and authoritative examples of different types of research have been presented along with the major explanatory factors considered, from the fields of both economics and psychology. In doing so, the necessity to develop more comprehensive models, incorporating all of the above-mentioned variables in a conceptually well-developed way is amply demonstrated. The present review shows that our present theoretical knowledge of and insight into the determinants of individual saving behaviour are far from complete. Only scattered parts of the process have been described in detail and have been studied empirically (compare Van Veldhoven and Groenland, 1993).

Recent methodological developments in the field point out the fruitfulness of a dynamic approach in which saving behaviour is viewed as a dynamically evolving process that may be highly unique to individuals or households and which is moulded by the influence of numerous repetitive internal and external events. This may represent the most promising avenue to arrive at the precise, concise and valid models needed in the coming era.

EDWARD A.G. GROENLAND

Bibliography

Duesenberry, J.S. (1949) *Income, Saving, and the Theory of Consumer Behavior,*

Cambridge, MA, Harvard University Press.

Friedman, M. (1957) *A Theory of the Consumption Function*, Princeton, NJ, Princeton University Press.

Groenland, E.A.G., Kuylen, A.A.A. and Bloem, J.G. (1996) 'The Dynamic Process Tracing Approach: Towards the Development of a New Methodology for the Analysis of Complex Consumer Behaviours', *Journal of Economic Psychology*, **17**: 809–25.

Katona, G. (1975) *Psychological Economics*, Amsterdam/New York, Elsevier .

Keynes, J.M. (1936) *The General Theory of Employment, Interest and Money*, London, Macmillan.

Lindqvist, A. (1981) 'The Saving Behavior of Households', Doctoral dissertation, Stockholm School of Economics.

Modigliani, F. and Brumberg, R. (1954) 'Utility Analysis and the Consumption Function: An Interpretation of Cross-Sectional Data', in Kurihara, K.K. (ed.) *Post-Keynesian Economics*, New Brunswick, NJ, Rutgers University Press: 388–438.

Ölander, F. and Seipel, C.M. (1970) *Psychological Approaches to the Study of Saving*, Urbana-Champaign, IL, University of Illinois.

Shefrin, H.M. and Thaler, R.H. (1988) 'The Behavioral Life-Cycle Hypothesis', *Economic Enquiry*, **66**: 609–43.

Sonuga-Barke, E.J.S. and Webley, P. (1993) *Children's Saving*, Hove, Erlbaum.

Van Veldhoven, G.M. and Groenland, E.A.G. (1993) 'Exploring Saving Behavior: A Framework and a Research Agenda', *Journal of Economic Psychology*, **14**: 507–22.

Wärneryd, K.-E. (1989) 'On the Psychology of Saving: An Essay on Economic Behavior', *Journal of Economic Psychology*, **10**: 515–41.

Search Processes

Studies focusing on the the search for information prior to purchase date back to the 1920s. Although recent investigations have been conducted from a variety of perspectives, it is widely recognized that to understand the search process, the essential research questions that need to be addressed are: who searches, what (information and sources), when, where, how much and why? (Srinivasan, 1990). This review focuses on three aspects of the literature on the consumers' information search process: first, the conceptualization of search as a stage of a complex decision process; second, the major theoretical approaches to search; and, finally, external search and its determinants.

Search as a stage of a decision cycle

Let us start with a simple example, that of a consumer who needs a new refrigerator. The consumer — who may be part of a multimember household — must first decide *which* information sources to search. This may be affected by information availability, ease of access to information sources and their credibility. For example, the consumer may consider whether *Consumer Reports* provides good enough information to justify time commitment and its cost, rather than simply relying upon advice from sales personnel in stores. For any source that is selected, the consumer must decide *when* to use it: should *Consumer Reports* be read before visiting appliance stores and seeking advice from sales personnel, or afterwards? Choice may be affected by changes consumers make in their sequences of searching information sources (Hauser, Urban and Weinberg, 1993). Once at a source, it is necessary to decide how long to spend using it as a source of information: when is it long enough with a refrigerator salesperson? Time spent is affected by the market environment, particularly the number, complexity and stability of alternatives. The division of time between different information sources may be affected by time pressure or its availability, perceptions of risk and of the extent of differences among alternatives, as well as the consumer's prior knowledge. The length of the search process will also be bound up with the consumer's attempt to work out when to buy the refrigerator, which may be affected by factors such as whether or not an old one is being replaced (is it still working or is it beyond repair?), financial pressure, the match between store loyalty/preference and what is in stock, and special buying opportunities. Information gathering does not always stop once a brand is selected and purchased, for the consumer may then set about looking around for further ways of justifying the choice, perhaps to eliminate cognitive dissonance.

Implied in this example is the idea that the consumer's search for information relevant to choice is a major component of a sequence of events leading to the purchase and use of a product. This is precisely how it is portrayed in most consumer-decision models (Beatty and Smith, 1987). Here, research tends to focus on how different quality goals lead to the use of different information search strategies for goal attainment. Whether or not the search process leads to a revision of the consumer's goals appears to be strongly related to the quality of the information search (Bettman, 1979; Srinivasan, 1990). Just as detailed models of decision cycles recognize that purchase decisions may not be successfully implemented or end up solving the consumer's initial problem, so search cycles within a larger decision cycle do not follow a rigid sequence; rather, search is a contingent, iterative activity in which the emerging pattern of information may lead the consumer to change the intended order and set the search tasks and revise the search goals.

Although models based on complex decision processes have for three decades provided a ready structure for many leading consumer behaviour textbooks, their recent editions tend, if somewhat unwillingly, to try to incorporate the view of Olshavsky and Granbois (1979) that purchasing frequently does *not* occur as a result of some type of decision process involving detailed prior search and evaluation. Rather, Olshavky and Granbois suggest (p. 98), 'a significant proportion of purchases may not be preceded by a decision process', and 'for many purchases a decision process never occurs, not even on the first purchase'. They go on to say (p. 99) that 'even when purchase behavior is preceded by a choice process, it is [often] very limited', involving 'the evaluation of few alternatives and criteria, little external search and simple evaluation process models'. In general, consumers appear to employ hybrid strategies: their purchases of 'necessities' may derive from 'culturally-mandated lifestyles' (p. 98); other items may be necessary elements of complex consumption systems; some may reflect 'preferences acquired in early childhood, simple conformity to group norms or from imitation of others'. Such information as is gathered may consist of recommendations gathered from personal or nonpersonal sources, often 'on a random or superficial basis' (p. 98). If consumers are operating in a haphazard manner, not particularly intent on gathering information about the wide range of alternatives that they might in principle consider, promotional campaigns may have a major role to play as a means for steering consumers at least towards asking particular questions and attracting their attention — here matters as simple as the height of a display in a supermarket may have a major influence on whether the consumer examines a product as suitable for purchase.

Theoretical approaches to search

The three major theoretical streams of search literature are: (i) the economic approach, (ii) the psychological/motivational approach, and (iii) the information-processing approach.

The *economic perspective* seeks to understand why consumers search for information, in terms of marginal costs and benefits of search. It conceives of consumers as if they compute their optimum amounts of search by equating expected marginal returns of search to the expected marginal costs of search. Since utility maximization may take into consideration any attribute(s) considered important, different consumers, each rationally maximizing their utility, may pursue different search strategies because of their different interests and prior beliefs about what the search process will uncover (Srinivasan, 1990).

Such a calculating approach to choice is questionable in situations where initially consumers have very little knowledge of the market in question. According to Hey (1982), causal empiricism and introspection suggest that consumers use *rules of thumb*, at both an individual and a market level, or mixtures of them — a consumer purchasing home and contents insurance, for example, might in this context use a rule such as 'choose the cheapest quotations from the first five familiar-sounding insurance companies that can offer prompt service over the telephone'. Hey uses experimental methods to uncover such rules and concludes that because of risk aversion and the uncertain returns to spending extra time on search, an increase in search costs will tend to reduce search for information. By contrast, an increase in the dispersion of prices offered by firms in the marketplace will tend to increase search activity.

The *psychological perspective* deals mainly with search in terms of the motivation to undertake it. Goal orientation and involvement are the major aspects of motivation. Accordingly, because of the diversity in reservation utilities that form the boundary between 'stop searching' and 'continue further search', consumers may have different motivation levels to search, even if the net utility is to be the same for both. Optimizers consider it worthwhile to continue searching as long as the expected net utility is positive whereas satisficers might choose an alternative whose utility may be less than the best possible choice and discontinue searching if an expected positive net utility is very small or considered 'not worthwhile'. Similarly, the higher the involvement, the higher would be the propensity to engage in search related to the concerned product class (Srinivasan, 1990).

Bettman (1979) proposes the *information-processing focus* on search. From this viewpoint, a consumer is perceived as being goal-orientated and as pursuing various subgoals during the various stages of information acquisition. In other words, there is a goal hierarchy that provides the motivation to pursue the search activity. The information acquisition and evaluation process occurs before a choice decision is made, and internal (memory) and external search constitute the subcomponents of this stage. Consequently, the information-processing approach decomposes search into two parts: internal and external search (Srinivasan, 1990).

External search
External search is 'the degree of attention, perception, and effort directed towards obtaining information related to the specific purchase under consideration' (Beatty and Smith, 1987). External search can also entail pre-purchase search and/or ongoing search (Bloch, Sherrell and Ridgway, 1986). In pre-purchase search, the major motive of consumers is to make better purchase decisions, using the market environment and situational factors as determinants. The possible outcomes of a pre-purchase search are increased product and market knowledge, better purchase decisions and increased satisfaction with purchase. Product involvement, market environment and situational factors determine consumers' ongoing information search. Building a bank of information for future use and experiencing fun and pleasure are the major motives to increase product and market knowledge leading to efficiencies in future buying and personal influence. Information banking involves increasing product expertise to optimize the outcome of a purchase. Expertise can also make

a consumer feel well-informed, enhance product care, add feelings of self-actualization, and improve the quality of future product selection. The bank is also a prerequisite for impulse buying, and its growth provides satisfaction as a result of the search (Bloch et al., 1986).

External search may be partially accounted for by the information-processing limitations of consumers (Srinivasan, 1990). Information processing entails cognitive costs due to limited capacity of human memory and capacity to retain information over time: the consumer's memory bank is rather akin to a leaky bucket. Even if the stored information is not also being rendered obsolete by changes in the external environment, consumers typically can retain only a few attributes and alternatives in memory to be retrieved for future choices. Hence Sheth and Parvatiyar (1995) predict continuity of external search efforts. Without this, ability to rely upon memorized information will decline because of decay in what is stored in the memory. Although ongoing external search may seem a Sisyphean activity, attempting to keep the memory topped up with potentially useful information makes sense because extensive external search carried out immediately prior to reaching a purchase decision can prove counterproductive: information overload may conflict with attempts to absorb the information into memory. Ongoing search and information overload can be avoided by the use of heuristics rather than systematic processing in choice behaviour. In the heuristic mode, decisions are based on a more superficial assessment of cues (Bettman, 1979; Bloch et al., 1986; Srinivasan, 1990). As noted earlier, Olshavsky and Granbois (1979) critically argue that often consumers simply end up using conformity, imitation and recommendations as their heuristics.

Determinants of external search
Choices concerning the problem-solving strategy that influence the type and amount of search seem, in turn, to depend particularly upon the following factors:

Perceived deficiency of information The amount of search can be conceptualized as having two components: breadth of search (the number of attributes about which information will acquired or processed) and depth of search (the amount of search devoted to each attribute) (Ozanne, Brucks and Grewal, 1992). An inverted-U relationship exists between the deficiency of attribute information and the breadth and depth of search: with a moderate level of perceived information deficiency, the breadth and depth of search are greatest. Similarly, an inverted-U shaped relationship exists between perceived deficiency of attribute information and the overall amount and time of search: at a moderate level of deficiency, the overall amount of information requested and the time spent searching are greatest

(Ozanne et al., 1992).

Time pressure Urgency and immediate need determine the time pressure impinging on the consumer, which is one of the major situational factors that shape search (Beatty and Smith 1987). Arguably, because time pressure increases the perceived costs of external search, consumers' motivation to search decreases, and consequently external search activity decreases. Furthermore, the consumer's perception of the availability of time is partly a function of this time pressure (Schmidt and Spreng, 1996). People who are rushed for time acquire slightly less information on each brand and on slightly fewer brands (Moore and Lehmann, 1980). Time availability, on the other hand, increases search time spent with retailers (phone calls/trips to retailers, number of visits, and consultation with salesperson/store employees), using media (advertisements, brochures), and neutral sources (consumer reports, news articles and other buying guides), much as it influences total search (Beatty and Smith, 1987). Time pressure often stems from product failure. If one's television succumbs to old age, then typically the search process would be shortened because of the aversion produced by not having a television, whereas a person in the market for a television for the first time may search more extensively (Schmidt and Spreng 1996).

Perceived risk Information search can also be considered as a risk-reduction strategy. Consumers use different search behaviours for situations with different levels of perceived risk (Beatty and Smith, 1987). Products high in perceived risk incite both move information search and a greater depth of search (Beatty and Smith, 1987; Moore and Lehmann, 1980).

Perceptions of risk during search processes involving unfamiliar/new products or brands may arise both at the beginning of a search for a new product/brand and at the time of the first visit to a store. Consumers may differ in terms of both levels of information about products/brands and search costs. An important question concerns the extent to which such differences in information and search costs create price differentials across buyers (Ozanne et al., 1992).

Within the pre-purchase search, the riskiness of the decision may be affected both by knowledge uncertainty (regarding a lack of information about alternatives), and by choice uncertainty (about which alternative to choose). Choice uncertainty appears to increase search, while knowledge uncertainty has a negative effect on search. High knowledge uncertainty is also associated potentially with a reduced ability to comprehend and use new information efficiently, which makes search a harder process. When consumers have brand-specific prior utility distributions, the existence of relative uncertainty between brands is necessary for search to be useful (Ozanne et al., 1992). Again, however, the critical perspective of Olshavsky and Granbois (1979) should be noted: it may well be that the more one searches, the more there is risk of information overload unless search clarifies the issues at hand, and opportunities may vanish if one spends a long time looking around for better alternatives.

Expertise Experts tend to try to gather more information, from more sources, than do novices. As compared to novices, they devote more effort to identification and definition of the problem and less effort to evaluation. They also use a strategy similar to deduction, formulating hypotheses and then testing these by acquiring relevant information, whereas nonexperts seem to use a strategy more similar to induction, that is, exploring information to look for differences and to generate propositions. The information search strategies of the two groups differ according to what drives the selection of information, and the ease with which the search is interrupted. Whereas novices seek information from limited sources in a rather incoherent manner, experts exhibit a more global search pattern guided by an overall planning strategy and are more efficient than novices in terms of search time, requiring significantly less time to perform the task.

Conclusion

In today's dynamic global environment, understanding search processes is of crucial importance for researchers, managers and policy makers because the effective functioning of an efficient and competitive market economy depends on buyers developing an awareness of price, quality and attribute differences of products. For researchers, consumers' search processes are a fertile area of research with important implications for different areas in marketing such as business-to-business marketing, marketing channels and relationship marketing. Because ability to search is intrinsic, managers should choose to reduce search costs (or increase benefits of search), thereby increasing consumers' motivation to search. For managers, understanding the determinants of information search is particularly critical for developing effective promotional strategies (Schmidt and Spreng, 1996). Also, in information-rich societies, understanding how consumers search and use information allows public policy makers to improve the quality and accessibility of information (Schmidt and Spreng, 1996; Srinivasan, 1990).

BÜLENT MENGÜÇ

Bibliography

Beatty, S.E. and Smith, S.M. (1987) 'External Search Effort: An Investigation Across Several Product Categories', *Journal of Consumer Research*, **14**: 83–95.

Bettman, J.R. (1979) *An Information Processing Theory of Consumer Choice*, Reading, MA, Addison-Wesley.

Bloch, P.H., Sherrell, D.L. and Ridgway, N.M. (1986) 'Consumer Search: An Extended Framework', *Journal of Consumer Research*, **13**: 119–26.

Hauser, J.R., Urban, G.L. and Weinberg, B.D. (1993) 'How Consumers Allocate Their Time When Searching For Information', *Journal of Marketing Research*, **30**: 452–66.

Hey, J.D. (1982) 'Search for Rules for Search', *Journal of Economic Behavior and Organization*, **3**: 65–81.

Moore, W.L. and Lehmann, D.R. (1980) 'Individual Differences in Search Behavior for a Nondurable', *Journal of Consumer Research*, **7**: 296–307.

Olshavsky, R.W. and Granbois, D.H. (1979) 'Consumer Decision-Making — Fact or Fiction?', *Journal of Consumer Research*, **6**: 93–100.

Ozanne, J.L., Brucks, M. and Grewal, D. (1992) 'A Study of Information Search Behavior During the Categorization of New Products', *Journal of Consumer Research*, **18**: 452–63.

Schmidt, J.B. and Spreng, R.A. (1996) 'A Proposed Model of External Consumer Information Search', *Journal of the Academy of Marketing Science*, **24**: 246–56.

Sheth, J.N. and Parvatiyar, A. (1995) 'Relationship Marketing in Consumer Markets: Antecedents and Consequences', *Journal of the Academy of Marketing Science*, **23**: 255–71.

Srinivasan, N. (1990) 'Pre-purchase External Search for Information', in Zeithaml, V.E. (ed.) *Review of Marketing*, Chicago, IL, American Marketing Association: 153–89.

Share Markets and Psychology

Traditionally the share market has been studied from an economic perspective which views it as a community of rational investors who perceive market information similarly and accurately. But investors rarely live up to the tenets of such a theory and economists and psychologists alike have investigated discrepancies between share market theory and market and investor behaviour.

This entry first presents the predominant economic theory of the share market, which views the investor as a rational utility maximizer, and then analyses the differences between the theory and investors' behaviour in the market.

Economic theory

The essential purpose of the share market ('stock market' in the US) is to raise capital, allocate it efficiently and provide an orderly liquid trading place. The economic value of a share is the sum of the expected discounted future dividend payments. However, the real difficulty in assessing the true value of a share can be seen in its price fluctuations. These daily price changes have been hypothesized to be a random walk. Essential to the random walk hypothesis is the premise that the market has no memory. This means that future share movement and value cannot be predicted on the basis of past market actions such as price or volume information. Consequently, investors will not consistently be able to achieve greater returns than market averages and therefore the best policy is to buy and hold.

A number of economists (notably Fama, 1965), using data from a variety of markets and a number of different techniques, found that successive price changes were essentially random. The explanation that evolved from this research was a stronger form of the random walk model, the efficient market hypothesis (EMH).

The EMH is built on the supply and demand model and presumes a number of requirements for an efficient market. EMH assumes: full, rapid and free information flow to all investors; low transaction costs and continuous trading so that any investor can immediately act on a decision to buy or sell; that the investor is a utility maximizer and rational; and within the limits of risk the individual is willing to assume, given available information, that the investor is capable of choosing the most effective way to maximize the return or profit (Schachter et al., 1986). In an efficient market any news is quickly and accurately assessed by the combined investors and immediately reflected in the price of shares. And as significant price changes occur only with the arrival of new information, which is by definition unpredictable, an investor cannot successfully predict share performance and thus continually outperform the market.

Acceptance of the EMH has additional implications. First, market prices will always reflect the correct value incorporating all relevant information — shares cannot be identified as either under- or overvalued. Second, share prices are highly elastic, the value of a share represents an equilibrium tradeoff with the associated risk. In an efficient market different shares should be almost perfect substitutes. Lastly, share prices are a consistently good economic indicator. They represent an informed economic consensus about future prospects. And again, as with the random walk hypothesis, the best strategy is simply to buy and hold a diversified portfolio of shares.

While evidence for the random walk hypothesis initially appeared compelling, the limited size of Fama's (1965) study, 30 shares observed between 1957 and 1962, has proved to be an inadequate basis for generalization about price movements on the share market. Price movements over other time periods and other locations have suggested different conclusions. If the time period is lengthened and the number of shares increased, new patterns emerge: one such pattern is mean reversion (De Bondt and Thaler, 1992). A price movement in any given direction is likely to be followed by a similar movement in the opposite direction. Mean reversion has been found to hold for daily, weekly, monthly, and periods all the way up to five years. The fact that prices are mean reverting implies that price movements do not behave in a purely random fashion.

A number of other market phenomena deviate from the prescriptions of the EMH. The following eight EMH departures are summarized from Duffee (1989), Maital, Filer and Simon (1986), De Bondt and Thaler (1992) and Ohanian (1996):

1. *Calendar effects*: The average returns on the New York Share Exchange (NYSE) for January are 3.5 per cent and 0.5 per cent in other months. The anomaly can only be partially explained by the sale of shares due to end of year tax considerations. There are similar seasonality effects in many other share markets around the world.
2. *Weekly effects*: Share prices typically rise on Fridays and fall on Mondays, although these effects are more pronounced in declining and stable markets than in an increasing market.
3. *Intraday effect*: Typically prices rise sharply during the first and last 45 minutes of the trading day.
4. *Holiday effect*: The NYSE increases 0.53 per cent the day before a holiday and 0.26 per cent for all other days.
5. *Volume of trade*: The volume of share market sales is far too high to be consistent with common and rational knowledge.
6. *Price earning effect*: Shares with low price to earnings ratios perform better than the market average, as do shares that have had recent large falls.
7. *Initial public offering anomalies*: For many initial public offerings the rate of return is enormous. In general the percentage increase on the first day of a float is more than 20 per cent which suggests that issuing firms deal with underwriters who underprice the value of the shares.
8. *Market volatility*: Share prices are too volatile to be explained by rational market forces such as dividends or real changes in investor discount rates.

A major reason for the discrepancies between the EMH and share market behaviour is that the psychology of investors is somewhat different to the axioms associated with the EMH. There are three main areas in which these divergences can occur — the information flow, the assumption that the investor behaves rationally, and the group behaviour of investors.

The flow of information
The EMH assumes that the investor can analyse market information and choose the utility-maximizing investments. However, investors receive share information from a number of sources including brokers, the media and prospective companies. All three have vested interests in share acquisitions which distort the information necessary for share valuation.

Sharebrokers' livelihoods depend on share trades. If they recommend a share that does not perform it is not bad for their standing if others make the same mistake, but a contrary opinion that does not perform could be quite devastating to their reputation (Scharfstein and Stein, 1990). Most brokers cannot afford to lose current clients because they promise future income. Thus, brokers typically recommend safe shares and those in fashion and as a result often underperform the market. Also, the institutional research that brokers base their opinion on has often been driven to recommend the shares institutions are pressured to buy (Dreman, 1977). Finally, professional brokers are as susceptible to individual biases (which are discussed later) as anyone else.

Information also comes to the investor through the media. But, generally speaking, the market is ahead of the news with information coming too late to the wider investing public to benefit (Tvede, 1990). Another problem with market information is the way companies deliver the information to the market. Their aim is to achieve the right intrinsic value for the company's shares and to lower price volatility by altering perceptions of risk — thus creating a more attractive investment (Hill, 1994).

Investor rationality

Essential to the EMH is that an individual's behaviour is rational. However, instead of our brain acting as a supercomputer, as required by the doctrine of EMH, it is better described as a personal computer, with a slow processor, little RAM, and a hard disk memory system that is not only small but at many times unreliable. The human mind simplifies information interpretation by using heuristics — or rules of thumb — such as representativeness and availability.

In the share market the 'representativeness' heuristic induces people to introduce order into randomness and imagine patterns in situations where they do not actually exist. A prime example of representativeness noted by Dreman (1995) was the reaction on the NYSE to the crash of 1987. Following the US share market crash of 1987 in one day the market dropped 23 per cent, following which the media and investors were quick to equate the recent collapse to the crash of 1929. Even though there was no great depression as had been the case in 1929 and the market had relatively strong fundamentals, many people stayed clear of the share market.

A second heuristic that investors often fall prey to is 'availability', in which only the most readily observable or available instances are used as a basis for judgement. For instance, when looking at the universe of available shares, many investors tend to focus on the well-known shares which readily spring to mind. However, a key finding in behavioural finance is that a portfolio of well-known current market favourites is normally outperformed by shares bought on a low price-to-earnings basis. In a similar vein, recent or dramatic, and hence available, events weight too heavily in judgments with people tending to put too much emphasis on them. For instance, a company's strong earning prospects and solid economic fundamentals can count for very little, in the decision to buy or sell, if the company reports a downturn in profit (Pennar, 1995). Thus, investors often anchor their appraisal of a share on its recent trading price rather than on the share's fundamentals (Dreman, 1995).

The 'hindsight bias' is where people view events as being predictable once they have already occurred. Any market failures can therefore easily be attributed to unforeseen factors that if the investor had known, they would not have bought, or would have sold the shares earlier. An excellent example of the hindsight bias in practice is shown in Shiller (1988), who surveyed investors after the 17 October 1987 crash inquiring whether they had been net buyers or sellers in the month leading up to the collapse. Later, in another survey, he asked of the same period whether the investor had considered the market to be overvalued in relation to market fundamentals. Surprisingly 68 per cent of private investors and 93 per cent of institutional investors buying prior to the crash had believed the market to be overvalued. In other words, the majority of investors buying shares before the crash believed that they were paying too much money for the shares they bought but purchased them anyway. A truly rational response if they had wished to lose money.

Another psychological failing is the way in which investors allocate their investments among shares, cash and other investments. Typically shares out-perform bonds and most other investments but investors tend to place greater weight on investments that appear safer than the share market. That is, people tend to view the short-term price fluctuations as a risk to the investment and forget that the market has risen for centuries (Dreman, 1995). Part of this failing is due to loss aversion — the tendency for people to view losses as worse than improvements or gains (Kahneman and Tversky, 1979).

Loss aversion affects investors' decisions in a number of ways. Many invest in mutual funds that offer protection against sharp falls in financial markets, even though this security comes at a cost, with most mutual funds performing worse than the market. In an analysis of the Standard and Poor's Index between 1981 and 1986 Shefrin and Statman (1986) discovered that 80 per cent of mutual funds performed worse than the market index. Thus an investor acting in a purely random way will perform better than most mutual funds. Loss aversion also affects investors through their reluctance to part with shares that have incurred losses. Kahneman and Tversky (1979) argue that this is due to the pain of regret that comes with the admission of a bad choice. Instead of accepting the situation for what it has become, investors' attention is focused upon restoring any loss. Even if recovery never comes, investors may in extreme cases escalate their commitment to a failing investment in order to maintain appearances (Drummond, 1994).

Group conformity

People also tend to behave irrationally in the share market by 'fitting in' with the beliefs and actions of other investors. Social psychology has demonstrated the great lengths people will take to fit in with others, with the majority of subjects indicating little awareness that their perceptions have been manipulated. Many studies have shown that people tend to move their opinions to fit in with group norms — even when faced with group opinion that is noticeably wrong. People are further influenced by groups holding authority. In the share market we can see these phenomena in the shares investors prefer: the currently high-profile companies that are in fashion; the shares often recommended by share brokers. But this strategy comes at the expense of more profitable opportunities.

One consequence of extreme conformity is share market bubbles and crashes. When a market bubbles it characteristically starts with strong economic fundaments and investor confidence which pushes prices of shares beyond the prevailing standards of value. More and more investors are drawn into the market and this speculation forces prices further up. Dreman (1977: 50) commented 'it is like a casino where the odds are suddenly in favour of the patrons'. Essentially, the market is experiencing a form of group think — an instance of mindless conformity and collective misjudgement. Once the crowd realizes the excesses of the bubble, there is a scramble to escape, resulting in panic which often carries values far below the point from which the mania began. Bubbles and crashes are not new. In Holland during the seventeenth century, tulip bulbs could command jewels, land, gold or whatever else was desired, but during January and February 1637 tulip bulbs slumped to be worth little more than onions.

Thus market values are fixed not only by balance sheets and income statements but by hopes, fears, greed, ambition, and numberless other causes (Pring, 1992). Because the market is controlled in part by these hopes and fears as well as by market fundamentals, the greatest chance of being successful is by first understanding ourselves and others. To make better than average gains an investor has to stand aside from popular thinking, ignoring the pressures leading to irrational behaviour and mindless conformity — a contrarian strategy. A good contrarian should not automatically do the opposite of the majority but learn to think in reverse, so that he or she can come up with reasons why the crowd may be wrong. Typically, contrarian strategies are successful because of the systematic over-reaction by investors. As has been noted, the psychological make-up of people is that they tend to overreact to recent data in making judgements.

Overall, the share market achieves its primary purpose, that of raising and allocating capital and providing a secure place to trade. However, the assertions that the market is random, investors are rational, and that only by luck can one outperform the market, do not hold when investors' psychological makeup is considered.

MICHAEL DUGGAN

Bibliography

De Bondt, W.F.M. and Thaler, R.H. (1992) 'A Mean Revering Walk Down Wall Street', in Thaler, R.H. (ed.) *The Winner's Curse: Paradoxes and Anomalies of Economic Life*, New York, Macmillan: 151–67.

Dreman, D.N. (1977). *Psychology and the Stock Market: Investment Strategy Beyond Random Walk.* New York, Amacom.

Dreman, D.N. (1995) 'Outpsyching the Market', *Forbes,* **155** (13): 162–68.

Drummond, H. (1994) 'The Pig-headed Way to Lose Your Money', *Personal Investor,* **9** (5): 54.

Duffee, G.R. (1989) 'The Importance of Market Psychology in the Determination of Stock Market Volatility', *Board of Governors of the Federal Reserve System Finance and Economic Discussion Series*: No. 109.

Fama, E.F. (1965) 'The Behavior of Stock Market Prices', *Journal of Business,* **38**: 34–105.

Hill, D. (1994) 'Follow the Leader', *Personal Investor,* **9** (6): 38.

Kahneman, D. and Tversky, A. (1979) 'Prospect Theory: An Analysis of Decision Making under Risk', *Econometrica,* **47**: 263–91.

Maital, S., Filer, R. and Simon, J.L. (1986) 'What do People Bring to the Stock Market (Besides Money)? The Economic Psychology of Stock Market Behavior', in Gilad, B. and Kaish, S. (eds) *Handbook of Behavioral Economics. Volume B. Behavioral Economics.* Greenwich, CT, JAI Press: 273–307.

Ohanian, L.E. (1996) 'When the Bubble Bursts: Psychology or Fundamentals?'. *Business Review* (Federal Reserve Bank of Philadelphia): 3–13.

Pennar, K. (1995) 'Why Investors Stampede', *Business Week,* 13 February, **3411**: 84–85

Pring, M.J. (1992) *Investment Psychology Explained*, New York, Wiley.

Schachter, S., Hood, D.C., Andreassen, P.B. and Gerin, W. (1986) 'Aggregate Variables in Psychology and Economics: Dependence and the Stock Market', in Gilad, B. and Kaish, S. (eds) *Handbook of Behavioral Economics. Volume B. Behavioral Economics.* Greenwich, CT, JAI Press: 237–72.

Scharfstein, D.S. and Stein, J.C. (1990) 'Herd Behavior and Investment', *American Economic Review,* **80**: 465–79.

Shefrin, H.M. and Statman, M. (1986) 'How Not to Make Money in the Stock Market', *Psychology Today,* **20**: 52–7.

Shiller, R.J. (1988) 'Investor Behavior in the October 1987 Stock Market Crash: Survey Evidence', *Yale Cowles Foundation Discussion Paper*: No. 853.

Tvede, L. (1990) *The Psychology of Finance*, Melbourne, Oxford University Press.

Tversky, A. and Kahneman, D. (1974) 'Judgement under Uncertainty: Heuristics and Biases', *Science,* **185**: 1124–30.

Shoplifting

Shoplifting is a pervasive, but little-studied aspect of consumer behaviour. While most individual acts of consumer theft are small, their aggregate impact is very large. In the United States, consumers shoplift an estimated $12–15 billion worth of merchandise a year. Evidence suggests that as many as 60 per cent of consumers have shoplifted at some time in their lives (Kraut, 1976; Klemke, 1992), prompting one investigator (Kraut, 1976) to label it a 'folk crime'.

Why do such a high percentage of consumers steal from retailers? Both Kraut (1976) and Cox, Cox and Moschis (1990) found that most shoplifters appear to have a fairly straightforward motive: shoplifting means getting desired merchandise without having to pay for it. Some researchers have argued that stores' efforts to stimulate consumer demand and impulse buying (for example, enticing displays which encourage customers to handle merchandise) may also unintentionally increase shoplifting. It is interesting to note that the same types of merchandise (for example, costume jewellery) are often listed both as frequent impulse purchases and as frequently shoplifted items.

In addition, many consumers seem ambivalent concerning the morality of shoplifting. Cameron (1964) observed that apprehended shoplifters 'generally [do] not think of themselves as thieves', or view their activity as a 'real crime'. Clinard and Meier (1979) note that shoplifters often argue that 'I buy a lot here anyway', that the stores 'expect' people to steal, or that a large corporation 'won't miss' an inexpensive item of merchandise. Similarly, Klemke (1992) presents data indicating that the shoplifting of an inexpensive item is widely viewed as less 'serious' than almost any other crime. In general, research has shown that individuals can more easily rationalize theft when it is targeted at large, impersonal organizations. Given this tendency, the continuing growth of national chains at the expense of local family-owned merchants may facilitate guilt-free consumer theft. Several decades ago, the sociologist Gregory Stone found that some consumers actually felt protective of stores owned by local individuals, but did not feel this way about large chains.

Finally, while shoplifting is certainly not riskfree, it may be perceived as less risky than many other crimes. Only about one in every 30 shoplifters is apprehended by store officials, and many stores are reluctant to press charges, especially for small thefts or those committed by very young offenders (Baumer and Rosenbaum, 1984).

As retail stores increasingly adopt self-service strategies, they become even more attractive targets for consumer theft. A lack of personal service may make stores seem 'faceless', making it easier for shoplifters to feel they are stealing from 'no one'. In addition, self-service operations typically have more difficulty monitoring customers' activity, thereby reducing shoplifters' risk of detection and punishment (Baumer and Rosenbaum, 1984).

Over the years, various writers have speculated that shoplifting (particularly that committed by middle-class women) is frequently the result of some form of mental pathology, such as kleptomania (in which a person compulsively steals items for which they have no inherent desire). However, while there have been individual case studies of shoplifters suffering from neurosis or psychosis, there is little systematic empirical evidence that these are common causes of shoplifting behaviour. Kleptomania, for example, while occurring frequently in popular films and novels, is reported in the psychiatric literature to be extremely rare. There is some indirect evidence that shoplifters tend to have an underdeveloped ability to delay gratification, and weigh the long-term consequences of their actions (for example, the fact, discussed below, that shoplifting activity becomes much less common as consumers enter adulthood). However, empirical studies indicate that shoplifters are no more (or less) likely to exhibit mental illness than the population as a whole.

Shoplifting peaks among adolescents

Shoplifting is a particularly common behaviour among adolescent consumers. Roughly 40 per cent of apprehended shoplifters are reported to be adolescents (Baumer and Rosenbaum, 1984) and anonymous self-report studies (for example, Klemke, 1992; Cox et al., 1990) also indicate widespread shoplifting among adolescents. Cox et al. (1990) found that nearly 40 per cent of adolescents admitted to shoplifting at least once in the previous 12 months.

Why does shoplifting peak among adolescents? To begin with, adolescents are prohibited from purchasing certain items, and this may prompt them to steal items an adult could simply purchase. More broadly, adolescents' apparently high rate of shoplifting relative to adults may be simply a function of maturation. One generally associates human maturation with increased impulse control (that is, ability to delay immediate gratification) as well as increased tendency to weigh the long run consequences, social impact and morality of one's actions. Research suggests that many individuals may simply 'grow out' of shoplifting as they enter adulthood.

Adolescents' high level of shoplifting may also be a function of opportunity. As juveniles age, the frequency of their independent shopping trips increases steadily, while trips with parents start declining after about age ten. By about the tenth grade, adolescents' independent store visits exceed those made in the company of their parents; at this age, a large proportion of American adolescents engage in frequent 'malling' (that is, hanging out at the local shopping mall; see, for example, Lo, 1994). Many adolescents make a sudden leap in independence at age 16, at which time they are typically permitted both to drive and to work for the first time. This also happens to be the approximate age at which adolescent shoplifting appears to peak.

Which adolescents are most likely to shoplift (and why)?

Adolescents are much more likely to shoplift if they have friends who shoplift (Klemke, 1992). The common interpretation for this has been that 'peer pressure' is a major cause of adolescent shoplifting. However, there may be other equally plausible interpretations. For example, adolescents who are already shoplifting may simply be attracted to each other ('birds of a feather'), or may find it convenient to work in tandem and seek out like-minded accomplices. Cameron (1964) notes that some shoplifters will work in teams of two or more, one distracting store personnel and the other stealing the merchandise. Knowing other shoplifters may also facilitate vicarious learning that crime may, in fact, pay. The actual odds of getting caught while shoplifting are quite low (some have estimated one in 30), and the chances of getting booked, convicted and punished are even lower. People who know other shoplifters (or see them in the act) may learn this and be tempted to join in. Seeing others shoplift (and get away with it) may also give the adolescent the impression that 'everybody does it', making the crime seem less serious. Further research is needed to more fully explain the social dimension of adolescent shoplifting.

Shoplifting and gender

Most empirical studies indicate that the majority of shoplifters are male (Cox et al., 1990; Klemke, 1992; Kraut, 1976). This finding would appear to contradict the popular view that shoplifting is a 'female crime', a view that has inspired some elaborate theories concerning females' supposed vulnerability to kleptomania and other larcenous impulses. While a few studies have shown a slight female majority among apprehended shoplifters, these have typically come from stores in which most shoppers are female. For example, Robin (1963) reported that 61 per cent of the shoplifters apprehended in three department stores were female; however, other research has found that 67 per cent of all department store shoppers were female. Thus, even among adults, a given male shopper is probably more likely to shoplift than a given female shopper. Why is this so? To begin with, males generally show a stronger tendency to bend or break rules, relative to females. This is reflected in crime statistics as well as unobtrusive observation of the sexes' rule-breaking behaviour. This tendency can probably be explained at least partially by the different social norms for the two sexes. Females may be socialized to be more conforming and compliant, while 'hell-raising' behaviour is tolerated more in boys; thus, young males' deviance is often dismissed with the statement, 'boys will be boys', but we seldom hear 'girls will be girls'. Whether there are also biological reasons for such gender differences is less clear.

Shoplifting and social class

Most self-report studies show only a weak relationship between consumers' social class and their likelihood of shoplifting. Why is this so? First, some of the reasons believed to lie behind at least adolescent shoplifting (for example, the desire for 'forbidden products', and peer influence) have little to do with family income or social class. Further, shoplifters tend to steal not necessities (à la Jean Valjean's loaf of bread) but luxuries. Cameron (1964: 164) notes that adult female shoplifters typically 'do not steal merchandise which they can rationalize purchasing: household supplies, husband's clothes, children's wear. But beautiful luxury goods for their own personal use can be purchased legitimately only if some other member of the family is deprived'. In general, the most frequently stolen items tend to be recreational products, such as candy, cigarettes, costume jewellery and CDs. Even some fairly affluent consumers may covet more such luxuries than they can afford to purchase, and for some, this unfulfilled desire leads to shoplifting.

ANTHONY D. COX AND DENA COX

Bibliography

Baumer, T. and Rosenbaum, D. (1984) *Combating Retail Theft: Programs and Strategies*, Stoneham, MA, Butterworth.

Cameron, M.O. (1964) *The Booster and the Snitch: Department Store Shoplifting*, New York, Free Press.

Clinard, M, and Meier, R. (1979) *Sociology of Deviant Behavior*, New York, Holt Rinehart & Winston.

Cox, D., Cox, A. and Moschis, G. (1990) 'When Consumer Behavior Goes Bad: An Investigation of Adolescent Shoplifting', *Journal of Consumer Research*, **17**: 149–59.

Klemke, L.W. (1992) *The Sociology of Shoplifting: Boosters and Snitches Today*, Westport, CT, Praeger.

Kraut, R.E. (1976) 'Deterrent and Definitional Influences on Shoplifting', *Social Problems*, **25**: 358–68.

Lo, L. (1994) 'Exploring Teenage Shoplifting Behavior: A Choice and Constraint Approach', *Environment and Behavior*, **26**: 613–39.

Robin, G. (1963) 'Patterns of Department Store Shoplifting', *Crime and Delinquency*, **9**: 163–72.

Smith, Adam

Adam Smith was the founding father of modern economics, writing in the second half of the eighteenth century but with a psychological perspective that goes well beyond what one finds in standard texts of the present day. For example, in 'An Essay on the History of Astronomy', Smith (1980) conceives science as a social activity motivated by psychological needs; science is given to the exercise of sentiments such as surprise, wonder and admiration. The unexpectedness of new appearances induces surprise and one is then led to wonder how the mysterious appearance came to occur in the first place. The human mind is then exercised by imagination to account for these appearances, to understand their underlying structure which in turn satisfies a desire to admire the coherent intellectual systems or theories subsequently constructed. Smith draws attention to the aesthetic dimension in scientific work: to the pleasure derived from constructing order and to the beauty of systematical arrangement of different observations connected by a few common principles (see Skinner, 1979). He also posits an intimate connection between theories of the world that the generality of mankind construct in their daily life (for example, in productive and consumptive activities and exchange relationships) and the generation and acceptance of scientific theories. The 'progress' of knowledge is a social construction not limited to the scientific community itself; it depends on the development of overall patterns and methods of world construction common to the layperson and the scientist.

Although better known for his writings on the division of labour and economic growth, his thinking in these areas relates to consumer behaviour since rising affluence and the introduction of new commodities opens up new consumption possibilities. In the *Wealth of Nations*, Smith expressly argues that the purpose of production is to provide for the consumer: 'Consumption is the sole end and purpose of all production'. He then introduces the principle of consumer sovereignty: 'the interest of the producer ought to be attended to, only so far as it may be necessary for promoting that of the consumer. The maxim is so perfectly self-evident, that it would be absurd to attempt to prove it' (1976a: 660) He defends the functional importance of consumption in a growing economy and the interests of the consumer in this context.

Human wants develop over time as the 'progress of opulence in different nations' is enhanced by international trade. Trade (and exchange in general) gives rise to a greater abundance and variety of commodities. For example, the 'surplus produce of America, imported into Europe, furnishes the inhabitants of this great continent with a variety of commodities which they could not otherwise have possessed, some for convenience and use, some for pleasure, and some for ornament, and thereby to increase their enjoyments' (Smith, 1976a: 591). However, Smith was not a utilitarian. The background for his discussion of consumer enjoyments in the *Wealth of Nations* is located in *The Theory of Moral Sentiments* (1976b). Here material well-being is in fact denigrated and the moral foundations of economic growth are highlighted. Production, trade and exchange augment the material means of human life and result in higher levels of consumption. Enjoyment or satisfaction from consuming commodities *per se* is not the sole purpose of consumer behaviour or the economic system as a whole. Moreover, the consumer does not generally accumulate wealth as an end in itself. The point of Smith's moral philosophy is that the real and hidden end of life is the acquisition of virtue.

Smith made limited use, in a range of applications, of a theory of demand based on consumer choice. For instance, he was aware of the complexity of the working-class budget and the role of relative prices in determining the commodity composition of the basket. Consumers substitute other goods in the place of relatively expensive items. In contemporary conditions (applauded by Smith) where real labour incomes were rising, he suggested that governments might, by judicious use of excise taxes, encourage the 'sober and industrious' to consume more 'necessaries' as opposed to luxuries (1976a: 869-70). This argument rested on the narrowly 'economic' mechanism of substitution in consumption and on the notion of civic virtue idealized in *The Theory of Moral Sentiments*. The unprecedented ability to consume made possible by rising incomes and declining costs of commodities in the last quarter of the eighteenth century, could potentially corrupt civic virtue (Muller, 1993: 28–34). Hence the need to limit consumption of luxuries.

Beyond basic human requirements wants are insatiable. The desire to consume, by contrast with the ability to consume, seems to be endless: the 'desire for food is limited by the capacity of the human stomach; but the 'desire for the conveniences and ornaments of building, dress, equipage, and household furniture, seem to have no limit' (Smith, 1976: 178, 181; 1976b: 184). We also have Smith's frankly stoical attack on consumer preferences. He objected to excessively high average consumption on moral grounds (see Hollander, 1973: 255). The 'great mob of mankind' indiscriminately follow the behaviour of the rich and powerful in forming their preferences, so some direction might be required in order to promote wisdom and virtue. He frequently refers to the 'frivolous and useless' trinkets and baubles which the well-endowed consume in order to gratify 'the most visible childish vanities' (1976a: 346). Here the putative link between commodity consumption and happiness is represented as a 'deception'. It is a deception, however, with positive unintended consequences for it 'rouses and keeps in continual motion the industry of mankind' (1976b: 183). A range of human qualities are thereby enhanced: thrift, enterprise, discipline, orderliness, punctuality and probity (see Rosenberg, 1968).

Instead of concentrating on isolated elements, Smith discussed the totality of the structure underlying consumer preference formation and satisfaction. The assumption of an independently given scale of preferences for individuals is not entertained. He considers the social determinants of consumption. The explanation of consumers' choices is not placed in the now familiar mechanical scheme of personal equilibrium, with given prices and budget constraints; it is broadened to include the influence exerted by foreign trading opportunities, producers, other consumers and prevailing customs and moral sentiments. The pattern of consumption is explained sociologically (see Reisman, 1976: 102–23). Consumption is a social activity enabling individuals to acquire symbols needed to achieve or identify social status. Propriety and obtrusive good taste take precedence over utility. Consumers spend much on 'conveniences which may be regarded as superfluities' but which appeal to a desire for vanity and distinction. Indeed 'emulation runs through all the different ranks of men' and it is the 'vanity not the ease or the pleasure', which attracts consumers. Consumers are motivated by a need to be noticed with 'sympathy and approbation' within their relevance reference groups (Smith, 1976b: 50). Demand patterns are socially stratified. Alternative preference sets are recognized for the typical consumer in the different social 'ranks'. For example, 'the frivolous accomplishments of that impertinent and foolish thing called a man of fashion' will enjoy the warmth of fellow-feeling from his peers as they sympathize with the propriety of one another's tastes. They should wear leather shoes and, to avoid contempt and ridicule, must don linen shirts. The costume wins respect and admiration; success and comfort must be conspicuously displayed in order to attract sympathy from spectators. By contrast, social convention dictates that wretchedness and misery be treated with disdain (1976b: 63, 144). Strong parallels have since been drawn between Adam Smith's and Thorstein Veblen's perspectives on consumer behaviour (see Sobel, 1979).

Rather than proceeding in his *Wealth of Nations* with a self-interested homo oeconomicus formulated as a deliberate, hypothetical abstraction, Smith proposes that self-interested actions, including economic actions pursing material wealth in commercial life, always have a social reference. The foundations for this perspective are established in *The Theory of Moral Sentiments* where the purpose of life is described in terms of a psychological propensity to 'better our condition'. By acting out this propensity, individuals enjoy the sympathy and approbation of others. Smith went further in maintaining that a person appears 'mean spirited' who does not follow the 'mean extraordinary and important objects of self-interest', contrasting the 'man of dull regularity' with the 'man of enterprise'. Only the latter receives esteem in a commercial society (1976b: 50, 173).

In the anonymous marketplace discussed in the *Wealth of Nations*, the social reference for human behaviour is downplayed but it is nevertheless always lurking in the background, providing the institutional stability for viable market exchanges. To be sure, the strategy involved in applying the profit motive in exchange is to succeed by addressing the 'self-love' and not humanity of fellow traders. It is not from the virtue of the butcher or baker that we should expect to obtain our dinner, but from their self-love (1976a: 26–7). While self-love meant pure ego, self-interest was a more inclusive notion because it mitigated self-love with a degree of virtue (see Fitzgibbons, 1995: 137–9). Smith understood self-interest in the wider sense by implanting an approving or disapproving spectator in the human breast: 'In the race for wealth he may run as hard as he can in order to outstrip his competitors. But if he should jostle, or throw down any of them, the indulgence of the spectators is entirely at an end. It is a violation of fair play, which they cannot admit of'. Some self-love is regarded as virtuous as long as it is constrained by a justice system based on natural liberty and combined, as the case demanded, with prudence and benevolence (Smith, 1976b: 83–173).

Altogether, the Smithian psychological drives to 'truck, barter and exchange one thing for another' in the market and the desire to 'better our condition' are postulated for a single value system. Consumer self-interest and the principles of moral virtue are inextricably linked in practice. The behaviour of Smith's sovereign consumer is not therefore activated by unadulterated greed. Smith was sanguine about the development of commerce and material well-being; he was not, however, an apologist for commercial or materialist interests. He thought that consumers would flourish if trade, production and hence economic growth were supported by an appropriate moral climate. That moral climate, as expounded by Smith , need not produce consumers who were vacuous, isolated, self-contained hedonists.

A.M. ENDRES

Bibliography
Fitzgibbons, A. (1995) *Adam Smith's System of Liberty, Wealth and Virtue*, Oxford, Clarendon Press.
Hollander, S. (1973) *The Economics of Adam Smith*, Toronto, Toronto University Press.
Muller, J.Z. (1993) *Adam Smith in His Time and Ours*, New York, Free Press.
Reisman, D. (1976) *Adam Smith's Sociological Economics*, London, Croom Helm.
Rosenberg, N. (1968) 'Adam Smith, Consumer Tastes and Economic Growth', *Journal of Political Economy*, **76**: 361–74.
Skinner, A.S. (1979) 'Adam Smith: An Aspect of Modern Economics?', *Scottish Journal of Political Economy*, **26**: 109–25.
Smith, A. (1976a) *An Inquiry Into the Nature and Causes of the Wealth of Nations*, edited by R.H. Campbell, A.S. Skinner and W.B. Todd, Oxford, Oxford University Press (first published 1776).
Smith A. (1976b) *The Theory of Moral Sentiments*, edited by D.D. Raphael and A.L. Macfie, Oxford, Oxford University Press (first published 1759).
Smith, A. (1980) 'An Essay on the History of Astronomy' (first published 1790) in his *Essays on Philosophical Subjects*, edited by W.P.D. Wightman and J.C. Bryce, Oxford, Oxford University Press.
Sobel, I. (1979) 'Adam Smith: What Kind of Institutionalist Was He?', *Journal of Economic Issues*, **13**: 347–68.

Soap Opera

Soap operas exist to entertain and to sell goods. These dual purposes, which may be unique to the soap opera genre, guided the development of radio's first serials in the 1930s. In the decades that followed, the broadcast media matured, and the demographic characteristics of soap opera audiences changed; none the less, entertainment and selling needs continue to inform the content of contemporary televised daytime dramas.

Working independently in Chicago during the early 1930s, Frank Hummert and Irna Phillips attempted to develop daytime radio programming that would appeal to a potential audience of 23 million US housewives. Hummert, a member of the Blackett–Sample–Hummert advertising agency, and Phillips, a writer for radio station WGN and later WMAQ, both recognized the need for programming that would allow consumer goods companies to reach their housewife customers. Indeed, Phillips wrote, 'any radio programme which is sponsored in order to be of utility to its sponsor, must actually sell merchandise; otherwise the object of radio advertising has failed' (Phillips, 1931–36).

In October 1930, Phillips introduced 'Painted Dreams', the first soap opera, to Chicago housewife listeners; two years later, Hummert aired 'Bob and Betty', the first daytime network serial. In developing their programmes, both Phillips and Hummert relied upon the format of continuing 15-minute narratives broadcast five days a week, which had proved successful for evening radio shows such as 'Amos 'n' Andy', but they adjusted story lines to gain the interest of female listeners. 'Painted Dreams', consequently, featured intergenerational conflict between an Irish-American mother and her 'modern' daughter, while 'Bob and Betty' recounted the difficulties of a simple secretary who married her rich boss.

The female audience rapidly and enthusiastically accepted soap operas, and by the end of 1933, Pillsbury, General Mills, and Procter and Gamble sponsored the national broadcast of three daily serials. As listeners followed the ongoing trials and tribulations of the serial characters, they were exposed to advertising messages, which consumed several minutes of each programme. In addition, the soap operas also directly stimulated sales by making special offers to listeners. When Pillsbury offered a history of 'Today's Children' (the successor of 'Painted Dreams') and a picture of its cast, more than 250 000 listeners sent in the flour label that was required for the premium; likewise, a million members of Procter and Gamble's 'Ma Perkins' audience responded to an offer of a package of flower seeds in return for an Oxydol box top and 10 cents.

The leading characters in early soap operas also acted as spokespersons for sponsor's products. Phillips, for example, positioned Mother Moynahan from 'Painted Dreams' — later renamed Mother Moran in 'Today's Children' — as an 'actual homemaker', and suggested that 'what she does not know about the home is not worth while [sic] knowing' (Phillips, 1931–66). This characterization permitted Mother Moran, in the context of the soap opera plots, to endorse Pillsbury's products, the company's flour sifter package, and the recipes appearing on the SnoSheen flour box (Lavin, 1995). Phillips even crafted a storyline that required Mother Moran to visit the Pillsbury test kitchen and report on the trip during several episodes. During an exchange with her daughter, she rhapsodized 'what a kitchen it is —- ah — they got everthin [sic] in it . . . that is where they test out the flour of all kinds . . . by bakin [sic] the proven recipes' (Phillips 1931–66).

By the early 1940s, more than 30 soap operas were broadcast each weekday from 10 a.m. to 6 p.m. to an audience of 20 million listeners (LaGuardia, 1974). The most prolific producers of radio daytime serials were Frank and Anne Hummert, who relied on a staff of dialogue writers to provide scripts for as many as 15 soap operas including 'Ma Perkins' and 'The Romance of Helen Trent'. The Hummerts retained ownership of their programmes, but produced them through the Blackett–Sample–Hummert Advertising Agency, which had general supervisory authority as well as responsibility for hiring actors, organist, director and announcer. Irna Phillips personally wrote each of her early soap operas, but she also owned each of her serials and had an arrangement, similar to that of the Hummerts, with the Hutchinson Advertising Agency and later the Compton Agency.

The popularity of soap operas led some educators and intellectuals in the 1940s to bemoan the 'social irresponsibility of commercial sponsorship' (Dennison, 1940). Louis Berg, a New York psychiatrist, was harshest in his condemnation of the serials. He argued that 'Pandering to perversity and playing out destructive conflicts, these serials furnish the same release for the emotionally distorted that is supplied to those who desire satisfaction from a lynching bee'. He also associated listening to soap operas with tachycardia, arrhythmias, gastrointestinal disturbances and a number of other maladies (LaGuardia, 1974).

Concerns about possible deleterious effects that might be associated with soap operas led to a survey of 100 listeners in the late 1930s. This research revealed that emotional release, wishful thinking and advice were the three most common reasons for soap opera loyalty. Respondents also indicated their dislike for direct advertising messages, because they took 'time away from the story', but accepted incorporation of the sponsor's product into serial plots. Of the 100 listeners surveyed, 61 reported buying sponsoring brands (Herzog, 1941). A larger survey of 10 000 women found that soap opera listeners were not more socially isolated than nonlisteners, but this research did reveal that listeners were more likely to live in rural areas and to be less educated than nonlisteners

(Kaufman, 1944).

In 1950, CBS launched the first televised daytime serial comedy, 'The First Hundred Years'. The next year, writer and advertising executive, Roy Winsor introduced two new soap operas, 'Search for Tomorrow' and 'Love of Life' on the same network. In 1952, CBS included in its daytime television schedule, 'The Guiding Light', a Phillips soap opera that had begun on radio in 1937, and, in 1954, the network added 'The Secret Storm'. During the mid-fifties, several soap operas including 'The Guiding Light', 'The Brighter Day', and 'Road of Life' were broadcast on both radio and television, but as the decade passed, serial programming shifted to the newer medium. In 1956, Phillips developed 'As the World Turns' for Procter and Gamble. The storyline of this first 30 minute soap opera proceeded at a much slower pace that did that of its 15 minute counterparts, and permitted the new serial to incorporate facial expressions and other visual effects possible on television. A second Procter and Gamble, half-hour serial, 'The Edge of Night', debuted in 1957. Three years later, in November 1960, the last six remaining serials on radio were terminated; none of these soap operas made the transition to television.

On television as on radio, audiences identify with soap opera characters, and blur the distinction between the actors and their serial roles. They call actors, in public settings, by their soap opera names, and they often have sent gifts to celebrate weddings and births occurring on the serials. In fact, when 'The Guiding Light' asked viewers to join in congratulating one character on his 65th birthday, they responded with 22 sacks of gifts and 39 000 cards and telegrams (LaGuardia, 1974).

Daytime soap opera was designed for a housewife audience, but by the late 1960s, feminist ideology and women's increasing participation in the workforce began to erode this viewership. In 1970, Nielsen reported that 20 million viewers a day watched daytime serials, and that 76 per cent of this audience were women 18 or older, 15 per cent were men, and 5 per cent were teens. By 1981, however, the percentage of women viewers had fallen to 70 per cent. In response to these changing demographics, soap opera producers and writers developed story lines that feature younger protagonists and that have considered such controversial topics as rape and incest. They have also recognized the importance of the sizeable African–American audience, and in recent years, have presented plots that give African–American characters primary importance (Passalacqua, 1997).

In the 1990s, the daytime soap opera audience declined to an estimated 16 million. Meanwhile, in 1996, Procter and Gamble, which alone owns three serials, spent an estimated $90 million producing their programmes. Commenting on this expenditure, one advertising executive stated, 'That is still how they reach a very large portion of their consumer base'. But he then went on to note, 'Certainly, it is not easy to reach women just by buying daytime anymore, and I'm not even sure it's the best way, but combined with other things it is very effective' (Canedy, 1997). This statement summarizes the conundrum facing contemporary soap opera producers. In the 1990s, daytime serials do continue to attract a sizeable following. That viewership, however, is not the relatively homogeneous housewife market for which first soap operas originated. As a consequence, in the present day, soap operas face the challenge of entertaining a wide range of viewers — most of whom are still women — but this audience includes large numbers outside the sponsor's target segment and excludes many potential buyers — most notably working women — who are either unable or unwilling to watch daytime serials.

While the audience for daytime soap operas has steadily eroded, the serial format, which features ensemble casts of actors and ongoing storylines, has become a popular staple of evening television programming in the 1980s and 1990s. Initially, programmes such as 'Dallas' and 'Coronation Street' merely transferred the daytime soap opera format to evening, albeit with more opulent production efforts. In more recent years, however, ongoing stories have characterized a wide range of both dramatic and comedy programmes including 'ER' and 'Caroline in the City'.

Finally, soap opera has even been successfully used as an advertising vehicle; that is, the advertisement itself has contained an on-going storyline. Perhaps the best known of these efforts is the series of Taster's Choice advertisements developed by the advertising agency McCann-Erickson Worldwide. These advertisements, which began in November 1990, feature Sharon and Tony, two neighbours in their forties who become romantically involved. The advertisements, which followed the couple's relationship for several years, gained cult status both in the US and in the UK. Moreover, within a year of the campaign's introduction, Taster's Choice also became the number one instant coffee (Rickard, 1994). The Taster's Choice advertisements, as well as similar efforts presented by Anchor Butter in New Zealand — new 'episodes' of which are themselves advertised — appear to reverse the roles of soap opera and advertising. Soap operas came into existence as a means of attracting an audience to an advertising message; the Taster's Choice and Anchor Butter advertisements, however, provide self-contained mini-entertainment.

MARILYN LAVIN

Bibliography

Canedy, D. (1997) 'P&G Is Seeking to Revive Soaps; Shaking Up TV Serials As Audiences Dwindle', *New York Times*, March 11, Sec. D: 1.

Dennison, M. (1940) 'Soap Opera', *Harper's*, **180**: 498–505.

Herzog, H. (1941) 'On Borrowed Experience: An Analysis of Listening to Daytime Sketches', in *Studies in Philosophy and Social Science*, Vol. 9, New York, Institute of Social Research: 65–95.

Kaufman, H. (1944) 'The Appeal of Specific Daytime Serials', in Lazarfield, P. and Stanton, F. (eds), *Radio Research, 1942-1943*, New York, Duell, Sloan & Pearce.

LaGuardia, R. (1974) *The Wonderful World of TV Soap Operas*, New York, Ballantine.

Lavin, M. (1995) 'Creating Consumers in the 1930s: Irna Phillips and the Radio Soap Opera', *Journal of Consumer Research*, **22**: 75–89.

Passalacqua, C. (1997) 'The Soaps: P&G's Fuller Canvas', *Newsday*, 28 July, Part II, B21.

Phillips, I (1931–66) Personal and Business Papers, Film and Manuscripts Archive, State Historical Society of Wisconsin, Madison.

Rickard, L. (1994) 'Taster's Choice Rolls Love Potion No. 9', *Advertising Age*, 13 June: 70.

Speculation

In essence, speculation is simply buying at a low price in the hope of selling later at a higher one. However, the concept is generally associated with quick, easy short-term profits and the people doing it being unconcerned with what they are buying and selling, but rather with the process itself. Consequently, negative perceptions of speculation as essentially greedy and parasitic are common. Speculation relates usually to dealings in financial assets (currencies, futures, bonds, equities) or property (real estate) rather than conventional goods and services. The intrinsic volatility of these markets facilitates the speculative process through the potential for massive profits (or losses) within a short period, often with a minimal cash or up-front investment.

Well-informed speculation in goods or shares can stabilize market conditions by evening out price differences between two or more different markets. In this vein, Keynes (1936) analysed the positive impact of 'stabilizing speculation' which is based on expert knowledge of supply, demand and overall market conditions. Indeed, in contrast to the statements in the above paragraph, speculators are sometimes perceived favourably for seeking out and developing weak or neglected sectors of the economy. But badly judged speculation may magnify price fluctuations to the detriment of the economy and individuals. Such processes exacerbate unfavourable sentiments towards speculators, when, for example, their activities bid property prices up and out of the range of low-income earners. Even worse, irrational, imprudent or compulsive waves of wild optimism or pessimism tend to cause severe fluctuations which obscure the more fundamental economic realities in a given market.

Speculation is thus heavily controlled by psychological factors as individuals act and react in relation to both perceived conditions in inherently volatile markets and to the behaviour of others with an interest in the same market. The greater the ratio of speculators to longer-term investors, the more volatile and crash-prone the market. As a market moves up into the boom phase, the proportion of speculators rises. Conversely, as it becomes clear that a market is receding, the speculators move out, often in large panic-stricken numbers.

Inevitably, therefore, the amount of speculation and its rationality vary considerably over the course of a business, property or financial-market cycle. Any given cycle may commence with full rationality from a neutral point which is neither particularly high nor low and gradually lose rationality as emotions become intensified and more speculators are drawn in. Furthermore, the speculation itself becomes more and more risky and, as indicated by Minsky (1986), entices participants with ever-lower levels of market expertise. Earl (1995: 281) concurs that buyers become 'less fussy' as a consequence of buoyant expectations. In addition, because fortunes can be made in a boom, individuals become progressively more voracious and there are invariably many unscrupulous operators who emerge to exploit this. People become 'blinded by greed' and thus ignore any warning signs in the market. Furthermore, no amount of moral suasion from officials or warnings in the media seems to curb the demand for fast money.

A further possible ingredient of speculation is that the process can provide participants with a 'rush' much in the manner of conventional gambling. Stone (1994: 112) comments that there is nothing like the thrill of speculating, and small investors 'who do not scare easy', love commodities. Intelligence or intellect are also no necessary prerequisite for success in volatile markets, because rationality may not prevail in (especially wildly) fluctuating and emotionally charged markets. Seemingly prudent, risk-averse approaches can prove disastrous. According to Wood (1988: 118), run-of-the-mill investors and money managers tend to follow the herd, whereas the most successful 'are probably the world's biggest prima donnas'. They are highly individualistic and 'live off their wits, sharing a common addiction to moving markets' (Wood, 1988: 118).

Some of the idiom used to describe speculators' reactions during cyclical phases is illuminating. The phrases and expressions used by Schluter (1933: 78–101) are loaded with psychological significance: 'intoxicated investors' with an 'overoptimistic discounting of future profits [which] acts like a dynamo in sucking funds' into the speculative system. In the 'phase of prosperity' of a booming economy or stock market the urge to consume 'with little or no solicitude for any abiding benefits to the masses biologically, psychologically or spiritually encourages profligacy'. Investment, finance and credit are 'caught in a feverish speculative whirl' and funds 'are distributed according to the whims and fancies of irrational speculation', it is 'a fool's paradise'. Even bankers become 'infected by the general ardent optimism'.

In referring to famous speculations of the past such as the Mississippi Company and tulipmania in Holland and so on, Röpke (1936: 39) refers to 'speculative mania' and 'excessive gambling that must have bordered on madness'. In the early eighteenth century, Crellius, a Dutch banker, commented that Exchange Alley resembled 'nothing so much as if all the lunatics had escaped out of the madhouse at once' (Wilson, 1941: 103). Garber (1989) refers to a 'final speculative frenzy' which 'terminated inexplicably'. He alludes to 'the orgy — unrestrained also from the moral point of view — of company promoting' and 'the delirium which centred round railways and the iron and steel industry'. Kindleberger (1989: 12) refers to the 'direct contagion of speculators'. More recently, Schwarz (1994) comments on derivative speculation being 'contagious and turning into a systemic risk'.

Mass psychology is particularly relevant to speculation and provides the key to understanding its excesses. The classic works of Sigmund Freud (1946), Elias Canetti (1962) and Gustav Le Bon (1921), on mass psychology, apply remarkably well to speculation. Le Bon argued that the communal soul erodes intellectual powers and individual personality. In a mass ambience, actions and emotions are so infectious that individual preferences are frequently sacrificed to those of the group. Furthermore, the mass is in a state of perpetual expectancy, which renders it highly susceptible to influence; it can easily be fooled. The mass is unresponsive even to irrefutable logical connections; it does not operate on a sophisticated level. Repetition is ultimately regarded as proof of veracity, and ideas, emotions and sentiments spread rapidly. This swift dissemination explains sudden panics, which are often quite out of proportion to imminent danger and frequently arise in response to relatively trivial stimulation. Furthermore, panic undermines the mass. When the collective emotional ties of the mass no longer bind it and individual intelligence is freed again, the mass disintegrates.

This concurs with Keynes's (1936) analysis of asset pricing and interest rates, in which he argues that under certain market conditions, prices are formed through an equilibrium-like balance of speculative behaviour and attitudes. Concerted, mass agreement on likely price movements will induce a movement in that direction until the process burns itself out as sceptics finally emerge in sufficient numbers to nullify or even reverse the trend. Smith and Williams (1992) consider further the causes, nature and inevitability of 'speculative bubbles' within the context of experimental replication of market behaviour.

According to Freud (1946), under conditions of heightened emotionalism, so typical of the mass, the individual is unwittingly impelled to follow the actions of others, in order to remain in consonance with the mass. This emotional charge moves it a step away from reality. As pointed out by Canetti (1962), the mass loves density. The smaller the distance between individuals, the more powerful their interactions. Therefore, electronic communication and the proximity of people in a dealing room, or even a town or city in a property boom are factors to consider. Add to this the pressure of time, large amounts of money involved, rapidly changing circumstances and information overload, and the situation is perfect for mass psychology to induce major and ill-considered speculative activity.

Undoubtedly, not everyone succumbs to the mass mindset. But as optimism and euphoria rise together with profits which begin to seem guaranteed, the pessimists are stunned into silence, so that this counterbalancing psychological mechanism is nullified. As Mueller (1995: 42) indicates, 'judgmental errors do not exact their normally expected penalties in good times; prosperity has a way of papering over mistakes'. This is a critical point, because it allows mass emotions to run riot, unchecked. Furthermore, even those who can see the speculative excesses, continue to participate, being quite convinced that they will be able to get out in time. Once again, Keynes (1936) explains why such optimism is unjustified for a large number of speculators. Further and lively insight into mass psychology through the process of cognitive dissonance and related elements of rationality are provided by Kaish (1986) and Maital, Filer and Simon (1986) on perceptions of risk.

When, ultimately, a panic occurs due the realization that there is not enough money around to enable everyone to sell at the top, the race out of real or long-term assets can turn into a stampede. Furthermore, stated Alfred Marshall, fierce rage and distrust work like an inferno even on assets and institutions that are intrinsically sound: 'as a fire spreads from one wooden house to another until even fireproof buildings succumb to the blaze of a great conflagration' (1965: 305). In the words of Röpke (1936: 207): 'once expansion has become the subject of mass cries and mass discussions it is in great danger of being executed under the worst possible circumstances in a crude and ill-considered manner'.

All the above considerations exert a very real impact on the economy. It is, therefore, not uncom.non for speculative behaviour to exacerbate the more 'real' trends inherent in a given market. Speculation is linked to and influences mainstream economic activity and the business cycle, also because it relates to the financial and property markets that are so basic to any economy. Minsky's seminal work (1986) on 'speculative finance', shows how lending patterns and mood swings thrust economies into steep booms or declines. Even more so in the computerized, globalized 1990s, the massive amounts of money that are potentially subject to speculation are undoubtedly sufficient to mould both national and international economic processes.

Under stable market conditions, attitudinal inputs into the market are individualistic and restrained; fundamentals rule, whereas when real processes begin to escalate, the human element becomes progressively more significant. Decision making diverges from rational norms as decisions are 'framed' in a context that is distinct from conventional, calculative economic consideration (Tversky and Kahneman, 1988). This ensures that booms and busts are relatively rapid by virtue either of speculation or of panic, whereas the more 'normal' periods last longer until, gradually, the psychology of the group changes and things start to accelerate.

Once emotions are really and truly heightened, the separation of the real from the psychological, not only in the mind(s) of the mass, but for all becomes ever more difficult. The very essence of speculative booms and the peaks and troughs of the business cycle is that they take on a psychological, perceived pseudo-reality which overrides the fundamentals underlying the trend. Prechter (1980) claims that this psychology forms the fundamentals rather than the other way round. The speculation–fundamental interaction is reciprocal. Intense and generally market-pervading perceptions work in tandem with economic fundamentals and the two reinforce each other mutually. Optimism can both instigate an improvement in economic conditions or enhance one that was there in the first place. Given that supply and demand, savings, investment and so on are all based on human conditions, perceptions and preferences, whatever factors bring about activity of any kind, have a real impact on the economy, whether or not they are founded on any concrete economic rationality. A speculative bubble is thus unlikely to burst without causing various nasty financial incidents that feed into the real economy.

In summary, speculation is a natural business and psychological phenomenon which both is facilitated by and is a cause of market instability and volatility. The rapidly rising and falling prices which occur, particularly in financial and property markets, attract people with a high-risk preference. Simultaneously, susceptibility to mass-psychology-induced panic and euphoria is to some degree inherent in the nature of the speculative process. When this occurs, speculation causes wild, destabilizing market swings which leave behind a series of winners and losers. The impact of this process on market fundamentals and economic activity can be serious. Although, at their best, speculators serve a useful purpose in identifying gaps in the market and shortfalls in supply, all too often, their short-term profit orientation and the concomitant psychological scenarios mutate the process into one that distorts the market and leads to a protracted period of disequilibrium.

BRIAN BLOCH

Bibliography
Canetti, E. (1962) *Crowds and Power*, London, Gollancz.
Earl, P.E. (1995) 'Liquidity Preference, Marketability and Pricing', in Dow, S.C. and Hillard, J. (eds) *Keynes, Knowledge and Uncertainty*, Aldershot, Edward Elgar: 269–92.

Freud, Sigmund. (1946) *The Ego and Mechanisms of Defence*, New York, International University Press.

Garber, P.M. (1989) 'Tulipmania', *Journal of Political Economy*, **97**: 535–60.

Kaish, S. (1986) 'Behavioral Economics in the Theory of the Business Cycle', in Gilad, B. and Kaish, S. (eds) *Handbook of Behavioral Economics*, Volume B, Greenwich, CT, JAI Press: 31–49.

Keynes, J.M. (1936) *The General Theory of Employment, Interest and Money*, London, Macmillan.

Kindleberger, C.P. (1989) *Manias, Panics and Crashes: A History of Financial Crises*, (2nd edn) Houndmills, Basingstoke, Macmillan.

Le Bon, G. (1921) *The Crowd: A Study of the Popular Mind*, London,: T.F. Unwin.

Maital, S., Filer, R. and Simon, J. (1986) 'What Do People Bring to the Stock Market (Besides Money)? The Economic Psychology of Stock Market Behavior', in Gilad, B. and Kaish, S. (eds) *Handbook of Behavioral Economics*, Volume B, Greenwich, CT, JAI Press: 273–307.

Marshall, A. (1965) *Money, Credit and Commerce*, New York, Augustus M. Kelly. (Originally published 1923).

Minsky, H.P. (1986) *Stabilizing an Unstable Economy*, New Haven, CT, Yale University Press.

Mueller, H.P. (1995) 'Cycles and the Credit Culture', *Journal of Commercial Lending*, **78**: (1), September.

Prechter, R. (1980) *The Major Works of R.N. Elliot*, Gainesville, GA, New Classics Library.

Röpke, W. (1936) *Crises and Cycles*, adapted from the German and revised by V.C. Smith, London, William Hodge & Company.

Schluter, W.C. (1933) *Economic Cycles and Crises*, New York, Sears Publishing Company.

Schwarz, A. (1994) 'Hedge or Speculate', *Far Eastern Economic Review*, **157**: 7 July.

Smith, V.L. and Williams, A.W. (1992) 'Experimental Market Economies', *Scientific American*, **267**: 72–7.

Stone, A. (1994) 'Futures: Dare You Defy the Odds?', *Business Week*, 28 February: 112–13.

Tversky, A. and Kahneman, D. (1988) 'Rational Choice and the Framing of Decisions', in Bell, D., Raiffa, H. and Tversky, A. (eds) *Decision Making: Descriptive, Normative, and Prescriptive Interactions*, Cambridge, Cambridge University Press.

Wilson, C. (1941) *Anglo-Dutch Commerce and Finance in the Eighteenth Century*, Cambridge, Cambridge University Press.

Wood, C. (1988) *Boom or Bust. The Rise and Fall of the World's Financial Markets*, London, Sidgewick & Jackson.

Tax Evasion

When completing an income tax return, taxpayers may consider doing this honestly, specifying all income they have received, and not claiming unwarranted deductions. On the other hand, they may think about fiddling, either by underdeclaring income, or by overstating deductions. At first sight, this seems to be an ideal field for applying standard rational choice theory. Applied to this context, rational choice theory states that the taxpayer will evaluate the expected outcomes of both choices, compare them, and prefer the option with the highest expected outcome. In the case of taxes, the expected outcomes are costs, namely, taxes to be paid. So a rational taxpayer chooses the option that costs less. The expected cost of the honest choice is simple: you have to pay the amount of tax T corresponding to your taxable income I, where the relation between T and I is formulated in the tax law. Let us denote T as $T = T(I)$, an increasing function of I. In a so-called flat tax system, $T = rI$ for some rate r between 0 and 1; in the common bracket-type tax systems $T(I)$ is a stepwise linear function of I, with steps corresponding with rates applicable to the successive brackets. Notice that the outcome of the honest choice is deterministic, given an income level I: the cost is fixed, no probabilities whatsoever play a role in the outcome. The expected result of the other, dishonest, choice is slightly more complex, as it is dependent on whether the tax inspector finds out that the taxpayer tries to cheat or not. Suppose that the taxpayer contemplates not declaring his or her real taxable income I, but instead to conceal an amount C, thus filing an income $I - C$. If the tax inspector finds out, at least the same amount of taxes $T(I)$ will be collected as in the honest case; in addition a fine, F, may be applied. In a number of tax administrations, the fine F is related to either the amount concealed C, or to the tax evaded $T(I) - T(I - C)$. In general, we denote the fine $F = F(I, C)$. If, however, the tax inspector fails to detect the underdeclaring altogether, the taxpayer pays only the amount $T(I - C)$ after all. If we assume that the probability of detection of the intended evasion is p (independent of the other parameters in the model), we see the expected costs of the choice of evading to be:

$$p * [T(I) + F(I, C)] + (1-p) * [T(I-C)]$$

which amounts to

$$T(I) + p * F(I, C) + (1-p) * [T(I-C) - T(I)].$$

According to rational choice theory, these expected costs must be compared with the (fixed) costs of the honest choice, $T(I)$. The rational taxpayer chooses to be honest if the difference D between those two costs,

$$D = p * F(I, C) + (1-p) * [T(I-C) - T(I)] \qquad (1)$$

is positive.

As the first term in (1) is positive, and the second negative, the sign of D is dependent on the various parameters. Essentially this model was proposed in the 1972 seminal paper by Allingham and Sandmo.

It is clear that D is an increasing function of p and of F, so a higher chance of detection and more severe punishment will increase the likelihood of an honest choice. The relation between D and either I or C is, however, much less clear, as it is critically dependent on the forms of the functions T and F. Allingham and Sandmo have already shown the rather anomalous result that for some fairly reasonable assumptions for F and T, the model specifies that the higher the tax rates are, the more evasion will occur, but for other, equally reasonable assumptions, on the contrary, the relation turns around: the higher the tax rates, the less the occurrence of evasion, which sounds rather counterintuitive.

This leads us to the question: 'How reasonable, after all, is the rational choice model for tax evasion?'. Let us first observe that in most tax administrations the probability of detecting evasion, p, is rather small. For reasons of workload, the vast majority of returns are only superficially looked into, or even not checked at all, in a given year. As a good example, in the US income tax system only a small percentage of returns is audited (thoroughly investigated), the others are accepted unchallenged (except for some correction of what are called 'mathematical and clerical errors'). Now this does not show that dishonest cases have the same low probability of being looked into, as that also depends on the ability of the tax administration to focus their audit process on dubious cases, but even if they are succesful in that, it remains the case that p is low. Moreover, in many tax systems (for instance in the Netherlands), often no fine is incurred at all. This is because tax officers face great difficulty when they have to discern between genuine, bona fide errors made by the taxpayer (which do not deserve fines) and intentional noncompliance (which is eligible for punishment). As modern tax systems tend to be overly complex, the generation of errors has been found to be abundant, provoking tax inspectors to be careful in issuing fines.

This state of affairs, low probability of detection and low or absent fines, implies that the difference D in expression (1) will be dominated by its second term, and therefore be negative. In other words, rational choice theory predicts that almost every taxpayer will evade. However, this is not the case in reality. Although estimates of the number of tax evaders vary wildly, most authors agree that honest tax declaration is by no means extinct. Moreover, low p and absent F would imply that the rational choice taxpayer will conceal *all* of his or her income, as that optimizes his or her cost saving. But this zero-declaration behaviour is almost never observed in the real tax world. Therefore, we have to conclude that there are serious defects in the Allingham and Sandmo model.

Of course, a number of adaptations have been proposed within the framework of rational choice theory (for example, Cullis and Lewis, 1997). It is not possible to enumerate all these possibilities, but three major trends are mentioned. One approach is to redefine the situation faced by the taxpayer. He or she simply gets more options to choose from when comparing expectations. Options proposed in this context range from relatively simple ones such as hiring a tax consultant or retiring to minimize income through to bribing the tax inspector or emigrating to a tax haven.

Another approach seeks to broaden the concept of expected outcome. We mention the introduction of other types of punishment than monetary fines (guilt, social disapproval, the costs of being marked by the tax authorities for following years) and of the possibility, particularly in poor nations, that evasion will be affected by knowledge of the probability that tax inspectors will be open to bribery (see, for example, Goswami et al., 1991)). There is the possibility of incorporating Kahneman-and-Tversky-type adaptations of valuing outcomes within the rational choice framework. Some authors propose not using the objective probability of detection, but a subjective variant, that is, what the taxpayers think the probability of detection will be. It is well documented that this subjective p is quite large among taxpayers. The majority of taxpayers believe that cases of evasion — as long as the concealed amount is not trivial — are fairly sure to be detected. On the other hand, a 'subjective probabilities rational choice model' is really quite at odds with the classical rational choice model that starts by assuming a fully informed rational taxpayer.

A third approach remodels the reaction of the tax service, for example, letting the probability of detection depend on the amount concealed, C, or possibly also on income, I. This may be rather more realistic than assuming a uniform probability.

A quite different line has been chosen by authors who challenge the assumption underlying the rational choice model, namely, that all taxpayers are alike in their drive to conceal income, if the expected costs are less than those of fully declaring income. These authors hold that some people have a stronger tendency to keep on the right side of the law than others. This school of thought tries to identify personal characteristics (sometimes called 'individual differences') that should explain why in exactly identical circumstances some people declare honestly, while others do not. The personal characteristics proposed are broadly to be divided into two classes: attitudes with respect to taxes on the one hand, and personality traits on the other hand.

Attitudinal explanations, in the line of Fishbein and Azjen's (1975) reasoned action model, hold that behaviour with respect to a given topic, for example, taxpaying, can be explained by attitudes towards the behaviour in question. An attitude is, in this context, an evaluative, emotional perspective on the pros and cons of that behaviour. A subjective social norm is the perception of the taxpayer of how he or she ought to behave according to his or her immediate environment or reference group. A number of attitudinal variables have been proposed in the tax field, such as the attitude with respect to the tax system in general, with respect to special features of the system (for instance certain deductions), with respect to taxpaying, with respect to tax evasion, with respect to the distribution of the tax burden over people ('equity', fairness), and with respect to the government's use of the tax gathered. Norms may vary according to what reference group the taxpayer is orientated towards. While in some environments tax evasion will be condemned, in others it will be at least tolerated, or thought of as comparatively 'normal', if not actually admired. It will be clear that this line of thought is close to the incorporation of guilt and social disapproval into the value function, as mentioned above. In the tax field the Fishbein approach has been used frequently (an overview of proposed models is given in Hessing et al., 1988).

Personality trait explanations focus on the the observation that people do differ in the extent that they feel obliged to follow rules (law abidingness, tolerance of deviance). As taxpaying can be seen as contributing to a common good at the expense of one's own free spending, a relevant personality trait is a subject's preferences when distributing goods, with respect to his or her own and other people's welfare (altruism, individualism, competition).

Empirical research into the above proposed explanations is complicated by the measurement problem: tax evasion is not overt behaviour. Basically there are two strategies of measurement: relying on tax returns or relying on self-reports of taxpayers. The former sets out to infer from the concrete traces of tax behaviour (filed returns) whether a taxpayer shows signs of evasion. Apart from the difficulty *per se* (skilful evasion is not easy to trace), we face the obstacle here of how to discern between bona fide errors and deliberate attempts to conceal income in a return: do these two processes leave different traces in a return? On the other hand, the latter measurement strategy, using self-reports, has to cope with a quite probable bias in the answers. People who claim to be honest as taxpayers may well be not honest in saying so, while those who claim to be noncompliant may be bragging. Moreover, research confronting the two measurement strategies (Elffers, 1991) has shown that rather different results emerge from the two ways of measuring tax evasion: self-reports tend to be related to attitudinal and deterrence variates, return-based measures with personality traits.

An integrating model of tax behaviour is Elffers's three-threshold model of *willing–being able–daring to undercomply*. In order to effectively underdeclare taxes the taxpayer must pass three thresholds successively: first, he or she has to feel the will to do so (and this may well be dependent on the above-mentioned attitudinal and personal variates). Second, if he or she feels a tendency to cheat, he or she then has to have an opportunity to do so in a way that is not immediately visible to the authorities (opportunity may be dependent on income structure, education, fiscal competence). If he or she has both the will and the opportunity, finally (s)he must not be deterred by the possibility of detection and punishment (here the rational choice model in the Allingham and Sandmo tradition comes into play again).

HENK ELFFERS

Bibliography

Allingham, M.G. and Sandmo, A. (1972) 'Income Tax Evasion: A Theoretical Analysis', *Journal of Public Economics*, 1: 323–38.

Cullis, J.G. and Lewis, A. (1997) 'Why People Pay Taxes: From a Conventional Economic Model to a Model of Social Convention', *Journal of Economic Psychology*, 18: 305–21.

Elffers, H. (1991) *Income Tax Evasion. Theory and Measurement*, Deventer, Kluwer.

Fishbein, M. and Azjen, I. (1975) *Belief, Attitude, Intention and Behaviour*, Reading, MA, Addison-Wesley.

Goswami, O., Sanyal, A. and Gang, I.N. (1991) 'Taxes, Corruption and Bribes: A Model of Indian Public Finance', in Roemer, M. and Jones, C (eds) *Markets in Developing Countries: Parallel, Fragmented and Black*, San Francisio, CA, ICS Press, for Harvard Institute of International Development: 201-213, 252-3.

Hessing, D.J., Kinsey, K.A., Elffers, H. and Weigel, R.H. (1988) 'Tax Evasion Research: Measurement Strategies and Theoretical Models', in Van Raaij, W.F., Van Veldhoven, G.M. and Wärneryd, K.E. (eds) *Handbook of Economic Psychology*, Dordrecht, Kluwer: 516–37.

Webley, P., Robben, H.S.J., Elffers, H. and Hessing, D.J. (1991) *Tax Evasion: An Experimental Approach*, Cambridge, Cambridge University Press.

Weigel, R.H., Hessing, D.J. and Elffers, H. (1987) 'Tax Evasion Research: A Critical Appraisal and Theoretical Model', *Journal of Economic Psychology*, 8: 215–35.

Time Use

In conventional microeconomic theory, the allocation of time to various activities is regarded in terms of the rational-choice paradigm. When their physiological needs are fulfilled, people can choose whether to allocate their time to leisure or to the production of goods and services, that is, work. This dichotomy is the basis of the canonical labour–leisure model, the theoretical framework underlying most time-use research of economists. The more complex household-production models (for example, Becker, 1965) further distinguish between productive activities performed in the labour market for pay and those taking place in one's own household yielding three general options of using one's time: leisure, work at home, and work in the market. According to the economic theory of consumption (Becker, 1965), an individual can attain utility (or happiness, satisfaction, well-being) only through two types of goods: leisure time and market goods one can buy with money. Their association with utility is not direct, though, but mediated through the generation of commodities to which they serve as input. A rational individual is, therefore, expected to maximize his or her utility given specific constraints by equating the marginal gain from time allocated to the market (that is, to enhancing the flow of goods) to the marginal gain from increased leisure.

In the process of commodity production, time and goods (money) have to be used in conjunction and can be substituted for each other. Possible combinations of income and leisure that yield equal utility are depicted graphically in indifference curves. The slope of such a curve represents the marginal rate of substitution, that is, the change in one dimension that is needed to hold utility constant when the other dimension changes by one unit. While all individuals should prefer a higher level of utility over a lower one, individuals differ with regard to the slope of their typical set of preferences.

The neglect of time use in conventional consumer theory notwithstanding, it is possible to distinguish consumer activities such as decision making, purchasing, consumption and disposal according to their time- or goods-intensiveness. Engaging in intensive information search and comparisons, for example, saves money. Consumers whose time is scarce and, therefore, highly valued, may be willing to pay more for the use of strategies or institutions that reduce transaction costs. As quality-screening mechanisms, for instance, they can use brands and prices or services such as brokers or travel agents who preselect information. Likewise, consumers rely on franchise chains not only for their fast delivery but also for consistent quality that does not have to be tested.

From a conceptual perspective, three aspects of the microeconomic approach seem problematic: its indebtedness to utility maximization, its conception of work as disutility that has to be compensated, and its focus on material commodities rather than well-being as final output. Since violations of the central axioms of rational choice are discussed elsewhere in this volume (for example, in the entries on Heuristics and Biases, Multiattribute Utility Models, Rationality, and Satisficing), suffice it here to point out the importance of the past in explaining our day-to-day behaviour. Longitudinal data are able to demonstrate that prior actions — cognitive and motor ones — are powerful predictors of present actions — be it as habits and routines, or in the form of sunk costs or increasing returns of acquired skills.

Many activities — productive as well as consumptive ones — are performed not only because they are instrumental in reaching desired objectives but also for their own sake because they are rewarding in themselves (joint dependence, Pollak and Wachter, 1975). Broader frameworks for analysing time-allocation data are able to incorporate concepts and outcome measures from other disciplines such as objective social indicators and subjective well-being (Juster and Stafford (eds), 1985: Ch. 6). An important aspect of subjective well-being is the range of immediate psychological consequences of engaging in an activity, that is, process benefits. They are afforded to a higher degree by paid work as compared to leisure activities. This finding may seem counterintuitive but can be explained by the fact that work provides opportunities for learning and using one's skills in addition to the social-interaction aspect emphasized by Juster. Competence is a prerequisite of enjoyment and, typically, more work- than leisure-related skills are acquired (Scitovsky, 1976). Evidence based on different psychological theories converges on the finding that the experience of competence plays an important role for self-regulation and, thereby, for mental health and well-being (the seminal article on competence is White, 1959). On the other hand, it has been demonstrated repeatedly that external rewards can undermine intrinsic motivation and enjoyment ('the hidden costs of reward' discussed by Lepper, Green and Nisbett, 1973).

From a methodological perspective, three problems of time-use data have to be tackled: the reliability and validity of their assessment, the fixed-resource approach, and possible dimensions of time use.

1. Time-use information can be collected in a number of fashions differing with regard to their costs. Direct observation is among the most time-intensive procedures and retrospective reports over periods up to a lifetime belong to the most economic ones. The efficiency of assessment comes with a price, however: the risk of cognitive and motivational factors compromising the validity of the responses. The accuracy of recall can be enhanced by minimizing selection, memory and aggregation requirements, as in time diaries (see Robinson and Godbey, 1997: Ch. 4).

2. Another problem is the treatment of parallel activities in recording and coding the data. Whereas common sense equates time and money as fixed resources a unit of which can only be spent once, workload research has shown that — with practice — multiple activities can take place in parallel. Typical combinations of activities may be as important to characterize the lifestyles of individuals or groups as the allocation of time *per se*. When

fractions of time allocated to different activities do not sum up to unity anymore, this has important research-practical as well as theoretical consequences since typically tradeoffs are investigated. So far, there is no satisfactory solution to this problem.

3. Time use can be described by several dimensions. While most time-use research is restricted to the duration of activities, frequency, sequence and variability, the participation in different life domains, rhythms and social entrainment are also important parameters.

Finally, from the themes prevailing in the recent literature, three are relevant in this context: scarcity of time, intertemporal time use and life-cycle patterns. The scarcity of time will be discussed first. From the last century on, market as well as household production were subject to the rule of time efficiency. In the market, this led to an increased time consciousness that stimulated, for example, the demand for time-management procedures such as time diaries. At the same time, examples of unintendedly wasted time are still abundant — particularly in connection with waiting — creating opportunities for the development of innovative goods and services that reduce system 'down-times' or make them usable. In the household, technical appliances have been employed to reduce time and effort. Up to now, however, no association has been found between household technology and reduced time spent on housework. In contrast, much evidence supports John Steinbeck's observation that most of our time is wasted trying to save time. In the case of housework, the time saved by technology seems to be offset by newly arising demands. For instance, as technical appliances become more complex more time is spent for their installation, operation and maintenance. In the domain of leisure, the scarcity of time resulted in a goods-intensive 'acceleration of consumption' (Linder, 1970), that is, the simultaneous enjoyment of various goods such as — to give a stereotypical example — listening to a German orchestra with a Danish hifi system, wearing French *haute couture* and a Swiss watch, drinking Italian wine, smoking a Cuban cigar while being stretched out on the rear seat of a car made in America and chauffeured by . . . and so on.

The second theme is intertemporal time use (for example, Hoch and Loewenstein, 1991). In the same way as consumers evaluate costs and benefits of durable goods over time in purchase decisions, they have to choose among possible outcome sequences resulting from time allocation to different (baskets of) activities. When time or money are spent now in order to save more time and money at a later point in time this is called an investment — equated to forgone immediate payoffs in the standard models of physical or human capital formation. Examples of investments are saving money, learning to use a technical device, or attending college. Being indebted to the discounted-utility model conventional economic analyses of outcome patterns assume positive time preference and diminishing marginal utility. To overcome myopia and align decisions with long-term preferences consumers may utilize strategies of attention-, emotion- and motivation-regulation such as (pre)commitments. There are, however, many examples of preference for improvement or negative time preference in the form of the proverbial 'saving the best for last'. In addition to the temporal dimension, there is also a social aspect to myopia: externalities of time-use decisions. Time-saving strategies in the course of producing and distributing as well as consuming a convenience good may be bound up with environmental costs that are not fully reflected in its market price. As a complement to the traditional concept of time efficiency, therefore, an 'ecology of time' has been suggested (for example, Kümmerer, 1996).

The last theme, life-cycle patterns, is related to the preceding one. While these patterns have been predicted from intertemporal time-use models, the narrow focus of research on the time use of paid, middle-aged, male workers has been extended only recently. Herzog et al. (1989), for instance, found that although the majority of Americans aged 65+ did not participate in the labour force any more, they clearly contributed to societal production at the same levels as young and middle-aged respondents through unpaid activities such as housework, maintenance and repair of possessions, informal help to family and friends, and volunteer work. Like consumptive activities, productive activities were a characteristic part of their everyday life.

In the generation of well-being, the allocation of time to activities appears to be at least as important as the allocation of money to material goods. Since a comprehensive theory has still to be developed, researchers can profitably allocate both time and money to this endeavour in the future.

PETRA L. KLUMB

Bibliography

Becker, G. (1965) 'A Theory of the Allocation of Time', *Economic Journal*, **75**: 493–517.
Herzog, A.R., Kahn, R.L., Morgan, J.N., Jackson, J.S. and Antonucci, T.C. (1989) 'Age Differences in Productive Activities', *Journal of Gerontology: Social Sciences*, **44**: S129—S138.
Hoch, S.J. and Loewenstein, G.F. (1991) 'Time-Inconsistent Preferences and Consumer Self-Control', *Journal of Consumer Research*, **17**: 492–507.
Juster, F.T. and Stafford, F.P. (eds) (1985) *Time, Goods and Well-being*, Ann Arbor, MI, Institute for Social Research.
Kümmerer, K. (1996) 'The Ecological Impact of Time', *Time and Society*, **5**: 209–35.
Lepper, M.R., Green, D. and Nisbett, R.E. (1973) 'Undermining Children's Intrinsic Interest with Extrinsic Rewards: A Test of the "Overjustification" Hypothesis', *Journal of Personality and Social Psychology*, **28**: 129–37.
Linder, S.B. (1970) *The Harried Leisure Class*, New York, Columbia University Press.

Pollak, R.A. and Wachter, M.L. (1975) 'The Relevance of the Household Production Function and Its Implications for the Allocation of Time', *Journal of Political Economy*, **83**: 255–77.
Robinson, J.P. and Godbey, G. (1997) *Time for Life — The Surprising Ways Americans Use their Time*, University Park, PA, Penn State University Press.
Scitovsky, T. (1976) *The Joyless Economy: An Inquiry into Human Satisfaction*, New York, Oxford University Press.
White, R.W. (1959) 'Motivation Reconsidered: The Concept of Competence', *Psychological Review*, **66**: 297–333.

Tourism, Psychology of

Tourism is the behaviour of people in touristic roles. As the study of mental processes and behaviour, psychology is ideally suited as a disciplinary base for the study of the complex phenomenon of tourism. However, despite this clear relevance, the application of psychology to the context of tourism has not been reflected widely in the psychology literature, and has a brief history, dating only to the late 1970s (Pearce, 1982, 1993b). As such, the psychology of tourism is an area that is brimming with underexploited research areas.

There are many ways of conceptualizing tourism and tourist behaviour. For the sake of discussing the psychology of tourism however, tourist behaviour will be conceptualized here as comprising five stages: (i) anticipation; (ii) travel to the site; (iii) on-site behaviour; (iv) return travel; and (v) recollection (Clawson and Knetsch, 1966; Fridgen, 1984). These five stages provide a convenient framework for considering the contributions that psychology has made to the understanding of tourism, as well as potential areas in which it can continue to advance. In the discussion below, stages (ii) and (iv) are considered together.

Anticipation
Before any individual engages in tourism a decision to travel must be made. What motivates people to become tourists is one area that has been examined widely from a psychological perspective, and several models of tourist motivation have been posited. Pearce (1993a) reviewed three frequently cited models of tourist motivation: Plog's (1991) personality theory in which travellers and nontravellers are presented as comprising a continuum from allocentric (more adventurous, self-confident travellers) to psychocentric (cautious, less-confident and security conscious travellers); Iso-Ahola's (1980) intrinsic motivation-optimal arousal perspective in which motivation for travel is seen as a result of opposing processes of escaping personal and interpersonal environments and seeking other environments (both personal and interpersonal) to achieve optimal levels of stimulation; and Pearce's (1993a) travel career ladder or

tapestry, which assumes that tourists are motivated by differing levels of need (similar to Abraham Maslow's hierarchy of needs) throughout their travel careers. Parrinello (1993) also reviewed several models of tourist motivation, extending them to examine motivation and anticipation as interrelated phenomena. She argued that there now exists a 'tourist culture' in which the cognitive and affective components of motivation and anticipation are deeply rooted. How potential tourists form images of a destination and how this affects their decisions to travel is another area that has been researched from a psychological perspective. Mansfeld's (1992) critical review provides a thorough discussion of all theoretical aspects of the destination-choice process.

The anticipation stage of tourist behaviour has been addressed widely in the psychology of tourism literature. The issues presented above have much in common with marketing and consumer behaviour, which perhaps accounts for the comparatively more comprehensive coverage in the psychology literature, particularly in the area of applied social psychology (see for example Mayo and Jarvis, 1981; Pearce, 1982, 1983, 1993b; Pearce and Stringer, 1991).

New areas which have relevance for applied social psychology and tourism continue to emerge. With the increasing advances in technology used at the anticipation stage (eg., personal computers, automated ticketing machines, 'ticket-less' travel) interesting questions can be raised about consumer reaction to technological advances and products and the psychology of responding to these changes. For example, how will access to information over the World Wide Web affect tourist motivations, decision making, image formation and attitudes? What are the psychological barriers to accessing these innovations?

Travel to and from the destination
Less prevalent in the psychology of tourism literature are aspects of the travel to and from stages of tourist behaviour. Despite this, there are several areas in which psychology has, and can continue, to contribute. For example, the process of travel imposes certain physical stresses on the human body which can be explored from a physiological psychology perspective. Long-haul flights transporting tourists across several time zones often result in the phenomenon of jet-lag. North–South travel can also be disruptive through changes to the sleep-wake cycle due to differences in the number of daylight hours. The interface between physiological psychology and medicine has made significant advances in addressing these aspects of travel. Motion sickness is another common condition which results from travelling to and from a destination. Physiological psychology, as well as the psychology of sense and perception, have contributed to the development of medications which anaesthetize the feedback from the inner ear to the brain, thus altering perceptions of balance and orientation to decrease motion sickness.

566

Psychology has also contributed to the type of transportation tourists use to get to and from a destination. Ergonomics, a branch of industrial and organizational psychology, along with the study of sense and perception, have contributed to a diversity of transportation considerations, ranging from jet aircraft cockpit design, the production of more comfortable aeroplane seats, information about how tourists utilize space on transportation, to road signs that are easier to read and comprehend. Rapid technological advances in transportation also have implications for psychology. As discussed above, the consumer reaction to technological changes and products is an important psychological consideration.

Moving from the hypothetical to the actual in terms of travelling to and from a destination, many individuals have clear psychological barriers to aspects of existing travel. The application of clinical psychological techniques to overcoming phobias (for example, fear of flying or driving) has enabled many people to travel who would not have done so otherwise.

On-site behaviour

The stage of behaviour most commonly associated with tourism is that of on-site behaviour. Given that psychology is essentially the study of mental processes and behaviour, it is interesting to note that there is relatively little in the psychology literature about the actual activities of tourists other than a few studies concentrating on tourists' time budgets. Social psychology, however, has been applied to other aspects of on-site tourist behaviour. One area, that of attitudes, has been prominent in tourism and psychology. Research has been conducted on how tourists form attitudes on site and what variables may affect their formation. Attitudinal change has also been well considered in the psychology of tourism literature. Factors which facilitate or hinder attitude change have been identified, as have factors which influence whether the change will be positive or negative (see, for example, Pearce's (1988) review of tourist attitudes in the natural environment and the discussion by Mayo and Jarvis (1981) of the influence of attitudes on individual travel behaviour).

Tourism is by nature a social activity. Whether tourists travel alone, or as part of a group, interpersonal social contact is an intrinsic part of the tourist experience. This raises social psychological issues such as the importance of understanding social dynamics on group tours and their relationship to satisfaction. Intergroup relationships are also important. How do tourists interact with members of the host community or other tourists? What are the outcomes of host–tourist or tourist–tourist interaction for both parties? How do these relate to satisfaction? Attitude formation? Attitude change? What social networks do tourists form? What role do they play in on-site tourist behaviour? Some of these questions have been addressed in the tourism and psychology literature (see, for example, the work of Fisher and Price (1991) on the linkages between travel motivations, level of intercultural interaction, vacation satisfaction and tourists' post-vacation attitudes, and Anastasopoulos' (1992) evaluation of attitude change as a result of tourist experience). However, the area is still relatively unexplored.

A great deal of tourism is undertaken in a cross-cultural context. This raises interesting cross-cultural psychological questions about how tourists adapt to new cultural environments and what may help facilitate successful adaptation. Cross-cultural adaptation has been explored widely from a cross-cultural psychological perspective. This research however, has focused primarily on longer-staying sojourner and migrant populations rather than tourists. How host nationals react and adapt to tourists is a concomitant and important consideration. There is a well-established, extensive literature on the sociocultural impacts of tourism for host nationals (mainly from the disciplines of sociology, anthropology and human geography). However, little has been done to extend the research to include psychological processes and effects.

In addition to a novel cultural context, tourists often find themselves in unfamiliar environments. This, too, has implications for tourism and psychology. Environmental psychology has contributed to the understanding of tourism through the consideration of how tourists perceive both time and space. Issues such as perceptions of crowding and their relationship to tourist satisfaction, the social meaning of interpersonal distance, the formation of environmental images and perceptions of risk are some of the areas that have been considered. Cognitive psychology has also contributed to the understanding of tourists' relationship with the environment. One area of cognitive psychology that has been widely applied to tourism is that which is concerned with the processing of maps and map information.

Related both to the cross-cultural aspects of tourism and to the novel environment in which tourists find themselves is the role of tour guides. Tour guides are often considered to be cultural or environmental interpreters who provide a supportive service to tourists in unfamiliar surrounds. Despite this important role that tour guides have to play, relatively little is known about their socio-psychological roles, whether they can affect attitudinal or behavioural changes in tourists, what psychological characteristics make for a effective guide and what are the relationships between tour guides and tourist satisfaction.

Recollection

Although no longer physically away from home, individuals are likely to recall, reflect on and remember their trips; so, in psychological term they could be considered still to be engaging in tourist behaviour. How tourists recall their travel experience, what role that plays in their life outside the tourism context and whether attitudinal (and subsequent behavioural change) is affected as a

568

result of travel are relatively unexplored in the tourism literature. The question of how recollection of previous travel experiences affects motivation and destination choice is another area that has much potential for future psychological research.

Conclusion

As can be ascertained from the brief discussion above, psychology has made several significant contributions to the understanding of tourism. These however, are minor in comparison to the potential contributions which psychology can make. Pearce (1993b: 873, 881), in comparing the psychology of tourism to a recently discovered landscape, summarized the current position of the psychology of tourism in the following statement, 'Regrettably there is a good deal of flat deserted terrain where few explorers have ventured. Nevertheless the total view is appealing and the area has vast potential for academic and applied settlement'.

TRACY BERNO

Bibliography

Anastasopoulos, P.G. (1992) 'Tourism and Attitude Change: Greek Tourists Visiting Turkey', *Annals of Tourism Research*, **19**: 629–42.

Clawson, M. and Knetsch, J.L. (1966) *Economics of Outdoor Recreation*, Baltimore, MD, Johns Hopkins Press.

Fisher, R.J. and Price, L.L. (1991) 'International Pleasure Travel Motivations and Post-vacation Cultural Attitude Change', *Journal of Leisure Research*, **23**: 193–208.

Fridgen, J. (1984) 'Environmental Psychology and Tourism', *Annals of Tourism Research*, **11**: 19–39.

Iso-Ahola, S.E. (1980) *The Social Psychology of Leisure and Recreation*, Dubuque, IA, W.C. Brown.

Mansfeld, Y. (1992) 'From Motivation to Actual Travel', *Annals of Tourism Research*, **19**: 399–449.

Mayo, E. and Jarvis, L. (1981) *The Psychology of Leisure Travel*, Boston, MA, CBI Publishing.

Parrinello, G.L. (1993) 'Motivation and Anticipation in Post-Industrial Tourism', *Annals of Tourism Research*, **20**: 233–49.

Pearce, P.L. (1982) *The Social Psychology of Tourist Behaviour*, Oxford, Pergamon.

Pearce, P.L. (1983) 'Fun, Sun and Behaviour: Social Psychologists and the Tourism Industry, *Australian Psychologist*, **18**: 89-95.

Pearce, P.L. (1988) 'Tourist Attitudes in Natural Environments', in Pearce, P. (ed.) *The Ulysses Factor: Evaluating Visitors in Tourist Settings*, New York, Springer-Verlag.

Pearce, P.L. (1993a) 'Fundamentals of Tourism Motivation' in Pearce, D.G. and Butler, R.W. (eds) *Tourism Research: Critiques and Challenges*, London, Routledge.

Pearce, P.L. (1993b) 'The Psychology ofTtourism' in Khan, M., Olsen, M. and Var, T. (eds) *VNR's Encyclopedia of Hospitality and Tourism*, New York, Van Nostrand

Reinhold.

Pearce, P.L. and Stringer, P.F. (1991) 'Psychology and Tourism', *Annals of Tourism Research*, **18**: 136–54.

Plog, S.C. (1991) Leisure Travel: Making it a Growth Market . . . Again', New York, Wiley.

Transformation in Eastern Europe

The transformation of the Eastern European economies from state-controlled to market orientated consisted of several actions that were quite painful for large groups of the population. The transformations included the abandonment of price control, cuts in government subsidies and strong restrictions on wages. In Poland these changes were implemented quite rapidly (shock therapy) while some other countries adopted more gradual changes. However, independently of the adopted strategy, the initial transformation brought about a serious deterioration in the standard of living for large groups of society.

In 1990, soon after the transformation in Poland began, J. Czapinski, B. Górecki , E. Gucwa-Lesny and T. Tyszka initiated a panel study of individual household budget data, indices of psychological well-being, and socioeconomic preferences of Poles. This entry is based mostly on the panel results, and thus largely describes the Polish experience. However, the phenomena revealed seem by and large to be representative of the transformation in Eastern Europe.

Material costs of transformation: changes in the objective quality of life

Statistics show that the first years of transformation brought about profound changes in the quality of life of various groups of the population. Real family income and consumption decreased. The number of people living in poverty increased rapidly. Similarly the rate of unemployment increased. Contrary to the general world trend, in many Eastern European countries the average life expectancy decreased.

How were these costs of transformation distributed among social groups? Panel studies of individual household budget data show that, overall, incomes did not become more unequal (Gucwa-Lesny, 1996). However, changes in income distribution were registered within some social groups. For example, income differentiation increased within the group of workers and employees (in which it had been stable over the previous three decades). According to the panel studies of individual household budget data, the material situation of younger families deteriorated much more than in older families (Górecki and Wisniewski, 1995). The data also show that the material status of families with large numbers of children deteriorated dramatically. As a result, in 1993 the poverty rate for families with two children was 40 per cent, for families with three children it was

58 per cent, and for families with four children 76 per cent (Górecki and Wisniewski, 1995).

Social and psychological costs of transformation

Apart from the material costs of transformation, statistics for the countries undergoing transformation show a tremendous increase of various kinds of social pathology: crime, alcoholism, drug addiction, and so on. Czapinski (1995) notes an increase of the mortality index from 1989 to 1993 in all Eastern European countries and an enormous increase in suicide and homicide rates from 1989 to 1993.

Perhaps there are grounds for some optimism concerning the psychological effects of transformation. Czapinski (1995), who in 1992 initiated in Poland an annual survey of psychological well-being, found that symptoms of depression and sense of hopelessness decreased systematically during 1993 and 1994. Thus, at least in Poland, some general improvement in psychological well-being has been observed since 1992. Moreover, Czapinski (1995) found that 'material and psychological costs of transformation do not go hand in hand'. Correlations between the material conditions of life and psychological indices of maladjustment (depression and sense of hopelessness) were low. In particular, while the material situation of younger families deteriorated more than that of older families, older members of the population felt more hopeless and more depressed than younger members. Indeed, in 1992 age was the strongest predictor of psychological depression and hopelessness symptoms. This suggests that money plays only a limited role in determining psychological well-being.

Perception of economics in post-communist countries

Inhabitants of Eastern European countries have doubtless had a different kind of experience with economic life than those living in countries with market economies. Most economic decisions were made centrally and ordinary people did not influence their economic life to a great extent. How has this different experience influenced people's cognitive representation of economics?

This question has been investigated in cross-country research on perception of economics by ordinary people. In one study (Verges, Tyszka and Verges, 1994) French and Polish students were asked to indicate 'who . . . plays an important role in the economy'. One of the most apparent differences in the answers of the two groups concerned the area of 'consumption'. 'Consumer' was one of the most frequently used words in the French sample, while it was completely absent from the Polish sample. This discrepancy can certainly be accounted for in terms of different economic experience. The lack of representation of 'consumers' in the thinking of the Polish students is predictable from their experiences: the centrally-planned communist economy, by its very definition, ignored consumption and consumers.

However, the differences which we found in this research were generally smaller and similarities stronger than we had expected. This suggests that, much cognitive representation of the economy is quite general and insensitive to past experience. Probably this is due to the uniformity of contemporary mass communication.

Similar conclusions can be drawn from research on the basic dimensions that ordinary people use when they evaluate various economic activities (Antonides et al., 1994). At issue was whether these dimensions would be the same across countries with different economic histories — Poland and Hungary versus the Netherlands and Great Britain. Again few differences between the former communist countries and the traditional market-economy countries were found. One example of such a difference concerned the evaluation of socially unacceptable activities — such as giving and receiving bribes, cheating on taxes and so on — on social-value scales. Those activities tended to be seen as less negative in the eyes of people living in the former socialist countries. This difference is probably due to many opportunities for corrupt practices in the previous state-controlled economic system. Moreover, the transition period with its unfixed rules of economic behaviour also favours these types of practices. As a result, when it became natural to participate in corrupt practices as a means of getting by, the attitudes to cheating and so on became less negative.

However, similar to the previous study, the country differences were generally small. Not only did the same perceptual space (factor structure) emerge in all four countries, but also the perception of the position of activities in this space turned out to be similar across country groups. Thus, cognitive representation of the economy seems to be quite general and insensitive to past experience.

Socioeconomic preferences and their changes

Starting from 1990, survey questionnaires have been carried out in Poland investigating socioeconomic preferences and their changes. These studies (Tyszka and Sokolowska, 1992; Sokolowska and Tyszka, 1996) show that in 1990, Poles' socioeconomic preferences appeared to be much closer to the socialist ideology of a welfare state than to the ideology of a market economy. The majority of respondents supported medical care, high unemployment benefits, high bottom wages and highly progressive taxes, and had no clear preference concerning privatization. It is hard to say how different these results are from those one would obtain in market economies of longer standing. For example, Kemp and Willetts (1995) found that New Zealanders, too, place a high value on state-supported medical care and many of the other features of the welfare state.

What was striking, however, was that at the same time there was relatively strong support for Leszek Balczerowicz's programme (known as shock therapy) for the rapid transformation of the Polish economy into a market system. Where did this inconsistency between declared support for rapid pro-market changes and detailed anti-market socioeconomic preferences come from? Tyszka and Sokolowska (1992) claimed that the general and detailed preferences were shaped by two opposite tendencies. On the one hand, the detailed preferences were influenced by the past experience of the socialist ideology of a welfare state. On the other, declared general support for transforming the Polish socioeconomic system into a market system was motivated by a positive attitude towards the political changes in the country.

This explanation is supported by the finding that the correlation between general endorsement of market transformation and detailed socioeconomic preferences was rather low. Naturally, those respondents who declared their support for system transformation displayed pro-market profiles more frequently than those who declared their disapproval for the programme. However, quite a substantial percentage of those supporting system transformation actually displayed anti-market profiles. Thus, the declared attitude towards system transformation was quite a poor predictor of actual attitudes towards a pro-market economy.

Analysis of Poles' socioeconomic preferences declared in subsequent years reveals a decrease in pro-market preferences:

1. The percentage of those supporting state control over the economy (over prices, wages, production profile, national product sales) has risen.
2. A decrease in support for privatization of educational institutions and for paid education has been observed.
3. As for the standard of living of the poorest, a systematic slight increase in the percentage of those voting for high unemployment benefits and high bottom wages has been noticed.
4. Similarly, a systematic increase in the percentage of respondents who supported limitations on private ownership has been observed.

Why this decrease in pro-market sympathy? As compared with 1990, the preferences declared in the subsequent years have become more and more experience based. Since this experience with the new economic system has frequently been painful, Poles have drifted away from their previous pro-market sympathy. Following these experiences with the new system, some of the former supporters of pro-market changes have become opponents. Thus, we think that the observed shift in Poles' socioeconomic preferences is caused by two reasons. One is that the preferences are now based less on ideology and more on personal experience. The other is that the drawbacks of the previous system are being forgotten while the newly-experienced drawbacks of the new system have become vivid and painful. This could be one reason for the victories of former communist politicians in recent elections in several East European countries.

What determines an individual's socioeconomic preferences? What impact do sociodemographic factors such as education, income, age, gender and profession have on these preferences? In all surveys a significant relationship has been found between preferences and education level. Well-educated respondents belonged more frequently to pro-market profiles than did poorly educated respondents. It has also been observed that affluent respondents more frequently belonged to pro-market profiles than did respondents with low income. However, the differentiation in preferences due to income has been less salient than the differentiation due to education level. Possibly this is because in Poland education is still a more salient determinant of social stratification than income.

Relationships between socioeconomic preferences and some psychological characteristics of individuals were also observed. One such characteristic was the need for achievement, that is, the motivation to improve one's own standards. McClelland (1961) claimed that achievement motivation is an essential element in entrepreneurial behaviour. In accordance with this claim we found that those who scored high in achievement motivation tended to belong to the pro-market socioeconomic profiles more often than those who scored low in achievement motivation. Also, the people who are more dynamic and economically more active (who try to improve their qualifications, invest in small businesses or in services, and claim to be looking for a well-paid job), preferred less state control over the economy, a more privatized economy, less egalitarian income distribution and less social security, as compared with those who are economically less active. This pattern seems to be logically consistent and implies that the number of supporters of the free-market economy solutions will increase with the number of people active economically.

TADEUSZ TYSZKA

Bibliography

Antonides, G., Farago, K., Ranyard, R. and Tyszka, T. (1994) 'Perceptions of Economic Activities. A Cross-Country Comparison', in Tyszka, T. (ed.) *Cognitive Representation of Economics*, Special Session of the IAREP/SABE Conference, Rotterdam, 10–13 July.

Czapinski, J. (1995) 'Money Isn't Everything: On the Various Social Costs of Transformation', *Polish Sociological Review*, **112**: 289–302.

Górecki, B. and Wisniewski, M. (1995) 'Economic Conditions of Polish Households, 1987–1993', paper presented at the 2nd East and Central European Conference, Warsaw, April.

Gucwa-Lesny, E. (1996) 'Four Years After the Velvet Revolution', manuscript at the Faculty of Economic Sciences, University of Warsaw, September.

Kemp, S. and Willetts, K. (1995) 'Rating the Value of Government-Funded Services: Comparison of Methods', *Journal of Economic Psychology*, **16**: 23–37.

McClelland, D.C. (1961) *The Achieving Society*, Princeton, NJ, Van Nostrand.

Sokolowska, J. and Tyszka, T. (1996) 'Preferencje spoleczno-ekonomiczne Polak w i ich zmiana w okresie transformacji polityczno-ekonomicznej' [Socioeconomic Preferences of Poles and their Change During the Transformation Period]. *Ekonomista*, **3**: 380–95.

Tyszka, T. and Sokolowska, J. (1992) 'Perception and Judgments of the Economic System', *Journal of Economic Psychology*, **13**: 421–48.

Verges, P., Tyszka, T. and Verges, P. (1994) 'Representation of Economics by French and Polish Students', in Tyszka, T. (ed.) *Cognitive Representation of Economics*, Special Session of the IAREP/SABE Conference, Rotterdam, 10–13 July .

Trust

The necessity of trust

It is impossible for people to achieve a state of absolute security. We are dependent on the actions of thousands of our fellow citizens, and not even the mightiest or richest people in the world can create perfect security systems for themselves. Even they have to rely on others. In the end, doubt is cast on all individual and public steps taken to guarantee safety and justice by the old question: 'Quis custodiet ipsos custodes?' (Who shall guard the guards themselves: Juvenal). Many people may lack *trust as a feeling* but they cannot avoid *expressing trust* in many of their actions; this entry deals with the latter phenomenon.

Let us also put to one side such meanings of trust as 'trust in the laws of physics' and concentrate on trust in persons, or groups of persons, or institutions. By trusting, we put our money, or our well-being or sometimes even our lives into the hands of others. There may be two reasons for doing so. First, because we presume that the trusted persons (or institutions) have a genuine interest in our well-being, as one's mother does, or because they have interests which are highly correlated with ours, as does the pilot of an aeroplane in which we are flying. Second, because we rely on reciprocity. (The expression of trust and reciprocity, particularly in long-term relationships, is sometimes called forbearance: see Buckley and Casson, 1988.) This is the most problematic kind of trust and the focal point of this entry.

Most sociologists and economists emphasize that reciprocity is the cornerstone of economic and social exchange. But in order to receive reciprocity we first have to trust! Lending money to a friend, putting it in an investment fund, or simply depositing it in a bank requires trust. We rely on the repairer of our TV set to carry out only the necessary repairs and to bill us only for those repairs that have been carried out. Our employer pays us possibly more than the 'equilibrium wage' and in turn expects us to work with more than a minimum of effort. This latter kind of reciprocity, a variant of the efficiency wage theory, apparently helps to avoid a prisoner's dilemma situation. Experiments by Fehr, Kirchsteiger and Riedl (1993) strongly support the existence of such a kind of reciprocity which survives even in a competitive market with an excess of workers. Fukuyama (1995), in his book on trust, discusses the hypothesis that business organizations in different cultures depend heavily on trust between employers and employees as well as between business partners. The amount of trust shapes economic relations in a society. The less we trust the higher is our need for information and control. This opinion can also be found in *The Economist* (13 July 1996: 19) which, in comparing Anglo-American and Continental owner–manager relations, states that '[a]t the heart of the difference is the issue of trust — the trust between those who supply capital and those who manage it'.

Vertical relations in markets with small numbers of participants are always threatened by opportunism. From transaction cost economics we know that complete contracts in such situations are practically impossible and enforcing the costs of written contracts often prohibitive (Williamson, 1993). Then trust is necessary and transaction costs are determined mainly by the exploitation risk. Incomplete or missing formal contracts are often called implicit contracts or relational contracts. The standard example is marriage, which requires a lot of trust as we all know. Another example is the cooperation of firms (Buckley and Casson, 1988; Kay, 1993). As in the case of individual cooperation, the possible duration of the relationship may be decisive for its success. Game theory tells us that in repeated games (with an infinite or unknown number of repetitions) cooperative strategies can be equilibria even if in one-shot games they are not. But, in reality, we find trust in one shot and even anonymous interactions, too: in Germany, as well as in other countries, it is sometimes possible to find baskets of fruit and vegetables together with a cash-box atop a post on a lonely country road.

Of course, trust is not necessarily rewarded: we all know of examples of people not paying their debts, of billing without corresponding repairs, and of employees unwilling to provide the services expected of them. Even worse, employees may defraud their firms; in Germany such cases of fraud are estimated to cost 10 billion Deutschmarks a year. Investors have lost billions of dollars to fund managers who may be fraudulent as well as incompetent. On the other hand, all this knowledge does not necessarily stop us from trusting others.

When to trust?
James Coleman (1990), a sociologist, suggested a simple cost–benefit approach
to the question of when to trust. If

$$(D) \text{ value of trusting} > \text{value of mistrusting}$$

one should trust, and vice versa. The value of mistrusting is usually determined
by an alternative action, that is, the opportunity costs of the trusting; the value of
trusting depends on the risk of being exploited.

$$(T) \text{ value of trusting} = (\text{probability of reciprocity}) \times (\text{value of reciprocity})$$
$$+ (\text{probability of exploitation}) \times (\text{value of exploitation}).$$

Let us take an example. For the sake of simplicity let us assume that the only
choice we have is to hide our money ($1000) under the mattress (where it is
completely safe) or to hand it over to an investment fund which may be reliable
(with probability $1 - p$) and earn the promised interest r, or may fall prey to a
deceptive manager (with probability p) in which case we lose all our money.
Thus we conclude that: value of trusting = $1000(1 + r)(1 - p)$ and value of
mistrusting = $1000. ($D$) tells us that we should trust if and only if $r - p > rp$. For
small r and p this means that the interest r should be larger than the risk p in
order to make us trust; otherwise we should mistrust.

Elsewhere (Bolle, 1995), I have called this simple decision structure the
Coleman Hypothesis on Trust. It is completely in line with the standard
economic theory of decision under risk (where the risk preference of the
decision-maker is incorporated in the valuation of situations). Implicitly, we have
assumed that all variables in (D) and (T), in particular p, are known to us. In
reality, this is far from clear. Nor is it clear whether people have the ability to
make the computations and comparisons required by (D) and (T). So, as a
descriptive theory, the Coleman Hypothesis should be subject to empirical tests.

In Figure 1, the results of several experiments with anonymous interactions
between two players (as in the example above) are displayed: note that negative
values of trust were possible, which results in net values from trust smaller than
$- 1$ in two cases. For the sources of the data and further details, see Bolle (1995).
Because rewards differed in magnitude and currency, the surplus of trusting has
been normalized as a multiple of the value of mistrust whereby mistrust always
got a sure reward. These results are mildly supportive of the Coleman
Hypothesis: if the value of trust is significantly higher than the value of mistrust,
we observe large frequencies of trust. There are only two cases where the value
of trust is significantly lower than the value of mistrust — these cases contradict
the Coleman Hypothesis because the related frequencies should be rather low. In

the majority of cases, however, we find the value of trust not significantly different from the value of mistrust. This is a surprising result and a challenge for theorists who model the possible emergence of trust. The latter is the topic of the next section. It is also interesting that, overall, the frequency of trust is rather high. This might be explained by an inclination to learn. In situations where the value of trust is about as large as the value of mistrust, more subjects chose the experience alternative 'trust' rather than the sure reward from mistrust.

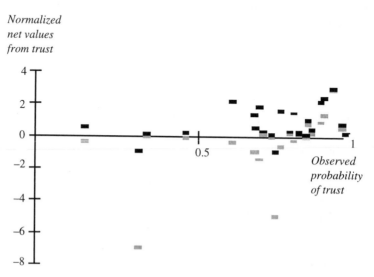

Source: From Bolle (1995).

Figure 1: Ninety per cent confidence intervals of normalized net value from trust and frequency of trust in 24 decision situations

The emergence of trust and reciprocity
A simple game-theoretic analysis of trust might result in the structure in Figure 2. This may be compared with the previous example by taking Player 1 as the investor and Player 2 as the fund manager, with the value of mistrusting = \$1000, V_1 (reciprocity) = \$$(1 + r)1000$, and V_1 (exploitation) = \$0.

Characteristic for a trust situation is that, if only objective values count, we find V_2 (exploitation) > V_2 (reciprocity). Then Player 2 would exploit Player 1, and if Player 1 knows this he or she will not trust. So, in one-shot interactions, we would never find trusting behaviour if Playes 2 evaluates situations only by his or her objective interest, possibly defined by monetary payoffs in an investment game or by the number of offspring in animal interactions. (At least in the case of lower animals we cannot expect calculative behaviour — although perhaps some learning — but mostly genetically determined actions.). Many people falsely conclude from this analysis that trust in one-shot interactions is impossible. The values of trusting in Figure 1, however, tell another story about Player 2's probability of reciprocating and therefore about his or her utility function V_2.

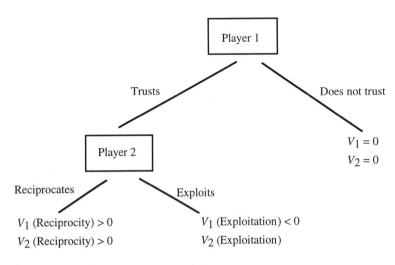

Figure 2: The game of trust: V_i = valuation of a situation by player i

If a behavioural norm of reciprocity reverts Player 2's payoff structure to V_2 (reciprocity) > V_2 (exploitation) then trust can emerge. In such a case V_2 may incorporate the values of a good or a bad conscience, a psychological notion which had long been rejected by most economists.

The crucial question is: why should a bad conscience emerge after exploiting someone else. Why should people act 'contrary to their own interest'? The simple answer is: otherwise they would not be trusted. We can describe the emergence of moral types of Player 2 (that is, types committed to reciprocity) using the notion of 'evolutionary stable strategies' (Güth and Kliemt, 1994). This is a kind of genetic learning of behaviour which is similar, in principle, for humans and animals. A necessary condition for such an emergence of trust and reciprocity, however, is a large enough probability of recognizing the moral types. So we have to hypothesize the coevolution of (i) reciprocity; (ii) signals indicating that an individual is committed to reciprocity; and (iii) trust. Among animals, the cooperation between a small cleaner fish and a big predator fish is a good example. The cleaner fish signal their identity by certain colours and 'dances'. Thus, cooperation usually works, that is, the predator fish gets a cleaning service of his mouth and gills and the cleaner fish gets food. There are, however, also imitators of cleaner fish which exploit the 'trust' they are given by biting pieces from the gills of the predator fish. It is clear that the success of such imitators must be limited — otherwise the cooperation between cleaner fish and their clients would break down.

What kinds of signals cause people to trust one another? Usually they do not even know themselves what made them decide one way or the other. We somehow get the impression that someone is trustworthy or not but it is rather difficult to say where this impression comes from; the evaluation process seems to work unconsciously and this is the reason why most experimental economists try to exclude (unobservable) signals and investigate anonymous interaction.

However, we can say something in principle about adequate signals. They must be easy to produce (that is, have low cost) by the moral types, and difficult to produce (that is, have high cost) by types not committed to reciprocity. Being a member of a religions congregation or working without payment in a social organization may be such a signal. Of course the strongest signal is previous behaviour (but even this might not guarantee reciprocity). Among firms, one such signal is the age of the firm. Deceitful firm owners who take their profit from exploiting their business partners often need to give up their business after a short time (and may reopen it under another name in another place). Behavioural norms are usually connected with strong emotions, and the existence or nonexistence of such emotions (or patterns of emotions) may help to identify moral people and be difficult to imitate (see Frank, 1988), which does not mean that this is impossible (see Ekman, 1985): all of us have more or less successful experiences in the faking of emotions. Signalling the reliability of goods and services is an important issue in marketing the products of a firm. Warranties as well as letters of endorsement from contented customers may serve this purpose. For further examples, see Kay (1993). In a way, however, signalling elevates the problem of trusting to another level: should we trust the signals?

Summary

Reciprocity and trust in reciprocity are necessary conditions for human and animal cooperation. Everyday experience and experimental evidence show that trust and reciprocity and, therefore, successful cooperation are found not only in repeated but also in one-shot transactions. There are hints that trust is given rationally, that is, on the basis of informative signals and expected values. The emergence of reciprocity and trust can be understood as genetically based developments of norms of behaviour. In long-term relationships (repeated games) between two or more agents — where previous behaviour is the most important signal — the incentives to reciprocate and therefore also the incentive to trust is strengthened by strategic considerations.

FRIEDEL BOLLE

Bibliography

Bolle, F. (1995) 'Does Trust Pay?', Discussion paper, Europa Universität Viadrina, Frankfurt (Oder).

Buckley, P.J. and Casson, M. (1988) 'A Theory of Cooperation in International Business', in Contractor, F.J. and Lorange, P. (eds) *Cooperative Strategies in International Business*, Lexington, MA, D.C. Heath: 31–53.

Coleman, J.S. (1990) *Foundations of Social Theory*, Cambridge, MA, Belknap Press of Harvard University Press.

Ekman, P. (1985) *Telling Lies*, New York, W.W. Norton & Company.

Fehr, E., Kirchsteiger, G. and Riedl, A. (1993) 'Does Fairness Prevent Market Clearing? An Experimental Investigation', *Quarterly Journal of Economics*, **108**: 437–59.

Frank, R.H. (1988) *Passions Within Reason: The Strategic Role of the Emotions*, New York, W.W. Norton & Company.

Fukuyama, F. (1995) *Trust — The Social Virtues and the Creation of Prosperity*, New York, Free Press.

Güth, W. and Kliemt, H. (1994) 'Competition or Co-operation: On the Evolutionary Economics of Trust, Exploitation and Moral Attitudes', *Metroeconomica*, **45**: 155–87.

Kay, J.A. (1993) *Foundations of Corporate Success*, Oxford, Oxford University Press.

Williamson, O.E. (1993) 'Calculativeness, Trust, and Economic Organization', *Journal of Law and Economics*, **36**: 453—86.

Unemployment and Well-Being

The adverse psychological consequences of exposure to unemployment were described as early as the 1930s by psychologists Jahoda, Lazarsdeld and Zeisel (1933), Bakke (1933) and Eisenberg and Lazarsfeld (1938). In a seminal piece of research Jahoda et al. conducted an in-depth study of a small Austrian village, Marienthal, beset by high unemployment. Their findings, based on interviews with families with an unemployed breadwinner in this one-factory village in rural Austria, were striking. Family members exhibited a marked deterioration in physical well-being and generally described themselves as psychologically broken. Their social interest diminished, apathy emerged and, somewhat surprisingly, political participation diminished. The interviews by Eisenberg and Lazarsfeld (1938) with unemployed persons in the US during the Great Depression revealed that, as the duration of unemployment lengthened, 'The individual's prestige is lost in his own eye, and as he imagines, in the eyes of his fellow man. He develops feelings of inferiority, loses self-confidence, and in general loses his morale' (p. 358).

Following the depression, growth in the availability of unemployment insurance and welfare programmes for the indigent has reduced the level of material deprivation that accompanies unemployment. Nevertheless, Jahoda (1982) believes that the psychological burden has not vanished, because of the heightened level of aspirations that characterized modern industrial societies. Indeed, using data from the early 1970s, there is evidence that social pathologies including suicides (Brenner, 1976) and admissions to mental hospitals (Catalano and Dooley, 1977) are inversely related to changes in the health of the economy. These findings were consistent with Jahaoda's view that the experience of unemployment in the postwar period is not fundamentally different from that of earlier periods.

A second wave of interest in the psychological consequences of unemployment began in the mid-1970s. This surge was fuelled by the extraordinarily levels of unemployment experienced in Europe and the US following the first oil crises. The high levels of unemployment that continue to plague most of Europe have sustained this research epoch.

Modern research on the relation between unemployment and psychological well-being has taken two forms. First, responding to the evidence provided by descriptive studies, prominent psychologists including Jahoda (1982), Warr (1987) and Feather (1990) have offered theories to explain why unemployment is likely to damage psychological health. Second, the focus of empirical work has shifted from describing the psychological state of the unemployed, to testing hypotheses generated by the theories.

Why might unemployment impair emotional health?

Social psychologists have developed a number of theories — often called models — relating work status to psychological well-being. These models draw the connection from unemployment to poorer psychological well-being in several distinct, but interrelated ways: as a consequence of lower self-esteem, as a result of a feeling that life is not under one's control leading to helplessness and depression, and as a loss of the social byproducts of participation in a work environment. We shall describe each of these below.

The self-esteem model asserts that opinions about 'self' are among the most treasured of our opinions and are a key aspect of personality. Psychologists treat self-esteem as multidimensional, comprising notions of worth, goodness, health, appearance, skills and social competence. Deficits in one area can be overcome by strengths in another. High self-esteem expresses the feeling that one is 'good enough', a 'person of worth'. Psychologists also envisage self-esteem to be a stable and enduring property of the individual, shaped during childhood. However, even proponents of this acknowledge that self-esteem may be altered by major life changes or traumatic events. Job loss could constitute such a traumatic event.

According to Erikson (1959), the founder of the life-span developmental theory, the healthy development of an individual's ego and self-esteem depends on successful completion of eight successive stages. During the fifth stage, Erikson's 'industry stage', an individual must move from adolescence to adulthood, a transition contingent upon attainment of a desirable occupational identity. Erikson postulated that in 'middle age' fulfilling life goals that involve career, family and society obligations are the developmental tasks that must be completed. Thus, lack of success in the labour market is likely to diminish an individual's sense of worth and emotional well-being.

One of the most commonly cited explanations for the deleterious effects of unemployment is the functional model attributed to Marie Jahoda (1982). Jahoda suggests that employment provides income and many valuable latent by-products, including a structured day, shared experiences, status and opportunities for creativity and mastery. She contends that unemployment is psychologically destructive primarily because it deprives an individual of these by-products of employment. Generally, leisure is unable to provide such by-products effectively.

Agency theory offers a third way in which joblessness can have far-reaching effects on one's emotional well-being and personality. Attribution theory postulates that people feel a need to seek out causes for what is happening to them. Individuals can assign cause to either self or situation if they understand their environment. Psychologists classify individuals either as 'internalizers', who believe they are masters of their own fates and thus responsible for what happens to them, or as 'externalizers', who generally believe that their life is controlled by outside forces and that they bear little or no responsibility for what happens to them.

Seligman (1975) postulated that experiences perceived as uncontrollable leave an individual with a sense of 'helplessness'. 'Helpless' people believe they have little influence over events in their lives. If unemployment leads people to believe that they are unable to affect their prospect of moving into employment, then it fosters feelings of helplessness and externality. Seligman also argued that one of the primary causes of depression is the realization that valued experiences such as meaningful work may be independent of efforts to obtain them. Of course, an individual's initial response to unemployment may be one of 'reactance' rather than helplessness. A reactant person actively seeks to reestablish control. However, helplessness is expected to emerge as the period of exposure to unemployment lengthens.

The conviction that the response to stressful events, such as unemployment, takes the form of a progression through stages is widespread in psychology. Indeed, Eisenberg and Lazarsfeld (1938) describe phased response of unemployment exposure to emotional well-being. First, there is shock, during which the individual is still optimistic and unbroken. Second, when all efforts to obtain work fail, the individual becomes pessimistic and suffers active distress. In the third stage, the individual becomes fatalistic and adapts pessimistically to his or her new state. In this latter stage, features of personality established earlier in life — such as locus of control and self-esteem — can alter and people are expected to exhibit poorer mental health due to greater depression, anxiety and alienation.

Finally, the life event model advanced by Brenner (1976) and Catalano and Dooley (1977) argues that any alteration in life circumstances is stressful and may hamper psychological health. Thus, mental health may be adversely effected by labour market developments such as changing employer, promotion, and unemployment.

What influences the link between unemployment and well-being?

Psychologists recognize that the connection between joblessness and psychological health may depend on a myriad of factors. For example, Peter Warr (1987) argues that previous job quality governs the magnitude of psychological distress for those who become unemployed. His vitamin model extends Jahoda's functional model by postulating that desirable features of the work environment — like vitamins — contribute to psychological health. Thus, the psychological consequence of job loss is contingent on the work environment — for sufficiently unappealing jobs, unemployment may improve a person's psychological health.

A related way to conceptualize the role of job quality in assessing the potential cost of unemployment is to consider forgone job satisfaction. According to Herzberg (1966) jobs have both intrinsic (variety, autonomy, use of skills) and extrinsic features. Warr (1983) reports that survey participants identified 'good' jobs as those high in intrinsic quality. Thus, loss of a desirable job — and satisfaction associated with the demands of that position — is expected to damage psychological well-being.

Robertson and Cochrane (1976) contend that a person's values may govern the psychological distress he or she experiences due to unemployment. They believe that a person whose values makes him or her more sensitive to social stresses will experience greater psychological harm from a bout of unemployment.

Furthermore, a number of psychologists believe that a person's occupation influences the strength of the association between unemployment and psychological health. People with greater commitment to work and involvement in the job — managers and skilled workers — are more likely to find unemployment traumatic. Job involvement may explain why age is often considered a factor that mediates the relation between job status and psychological well-being. Young people often change jobs to sample work options. Their low commitment to a particular employer may act as a buffer between unemployment and mental health. On-the-job training providing a person with skills that are portable between jobs and employers also may act as a cushion against the detrimental effects of unemployment.

Furnham (1988) claims that although unemployment may alter subsequent locus of control — one aspect of psychological health — a person's locus of control when he or she becomes unemployed will influence the impact of unemployment on many facets of his or her psychological well-being. However, how a person's control ideology intervenes in the relation between unemployment and mental health is unclear and may differ across individuals. A person with an internal locus may blame him- or herself for becoming unemployed, leading to substantial psychological distress. On the other hand, such persons may see little reason to worry since they tend to be highly motivated (for example, expectancy-value theory) and perceive a close link between their actions and desired outcomes. In their view, a short and successful job search is likely.

Social support may help the unemployed cope with their situation and thus mitigate the psychological distress. Effective support can come from a close, confiding, relationship with a person capable of responding to the needs elicited by a stressful event. Support can also arise from the social network, and roles that evolve with integration into a community at large.

Quantifying the connection between unemployment and well-being

Psychologists have developed inventories of questions designed to measure an individual's self-esteem, locus of control and mental health. These measures, constructed from self-reported evaluations collected in the form of responses to survey questions, can be used to evaluate the hypothesis that unemployment damages psychological well-being. However, proper evaluation of this hypothesis poses a number of challenges.

Measurement

The 'anchoring' problem arises because individuals might 'anchor' their scale at different levels, making interpersonal comparisons of subjective responses difficult to interpret. The 'anchoring' issue can be addressed by careful construction of the response options for questions in a scale used to represent a psychological construct (Goldsmith, Veum and Darity, 1996a).

A second issue is whether components of a person's psychological status such as self-esteem and depression can be measured accurately. Psychologists assess the usefulness of scales developed to measure a psychological construct by examining three features: convergent validity, reliability and stability.

Convergent validity is a criterion that considers whether an alternative scale seeking to measure the same construct yields a similar assessment. For instance, would a person rated as high in self-esteem using Rosenberg's self-esteem scale score correspondingly high on Coopersmith's self-esteem inventory? A scale is reliable when the questions that comprise the scale all probe similar or related features of an individual's makeup. Finally, a scale is considered stable if a similar assessment is generated by administering the same scale a short time in the future. Studies reveal that existing scales designed to gauge an individual's self-esteem, locus of control and mental health meet all three criteria used to evaluate measurement quality. Robinson and Wrightsman (1991) provide an excellent description and psychometric evaluation of the most commonly used measurement instruments for the full range of psychological constructs.

Model specification

Psychologists have conducted both cross-section and longitudinal studies to evaluate the impact of unemployment on psychological well-being, and to test hypotheses aimed at identifying the set of variables that mediate this relation. The methodologies adopted by psychologists to examine the influence of unemployment on subjective well-being are described below. In cross-section studies — if self-esteem is used to measure psychological health — then at a given point in time, self-esteem data obtained from unemployed respondents is compared with self-esteem data obtained from respondents with a job. The self-esteem level of people is tracked over time as they move into and out of

586

employment in longitudinal studies. Because there may be a lag between exposure to unemployment and its subsequent impact on self-esteem, longitudinal data is especially useful to investigate this relationship. In addition, longitudinal data are necessary to control for the possibility that individuals already suffering from poor mental health may be those most likely to become unemployed.

In longitudinal studies, individuals are interviewed initially at some baseline date, to collect information on labour force status and self-esteem. A follow-up interview is conducted to obtain additional measures of self-esteem, and individuals are once again classified by their labour force status such as employed, unemployed and attending school. Although the raw data are collected for each person in the sample, a tradition has developed in the psychology literature of analysing variations in group data rather than individual data. Thus, investigators expect self-esteem to decline between the baseline and follow-up periods for the group that is unemployed at follow-up, regardless of their initial labour force status. Moreover, at follow-up, on average, the unemployed are expected to exhibit a less-favourable view of self than the employed.

The stylized facts
The literature on the relationship between unemployment and various measures of subjective well-being has been reviewed by Feather (1990), Warr (1987), and Winefield et al. (1993). These reviews reveal that unemployment generally is found to be correlated negatively with psychological well-being in studies using cross section data. Moreover, in most cross-section studies psychological health is poorer the longer a person's exposure to unemployment. However, emotional well-being ceases to deteriorate after six months of unemployment. Investigators have attempted to determine which factors govern the relationship between unemployment and psychological health but much research remains to be done in this area. A cursory review of the available evidence is provided below.

There are indications in the literature (Korpi, forthcoming) that the negative association between unemployment and well-being is stronger for middle-aged persons compared to youths, among men than among women, for those without unemployment insurance, and for those with less job-based training prior to unemployment. Studies evaluating the vitamin model have found that people employed in jobs they view as unsatisfactory were no different from the unemployed on various measures of mental health. Thus, job quality appears to mediate the relation between unemployment and emotional health — losing a poor quality job generates less of a psychological burden. Social support, both from personal relations and contacts in the community reduce the psychological costs of joblessness. Although there is evidence that locus of control is negatively associated with unemployment, future research needs to address whether those with a more external outlook prior to unemployment are better able to maintain their psychological health when exposed to unemployment. Investigators also need to identify the values that cushion the psychological distress of unemployment.

The early studies using longitudinal data were unable to offer clear support for the hypothesis that unemployment damages psychological well-being. For instance, three different findings on the relation between unemployment and self-esteem, are present in the literature (Winefield et al., 1993; Goldsmith et al., 1996a). First, many studies find that people who are unemployed hold a less-favourable view of self than comparable but employed persons. Second, there are studies reporting that self-esteem is independent of labour force status. Finally, investigators have found that employment leads people to possess greater self-esteem, while unemployment fails to influence this aspects of psychological well-being. For a review of this literature, as well as the inconsistent results for the impact of unemployment on subsequent locus of control, see Goldsmith, Veum and Darity (1996a, 1996b).

Methodology and the stylized facts revisited

The failure of a consensus to emerge regarding the impact of unemployment on subjective psychological well-being from the first wave of longitudinal studies may be due to statistical problems — omitted variables, and a methodological problem — and improper data selection. These problems are discussed below along with the results of studies that avoid these pitfalls.

People who dropped out of the labour force are generally not included in data in sets constructed by investigators, since these individuals were not officially 'unemployed'. However, there are large monthly movements between unemployment and out-of-labour force status, leading many economists to claim that being unemployed and being out of the labour force are not distinctly different states. Moreover, labour force drop outs may be the individuals whose psychological well-being is affected most adversely by joblessness. In addition, the data sets used typically lack detailed information on labour force histories such as prior job training or personal characteristics expected to influence either psychological well-being or both the likelihood of becoming unemployed and psychological health. Without these data, the associated variables are omitted from the models estimated leading to inconsistent — inaccurate — estimates of the relations examined.

The latest wave of longitudinal research addressed the shortcomings of the earlier studies and has produced more reliable findings. These studies reveal that emotional well-being is indeed damaged in a substantial way by joblessness. For instance, Korpi (1998) found that current unemployment significantly increases an index of emotional distress for youths in Stockholm, Sweden, but youths recover over time, they are 'blemished' rather than 'scarred'. Winkelmann and Winkelmann (1998) find 'life satisfaction' among German men is diminished significantly by unemployment. Finally, using data on youths in the United States, Goldsmith et al. (1996a, 1996b) find that unemployment fosters feelings of externality and that joblessness, due either to unemployment or to time spent out of the labour force, damages self-esteem and scars a person's view of self.

The importance of evidence indicating that unemployment damages psychological well-being cannot be understated. These personal costs spill over not only on to family members, friends, and former business associates but have an aggregate economic impact as well. Economists now believe that the most plausible explanation for the European experience of persistently high unemployment for the past two decades is one based on hysteresis, but they contend that evidence on various economic channels for hysteresis is weak. However, a social psychological channel for hysteresis exists (Darity and Goldsmith, 1996). There is evidence (Goldsmith, Veum and Darity, 1997) that psychological well-being directly influences personal productivity. Therefore, when unemployment damages an individual's psychological well-being, it reduces his or her subsequent productivity as well. Thus, employers can be expected to move slowly in hiring from the pool of the unemployed, leading to unemployment hysteresis.

WILLIAM A.DARITY, JR, ARTHUR H. GOLDSMITH AND JONATHAN R. VEUM

Bibliography

Bakke, E.W. (1933) *The Unemployed Man: A Social Study*, London, Nisbett.

Brenner H. (1976) 'Estimating the Social Costs of National Economic Policy: Implications for Mental and Physical Health', in *Achieving the Goals of the Employment Act of 1946*, **1** (5), US Congress Joint Economic Committee.

Catalano, R., and Dooley, C. (1977) 'Economic Predictors of Depressed Mood and Stressful Life Events', *Journal of Health and Social Behaviour*, **18**: 292–307.

Darity, W., Jr and Goldsmith, A.H. (1996) 'Social Psychology, Unemployment and Macroeconomics', *Journal of Economic Perspectives*, **10**: 121–40.

Eisenberg, P. and Lazarsfeld, P. (1938) 'The Psychological Effects of Unemployment', *Psychological Bulletin*, **35**: 358–90.

Erikson, E.H. (1959) 'Identity and the Life Cycle', *Psychological Issues*, **1**: 50–100.

Feather, N.T. (1990) *The Psychological Impact of Unemployment*, New York, Springer-Verlag.

Furnham, A.F. (1988) 'Unemployment', in van Raaij, W.F., van Veldhoven, G.M. and Wärneryd, K.E. (eds), *Handbook of Economic Psychology*, Amsterdam, Elsevier.

Goldsmith, A.H., Veum J.R. and Darity, W., Jr. (1995) 'Are Being Unemployed and Being Out of the Labor Force Distinct States?: A Psychological Approach', *Journal of Economic Psychology*, **16**: 275–95.

Goldsmith, A.H., Veum J.R. and Darity, W., Jr. (1996a) 'The Impact of Labor Force

History on Self-Esteem and its Component Parts, Anxiety, Alienation, and Depression', *Journal of Economic Psychology*, **17**: 183–220.

Goldsmith, A.H., Veum J.R. and Darity, W., Jr. (1996b) 'The Psychological Impact of Unemployment and Joblessness', *Journal of Socio-Economics*, **25**: 333–58.

Goldsmith, A.H., Veum, J.R. and Darity, W., Jr. (1997) 'The Impact of Psychological and Human Capital on Wages', *Economic Inquiry*, **35**: 815–29.

Herzberg, F. (1966) *Work and the Nature of Man*, Cleveland, OH, Word Publishing Company.

Jahoda, M. (1982) *Employment and Unemployment: A Social-Psychological Analysis*, Cambridge, Cambridge University Press.

Jahoda, M., Lazarsdeld, P., and Zeisel, H. (1933) *The Sociography of an Unemployed Community*, London, Tavistock.

Korpi, T. (forthcoming) 'Employment, Unemployment, Labor Market Policies, and Subjective Well-Being among Swedish Youth', *Labour Economics*.

Robertson, A. and Cochrane, R. (1976) 'Attempted Suicide and Cultural Change: An Empirical Investigation', *Human Relations*, **9**: 863–83.

Robinson, J. and Wrightsman, L. (1991) *Personality and Social Psychological Attitudes*, Boston, MA, Harcourt Brace Jovanovich.

Seligman, M.E.P. (1975) *Helplessness: On Depression, Development and Death*, San Francisco, CA, W.H. Freeman.

Warr, P.B. (1983) 'Work, Jobs, and Unemployment', *Bulletin of the British Psychological Society*, **36**: 305–11.

Warr, P.B. (1987) *Work, Unemployment, and Mental Health*, Oxford, Clarendon Press.

Winefield, A.H., Tiggemann, H.R., Winefield, H.R. and Goldney, R.D. (1993) *Growing Up With Unemployment*, London, Routledge.

Winkelmann, L. and Winkelmann, R. (1998) 'Why Are the Unemployed So Unhappy? Evidence from Panel Data', *Economica*, **65**: 1–15.

Utility

The concept of utility in economics refers to the pleasure, or relief of pain, associated with the consumption of goods and services. The terminology is derived from the utilitarian theory of social choice proposed by Jeremy Bentham in the eighteenth century. Disregarding the difficulties of constructing a numerical measure of utility, Bentham based his utilitarian theory on the proposition that political organizations should be organized to achieve 'the greatest good of the greatest number' by maximizing the sum of individual utilities.

The concept of utility played a critical role in the development of the neoclassical theory of value, price and welfare in the late nineteenth century. In the first half of the twentieth century, analysis based on the concepts of preference and indifference, referred to as 'the New Welfare Economics', displaced the notion of utility from welfare economics. However, the concept of utility proved indispensable in the analysis of choice under uncertainty and in the allocation of consumption over time. As a result, utility models have returned to a central role in welfare economics. Because utility concepts lead naturally to egalitarian policy conclusions, their recent resurgence may have significant political implications in the long run.

Cardinal utility and the marginal revolution

Although utilitarianism, with its emphasis on rational optimization, was compatible with the spirit of classical economics, economists made little use of utility concepts until the neoclassical 'marginalist revolution', associated with the names of W.S. Jevons, Carl Menger and Léon Walras. Their central insight was that the terms on which individuals were willing to exchange goods depended not on the total utility associated with consuming those goods, but on the utility associated with consuming the last or 'marginal' unit of each good. The critical point is the principle of diminishing marginal utility, based on the observation that consumption of any commodity, such as water, is first directed to essential needs, such as quenching thirst, and then to less important purposes, such as hosing down pavements.

It is the utility associated with the marginal use of the commodity that determines willingness to engage in trade at any given prices. The use of the principle of diminishing marginal utility led to a resolution of the classical 'paradox of value', exemplified by the observation that wherever water is plentiful and diamonds are not, diamonds are more valuable than water, even though water is essential to life and diamonds are purely decorative.

The principle of diminishing marginal utility had egalitarian implications which Bentham almost certainly did not anticipate. If the marginal utility from consumption of an additional unit of each individual commodity is diminishing, the marginal utility from an additional unit of wealth must also be diminishing. If utility is represented as a real-valued function of wealth, diminishing marginal utility of wealth is equivalent to downward concavity of the utility function. If all utility functions are concave then, other things being equal, an additional unit of wealth yields more utility to a poor person than to a rich one, and a more equal distribution of wealth will yield greater aggregate utility.

All of this analysis rests on the assumption that utility can be treated as a cardinal quantity or, more precisely, one measurable on an interval scale. Using an interval scale, statements like 'the difference in utility between commodity bundles A and B is greater than the difference in utility between commodity bundles C and D' are meaningful. Krantz et al. (1971) discuss measurement issues in more detail.

Ordinalism and the New Welfare Economics

The rise of positivism and behaviourism in the early twentieth century reduced the appeal of theoretical frameworks based on the unobservable concept of utility. The New Welfare Economics developed by Hicks (1939) and others, showed that ordinal concepts of utility, requiring only the use of statements like 'commodity bundle *A* yields higher utility than commodity bundle *B*' were sufficient for all the ordinary purposes of demand theory and could be used to derive a welfare theory independent of cardinal utility. An ordinal utility function allows the ranking of commodity bundles, but not comparisons of the differences between bundles.

Opponents of egalitarian income redistribution also attacked the use of cardinal utility theories to make judgements about the welfare effects of economic policies. Robbins's (1938) claim that all interpersonal utility comparisons were 'unscientific' was particularly influential in promoting the idea that cardinal utility concepts should be avoided. The basic difficulty is that there is no obvious way of comparing utility scales between individuals, and, in particular, no way of showing that two people with similar income levels get the same additional utility from a given increase in income.

The apparent *coup de grâce* was given by Samuelson's (1947) recasting of welfare economics in terms of revealed preference. Samuelson showed that the standard theory of consumer demand could be constructed without any overt reference to utility. Even the use of ordinal utility, Samuelson suggested, was purely a matter of expositional convenience. The analysis of consumer demand can be undertaken using only statements about preferences. Samuelson's claim is correct in a formal sense. However, consumers will have well-defined demand functions only if preferences over bundles of goods are convex, that is, if a bundle containing an appropriate mixture of two goods is preferred to either of two equally valued bundles each containing only one of the goods. The only plausible basis for postulating this kind of convexity of preferences is the principle of diminishing marginal utility.

Expected utility and choice under uncertainty

Just as the New Welfare Economics appeared to eliminate cardinal utility concepts from demand theory, however, the concept of cardinal utility theory was revived by von Neumann and Morgenstern (1944) in their analysis of behaviour under uncertainty, and its application to game theory, based on the idea of expected utility maximization. When faced with an uncertain prospect, under which any of a set of outcomes could occur with known probability, von Neumann and Morgenstern suggested attaching a numerical utility to each outcome and evaluating the prospect by calculating the mean value of the utilities. This procedure is feasible only for cardinal measures of utility.

Von Neumann and Morgenstern denied that the cardinal nature of the utility function they used had any normative significance, and most advocates of expected utility agreed. Savage (1954) warned against confusing the von Neumann–Morgenstern utility function with 'the now almost obsolete notion of utility in riskless situations'. Arrow (1951) described cardinal utility under certainty as 'a meaningless concept'. However, as Wakker (1991: 10) observes,

> The same cardinal function that provides an expectation representing individuals' preferences over randomized outcomes is also used to provide the unit of exchange between players. The applicability of risky utility functions as a means of exchange between players is as disputable as their applicability to welfare theory, or to any other case of decision making under certainty.

This view was adopted by Allais (1953, 1987), the most prominent critic of the expected utility model. Allais argued that a proper analysis of choice under risk required both a cardinal specification of utility as a function of wealth under certainty and a separate specification of attitudes towards uncertainty. Allais's position has been strengthened by the development of the rank-dependent family of generalizations of the expected utility model (Quiggin, 1982), in which there is a clear separation between diminishing marginal utility of wealth and risk attitudes derived from concerns about the probability of good and bad outcomes.

Intertemporal choice

Utility functions identical in form to those of von Neumann–Morgenstern are found in the context of intertemporal choice. The same functional forms are found to be useful and the interpretations given to the parameters of the utility functions are strikingly similar. Individuals seek to smooth consumption over time, and show a strong aversion to large reductions in consumption, even if they are offset by subsequent increases in consumption. The most natural basis for such an aversion is diminishing marginal utility of wealth (Bailey, Olson and Wonnacott, 1980).

Intertemporal objective functions also contain a discount factor, reflecting the assumption, dating back to Bentham, that the utility of anticipated pleasures is diminished the further in the future they lie. In formal terms, this discount factor is similar to the probability weights of rank-dependent expected utility (Quiggin and Horowitz, 1995). Probability weights may also be used to separate aversion to intertemporal variations in income from aversion to risk *per se*. This idea has been used by Epstein and Zin (1990) as a partial explanation of the 'equity premium puzzle', that is, the surprisingly large difference between the rate of return for equities observed in security markets and the rate of interest on high-quality bonds, observed by Mehra and Prescott (1985).

Social choice

The use of objective functions incorporating a cardinal utility function concave in wealth is now standard practice in the analysis of choice under uncertainty and over time. The formal analogy between choices involving allocation of income over time, over states of the world and between individuals has encouraged the use of similar models in the analysis of social choices.

The use of cardinal utility models of social choice has been encouraged by the popularity of contractarian models such as that of Rawls (1971). Rawls introduces the device of a 'veil of ignorance' behind which individuals choose social arrangements without knowing what place they will occupy in those arrangements. Rawls argues, largely on the basis of intuition about choices under uncertainty, that rational individuals will adopt a 'maximin' criterion, focusing on the worst possible outcome. This is an extreme form of the decision-weighting process represented in rank-dependent expected utility. From the maximin criterion of choice under uncertainty, Rawls derives his theory of justice based on concern for the worst-off members of the community. The approach used by Harsanyi (1953) may be interpreted in similar terms. Unlike Rawls, Harsanyi assumes that rational individuals seek to maximize expected utility. He therefore derives the conclusion that they will prefer utilitarian social arrangements.

JOHN QUIGGIN

Bibliography

Allais, M. (1953) 'Le Comportement de l'Homme Rationel Devant le Risque, Critique des Postulates et Exiomes de l'École Americane' (The Behaviour of the Rational Man in the Face of Risk: Critique of the Postulates and Axioms of the American School), *Econometrica*, **21**: 503–46.

Allais, M. (1987) *The General theory of Random Choices in Relation to the Invariant Cardinal Utility Function and the Specific Probability Function: The* (U, q) *Model — A General Overview*, Paris, Centre National de la Recherche Scientifique.

Arrow, K. (1951), 'Alternative Approaches to the Theory of Choice in Risk-taking Situations', *Econometrica*, **19**: 404–37.

Bailey, M., Olson, M. and Wonnacott, P. (1980), 'The Marginal Utility of Income does Not Increase: Borrowing, Lending and Friedman–Savage Gambles', *American Economic Review*, **70**: 372–9.

Epstein, L.G. and Zin, S.E. (1990) '"First-Order" Risk Aversion and the Equity Premium Puzzle', *Journal of Monetary Economics*, **26**: 387–407.

Harsanyi, J. (1953) 'Cardinal Utility in Welfare Economics and in the Theory of Risk Taking', *Journal of Political Economy*, **61**: 434–5.

Hicks, J.R. (1939) *Value and Capital*, Oxford, Oxford University Press.

Krantz, D., Luce, R., Suppes, P. and Tversky, A. (1971) *Foundations of Measurement*, Volume I, New York, Academic Press.

Mehra, R. and Prescott, E.C. (1985) 'The Equity Premium: A Puzzle', *Journal of Monetary Economics*, **15**: 145–61.

Quiggin, J. (1981) 'Risk Perception and Risk Aversion among Australian Farmers', *Australian Journal of Agricultural Economics*, **25**: 160–69.

Quiggin, J. (1982) 'A Theory of Anticipated Utility', *Journal of Economic Behavior and Organization*, **3**: 323–43.

Quiggin, J. and Horowitz, J. (1995) 'Time and Risk', *Journal of Risk and Uncertainty*, **10**: 37–55.

Rawls, J. (1971) *A Theory of Justice*, Oxford, Clarendon Press.

Robbins, L. (1938) 'Interpersonal Comparisons of Utility: A Comment', *Economic Journal*, **48**: 635–41.

Samuelson, P.A. (1947) *Foundations of Economic Analysis*, Cambridge, MA, Harvard University Press.

Savage, L.J. (1954) *Foundations of Statistics*, New York, Wiley.

von Neumann, J. and Morgenstern, O. (1944) *Theory of Games and Economic Behavior*, Princeton, NJ, Princeton University Press.

Wakker, P. (1991) 'Separating Marginal Utility and Probabilistic Risk Aversion', Paper presented at University of Nijmegen, Nijmegen.

Utility of Public Goods

Utility is the value received from the consumption or employment of a good or service. Despite the importance of the concept to economic theory, it is often thought by economists to be unmeasurable in any direct way because of its essentially subjective nature. Thus, typically in economics ordinal utility is inferred from people's behaviour. If, for example, I regularly buy good *A* rather than the similarly priced good *B*, it is reasonable to infer that the utility of *A* for me exceeds that of *B*.

For many purposes such indirect inference of utilities is perfectly adequate. Moreover, while the measurement of subjective dimensions such as utility has been an important part of psychology since Gustav Fechner published his *Elemente der Psychophysik* in 1860, debate on both the correct techniques for such measurement and how the results should be interpreted has also been a constant theme in psychology. It is also well known that deriving behavioural predictions from knowledge of people's apparent mental states is often problematic. Thus, the economist's attitude is not an unreasonable one.

None the less, there are a number of goods and services whose utility cannot be inferred simply from people's behaviour. One obvious example is when the good or service has not yet been developed or marketed. Another is when the good is a public one. Such goods are provided or administered by a government or other authority and paid for by taxation rather than by the individual consumers. A few of the many examples are: parks and nature reserves, immigration control, hospitals, schools and street lighting. There is a vast variety of such goods, and their provision differs greatly between different countries and regions.

Usually, the utility of public goods cannot be inferred from people's purchasing behaviour because the good is not purchased at all. Nor is people's use of a public good for which no charge is made necessarily an indication of how much utility they derive from it (although they must derive some). Yet knowing these utilities is clearly important for decisions about how to allocate resources, and so a number of methods have been suggested to measure them.

Estimation methods

Both indirect and direct methods have been used to assess the utility of public goods. The principle of the former is that the utility of the goods is inferred from observable behaviour of some kind. An important point here is that even public goods for which no charge is made often have an estimable cost of some kind. For example, the cost of travel to nature reserves has sometimes been taken as a minimum indicator of the value of these reserves to visitors. Brookshire et al. (1981) used property values of different areas in the Los Angeles basin to estimate the value of clean air.

The behaviours observed in indirect methods are not usually sufficient on their own to enable utilities to be inferred, and additional assumptions, controls or observations are necessary. If, for example, a suburb with clean air has property values that average $50 000 more than another suburb with polluted air, one cannot simply conclude that the value of clean air to people living in the area is $50 000 since suburbs differ on other dimensions besides clean air, and these other dimensions need to be controlled for.

Indirect approaches are often rather piecemeal, applicable perhaps to one but not to a range of public goods. However, one indirect approach which does enable a range to be examined and compared, and one which has received considerable attention from public choice theorists (for example, Tullock, 1976; Schram, 1991), is to take people's votes for different political parties as the observable behaviour.

The task of inferring the utilities assigned to the whole range of public goods from a vote for a particular political party is necessarily assumption laden and the approach is usually an axiomatic one, from which various predictions have been derived. For example, Tullock (1976) concludes that in a democracy the amount of a public good supplied should be that desired by the median voter, unless there are unusual preference distributions or unless groups organized in support of a single good can coalesce with other single-interest groups to ensure its provision.

Direct methods, by contrast, simply entail asking respondents to value different public goods. The assumption here is that people are both in some sense

596

aware of their own utilities and choose to report on them honestly. Moreover, the methods seem to be subject to some systematic biases. For example, it is often found that the methods show insensitivity to quantity: the total value of a number of public reserves may be little higher than that of one such reserve (Baron, 1997).

Direct methods differ among themselves chiefly in the way people are asked to report their values. The most commonly used direct method is probably contingent valuation, in which people are asked how much they would be prepared to pay for the good or service if it was not free. Such methods (see the entry on Contingent Valuation in this volume for more information) have been used mainly to identify the value of environmental goods, clean air or unpolluted waterways, for example, and normally the value of one public good at a time rather than a range of them. However, in De Groot and Pommer's (1989) 'budget game', respondents assign their desires for government spending to a range of public goods.

In contingent valuation, people's valuations are made on a continuous cardinal scale. Another approach has been to present respondents with a range of public goods and to ask whether they wish to spend more, the same or less on the good (for example, Lewis and Jackson, 1985). This approach has the merit of simplicity, but the interpretation of the results is not always clear, since if more people choose higher spending on good *A* than on good B, this does not necessarily imply anything about the level of increased spending that is desired.

Category rating, in which people simply rate the utilities of different services on a scale from, say, one to ten, provides a measure — often claimed to be an interval scale — that is between those of the two previous methods in complexity. Category rating is commonly used in psychological measurement and has occasionally been used to measure the utility of public goods as well (for example, Kemp and Willetts, 1995 a, 1995b).

General results

Both indirect and direct methods have been used to value specific public goods, sometimes in combination (for example, Brookshire et al., 1981). Research carried out with the direct methods has also produced some interesting general results.

First, while different respondents often produce quite different utility estimates, these individual differences are rather poorly explained by demographic variables such as age, sex, political party supported or income. Thus, for example, while Kemp and Willetts (1995b) found that retirement-age respondents believed state pensions for the elderly to be more useful than did younger respondents, the differences were small. Other researchers using other direct methods have found similarly small effects (for example, De Groot and

Pommer, 1989). An implication of the result is that people's estimates of the utility of public goods by and large do not reflect their narrow self-interest. Instead they may contain a component of altruism (Hudson and Jones, 1994), paternalism, or concern for public order. For example, reducing unemployment is often thought to be a means of reducing crime.

Second, people seem to think about the utility of public goods in a rather simple way, and their responses appear to be 'generated to a large extent by very general notions on the (un)desirability of public goods: "defence is bad, education and health care are good"' (De Groot and Pommer, 1989: 131). Baron (1997) suggests that people's valuations of public goods are based mainly on their notions of how important they think the different goods are. Kahneman et al. (1993) found contingent valuations of a range of public goods to be well predicted by simple attitude measures. Moreover, while respondents using category ratings distinguish the marginal and total utilities of market-supplied goods, these utilities are not distinguished for public goods (Kemp and Willetts, 1995a). Such results indicate considerable differences between lay economic thinking about public goods and that of economists (see also the entry on Lay Economic Beliefs in this volume).

Third, it is not unusual to find examples of comparatively costly public goods which are held to be of rather low utility by respondents. Hence, for example, the survey of New Zealanders by Kemp and Willetts (1995b) revealed that the relatively costly good of defence received low-rated utility. Moreover, it was not possible to identify any demographic group (for example, elderly or conservative voters) who did accord it a high utility. Findings like these are interesting because they raise the general question of how such policies can survive in a democracy, and incidentally appear to contradict the idea that democratic policies should reflect the preferences of the median voter.

Practice and prospects
Huge sums of money are spent on public goods worldwide, and one might expect that trying to estimate the benefits that actually arise from this expenditure would be a matter of some priority to national and local governments. To date, however, while most governments have well-established audit procedures for checking that money is spent on the projects it is intended for, the utility that people derive from spending it has been evaluated only sporadically by any of the methods developed to date.

One area in which there has been recent progress towards assessing benefits with some rigour is in health economics, where it is becoming common to try to weigh up the benefits in terms of improved quality of life produced by spending money on different medical procedures (for example, McDowell and Newell, 1996). It is possible that in the future such accounting, either using the methods outlined above or others yet to be developed, will become more important for other types of public good as well.

SIMON KEMP

Bibliography
Baron, J. (1997) 'Biases in the Quantitative Measurement of Values for Public Decisions', *Psychological Bulletin*, **122**: 72–88.
Brookshire, D.C., d'Arge, R.C., Schulze, W.D. and Thayer M.A. (1981) 'Experiments in Valuing Public Goods', *Advances in Applied Microeconomics*, **1**: 123–72.
De Groot, H. and Pommer, E. (1989) 'The Stability of Stated Preferences for Public Goods: Evidence from Recent Budget Games', *Public Choice*, **60**: 123–32.
Hudson, J. and Jones, P.R. (1994) 'The Importance of the "Ethical Voter": An Estimate of "Altruism"', *European Journal of Political Economy*, **10**: 499–509.
Kahneman, D., Ritov, I., Jacowitz, K.E. and Grant, P. (1993) 'Stated Willingness to Pay for Public Goods: A Psychological Perspective', *Psychological Science*, **4**: 310–15.
Kemp, S. and Willetts, K. (1995a) 'Rating the Value of Government-Funded Services: Comparison of Methods', *Journal of Economic Psychology*, **16**: 1–21.
Kemp, S. and Willetts, K. (1995b) 'The Value of Services Supplied by the New Zealand Government', *Journal of Economic Psychology*, **16**: 23–37.
Lewis, A. and Jackson, D. (1985) 'Voting Preferences and Attitudes to Public Expenditure', *Political Studies*, **33**: 457–66.
McDowell, I. and Newell, C. (1996) *Measuring Health: A Guide to Rating Scales and Questionnaires*, Oxford, Oxford University Press.
Schram, A.J.H. C. (1991) *Voter Behavior in Economic Perspective*, Berlin, Springer.
Tullock, G. (1976) *The Vote Motive*, London, Institute of Economic Affairs.

Utility Theory

In the literature of economics, utility has been used variously to signify pleasure, satisfaction, happiness, the capacity of goods to contribute to consumers' well-being or to yield satisfaction. Jeremy Bentham and later W.S. Jevons, for instance, defined total utility of a thing as the total pleasure it yields to a consumer.

In early stages of the development of the concept, utility was identified with the pleasure felt during consumption, but it was not given an explicit psychological basis. Nevertheless, under the editor's heading: 'The Psychology of Economic Man', a section of Bentham's *Economic Writings* refers to

an isolated individual's enjoyment of utility. That enjoyment emanated from a propensity in human nature, by which . .. every human being is led to pursue a line of conduct which . . . will be in the highest degree contributory to his own greatest happiness, whatsoever be the effect of it, in relation to the happiness of other similar beings. (Bentham, 1954: 421)

Bentham's hedonistic psychology, if it may be called that, was extended in the work of Hermann H. Gossen in the 1850s. From the general principle that every human being aims to maximize pleasure, two laws are derived. First, the principle of diminishing marginal utility is established on the observation that wants decline successively in intensity when met by continuous, uninterrupted satisfaction, until satiation is reached. In other words, the increment of utility gained from a stock of goods consumed in a given time period declines with every addition to the stock. The second law formulated an equimarginal principle: that in order to maximize utility, a consumer should satisfy at a given time only a portion of each competing want with a view to equalizing their contribution to total utility. Later these insights were expressly connected with rational economic behaviour predicated upon equalizing utility at the margin for desired goods given a resource or income constraint. According to Jevons for example, total utility was maximized when for all goods purchased and consumed out of a given income, the marginal utilities weighted by their prices were equalized. These principles were underwritten by the assumption that the consumer's mind subdivides wants and goods into infinitesimally small fractions when deliberating over a choice.

By contrast, the Austrian economist, Carl Menger, claimed that consumers were generally incapable of making finely calculated decisions in pursuit of utility. Maximization of total utility from a mix of consumers' goods was not very meaningful when those goods were applied to wants which were ordered in a Maslowian type of hierarchy. Menger provided precursory foundations for a lexicographic choice model which in principle seemed to preclude the adding-up of utilities (see Endres, 1997: Ch. 3).

When Jacob Viner (1925: 369) referred to the 'psychological law of diminishing utility' he was reflecting on extensive debate in economics and psychology from the 1870s on the behavioural foundations of the utility theory of value and price. The 'marginal revolution' in economics during the 1870s linked utility with market demand and maintained that utility, and especially marginal utility, was the ultimate determinant of exchange value. The early marginalists, Jevons and Léon Walras, were able loosely to link utility schedules with demand schedules: by measuring utility in monetary terms, they reasoned from equivalence of a list of demand prices (that is, the amounts consumers were willing and able to pay) for particular quantities of a good to equivalence of marginal utilities enjoyed by those consumers. In addition, under the influence of F.Y. Edgeworth, Alfred Marshall and Philip Wicksteed, disutility or pain cost of producing goods for consumption was included as an influence on the amounts producers were willing and able to supply for every price.

Utility and marginal utility focused attention on demand, which was recognized as the driving force behind economic activity. It was supposed that utility theory carried the analysis of consumers' demand patterns beyond the surface, objective phenomena of price quantity — that it explains demand behaviour. For example:

> Utility is taken to be correlative to Desire or Want. It has been already argued that desires cannot be measured directly, but only indirectly by the outward phenomena to which they give rise: and that in those cases with which economics is chiefly concerned the measure is found in the price which a person is willing to pay for the fulfilment or satisfaction of his desire. He may have desires and aspirations which are not consciously set for any satisfaction: but for the present we are concerned chiefly with those which do so aim; and we assume that the resultant satisfaction corresponds in general fairly well to that which was anticipated when the purchase was made. (Marshall, 1920: 78)

Here utility theory is supported by two assumptions: stable desires (tastes) and consumption expectations being fulfilled. Diminishing 'desire' need be referred to only when explaining diminishing demand price (that is, the diminishing price consumers are willing to pay as they contemplate consuming greater quantities). The utility concept was to be de-psychologized. By the turn of the century, Marshall, Irving Fisher, Wicksteed and Eugen von Böhm-Bawerk had all submitted that utility was independent of psychological hedonism, or any other psychological proposition for that matter. However, terminological changes in themselves (for example, from utility to 'desire') did not remove hedonistic associations (see Sweezy, 1934). On these issues there was much disagreement and the keenest controversy.

Psychologists and American institutionalist economists, notably Thorstein Veblen, argued that consumer behaviour was not under the constant guidance of careful, finely calibrated hedonic calculations. Consumers' choices were the product of unstable, irrational, complex instinctual impulses, habits and even hysteria. A.W. Coats (1976: 46) captured the intellectual context as follows:

> During the second half of the nineteenth century the development of new ideas and experimental methods in psychology led to the formulation of three major new approaches in the USA, each of which seemed directly applicable to economics: namely, William James's conception of the psychological and biological determinants of human behaviour; William McDougall's instinct theory; and John Broadus Watson's behaviourism. At about the same time, the new 'subjective' theories of value commonly associated with the so called 'marginal revolution' of the 1870s were being assimilated, not without difficulty, into the central corpus of economic theory. In retrospect it seems hardly surprising that the trend towards objectivisim in psychology should clash with an apparently

contradictory trend in economics.

In its attempt to explain exchange value, utility theory referred back to subjective scales of valuation which were supposed to reside in the consumer's mind. As long as economists insisted on explaining demand they could not easily escape by concentrating on the overt 'facts' (for example, schedules of demand price); they needed to offer a theory of the motivational bases of choice and the process of want formation. As the utility concept was employed in economics, it did not prove adequate to these tasks (see Lewin, 1996: 1301–4). It ended in a tautology: the fact that something is consumed at the margin must mean that it yields the highest marginal utility per unit of income spent.

There were some important differences among leading marginalists in respect of their reference to psychological assumptions. Jevons began with a theory of pleasure and pain; he derived a theory of utility from a theory of pleasure and used marginal utility — a ratio not a quantity of feeling — as a central concept in the analysis of exchange value. Walras began with price and worked back to final demand, making no 'psychological' reflections whatsoever. The only allusion to psychology in Walras is the supposition that individuals can measure the intensity of their wants of the same and different kinds and on this basis Walras developed the notion of marginal utility which he called *rareté*. These formulations did not really explain the basis of consumer demand schedules. The outside observer cannot know after choice whether the subject performed in such a way as to realize maximum possible utility and it was not possible to repeat choices experimentally with controlled variations following, for example, Marshall's well-known *ceteris paribus* rule.

Some economists, notably Edgeworth in his *Mathematical Psychics* (1881) and later Dickinson (1922), offered a more sophisticated *ex post* psychological rationalization for diminishing marginal utility by invoking Fechner's law (after Gustav Fechner). The latter turns on the proposition that sensation in general bears, within limits, a continuing diminishing ratio to physical stimulus; as stimulus increases at a geometric rate, sensation increases at a simple arithmetic rate. In accordance with this principle, as one 'consumes' music for instance,

> dormant responses are aroused, and distracting impulses subside, so that [one's] total inclination toward the music is presently stronger than it was at first. But if we could dissect out one of the constituent responses and watch it in isolation we should find its energy diminishing from the beginning, if the stimulus remained constant. . . . This proposition can be put into the form familiar to economists by saying there is diminishing sensibility per [degree] of stimulus. The fundamental cause of the phenomenon is presumably fatigue of the response-mechanism or adaptation in the sense organ. (Dickinson, 1922: 232–3)

Resemblance between Fechner's law and diminishing marginal utility was noticed by economists only in the breach. Connections to results in experimental psychology were tenuous, and brought in belatedly. Utility analysis in economics was not dependent on psychological theorems or categories (see Max Weber, 1908). Economic theory did not break down the internal experimental correlates of everyday consumer experience into psychical elements (stimulus, sensation, reactions, feelings and so on). Instead, utility theory sought to understand certain adaptations of consumers' external behaviour to outside constructs (income, prices, given tastes). This is precisely Lionel Robbins's position in his influential 1932 work *An Essay on the Nature and Significance of Economic Science*, as Sweezy (1934: 181–2) points out.

The Austrian economists, especially Menger and Friedrich Wieser, did not declare independence from psychology, broadly conceived. They welcomed the insights of psychology into their studies of the nature, structure and growth of wants, although it was an everyday form of psychology. Wieser explained Gossen's laws by appealing to what he called the 'psychological' method of introspection. There was at least an attempt made among Austrian economists to inquire into the deeper substance of the consumer choice process which yielded utility. Diminishing marginal utility and the negative-sloping demand curve became inferences from experience. The consciousness of the economizing individual is accessible because it derives from everyday experience shared by observer and the observed. For Menger, the consumer's perceived relationship between goods and subjectively felt human wants could be 'observed' by introspection; Menger's introspective observation was that these perceptions were inherently subject to error. Wieser compared the importance of the marginal utility principle with the principle of gravity in mechanics. However, the observation which discovered diminishing marginal utility was the result of an intuitive understanding of other human beings. Moreover, our thinking about consumer choice must conform to commonsense introspection and intelligible inter-communication with our subject matter. The motives behind choice, the reasons for consumer behaviour, can also be observed by introspection; there was thought to be no need to resort to formal, professional psychological analysis for support. These insights were later extended by Max Weber and Frank Knight, who criticized positivist approaches to consumer theory because they relied on sterile behaviourism and deprived the concepts of utility and the utility theory of value of their *raison d'être* (Weber, 1908; Lewin, 1996: 1298–9, 1313–14).

In developing the utility concept, economists were always seeking to be freed from the 'embarrassments' of pure psychological reasoning, and have on occasion with impunity overridden the complaints of psychologists. Psychological research was not used to provide the background when the utility theory of exchange value was constructed. That economists generally evaded the

Vanity

Two dominant themes in Western culture are a fixation with physical appearance and achievement of personal goals. These two themes reflect aspects of 'vanity'. Because vanity has contributed to, or is reflected in, the development of countless products and services, insights into the vanity construct have important implications for consumer behaviour.

The term 'vanity' has been used in numerous contexts and has varying definitions across the sociology, psychology, philosophy and consumer behaviour literatures. However, two recurring themes are evident in these bodies of literature: first, vanity encompasses a physical appearance aspect; and second, vanity encompasses an achievement aspect. We view 'vanity' as having four components — two physical and two achievement: (i) a concern for physical appearance; (ii) a positive (and perhaps inflated) view of physical appearance; (iii) a concern for achievement; and (iv) a positive (and perhaps inflated) view of achievement.

Physical aspects of vanity

In the past decade or so, both the popular and academic press have been replete with books and articles relating to physical appearance and its impact on consumer demand for products and services. Consider the following examples. In 1992, 53 million Americans went 'on a diet' (of course, part of this is due to health concerns), and $36 billion was spent on dieting and programmes/products. Sales of dieting-related products were more than $50 billion in 1995. Retail sales of cosmetics exceed $20 billion annually. A *Psychology Today* survey has tracked perceptions of body-image and physical appearance in 1972, 1985, and 1997. It reports the following statistics: in 1972, 25 per cent of the female respondents and 15 per cent of male respondents said they were 'dissatisfied with their overall physical appearance'; in 1985, 38 per cent of the female respondents and 34 per cent of the male respondents were 'dissatisfied with their overall physical appearance'; in 1997, 56 per cent of female respondents and 43 per cent of male respondents were 'dissatisfied with their overall physical appearance'. Another 1994 *Psychology Today* survey reported that 25 per cent of men approved of five different elective cosmetic surgery procedures (that is, nose, eyelid, liposuction, face-lift and ear-pinning) for men, and 37 per cent of men approved of these procedures for women; 22 per cent of women approved of these procedures for men, and 33 per cent of women approved of these procedures for women. In fact, the occurrence of cosmetic surgery has risen dramatically in the past ten years, and 80 per cent of these surgeries are elective (Brownell, 1991). Some potential negative consequences of physical vanity are also apparent. Despite repeated warnings from the medical community, an estimated 1 million Americans, half of them adolescents, use black market steroids to improve their physique, and, while new cases of skin cancer have risen 50 per cent from 1985 to 1990, approximately 29 per cent of white Americans still intentionally suntan. These are but a few examples cited in the popular press relating to the emphasis on physical appearance.

A growing body of academic research has also been devoted to physical appearance and its effect on consumer behaviour. It has been suggested that outward physical appearance is important for establishing and maintaining one's self-concept. This is supported by the proliferation of, and demand for, appearance-related products such as cosmetics and clothing (Solomon, 1997). It has also been suggested that concern for physical attractiveness leads not only to positive consumption behaviours (for example, exercising, healthier eating habits), but to negative behaviours as well (for example, eating disorders, numerous elective cosmetic surgeries, steroid use) (Solomon, 1997). In fact, clinical psychologists have long proposed a link between physical appearance and eating/body disturbance disorders (Stice, 1994).

Achievement aspects of vanity

Consumption behaviours related to achievement vanity have been proposed for decades. 'Conspicuous consumption', which reflects the purchase of prestige and luxury products for social consequences, has historical links to vanity as far back as the mid-1800s (Mason, 1981). Early theorists, such as John Rae (1834/1905), contended that 'vanity' and self-indulgence were driving forces behind the consumption of luxuries. Others suggest that conspicuous consumption was necessary for those seeking higher status or prestige within their communities, that is, the 'Veblen Effect' (Mason, 1981). Regardless of whether driven by self-indulgence or the Veblen Effect, achievement vanity has links to conspicuous consumption.

More recently, both theoretical and empirical links between personal achievements and product consumption have been established. Using the VALS typology on data from a large-scale national survey, Mitchell (1983) classified 22 per cent of respondents as 'achievers' — those concerned with personal goals, and another 9 per cent as 'emulators' — those aspiring to be achievers. Another national classification, the list of values (LOV), found that about 16 per cent of people surveyed endorsed 'a sense of accomplishment' as the value most important to them. It has been suggested that these groups often conspicuously consume to convey their success/status (Solomon, 1997).

Several other researchers believe that personal and career goals are strongly associated with consumer aspirations. Hirschman (1990) contends that a dominant theme in our culture is the documentation of personal achievement via consuming in a prescribed way (for example, status is exemplified by 'showing off' material possessions). Richins and Dawson (1992) also show evidence that materialism is used as a symbol of achievement. Lastly, vanity is important from a marketing practitioner perspective. Consider the advertising industry. Numerous products are advertised with claims of enhancing one's appearance and/or the benefits associated with being considered physically attractive (Solomon, 1997). Advertising themes are replete with achievement and status symbol consumption. For instance, the VALS/LOV-inspired advertisements rely heavily on an entitlement-achievement theme of 'you are successful — so you deserve it,' and that 'having and showing more' is a reflection of social status and achievement-related vanity (Pollay, 1986). Perhaps David Ogilvy summed it up best in *Ogilvy on Advertising* (1983: 7):

> Meanwhile, most of the advertising techniques which worked when I wrote *Confessions of an Advertising Man*, still work today. Consumers still buy products whose advertising promises them value for the money, *beauty* [emphasis added], nutrition, relief from suffering, *social status* [emphasis added], and so on — ALL OVER THE WORLD.

Some empirical results and suggestions for future research

Scales measuring the four aspects of vanity have been developed and validated (Netemeyer, Burton and Lichtenstein, 1995). Numerous studies have demonstrated the importance and relevance of the vanity constructs to consumer behaviour, and more generally, to social behaviour. Consumer-based constructs related to the physical aspects of vanity include cosmetics use, clothing concern, dieting, exercise, consideration of elective cosmetic surgery, sunbathing frequency, neuroticism, depression, and eating disorder symptomology (Burton, Netemeyer and Lichtenstein 1995; Netemeyer et al., 1995).

The results pertaining to the achievement aspects of vanity also reinforce the notion that achievement vanity has important implications for numerous consumer behaviour and marketing activities, such as advertising appeals and materialistic pursuits. The achievement aspects of vanity were found to be related to materialism, price-based prestige sensitivity, clothing concern, country club membership, narcissism, grandiosity, concern for social status, importance of money and education level. Thus, achievement vanity should also be a useful construct for studying consumption behaviour.

The aspects of vanity and the empirical findings related to these aspects suggest several avenues for future research. First, it is clear that we live in a consumption-orientated society. This notion is constantly reinforced by marketers who advertise products that promote achievement status and physical appearance with attractive spokespeople and models. These advertising/media images appeal to the vanity traits we have delineated, and many researchers feel that these images of wealth and physical perfection are likely to be unattainable for the general populace (Pollay, 1986; Richins, 1991). Relevant questions include: (i) 'Does the consumption-oriented society we live in promote vanity to the point that consumers engage in unhealthy/addictive behaviours?', and if so, (ii) 'Do advertisers and marketers in general have a social responsibility related to the promotion of vanity?'. For example, recent studies in clinical psychology suggest that an overconcern for physical appearance and the 'perfect body' images projected by some of the media (that is, fashion magazines, TV shows and commercials), influence young women to engage in unhealthy eating habits that can lead to anorexia and bulimia nervosa (see Stice (1994) for a review). In fact, empirical results over several studies show a substantial correlational link between physical aspects of vanity, body image disturbance, eating disorder symptomology, and the images of women (that is, thin and attractive) portrayed in the media (for example, Guidry, Williamson and Netemeyer, 1997). Thus, studies assessing the potential impact of physical vanity and the media on the development of maladaptive consumer behaviours are of interest. Given the relations between the achievement vanity scales and narcissism and grandiosity, high levels of concern for achievement may have negative social consequences. These negative social consequences can manifest themselves in negative consumer behaviours. Possible 'dark-side' consequences of a very high concern for achievement (for example, unethical behaviours) are of interest to researchers.

Various other research areas related to the vanity constructs should also be fruitful. Studying groups based on age, gender, and culture seem appropriate. For example, at what age does attention and concern for physical appearance emerge? In a study of 1000 adolescents, Guber (1987) found that, as early as 12 years old, girls want to be thin and attractive and boys want to be muscular. This attention to physical appearance may go back even further to early childhood as it has been suggested that television may teach children, particularly little girls, a desire for thinness, beauty and youth. This could translate into concerns and perceptions pertaining to physical appearance.

As for gender, an interesting question is 'do the four vanity measures relate differentially for males versus females?'. It has been suggested that women's orientation to achievement is more heavily tied to their physical appearance than men's, that is, a woman's physical appearance may be viewed as an instrument of career achievement in a man's world (Burton et al., 1995). In fact, one study reports that many women felt that being good-looking was a form of accomplishment, and 61 per cent of them said that looking attractive made them feel more successful in their careers.

Studies could assess the prevalence of vanity in Western versus eastern cultures. Some empirical evidence suggests that Western societies such as the US value beauty and physical appearance more than Eastern cultures such as China and India (for example, Schwartz and Bilskey, 1987). These same studies suggest that Western cultures are more success/achievement orientated than their Eastern counterparts. Research assessing the cross-cultural applicability of the aspects of vanity should be of interest.

RICHARD G. NETEMEYER, SCOT BURTON AND DONALD R. LICHTENSTEIN

Bibliography

Brownell, K.D. (1991) 'Dieting and the Search for the Perfect Body: Where Physiology and Culture Collide', *Behavior Therapy*, **22**: 1–12.

Burton, S., Netemeyer, R.G. and Lichtenstein, D.R. (1995) 'Gender Differences for Appearance-related Attitudes and Behaviors: Implications for Consumer Welfare', *Journal of Public Policy and Marketing*, **13**: 60–75.

Guber, S.S. (1987) 'The Teenage Mind', *American Demographics*, August: 42–4.

Guidry, S.-V., Williamson, D.A. and Netemeyer, R.G. (1997) 'Structural Modeling Analysis of Body Dysphoria and Eating Disorder Symptoms in Preadolescent Girls', *Eating Disorders: Journal of Treatment and Prevention*, **5**: 15–27.

Hirschman, E.C. (1990) 'Secular Immortality and the American Idealogy of Affluence', *Journal of Consumer Research*, **17**: 31–42.

Mason, R.S. (1981) *Conspicuous Consumption: A Study of Exceptional Consumer Behavior*, New York, St. Martin's Press; Farnborough, Gower.

Mitchell, A. (1983) *The Nine American Lifestyles: Who We Are and Where We're Going*, New York, Macmillan.

Netemeyer, R.G., Burton, S. and Lichtenstein, D.R. (1995) 'Trait Aspects of Vanity: Measurement and Relevance to Consumer Behavior', *Journal of Consumer Research*, **21**: 612–26.

Ogilvy, D. (1983) *Ogilvy on Advertising*, New York, Crown Publishers.

Pollay, R.W. (1986) 'The Distorted Mirror: Reflections on the Unintended Consequences of Advertising', *Journal of Marketing*, **50**: 18–36.

Rae, J. (1905) *The Sociological Theory of Capital*, New York, Macmillan (first published in 1834).

Richins, M. (1991) 'Social Comparison and the Idealized Images of Advertising', *Journal of Consumer Research*, **18**: 71–83.

Richins, M. and Dawson, S. (1992) 'A Consumer Values Orientation for Materialism and its Measurement: Scale Development and Validation', *Journal of Consumer Research*, **19**: 303–16.

Schwartz, S.H. and Bilskey, W. (1987) 'Toward a Universal Psychological Structure of Human Values', *Journal of Personality and Social Psychology*, **53**: 550–62.

Solomon, M.R. (1997) *Consumer Behavior: Buying, Having, and Being*, Englewood Cliffs, NJ, Prentice-Hall.

Stice, E. (1994) 'Review of the Evidence for a Sociocultural Model of Bulimia Nervosa and an Exploration of the Mechanisms of Action', *Clinical Psychology Review*, **14**: 633–61.

Variety-Seeking Behaviour

Basic models

Choice models and their extensions have always played a significant role in the description and prediction of consumer behaviour, providing important information in terms of switching behaviour, segmentation and partitioning. It was not until much later that the issue of *why* people switch was explicitly addressed in the stochastic choice literature. Varying choice behaviour could, in fact, be due to any number of reasons: coupon availability, budget constraints, locational convenience, stock outs and so on. However, in 1972, Bass, Pessemier and Lehmann noted that even in the absence of such external factors, considerable brand-switching behaviour could be observed in consumer purchase patterns. Furthermore, while switching to similar products was more frequent, there was also considerable switching to dissimilar brands, even when stated preferences remained the same. Bass et al. thus postulated that one possible reason for consumers to switch away from a preferred brand could be an internal need for variety. This led to a stream of modelling literature, first appearing in 1978, which dealt with the issue of switching behaviour observed regardless of any external influence.

This motivation to switch — that is, an internal need to seek variety — needs to be distinguished from other forms of motivation such as information seeking. Thus researchers studying variety-seeking behaviour tend to study categories such as soft drinks (see Bass et al., 1972; Trivedi, Bass and Rao, 1994) — a mature category with brands that are generally well known — while information-seeking research may use a category involving a technical product where information regarding the product is critical to its selection. Clearly, these two types of purchase behaviour have a sufficiently different impact and implications as to require separate treatment.

In a different vein, the study of variety seeking has also been of great interest to researchers in areas such as economics and psychology, for the last four decades. In fact, much of the modelling literature looks to the attribute-based models proposed by Lancaster (1966) in economics to determine brand similarities and, subsequently, to evaluate the level of variety offered by each pair of brands. In an application of this to the marketing literature, Ratchford (1975) shows that multiple-brand purchase behaviour is very much the norm and is done as a means of achieving an optimal mix of attributes (or characteristics).

The psychology literature also addresses the issue of variety seeking (or sensation seeking, arousal seeking and so on). Researchers have offered a number of different attitudinal scales and theories (see Zuckerman, 1979) in an effort to understand the various aspects of variety-seeking behaviour. While both the psychology and marketing streams of research study the same underlying dimension of variety seeking, the similarity appears to end there. Marketing modellers use sequential purchase data to derive models of purchase behaviour, and the latter develop constructs and obtain responses to scales regarding attitudes. Unfortunately, the inability to infer behaviour and thus develop managerial implications limit the marketing applications of such work.

The study of variety seeking has thus offered a useful and intuitive means of explaining and modelling the phenomenon of what is technically termed 'nonzero-order behaviour' — that is, behaviour which implies that there is some memory in the system and that what one buys now depends on what one has purchased earlier, in contrast to 'zero-order behaviour' which implies that each purchase is independent of previous purchases. Several models of variety-seeking behaviour were offered by various researchers, based on how the shift from zero order to nonzero order was accomplished. Most such models fall under the category of *constant parameter models*, whereby the shift from zero order to nonzero order purchase probabilities is by a constant amount for each choice alternative. The implication is that the variety sought by the consumer is constant for each purchase occasion. One trend of research in this area used the underlying notion of dynamic attribute satiation (Lattin and McAlister, 1985). That is, the modelling is based on the premise that individuals experience 'satiation' on attributes provided by consumed brands. Thus, they would look less for these same attributes in their next purchase. This effect would depend on the individual's ideal attribute level and the rate at which the inventory of accumulated attribute levels decay. This is, in fact, a variation on Ratchford's (1975) theory referred to above.

Lattin (1987), on the other hand, designed a variety-seeking model using the theory that attributes can be divided into four categories — those which an individual equibalances, counterbalances, finds desirable and finds undesirable. Utility is then measured as the weighted sum of the above four sets of attributes. Alternatively, the *constant parameter learning models* (such as Bawa, 1990) allow for different types of choice behaviour over a purchase history, but the shift from zero order to non zero order probabilities is deterministic.

More recently, a new class of stochastic variety-seeking models — *random parameter models* — has been proposed (Trivedi et al., 1994), whereby the shift from zero-order to nonzero-order purchase probabilities is by a random amount for each choice alternative. This theory holds that each individual has an internal, inherent need for variety which may vary in intensity and consistency over different individuals. Variety is thus modeled as a random variable which follows a beta distribution over a sequence of purchases for a given individual. In other words, on each purchase occasion, the level of variety sought is a random variable. (In keeping with the concept of stochastic choice behaviour, variety seeking — which we incorporate to drive choice — is modelled as a stochastic random variable.) While the individual does not on each occasion consciously seek out this degree of need and then make a purchase, the sequence of purchases will reflect the intensity and consistency of this need. The stochastic element in this type of variety-seeking model therefore has the important property of allowing the individual to choose nonuniform levels of variety on each purchase occasion without enforcing a completely random pattern of purchase behaviour. By suitable parameterization of the distribution, a wide variety of individual behaviour can be accommodated. The model thus incorporates similarity between brands, while allowing individuals to choose a dissimilar product as a function of the degree to which they seek variety.

The model was tested empirically using a sample of individuals from a geographically concentrated area. Choice data over three product categories, as well as perceived similarity data between products, is collected from the sample over a period of two to three months in order to calibrate the model. A comparison of results over several models shows that the stochastic variety-seeking model offers an improved fit, especially when the data are strongly variety seeking (Morgan and Trivedi, 1996). Results suggest a rich set of implications for brand managers in terms of understanding consumer responses, and determining product and line extension strategies.

Extensions
Since a manager's interest would lie primarily in the application of such variety-seeking models to brand strategy issues, a considerable amount of research has recently focused on the influence of variety seeking on marketing-mix variables such as promotions. The issue of whether a brand can use price promotions to attract specific market segments is an extremely interesting one. Differential responses to marketing actions such as pricing, advertising, promotions and merchandising can allow managers to efficiently target each segment and maximize returns on efforts.

Using the unidimensional constant parameter models for segmenting consumers, researchers studied the impact of promotions on purchase response behaviour. Findings of differences in promotion sensitivity among variety-seeking segments, however, have been somewhat mixed. In their simulation and experimental studies, Feinberg, Kahn and McAlister (1992: 234) found that variety seeking flattens out the promotional response: 'less preferred brands are helped and more preferred brands are hurt by variety seeking'. At the same time, Kahn and Raju (1991) found that the gains by major brands from promoting come mainly from variety seekers, while the gains by minor brands come mainly from brand-loyal consumers. Krishnamurthi and Raj (1991), alternatively, found that loyal/inert consumers are relatively insensitive to price changes of their favourite brand.

The use of the stochastic parameter model, rather than the constant parameter model to segment consumers offered a different kind of segmentation scheme (Morgan and Trivedi, 1996). Since the stochastic variety-seeking model yielded two parameters on which to calibrate variety-seeking behaviour, a new dimension was added to describe variety seeking: in addition to the 'extent' (or amount) of variety seeking studied so far in the literature, the notion of the 'intensity' with which variety is sought was also considered. In this characterization of variety seeking, the extent was interpreted as the mean amount of variety sought, while the intensity of variety seeking was the likelihood of engaging in the behaviour represented by the mean (similar to a variance). Thus, whether the purchase pattern of individuals classified their behaviour as zero order, variety seeking or brand loyal, the intensity parameter defined the consistency with which they would maintain this pattern. They showed that individuals with a lower intensity of behaviour (and therefore a lower consistency in maintaining their purchase pattern) would be more susceptible to externalities (such as marketing-mix effects), relative to high-intensity individuals seeking a specific pattern of behaviour with greater consistency.

The future of variety seeking and variety-seeking models is bright. Recent models give proof to claims of superior fit and flexibility, and are more focused in addressing application-orientated managerial concerns. Furthermore, they represent a unique blend (and a much-needed link) between two fairly distinct and thus far non-overlapping areas of marketing — the behavioural and the quantitative modelling areas.

MINAKSHI TRIVEDI

Bibliography

Bass, F.M., Pessemier, E.A. and Lehmann, D.R. (1972) 'An Experimental Study of Relationships between Attitudes, Brand Preference and Choice', *Behavioral Science*, **17**: 532–41.

Bawa, K. (1990) 'Modeling Inertia and Variety Seeking Tendencies in Brand Choice Behavior', *Marketing Science*, **9**: 263–78.

Feinberg, F., Kahn, B.E. and McAlister, L. (1992) 'Market Share Response When Consumers Seek Variety', *Journal of Marketing Research*, **29**: 227–7.

Kahn, B.E. and Louie, T.A. (1990) 'The Effects of Retraction of Price Promotions on Brand Choice Behavior for Variety Seeking and Last Purchase Loyal Consumer', *Journal of Marketing Research*, **27**: 279–89.

Kahn, B.E. and Raju, J.S. (1991) 'The Effects of Price Promotions on Variety Seeking and Reinforcement Behavior', *Marketing Science*, **10**: 316–38.

Krishnamurthi, L. and Raj, S.P. (1991) 'An Empirical Analysis of the Relationship Between Brand Loyalty and Consumer Price Elasticity', *Marketing Science*, **10**: 172–83.

Well-Being

The concept of well-being lies at the foundations of both neoclassical economics and many of the main criticisms of that approach deriving from economic psychologists.

Within positive neoclassical economics, well-being joins the long list of synonyms which have been applied to the maximization model: utility, happiness, desire fulfilment, satisfaction, welfare, ophelimity, pleasure, well-being, all terms used to describe that presumably well-established whatever-it-might-be which individuals are assumed to be so effective at maximizing. Within the normative domain of modern welfare economics, the goal of economic efficiency is paramount. As it is usually operationalized, there is an efficiency improvement if, across all individuals in the society, the total of the gains from a change exceeds the total of losses. Efficiency is based on the presumption that the social value we attach to gains and losses is the value that individuals voluntarily associate with them, thereby making more explicit the presumption that utility (which individuals are assumed to maximize) is a euphemism for well-being.

Many critics of this approach feel that there is much to be said for our commonsense doubt that the term utility can mean all these things simultaneously: wants and needs are not the same; preferences need not correspond with welfare; happiness and satisfaction are not identical; and what gives pleasure is not necessarily compatible with our well-being. Sen (1977) famously remarked that anyone who accepts the equivalences among concepts implied by the neoclassical theory of utility maximization is a 'rational fool'. However, once it is accepted that these various terms may refer to different things, the questions arise whether there is any reasonably precise way to distinguish among them, and how they relate to one another. Lane (1991: Part VII) provides a very thorough and stimulating discussion of the economists' notion of utility and how it relates to concepts such as satisfaction, happiness and well-being. Well-being is arguably the most fundamental of the concepts. While greater satisfaction or more happiness may be appealing, when it comes down to it, would not improved well-being be what we really want as individuals and for society?

Critics of the neoclassical approach have argued that individuals are aware of these distinctions, and that they do affect behaviour. The literature on multiple selves and economic decision making, for instance, suggests that individuals frequently have a number of different preference orderings, depending upon the perspective they take, some of the orderings reflecting a more careful and thoughtful consideration of the individual's interests, others betraying an impulsive concentration on immediate self-gratification (Elster (ed.), 1985). This approach removes well-being as the single objective underlying individuals' economic behaviour. But it also implies that well-being is one of the things we care about, and that, at least in some circumstances, our behaviour is affected by what we think will further it. This view is consistent with approaches which suggest that individuals may have a meta-preference ordering over the various subsidiary preference orderings which drive our behaviour, and which reflects an assessment of what we would ideally like our values to be. It also ties into the view held by some (but not all) psychologists that, contrary to the behaviour we may often exhibit, we basically desire to be healthy in mind and body.

However, this addresses only indirectly the question of what is meant by well-being. To pose the question directly implies a shift in focus, away from the simplifying assumptions of neoclassical economics, into more disputatious realms of psychology and moral philosophy.

A pragmatic, but ultimately unsatisfying, suggestion is that well-being is a multifaceted concept, which is separable into numerous components. One can then speak of what might be called *hyphen*-well-being, where the *hyphen* might be *material* or *economic* or *mental* or *psychological* or *social* or *community* or *ecological* or *moral* or *spiritual* or what-you-will. The suggestion that well-being is multifaceted may be entirely reasonable, but separability is more problematic. Consider, for example, the suggestion that the focus of economics should be on *economic*-well-being, with other components of well-being left unexplored. One might be drawn, for instance, to the supposition that a higher real income implies more *economic*-well-being, because it provides more access to whatever can be bought. However, while one may say that 'what I really mean by *economic*-well-being is higher income', there is ample evidence that any meaningful link with general well-being has been severed. We know that when people list what they say they value, or think they should value, they rarely put material possessions at the top; that levels of income seem very imperfectly correlated with measures of happiness; that what people regret not having done often does not involve great expense. Thus, while there are many reasons to study individual behaviour in relation to economic resources, the suggestion that this can capture a meaningful and discrete component of our well-being seems misguided. A multifaceted definition of well-being, however appealing, is problematic and will require much more research on its possible component parts before such a composite will be widely accepted.

If, however, we view well-being as a holistic concept, we must still consider what exactly it is. The question has attracted numerous theologians and moral philosophers, since what furthers our well-being is tied to what we should be doing with our lives. Debate is often organized around several possible dimensions of well-being. For example, are *social*- and *individual*-well-being different and important concepts? Most economists and psychologists have been inclined to see well-being as relating to the individual, while recognizing that we are social beings, living in a natural world. The idea that one can ascribe meaning to the well-being of society, other than in terms of individual assessments, has been less readily accepted; expressed in other terms, the well-being of society is not seen as residing in society itself, but as reflecting some aggregate of interactive, but still individual, levels of well-being. While this reflects a perspective of methodological individualism, as commonly adopted by economists and psychologists, it is fair to note that this conclusion is less accepted in some of the other social sciences, and by ecologists.

A second important distinction in assessments of well-being relates to whether it is essentially 'objective' or 'subjective'. Does well-being lie in a specific set of behaviours which apply to all people, or does it lie in the psyche, in a manner unique to each individual? Much early philosophy, and many theological views, argued for an objective definition, with the desired behaviours derived from divine revelation or some specific idea of what constitutes the good life. In recent centuries, there has been much more emphasis upon a subjective view of well-being. At one level this simply recognizes the existence of interpersonal differences in factors such as physiology, intelligence, personality and family and cultural background. It also corresponds with the shift from a reliance on external forms of authority to define meaning in our lives, to the view that this is one of the responsibilities of the self (Taylor, 1989). However, to opt for a definition of well-being as subjective does not clarify its source: do we rely on a hedonistic view, counting pleasures and pains, or on a broader assessment of people's mental state, or does it include various desires people may have apart from any direct effect on their own mental state? Griffin (1986) in his careful assessment of these possibilities argues quite convincingly for a 'full prudential value theory'. Here well-being derives from a careful assessment of all that an individual feels bears upon his or her self-interest; expressed in other terms, well-being stems from the fulfilment of informed desire. This may suggest a return to the view common in economics, but the stringency of the requirement that desires must be informed, considered and rational, is critical. Further, a prudential value theory points out that well-being is not something which simply happens; rather it results from the application of effort to our life situation and our understanding of that situation and ourselves.

Emphasis upon individualistic, and subjective, interpretations of well-being provides an obvious link to psychological perspectives. In some respects the diverse psychological approaches mirror those from philosophy. It is possible, for instance, to interpret Abraham Maslow's famous needs hierarchy rather less as a description of how individuals actually satisfy needs as their resources increase, and rather more as an objective list of what is necessary to generate well-being, including the satisfaction of basic physiological requirements and progressing through to activities which are self-actualizing. A more common approach in psychology, and in the vast quality of life literature, has been to question people about exactly what it is that provides a feeling of well-being, thereby clearly taking a subjective stance. The research is wide-ranging (Stack, Argyle and Schwartz (eds), 1991), with surveys focusing on a number of different variables, ranging from the general (happiness, satisfaction and quality of life) to the more specific (work satisfaction); from variables which quite clearly have positive valence to ones which express an absence of negative valence (for example, absence of depressive symptoms). One interpretation is that such studies are assessing quite different things, and most of them are not general well-being. However, there are certain common findings. Lane (1991) suggests that in their evaluation of what constitutes well-being, people emphasize factors which derive, in somewhat different ways, from a desire for satisfaction and from a wish to be happy; the former has a strong cognitive, evaluative component, the latter an emotional one.

Tensions between the cognitive and the emotional raise possible difficulties for a prudential value view of well-being. Thus, for example, a requirement that we be well informed about the world we live in and our place in it rests uneasily with the finding that those who are unrealistically optimistic tend to be happier. While the individual's economic situation (standard of living, income level, wealth) is among the specific factors cited as underlying a feeling of well-being, it is not given top ranking by most people, who place greater emphasis upon family and social relations, and having a sense of personal control and accomplishment. This provides a link to the views of the economist Tibor Scitovsky (1976) who, drawing on Daniel Berlyne's theory of arousal, argued that access to material resources might well be capable of increasing our level of comfort, but that we also have need for stimulation (or joy) and that this seems much less clearly related to our ability to purchase goods and services. Scitovsky's view fits well into the prudential value approach, implying that careful evaluation is necessary to find the optimal balance between comfort and joy, and that considerable effort may be required in order to secure the requisite level of stimulation.

If we relate the psychological literature to Griffin's (1986) emphasis upon informed desires, it is necessary to ask whether what is expressed through individual surveys reflects a rational assessment of the individual's best interests. The question arises, in part, because what people say matters most to them often differs from what their behaviour implies. This may be taken as an indication that assessments of what provides well-being do in fact reflect more careful analysis than is seen in the impulsiveness of daily decisions. On the other hand, it seems likely that the cognitive biases which plague other human actions and judgement tasks would also affect individuals' assessments of what contributes to their well-being. Thus, while one might accept that the concept of well-being derives from a subjective evaluation of what is desirable, the question of how this is determined is still controversial. Can we derive it from individuals' own judgements, or does a requirement of informed opinion move us back towards an objective list of what underlies well-being?

In the end, one can perceive two somewhat different judgements about the value of the concept of well-being. Some authors (Lane, 1991; Griffin, 1986) feel that we know enough about well-being that it can play a useful role in our assessment of individual behaviour and government policies. Others feel that the term well-being has so many different meanings to different people (or even the same person), and by its very nature must have, that some other criteria is necessary. In these circumstances one might turn to restrictive measures, which are recognized as providing a narrow and incomplete measure of social desirability, such as welfare economics' criterion of economic efficiency, or an operationalized version of some presumed component of general well-being (for example, economic well-being). Alternatively reliance might be placed on a concept which has the breadth of focus of well-being, but derives from a different frame of reference; Sen's (1985) emphasis on functioning and capabilities is an example. Most such approaches would argue that the well being of individuals is a relevant concern, but question whether the concept is sufficiently well defined and practicable that it can play a useful role in economic analysis.

ALAN J. MACFADYEN

Bibliography

Elster, J. (ed.) (1985) *The Multiple Self*, Cambridge, Cambridge University Press.
Griffin, J. (1986) *Well-Being: Its Meaning, Measurement and Moral Importance*, Oxford, Clarendon Press.
Lane, R.E. (1991) *The Market Experience*, Cambridge, Cambridge University Press.
Scitovsky, T. (1976) *The Joyless Economy*, Oxford, Oxford University Press.
Sen, A. (1977) '"Rational Fools": A Critique of the Behavioral Foundations of Economic Theory', *Philosophy and Public Affairs*, **6**: 317–44.
Sen, A.K. (1985) *Capabilities and Commodities*, Amsterdam, North-Holland.
Stack, F., Argyle, M. and Schwartz, N. (eds) (1991) *Subjective Well-Being: An Interdisciplinary Perspective*, Oxford, Pergamon.
Taylor, C. (1989) *Sources of the Self: The Making of Modern Identity*, Cambridge, MA, Harvard University Press.

Women in Advertising

The resurgence of feminist activity in the late 1960s and early 1970s, now often referred to as 'the Second Wave', brought an impassioned critique of the depiction of women in advertisements. At that time, feminists objected most frequently to the exclusive picturing of women as either housewives or 'sex objects', rather than as workers, professionals or political leaders. A number of studies were quickly undertaken by both academics and advertising agencies in response to this criticism. The findings generally substantiated the complaints of women's groups: women were, indeed, pictured almost exclusively as either housewives or as desirable sexual partners (Belkaoui and Belkaoui, 1976; Courtney and Lockeretz, 1971; Courtney and Whipple, 1983; Wagner and Banos, 1973; Sexton and Haberman, 1974; Venkatesan and Losco, 1975). Two empirical studies investigated the responses of real women to various representations of female roles in advertising: both Wortzel and Frisbie (1974) and Duker and Tucker (1977) found that feminists and nonfeminists did not differ in their evaluations of images of women, whether the roles depicted were traditional or nontraditional. No studies were undertaken that attempted to verify more general feminist claims that advertising imagery lowered women's self-esteem, made them more compliant, or limited their horizons.

Over the next few years, advertising images of women changed substantially (Scott, forthcoming). Pictures of working women professionals proliferated in the fashion and women's service magazines. Women in other nontraditional jobs, particularly in the military, and women in political roles can be also be observed in the advertisements of the 1970s. The sudden reorientation of imagery resulted in a fresh complaint from feminist leaders and lecturers: that advertisers had created a new monster, the 'Superwoman'. This role model, it was said, not only portrayed real women's lives unrealistically, it also intimidated women by making them feel inadequate and insecure. Thus, having responded to the demand that advertisements present a new ideal, advertisers found themselves condemned for establishing an unrealistic role model.

Since the 1970s, only one study has counted the types of female images that appear in the popular press (Lazier-Smith and Kendrick 1993). Lazier-Smith's (1988) unpublished doctoral dissertation found that the depiction of either housewives or working professionals had dwindled substantially, leaving mostly pictures of pretty women whose work roles were unstipulated. Pictures of pretty women who were not clearly engaged in either work or home-making were counted as 'sex objects' by Lazier, whether the imagery was overtly sexual or not. Not surprisingly, she found that the decline in working women and housewives had been replaced by a remarkably strong rise in the number of 'sex objects'. From the advertiser's viewpoint, however, a reasonable response to the experience of the 1970s might have been to avoid identifying women by employment at all. With this proviso, the only ways for an advertiser to escape the 'sex object' category would have been to show only unattractive women or to omit pictures of women entirely. Again, it is less than amazing that Lazier also found a notable increase in the number of advertisements that had no pictures of women at all.

Between the late 1970s and the mid-1990s, a plethora of essays, videos, speeches and books on the topic of women in advertising imagery appeared. These range in sophistication from the purely polemical to the highly theoretical (Judith Williamson's *Decoding Advertisements* is an example of the latter). Recent works have included bestsellers like Naomi Wolf's *The Beauty Myth* and widely-read academic works, such as Susan Bordo's *Unbearable Weight* and Diane Barthel's *Putting on Appearances*. These works vary somewhat in the details of their argumentation and the sophistication of their rhetoric, but little in tone or evidence. All these treatises are aggressive and hyperbolous in tone, asserting dark mysteries behind marketing powers that compel and enforce a system of violent degradation against women. These works use only advertisements themselves as data, but do not contextualize their examples in terms of their representativeness in the overall discourse. Social problems such as rape, eating disorders and child abuse are routinely attributed to the images in advertisements, without any evidence of causality except the logic of assertion.

One study has attempted to assess empirically the responses of real women to the beautiful images in advertisements. Richins (1991) exposed college students to photographs of models, expecting a decline in self-esteem to result, but her findings were mixed. While respondents did seem to use the models to set their standards for a good appearance, their perceptions of their own attractiveness were unaffected by the exposure to images of beautiful women. Thus, a general claim that advertising images of beautiful women lowered the self-esteem of viewers could not be supported.

At the century's end, therefore, the issue of female depictions in advertising has engendered a highly-charged political battle upon very little concrete evidence. Several writers, such as Ann Simonton (1995) and Marilyn French (1992), actually assert that advertising images are the primary cause for the oppression of women. Such arguments seem to be accepted unquestioned by feminists from a range of philosophical viewpoints. Yet every documented society, including those where advertising imagery does not exist, has discriminated against women — and those societies where advertising imagery is most pervasive are also those where feminist movements have had the greatest success. The current excessive emphasis on advertising imagery, therefore, presents a puzzle in political proportions. Why is it that this one issue has so thoroughly captured the imagination of feminists, when the oppression of women along so many other fronts continues?

When such disproportionate claims characterize a social issue, there are usually other fears and prejudices at work. In the United States, the mistrust of advertising images results from a long tradition that affects even academic research on the topic (see the entry for Images in Advertising). From the Puritan founders, whose hatred of images was linked to their hatred of Roman Catholics, to the pop theorists of the 1950s, whose conspiracies of subliminal control were spun from Cold War paranoia and vulgar Freudianism, Americans have produced a folklore about images, particularly in advertising, that is remarkable for its sheer iconophobia. The feminist critique of advertising images, while more recent and often dressed in contemporary theory, draws its power from these traditions.

Criticism of advertising images first appears in the feminist literature with Betty Friedan's (1963/71) *The Feminine Mystique*. Friedan mentions the representations of housewives in advertisements as one piece of a substantial array of evidence supporting her claim that a major ideological shift occurred in the postwar period with regard to the proper role of women. Though she identifies several possible causes, Friedan does argue that the need to find new and larger markets for consumer goods after the economy shifted away from wartime demands spurred advertisers to manipulate women in subterranean ways. Following Vance Packard and others of her period, Friedan attributes dark, vaguely Freudian powers to the images in advertising. She substantiates her claims by quoting interviews with unnamed advertising professionals. One of these was almost certainly Ernest Dichter, the founder of (now discredited) motivation research, and another was probably James Vicary, the perpetrator of the subliminal advertising hoax of the late 1950s.[1] Although the sources are suspect — and despite Friedan's dismissal of Freud in nearly every other chapter

---

[1]   Vicary announced to the US press in 1957 that he had influenced the concession purchases of a movie audience using messages spliced into film in a manner too rapid to be perceived. Over the next ten months, the unemployed market researcher collected retainers from major manufacturers to apply his new 'subliminal advertising' to a variety of consumer products, but his story slowly fell apart. The owner of the theatre at which the initial study purportedly took place announced there had been no test. A demonstration demanded by the Federal Communications Commission failed to produce any effect. The government, the press and the marketing community began to ask difficult questions and Vicary began to back-pedal. Suddenly, in June 1958, Vicary disappeared, leaving no clothes in his closet or money in his bank account — including the estimated $22 million in today's dollars he had taken in fees from advertisers. He was never heard from again. In the 40 years since Vicary's infamous 'popcorn and cola' experiment, no researchers have ever been able to replicate the study. Yet the legend lives on as folklore. Source: Stuart Rogers, 'How a Publicity Blitz Created the Myth of Subliminal Advertising,' *Public Opinion Quarterly* (Winter 1992–3): 12–17.

622

of her book — the advertising critique in *The Feminine Mystique* set the tone for the discourse that followed.

Although the feminist movement prior to Friedan did not address the issue of advertising images directly, it often exhibited anxiety and disapproval over a number of related phenomena: mass-produced images, sexual or nude images of any kind, commerce, pleasure or license in a variety of arenas. The first-generation feminists in America were from the rural gentry, a group stripped of their power in the social restructuring and burst of commercial activity following the Revolution. Feminist historians note that the 'founding feminists' were nearly all Yankee Puritans or Quakers and thus shared an ethnic tradition of mistrust of pictures, pleasure and theatre. Like the men of their social group, these women were active in a variety of social movements aimed at controlling the behaviours of the growing working class, especially the new immigrants flooding in from Europe.

Several historians of feminism have noted the way xenophobia and status deprivation influenced the early feminists' strategies, agendas and activities. Leading feminists were prominently involved in movements to censor the popular press and the arts where display of attractive women was concerned, and often showed little regard for intention or context. The same women were also involved in dress and recreational reforms that aimed to draw Americans of lesser social standing away from their 'commercial amusements', such as popular theatre, fashion magazines, dance halls, amusement parks and pubs.

Between the rise of American feminism in the mid-nineteenth century and the granting of suffrage in 1920, rising commercial elites from the new publishing industry, the theatre, fashion, and, eventually, the movies, repeatedly challenged the rights of the former Yankee gentry to police daily life in America. Among these new elites were many women (including, for instance, actress Lillian Russell, cosmetics magnate Elizabeth Arden, advertising agent Helen Resor, designer Ellen Demorest, and fashion editor Jane Cunningham Croly), who were active in the suffrage movement — but who were also heavily involved in the emerging culture of commerce, consumption and imagery. Today, feminist activism among early female entrepreneurs, actresses, and publishers has been almost entirely omitted from histories of feminism. This very absence suggests the degree to which the old Protestant leisure class view has dominated our understanding of the origins of the women's movement, as well as the basic premises of feminist policy. The Friedan critique, therefore, tapped into a tradition in feminism that was characteristically iconophobic and anti-commercial. This tradition, however, was rooted in xenophobia and class prejudice rather than in the enlightened leftist thinking commonly attributed to feminism today.

As the ideas about advertising that first appeared in *The Feminine Mystique* proliferated into a huge stream of criticism, feminist involvement among designers, editors, actresses and even advertising agents continued. Many staunch supporters of the Second Wave, such as Helen Gurley Brown, Mary Ayres, Phyllis Robinson and Rena Bartos, had high profiles in the commercial world. Their business ties, as well as their involvement with images, sexuality, fashion and pleasure, have resulted in their efforts being either discredited or ignored by feminist historians and intellectuals, however.

Today, in spite of the long strides made by women in many areas of American life, including advertising and commerce, the feminist movement continues to display an unabated anticommercialism and a truly irrational fear of images. Of late, several women with feminist sympathies, such as Christina Hoff Sommers (1994) and Elizabeth Fox-Genovese (1997), have written books challenging some basic assumptions that have come to characterize the feminist critique, arguing that feminist rhetoric on issues like sexuality and pleasure put the leadership at odds with the greater majority of American women, thus unnecessarily undermining the movement. Perhaps such challenges will open up the debate on images and commerce, allowing some of the more sweeping claims to be critically reexamined.

Two areas seem most in need of empirical research. One is to document the images of women in the advertising discourse since 1970 in ways that more fully describe the incidence of egregious stereotyping, implicit violence, and the like. Further, categories established by earlier studies, such as 'sex object', need to be refined in ways that better describe the images found. As it currently stands, for instance, the many images of athletes that appear in advertisements between the early fitness craze of the 1980s and the Olympics of 1996 would all have to be characterized as 'sex objects', since the old typology does not provide any other slot for attractive women who are not either housewives or businesswomen. The second, but perhaps more morally pressing, research imperative is to study empirically the actual effects of advertising imagery on women. Given the tone of heated certainty that characterizes charges about the effects of advertising imagery on women, it is surprising to see that, in fact, there has been almost no empirical research on the topic. If, indeed, the claimed effects do occur, then surely substantiating research would be an important aid to the empowerment of women throughout the global consumer culture. If, however, women's actual responses to advertising imagery are not in keeping with the dire claims that have been made, then it would be well to provide support for a shift in emphasis towards issues that are, arguably, more concretely threatening to women's welfare, such as the availability of birth control, employment and educational rights, freedom from harassment, and protection from violence.

LINDA M. SCOTT

Women in Advertising

Bibliography

Barthel, D. (1988) *Putting on Appearances: Gender and Advertising*, Philadelphia, PA, Temple University Press.

Belkaoui, A. and Belkaoui, J.M. (1976) 'A Comparative Analysis of the Roles Portrayed by Women in Print Advertisements: 1958, 1970, 1972', *Journal of Marketing Research*, **8**: 168–72.

Bordo, S. (1993) *Unbearable Weight: Feminism, Western Culture and the Body*, Berkeley, CA, University of California Press.

Courtney, A.E. and Lockeretz, S.W. (1971) 'A Woman's Place: An Analysis of the Roles Portrayed by Women in Magazine Advertisements', *Journal of Marketing Research*, **8**: 92–5.

Courtney, A.E. and Whipple, T.W. (1983) *Sex Stereotyping in Advertising*, Lexington, MA, Lexington Books.

Duker, J.M. and Tucker, L.R., Jr (1977) 'Women's Lib-ers Versus Independent Women: A Study of Preferences for Women's Roles in Advertisements', *Journal of Marketing Research*, **14**: 469–75.

Fox-Genovese, E. (1997) *Feminism Is Not the Story of My Life: How Today's Feminist Elite Has Lost Touch with the Real Concerns of Women*, New York, Anchor Books.

French, M. (1992) *The War Against Women*, New York, Ballantine Books.

Friedan, B. (1963/71) *The Feminine Mystique*, London, Golllancz.

Lazier-Smith, L. (1988) 'The Effect of Changes in Women's Social Status on Images of Women in Magazine Advertising', Unpublished PhD dissertation, Indiana University.

Lazier-Smith, L. and Kendrick, A.G. (1993) 'Women in Advertisements: Sizing Up Images, Roles, and Functions', in Creedon, P.J. (ed.) *Women in Mass Communication*, Thousand Oaks, CA, Sage.

Richins, M.L. (1991) 'Social Comparison and the Idealized Images of Advertising', *Journal of Consumer Research*, **18**: 71–83.

Scott, L.M. (forthcoming) *Fresh Lipstick: Redressing Fashion and Feminism*, Urbana, IL, University of Illinois Press.

Sexton, D.E. and Haberman, P. (1974) 'Women in Magazine Advertisements', *Journal of Advertising Research*, **14**: April.

Simonton, A.J. (1995) 'Women for Sale', in Lont, C.M. (ed.) *Women and Media*, New York, Wadworth.

Sommers, C.H. (1994) *Who Stole Feminism? How Women Have Betrayed Women*, New York, Simon & Schuster.

Venkatesan, M. and Losco, J. (1975) 'Women in Magazine Ads 1959–1971', *Journal of Advertising Research*, **17**: October.

Wagner, L.C. and Banos, J.B. (1973) 'A Woman's Place: A Follow-Up Analysis of the Roles Portrayed by Women in Magazine Advertisements', *Journal of Marketing Research*, **10**: 213–14.

Williamson, J. (1978) *Decoding Advertisements: Ideology and Meaning in Advertising*, London, Boyars.

Wolf, N. (1991) *The Beauty Myth: How Images of Beauty are Used Against Women*, New York, Morrow.

Wortzel, L.H. and Frisbie, J.M. (1974) 'Women's Role Portrayal Preferences in Advertisements: An Empirical Study', *Journal of Marketing*, **38**: 41–46.

Work Effort

> I remind you again that workers are not peanuts. (Frank H. Hahn 1981: 66)

The idea that social factors are important to economic behaviour, especially the social context of economic actions, can be traced back to Adam Smith (1759, 1776). In addition, the analysis of work effort and labour productivity has been the subject of interest in the fields of organisational behaviour and psychology (see. for example, Taylor, 1912/1947, Mayo, 1933, and Vroom, 1964). However, significant contributions to the formal economic analysis of the role of socio-psychological factors in the labour market, especially the formal treatment of labour effort within the neoclassical modelling framework were not made until much later, in the 1970s and the 1980s (see, for example, Leibenstein, 1976; Akerlof, 1982; and Akerlof and Yellen, 1990). While the assumptions of homogeneity of labour and the independence of units of labour have allowed major simplifications in the analysis of the theory of the firm, the treatment of labour *effort* as a variable input resulting in heterogeneous *effective* labour units, and allowing *social interactions* among workers resulting in effort outcomes have been major developments in presenting more realistic theories of labour as an input of production. This review focuses on developments in the economic analysis of work effort.

Work effort as a variable factor of production

The idea that utility maximization by workers may be analysed as a function of the level of 'effort' exerted received significant attention in the work of Leibenstein (1976), in a model of labour supply with *effort* as a variable input. In this analysis, two major changes to the usual assumptions were, first, that work effort is variable in all instances, and, second, that work contracts are incomplete and open, such that workers exert volition over their effort in production. Although effort was defined as reflecting harder work at given times, four components were identified regarding the choice of *activities*, the *pace*, the *quality* and the *time* pattern or the length of each activity. This *activity–pace–quality–time* (APQT) bundle was now potentially variable across individuals, as influenced by personal motivation and incentives in the work environment.

The worker's utility as a function of effort was assumed to follow an inverse U-shape, since having a job and some effort was preferred to no effort, but beyond some point, exerting additional effort would decrease worker utility. Leibenstein, therefore, hypothesized that the relationship between worker effort and utility reached its maximum with a flat top, representing 'a comfortable effort range' available to each individual. The combined effect of earnings and effort on utility was further to flatten the utility-effort curve, resulting in a wider 'comfortable effort range' when increased effort increases earnings through factors such as bonuses. One of the important implications of this analysis was that it extended the theories of the firm and labour supply to incorporate the variable nature of effort. This, combined with theories of inert areas and *X*-efficiency, provided a closer link between models of organizational behaviour in management, and the theory of the firm in economics, as regards productivity of labour. Furthermore, this provided a means of analysing labour productivity due to worker volition, complementing the conventional role assigned to physical and human capital. This meant that economic analysis could formally incorporate increases in labour productivity while units of capital and the wage rate were kept constant, due to a sense of purpose. It also facilitated the analysis of voluntary work, perfectionism, or, as in Etzioni's (1988) work, the exertion of effort due to moral and ethical convictions. This can explain personal commitment towards the quality of performance or customer care beyond the profit motive — for example, Dore (1986) notes the role of ethical and moral/duty convictions of employees in Japan, in relation to lifetime employment contracts, openness to change and the treatment of customers.

Social and psychological aspects of work effort
Further developments in the microeconomic analysis of work effort were made by Akerlof (1982), Solow (1990) and Yellen (1984), who constructed models in which worker effort is influenced by social interactions at work and social norms regarding a fair day's work. These studies, and a number of others that followed, further and formally incorporated effort as a variable factor into the objective functions of the firm and the worker. In addition to allowing the optimal level of effort to be different across workers, a contribution to the theory of the firm as a common characteristic of these studies was that the labour market was treated as a *social institution*, where worker productivity is influenced by the interactions of the working group. This approach, thereby, allowed further asymmetries in the treatment of capital and labour in the theory of the firm, by incorporating the potential effect of worker–employer and work-group interactions on the quantity and quality of work performed by workers. Two key concepts in this social/psychological treatment of worker effort are *gift exchange* and the concept of a *fair wage*.

Labour contracts as gift exchange
In standard economic theory, the incompleteness of employment contracts makes many different standards of performance possible, but when a firm hires a

worker there is an expectation that certain minimum standards must be met. In models of long-term expected employment, the worker–employer contract is partly implicit in nature. In these employment settings, especially when promotion mechanisms are at work, a worker's effort may correspond to long-term rewards, and need not be compensated in every time period, as compensation can occur at a later time period.

The idea of promotion incentives or job ladders has been a salient feature of several other models, such as the theories of internal labour markets. However, observations that workers who had no expectations of future promotions consistently produced more than the minimum required output levels (for example, cash register workers of the Eastern Utility Co.) led Akerlof (1982) to explore alternative explanations as to why the firm did not raise the minimum performance requirements, or why workers did not reduce their effort level. He concluded that an explanation of either the firm's behaviour or the workers' behaviour must depend either on maximization of something other than profits by the firm or on interaction of the workers with each other and with the firm that alters their utility function. An answer to this question was that a part of the exchange between the employer and employees is in the form of a *gift* of effort in exchange for a fair treatment.

A *fair* treatment by the employer is traded for the *loyalty* of the employee as reflected by greater effort beyond the minimum requirements. The nature of this exchange, or implicit contract, was characterized as somewhat like Christmas *gift giving,* such that in repeated exchanges over extended time periods workers will adjust their effort level to reciprocate the employer's treatment (Akerlof, 1982). Work standards are only one dimension of the treatment of workers, while the wage rate is the other. Therefore, a part of the work standards and wage-effort relationship between employers and employees is more loosely determined, as in the form of gift exchange (efficiency wages). If wages are sufficiently low, workers will feel unfairly treated, leading to decreased job satisfaction and either decreased effort levels or exit behaviour by them.

In this context, worker effort depends on the workplace norms as to what determines a fair day's work. This is often different from the minimum standards set by the employer and is guided by standards set by work groups.

The *fair wage* hypothesis of how employer–worker relationships result in worker effort was developed around the same time as alternative *shirking* models, in which it is assumed employers are concerned about worker shirking behaviour, particularly in industries where monitoring is difficult. Therefore, to discourage shirking behaviour and ensure increased effort, employers would pay workers more (efficiency wages) either currently or through promotion prospects to increase the cost of shirking.

Work groups

Detailed examinations of worker effort — that began with the Hawthorne Works study of the 1930s and which have been exemplified more recently by Burawoy's (1979) study of a piecework machine shop — have shown considerable support for worker autonomy in determining output levels and worker interactions in setting output level norms. This evidence further showed that workers had turned their jobs and output levels into something like a game in which they could score. Akerlof (1982) concluded that in this framework, where adherence to authority is not complete, the loyalty of employees is one contributor to high productivity. In this setting, workers' perception of a fair treatment, such as a fair day's work, or a fair pay, is partly determined by work group norms.

Effort and conformism

The effect of work groups and worker social interactions in determining a workers level of output was further incorporated by Jones (1984) into a neoclassical setting in the economics of conformism. In his model, workers are heterogeneous regarding their tastes, ability and the disutility of effort, but a worker's productivity within a firm is influenced by conformism to group norms. Conformism is a widespread phenomenon, as evidenced in work places, schools, the military, and social psychology laboratories. A number of studies surveyed by Jones lend support to the idea that group interactions affect the effort and output of workers, not only by putting pressure on the faster workers to slow down but also by producing siutations where sentiments for coworkers may induce greater effort. In complementary work that focuses on the costs of deviance, Earl (1983: 182–3) suggests that guilt may prevent workers from offering only the minimum acceptable contribution, while upper bounds of effort levels may be shaped by expectations that attempts to enhance promotion prospects by working harder might result in a fruitless 'effort war' with their equally promotion-hungry rivals.

Equity and relative deprivation

The relation between worker effort and perceptions of receiving a fair wage was further developed in a second generation of efficiency wage models (Akerlof and Yellen, 1990), where perceptions of fairness are formed on the basis of comparisons to salient others or a reference group, either in the same firm or in the same occupation in other firms. The fair wage may not correspond closely with the market-clearing wage, but there is clear evidence that market forces do influence the wages level that people consider to be fair. The importance of relativities in wage determination is consistent with observed behaviour in individual wage setting and union negotiations (see Wood, 1978). Blinder and

Choi (1990) also find supporting evidence for the fair wage hypothesis based on survey data of employers. The evidence presented by Akerlof and Yellen (1990) further supports the hypothesis that when wages are below the perceived fair wage, workers experience feelings of relative deprivation, resulting in the withdrawal of effort. Decreased effort represents a worker's attempt to get even with the firm. This is consistent with Adams's (1963) theory of equity which predicts that in social exchange between two agents, the ratio of the perceived value of the inputs to the outcomes would be equal.

Efficiency wages and work effort
One of the implications of incorporating effort into firm and individual objective functions has been the feedback effect of the wage rate on labour productivity, or the marginal product of labour for a given quantity of labour. This has provided new explanations as to why firms may voluntarily pay workers 'above the market-clearing wage rate' (efficiency wages) in exchange for worker loyalty, increased effort levels and productivity.

Efficiency wage theories, developed in the 1980s, have provided alternative explanations for the existence of involuntary unemployment due to nonmarket clearing wages. This has been the subject of scrutiny and debate in the field of unemployment. For example, Carmichael (1990) surveys efficiency wage models and concludes that they fail to explain wage rigidity or persistent involuntary unemployment.

While the social and psychological aspects of worker effort, work groups and the idea of a fair wage are consistent with observed behaviour and empirically supported through direct observations, the empirical establishment of the existence of efficiency wages or their link to labour productivity and involuntary unemployment has posed significant challenges. This is because the efficiency wage, or the gift component of observed salaries, cannot be conclusively isolated from other components of salaries in micro-level data sets. Therefore, indirect measurement and a process of elimination have been features of this empirical literature. Most notably, for example, Krueger and Summers (1988) have provided evidence, by elimination, that interindustry wage differentials are prominent in the US, based on individual-level data sets which control for a wide range of worker, occupational, firm and job characteristics. The extent to which interindustry wage differentials comprise *efficiency wages* is, however, open to debate. An alternative method has been to directly examine firm- or establishment-level data on worker earnings, and on labour productivity as a measure of worker effort. This approach has provided supportive evidence for the link between incentives, perceptions of a fair wage, and worker effort. While efficiency wage models do not appear to have provided breakthroughs in the theory of unemployment to the degree that was initially anticipated, their contributions, especially the developments in the analysis of work effort, remain prominent.

Alternatively, *insider–outsider* models of unemployment (Lindbeck and Snower, 1988; Solow, 1985) have provided further developments in economic theory based on worker group behaviour and effort levels. In these models, employed workers comprise insiders in a firm, downgrading the influence of outsiders in the face of unemployment. Outsiders can exert less downward influence on wages, since replacing existing workers by lower-paid unemployed workers would result in decreased effort and less cooperation by the existing workers, resulting in decreased productivity. Empirical work in the UK and Australia is consistent with this hypothesis (Nickell and Andrews, 1983).

SHOLEH A. MAANI

Bibliography

Adams, J.S. (1963) 'Toward an Understanding of Inequality', *Journal of Abnormal and Social Psychology*, **67**: 422–36.

Akerlof, G.A. (1982) 'Labor Contracts as Partial Gift Exchange', *Quarterly Journal of Economics*, **92**: 543–69.

Akerlof, G.A. and Yellen, J.L. (1990) 'The Fair Wage–Effort Hypothesis and Unemployment', *Quarterly Journal of Economics*, **90**: 255–68.

Blinder A.S. and Choi, D.H. (1990) 'A Shred of Evidence on Theories of Wage Stickiness', *Quarterly Journal of Economics*, **90**: 1003–15.

Burawoy, M. (1979) *Manufacturing Consent*, Chicago, University of Chicago Press.

Carmichael, H.L. (1990) 'Efficiency Wage Models of Unemployment — One View', *Quarterly Journal of Economics*, **90**: 269–95.

Dore, R. (1986) *Flexible Rigidities*, London, Athlone Press.

Earl, P.E. (1983) *The Economic Imagination: Towards a Behavioural Analysis of Choice*, New York, M.E. Sharpe.

Etzioni, A. (1988) *The Moral Dimension: Toward A New Economics*, New York, Free Press.

Hahn, F.H. (1981) *Money and Inflation*, Oxford, Basil Blackwell.

Jones, S.R.G. (1984) *The Economics of Conformism*, Oxford, Basil Blackwell.

Krueger A. and Summers, L. (1988) 'Efficiency Wages and the Inter-industry Wage Structure', *Econometrica*, **56**: 259–93.

Leibenstein, H. (1976) *Beyond Economic Man: A New Foundation for Microeconomics*, Cambridge, MA, Harvard University Press.

Lindbeck A. and Snower, D. (1988) 'Cooperation, Harassment, and Involuntary Unemployment: An Insider–Outsider Approach', *American Economic Review*, **78**: 167–88.

Mayo, E. (1933) *The Human Problems of an Industrial Civilization*. New York, Macmillan.

Nickell, S.J. and Andrews, M. (1983) 'Trade Unions, Real Wages, and Employment in Britain: 1951–79', *Oxford Economic Papers*, **35**: 507–30.

Smith, A. (1759) *The Theory of Moral Sentiments* (1976 edn), edited by D.D. Raphael, and A.L. Macfie, Oxford, Clarendon Press.

Smith, A. (1776) *The Wealth of Nations* (reprinted 1974), Harmondsworth, Penguin.

Solow, R.M. (1985) 'Insiders and Outsiders in Wage Determination', *Scandinavian Journal of Economics*, **87**: 411-28.

Solow, R.M. (1990) *The Labour Market as a Social Institution*, Cambridge, MA, Basil Blackwell.

Taylor, F.W. (1947) *Scientific Management*, New York, Harper & Row (Original work published 1912).

Vroom, V.H. (1964) *Work and Motivation*, New York, Wiley.

Wood, A. (1978) *A Theory of Pay*, Cambridge, Cambridge University Press.

Yellen, J.L. (1984) 'Efficiency Wage Models of Unemployment', *American Economic Review*, **74**: 200–205.

Index